T0210660

Lecture Notes in Computer Science 9483

Commenced Publication in 1973
Founding and Former Series Editors:
Gerhard Goos, Juris Hartmanis, and Jan van Leeuwen

More information about this series at http://www.springer.com/series/7409

Zhiqiu Huang · Xingming Sun
Junzhou Luo · Jian Wang (Eds.)

Cloud Computing and Security

First International Conference, ICCCS 2015
Nanjing, China, August 13–15, 2015
Revised Selected Papers

 Springer

Editors

Zhiqiu Huang
Nanjing University of Aeronautics
    and Astronautics
Nanjing
China

Xingming Sun
Nanjing University of Information Science
    and Technology
Nanjing
China

Junzhou Luo
Nanjing University
Nanjing, Jiangsu
China

Jian Wang
Nanjing University of Aeronautics
    and Astronautics
Nanjing, Jiangsu
China

ISSN 0302-9743   ISSN 1611-3349   (electronic)
Lecture Notes in Computer Science
ISBN 978-3-319-27050-0   ISBN 978-3-319-27051-7   (eBook)
DOI 10.1007/978-3-319-27051-7

Library of Congress Control Number: 2015955894

LNCS Sublibrary: SL3 – Information Systems and Applications, incl. Internet/Web, and HCI

Printed on acid-free paper

This Springer imprint is published by SpringerNature
The registered company is Springer International Publishing AG Switzerland

Preface

This volume contains the papers presented at ICCCS 2015: the First International Conference on Cloud Computing and Security held during August 13–15, 2015, in Nanjing, China. The conference was hosted by the College of Computer Science and Technology at the Nanjing University of Aeronautics and Astronautics, who provided the wonderful facilities and material support. We made use of the excellent EasyChair submission and reviewing software.

The aim of this conference is to provide an international forum for the latest results of research, development, and applications in the field of cloud computing and information security. This year we received 158 submissions from eight countries, including the USA, China, Japan, UK, India, Slovenia, Bangladesh, and Vietnam. Each submission was allocated to three Program Committee (PC) members and each paper received on average 2.2 reviews. The committee decided to accept 47 papers.

The program also included four excellent and informative invited talks: "Domain Identity: Tools for Privacy-by-Design in Cloud Systems" by Prof. Miroslaw Kutylowski, Wroclaw University of Technology, Poland; "Cloud Security: Challenges and Practice" by Prof. Hai Jin, Huazhong University of Science and Technology, China; "Cloud-Centric Assured Information Sharing for Secure Social Networking" by Prof. Bhavani Thuraisingham, University of Texas at Dallas, USA; "New Trends of Cloud Computing Security" by Prof. Zhenfu Cao, Shanghai Jiao Tong University, China.

We would like to extend our sincere thanks to all authors who submitted papers to ICCCS 2015, and all PC members. It was a truly great experience to work with such talented and hard-working researchers. We also appreciate the external reviewers for assisting the PC members in their particular areas of expertise. Finally, we would like to thank all attendees for their active participation and the organizing team, who nicely managed this conference. We look forward to seeing you again at next year's ICCCS.

August 2015   Zhiqiu Huang
                                                               Xingming Sun

Organization

General Chairs

Elisa Bertino	Purdue University, USA
Zhiqiu Huang	Nanjing University of Aeronautics and Astronautics, China
Xingming Sun	Nanjing University of Information Science and Technology, China

Program Committee

Co-chairs

Junzhou Luo	Southeast University, China
Kui Ren	State University of New York Buffalo, USA

Members

Arif Saeed	University of Algeria, Algeria
Zhifeng Bao	University of Tasmania, Australia
Elisa Bertino	Purdue University, USA
Jintai Ding	University of Cincinnati, USA
Zhangjie Fu	Nanjing University of Information Science and Technology, China
Lein Harn	University of Missouri – Kansas City, USA
Jiwu Huang	Sun Yat-sen University, China
Yongfeng Huang	Tsinghua University, China
Hai Jin	Huazhong University of Science and Technology, China
Jiwu Jing	Institute of Information Engineering CAS, China
Jiguo Li	Hohai University, China
Li Li	Hangzhou Dianzi University, China
Qiaoliang Li	Hunan Normal University, China
Xiangyang Li	Institute of Illinois Technology, USA
Quansheng Liu	University of South Brittany, France
Mingxin Lu	Nanjing University, China
Yonglong Luo	Anhui Normal University, China
Yi Mu	University of Wollongong, Australia
Shaozhang Niu	Beijing University of Posts and Telecommunications, China
Xiamu Niu	Harbin Institute of Technology, China
Jiaohua Qin	Central South University of Forestry and Technology, China
Yanzhen Qu	Colorado University of Technology, USA

Jian Shen	Nanjing University of Information Science and Technology, China
Yun-Qing Shi	New Jersey Institute of Technology, USA
Takagi Tsuyoshi	Kyushu University, Japan
Shaohua Tang	South China University of Technology, China
Xianping Tao	Nanjing University, China
Tobe Yoshito	Aoyang University, Japan
Hongxia Wang	Southwest Jiaotong University, China
Huaxiong Wang	Nanyang Technological University, China
Jian Wang	Nanjing University of Aeronautics and Astronautics, China
Liangming Wang	Jiangsu University, China
Xiaojun Wang	Dublin City University, Ireland
Aiming Yang	Guandong University of Foreign Studies, China
Ming Yang	Southeast University, China
Xinchun Yin	Yangzhou University, China
Jiabin Yuan	Nanjing University of Aeronautics and Astronautics, China
Futai Zhang	Nanjing Normal University, China
Mingwu Zhang	Hubei University of Technology, China
Youwen Zhu	Nanjing University of Aeronautics and Astronautics, China
Wei Zhang	Nanjing University of Posts and Telecommunications, China
Xinpeng Zhang	Shanghai University, China
Yao Zhao	Beijing Jiaotong University, China
Chi Cheng	Kyushu University, Japan

Organizing Committee

Chair

Jian Wang	Nanjing University of Aeronautics and Astronautics, China

Members

Dechang Pi	Nanjing University of Aeronautics and Astronautics, China
Yu Zhou	Nanjing University of Aeronautics and Astronautics, China
Youwen Zhu	Nanjing University of Aeronautics and Astronautics, China
Juan Xu	Nanjing University of Aeronautics and Astronautics, China
Liming Fang	Nanjing University of Aeronautics and Astronautics, China
Xiangping Zhai	Nanjing University of Aeronautics and Astronautics, China
Mingfu Xue	Nanjing University of Aeronautics and Astronautics, China

Contents

Data Security

VH: A Lightweight Block Cipher Based on Dual Pseudo-random
Transformation 3
  Xuejun Dai, Yuhua Huang, Lu Chen, Tingting Lu, and Fei Su

Security Against Hardware Trojan Attacks Through a Novel Chaos FSM
and Delay Chains Array PUF Based Design Obfuscation Scheme 14
  Mingfu Xue, Jian Wang, Youdong Wang, and Aiqun Hu

Secure and Efficient Protocol for Outsourcing Large-Scale Systems
of Linear Equations to the Cloud 25
  Cheng Qian and Jian Wang

A Provably Secure Ciphertext-Policy Hierarchical Attribute-Based
Encryption 38
  Ziying Wang and Jian Wang

Privacy-Preserving Multidimensional Range Query on Real-Time Data 49
  Zhong Ting, Han Xiao, Yang Yunshuo, and Zhu Aixiang

ARM-Based Privacy Preserving for Medical Data Publishing 62
  Zhang Fengli and Bai Yijing

Attribute-Based Encryption Without Key Escrow 74
  *Xing Zhang, Cancan Jin, Zilong Wen, Qingni Shen, Yuejian Fang,
  and Zhonghai Wu*

An Efficient Access Control Optimizing Technique Based on Local Agency
in Cryptographic Cloud Storage 88
  Shidong Zhu, Liu Jiang, and Zhenliu Zhou

Complete Separable Reversible Data Hiding in Encrypted Image 101
  Yin Zhaoxia, Wang Huabin, Zhao Haifeng, Luo Bin, and Zhang Xinpeng

Multi-threshold Image Segmentation Through an Improved
Quantum-Behaved Particle Swarm Optimization Algorithm 111
  Wang Jiali, Liu Hongshen, and Ruan Yue

Coverless Image Steganography Without Embedding. 123
  Zhili Zhou, Huiyu Sun, Rohan Harit, Xianyi Chen, and Xingming Sun

Coverless Information Hiding Method Based on the Chinese
Mathematical Expression   133
   Xianyi Chen, Huiyu Sun, Yoshito Tobe, Zhili Zhou, and Xingming Sun

System Security

Network Information Security Challenges and Relevant Strategic Thinking
as Highlighted by "PRISM"   147
   Jing Li

A Lightweight and Dependable Trust Model for Clustered Wireless
Sensor Networks   157
   Nannan Shao, Zhiping Zhou, and Ziwen Sun

The Optimization Model of Trust for White-Washing   169
   Zhidan Wang, Jian Wang, and Yanfei Zhao

Malware Clustering Based on SNN Density Using System Calls   181
   Wang Shuwei, Wang Baosheng, Yong Tang, and Yu Bo

Analyzing Eventual Leader Election Protocols for Dynamic Systems
by Probabilistic Model Checking   192
   Jiayi Gu, Yu Zhou, Weigang Wu, and Taolue Chen

A Dynamic Resource Allocation Model for Guaranteeing Quality
of Service in Software Defined Networking Based Cloud
Computing Environment   206
   Chenhui Xu, Bing Chen, Ping Fu, and Hongyan Qian

Research and Development of Trust Mechanism in Cloud Computing   218
   Jun Xu, Feng Xu, Wenna Chang, and Haiguang Lai

Analysis of Advanced Cyber Attacks with Quantified ESM   230
   Blaž Ivanc and Tomaž Klobučar

A Web Security Testing Method Based on Web Application Structure   244
   Xueyong Yu and Guohua Jiang

An Improved Data Cleaning Algorithm Based on SNM   259
   Miao Li, Qiang Xie, and Qiulin Ding

Enhancing Security of IaaS Cloud with Fraternal Security Cooperation
Between Cloud Platform and Virtual Platform   270
   Jie Yang, Zhiqiang Zhu, Lei Sun, Jingci Zhang, and Xianwei Zhu

Cloud Platform

Cluster Analysis by Variance Ratio Criterion and Quantum-Behaved PSO . . .   285
  Shuihua Wang, Xingxing Zhou, Guangshuai Zhang, Genlin Ji,
  Jiquan Yang, Zheng Zhang, Zeyuan Lu, and Yudong Zhang

Failure Modes and Effects Analysis Using Multi-factors Comprehensive
Weighted Fuzzy TOPSIS   294
  Wenjun Zhang and Fenglin Zhang

Efficient Query Algorithm of Coallocation-Parallel-Hash-Join
in the Cloud Data Center   306
  Yao Shen, Ping Lu, Xiaolin Qin, Yuming Qian, and Sheng Wang

Dynamic Data Driven Particle Filter for Agent-Based Traffic State
Estimation   321
  Xiang-wen Feng, Xue-feng Yan, and Xiao-lin Hu

An Improved Dynamic Spectrum Access Scheme in Cognitive Networks. . . .   332
  Qingwei Du and Yinmeng Wang

The Design and Implementation of a Dynamic Verification System of Z   344
  Jun Wang, Yi Zhuang, and Siru Ni

Maximizing Positive Influence in Signed Social Networks   356
  Huanhuan Wang, Qun Yang, Lei Fang, and Weihua Lei

OpenFlow-Based Load Balancing for Wireless Mesh Network   368
  Hanjie Yang, Bing Chen, and Ping Fu

SPEMS: A Stealthy and Practical Execution Monitoring System
Based on VMI   380
  Jiangyong Shi, Yuexiang Yang, Chengye Li, and Xiaolei Wang

A Total Power Control Cooperative MAC Protocol for Wireless
Sensor Networks.   390
  Xiongli Rui, Xuehong Cao, and Jie Yang

Parallel Processing of SAR Imaging Algorithms for Large Areas
Using Multi-GPU   404
  Xue Wang, Jiabin Yuan, and Xingfang Zhao

An Extreme Learning Approach to Fast Prediction in the Reduce Phase
of a Cloud Platform.   417
  Qi Liu, Weidong Cai, Jian Shen, Baowei Wang, Zhangjie Fu,
  and Nigel Linge

Data Analysis in Cloud

Wind Speed and Direction Predictions Based on Multidimensional Support
Vector Regression with Data-Dependent Kernel 427
  Dingcheng Wang, Yujia Ni, Beijing Chen, Zhili Cao, Yuhang Tian,
  and Youzhi Zhao

Research on Rootkit Detection Model Based on Intelligent Optimization
Algorithm in the Virtualization Environment 437
  Lei Sun, Zhiyuan Zhao, Feiran Wang, and Lei Jin

Performance Analysis of (1+1)EA on the Maximum Independent
Set Problem 448
  Xue Peng

A Robust Iris Segmentation Algorithm Using Active Contours
Without Edges and Improved Circular Hough Transform 457
  Yueqing Ren, Zhiyi Qu, and Xiaodong Liu

An Adaptive Hybrid PSO and GSA Algorithm for Association
Rules Mining 469
  Zhiping Zhou, Daowen Zhang, Ziwen Sun, and Jiefeng Wang

Sequential Pattern Mining and Matching Method with Its Application
on Earthquakes 480
  Jiang Zhu, Dechang Pi, Pan Xiong, and Xuhui Shen

Teaching Quality Assessment Model Based on Analytic Hierarchy
Process and LVQ Neural Network 491
  Shuai Hu, Yan Gu, and Hua Jiang

Fast Sparse Representation Classification Using Transfer Learning 501
  Qi Zhu, Baisheng Dai, Zizhu Fan, and Zheng Zhang

Probing the Scheduling Algorithms in the Cloud Based on OpenStack. 510
  Yang Luo, Qingni Shen, Cong Li, Kang Chen, and Zhonghai Wu

Top-k Distance-Based Outlier Detection on Uncertain Data 521
  Ying Zhang, Hongyuan Zheng, and Qiulin Ding

An Airport Noise Prediction Model Based on Selective Ensemble
of LOF-FSVR 536
  Haiyan Chen, Jiajia Deng, Bo Sun, and Jiandong Wang

Application of Semantic-Based Laplacian Eigenmaps Method in 3D Model
Classification and Retrieval 550
  Xinying Wang, Fangming Gu, Gang Liu, and Zhiyu Chen

Author Index 561

Data Security

VH: A Lightweight Block Cipher Based on Dual Pseudo-random Transformation

Xuejun Dai[1(✉)], Yuhua Huang[1], Lu Chen[1], Tingting Lu[2], and Fei Su[3]

[1] College of Computer Science and Technology, Nanjing University
of Aeronautics and Astronautics, Nanjing 210016, China
{daixuemai,hyuhua2k}@163.com, 815720399@qq.com
[2] College of Civil Aviation, Nanjing University
of Aeronautics and Astronautics, Nanjing 211106, China
1121789817@qq.com
[3] Suzhou Chinsdom Co. Ltd., Suzhou 215500, China
Sophy_su@126.com

Abstract. In this paper, we propose a new lightweight block cipher based on dual pseudo-random transformation called VH. Similar to many other lightweight block ciphers, the block size of VH is 64-bit and the key size is 80-bit. Our security evaluation shows that VH can achieve enough security margin against known attacks, such as differential cryptanalysis, linear cryptanalysis, and impossible differential cryptanalysis etc. Furthermore, VH can be implemented efficiently not only in hardware environments but also in software platforms such as 8-bit microcontroller. Our hardware implementation of VH requires about 3182 GE on 0.18 μm technology with a throughput of 200 Kbps at 100 kHz. The software implementation of VH on 8-bit microcontroller requires about 44.47 Mb/s to encrypt a plaintext block. The implementation efficiency of both software and hardware based on VH algorithm is higher than CLEFIA algorithm, which is the international standard also oriented to 8-bit platform.

Keywords: Block cipher · Lightweight · Hardware efficiency · Cryptanalysis

1 Introduction

In recent years, a number of security and high performance block cipher have been designed to promote the development of cryptography [1]. For example, AES, Camellia and SHACAL, etc. [2–4]. However, with the development of wireless network technology, ordinary block cipher is difficult to meet the mobile terminal resource-constrained, lightweight cryptographic algorithms required to meet hardware and software, computing power and energy consumption and other resource-constrained needs

College of Computer Science and Technology, Nanjing University of Aeronautics and Astronautics, Nanjing, China. The subject has been supported by the Science & Technology Support Plan of Jiangsu Province under Grant No. BE2013879 and the NUAA Research Funding under Grant No. NS2010097.

© Springer International Publishing Switzerland 2015
Z. Huang et al. (Eds.): ICCCS 2015, LNCS 9483, pp. 3–13, 2015.
DOI: 10.1007/978-3-319-27051-7_1

of the terminal. CLEFIA and PRESENT as an outstanding representative of the light-weight block cipher, provides us with a good opportunity based on the most advanced technologies designed for mobile terminals with limited resources [5–8]. The block cipher refers to a mathematical manipulation which the plain text is coded using the binary digital sequence $x_1, x_2, \ldots$ and partitioned into the blocks $x = (x_1, x_2, \ldots, x_m)$ with a length of m. The blocks are then converted into the equal length digital sequences $y = (y_1, y_2, \ldots, y_n)$ using the key of $k = (k_1, k_2, \ldots, k_t)$. This process can be represented with the model in Fig. 1.

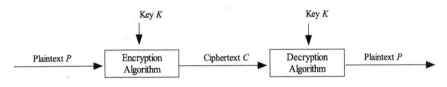

Fig. 1. The mathematical model of block cipher

In this paper, we propose a new 64-bit block cipher lightweight VH, namely Vertical Horizontal. It expressly refers to the 64 bits plaintext arranged in 8 bytes * 8 bits of matrix, pseudo random transformation for each row and column of the matrix, supporting key lengths of 64, 80, 96, 112 and 128 bits. One novel design methods of VH is the use of SP structure, with a pseudo-random transformation to construct 256-byte encryption transformation table and decryption transformation table, simplified S-box design, which fully reflects the realization of lightweight block cipher to achieve small space occupied. In addition, VH after P permutation, have been purged diagonal pseudo-random data transformation, and improve its security. VH on currently known attack methods to achieve adequate immunity and exhibits efficiency in hardware and software on consumption. VH-80's hardware implementation requires 3182 GE [9]. The software efficiency of VH-80 is computed to be 44.47 Mb/s. However, the hardware implementation of CLEFIA reaches 5979 GE and the software efficiency is computed to be 33.90 Mb/s. We believe that the software and hardware efficiency of VH algorithm is higher than the same platform for the eight international standards CLEFIA algorithm. VH in the safety and performance achieves excellent balance, which, on the basis of meeting the security, improves the efficiency of the software, at the same time takes into account hardware efficiency. So the thus is more feasible.

2 Specification of VH

2.1 Notations

The following notations are used throughout this paper.

- P: 64-bit plaintext
- Key: Master key

- C: 64-bit cipher text
- $S[256]$: Encryption transformation table
- $S^{-1}[256]$: Decryption transformation table
- E_K: Encryption transformation
- D_K: Decryption transformation
- $|$: Connect operation
- $\oplus$: Bitwise exclusive-OR operation
- $\&$: And operation
- DS: Differential active S-boxes
- LS: Linea active S-boxes

2.2 VH Algorithm Description

VH adopts the SP structure [1], has a block length of 64 bits, and supports the keys of 64, 80, 96, 112 and 128 bits. The number of rounds is $r = 10, 11, 12, 13$ and 14, respectively. VH has three parameters: 64-bit plain text P, key K and the 64-bit cipher text C. Let $C = E_K(P)$ denote the encryption transformation and $P = D_K(C)$ denote the decryption transformation. The encryption and decryption steps of VH are as follows:

(1) Encryption Transformation Table And Decryption Transformation Table

The encryption and decryption S-box is generated via pseudorandom transformation. We first compute $T(i) = \lfloor |256 \sin(i)| \rfloor$, where $\lfloor \rfloor$denote the round-down operation; to generate 256 non-repetitious bytes, i ranges from 1 to 30000, eliminating repetitions that occur. The encryption transformation table $S[256]$ and decryption transformation table $S^{-1}[256]$ are a pseudorandom combination of 256 bytes, which is obtained by alternating bytes in T: $S[T(j)] = T(j+1)$, $S[T(255)] = T(0)$; $S^{-1}[T(j+1)] = T(j)$, $S^{-1}[T(0)] = T(255)$; where $0 \leq j \leq 254$.

(2) Key Schedule

Key scheduling is achieved via iterations, so the L-byte key K is expanded to $8(r + 1)$ bytes: the expanded key $\text{Key} = K_0|K_1|\ldots|K_i|\ldots|K_r = k_0|k_1|\ldots|k_i|\ldots|k_{8r+7}$, where each K_i has 8 bytes, $0 \leq i \leq r$, each k_i has a unit byte, $0 \leq i \leq 8r + 7$. For the key K with 8, 10, 12, 14 and 16 bytes, the number of rounds is $r = 10, 11, 12, 13$, and 14. The first L bytes of the expanded key is the key K: $K = k_0|k_1|\ldots|k_{L-1}$. In the case of $L \leq i \leq 8r + 7$, k_i in the expanded key is obtained via recursion of k_{i-L} and k_{i-1}, i.e. $k_i = S[k_{i-1}] \oplus k_{i-L}$.

(3) Data Encryption Process

The encryption process of VH is shown in Fig. 2. At the first, we get the results of the initial key K_0 and plaintext by XOR. Then, through further r-round to encrypt the result of the previous step, each round of encryption including S-box transformation, P permutation and round key XOR. The output is the next round of input. Finally we get final cipher text C.

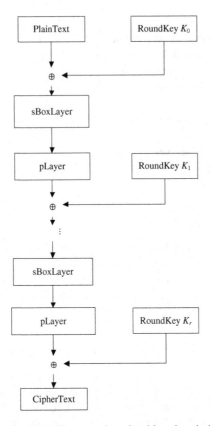

Fig. 2. The VH encryption algorithm description

- *Initial Encryption*

  The initial cipher text $C_0 = P \oplus K_0$, where P is the 64-bit initial plain text, K_0 is the first 8 bytes of the key K.

- *r-round Encryption*

  For i within $[1, r]$, each round of iteration has the following three steps:

  Firstly, perform pseudorandom transformation on each byte of the data using the encryption S-box: $M_i(j) = S[C_{i-1}(j)]$, where i range from 1 to r, $X_i(j)$ denotes the j byte of X_i, $0 \leq j \leq 7$.

  Secondly, arrange the 64-bit data M_i into a 8 * 8 matrix, perform pseudorandom transformation on each diagonal line of M_i using the encryption S-box.

$$P_i(0) = S\{[M_i(0)\&128|[M_i(1)\&64]|[M_i(2)\&32]|[M_i(3)\&16]$$
$$|[M_i(4)\&8]|[M_i(5)\&4]|[M_i(6)\&2]|[M_i(7)\&1]\}$$

$$P_i(1) = S\{[M_i(1)\&128|[M_i(2)\&64]|[M_i(3)\&32]|[M_i(4)\&16]$$
$$|[M_i(5)\&8]|[M_i(6)\&4]|[M_i(7)\&2]|[M_i(8)\&1]\}$$

$$P_i(2) = S\{[M_i(2)\&128|[M_i(3)\&64]|[M_i(4)\&32]|[M_i(5)\&16]$$
$$[M_i(6)\&8]|[M_i(7)\&4]|[M_i(0)\&2]|[M_i(1)\&1]\}$$

$$P_i(3) = S\{[M_i(3)\&128|[M_i(4)\&64]|[M_i(5)\&32]|[M_i(6)\&16]$$
$$|[M_i(7)\&8]|[M_i(0)\&4]|[M_i(1)\&2]|[M_i(2)\&1]\}$$

$$P_i(4) = S\{[M_i(4)\&128|[M_i(5)\&64]|[M_i(6)\&32]|[M_i(7)\&16]$$
$$[M_i(0)\&8]|[M_i(1)\&4]|[M_i(2)\&2]|[M_i(3)\&1]\}$$

$$P_i(5) = S\{[M_i(5)\&128|[M_i(6)\&64]|[M_i(7)\&32]|[M_i(0)\&16]$$
$$|[M_i(1)\&8]|[M_i(2)\&4]|[M_i(3)\&2]|[M_i(4)\&1]\}$$

$$P_i(6) = S\{[M_i(6)\&128|[M_i(7)\&64]|[M_i(0)\&32]|[M_i(1)\&16]$$
$$|[M_i(2)\&8]|[M_i(3)\&4]|[M_i(4)\&2]|[M_i(5)\&1]\}$$

$$P_i(7) = S\{[M_i(7)\&128|[M_i(0)\&64]|[M_i(1)\&32]|[M_i(2)\&16]$$
$$|[M_i(3)\&8]|[M_i(4)\&4]|[M_i(5)\&2]|[M_i(6)\&1]\}$$

Finally, obtain the cipher text of the current iteration by performing XOR operation on the output P_i above and the sub-key K_i of the current iteration: $C_i = P_i \oplus K_i$, where r range from 1 to r. The result output in the last round is the final cipher text C.

(4) Data Decryption Process

- *Initial Decryption*

$P_r = C \oplus K_r$, where C is the 64-bit cipher text, K_r is the last 8 bytes of the expanded key.

- *r-round Decryption*

For i within $[1, r]$, each round of iteration has the following three steps:

Firstly, perform pseudorandom transformation on each byte of the data using the decryption S-box: $M_i(j) = S^{-1}[P_{i+1}(j)]$, where i range from 1 to r, $X_i(j)$ denotes the j byte of X_i, $0 \le j \le 7$.

Secondly, arrange the 64-bit data M_i into a 8 * 8 matrix, perform pseudorandom transformation on each diagonal line of M_i using the decryption S-box

$$C_i(0) = S^{-1}\{[M_i(0)\&128|[M_i(7)\&64]|[M_i(6)\&32]|[M_i(5)\&16]$$
$$|[M_i(4)\&8]|[M_i(3)\&4]|[M_i(2)\&2]|[M_i(1)\&1]\}$$

$$C_i(1) = S^{-1}\{[M_i(1)\&128|[M_i(0)\&64]|[M_i(7)\&32]|[M_i(6)\&16]$$
$$|[M_i(5)\&8]|[M_i(4)\&4]|[M_i(3)\&2]|[M_i(2)\&1]\}$$

$$C_i(2) = S^{-1}\{[M_i(2)\&128|[M_i(1)\&64]|[M_i(0)\&32]|[M_i(7)\&16]$$
$$|[M_i(6)\&8]|[M_i(5)\&4]|[M_i(4)\&2]|[M_i(3)\&1]\}$$

$$C_i(3) = S^{-1}\{[M_i(3)\&128|[M_i(2)\&64]|[M_i(1)\&32]|[M_i(0)\&16]$$
$$|[M_i(7)\&8]|[M_i(6)\&4]|[M_i(5)\&2]|[M_i(4)\&1]\}$$

$$C_i(4) = S^{-1}\{[M_i(4)\&128|[M_i(3)\&64]|[M_i(2)\&32]|[M_i(1)\&16]$$
$$|[M_i(0)\&8]|[M_i(7)\&4]|[M_i(6)\&2]|[M_i(5)\&1]\}$$

$$C_i(5) = S^{-1}\{[M_i(5)\&128|[M_i(4)\&64]|[M_i(3)\&32]|[M_i(2)\&16]$$
$$|[M_i(1)\&8]|[M_i(0)\&4]|[M_i(7)\&2]|[M_i(6)\&1]\}$$

$$C_i(6) = S^{-1}\{[M_i(6)\&128|[M_i(5)\&64]|[M_i(4)\&32]|[M_i(3)\&16]$$
$$|[M_i(2)\&8]|[M_i(1)\&4]|[M_i(0)\&2]|[M_i(7)\&1]\}$$

$$C_i(7) = S^{-1}\{[M_i(7)\&128|[M_i(6)\&64]|[M_i(5)\&32]|[M_i(4)\&16]$$
$$|[M_i(3)\&8]|[M_i(2)\&4]|[M_i(1)\&2]|[M_i(0)\&1]\}$$

Finally, obtain the plain text of the current iteration by performing XOR operation on the output C_i above and the sub-key K_i of the current round: $P_i = C_i \oplus K_i$, where i range from 1 to r. The result output in the last round is the final plain text P_0.

3   Performance Evaluation

3.1   Software Implementations

The implementation performance of VH with the 80-bit key is tested by using the C language in the environment of Intel(R) Core(TM) i7-3610QM 2.3 GHz CPU and 8 GB memory. Six million bits of data is selected from 1 million bits of data. The time consumption of VH-80 is shown in Fig. 3. The software efficiency of VH-80 is computed to be 44.47 Mb/s.

From the comparison with existing lightweight block cipher algorithms MIBS, CLEFIA and PRESENT, it can be seen that the software implementation of VH consumes much less time than other algorithms [10, 11]. The software efficiency of VH-80, MIBS, CLEFIA-128 and PRESENT is 44.47 Mb/s, 33.26 Mb/s, 33.90 Mb/s and 0.98 Mb/s respectively, which are shown in Table 1. It can be observed that VH-80 outperforms other algorithms in terms of software efficiency.

3.2   Hardware Performance

Efficiency of hardware implementation is usually measured by the equivalent number of GE. The number of GE needed to achieve hardware implementation of CLEFIA-128 was estimated in reference [5]. The authors reported that 5979 GE were required to

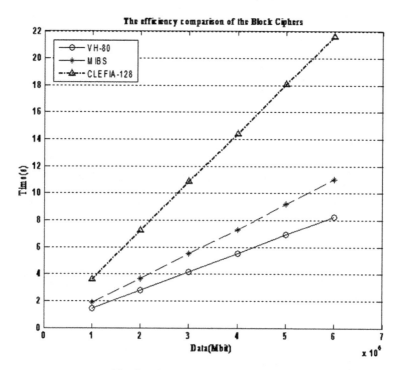

Fig. 3. Time consumption of VH-80

implement CLEFIA-128, neglecting the effect of different ASIC libraries. The authors in reference stated that 6 GE were needed to store 1 bit, and 2.67 GE were required for a XOR operation [9].

For key expansion of VH-80, it requires 8 XOR gates or 21.36 GE to perform a XOR operation; a 64-bit sub-key needs to be stored during each round, totaling 384 GE. It requires 384 GE to store the 64-bit plain text during encryption; the S-box demands 200 GE; 384 GE are needed to store the 64-bit cipher text generated during each round; the encryption process requires 704 AND gates, totaling 936.32 GE; 616 OR gates are used, totaling 819.28 GE; the XOR operation needs to be performed on the cipher text and the sub-key during each round, demanding 12 XOR gates, totaling 53.4 GE. The number of gate circuits needed by VH and other lightweight block cipher algorithms is given in Table 2. Compared with CLEFIA which needs 5979 GE for hardware implementation, VH only demands 3182 GE. It demonstrates that hardware

Table 1. Comparison of lightweight block cipher implementations

Algorithm	Software efficiency (Mb/s)	Hardware efficiency (GE)
VH-80	44.47	3182
MIBS	33.26	1400
CLEFIA-128	33.90	5979
PRESENT	0.98	1570

efficiency of VH is higher than CLEFIA which is an international standard also designed for the 8-bit platform.

4 Security Evaluation

4.1 Differential Cryptanalysis and Linear Cryptanalysis

Differential cryptanalysis and linear cryptanalysis have been the most effective attack against block cipher [12–14]. Hence, it is absolutely necessary to determine the maximum portability of differential a cryptanalysis and linear cryptanalysis to evaluate the security of a block cipher. Currently, any new block cipher algorithm is expected to have the ability to resist these two attacks. Differential cryptanalysis and linear cryptanalysis have been extensively studied since their birth. The authors in reference detailed the method for evaluating a cipher's resistance against differential and linear cryptanalysis, and proposed to compute the maximum differential and linear probability by counting the number of dynamic S-boxes [15–19]. This method was used by reference to evaluate CLEFIA [5]. Evaluation of other block cipher algorithms like AES and Camellia is also based on this method.

The maximum differential probability of VH's S-box is computed to be $2^{-4.415}$. The number DS of dynamic S-boxes for the first ten rounds of VH with a key of 80-bit long, is computed by using the program, which is shown in Table 2. It can be observed that the 4-round maximum differential probability of VH is $DCP^{4r}_{max} \leq 2^{21*(-4.415)} = 2^{-67.92} \leq 2^{-64}$. When the number round is larger than 4, no effective differential characteristic is found for cryptanalysis. So the full-round VH can resist differential cryptanalysis.

The maximum linear probability of VH's S-box is computed to be $2^{-2.83}$. The number LS of dynamic S-boxes for the first ten rounds of VH with a key of 80-bit long, is computed by using the program, which is shown in Table 2. It can be observed that the 4-round maximum linear probability of VH is $LCP^{4r}_{max} \leq 2^{24*(-2.83)} = 2^{-67.62} \leq 2^{-64}$. When the number of round is larger than 4, no effective linear characteristic is found for cryptanalysis. So the full-round VH can resist linear cryptanalysis.

Table 2. Guaranteed number of active S-boxes of VH

Rounds	DS	LS	Rounds	DS	LS
1	0	0	6	35	40
2	7	8	7	42	48
3	14	16	8	49	56
4	21	24	9	56	64
5	28	32	10	63	72

4.2 Impossible Differential Cryptanalysis

Impossible differential cryptanalysis is a very effective attack against VH. J. Kim proposed a moment algorithm $\mu - method$ to perform impossible differential cryptanalysis of the structure of the block cipher [20–22]. Their method can find different impossible differential paths. Impossible differential cryptanalysis of VH is carried out by using this method, determining the maximum number of rounds is 6, finding 8 non-differential paths.

$$0,0,0,\alpha,0,\alpha,\alpha,\alpha \xrightarrow{6r}_{\not\rightarrow} (0,0,0,0,\alpha,\alpha,\alpha,\alpha) \quad p=1$$

$$0,0,\alpha,0,\alpha,\alpha,\alpha,0 \xrightarrow{6r}_{\not\rightarrow} (0,0,0,0,\alpha,\alpha,\alpha,\alpha) \quad p=1$$

$$0,\alpha,0,\alpha,\alpha,\alpha,0,0 \xrightarrow{6r}_{\not\rightarrow} (0,0,0,\alpha,\alpha,\alpha,\alpha,0) \quad p=1$$

$$0,\alpha,\alpha,\alpha,0,0,0,\alpha \xrightarrow{6r}_{\not\rightarrow} (0,\alpha,\alpha,\alpha,\alpha,0,0,0) \quad p=1$$

$$\alpha,0,0,0,\alpha,0,\alpha,\alpha \xrightarrow{6r}_{\not\rightarrow} (\alpha,\alpha,0,0,0,0,\alpha,\alpha) \quad p=1$$

$$\alpha,0,\alpha,\alpha,\alpha,0,0,0 \xrightarrow{6r}_{\not\rightarrow} (0,0,\alpha,\alpha,0,0,0,0) \quad p=1$$

$$\alpha,\alpha,0,0,0,\alpha,0,\alpha \xrightarrow{6r}_{\not\rightarrow} (\alpha,\alpha,\alpha,0,0,0,0,\alpha) \quad p=1$$

$$\alpha,\alpha,\alpha,0,0,0,\alpha,0 \xrightarrow{6r}_{\not\rightarrow} (\alpha,\alpha,\alpha,\alpha,0,0,0,0) \quad p=1$$

Where $\alpha \in GF(2^8)$ denotes the non-zero differential. Therefore, impossible differential cryptanalysis is invalid for VH.

5 Conclusion

A new lightweight block cipher based on dual pseudo-random transformation is proposed in this paper for the low-cost embedded mobile terminals in wireless communication. The encryption transformation table $S[256]$ is generated to perform row wise pseudo-random transformation and diagonal pseudo-random transformation, achieving confusion and diffusion. Comparison with other lightweight block cipher algorithms (i.e. MIBS, CLEFIA, and PRESENT) in software implementation shows that VH performs much better. Comparison with other lightweight block cipher algorithms in hardware implementation indicates that VH needs 3182 GE, less than 5979 GE of the international standard CLEFIA. In terms of software and hardware efficiency, VH outperforms the international standard CLEFIA also designed for the 8-bit platform overall. Security of VH is analyzed and verified by performing dependence test, differential and linear cryptanalysis as well as impossible differential cryptanalysis.

References

1. Wu, W., Feng, D., Zhang, W.: Design and Analysis of Block Cipher (in Chinese). TsingHua University Press, Beijing (2009)
2. Daemen, J., Rijmen, V.: The Design of Rijndael: AES-the Advanced Encryption Standard. Springer, Heidelberg (2002)
3. Feng, D., Zhang, M., Zhang, Y.: Study on cloud computing security (in Chinese). J. Journal of Software. **22**, 71–83 (2011)
4. Lu, F., Wu, H.: The research of trust evaluation based on cloud model. J. Eng. Sci. **10**, 84–90 (2008)
5. Shirai, T., Shibutani, K., Akishita, T., Moriai, S., Iwata, T.: The 128-Bit Blockcipher CLEFIA (Extended Abstract). In: Biryukov, A. (ed.) FSE 2007. LNCS, vol. 4593, pp. 181–195. Springer, Heidelberg (2007)
6. Tsunoo, Y., Tsujihara, E., Shigeri, M., Saito, T., Suzaki, T., Kubo, H.: Impossible differential cryptanalysis of CLEFIA. In: Nyberg, K. (ed.) FSE 2008. LNCS, vol. 5086, pp. 398–411. Springer, Heidelberg (2008)
7. Juels, A., Weis, S.A.: Authenticating pervasive devices with human protocols. In: Shoup, V. (ed.) CRYPTO 2005. LNCS, vol. 3621, pp. 293–308. Springer, Heidelberg (2005)
8. Bogdanov, A.A., Knudsen, L.R., Leander, G., Paar, C., Poschmann, A., Robshaw, M., Seurin, Y., Vikkelsoe, C.: PRESENT: an ultra-lightweight block cipher. In: Paillier, P., Verbauwhede, I. (eds.) CHES 2007. LNCS, vol. 4727, pp. 450–466. Springer, Heidelberg (2007)
9. Özen, O., Varıcı, K., Tezcan, C., Kocair, Ç.: Lightweight block ciphers revisited: cryptanalysis of reduced round PRESENT and HIGHT. In: Boyd, C., González Nieto, J. (eds.) ACISP 2009. LNCS, vol. 5594, pp. 90–107. Springer, Heidelberg (2009)
10. Izadi, M., Sadeghiyan, B., Sadeghian, S.: MIBS: a new lightweight block cipher. In: Garay, J.A., Miyaji, A., Otsuka, A. (eds.) CANS 2009. LNCS, vol. 5888, pp. 334–348. Springer, Heidelberg (2009)
11. Bay, A., Nakahara Jr., J., Vaudenay, S.: Cryptanalysis of reduced-round MIBS block cipher. In: Heng, S.-H., Wright, R.N., Goi, B.-M. (eds.) CANS 2010. LNCS, vol. 6467, pp. 1–19. Springer, Heidelberg (2010)
12. Biham, E., Shamir, A.: Differential Cryptanalysis of The Data Encryption Standard. Springer, New York (1993)
13. Su, B., Wu, W., Zhang, W.: Differential cryptanalysis of SMS4 block cipher. In: IACR, Cryptology Eprint Archive (2010)
14. Matsui, Mitsuru: Linear Cryptanalysis Method for DES Cipher. In: Helleseth, Tor (ed.) EUROCRYPT 1993. LNCS, vol. 765, pp. 386–397. Springer, Heidelberg (1994)
15. Kanda, M., Takashima, Y., Matsumoto, T., Aoki, K., Ohta, K.: A strategy for constructing fast round functions with practical security against differential and linear cryptanalysis. In: Tavares, S., Meijer, H. (eds.) SAC 1998. LNCS, vol. 1556, pp. 264–279. Springer, Heidelberg (1999)
16. Kanda, M.: Practical security evaluation against differential and linear cryptanalysis for Feistel ciphers with SPN round function. In: Stinson, D.R., Tavares, S. (eds.) SAC 2000. LNCS, vol. 2012, pp. 324–338. Springer, Heidelberg (2012)
17. Hong, S.H., Lee, S.-J., Lim, J.-I., Sung, J., Cheon, D.H., Cho, I.: Provable security against differential and linear cryptanalysis for the SPN structure. In: Schneier, B. (ed.) FSE 2000. LNCS, vol. 1978, pp. 273–283. Springer, Heidelberg (2001)

18. Liu, F., Ji, W., Hu, L., Ding, J., Lv, S., Pyshkin, A., Weinmann, R.-P.: Analysis of the SMS4 block cipher. In: Pieprzyk, J., Ghodosi, H., Dawson, E. (eds.) ACISP 2007. LNCS, vol. 4586, pp. 158–170. Springer, Heidelberg (2007)

19. Ojha, S.K., Kumar, N., Jain, K., Sangeeta, : TWIS – a lightweight block cipher. In: Prakash, A., Sen Gupta, I. (eds.) ICISS 2009. LNCS, vol. 5905, pp. 280–291. Springer, Heidelberg (2009)

20. Biham, E., Biryukov, A., Shamir, A.: Cryptanalysis of Skipjack reduced to 31 rounds using impossible differentials. In: Stern, J. (ed.) EUROCRYPT 1999. LNCS, vol. 1592, pp. 12–23. Springer, Heidelberg (1999)

21. Zhang, W., Wu, W., Zhang, L., Feng, D.: Improved related-key impossible differential attacks on reduced-round AES-192. In: Biham, E., Youssef, A.M. (eds.) SAC 2006. LNCS, vol. 4356, pp. 15–27. Springer, Heidelberg (2007)

22. Kim, J.-S., Hong, S.H., Sung, J., Lee, S.-J., Lim, J.-I., Sung, S.H.: Impossible differential cryptanalysis for block cipher structures. In: Johansson, T., Maitra, S. (eds.) INDOCRYPT 2003. LNCS, vol. 2904, pp. 82–96. Springer, Heidelberg (2003)

Security Against Hardware Trojan Attacks Through a Novel Chaos FSM and Delay Chains Array PUF Based Design Obfuscation Scheme

Mingfu Xue[1,2,3]([⊠]), Jian Wang[1], Youdong Wang[2], and Aiqun Hu[2]

[1] College of Computer Science and Technology,
Nanjing University of Aeronautics and Astronautics, Nanjing 210016, China
{mingfu.xue,wangjian}@nuaa.edu.cn
[2] School of Information Science and Engineering,
Southeast University, Nanjing 210096, China
sniper1432@163.com, aqhu@seu.edu.cn
[3] Information Technology Research Base of Civil Aviation Administration
of China, Civil Aviation University of China, Tianjin 300300, China

Abstract. Hardware Trojan has emerged as a major security concern for integrated circuits. This paper presents a novel design obfuscation scheme against hardware Trojan attacks based on chaos finite state machine (FSM) and delay chains array physical unclonable function (PUF). We exploits the pseudo-random characteristics of the *M-sequences* to propose a chaos FSM design method which can generate exponentially many random states and transitions to obfuscate the chip's functional states with low overhead. The chip's functionalities are locked and obfuscated and would not be functional without a unique key that can only be computed by the designer. We also propose a new PUF construction method, named delay chains array PUF (DAPUF), to extract the unique power-up state for each chip which is corresponding to a unique key sequence. We introduce confusions between delay chains to achieve avalanche effects of the PUF outputs. Thus the proposed DAPUF approach can provide large number of PUF instances with high accuracy and reverse-engineering resistant. Through the proposed obfuscation scheme, the designer can control the IC's operation modes (*chaos mode* and *normal mode*) and functionalities, and can also remotely disable the chips when hardware Trojan insertion is revealed. The functional obfuscation prevents the adversary from understanding the real functionalities of the circuit as well as the real rare events in the internal nodes, thus making it difficult for the adversary to insert hard-to-detect Trojans. It also makes the inserted Trojans become invalid since the Trojans are most likely inserted in the *chaos mode* and will be activated only in the *chaos mode*. Both simulation experiments on benchmark circuits and hardware evaluations on FPGA show the security, low overhead and practicality of the proposed method.

Keywords: Hardware Trojan · Design obfuscation · Chaos FSM · Delay chains array PUF

© Springer International Publishing Switzerland 2015
Z. Huang et al. (Eds.): ICCCS 2015, LNCS 9483, pp. 14–24, 2015.
DOI: 10.1007/978-3-319-27051-7_2

1   Introduction

Hardware Trojan attacks have emerged as a major threat for integrated circuits (ICs) [1–3]. A design can be tampered in untrusted design houses or fabrication facilities by inserting hardware Trojans. Hardware Trojans can cause malfunction, undesired functional behaviors, leaking confidential information or other catastrophic consequences in critical systems. Methods against hardware Trojan attacks are badly needed to ensure trust in ICs and system-on-chips (SoCs).

However, hardware Trojans are stealthy by natures which are triggered under rare conditions or specific conditions that can evade post-manufacturing test. Moreover, there are large number of possible Trojan instances the adversary can exploit and many diverse functions of Trojans which makes hardware Trojan detection by logic testing extremely challenging.

Many side-channel signal analysis approaches [4–6] have been proposed to detect hardware Trojans by extracting the parameters of the circuits, e.g. leakage current, transient current, power or delay. However, these methods are very susceptible to process variations and noises. Moreover, the detection sensitivity is greatly reduced for small Trojans in modern ICs with millions of gates. A few regional activation approaches were proposed to magnify Trojan's contributions [7, 8]. However, large numbers of random patterns were applied during detection, while computationally consuming training processes were also used for pattern selection. Besides, these approaches need to alter the original design and add more circuits during design phase which will increase the complexity of the design process and produce a considerable overhead for large designs.

Most of the existing works require golden chips to provide reference signals for hardware Trojan detection. However, obtaining a golden chip is extremely difficult [9]. The golden chips are supposed to be either fabricated by a trusted foundry or verified to be Trojan-free through strict reverse engineering. Both methods are prohibitively expensive. In some scenarios, the golden chips even don't exist, e.g., if the mask is altered at the foundry. Recently, a rare few methods are proposed to detect HT without the golden chips by using self-authentication techniques [9–11]. However, these methods are not without limitations [12]. They always need expensive computations, sophisticated process variation models and a large number of measurements to ensure accuracy for large deigns.

R.S. Chakraborty et al. propose an application of design obfuscation against hardware Trojan attacks [13, 14]. However, the key sequence is the same for all the chips from the same design which makes the approach itself vulnerable to various kinds of attacks, e.g. the fab can use the key to unlock all the chips and then tamper or overbuild the chips arbitrarily. The fab or the user can also release the key sequence of the design in the public domain which makes the chip vulnerable to reverse-engineering attacks. Besides, the procedure of determination of unreachable states is also time consuming and computationally complex.

This paper presents a novel design obfuscation scheme against hardware Trojan attacks based on chaos finite state machine (FSM) and delay chains array physical unclonable function (PUF). The obfuscation scheme is realized by hiding and locking the original FSM using exponentially many chaotic states. We exploits the pseudo-random characteristics of the *M-sequences* [15] to propose a chaos FSM design method which can generate many random states and transitions with low overhead. The chip is obfuscated and would not be functional without a unique key that can only be computed by the designer. We also propose a new PUF construction method, named delay chains array PUF (DAPUF), to extract the unique signature of each chip. Each chip has a unique key sequence corresponding to the power-up state. We introduce confusions between delay chains to achieve avalanche effects of the PUF outputs. Thus the proposed DAPUF can provide large number of PUF instances with high accuracy and reverse-engineering resistant. Through the proposed scheme, the designer can control the IC's operation modes (*chaos mode* and *normal mode*) and functionalities, and can also remotely disable the chips when hardware Trojan is revealed. The functional obfuscation prevents the adversary from understanding the real functionalities of the circuit as well as the real rare events in the internal nodes, thus making it difficult for the adversary to insert hard-to-detect Trojans. It also makes the inserted Trojans become invalid since the Trojans are most likely inserted in the *chaos mode* which will be activated only in the *chaos mode*. Both simulation experiments on benchmark circuits and hardware evaluations on FPGA platforms show the security, low overhead and practicality of the proposed method.

2 Overall Flow

First, the designer exploits the high level design description to form the FSM. Then, the original FSM is modified based on the nonlinear combination of the *M-sequences* to generate the chaos FSM which adds exponentially many random states and transitions to obfuscate the functional states. Then, the DAPUF module is constructed to generate the unique signature of each IC. After the subsequent design procedures are performed, the foundry will receive necessary information to fabricate the chips. Each chip is locked upon fabrication. In the proposed chaos FSM construction scheme, up to 2^{20} chaotic states are added, so the functional states of the chip are submerged in a large number of chaotic states. When the chip is powered on, it will be a great probability to fall into the chaotic states thus is non-functional, named *chaos mode*.

Then, the foundry applies the set of challenge inputs to the PUF unit on each chip and sends the PUF response to the designer. Each PUF response is corresponding to a unique power-up state. The designer who masters the *M-sequences* and transition table is the only entity who can compute the passkey to make the chip enter into functional states. After applying the passkey, the locked IC will traverse a set of transitions and reach to the functional reset state. Then the IC is unlocked and becoming functional, called *normal mode*.

Figure 1 shows the proposed design obfuscation scheme. In this sample, there are 8 states in the original FSM. 24 chaotic states are generated adding to the original FSM. 4 black hole states are introduced to enable the designer to disable the chips when needed. The DAPUF module generates a unique identifier for each chip corresponding to a unique power-up state. The power-up state is most likely to fall into the chaos FSM making the chip nonfunctional until an IC-unique passkey is applied. The passkey can make the chip traverse through a set of transitions and reach to the functional reset state.

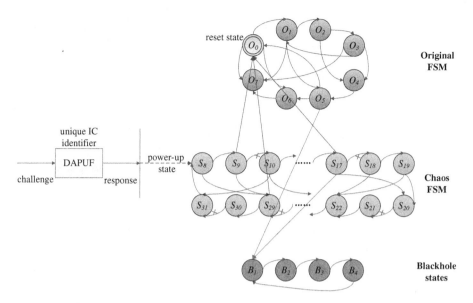

Fig. 1. The chaos FSM and DAPUF based design obfuscation scheme against hardware Trojans

3   Chaos FSM Construction

We define the following symbols for discussion:

$O_0, O_1, O_2 \ldots, O_{n_o - 1}$	The original FSM states (O_0 is the reset state)
$S_{n_o}, S_{n_o + 1}, \ldots, S_{n_0 + 2^L - 1}$	The added chaotic states
K_{ij}	The required key for traversing from state i to state j
C_{ij}	The connected transition path from state i to state j
D_{ij}	The disconnected path from state i to state j

In this paper, we nonlinearly combine the outputs of the *M-sequences* to generate exponentially many random states and transitions with low overhead. First, we exploit the *M-sequences* to construct a circular state transition graph (STG). A simple illustration is shown in Fig. 2. For simplicity, there are only seven chaotic states and one reset state in this illustration while the original FSM are omitted. The state transition paths are denoted as $C_{12}, C_{23} \ldots, C_{ii+1}$, where i is the i_{th} state of the chaotic states generator. There are n_o states in the original FSM of the design. We assume the order of the chaotic states generator has a large value L to ensure $2^L > > n_o$, thus there are $n_o + 2^L$ states in total. When the chip is powered on, it only has a probability of $\frac{n_o}{n_o + 2^L}$ to fall into the functional states. Obviously, this probability is nearly zero.

Second, we perform chaos process of the STG which needs to satisfy the following principles: (1) for any chaotic state S_k, there is at least one transition path C_{ak} to ensure that all the chaotic states are reachable, where a is an arbitrary value; (2) there is a set of transition paths $C_{pi_1}, C_{i_1 i_2}, \ldots, C_{i_m q}$ to ensure that any two chaotic states S_p, S_q can be

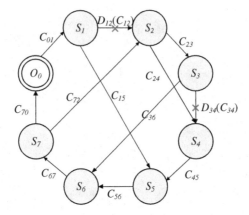

Fig. 2. The state transition graph of the chaos FSM

connected; (3) there is at least one chaotic state can reach the reset state O_0 through one transition C_{iO_0}.

The first step of the chaos process is to add new random transition paths to the existing circular STG. In Fig. 2, that is, adding new C_{ij} where $j \neq i+1$, such as $C_{15}, C_{24}, C_{36}, C_{72}$. The second step is to disconnect several transition paths randomly, that is, replacing C_{ij} with D_{ij}, such as D_{12} and D_{34}. Each time a D_{ij} is added, we should check the connectivity between state i and state j, which means, there is at least one transition path $C_{ii_1}, C_{i_1 i_2}, \ldots, C_{i_m j}$ to connect state i and state j. Otherwise, one need to add the corresponding $C_{i_n i_m}$ to ensure the connectivity.

Suppose the power-up state is S_n, there is one transition path $C_{S_n i_1}, C_{i_1 i_2}, \ldots, C_{i_m O_0}$ to ensure that the power-up state and the reset state O_0 is connected. We can get $O_0 = F\{F \ldots \{F\{S_n, C_{ni_1}, K_{S_n i_1}\} C_{i_1 i_2}, K_{i_1 i_2}\} \ldots C_{i_m O_0}, K_{i_m O_0}\}$. To unlock the chip, the transition key $K_{S_n i_1}, K_{i_1 i_2}, \ldots, K_{i_m O_0}$ is needed. The designer can increase the number of required transition keys to increase the complexity of the key space. Since there is a huge number of chaotic states, adding one transition path will exponentially increase the key space while the added overhead is negligible.

In the chaos FSM construction, the designer can also create black hole states to disable the chip when needed [16]. Black hole states are the states that can't return to functional states regardless of the input sequences. When the fab provide the power-up state to the designer asking for the unlock passkeys, the designer may deliberately provide a specific input sequence to make the chip enter into black hole states rather than reset state once hardware Trojan insertion is revealed.

4   Delay Chains Array PUF Implementation

The changes of chip's operating conditions, including temperature and voltage, etc., will affect physical characteristics of the chip, thus affecting the PUF. The traditional solution is to add redundancy or use the error correcting codes. Two advantages of the proposed DAPUF construction method compared to traditional PUF approaches are: (1) exploiting relative value algorithm rather than absolute value to analyze the results, thus can overcome the impact of chips' working conditions; (2) introducing confusions between delay chains which can result in avalanche effects of the PUF output, thus can generate large number of PUF instances with reverse-engineering resistant.

Zou J. et al. use the delay chain to obtain FPGA gate-level timekeeping and the precision of such delay chain can reach to 1 ns [17]. In this paper, we propose a PUF implementation approach based on delay chains array, named DAPUF.

First, let's consider the one-dimensional delay chain PUF (DPUF). As shown in Fig. 3, the DPUF is constructed by cascading the buffers and the D flip-flops. We use symbol $start$ to represent the high level of the D flip-flop's input signal, while using symbol end to represent the high level of the buffer's input signal. The delay of the buffer is denoted as t_B and the delay of the D flip-flop is denoted as t_D, thus the delay difference between the D flip-flop and the buffer is $\Delta t = t_D - t_B$ (note that $t_D > t_B$). At the beginning, both the input of the D flip-flop chain and the input of the buffer chain are at low level. When the first high level signal $start$ comes, this high level signal will propagate through the D flip-flop chain. After a certain delay T, the end signal will come and propagate along the buffer chain. Because of the delay difference Δt between the D flip-flop and the buffer, when propagating through every stage, the propagation time difference between the $start$ signal and the end signal will reduce Δt. At a certain time, the end signal will catch up with and surpass the $start$ signal.

Due to the intrinsic process variations, each chip has different t_B and t_D. Even within one chip, the delays of different D flip-flops (or buffers) also have tiny differences. Thus, we can define t_{Bn} as the inherent delay of the n_{th} buffer while t'_{Bn} is the difference between t_{Bn} and the expected mean value t_B. Similarly, we define t_{Dn} as the inherent delay of the n_{th} D flip-flop while t'_{Dn} is the difference between t_{Dn} and the expected mean value t_D. Denote σ as the random noise. Generally, Δt_n, σ satisfy the normal distribution with a certain expectation, thus we can get $t_{Bn} = t_B + t'_{Bn} + \sigma$ and $t_{Dn} = t_D + t'_{Dn} + \sigma$ under noise condition. Further more, we can get:

$$\sum_{n=1}^{k_B} (t_B + t'_{Bn} + \sigma) + T = \sum_{n=1}^{k_D} (t_D + t'_{Dn} + \sigma) \tag{1}$$

In which, k_B and k_D are the number of propagated buffers and the number of propagated D flip-flops when the end signal catches up with the $start$ signal. We can obtain the tuple (k_B, k_D) through the time discriminator. This tuple (k_B, k_D) is unique for each chip and physically stochastic.

We define m groups of input signals as $\{X_1, Y_1, T_1\}, \ldots, \{X_m, Y_m, T_m\}$, where $X_1, X_2, \ldots, X_m$ represent the high level input signals of the D flip-flop, $Y_1, Y_2, \ldots, Y_m$ represent the high level input signals of the buffer, and $T_1, T_2, \ldots, T_m$ represent the time difference between input signal X_g and Y_g, $1 \leq g \leq m$. Let's define:

$$(k_{gB}, k_{gD}) = W\{X_g, Y_g, T_g\} \tag{2}$$

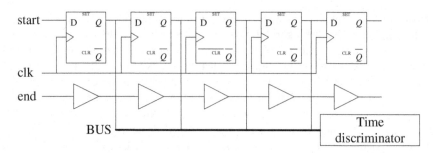

Fig. 3. The structure of the one-dimensional delay chain PUF (DPUF)

where $W\{X_g, Y_g, T_g\}$ represents the delay chain's response to the g_{th} group of input signals. k_{gB} and k_{gD} are the number of propagated buffers and the number of propagated D flip-flops when the signal Y_g catches up with the signal X_g. Thus, we can obtain a group of tuples $\{(k_{1B}, k_{1D}), (k_{2B}, k_{2D}), \ldots, (k_{mB}, k_{mD})\}$ based on the response of the DPUF. Then, we can extract the PUF characteristic vector:

$$
\vec{E} = [(k_{2B}, k_{2D}) - (k_{1B}, k_{1D}), (k_{3B}, k_{3D}) - (k_{2B}, k_{2D}), \ldots, (k_{mB}, k_{mD}) \\
- (k_{(m-1)B}, k_{(m-1)D})]
$$

(3)

In which, $\vec{E}$ is the power-up state of the chip. Generally, one can consider that the working conditions of different regions within one chip are the same. We use relative value for characterization can eliminate the effect of working conditions.

However, there are some shortages if we only use one-dimensional delay chain PUF (DPUF). Since the precision is only 1 ns, the physical unique characteristic of each chip is quantified by this precision. Thus, the number of possible PUF instances is reduced due to this limitation. However, less PUF instances may cause the collision problem, which means two chips with different characteristics may have the same DPUF after quantified. Therefore, this paper proposes delay chains array PUF (DAPUF) which can magnify the delay differences thus significantly increase the number of PUF instances.

The block diagram of the proposed DAPUF is shown in Fig. 4. $I_1, I_2, \ldots, I_{2h}$ represent the rising edges of the input signals, in which, h is the number of delay chains. We add confusions between delay chains by the configuration of Con_{ij}. Con_{ij} represents whether the node in row i column j is connected. In other words, it satisfies:

$$
Con_{ij} = \begin{cases} 1 \ connected \\ 0 \ disconnected \end{cases}
$$
. Obviously, the coming moment of the rising edge in each

node $P_{i_0 j_0}$ depends on the values of all $Con_{ij}(i < i_0, j < j_0)$. It's illustrated in a simple example, as shown in Fig. 4, since $Con_{11}, Con_{22}, Con_{31}$ are 1, the time of the rising edge in node P_{23} is affected by I_1, I_2 and I_3. The time discriminator will detect the first (k_B, k_D) rising edges of each delay chain, and extract the corresponding characteristic vector $\vec{E}$. The final DAPUF characteristic vector is $\{\vec{E}_1, \vec{E}_2, \cdots, \vec{E}_h\}$. Obviously, the configurations of the Con_{ij} significantly magnify the delay differences between delay chains and greatly increases the number of PUF instances with avalanche effects.

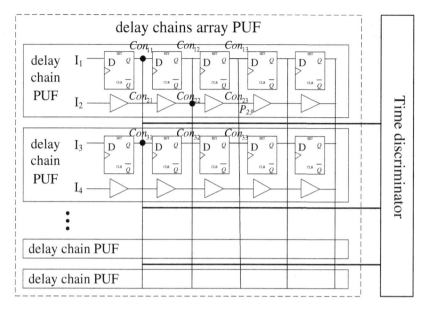

Fig. 4. The structure of the proposed delay chains array PUF (DAPUF)

5   Simulation and Hardware Implementation Evaluation

Simulation experiments are performed on a set of ISCAS89 benchmark circuits while the hardware evaluations are based on the CC1200 wireless transmitter control circuit implemented on Altera EP2C8Q208C8 FPGA platforms.

Figure 5 shows the test waveforms of the one-dimensional DPUF. The rising edges are the *start* signal propagating in the D flip-flop chain and the *end* signal in the buffer chain, respectively. Obviously, at a certain moment, the *end* signal catches up with and surpasses the *start* signal. We can get the tuple (k_B, k_D) of this moment through the time discriminator.

There are m groups of input signals in each delay chain thus there are m groups of (k_B, k_D) and we can calculate $\vec{E}$ of the DPUF. For the delay chains array PUF (DAPUF), there are h delay chains in total and we can obtain $m \cdot h$ groups of (k_B, k_D) through the time discriminator and we can calculate the characteristic vector $\{\vec{E}_1, \vec{E}_2, \cdots, \vec{E}_h\}$. The characteristic vector is corresponding to the unique power-up state of the chip.

Figure 6 shows the test waveforms of the proposed obfuscation scheme. Note that, the state transition waveform is only a simple illustration to show the chaotic states transitions, which contains only seven chaotic states and one reset state. The real chaos FSM is much bigger than this sample thus is not convenient to present in this waveform. As shown in the figure, when the chip is powered on, it falls into a chaotic state and will traverse in the chaos FSM. The states of the chaos FSM are chaotic and unpredictable. When a wrong passkey is applied, the module starts to perform passkey identification. Since this is a wrong passkey, after the passkey identification, the chip continues to traverse in the chaos FSM until the correct passkey (00010100100100 001100111100000001) is applied. Then the module performs passkey identification again. The chaos FSM will traverse to the reset state "000" through several transition paths and the chip is unlocked. Then, the chip will enter into the *normal mode*.

Table 1 shows the overhead of the proposed scheme on ISCAS89 benchmark circuits as well as the CC1200 wireless transmitter control circuit. The overhead has two main parts, the DAPUF construction and the chaos FSM implementation. The DAPUF module in our experiments consists of 28 delay chains with each delay chain contains 10 buffers and 8 D flip-flops. The results show that this DAPUF module costs 156 logic elements (LE). We use a large scale DAPUF in the experiment to ensure obtaining massive PUF instances and strong avalanche effects. The overhead of the chaos FSM implementation mainly comes from the polynomial coefficients of the *M-sequences*, the added transition paths table, and the storage of the passkeys. In this paper, there are 2^{20} chaotic states and the unlocking process needs 4 passkeys with each key is 128 bit long. Note that, in related works, the PUF weren't included in the evaluations. If we remove the overhead of the DAPUF, the overhead of the scheme is rather small. It is shown that when the circuit's size becomes larger, the overhead becomes much smaller. For modern circuits with millions of gates, the overhead of the scheme is negligible.

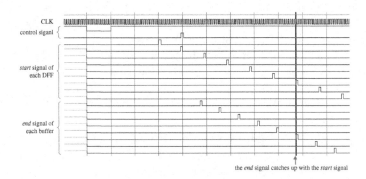

Fig. 5. The test waveform of the DPUF

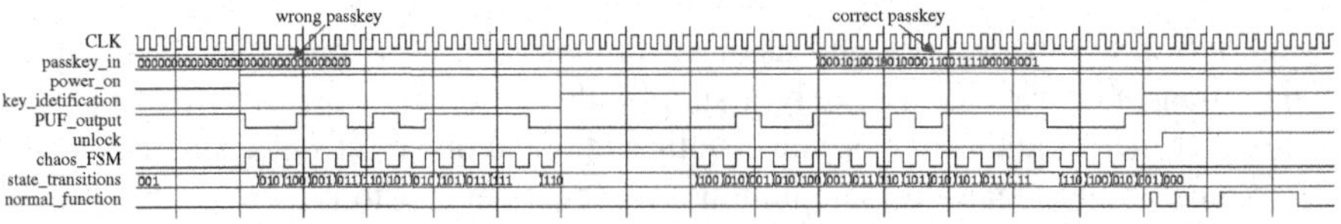

Fig. 6. The test waveform of the proposed obfuscation scheme

Table 1. Overhead of the proposed obfuscation scheme

Circuit	Orig. LE	Overall added LE	Overall overhead (%)	Added LE without PUF	Overhead without PUF (%)
s526	35	232	662.9	76	217.1
s1494	175	248	141.7	92	52.6
s5318	417	226	54.2	70	16.8
s15850	796	256	32.2	100	12.6
s38584	2207	252	11.4	96	4.3
CC1200 cir.	5508	266	4.8	110	2

6 Conclusion

We have developed a novel design obfuscation scheme against hardware Trojan attacks based on chaos FSM and DAPUF. We propose a chaos FSM design method which can generate many random states to obfuscate the original FSM. We also propose a new PUF construction method obtaining large number of PUF instances with avalanche effects. Through the proposed scheme, the designer can control the IC's operation modes and functionalities, and can remotely disable the chips. The obfuscation prevents the adversary from understanding the real function and the real rare events of the circuit, thus making it difficult to insert Trojans. It also makes the inserted Trojans become invalid since they are most likely inserted in the *chaos mode* which will be activated only in the *chaos mode*.

Acknowledgments. This work is supported by Natural Science Foundation of Jiangsu Province, Chinese Postdoctoral Science Foundation, Jiangsu Province Postdoctoral Science Foundation, and Open Project Foundation of Information Technology Research Base of Civil Aviation Administration of China (NO. CAAC-ITRB-201405).

References

1. Bhunia, S., Hsiao, M.S., Banga, M., Narasimhan, S.: Hardware Trojan attacks: threat analysis and countermeasures. Proc. IEEE **102**(8), 1229–1247 (2014)
2. Rostami, M., Koushanfar, F., Karri, R.: A primer on hardware security: models, methods, and metrics. Proc. IEEE **102**(8), 1283–1295 (2014)
3. Bhunia, S., Abramovici, M., Agarwal, D., Bradley, P., Hsiao, M.S., Plusquellic, J., Tehranipoor, M.: Protection against hardware Trojan attacks: towards a comprehensive solution. IEEE Des. Test **30**(3), 6–17 (2013)
4. Agrawal, D., Baktır, S., Karakoyunlu, D., Rohatgi, P., Sunar, B.: Trojan detection using IC fingerprinting. In: Proceedings of IEEE Symposium on Security and Privacy (SP 2007), pp. 296–310. Berkeley, California, 20–23 May 2007
5. Nowroz, A.N., Hu, K., Koushanfar, F., Reda, S.: Novel techniques for high-sensitivity hardware Trojan detection using thermal and power maps. IEEE Trans. Comput.-Aided Des. Integr. Circuits Syst. **33**(12), 1792–1805 (2014)

6. Potkonjak, M., Nahapetian, A., Nelson, M., Massey, T.: Hardware Trojan horse detection using gate-level characterization. In: 46th Design Automation Conference (DAC 2009), pp. 688–693. San Francisco, California, USA, 26–31 July 2009
7. Banga, M., Hsiao, M.S.: A region based approach for the identification of hardware Trojans. In: IEEE International Workshop on Hardware-Oriented Security and Trust (HOST 2008), pp. 40–47. Anaheim, CA, 9–9 June 2008
8. Wei, S., Potkonjak, M.: Scalable hardware Trojan diagnosis. IEEE Trans. Very Large Scale Integr. VLSI Syst. **20**(6), 1049–1057 (2012)
9. Davoodi, A., Li, M., Tehranipoor, M.: A sensor-assisted self-authentication framework for hardware Trojan detection. IEEE Des. Test **30**(5), 74–82 (2013)
10. Wei, S., Potkonjak, M.: Self-consistency and consistency-based detection and diagnosis of malicious circuitry. IEEE Trans. Very Large Scale Integr. VLSI Syst. **22**(9), 1845–1853 (2014)
11. Xiao, K., Forte, D., Tehranipoor, M.: A novel built-in self-authentication technique to prevent inserting hardware Trojans. IEEE Trans. Comput. Aided Des. Integr. Circuits Syst. **33**(12), 1778–1791 (2014)
12. Cao, Y., Chang, C.-H., Chen, S.: A cluster-based distributed active current sensing circuit for hardware Trojan detection. IEEE Trans. Inf. Forensics Secur. **9**(12), 2220–2231 (2014)
13. Chakraborty, R.S., Bhunia, S.: Security against hardware Trojan through a novel application of design obfuscation. In: IEEE/ACM International Conference on Computer-Aided Design (ICCAD), pp. 113–116. San Jose, California, 2–5 November 2009
14. Chakraborty, R.S., Bhunia, S.: Security against hardware Trojan attacks using key-based design obfuscation. J. Electron. Test. **27**, 767–785 (2011). Springer
15. Klapper, A., Goresky, M.: 2-Adic shift registers. In: Anderson, R. (ed.) FSE 1993. LNCS, vol. 809. Springer, Heidelberg (1994)
16. Alkabani, Y.M., Koushanfar, F.: Active hardware metering for intellectual property protection and security. In: Proceedings of USENIX Security Symposium, pp. 291–306. Berkeley, CA, USA (2007)
17. Zou, J., Yu, W., Chen, Q.: Resolution of time-interval measurement based on chain delay difference of FPGA (in Chinese). Opt. Optoelectron. Technol. **12**(5), 43–45 (2014)

Secure and Efficient Protocol for Outsourcing Large-Scale Systems of Linear Equations to the Cloud

Cheng Qian[1,2]([✉]) and Jian Wang[1]

[1] College of Computer Science and Technology,
Nanjing University of Aeronautics and Astronautics, Nanjing 210016, China
{SX1316062,wangjian}@nuaa.edu.cn
[2] Information Technology Research Base of Civil Aviation Administration of China,
Civil Aviation University of China, Tianjin 300300, China

Abstract. Cloud services enables clients using their limited resources to economically enjoy the massive computational power and storage of the public cloud. Nevertheless, this promising computing services inevitably brings in new threats and challenges, for example, input and output data privacy and cheating detection. Since large-scale systems of linear equations(LSLE) is widely rooted in many engineer and scientific applications. In this paper, for the first time, we utilize two non-colluding cloud servers to propose practical protocol for secure outsourcing LSLE in the fully malicious model. The new approach employs some efficient linear transformations but no expensive homomorphic encryptions system. Extensive theoretical analysis and the experimental evaluation demonstrates the correctness, efficiency, security and checkability of the method. In addition, compared with the existing algorithms, the protocol is superior in both efficiency and security.

Keywords: Cloud computing · Privacy · Secure outsourcing · Linear equations

1 Introduction

With the rapid development of cloud services in business and scientific application, it has become an increasingly important trend to provide service-oriented computing service, which is more economical than traditional IT service. Computation outsourcing enables a client with relatively weak computing power to give out a hard computational task to some servers with more powerful computing power and sufficient computing resources. Then the servers are expected to fulfill the computation and return the result correctly. Such a computing model is especially suitable for cloud computing, in which a client can buy a computation server from a cloud server provider in a pay-per-go [1] manner. This computational framework enables customers receive the correct results, rather than purchasing, provisioning, and maintaining their own computing resources.

© Springer International Publishing Switzerland 2015
Z. Huang et al. (Eds.): ICCCS 2015, LNCS 9483, pp. 25–37, 2015.
DOI: 10.1007/978-3-319-27051-7_3

Linear Equations computation (LSLE) $Ax = b$ [2]is one of the most basic computation problems in linear algebra computations and widely used in many scientific and engineering fields. For example, LSLE plays a significant role in computer graphics, such as 3D graphics rendering and 3D simulations [15], and LSLE is employed to model linear system [16]. In practice, there are many realistic applications can generate enormous scale and extremely dense systems of linear equations with up to hundreds of thousands or even millions unknown variables. For example, if each element of the matrix for 8 byte, a typical double-precision $100,000 \times 100,000$ system matrix produced by image processing application would enlarge to 80 GB. Hence, the storage requirements of the extraordinarily large system of coefficient matrix may easily excess the available memory of the consumer's computing equipment such as a mobile device or a sensor node in a wireless sensor network. With the limited computing resources, client cannot handle such expensive $(\mathcal{O}(n^\rho)(2 < \rho \leq 3)$ computation locally. Hence it makes perfect sense that the client resorts to cloud servers for solving the LSLE computation problem.

However, outsourcing computational problems to the commercial public cloud service provider will brings some security issues [3]. The most important one is the data privacy issue, the computation problems often contain some sensitive knowledge that should not be exposed to the public cloud servers. Such as business financial records, personally identifiable health information, engineering data, or proprietary asset data, etc. In order to protect these private information, the original computational problem should be encrypted before outsourcing. Therefore, the first security challenge is the security of client's input/output data. Sometimes, the third party may be lazy in the computation and return an invalid result. In some cases, some possible softwares bugs and hardware errors may also get a wrong computation result. The cloud may also want to recover some meaningful knowledge of the consumer's data by responding an incorrect answer. Consequently, the proposed protocol must have a way to detect whether the returned answer is correct or not. Thus , the second security challenge is result verification. Another important requirement is that the total of local work cost by the client must be substantially smaller than the time needed if the client chooses to handle the computational problem locally. To sum up, an outsourcing computation algorithm should satisfy four conditions:correctness,verifiability, security, and efficiency.

1.1   Related Works

The problem of computation outsourcing has attracted a lot of attention in the theory community, cryptography community and security. Abadi M et al. [4] firstly proved the impossibility of secure outsourcing an complicated computation while the client does only polynomial time work. And then, the theoretical computer science community showed increasingly solicitude for the tasks of how to efficiently and securely outsource different expensive computational problems. We review some most recent works here.

In order to address this problems, outsourced data is usually encrypted to ensure client-to-provider data confidentiality and privacy. However, the cloud servers are unable to perform any meaningful computation on the encrypted data. An alternative solution to this problem is to employ fully homomorphic encryption [5] that incurs heavy processing overhead, which is not yet efficient enough for practical application. The proposed protocol [6] required client and agent to carry out expensive cryptographic computations. Algorithms [7,8]are all require the expensive operations of homomorphic encryptions.

The common drawback of the early protocols on secure outsourcing is that they are often short of detailed security analysis and efficiency evaluation. Also, lack of the important case of result verification. And after then, two algorithms [7, 13] are proposed for solving secure matrix multiplication outsourcing. Recently, caring about the engineering and scientific computing problems LSLE, plenty of researchers investigates secure outsourcing for large-scale systems of linear equations(LSLE). Then, algorithm [9] proposed a secure outsourcing algorithm for LSLE based on the Jacobi iterative approach [10], however, it is not only requires multi-round iteractions between the client and the cloud server, but also requires expensive cryptographic computations, and thus is impractical. Chen F et al. [11] proposed the security problem of [10]. The weakness of the protocol lies in an inappropriate use of the paillier public-key cryptosystem that the attack can recover partial of the client's input data. In order to solve this problem , Chen F et al. [11] proposed a more efficient algorithm to securely outsource large-scale linear equations to cloud. However, an evident disadvantage of the algorithm is that the third-party can easily distinguish the ciphertext of different plaintext by the computation of zero-elements in the matrix, because the randomization of the scheme does not change the zero-elements in the original matrix. The other disadvantage of the algorithm is that the use of simple multiple obfuscation techniques can not secure the sensitive data of client. Recently, Chen et al. [12] proposed a secure outsourcing program for solving large-scale systems of linear equations based on multiple obfuscation techniques, whereas it required client to carry out expensive matrix multiplication that incurs low efficiency of the client.

1.2 Our Contributions

This paper addresses the issue of how to outsource LSLE $Ax = b$ to the public cloud, while ensuring correctness, maintaining data input/output privacy, realizing result verifiability, and improving computational efficiency. Our proposed algorithm works with two non-colluding cloud servers, this two non-colluding cloud servers framework is also employed in the previous scheme (e.g. [13,14]). Our contributions are 3 folds:

1. We propose practical protocol for secure outsourcing of LSLE based on randomization techniques. With the uncertainty of the vector splitting procedure, the vector encryption method that we employed provides non-deterministic encryption.
2. We show that our algorithm can achieve goals of correctness, high-security, efficiency, and cheating detection . Compared with Wang's algorithm [9] our protocol is superior in both efficiency and security, and more effective than Chen' algorithm [12].

3. Our protocol algorithm only requires one round communication between the consumer and cloud servers, and the client can detect the misbehave of servers with the probability 1. Further more, theoretical analysis and experimental evaluation show that our protocol can be deployed in practical applications immediately.

1.3 Organization

The following of the paper is organized following: In Sect. 2, security definitions are depicted. Outsourcing LSLE is described with detailed techniques in Sects. 3 and 4 gives some security analysis and performance evaluation. The experimental evaluation of the proposed algorithm is given in Sect. 5. And the paper is concluded in Sect. 6.

2   Our Framework

2.1   System Model

We consider a computation outsourcing model including cloud client and cloud servers depicted in Fig. 1. The LSLE task $Ax = b$ need to be solved by the client, denoted as $\Phi = (A, b)$. Due to the limited computing power, the client wants to outsource problem Φ to the cloud. To protect privacy, it is firstly transformed to another problem $\Phi' = (A', b')$(which has the same answer to the original $Ax = b$), then, the new LSLE problem Φ' will be encrypted into two LSLE problems $\Phi'_{k_1} = (H, c_1)$ and $\Phi'_{k_2} = (H, c_2)$ with the secret key K, and then sent to the two non-collude cloud servers respectively for finding solutions. The cloud servers solve the encrypted LSLE problems, and return the solutions to the client. Using the secret key K, the client verifies the solutions, if they are correct, the client decrypts them and interpolates the two answers to learn the solutions of $\Phi = (A, b)$. If not, the client rejects the solutions.

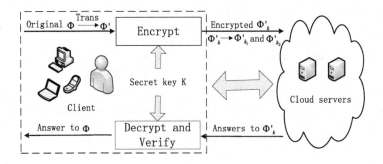

Fig. 1. LSLE outsourcing system model.

2.2   Security Model and Formal Definition

In this paper, the security threats are primarily come from the cloud servers. There are two forms of threat models in outsourcing computations in general: semi-honest model and fully malicious model. Goldreich et al. [17] firstly introduced the semi-honest mode. In this model, both the parties are guaranteed to properly execute a prescribed protocol, however, the cloud records all the knowledge it can access, and attempts to try his best to retrieve some sensitive information such as the secret input and output of client. Fully malicious model is the strongest adversarial model. In many applications, we must consider the case that servers are attackers. For example, servers can intentionally send a computationally indistinguishable result to mislead client.

Hobenberger and Lysyanskaya [18] first introduced a model called "two untrusted problem model". In the two untrusted program model, there are two non-colluding servers and we assume at most one of them is adversarial while we cannot know which one. besides, the misbehavior of the dishonest server can be detected with an overwhelming probability. Recently, this two non-colluding cloud servers framework is employed in the previous scheme (e.g. [13,14]).

Propositions 1.(α-Efficiency [18]): A pair of algorithms (U, S) is said to be an α-efficiency implementation of LSLE outsourcing if U^S (denotes that U is given oracle access to S) correctly implements LSLE outsourcing and for all matrix of LSLE, the costly time of user is smaller an α-multiplicative factors of the costly of LSLE outsourcing.

Propositions 2.(β-Checkability [18]): A pair of alogorithms (U, S) is said to be a β-Checkability implementation of LSLE outsourcing if U^S correctly implements LSLE outsourcing and for all matrix A of LSLE, if a malicious server break its correct functionality during the execution of U^S(A), user have a way to detect the threat with probability no less than β.

2.3   Mathematical Preparation

In this paper, permutation function is well used to achieve randomization and unpredictability. In cauchy's two-line notation, This notation lists each of the elements of M in the first row, and for each preimage element lists its image under the permutation below it in the second row. In this paper, the $M = \{1, 2, ..., n\}$, Then,

$$\begin{pmatrix} 1 \ ... \ n \\ p_1 \ ... \ p_n \end{pmatrix} \tag{1}$$

We use p as the permutation of the set M, and a permutation function $\pi_{(i)} = p_i$, where $i = 1, \ldots, n$, to denote (1). We write $\{k_1, \ldots, k_n\} \leftarrow \kappa$ to denote $k_1, \ldots, k_n$ are all randomly chosen from the key space κ.

The entry in ith row and jth column in matrix A are denoted as $A(i,j), a_{i,j}$, or a_{ij} where i and j are indexed from 1 to n.

3   The Protocol

We have done extensive analysis of the existing techniques, and based on the analysis, we propose a new secure protocol to secure outsource LSLE to the cloud. Our approach is non-interactive and requires less computational effort from the client side.

Propositions 3. A securely outsourcing of LSLE computation scheme consist of five algorithms: (1) the algorithm for key generation **KenGen**; (2) the algorithm to encrypt the original problem $\Phi = (A, b)$ **ProGen**; (3) the **Compute** to solve Φ_{k_1} and Φ_{k_2} problem; (4) the algorithm for LSLE decryption **Solve**; (5)the algorithm for result verification **Verify**.

Each part of the framework will be individually solved as follows:

3.1   Secret Key Generation (KeyGen)

The input of original LSLE problem is a coefficient matrix $A \in \mathbb{R}^{n \times n}$ and a coefficient vector $b \in \mathbb{R}^n$ such that $Ax = b$. The client with relatively weak computing power wants to secure outsource the task of LSLE to the public cloud. The protocol invokes Algorithms 1 and 2 to set up the secret key.

Algorithm 1. Procedure Key Generation

Input: a security parameter λ.
Output: encryption key: $\{\alpha_1, \ldots, \alpha_n\}$, $\{\beta_1, \ldots, \beta_n\}$, $\{\gamma_1, \ldots, \gamma_n\}$, and $\{\theta_1, \ldots, \theta_n\}$, $\pi_1, \pi_2, \pi_3, \pi_4, \pi_5$.
  1: Input a security parameter λ, it specifies the key space $\kappa_\alpha, \kappa_\beta, \kappa_\gamma$, and κ_θ. The client picks five sets of random numbers: $\{\alpha_1, \ldots, \alpha_n\} \leftarrow \kappa_\alpha$, $\{\beta_1, \ldots, \beta_n\} \leftarrow \kappa_\beta$, $\{\gamma_1, \ldots, \gamma_n\} \leftarrow \kappa_\gamma$, and $\{\theta_1, \ldots, \theta_n\} \leftarrow \kappa_\theta$, where $0 \notin \kappa_\alpha \bigcup \kappa_\beta \bigcup \kappa_\gamma \bigcup \kappa_\theta$
  2: Then, the client invokes Algorithm 2 to generate five random permutations $\pi_1, \pi_2, \pi_3, \pi_4,$ and π_5.

Algorithm 2. Procedure Random Permutation

  1: We first set π to be an identical permutation where $\pi = I_n$.
  2: **For** $i = n$ down to 2
  3:     To set $\pi_{[j]}$ where j is a random integer meet $1 \leq j \leq i$;
  4:     Then swap $\pi_{[j]}$ and $\pi_{[i]}$;
  5: **End For**

3.2   Procedure LSLE Encryption (ProGen)

Then, we describe the procedure LSLE encryption scheme with detailed techniques.

Algorithm 3. LSLE Random Transformation

Input: .The original matrix A and the secret key K:$\{\alpha_1, \ldots, \alpha_n\}$, $\{\beta_1, \ldots, \beta_n\}$, $\{\gamma_1, \ldots, \gamma_n\}$ $\{\theta_1, \ldots, \theta_n\}$, π_1, π_2, π_3.

Output: .The new transformed LSLE problem $A'x = b'$, where $A' = E + D^{-1}F$, $b' = D^{-1}b$.

1: The client generates two unit matrices, E_1, E_4, where $E_1 \in \mathbb{R}^{\lfloor \frac{n}{2} \rfloor \times \lfloor \frac{n}{2} \rfloor}$, $E_4 \in \mathbb{R}^{\lceil \frac{n}{2} \rceil \times \lceil \frac{n}{2} \rceil}$

2: The client generates a random sparse matrix P_2, $P_2 \in \mathbb{R}^{\lfloor \frac{n}{2} \rfloor \times \lceil \frac{n}{2} \rceil}$. We assume that there is at most γ ($\gamma \ll n$) non-zero elements for each row(or column) of P_2, and all of the non-zero elements are set to 1.(We assume that γ in this algorithm is 10).

3: The client generates matrix $D \in \mathbb{R}^{n \times n}$,

$$D = \begin{pmatrix} A_1 & A_2 \\ 0 & A_4 \end{pmatrix} \qquad (2)$$

where $A_1(i,j) = \alpha_i E_1(\pi_1(i), j)$, $A_2(i,j) = (\beta_i \gamma_j) P_2(\pi_2(i), j)$, $A_4(i,j) = \theta_i E_4(\pi_3(i), j)$.

4: To additively split the original matrix A, $(A = D + F)$, where $F = A - D$.

5: The client computes $D^{-1}Ax = D^{-1}b$, where $A = D + F$, we can get $(E + D^{-1}F)x = D^{-1}b$.

6: The original LSLE can be finally rewritten as $A'x = b'$, where $A' = E + D^{-1}F$, $b' = D^{-1}b$.

Lemma 1. In LSLE Random Transformation, matrix D is invertible.

Proof. Since $0 \notin \kappa_\alpha \bigcup \kappa_\theta$, The determinants of E_1, E_4 satisfy $det(E_1) \neq 0$, $det(E_4) \neq 0$. Hence, A_1 and A_4 are invertible. Because $det(D) = det(A_1) \times det(A_4) \neq 0$. Hereafter, the proof is straightforward.

Lemma 2. The client can efficiently computes D^{-1} and $D^{-1}F$

Proof. As we see:

$$D^{-1} = \begin{pmatrix} A_1^{-1} & -A_1^{-1}A_2A_4^{-1} \\ 0 & A_4^{-1} \end{pmatrix} \qquad (3)$$

The computational complexity of A_1^{-1} and A_4^{-1} is $O(n)$, then the calculation of $-A_1^{-1}A_2A_4^{-1}$ takes at most γn multiplications. That is, the computational complexity is $O(n)$, Thus, the client can efficiently computes D^{-1}. Obviously, the D^{-1} is also a sparse matrix, since the constant $\gamma \ll n$, the computational complexity of $D^{-1}F$ is $O(n^2)$. Hereafter, the proof is straightforward.

3.3 Solved in the Cloud (Compute)

The cloud servers receive the encrypted LSLE problems from the client and responds with the solutions y_1 and y_2.

$$y_1 = H^{-1}c_1 = N^{-1}A'^{-1}M^{-1} \cdot Mb'_1 = N^{-1}A'^{-1}b'_1 \qquad (5)$$

$$y_2 = H^{-1}c_1 = N^{-1}A'^{-1}M^{-1} \cdot Mb'_2 = N^{-1}A'^{-1}b'_2 \qquad (6)$$

Algorithm 4. Procedure LSLE Encryption

Input: .The new transformed LSLE problem $A'x = b'$ and the Secret key: π_4, π_5.
Output: .The new encrypted LSLE problems $Hy = c_1$ and $Hy = c_2$.
1: The client chooses two random tri-diagonal matrices, Q_1, Q_2, where $Q_1, Q_2 \in \mathbb{R}^{n \times n}$.
2: The client generates two matrices M, N, where $M(i,j) = Q_1(\pi_4(i), j)$, $N(i,j) = Q_2(\pi_5(i), j)$
3: The client computes $H = MA'N$.

$$H(i,j) = Q_1(\pi_4(i), j)A'Q_2(\pi_5(i), j) \tag{4}$$

4: The client picks a random blinding coefficient vector b'_1, and substract it from b' to obtain b'_2: $b' = b'_1 + b'_2$. Then, the client computes $c_1 = Mb'_1$ and $c_2 = Mb'_2$.
5: The transformed LSLE problem $A'x = b'$ can be encrypted to two LSLE problems $Hy = c_1$ and $Hy = c_2$.
6: Later, the client sends (H, c_1) to the server1, and sends (H, c_2) to the server2, and cloud servers responds with the solutions to the problem $Hy_1 = c_1$ and $Hy_2 = c_2$.

3.4 LSLE Verification (Verify)

The client verifies whether the returned solutions to linear equations $Hy_1 = c_1$, and $Hy_2 = c_2$ are correct.

3.5 LSLE Decryption (Solve)

If Verify=1, the client interpolates the returned vector y_1 and y_2 to obtain x

$$x = N(y_1 + y_2) = N(N^{-1}A'^{-1}b'_1 + N^{-1}A'^{-1}b'_2) = A'^{-1}(b'_1 + b'_2) = A'^{-1}b' = A^{-1}b \tag{7}$$

4 Security and Efficiency Analysis

4.1 Security Analysis

First, we want to remind that our protocol is similar to the one-time pad encryption scheme. A new secret key is used every time the protocol is run. Thus, there is no know-plaintext attack or chosen-plaintext attack. Now we discuss the privacy issue of the proposed protocol. Suppose the original LSLE problem is $\Phi = (A, b)$ and the encrypted problem is $\Phi'_{k_1} = (H, c_1)$ and $\Phi'_{k_2} = (H, c_2)$.

Theorem 1. *Input Privacy Analysis*: In the fully malicious model, the protocol is privacy for A and b.

Proof: From above protocol instantiation, we can see that throughout the whole process, the cloud two servers only sees the disguised data (H, c_1) and (H, c_2) respectively. We first prove the privacy for input b, for hiding the privacy of b, we use the operations of Multiplicative encryption and Additive splitting. The original b first multiplies a random special matrix D^{-1}: $b' = D^{-1}b$, and then for hiding the b', we additively split it into two matrices b'_1 and b'_2: $b' = b'_1 + b'_2$ using the Additive splitting. This operation is secure since b'_1 is undistinguishable. Server1 cannot recover the vector b' because he has only one point b'_1, it can be analyzed in the same way with that of Server2. With the assumption these two servers non-colluding that the original value of b is well protected.

We prove the privacy for input data A of LSLE. The matrix A is transformed to A' firstly, $A' = E + D^{-1}F$, where $A = D + F$. Moreover, we choose two sparse matrices M and N, and the A' is transformed to $H = MA'N$. In order to thwart the brute force attack, the size of non-zero elements in each row of M and N are set to three for medium security and a choice of large key space κ_α, κ_β, κ_γ, and κ_θ. Given the H, there are a lot of choices for the secret key $D \in \mathbb{R}^{n \times n}$, $M \in \mathbb{R}^{n \times n}$ and $N \in \mathbb{R}^{n \times n}$. Suppose each entry of the matrix is an s-bit number. Since D is an special sparse matrix, there are roughly $5ns$ bit information for D. Thus, there are 2^{5ns} possibilities for choice for D. Since M and N are random tri-diagonal matrices. Similarly, there $2^{(3n-2)s}$ possible choices for M and N respectively. Thus, given H there are $2^{(11n-4)s}$ possibilities for the client's data, which is an exponential number on n. But notice that the protocol generates a new secret key whenever the protocol is run. Therefore, the cloud servers cannot find meaningful knowledge about the client's data A even for a computationally unbounded cloud. Therefore, the original value of A is well protected too.

Theorem 2. *Output Privacy Analysis*: In the fully malicious model, the protocol is privacy for x.

Proof: The Server1 can not recover the value x (the solution of the original LSLE problem $Ax = b$) by y_1 (the solution to $Hy_1 = c_1$), and Server2 can not recover the value x (the solution of the original LSLE problem $Ax = b$) by y_2 (the solution to $Hy_2 = c_2$). With the assumption these two servers non-colluding that the solution value x is well protected.

Theorem 3. *Robust Cheating resistance*: In the fully malicious model, the protocol is a 1-checkable implementation of LSLE.

Proof: Given a solution y, the client can verifies whether the equations $Hy = c$ hold efficiently because the computational complexity for Hy is $O(n^2)$. No Invalid result from a malicious cloud server can pass the client's verification with probability 1.

4.2 Efficiency Analysis

Theorem 4: Our protocol is an $O(\frac{1}{n})$-efficient implementation of LSLE.

Proof: The client costly is generated by handle four algorithms: KeyGen, ProGen, Verify and Solve. There is no doubt that KeyGen takes time $O(n)$.

In ProGen, the computational complexity of multiplies D^{-1} is $O(n^2)$, and the inverse computational of D is $O(n)$, besides Client also needs to compute $H = MA'N$, c_1, and c_2, which also takes $O(n^2)$. On the other hand, it takes $O(n^3)$ computations in order to solve the linear equations directly. Thus, our protocol is an $O(\frac{1}{n})$-efficient implementation of LSLE. Table 1 shows the summarization of the theoretical consume.

Table 1. Theoretical performance of our protocol

Algorithms	Our protocol
KeyGen	$O(n)$
ProGen	$O(n^2)$
Verify	$O(n^2)$
Solve	$O(n)$

5   Experiment and Results Analysis

Theoretical analysis shows that our proposed algorithm indeed benefits the client. We further conduct numerical experiments to verify the practical efficiency of our protocol. The client and cloud servers computations in the experiments are both implemented on the same workstation. We conduct it using MATLAB R2013b on a workstation equipped with Intel(R)Core(TM) i3–3220 CPU 3.30 GHz and 4 GB RAM. Additionally, we do not take into account of the communication time costly between the client and the cloud servers in this paper since cloud storage is the only choice for weak client with limited local storage and the task solving computation dominates the costly time which is shown in our experiments.

We focus our attention on verifying whether the client has a computational gain by outsource the problem. Then, the main performance indicator is a ratio of the time of client costly locally and computation outsourcing. The definition of parameters are clear depicted in Table 2. Then, the performance gain by outsource the LSLE problem can be reflected by $\frac{t_{original}}{t_{client}}$.

Table 2. Notations

Notations	Our Means
$t_{original}$	Client solves the original LSLE locally
$t_{server1}$	Cloud server1 computes the LSLE $Hy_1 = c_1$
$t_{server2}$	Cloud server2 computes the LSLE $Hy_2 = c_2$
$t_{client1}$	Client generates the secret key and encrypts the original LSLE
$t_{client2}$	Client decrypts and verifies the returned results
t_{client}	$t_{client} = t_{client1} + t_{client2}$

Table 3. Performance of the our protocol

No	Dimension	Storage	$t_{original}$	$t_{client1}$	$t_{client2}$	t_{client}	$t_{server1}$	$t_{server2}$	$\frac{t_{original}}{t_{client}}$
1	250	0.5MB	0.3006	0.0216	0.0023	0.0239	0.3044	0.3047	12.5774
2	500	2MB	1.6986	0.0860	0.0039	0.0899	1.6873	1.6754	18.8943
3	1000	8MB	11.5324	0.4729	0.0097	0.4825	11.0807	11.1252	23.8980
4	1500	18MB	46.0798	1.7123	0.0261	1.7384	47.4675	47.4587	26.5070
5	2000	32MB	114.1304	3.8355	0.0456	3.8811	113.6327	113.5908	29.4067
6	2500	50MB	229.3545	7.4749	0.0752	7.5501	228.6259	228.5899	30.3776

Table 4. Performance of Chen' Algorithm [12]

No	Dimension	Storage	$t_{original}$	t_{client}	t_{server}	$\frac{t_{client}}{t_{original}}$
1	250	0.5MB	0.3146	0.0338	0.3897	9.3077
2	500	2MB	1.6845	0.1188	1.6845	14.1793
3	1000	8MB	11.6785	0.6258	11.6785	18.6617
4	1500	18MB	46.2345	2.2102	46.2345	20.9187
5	2000	32MB	114.0097	4.8429	114.0097	23.5416
6	2500	50MB	229.1120	9.0405	229.1120	25.3428

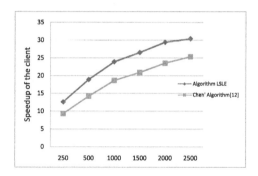

Fig. 2. Comparison of client speedup.

For secure linear equation outsourcing, the experimental results are shown in Table 3. All time is measured in seconds. In our experiment, the Guass-Jordan elimination, the most commonly used schoolbook matrix computation algorithm is employed by the cloud servers.

For the sake if completeness, we investigate the superiority of our algorithm by making an experimental comparison with [12]. To give a fair comparison, we implement Chen' algorithm [12] on our workstation, and the experiment results are shown in Table 4. As expected in Fig. 2, the experiment results shows that our protocol is much efficient than that in Chen's algorithm [12].

For our main concern on the client's computational gain, Table. 3 indicates that the gain is considerable and does increase with the dimension of the coefficient matrix. In practice, there may be more performance gains. For example, the cloud have more computational resources, e.g. memory. If the scale of the LSLE problem becomes large, there will be a lot of input/ output operations for matrix computations. For the client with poor memory, a lot of additional cost is needed to move data in and out of the memory. However, the cloud can handle this problem more easily with a large memory.

6   Conclusion Remarks

In this paper, we proposed an efficient outsource-secure protocol for LSLE, which is one of the most basic and expensive operations in many scientific and business applications. We have proved that our protocol can fulfills goals of correctness, security, checkability, and high-efficiency. Our protocol is suitable for any nonsingular dense matrix in the fully malicious model. Furthermore, the use of effective additive splitting technique and two non-colluding cloud servers program model enables our protocol more secure and efficient than Chen' Algorithm [12].

Acknowledgments. This work is partly supported by the Fundamental Research Funds for the Central Universities (No. NZ2015108), and the China Postdoctoral Science Foundation funded project (2015M571752), and the Jiangsu Planned Projects for Postdoctoral Research Funds (1402033C). and Open Project Foundation of Information Technology Research Base of Civil Aviation Administration of China(NO.CAAC-ITRB-201405).

References

1. Armbrust, M., Fox, A., Griffith, R.: A view of cloud computing. Commun. ACM **53**(4), 50–58 (2010)
2. Benzi, M.: Preconditioning techniques for large linear systems: a survey. J. Comput. Phy. **182**(2), 418–477 (2002)
3. Brunette G., Mogull R.: Security guidance for critical areas of focus in cloud computing v2. 1. Cloud Security Alliance, pp. 1–76 (2009)
4. Abadi M., Feigenbaum J., Kilian J.: On hiding information from an oracle. In: Proceedings of the Nineteenth Annual ACM Symposium on Theory of Computing, pp. 195–203. ACM (1987)
5. Gentry, C.: Fully homomorphic encryption using ideal lattices. STOC **9**, 169–178 (2009)
6. Rivest, R.L., Adleman, L., Dertouzos, M.L.: On data banks and privacy homomorphisms. Found. Sec. Comput. **4**(11), 169–180 (1978)
7. Benjamin, D., Atallah, M.J.: Private and cheating-free outsourcing of algebraic computations. In: Sixth Annual Conference on Privacy, Security and Trust, PST 2008, pp. 240–245. IEEE (2008)
8. Blanton, M., Atallah, M.J., Frikken, K.B., Malluhi, Q.: Secure and efficient outsourcing of sequence comparisons. In: Foresti, S., Yung, M., Martinelli, F. (eds.) ESORICS 2012. LNCS, vol. 7459, pp. 505–522. Springer, Heidelberg (2012)

9. Urs, K.M.R.: Harnessing the Cloud for Securely Outsourcing Large-scale Systems of Linear Equations

10. Saad, Y.: Iterative methods for sparse linear systems. Siam (2003)

11. Chen, F., Xiang, T., Yang, Y.: Privacy-preserving and verifiable protocols for scientific computation outsourcing to the cloud. J. Parallel Distrib. Comput. **74**(3), 2141–2151 (2014)

12. Xiaofeng, C., Xinyi, H., Jin, L., Jianfeng, M., Wenjing, L., Wong D.: New Algorithms for Secure Outsourcing of Large-scale Systems of Linear Equations (2015)

13. Atallah, M.J., Frikken, K.B.: Securely outsourcing linear algebra computations. In: Proceedings of the 5th ACM Symposium on Information, Computer and Communications Security, pp. 48–59. ACM (2010)

14. Elmehdwi, Y., Samanthula, B.K., Jiang, W.: Secure k-nearest neighbor query over encrypted data in outsourced environments. 2014 IEEE 30th International Conference on Data Engineering (ICDE), pp. 664–675. IEEE (2014)

15. Gibson, S.F.F., Mirtich, B.: A survey of deformable modeling in computer graphics. Technical report, Mitsubishi Electric Research Laboratories (1997)

16. Oppenheim, A.V., Willsky, A.S., Nawab, S.H.: Signals and systems. Prentice-Hall, Englewood Cliffs (1983)

17. Goldreich O., Micali S., Wigderson A.: How to play any mental game. In: Proceedings of the Nineteenth Annual ACM Symposium on Theory of Computing, pp. 218–229. ACM (1987)

18. Hohenberger, S., Lysyanskaya, A.: How to securely outsource cryptographic computations. In: Kilian, J. (ed.) TCC 2005. LNCS, vol. 3378, pp. 264–282. Springer, Heidelberg (2005)

19. Goldreich, O.: Computational complexity: a conceptual perspective. ACM SIGACT News **39**(3), 35–39 (2008)

A Provably Secure Ciphertext-Policy Hierarchical Attribute-Based Encryption

Ziying Wang[1,2(✉)] and Jian Wang[1]

[1] College of Computer Science and Technology,
Nanjing University of Aeronautics and Astronautics, Nanjing 210016, China
`wangziying1008@126.com`, `wangjian@nuaa.edu.cn`
[2] Information Technology Research Base of Civil Aviation Administration
of China, Civil Aviation University of China, Tianjin 300300, China

Abstract. With the booming growth of network technology, the problems of information disclosure are becoming more and more serious. The attribute-based encryption has been one of hotspots for the advantage of fine-grained access control. In this paper, a provably secure ciphertext-policy hierarchical attribute-based encryption is proposed, which can satisfy the need of attribute hierarchy in attribute-based encryption and overcome the shortage of access control policies in the logic operations. We give a solution to the problem of hierarchical relationship between attributes in the same category in attribute-based encryption and provide a more expressive description of the access control structure. The security of the proposed CP-HABE scheme is proved in the standard model on the basis of decisional l parallel-BDHE assumption. Also the performance analysis is provided.

Keywords: Attribute–based encryption · Hierarchical attribute · Ciphertext-policy · Access control

1 Introduction

Much attention has been payed to information security issues, with the increasing development of network technology. Traditional PKC ensures data confidentiality, but limits the flexibility of access control [1]. Sahai and Waters [2] proposed the concept of attribute-based encryption (ABE) for a more flexible and fine-grained access control. Sets of descriptive attributes are used to describe files and users in ABE. A certain user can decrypt his ciphertext, when the concerned access control policy is satisfied by his attributes. ABE can be divide into 2 categories: key-policy (KP-)ABE and ciphertext-policy (CP-)ABE. The system labels each ciphertext in KP-ABE with the descriptive attributes sets; access control policies are related to the secret key of the user. CP-ABE is similar to KP-ABE, except that a secret key is related to the user's attributes and the system labels access control policies with each ciphertext.

1.1 Motivation

However, the hierarchy relationships among the attributes in the same category are often overlooked. For example, according to the Academic Title Evaluation, university

© Springer International Publishing Switzerland 2015
Z. Huang et al. (Eds.): ICCCS 2015, LNCS 9483, pp. 38–48, 2015.
DOI: 10.1007/978-3-319-27051-7_4

teachers can be divided into professors, associate professors, lecturers, teaching assistants. {teaching assistant}, {university teacher}, {lecturer}, {associate professor} and {professor} are five attributes in the same category, among which there are hierarchy relationships: Teaching assistant, lecturer, associate professor and professor are all university teachers. Assume that the user who has the attribute {university teacher} can access the system, then one user who holds any attribute of the set {professor, associate professor, lecturer, teaching assistant} can do access. The above example shows that, the hierarchy relationships among the attributes in the same category leads to a higher demand for access control in the system.

Jin Li et al. [3] created the concept of hierarchical ABE (HABE) in 2011, and gave a specific HABE scheme consideration of a tree hierarchy structure among the attributes, which is the first research result along this direction. But it lacks a description of the structure of access control. In these schemes [4–6], the users are organized in a hierarchical tree but all attributes are at the same level. They use DNF and CNF formula to describe the access structure, which means that the formal expression ability is limited, and it lacks the evidence of formal security, because only when in random oracle models were they proved to have security. Indeed, they focus on adapting ABE schemes for specific applications. A new HABE scheme in [7], which is essentially a hierarchical identity-based encryption scheme, aims mainly to solve delegation problems and is not able to reflect the logical relationships between access control policies.

1.2 Our Contribution

We put forward a novel construction for ciphertext-policy hierarchical attribute-based encryption (CP-HABE) scheme, consider the hierarchy relationships among the attributes in the same category and the logical relationships between access control policies. This paper constructs access control policy based on sets of attribute paths, which are defined by constructing attribute trees. And we use Linear Integer Secret Sharing (LISS) to express access control policies by a $d \times e$ distribution matrix M. Only when one user's attributes meet the demand of the access control policies, can the ciphertext be decrypted. In the standard model, the proposed scheme has been proved to be secure on the basis of Decisional l-parallel Bilinear Diffie–Hellman Exponent (l-BDHE) Assumption. Comparing with the scheme in [7], our HABE scheme achieves significantly better performance.

1.3 Related Work

In 2005, Sahai and Waters [2] created the notion, ABE. Goyal et al. [8] provided the first KP-ABE to support monotone access trees. Bethencourt et al. [9] were the first to propose CP-ABE notion. It uses the method of threshold secret sharing in order to implement the corresponding policies in the stage of encryption. Since then, there were numerous studies on ABE [10–13]. Waters [14] proposed in 2011 an expressive and efficient CP-ABE, where a distribution matrix of Linear Secret Sharing Scheme (LSSS) is on behalf of access control policies. Balu and Kuppusamy [15] adopted Linear Integer Secret Sharing (LISS) so that it can represent access control policies, implementing the logic operations between the access control policies, making a more flexible access control structure.

The term of HABE appears in several recent schemes in different senses. In 2011, the notion of hierarchical ABE (HABE) [3] was put forward, after which a lot of schemes [4–6] based on HABE are proposed. Recently, a new HABE scheme in [7] has been proposed which aims mainly to solve delegation problems.

2 Preliminaries

2.1 Linear Integer Secret Sharing(LISS)

It selects the secret from an open interval of integers, each of which is a linear combination of a series of integers randomly selected by the secret distributor. It accomplishes the secret reconstruction. It is by means of computing the linear combination consisting of integer coefficients coming from a qualified set.

Detailed introductions are in [15, 17].

2.2 Bilinear Maps

Let G_1, G_2 be two multiplicative cyclic groups of prime order p; g, G_1's generator; $e : G_1 \times G_1 \to G_2$, a bilinear map. e has the following properties [16]:

1. Bilinear: $\forall u, v \in G_1$, $\forall a, b \in Z_p$, $e(u^a, v^b) = e(u, v)^{ab}$.
2. Non-degenerate: $e(g, g) \neq 1$.
3. Symmetric: $e(g^b, g^a) = e(g, g)^{ab} = e(g^a, g^b)$.

2.3 Decisional Bilinear Diffie–Hellman Exponent Assumption

Decisional l-parallel Bilinear Diffie–Hellman Exponent problem: Choose a group G is of prime order p. Let $a, s \in Z_p$ be randomly selected and g be a generator of G. It must be kept difficult to tell $T = e(g^s, y_{l+1}) \in G_1$ from an element R randomly chosen from G_1 given that an adversary knows that $Y = (g, g^s, y_1, y_2, \ldots, y_l, y_{l+2}, \ldots, y_{2l})$, in which $y_k = g^{a^k}$ for $1 \leq k \leq 2l$.

If

$$|\Pr[B(Y, e(g^s, y_{l+1})) = 0] - \Pr[B(Y, R) = 0]| \geq \varepsilon$$

The algorithm B, which can output $z \in \{0, 1\}$, has the advantage ε to handle decisional l-parallel BDHE problem in G.

Definition 1. The (decisional) l parallel-BDHE assumption establishes that no polynomial time algorithm has a non-negligible advantage to solve decisional l-parallel BDHE problems.

3   The CP-HABE Scheme

3.1   Attribute Tree

Attributes are firstly sorted in the CP-HABE scheme based on the relationships justified in the access control system. The rest of the attributes are independent and can be seen as trees with only roots. Assume that there are d trees with roots $a_{10}, a_{20}, \ldots, a_{n0}$ formed by N attributes. We suppose that the tree depth with root a_{i0} to be l_i, and $e = \max\{l_1, l_2, \ldots, l_n\}$. In the ith attribute tree, let a be an attribute in k depth. We define attribute path from root a_{i0} to be $(a_{i0}, a_{i1}, \ldots, a_{i,k-1}, a_{ik})$, in which $a_{ik} = a$. If $a_{i\theta} = a'_{j\theta}$ for $0 \leq \theta \leq k$, then we say that with attribute path $(a'_{j0}, a'_{j1}, \ldots, a'_{j,\theta-1}, a'_{j\theta})$, a' is covered by a. If a' is covered by a, it means that in the system of access control, a has a higher level of priority than a'. Assume that the user who has the attribute a' can access the system, then one user who holds the attribute a can do access.

3.2   Access Control Structure

We compute shares of the attributes using a distribution matrix M after converting the access control policy into the distribution matrix M in our CP-HABE construction. Then message m is encrypted, and through the attribute shares, we encrypte the concerned attributes in policies of access control. The user who meets the demand of access control policies can decrypt the ciphertext.

Access Control Policy. In our paper, the attribute paths construct one access control policy. Then it can be divided into the following two kinds of situations.

(1) **Poly-attribute**

Assume that it needs to hold the attribute a in the k depth, which is of the ith attribute tree, then the attribute path is expressed as $R_a = (a_{i0}, a_{i1}, \ldots, a_{ik})$, where $a_{ik} = a$.
Then, access control policy can be expressed by $P = R_a$.

(2) **Multi-attribute**

OR-term: $a_1 \vee a_2 \vee \ldots \vee a_n$, the attribute paths of $a_1, a_2, \ldots, a_n$ are represented as $R_{a_1}, R_{a_2}, \ldots, R_{a_n}$ respectively. Access control policy is $P = R_{a_1} \vee R_{a_2} \vee, \ldots, \vee R_{a_n}$.

AND-term: $a_1 \wedge a_2 \wedge \ldots \wedge a_n$, the attribute paths of $a_1, a_2, \ldots, a_n$ are represented as $R_{a_1}, R_{a_2}, \ldots, R_{a_n}$ respectively. Access control policy can be expressed by $P = R_{a_1} \wedge R_{a_2} \wedge, \ldots, \wedge R_{a_n}$.

OR-AND-term: assume $(a_1 \vee a_2) \wedge (a_3 \vee a_4)$, the attribute paths of a_1, a_2, a_3, a_4 are respectively $R_{a_1}, R_{a_2}, R_{a_3}, R_{a_4}$. Access control policy can be expressed by $P = (R_{a_1} \vee R_{a_2}) \wedge (R_{a_3} \vee R_{a_4})$.

3.3   Formation of Access Control Policy Matrix M

Let $M_u \in Z^{1 \times 1}$ be a single entry matrix, which is one, that is to say, $M_u = [1]$. Given a matrix $M_a \in Z^{d_a \times e_a}$, it forms $r_a \in Z^{(d_a-1) \times e_a}$ on behalf of all columns except for the first one in M_a and $c_a \in Z^e$ for the first column in M_a.

The matrix M is constructed by the following three rules [15].

(1) **Rule 1**

   M_u can express any variable R_i in the access control policy P.

(2) **Rule 2**

   For any OR-term $P = P_a \vee P_b$, $M_a \in Z^{d_a \times e_a}$ and $M_b \in Z^{d_b \times e_b}$ express the formula P_a and P_b respectively. P is expressed by a matrix $M_{OR} \in Z^{(d_a+d_b)(e_a+e_b-1)}$ constructed by

$$M_{OR} = \begin{matrix} c_a & r_a & 0 \\ c_b & 0 & r_b \end{matrix}$$

(3) **Rule 3**

   For any AND-term $P = P_a \wedge P_b$, $M_a \in Z^{d_a \times e_a}$ and $M_b \in Z^{d_b \times e_b}$ express the formula P_a and P_b respectively. A matrix $M_{AND} \in Z^{(d_a+d_b)(e_a+e_b)}$ expresses P and is constructed by

$$M_{AND} = \begin{matrix} c_a & c_a & r_a & 0 \\ 0 & c_b & 0 & r_b \end{matrix}$$

3.4   The Construction

Assume N attributes are divided into d trees. Consider a bilinear group G with prime order p, g, its one generator. Also, take $H : \{0,1\}^* \to Z_p^*$ as a hash function to resist collusion attacks, $e : G \times G \to G_1$ as a bilinear mapping. Our CP-HABE scheme will be described below.

Setup (1^λ): Choose a random vector $U = (u_i)_{1 \le i \le e}$ of length e, random elements $\alpha, a \in Z_p^*$, and a random d-length vector $H = (h_j)_{1 \le j \le d}$, whose elements are randomly chosen from G. We present the expressions for public parameters, *params*, as well as for master key *mk* here:

$$params = (g, g^a, e(g,g)^\alpha, U, H), \quad mk = g^\alpha$$

KeyGen $(A', params, mk)$: Input A', which is a set of given attributes, the expressions for master key *mk* as well as for the public parameters *params*, then select $t \in Z_p^*$ randomly then perform the following:

(1) Compute $d_0 = g^t$.
(2) For each attribute $a \in A'$, $1 \le i \le d$, compute $d_1 = g^\alpha g^{at} \left(h_i \prod_{\delta=1}^e u_\delta \right)^t$, $d_2 = h_i^t$,
(3) The secret key is $d_{A'} = \left(d_0, \{d_1, d_2\}_{a \in A'} \right)$.

Enc $(m, P, params)$**:** Input the access control policy P, a message $m \in G_1$ to encrypt and the public parameters *params*.

(1) Choose a random element $s \in [-2^L, 2^L]$. The above method for the access control policy P constructs distribution matrix M. A is a set containing attributes in the access control policy P. Choose $\rho = (s, \rho_2, \ldots, \rho_e)^T$, in which $\rho'_i s$ are uniformly randomly selected integers in $[-2^{L_0+k}, 2^{L_0+k}]$. Compute $M \cdot \rho = (s_1, \ldots s_d)^T$.

(2) Compute $CT_1 = me(g, g)^{\alpha s}, CT_2 = g^s$.

(3) For each attribute in P, compute $CT_3 = \left(h_i \prod_\theta^e u_\theta\right)^s$, $CT_4 = g^{as_i} h_i^{-s}, 1 \le i \le d$.

The ciphertext is published as

$$CT = \left(CT_1, CT_2, \{CT_3, CT_4\}_{a \in A}\right)$$

Dec $(CT, params, d_{A'})$**:** Input a ciphertext CT and the secret key for set $A^*(A^* \subseteq A')$.

The algorithm begins to match attributes first. Traverse attribute path set R_{A^*} in which attributes belong to user attribute set A^* and attribute path set R_P in access control policy P. If there is a path present in R_{A^*} which does not cover paths of R_P, the ciphertext cannot be decrypted.

Assume that all attribute paths of the set A^* cover those in the access control policy P, that is to say, A^* meets the access control policy P, then there exists a vector $\lambda_{A^*} \in Z^{d_{A^*}}$ that satisfies $M_{A^*}^T \lambda_A = \xi$. Reconstruct the secret using $\sum_{i \in A^*} \lambda_i s_i = s$, the decryption algorithm calculates

$$CT_1 \cdot \frac{\prod_{i \in A^*} \left\{ e(CT_3, d_0) \cdot e(CT_2, d_2) \cdot [e(CT_4, d_0)]^{\lambda_i} \right\}}{\prod_{i \in A^*} e(CT_2, d_1)}$$

$$= me(g, g)^{\alpha s} \cdot \frac{\prod_{i \in A^*} \left\{ e\left(\left(h_i \prod_\theta^e u_\theta\right)^s, g^t\right) \cdot e(g^s, h_i^t) \cdot \left[e(g^{as_i} h_i^{-s}, g^t)\right]^{\lambda_i} \right\}}{\prod_{i \in A^*} e\left(g^s, g^\alpha g^{at} \left(h_i \prod_{\delta=1}^e u_\delta\right)^t\right)}$$

$$= me(g, g)^{\alpha s} \cdot \frac{\prod_{i \in A^*} e\left(h_i \prod_\theta^e u_\theta, g\right)^{st} \cdot e(g^s, h_i^t) \cdot e(g^{as_i \cdot \lambda_i} h_i^{-s}, g^t)}{e(g^s, g^\alpha) \cdot e(g^s, g^{at}) \prod_{i \in A^*} e\left(g, h_i \prod_{\delta=1}^e u_\delta\right)^{st}}$$

$$= m \frac{\prod_{i \in A^*} e\left(g^s, h_i^t\right) \cdot e\left(g^{as} h_i^{-s}, g^t\right)}{e(g, g)^{ast}}$$

$$= m \frac{\prod_{i \in A^*} e\left(g^s, h_i^t\right) \cdot e(g^{as}, g^t) \cdot e\left(h_i^{-s}, g^t\right)}{e(g, g)^{ast}}$$

$$= m \frac{\prod_{i \in A^*} e(g, h_i)^{st} \cdot e(h_i, g)^{-st} \cdot e(g, g)^{ast}}{e(g, g)^{ast}}$$

$$= m$$

4   Security Analysis

4.1   Security Model

Refering to [14], we firstly give our CP-HABE security model. We model the semantic security model opposed to chosen-plaintext attack (CPA) based on selective attribute (sAtt) model. We now present a game, which is played in two players: a challenger C plus an adversary A. This game defines the concept of semantic security in the CP-HABE scheme.

Init: Firstly A chooses the challenge access control policy Γ^*, which is given to C.

Setup: With a security parameter 1^λ chosen by C and is large enough, C can calculate the algorithm **Setup** to acquire mk, the master key, as well as $params$, the public parameters. C gives A $params$ but maintain mk herself.

Phase 1: A requests for a bounded number in polynomial of any attribute set A_i not satisfying Γ^*. C returns **KeyGen**.

Challenge: A submits m_1 and m_0, two messages having the same length. Randomly, C chooses $b \in \{0, 1\}$, then encrypts m_b over Γ^*. After that, the challenge ciphertext CT^* is sent to A.

Phase 2: Similar to **Phase 1**.

Guess: A gives $b' \in \{0, 1\}$, a speculation of b. A beats C if $b = b'$. A's advantage is

$$Adv_{CP-HABE,A} = |\Pr[b = b'] - 1/2|$$

Definition 2. If no adversary holds a non-negligible advantage in polynomial time, then the CP-HABE scheme is secure.

Security proof.

Theorem 1. No adversary is able to break our construction selectively in polynomial time if the decisional l-parallel BDHE assumption holds.

The above theorem can ensure the security of our CP-HABE scheme.

Proof. In the security game, Assume that we have an adversary A with a non-negligible advantage $\varepsilon = Adv_{CP-HABE,A}$. Below we will show you how to use adversary A to construct B, which is a simulator playing the decisional l-parallel BDHE problem.

Init: Given $(G, G_1, e, g, g^s, y_1, y_2, \ldots, y_l, y_{l+2}, \ldots, y_{2l}, T)$, in which $y_i = g^{a^i}$, then we let $Y = (g, g^s, y_1, y_2, \ldots, y_l, y_{l+2}, \ldots, y_{2l})$. A chooses a challenge access control policy (M^*, ρ^*), in which M^* is a $d^* \times e^*$ matrix, $e^* \leq l$, and B receives it.

Setup: B chooses at random $\alpha' \in Z_p^*$, let $W = e(y_1, y_l) \cdot e(g, g)^{\alpha'} = e\left(g^a, g^{a^l}\right) \cdot e(g, g)^{\alpha'} = e(g, g)^{\alpha' + a^{l+1}}$. For each a_i for $1 \leq a_i \leq U^*$, it firstly selects a value $Z_i \in Z_p^*$ randomly, and U^* being the sets of attributes in the access control policy. If $a_i \notin P^*$, set $h_i = g^{z_i} \prod_{j=1}^{e^*} y_j^{M_{i,j}^*}$, otherwise let $h_i = g^{z_i}$. For $1 \leq k \leq e^*$, it chooses at random $\delta_0, \delta_1,$

$\ldots, \delta_{e^*} \in Z_p^*$, let $u_k = g^{\delta_k} y_{l-k+1}^{-1}$. B sends public parameters $params = (G, G_1, g, e, W,$
$(h_i)_{1 \leq i \leq d^*}, (u_j)_{1 \leq j \leq e^*})$ to A, while keeping the master key $mk = g^{\alpha^l + a^{l+l}}$ for itself.

Phase 1: A requests for a number bounded in polynomial of any attribute set A^* not meeting the needs of challenge access control policy (M^*, P^*) in this phase. By the definition of LSSS, there must exist a vector $K = (k_1, k_2, \ldots, k_{e^*}) \in Z^e$ such that $M^* \cdot K = 0$ with $k_1 = -1$. B selects $t' \in Z_p^*$ randomly, sets $t = t' + \sum_{j=1}^{e^*} k_j a^{l-j+1}$, then computes:

$$d_0 = g^t = g^{t' + \sum_{j=1}^{e^*} k_j a^{l-j+1}} = \prod_{j=1}^{e^*} y^{l-j+1} g^{t'}$$

$$d_1 = g^\alpha g^{at} \left(h_i \prod_{\delta=1}^e u_\delta \right)^t$$

$$= g^{\alpha^l + a^{l+1}} g^{a\left(t' + \sum_{j=1}^{e^*} k_j a^{l-j+1} \right)} \left(h_i \prod_{\delta=1}^e u_\delta \right)^{\left(t' + \sum_{j=1}^{e^*} k_j a^{l-j+1} \right)}$$

$$= g^{\alpha^l} g^{a^{l+1}} g^{at'} g^{a \sum_{j=1}^{e^*} k_j a^{l-j+1}} \left(h_i \prod_{\delta=1}^e u_\delta \right)^{t'} \left(h_i \prod_{\delta=1}^e u_\delta \right)^{\sum_{j=1}^{e^*} k_j a^{l-j+1}}$$

$$= g^{\alpha^l} g^{a^{l+1}} g^{at'} g^{-a^{l+1}} g^{\sum_{j=2}^{e^*} k_j a^{l-j+2}} \left(g^{z_i} \prod_{j=1}^{e^*} y_j^{M_{i,j}^*} \prod_{k=1}^e g^{\delta_k} y_{l-k+1}^{-1} \right)^{\sum_{j=1}^{e^*} k_j a^{l-j+1}} \left(h_i \prod_{\delta=1}^e u_\delta \right)^{t'}$$

$$= g^{\alpha^l} g^{at'} \prod_{j=2}^{e^*} y_{l-j+2}^{k_j} g^{z_i \sum_{j=1}^{e^*} k_j a^{l-j+1}} \left(\prod_{k=1}^e g^{\delta_k} y_{l-k+1}^{-1} \right)^{\sum_{j=1}^{e^*} k_j a^{l-j+1}} \left(h_i \prod_{\delta=1}^e u_\delta \right)^{t'}$$

$$= g^{\alpha^l} g^{at'} \left(\prod_{j=2}^{e^*} y_{l-j+2}^{k_j (z_i + 1)} g^{-a^l z_i} \right) \left(\prod_{k=1}^e g^{\delta_k} y_{l-k+1}^{-1} \right)^{\sum_{j=1}^{e^*} k_j a^{l-j+1}} \left(h_i \prod_{\delta=1}^e u_\delta \right)^{t'}$$

$$= \left[\left(\prod_{j=2}^{e^*} y_{l-j+2}^{k_j (z_i + 1)} g^{-a^l z_i} \right) \left(\prod_{k=1}^e g^{\delta_k} y_{l-k+1}^{-1} \right)^{\sum_{j=1}^{e^*} k_j a^{l-j+1}} \right] g^{\alpha^l} g^{at'} \left(h_i \prod_{\delta=1}^e u_\delta \right)^{t'}$$

$$d_2 = h_i^t = \left(g^{z_i} \prod_{j=1}^{e^*} y_j^{M_{i,j}^*} \right)^{t' + \sum_{j=1}^{e^*} k_j a^{l-j+1}} = \left(g^{z_i} \prod_{j=1}^{e^*} y_j^{M_{i,j}^*} \right)^{\sum_{j=1}^{e^*} k_j a^{l-j+1}} h_i^{t'}$$

$$= g^{z_i \sum_{j=1}^{e^*} k_j a^{l-j+1}} h_i^{t'} = \prod_{j=1}^{e^*} y_{l-j+1}^{z_i k_j} h_i^{t'}$$

B sends the secret key $d = (d_0, \{d_1, d_2\}_{a \in A^*})$ to A.

Challenge: Two messages $m_0, m_1 \in G_1$ are submitted by A. B chooses $b \in (0, 1)$, and encrypts m_b for $1 \leq i \leq d^*$ as follows:

$$CT_1 = m_b T e \left(g^s, g^\alpha \right), \quad CT_2 = g^s, \quad CT_3 = \left(h_i \prod_\theta^e u_\theta \right)^s$$

Intuitively, B then chooses uniformly random integers $\rho_2', \ldots, \rho_{e^*}' \in [-2^{L_0 + k}, 2^{L_0 + k}]$ and shares the secret s using the vector $\rho^* = (s, sa + \rho_2', \ldots, sa^{e^* - 1} + \rho_{e^*}')$ with $\rho_1' = 0$.

Let $s_i = M^* \cdot \rho^* = \sum_{j=1}^{e^*} \left(sa^{j-1} M_{i,j}^* + \rho_j' M_{i,j}^* \right)$, then the corresponding challenge ciphertext is computed as follows:

$$CT_4 = g^{as_i}h_i^{-s} = g^{a\sum_{j=1}^{e^*}\left(sa^{j-1}M_{i,j}^* + \rho_j'M_{i,j}^*\right)}h_i^{-s}$$

$$= \prod_{j=1}^{e^*} g^{sa^j M_{i,j}^*} g^{a\rho_j' M_{i,j}^*} \left(g^{z_i}\prod_{j=1}^{e^*} y_j^{M_{i,j}^*}\right)^{-s}$$

$$= \prod_{j=1}^{e^*} g^{sa^j M_{i,j}^*} g^{a\rho_j' M_{i,j}^*} (g^{z_i})^{-s}\prod_{j=1}^{e^*} y_j^{-sM_{i,j}^*}$$

$$= \prod_{j=1}^{e^*} y_j^{sa M_{i,j}^*} g^{a\rho_j' M_{i,j}^*} (g^{z_i})^{-s}\prod_{j=1}^{e^*} y_j^{-sM_{i,j}^*}$$

$$= g^{a\rho_j' M_{i,j}^*} (g^{z_i})^{-s}$$

A receives the challenge ciphertext $CT^* = \left(CT_1, CT_2, \{CT_3, CT_4\}_{a\in A}\right)$.

Phase 2: Similar to **Phase 1.**

Guess: Finally, A give b'. B outputs 0 to assume that $T = e(g^s, y_{l+1}) = e(g,g)^{sa^{l+1}}$ if $b' = b$; or else outputs 1 in order to indiciate that it considers T as a random element in group G_1.

B shows a perfect simulation when $CT_1 = m_b Te(g^s, g^{\alpha'}) = m_b e(g,g)^{s(\alpha' + a^{l+1})} = m_b e(g,g)^{\alpha s}$ and $T = e(g^s, y_{l+1})$, then the advantage is $\Pr[B(Y, e(g^s, y_{l+1})) = 0] = \frac{1}{2} + Adv_{CP-HABE,A}$. Otherwise the advantage is $\Pr[B(Y,R) = 0] = \frac{1}{2}$ if T is a random group element R in G_1.

All the analysis shows that

$$|\Pr[B(Y, e(g^s, y_{l+1})) = 0] - \Pr[B(Y,R) = 0]| \geq \left|(\frac{1}{2}\pm\varepsilon) - \frac{1}{2}\right| = \varepsilon$$

We have completed the proof of Theorem 1.

5 Performance Evaluation

Comparing with the scheme in [7], the following tables show the results based on the comparsion of storage cost and computation cost respectively.

Table 1. Comparsion of storage cost

Scheme	Public parameters	Secret key	Ciphertext
[7] scheme	$(L+D+3)l_1 + l_2$	$[(l-k+1)|S|+2]l_1$	$(3l+2)l_1$
Our scheme	$(L+D+2)l_1 + l_2$	$(2|S|+1)l_1$	$(2l+2)l_1$

In these two tables, L and D indicate the number of rows and number of columns of the attribute matrix in [7] scheme respectively, the maximum depth and the number of the attribute trees in our scheme. k is the depth of the user ($k \leq L$), l_1, l_2 the bit lengths of the elements of group G, G_1, respectively, and l and n the numbers of rows and columns, respectively, of the share-generating matrix. Exponentiation, choosing a random element and computing a bilinear pairing are denoted by τ_e, τ_r and τ_p. $|S|$ and $|S^*|$ are the number of attribute vectors of the set meeting the access structure related to a ciphertext as well as the number related to a user, respectively.

Table 2. Comparsion of computation cost

Scheme	Encrypt	Decrypt
[7] scheme	$[(4+k)l+2]\tau_e + (n+l)\tau_r$	$|S^*|\tau_e + (3|S^*|+1)\tau_p$
Our scheme	$[(l+3)n+2]\tau_e + (n+l)\tau_r$	$|S^*|\tau_e + (3|S^*|+1)\tau_p$

We give the comparison of the scheme in [7] with our scheme in terms of storage cost and computation cost in Tables 1 and 2. Our CP-HABE scheme has significantly better performance than the scheme in [7].

Additionally, the scheme in [7] is essentially a hierarchical identity-based encryption scheme. However, our scheme is a truly hierarchical attribute-based encryption scheme, which can reflect the hierarchy relationships among the attributes in the same category, so that it can achieve the purpose of simplifying access control rules.

What's more, access control structure in our CP-HABE scheme can reflect the logical relationships between access control policies, which is more expressive.

6 Conclusion

We put forward a new kind of ciphertext-policy hierarchical attribute-based encryption scheme based on LISS, which reflects the logical relationships between access control policies and hierarchy relationships between the attributes in the same category. In the standard model, this scheme has been proved to be secure on the basis of decisional l-BDHE assumption. Comparing with the scheme in [7], our HABE scheme achieves significantly better performance.

Acknowledgements. This work is partly supported by the Fundamental Research Funds for the Central Universities (No. NZ2015108), and the China Postdoctoral Science Foundation funded project (2015M571752), and the Jiangsu Planned Projects for Postdoctoral Research Funds (1402033C), and Open Project Foundation of Information Technology Research Base of Civil Aviation Administration of China(NO.CAAC-ITRB-201405).

References

1. Guo, L., Wang, J., Wu, H., Du, H.: eXtensible Markup Language access control model with filtering privacy based on matrix storage. IET Commun. **8**, 1919–1927 (2014)
2. Sahai, A., Waters, B.: Fuzzy identity-based encryption. In: Cramer, R. (ed.) EUROCRYPT 2005. LNCS, vol. 3494, pp. 457–473. Springer, Heidelberg (2005)
3. Li, J., Wang, Q., Wang, C., Ren, K.: Enhancing attribute-based encryption with attribute hierarchy. Mob. Netw. Appl. **16**, 553–561 (2011)
4. Wang, G., Liu, Q., Wu, J., Guo, M.: Hierarchical attribute-based encryption and scalable user revocation for sharing data in cloud servers. Comput. Secur. **30**, 320–331 (2011)
5. Wan, Z., Liu, J.E., Deng, R.H.: HASBE: a hierarchical attribute-based solution for flexible and scalable access control in cloud computing. IEEE Trans. Inf. Forensics Secur. **7**, 743–754 (2012)

6. Liu, X., Xia, Y., Jiang, S., Xia, F., Wang, Y.: Hierarchical attribute-based access control with authentication for outsourced data in cloud computing. In: 2013 12th IEEE International Conference on Trust, Security and Privacy in Computing and Communications (TrustCom), pp. 477–484. IEEE (2013)

7. Deng, H., Wu, Q., Qin, B., Domingo-Ferrer, J., Zhang, L., Liu, J., Shi, W.: Ciphertext-policy hierarchical attribute-based encryption with short ciphertexts. Inf. Sci. **275**, 370–384 (2014)

8. Goyal, V., Pandey, O., Sahai, A., Waters, B.: Attribute-based encryption for fine-grained access control of encrypted data. In: Proceedings of the 13th ACM Conference on Computer and Communications Security, pp. 89–98. ACM (2006)

9. Bethencourt, J., Sahai, A., Waters, B.: Ciphertext-policy attribute-based encryption. In: IEEE Symposium on Security and Privacy, 2007, SP 2007, pp. 321–334. IEEE (2007)

10. Cheung, L., Newport, C.: Provably secure ciphertext policy ABE. In: Proceedings of the 14th ACM Conference on Computer and Communications Security, pp. 456–465. ACM (2007)

11. Goyal, V., Jain, A., Pandey, O., Sahai, A.: Bounded ciphertext policy attribute based encryption. In: Aceto, L., Damgård, I., Goldberg, L.A., Halldórsson, M.M., Ingólfsdóttir, A., Walukiewicz, I. (eds.) ICALP 2008, Part II. LNCS, vol. 5126, pp. 579–591. Springer, Heidelberg (2008)

12. Kapadia, A., Tsang, P.P., Smith, S.W.: Attribute-based publishing with hidden credentials and hidden policies. In: NDSS, pp. 179–192 (2007)

13. Boneh, D., Waters, B.: Conjunctive, subset, and range queries on encrypted data. In: Vadhan, S.P. (ed.) TCC 2007. LNCS, vol. 4392, pp. 535–554. Springer, Heidelberg (2007)

14. Waters, B.: Ciphertext-policy attribute-based encryption: an expressive, efficient, and provably secure realization. In: Catalano, D., Fazio, N., Gennaro, R., Nicolosi, A. (eds.) PKC 2011. LNCS, vol. 6571, pp. 53–70. Springer, Heidelberg (2011)

15. Balu, A., Kuppusamy, K.: An expressive and provably secure ciphertext-policy attribute-based encryption. Inf. Sci. **276**, 354–362 (2014)

16. Boneh, D., Franklin, M.: Identity-based encryption from the weil pairing. In: Kilian, J. (ed.) CRYPTO 2001. LNCS, vol. 2139, pp. 213–229. Springer, Heidelberg (2001)

17. Damgård, I.B., Thorbek, R.: Linear integer secret sharing and distributed exponentiation. In: Yung, M., Dodis, Y., Kiayias, A., Malkin, T. (eds.) PKC 2006. LNCS, vol. 3958, pp. 75–90. Springer, Heidelberg (2006)

Privacy-Preserving Multidimensional Range Query on Real-Time Data

Zhong Ting[✉], Han Xiao, Yang Yunshuo, and Zhu Aixiang

School of Information and Software Engineering,
University of Electronic Science and Technology of China,
Chengdu, China
zhongting@uesct.edu.cn

Abstract. We propose a scheme for realizing privacy-preserving multidimensional range query on real-time data. This is motivated by the scenario where data owner (DO) stores its real-time data that are periodically submitted by its subordinate data collectors (DCs) on cloud service provider (CSP) in encrypted form and sometimes executes range query. The semi-trusted CSP is curious about the data and may return incomplete query results to DO. We divide time into N epochs and adopt key-insulated technology which supports periodical key update to bucketization method. Our scheme radically reduces the cost of DO and is more secure in the sense that keys for up to $m < N$ epochs can be compromised without jeopardizing the security of whole system. Moreover, we realize the integrity verification of query results. Experiment results show that the cost of our scheme is acceptable, particularly for the scenario where each DC collects small amount of real-time data in each epoch.

Keywords: Multidimensional range query · Real-time data · Key-insulated technology · Privacy-preserving · Storage security

1 Introduction

Motivation: In some data outsourcing scenarios, the data owner (DO) may store its real-time data that are periodically submitted by its subordinate data collectors (DCs) on cloud service provider (CSP) in encrypted form. For a typical example, Fig. 1 shows a radiation detection scenario where DCs which manage sensing devices periodically upload the data they collected to CSP, and the data they collected are related with three dimensions: the time, the geographic location of the road (denoted by GPS coordinates) and the local radiation level. Environmental Protection Agency (DO) sometimes may query the CSP to get radiation levels of roads. Moreover, there are many other similar scenarios, such as traffic accident monitoring system where Traffic Management Agency often requests pictures of accidents stored on CSP. In these scenarios, the privacy of those data which DCs upload to the CSP should be respected. We note that CSPs in these scenarios is semi-trusted and curious. The CSP can correctly implement various operations by rules but may omit some query results and it is curious about the data they store. In addition, the CSP may omit some query results.

© Springer International Publishing Switzerland 2015
Z. Huang et al. (Eds.): ICCCS 2015, LNCS 9483, pp. 49–61, 2015.
DOI: 10.1007/978-3-319-27051-7_5

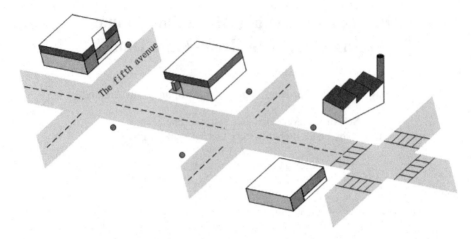

Fig. 1. Radiation detection scenario

We aim to realize multidimensional range query on real time data with privacy-preserving in the above scenarios. Generally, it is necessary to store these sensitive data in encrypted form and the keys are kept secret from CSP all the time. In the trivial approach, DCs upload data to DO in real time first. Then DO encrypts the data and generates indexes itself and finally uploads them to CSP. Also, DO may sometimes query the data that are stored in CSP. Note that symmetric cryptosystem, such as AES, is used in the trivial approach, and the key keeps unchanged.

Since data that DCs upload to DO is real-time, the trivial approach is very ineffi-cient. DO needs to frequently upload newly collected data to the CSP and frequently updates index structure on the CSP, which lead to very high cost at DO.

For the scenario mentioned above, we propose a scheme to realize privacy-preserving multidimensional range query based on bucketization scheme on real-time data for cloud storage. Since we are dealing with real time data, we divide time into N epochs and adopt an asymmetric key-insulated method to automatically update the key at each epoch. Thus DO only need to issue keys to DC every N epochs and query the CSP when necessary. DCs directly upload the collected real time data and indexing information to the CSP. Furthermore, since the CSP is semi-trusted and may submit forged or incomplete query results to DO, it is necessary to guarantee the integrity of query result.

Our Contributions: For the scenario mentioned above, we propose a scheme to realize privacy-preserving multidimensional range query based on bucketization scheme on real-time data for cloud storage. To summarize, the contributions of this paper are: (1) We divide time into N epochs and adopt key-insulated technology which is based on public key cryptosystem and supports periodical key update to bucketization method. Compared with the trivial approach, there are two advantages: (i) DCs undertake most of the work including collecting data, generating indexes and uploading data and thus radically reduce the cost of DO in the trivial approach. (ii) Key distri-bution is simple, because keys of each epoch can be calculated from keys of the previous epoch and the cycle for key distribution are N epochs where N is a parameter of the key-insulated technology. (2) Our scheme supports the integrity verification of query result, and can verify whether CSP who is semi-trusted omits some query results or not and thereby avoid the query-result incompleteness.

Organization: Section 2 introduces related works. Our scheme is presented in Sect. 3 and security analysis is exhibited in Sect. 4. Experiment results are provided in Sect. 5. Section 6 is the conclusion and Sect. 7 is the acknowledgements of this paper.

2 Related Work

2.1 Solutions for Multidimensional Range Query

So far, there are mainly three types of solutions for multidimensional range queries:

(1) Methods that use some specialized data structures [1–3]: The performance of these methods often gets worse as the dimension of data increases. Shi et al. [1] proposes a binary interval tree to represent ranges efficiently and applies it to multidimensional range queries, but their scheme cannot avoid unwanted leakage of information because of adapting one-dimensional search techniques to the multidimensional case. A binary string-based encoding of ranges is proposed by Li, J. et al. in [3]. However, since each record in their scheme has to be checked by the server in query processing, the access mechanism of their scheme is inefficient. (2) Order-preserving encryption-based techniques (OPE) [4, 5]: the order of plaintext data in OPE is preserved in cipher text domain. But it is susceptible to statistical attacks as the encryption is deterministic (i.e., the encryption of a given plaintext is identical, thus the frequency of distinct value in the dataset often be revealed). (3) Bucketization-based techniques [6–8]: Since it partitions and indexes data by simple distributional properties, it can realize efficient query and keep the information disclosure to a minimum. Hacigumus et al. [6] first propose the bucketization-based representation for query processing, and afterward many researchers adopted Bucketization-based techniques for multidimensional range queries [7–10].

2.2 Key-Insulated Technology

Key-insulated technology [9, 10, 11–13] is based on public key cryptosystem. We call a scheme is (m, N)-key-insulated [10] if it satisfies the following notion: we assume that the exposures of secret keys for decrypting data are inevitable and up to $m < N$ epochs can be compromised. Secret key which is used to decrypt the data encrypted by public key is refreshed at discrete time epochs via interaction with a secure device; public key update can be done independently. The security objective is to minimize the affect caused by compromised epochs, and the only thing an adversary can do is to destroy the security of the data in the epochs that are compromised.

3 Privacy-Preserving Multidimensional Range Query

In this section, we present a scheme for privacy-preserving multidimensional range query which can be applied in the case where data are submitted in real time.

We describe real-time data as a tuple of attribute values $\{A_1, A_2, \cdots, A_d\}$, where $d \geq 1$ denotes the number of attributes of data and this data is referred to as multidimensional data. We consider the following type of multidimensional range query:

$$(epoch = t) \wedge (l_a \leq A_j \leq l_b), j \in [1, d],$$

Where t denotes the interested epoch ($t \in [1, N]$), $[l_a, l_b]$ denotes the wanted range of attribute A_j. Moreover, this type of range query can be extended to the type of multiple range queries that involve several epochs and the union of several attributes.

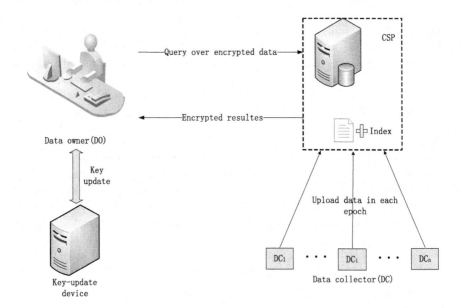

Fig. 2. System model

3.1 Our System Model

Figure 2 shows our system model. We assume that DO, DCs and the key-update device are trusted, while the CSP is semi-trusted and curious. The key-update device is physically-secure but computationally-limited, it is applied only to key updates and not applied to the actual cryptographic computations.

As for setup of the system, DO generates an initial decryption key, a master encryption key and a master key for each DC. Then it distributes master encryption keys to corresponding DCs, and distributes master keys to the key-update device. We will provide detailed system setup in Sect. 3.2.

At the end of each epoch, each DC generates an encryption key by its master encryption key to encrypt the data it collected in that epoch. In addition to partitioning the data to buckets by bucketization-based method, each DC also generates some verifying numbers for empty buckets (the buckets that have no data in them) which are used in our integrity verification processing of query result. The data which consists of bucket IDs, encrypted data and verifying numbers are finally uploaded to the CSP by each DC at each epoch. Detailed data processing in each epoch is provided in Sect. 3.3.

DO sometimes needs to query the data stored on the CSP. DO first translates plaintext queries to bucket IDs and sends them to the CSP. Then the CSP returns a set of encrypted results, it also returns a proof that is generated using corresponding verifying numbers. Once DO receives the results, it first verifies query-result integrity by the proof. If it succeeds, DO will update the decryption key(s) by interacting with the key-update device to decrypt the encrypted results and then filter them to get wanted query results. Note that in our scheme, initial decryption keys are used only one time when DO generates decryption keys of the first epoch ($t = 1$) and DO can update the to the decryption keys of any desired epoch on "one shot". Detailed query processing is shown in Sect. 3.4.

3.2 System Setup

For DC_i, DO generates master encryption keys, initial decryption keys and master keys by the key generation algorithm $\mathcal{G}(1^k, m, N) \rightarrow (PK_i^*, SK_i^*, SK_{i,0})$.

In detail, given a security parameter 1^k, the maximum of acceptable exposure epoch m and the number of epochs N, DO does following steps for DC_i:

Step 1. It randomly chooses a prime $q(|q| = k)$ and a prime $p = 2q + 1$. Let $\mathbb{G} \subset \mathbb{Z}_p^*$ of size q be a unique subgroup. And we assume that $\mathbb{G}$ holds the DDH assumption. Then it chooses $g, h \in \mathbb{G}$ at random.

Step 2. It selects $x_0^*, y_0^*, \cdots, x_m^*, y_m^*$ by $\mathbb{Z}_q$;

Step 3. It computes $z_0^* = g^{x_0^*} h^{y_0^*}, \cdots, z_m^* = g^{x_m^*} h^{y_m^*}$;

Step 4. Finally, it outputs:

the master encryption key, $PK_i^* = (g, h, z_0^*, \cdots, z_m^*)$;

the initial decryption key, $SK_{i,0} = (x_0^*, y_0^*)$;

the master key, $SK_i^* = (x_1^*, y_1^*, \cdots, x_m^*, y_m^*)$.

Step 5. It distributes the master encryption key PK_i^* to DC_i, and distributes master key SK_i^* to the key-update device.

3.3 Data Processing in Each Epoch

Each DC partitions the data it collected into buckets by bucketization based method [14]. Note that we denote by bucket ID the index in our scheme. Due to space constraints, we do not describe bucketization based method in detail. For convenience, we make the following assumptions:

- We denote by Ω the set of all buckets including non-empty buckets and empty buckets that DC_i generated in epoch t.
- We define the number of non-empty buckets DC_i generated in epoch t with $Y_{i,t}$, the non-empty buckets DC_i generated in epoch t are denoted by $\mathbf{B}_{i,t} = \{b_1, b_2, \cdots, b_{Y_{i,t}}\} \subseteq \Omega, j \in [1, Y_{i,t}]$.

At the end of each epoch, each DC generates the corresponding encryption key for the epoch by its master encryption key and uses it to encrypt all the non-empty buckets that have data in them. Let's consider the encryption work that DC_i does at the end of epoch t. Given master encryption key $PK_i^* \equiv (g, h, z_0^*, \cdots, z_m^*)$ and epoch value t, DC_i does:

Step 1. It computes $PK_{i,t} = \prod_{l=0}^{m} (z_l^*)^{t^l}$;

Step 2. It selects $r \in \mathbb{Z}_q$ at random, and computes the cipher text of data D_j falling into the bucket b_j: $\left(\{D_j\}_{PK_{i,t}}\right) = \left(g^r, h^r, (PK_{i,t})^r \cdot (D_j)\right)$.

Although the above encryption method can ensure data confidentiality (as the CSP does not know decryption key), the CSP may still omit some data which satisfy the query, leading to query-result incompleteness. Our solution is that DC_i generates verifying number $num(b_k, i, t)$ for each empty bucket $b_k \in \Omega \backslash \mathbf{B}_{i,t}$ at the end of epoch t: $num(b_k, i, t) = h_a(i \parallel t \parallel b_k \parallel PK_{i,t})$, where $h_a(\cdot)$ denotes a hash function of a bits. Finally, DC_i uploads to the CSP all encrypted non-empty buckets and verifying numbers with their respective bucket IDs as follows:

$$i, t, \left\{b_j, \{D_j\}_{PK_{i,t}} | b_j \in \mathbf{B}_{i,t}\right\}, \left\{b_k, num(b_k, i, t) | b_k \in \Omega \backslash \mathbf{B}_{i,t}\right\}.$$

3.4   Query Processing

3.4.1   Decryption Key Update

The key update here is semantic secure which can be proved under the DDH assumption. We note that the key-update device is unnecessary for key update in the scenario where the storage of DO is secure (decryption keys cannot be exposure). Here, we assume that the exposures of decryption keys are inevitable and up to $m < N$ epochs can be compromised (where m is a parameter). Adversary is not sufficient to derive any decryption keys even it compromise the key-update alone.

Let's consider the update from the decryption key $SK_{i,t}$ which can decrypt the data uploaded by DC_i in epoch t to the decryption key $SK_{i,t'}(t, t' \in [1, N], t < t')$.

First, the key-update device generates a partial decryption key $SK'_{i,t'}$ of epoch t' by the device key-update algorithm $\mathcal{DKU} \ominus (t', SK_i^*) \rightarrow \left(SK'_{i,t'}\right)$, which inputs epoch value t' and the master key $SK_i^* = (x_1^*, y_1^*, \cdots, x_m^*, y_m^*)$ and finally outputs partial decryption key $SK'_{i,t'} = (x'_{t'}, y'_{t'})$ by computing $x'_{t'} \equiv \sum_{l=1}^{m} x_l^* \left((t')^l - t^l\right)$ and $y'_{t'} \equiv$

$\sum_{l=1}^{m} y_l^* \left((t')^l - t^l\right)$. We assume that the exposure of partial decryption key occurs less likely than the exposure of decryption key.

Second, DO uses the partial decryption key $SK_{i,t'}'$ to generate the decryption key $SK_{i,t'}$ by the DO key-update algorithm $\mathcal{DOKU}\left(t', SK_{i,t}, SK_{i,t'}'\right) \rightarrow \left(SK_{i,t'}\right)$, which inputs epoch value t', the decryption key of epoch t $SK_{i,t} = (x_t, y_t)$ and the partial decryption key $SK_{i,t'}' = (x_{t'}', y_{t'}')$ and finally outputs the decryption key $SK_{i,t'} = (x_{t'}, y_{t'})$ by computing $x_{t'} = x_t + x_{t'}'$ and $y_{t'} = y_t + y_{t'}'$.

3.4.2 Query and Verification

Here, we make the following assumptions for convenience: (1) We denote by α the average number of non-empty buckets generated by all DCs in each epoch; (2) $\langle t, Q_t \rangle$ denotes a query, where Q_t represents the set of queried bucket IDs.

When DO wants to query some data, it first translates the plaintext query to $\langle t, Q_t \rangle$ by the bucketization based partition method. After receiving $\langle t, Q_t \rangle$, CSP queries the data that are uploaded by DCs in epoch t to get all the buckets satisfying Q_t and then it computes a hash by the concatenated verifying numbers from all DCs which corresponding empty bucket IDs interacts with Q_t:

$$NUM_{Q_t} = h_b\left(\underset{b_k \in Q_t \cap \Omega \backslash \mathbf{B}_{i,t}, i \in [1,n], t \in [1,N]}{||} num(b_k, t)\right),$$

Where $h_b(\cdot)$ is a hash function with b bits. And afterwards the CSP returns query results as follows:

$$i, t, \left\{b_j, \{D_j\}_{PK_{i,t}} | b_j \in Q_t \cap \mathbf{B}_{i,t}\right\}, \left\{b_k, NUM_{Q_t} | b_k \in Q_t \cap \Omega \backslash \mathbf{B}_{i,t}, i \in [1,n], t \in [1,N]\right\}.$$

Since DO knows PK_i^*, it can compute all the corresponding verifying numbers and then computes a NUM_{Q_t}'. If $NUM_{Q_t}' = NUM_{Q_t}$, DO considers that CSP did not omit query results (otherwise it did) then uses corresponding decryption key(s) to decrypt the results by computing $D_{i,j} \equiv \{D_j\}_{PK_{i,t}} \Big/ g^{rx_t} h^{ry_t}$. We note that DO can query the data that are uploaded by several DCs in several epochs.

However, the query results always contain some superfluous data items (false positives) that DO does not really want (as the interested ranges may not exactly span full buckets). Using finer buckets can reduce such false positives, but this brings the problem that the data distribution may be more accurately estimated by adversary and thus increase the risk of information disclosure in bucketization. For this problem, we can adopt the maximum entropy principle to each bucket to uniform the distribution of sensitive attributes in each bucket, whereby minimize the risk of disclosure. And we also can refer to [15, 16] for optimal bucketing strategies which can achieve a good balance between reducing false positives and reducing the risk of information disclosure.

4 Security Analysis

4.1 Analysis on Integrity Verification

As we discussed above, the CSP may omit some query results, leading to incompleteness of query. Let's consider the probability that the misbehavior of the CSP can be detected. We assume that each of α non-empty bucket is queried with probability γ and omitted with probability δ, so the total number of omitted buckets generated by all DCs is $\alpha\gamma\delta$. To escape the detection by DO, the CSP must return a correct NUM'_{Q_t} corresponding to the incomplete query results. And the probability of guessing a correct NUM'_{Q_t} is 2^{-a}. So the probability that the misbehavior of the CSP can be detected is:

$$P_{\text{det}} = 1 - 2^{-a\alpha\gamma\delta}.$$

It is more likely to successfully detect the misbehavior of the CSP as $a\alpha\gamma\delta$ is larger.

4.2 Analysis on Impact of Compromised DCs

In this section, we analyze the case that adversary may additionally compromise some DCs to help the CSP escape our query-result integrity verification. With the master encryption keys revealed by these compromised DCs, the CSP can derive all the corresponding verifying numbers and omit the buckets which are uploaded by compromised DCs without being detected. Note that the behaviors of compromised DCs can not affect non-compromised DCs, so the performance of the integrity verification method will not be affected when non-compromised DCs are always the majority.

Specially, we assume that each DC is compromised with probability $p_c \ll 1/2$. Let's consider following case: the CSP omits some buckets generated by $n' = (1 - p_c)n$ non-compromised DCs which totally generate $\alpha' = \alpha(1 - p_c)$ non-empty buckets. The analysis on integrity verification still holds after replacing n with n' and α with α'.

4.3 Attacks on the (M, N)-Key-Insulated Method

Let's analyze the impact of compromised DO with an insecure storage and compromised key-update device. To model key exposure attacks, it assumed that adversary has right to access key exposure oracle (which inputs t and returns the temporary decryption key), left-or-right encryption oracle [17] (which inputs epoch value and plaintext data and then returns cipher text) and decryption oracle (which inputs epoch value and cipher text then returns plaintext).

Under the DDH assumption, the (m, N)-key-insulated method is semantically secure. The authors in [10] proved that the (m, N)-key-insulated method can against following three types of key exposure, and we omit the proof for space constraint: (1) Ordinary key exposure: it occurs when adversary compromise the insecure storage of DO (i.e., $SK_{i,t}$ is leaked); (2) Key-update exposure: it occurs when adversary break into the insecure storage of DO in key updating step (i.e., between epoch $t - 1$ and epoch t) to get $SK_{i,t-1}$, $SK'_{i,t}$ so as to generate $SK_{i,t}$; (3) Master key exposure: it occurs when adversary compromise the key-update device (i.e., leakage of SK_i^*).

5 Experiment

To evaluate the performance of our scheme, we compare it with the trivial approach described in Sect. 1. We assume that DO in the trivial approach adopts AES-128 algorithm and the same bucketization-based methods as in our scheme. In both approaches, time is divided into epochs. The cost of generating bucket IDs in both schemes can be ignored due to its simplicity. Let k be the total number of buckets in each epoch and λ be the percentage of non-empty buckets among all buckets. We denote the probability of each bucket being queried by γ. Since the duration for each epoch is not long and the data collected in each epoch and each bucket won't be much, we suppose that the size of data in each non-empty bucket and each epoch is 4096bit for simplicity.

Primitive Operations: The main (primitive) operations used in our scheme including

(1) Modular exponentiation;
(2) Modular multiplication;
(3) SHA-256 computation of 1024-bit integers.

The time needed for these operations was benchmarked in [18] as following:

(1) The average time for computing the power of a 1024-bit number to a 270-bit exponent and then reducing modulo was found to be $t_1 = 1.5$ ms;
(2) Multiplication of 270-bit numbers modulo was found to be $t_2 = 0.00016$ ms;
(3) The average time to compute the 256-bit digest of a 1024-bit number was found to be $t_3 = 0.01$ ms.

For efficiency, we can adopt AES-128 algorithm to encrypt the data in buckets and then use the keys generated by (m, N)-key-insulated method to encrypt symmetric keys in our scheme. Since AES-128 algorithm in the trivial approach and our scheme is efficient and the amount of data that are encrypted using AES-128 algorithm is same, we do not consider the cost of AES-128 algorithm when comparing the performance of the trivial approach and our scheme.

Next, we will compare the cost of the trivial approach and our scheme, including cost of the system setup, data processing work in each epoch and query processing. t'' is the number of queried epochs.

System Setup. DO in our scheme generates an initial decryption key, a master encryption key and a master key for each DC, while DO in the trivial approach only generates a key which is used in the AES-128 algorithm. In addition, DO in our scheme then distributes the master encryption key and the master key to the corresponding DC and key-update device respectively. We can ignore the transmission time, and the time of system setup for each DC is $2(m + 1)t_1 + (m + 1)t_2$. And the cost of system setup in

Table 1. The comparison between the trivial approach and our scheme in each epoch

		DO in trivial approach	DO in our scheme	DC in our scheme
In system setup	Generating keys	$O(1)$	$O(mn)$	\
In each epoch	Encryption	$O(\lambda k)$	\	$O(k/n)$
	Key update	\	\	$O(m)$
	Generating verifying numbers	\	\	$O(k(1-\lambda)/n)$
	Communication cost	$O(k)$	\	$O(k/n)$
In query processing	Key update	\	$O(mt'')$	\
	Decryption	$O(\gamma k)$	$O(\gamma k)$	\
	Verification	\	$O(k(1-\lambda)\gamma/n)$	\

our scheme is acceptable for the following two reasons: (i) The cost is linearly related to m which can be very small even for high security requirements. (ii) DO only needs to generate these keys for every N epochs.

Data Processing in Each Epoch. DO in the trivial approach needs to encrypt and generate bucket IDs for the data that are uploaded by all DCs, and it also need frequently upload these encrypted data and bucket IDs to CSP. The communication cost of DO would be high for real-time data. However, in our scheme, each DC undertakes these works for its data and DO don't need to do anything for data processing. Additionally, each DC in our scheme needs to generate its encryption key for current epoch and the time for key generation is $2(m+1)t_1 + mt_2$ (it is acceptable for the small value of m). And each DC in our scheme also generates verifying numbers for empty buckets and this is to improve security against semi-trusted CSP which the trivial approach doesn't consider. The averaged time that each DC in our scheme encrypts $\lambda k/n$ non-empty data buckets and generates verifying numbers for $(1-\lambda)k/n$ empty buckets in each epoch is $(3t_1 + t_2)\lambda k/n + (1-\lambda)kt_3/n$. It is worthwhile for DCs in our scheme to spend additional time for verifying numbers generation and encryption key update because this also improves security of the system. And the total time of data processing in each epoch for each DC is as follows:

$$2(m+1)t_1 + mt_2 + (3t_1 + t_2)\lambda k/n + (1-\lambda)kt_3/n$$

Results are showing in Fig. 3. There are four lines that denote the time for data upload work with $k = 1000$, $k = 2000$, $k = 3000$ and $k = 4000$, respectively. The time is increasing as λ increasing. Experiment results show that the cost of data processing work in each epoch for each DC is acceptable.

Query Processing. In addition to transforming query and decrypting query results, DO in our scheme need update decryption keys and verify the integrity of query results.

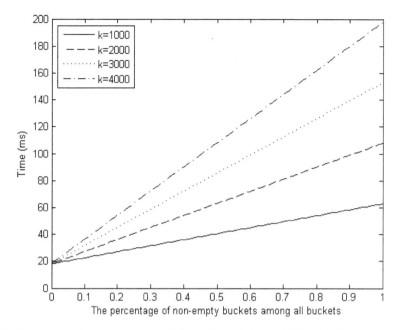

Fig. 3. The time for data processing work in each epoch for each DC with different amount of buckets ($n = 100$, $m = 5$).

But these only occur when DO wants to query the data. Here, let's first consider the case that DO queries the data that are uploaded by one DC in one epoch. The query results contain $k\lambda\gamma/n$ non-empty buckets, and the time for decrypt the query results is $2\lambda\gamma k(t_1 + t_2)/n$. Moreover, the time for key update is $4m(t_1 + t_2)$, and the time for computing NUM_{Q_t} is $(1 - \lambda)\gamma kt_3/n$. So the total time is below:

$$4m(t_1 + t_2) + 2\lambda\gamma k(t_1 + t_2)/n + (1 - \lambda)\gamma kt_3/n.$$

Results are shown in Fig. 4. There are four lines that denote the time for querying the data which are submitted by DC_i in one epoch with $k = 1000$, $k = 2000$, $k = 3000$ and $k = 4000$, respectively. Obviously, the query time increases with the number of buckets. In actual scenarios, such as radiation detection and traffic monitoring, DO often queries the data that are collected by sensing devices in specific area and limited number of epochs. Therefore, the cost of query processing in our scheme is acceptable.

Table 1 is the comparison between our scheme and the trivial approach. Note that the value of m is small in actual applications. In addition, the cost of DO in our scheme is radically reduced for the work of data processing are shared by n DCs. Additionally, since we adopt (m, N)-key-insulated method to update keys in each epoch, the data in our scheme is more secure compared with the data in the trivial approach that are encrypted by unchanged key during N epochs. Furthermore, our integrity verification method can verify that the semi-trusted CSP whether omit query results or not. The additional cost of key update and integrity verification are acceptable.

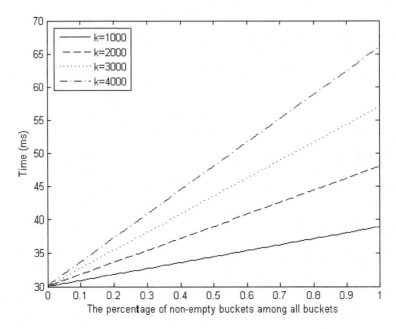

Fig. 4. The time for query processing with different amount of buckets ($n = 100$, $m = 5$, $\gamma = 0.3$).

6 Conclusion

In this paper, we are the first to construct a scheme for realizing multidimensional range query for real-time data. We adopt (m, N)-key-insulated method to bucketization method and radically reduce the cost of DO. In our scheme, DO don`t need to do anything at data processing in each epoch, and it only executes query when it wants. Each DC undertakes the work of updating encryption keys, encrypting and generating verifying numbers for its data in each epoch, and experiments show that the cost for each DC to do these works is acceptable for practice. By using (m, N)-key-insulated method which is semantically secure under the DDH assumption, we improve the security of data (an adversary who compromises at most m epochs can only destroy the security of the data in the epochs that are compromised) and also simplify the key distribution of DO. Furthermore, we can verify whether the semi-trusted CSP omits some query results or not and thereby ensure query-result integrity. Because of space constraints, we leave further research on the optimal method for reducing false positives and the risk of information disclosure for the future.

Acknowledgements. Our work is sponsored by the national natural science foundation of China (research on privacy protecting cipher text query algorithm in cloud storage, No. 61472064), the science and technology foundation of Sichuan province (research and application demonstration on trusted and safety-controllable privacy protecting service architecture for cloud data, 2015GZ0095) and the fundamental research funds for the central universities (research on some key technology in cloud storage security, YGX2013J072).

References

1. Shi, E., Bethencourt, J., Chan, H.T.-H., Song, D.X., Perrig, A.: Multi-dimensional range query over encrypted data. In: IEEE S&P (2007)
2. Boneh, D., Waters, B.: Conjunctive, subset, and range queries on encrypted data. In: Vadhan, S.P. (ed.) TCC 2007. LNCS, vol. 4392, pp. 535–554. Springer, Heidelberg (2007)
3. Li, J., Omiecinski, E.R.: Efficiency and security trade-off in supporting range queries on encrypted databases. In: Jajodia, S., Wijesekera, D. (eds.) Data and Applications Security 2005. LNCS, vol. 3654, pp. 69–83. Springer, Heidelberg (2005)
4. Agrawal, R., Kiernan, J., Srikant, R., Xu, Y.: Order-preserving encryption for numeric data. In: Proceedings of the 2004 ACM SIGMOD International Conference on Management of Data, pp. 563–574. ACM (2004)
5. Boldyreva, A., Chenette, N., Lee, Y., O'Neill, A.: Order-preserving symmetric encryption. In: Joux, A. (ed.) EUROCRYPT 2009. LNCS, vol. 5479, pp. 224–241. Springer, Heidelberg (2009)
6. Hacigümüş, H., Lyer, B., Li, C., Mehrotra, S.: Executing SQL over encrypted data in the database-service-provider model. In: Proceedings of the 2002 ACM SIGMOD International Conference on Management of Data, pp. 216–227. ACM (2002)
7. Hore, B., Mehrotra, S., Tsudik, G.: A privacy-preserving index for range queries. In: Proceedings of the Thirtieth International Conference on Very Large Data Bases, vol. 30, pp. 720–731. VLDB Endowment (2004)
8. Hore, B., Mehrotra, S., Canim, M., Kantarcioglu, M.: Secure multidimensional range queries over outsourced data. Int. J. Very Large Data Bases 21, 333–358 (2012)
9. Girault, M.: Relaxing tamper-resistance requirements for smart cards by using (auto-) proxy signatures. In: Quisquater, J.-J., Schneier, B. (eds.) CARDIS 1998. LNCS, vol. 1820, pp. 157–166. Springer, Heidelberg (2000)
10. Dodis, Y., Katz, J., Xu, S., Yung, M.: Key-insulated public key cryptosystems. In: Knudsen, L.R. (ed.) EUROCRYPT 2002. LNCS, vol. 2332, pp. 65–82. Springer, Heidelberg (2002)
11. Tzeng, W.-G., Tzeng, Z.-J.: Robust key-evolving public key encryption schemes. In: Deng, R.H., Qing, S., Bao, F., Zhou, J. (eds.) ICICS 2002. LNCS, vol. 2513, pp. 61–72. Springer, Heidelberg (2002)
12. Lu, C.-F., Shieh, S.-P.: Secure key-evolving protocols for discrete logarithm schemes. In: Preneel, B. (ed.) CT-RSA 2002. LNCS, vol. 2271, pp. 300–309. Springer, Heidelberg (2002)
13. Hanaoka, G., Hanaoka, Y., Imai, H.: Parallel key-insulated public key encryption. In: Yung, M., Dodis, Y., Kiayias, A., Malkin, T. (eds.) PKC 2006. LNCS, vol. 3958, pp. 105–122. Springer, Heidelberg (2006)
14. Zhang, R., Shi, J., Zhang, Y.: Secure multidimensional range queries in sensor networks. In: Proceedings of the Tenth ACM International Symposium on Mobile Ad Hoc Networking and Computing, pp. 197–206. ACM (2009)
15. Phan Van Song, Y.-L.: Query-optimal-bucketization and controlled-diffusion algorithms for privacy in outsourced databases. Project report, CS5322 Databases Security-2009/2010
16. Hore, B., Mehrotra, S., Tsudik, G.: A privacy-preserving index for range queries. In: Proceedings of the Thirtieth International Conference on Very Large Data Bases, vol. 30, pp. 720–731. VLDB Endowment (2004)
17. Bellare, M., Desai, A., Jokipii, E., Rogaway, P.: A concrete security treatment of symmetric encryption. In: Foundations of Computer Science, pp. 394–403 (1997)
18. Papamanthou, C., Tamassia, R., Triandopoulos, N.: Authenticated hash tables. In: Proceedings of the 15th ACM Conference on Computer and Communications Security, pp. 437–448. ACM (2008)

ARM-Based Privacy Preserving
for Medical Data Publishing

Zhang Fengli[⊠] and Bai Yijing

School of Information and Software Engineering,
University of Electronic Science and Technology of China,
Chengdu, China
yijing_1111@163.com

Abstract. The increasing use of electronic medical records (EMR) makes the medical data mining becomes a hot topic. Consequently, medical privacy invasion attracts people's attention. Among these, we are particularly interested in the privacy preserving for association rule mining (ARM). In this paper, we improve the traditional reconstruction-based privacy preserving data mining (PPDM) and propose a new architecture for medical data publishing with privacy preserving, and we present a sanitization algorithm for the sensitive rules hiding. In this architecture, the sensitive rules are strictly controlled as well as the side effects are minimized. And finally we performed an experiment to evaluate the proposed architecture.

Keywords: Medical data · Privacy preserving data mining · Association rule mining

1 Introduction

As the size of healthcare data increase dramatically, more and more medical information system are using digitalized technology to realize the storage of the big data. The electronic form of healthcare data is called EMR (electronic medical records). The storage of these information are all precious wealth of human being. These medical information resources are very valuable for disease treatment, diagnosis and medical research. And data mining, that is to find the valuable knowledge hidden in these massive medical data resources, has become a very important research topic. One of the typical application conditions of data mining is association rule mining(ARM). ARM is to find a rule set such that the support and confidence value of each rule is bigger than the giving threshold.

Despite that a great number of valuable knowledge are discovered by ARM, these rules may include some privacy information for the patients and medical department, people have shown increasing concern about privacy violation brought by the technology. Because there are person-specific information contained in the medical system, publish of data will cause unconscious privacy leakage, which may bring some bother to victim. Typically privacy information can be classified into two categories [1]: one is that you can get directly from the original data, which can be protected by the methodologies like perturbation, sampling, generalization/suppression, transformation,

Z. Huang et al. (Eds.): ICCCS 2015, LNCS 9483, pp. 62–73, 2015.
DOI: 10.1007/978-3-319-27051-7_6

or anonymity technology etc. The other is sensitive knowledge patterns, which is hidden in the data. You can get them only in the results of data mining. To avoid the disclosure, you have to use privacy-preserving data mining (PPDM).

Take the medical data publishing as example: a typical EMR(Electronic Medical Record) template in China contains <Name, ID Number, Gender, Age, Birth Place, Nationality, Symptoms, Physical Examination, Diagnosis,...>. We suppose there is a medical institution negotiating with a medical factory. The medical factory offers the institution with a reduced-price products if they publish their database of EMR to the factory. The medical institution accepts the deal and preprocesses data to hide the sensitive information like name, ID number etc. However factory starts mining the data using ARM, they find a woman who bought Zyban is most likely pregnant. The female customers who has bought Zyban in the medical factory would receive some promotion of maternal medicine from the factory, and some of them are indeed pregnant, then they will feel a strong privacy invasion. And how to hide these sensitive association rules in order to avoid this kind of privacy invasion is this paper mainly focuses on.

Privacy preserving of ARM is to process the original medical dataset to get a new dataset, so that the sensitive association rules cannot be mined from the new dataset but all the non-sensitive rules can still be mined from it.

To complete the above process, we propose a new architecture of privacy preserving for medical data publishing. The rest of this paper will be organized as follows: we describe the related work in Sect. 2. Section 3 provides the system architecture we proposed and some preliminary we use in this paper. The specific procedure of the architecture and all of the algorithm details in each step are described in Sect. 4. Section 5 discusses performance evaluation of our architecture and algorithms.

2 Related Works

Since the concept of PPDM was first proposed in 1999 by Agrawal [2], there were a great number of achievements in this field by now [3–5]. Data mining technology is an inter-discipline includes lots of data analysis techniques like statistics and machine learning, and hence the diversity of privacy-preserving techniques on it.

Lei Chen identifies the incompatibilities between the traditional PPDM and the typical free text Chinese EMR. And he proposed a series of new algorithms to solve the problem in [6]. Then he also designed a new framework of privacy preserving for healthcare data publishing based on the method in [7]. There are also some achievements for medical data protection in [8, 9].

Typically, privacy-preserving technology in the field of data mining can be divided into two categories. For one kind is to protect the sensitive data itself, like name, ID number. For medical data, the Health Insurance Portability and Accountability Act (HIPAA) was enacted in US in 1996 [10]. The Act announced the personal health information privacy standards and guidelines for implementation. There are many kinds of technologies to protect it. The most common one is anonymization, including k-anonymity [11], l-diversity [12], t-closeness [13]. In [14] Aristides Gionis and Tamir Tassa extended the framework of k-anonymity to include any type of generalization operators and define three measures to count the loss of information more accurately.

They also proved that the problem of k-anonymity with minimal loss of data is NP-hard. And then proceed to describe an approximation algorithm with an approximation guarantee of O(ln k).

Another kind of category is to protect the sensitive data mining results that were produced in the process of data mining [15]. Generally, these techniques are focusing on the improvement of data mining algorithms. Among them, we are particular interested in approaches proposed to perform association rule hiding [16, 17]. In [18] a new algorithm for hiding sensitive rules using distortion techniques are proposed by Jain. The confidence of the sensitive rules are reduced by altering the position of them. In [19] Le proposed a heuristic algorithm to identify the items which has the least impact on the mining results, and remove these items from the original data set. There are also many achievements in [20–22]. In [23] Verykios proposed three groups of algorithms to hide the sensitive rules based on reducing the support and confidence values, which can be seen as the precursors to the algorithms we proposed in this paper.

3   Arm-Based System Architecture of Privacy-Preserving for Medical Data Publishing

As showed in Fig. 1, in our architecture, there are three types of data characters: data owner, data collector, and data user. Data owner provides the original medical dataset and privacy definition and policy; data collector processes ARM and sanitization algorithm and publishes new dataset to data user. And we assume that data collector and network communications are reliable.

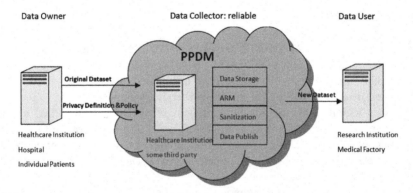

Fig. 1. ARM-based system architecture of privacy preserving for medical data publishing

Data owner could be a healthcare institution, hospital or individual patients, who has a collection of medical data provided to data collector. We use notation $D = \{T_1, T_2, T_3, \ldots, T_m\}$ to represent original medical dataset, and $I = \{i_1, i_2, i_3, \ldots, i_n\}$ to represents a set of items, $T_i \subseteq I$ is a transaction. We use TID to identify every transaction.

Data collector could be a healthcare institution or some third party(sometimes data owner and data collector could be the same one). Data collector's work includes: data storage, data processing(ARM and sanitization algorithm), and data publish. In this paper, we suppose that data storage and data publish are finished, and we only consider the data processing.

Data collector applied ARM algorithm on the dataset provided by data owner. We use r or $X => Y$ to denote a rule, where $X \subset I, Y \subset I$, and $X \cap Y = \emptyset$. Given an itemset X, support of an itemset is the number of transactions that contains the itemset, which is denoted as $s(X)$. $X => Y$ means the number of occurrence of Y on condition of occurrence of X. Given an rule r(or $X => Y$), X is denoted as r_1, and Y is r_r, support of the rule is the number of transactions that contain both X and Y, $s(X => Y) = s(X \cup Y)$. Confidence of a rule is the frequent of itemsets that contain Y appear in transactions that contain X, $c(X => Y) = P(Y|X) = P(X \cup Y)/P(X)$. We define two threshold: α for minimum support value, ε for minimum confidence value. And ARM is to find all the rules that satisfy $s(X => Y) \geq \alpha, c(X => Y) \geq \varepsilon$. We use $R = \{r|$all rules such that $s(r) \geq \alpha$ and $c(r) \geq \varepsilon\}$ to denote the mining result.

Then data collector identifies the privacy rules according to the privacy definition and policy. Here let Rh be a set of sensitive rules to be hidden, $Rh \subset R$.

And finally data collector clean Rh directly from original dataset by sanitization algorithm. For a rule $r \in R$, we use Tr to denote a set of transactions that r appears, $Tr = \{t \in D|r \subseteq t\}$. If there exists a rule $r' \in R$ such that, the number of items appears both in r and r' is larger than $|r|/2$ and $|r'|/2$, as well as r and r' both appear in one or more transaction, $Tr \cap Tr' \neq \emptyset$, we call r and r' are brother rules. We use Rb to denote a set of brother rules, $Rb = \{r'|r' \in R, r'$ and r are brother rules$\}$. After the sanitization algorithm, we got a new data set $D' = \{T'_1, T'_2, T'_3, \ldots, T'_n\}$. D' is a "clean" dataset that satisfy the condition: no rules in Rh can be mined from D', but all rules in (R-Rh) can still be mined from it.

Data user could be research institution, pharmaceutical factory etc. We consider data user is unreliable. The new dataset D' is the final dataset to be published to data user.

4   Processing of the Archetecture

The process of the architecture is showed in Fig. 2. Data owner provides original datasets D and privacy definition and policy. Data collector is the main part of the procedure who transforms the original datasets D into a "clean" datasets D' by applying a series a privacy-preserving algorithms, and finally publishes D' to data user.

The procedure of the framework is as follows:

step 1: Data owner provides the original datasets $D = \{T_1 T_2, T_3, \ldots, T_m\}$ and privacy definition and policy to data collector.
step 2: Data collector uses ARM algorithm to generate association rule set R.
step 3: Data collector identifies corresponding sensitive association rules Rh for different data users according to the privacy definition and policy.

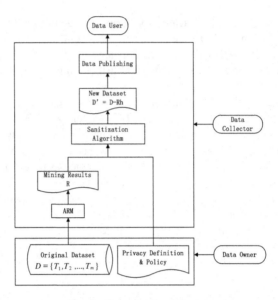

Fig. 2. Process of architecture

step 4: Data collector performs sanitization algorithm to hide the rules in Rh from the dataset.

step 5: Step 2 to step 5 is repeated until there are no sensitive rules could be found in the mining results. The rest of the dataset are "clean".

step 6: The new dataset D' with no sensitive patterns will be published to data user.

As depicted in Fig. 2, we do not use a reconstruction algorithm after sanitization as traditional framework does. Because it has been proven that the relationship between the transactions and their k-itemsets is one to one correspondence [24]. That is to say, direct modification in dataset D during sanitization algorithm, or cleaning sensitive rules from k-itemsets and then reconstructing a new dataset D' using the clean k-itemsets, we can get the same result. In order to improve the efficient of our architecture, we hide rules directly from dataset D.

4.1   Applying Framework on Medical Data

A typical EMR(Electronic Medical Record) template in China contains <Name, ID Number, Gender, Age, Birth Place, Nationality, Symptoms, Physical Examination, Diagnosis,...>. For most of healthcare institution, the datasets stored in the system are in free text form instead of structured data. In order to apply the architecture on datasets, we shall label the EMRs at first place. Because our algorithms process involve only the patterns of datasets rather than specifics, it's OK to use just numbers to label the records.

Take the heart diseases diagnosis dataset as example, few samples of labeling EMRs is described in Tables 1 and 2.

Table 1. Sample of physical examination and Symptoms labeling

Code	Physical examination	Code	Symptoms
1	High blood cholesterol	31	Palpitation
2	High blood pressure	32	Dizzy
3	Subclinical atherosclerosis	33	Chest tightness
...	...	...	...

Table 2. Sample of age and diagnosis labeling

Code	Age	Code	Diagnosis
51	[0,5)	71	No heart disease
52	[5,10)	72	Heart disease
...	...	...	...

After the labeling, an item can be transformed into a transaction format as shown in the Table 3. The first column represents transaction ID, namely the patient number. The second column represents all the items recorded in his(her) EMR. The set of items $I = \{1, 2, 3, 4, 5, 6, ...\}$. Our medical datasets can be transformed into a transaction format $D = \{T_1 T_2, T_3, ..., T_m\}$. After the labeling, our framework can be easily used on the medical data.

4.2 Sanitization Algorithm

After ARM process, we have the association rule set R and the support, confidence values of each rule. In this part, we will use the sanitization algorithm to hide the sensitive patterns Rh by altering the support or confidence values of related items. The algorithm is depicted in the following codes. It starts by generating the transaction set Tr where the rule r comes from, and sort Tr in ascending order of transaction size $|t|$. Then it determines whether there exists brother rules of r in Rh. If there are brother rules, it would compute the loop_num of each rule in Rb and choose one of them to represent the Rb to be hidden in order to minimize the impact on the database. If there are no brother rules in Rh, it would compute the loop_num of rule r, and choose the smallest transaction t in Tr. Then it deletes the r_r of rule r from t. When the rule r is hidden, another rule is selected from set Rh. In the following codes, symbol [x] means the minimal integer that larger than but not equal to x.

Table 3. Sample of datasets D

TID	Records
1	1-2-31-55-72
2	1-2-3-34-58-72
3	5-11-40-64-71
...	...

```
Algorithm: Sanitization algorithm
Input: D, Rh, α, ε
Output: D'
Begin
  Foreach rule R ⊆ Rh do
  {
    Tr={t∈D| R⊆ t}
    //sort Tr in ascending order of |t|
    sort(Tr)
    if there exists brother rules of r in Rh
    {
      Tr = { t∈D| ∀r ∈ Rb , r⊆ t}
      Foreach rule r ∈ Rb do
      {
        Loop_supp = [S(r)-α)
        Loop_conf = [S(r)-ε*S(r₁))
        Num = min(Loop_supp, Loop_conf)
      }
      Loop_num = maximal Num among Rb
      R' = {r| r∈ Rb, r.Loop_num is the largest}
      if |R'| >= 2
        R is the one in R' who has the shortest r_r
      else
        R = R'
        delete(Rb-{R}, Rh)
    }
    else
    {
      Loop_supp = [S(r)-α)
      Loop_conf = [S(r)-ε*S(r₁))
      Loop_num = min(Loop_supp, Loop_conf)
    }
    For i=1 to Loop_num do
    {
      t = pop(Tr)
      delete(R.r_r, t)
      delete(t, Tr)
    }
    delete(R, Rh)
  }
end
```

In our architecture, the sanitization algorithm will be repeated until there exists no sensitive patterns in the discovered rules. This will ensure that no unexpected information from Rh will be published to unreliable party.

5 Performance Evaluation

In this part, we perform our framework on a computer running windows server 2008 R2 operating system. The dataset we use is generated by ourselves as shown in the Table 4. In order for a more realistic simulation, we make the length of a transaction ranges from 2 to 7. All the performance are implemented on matlab R2012b.

We use three criteria to evaluate the performance of our framework: 1. time required of sanitation algorithm. 2. Number of lost rules. 3. Number of new rules. Lost rules are the non-sensitive rules that can be mined before the sanitization algorithm and lost after that. New rules are the non-sensitive rules that cannot be mined before the sanitization algorithm and being introduced to the mining result after that. Rules hiding would have some side effect on the mining result. Number of lost rules and new rules are used to evaluate the side effect of our sanitization algorithm.

5.1 Time Requirement

The main contribution of our framework is on the sanitization algorithm component, so we only consider the time requirement of that part. As shown in Fig. 3, the time required by sanitization algorithm is linear in $|D|$.

5.2 Lost Rules

Figure 4 shows the number of lost rules in different size of dataset. We can see it is almost a horizontal line except two peaks of 25 k and 50 k. By looking at the five hiding rules of the two dataset can explain the peaks.

As Table 5 shows that, in 25 k dataset, the first hiding rule [14,22,23=>5] and second hiding rule [5,22,23=>14] are brother rules. As depicted in our sanitization algorithm, only one of the two will represent the Rb to be hidden. Because they come from the same transactions, hiding one of them will cause the hiding of the other. That is to say, we only hide four rules in the 25 k dataset, which causes the lower values than other datasets. Then we look at the hiding rules in the 50 k dataset. The first hiding rule [9,27=>8] has a support value of 6, which is much larger than other support values. According to our sanitization algorithm, it has to make four loops to hide the rule. This is why the 50 k dataset has a much larger number of lost rules. Now we know that the number of lost rules does not depend on the volume of dataset, but the number of hiding rules and how many times the loop is performed. And proposing the concept of "brother rules" can effectively reduce the number of hiding rules, and in consequence of reducing number of lost rules.

Table 6 shows a comparison between hiding rules and lost rules of the 25 k dataset. It is obviously that almost all the lost rules are brother rules of the hiding rules except the last one [8,23=>5]. Actually [8,23=>5] and the hiding rules [14,22,23=>5], [5,22,23=>14] are very much alike though they are not brother rules. And in realistic EMR condition, for example, rule [12,22,23=>5] is sensitive rule, then rule

Table 4. Data set used in experiment

|D|	|I|	TL	|Rh|
15 k	50	2 ~ 7	5
20 k	50	2 ~ 7	5
25 k	50	2 ~ 7	5
30 k	50	2 ~ 7	5
35 k	50	2 ~ 7	5
40 k	50	2 ~ 7	5
45 k	50	2 ~ 7	5
50 K	50	2 ~ 7	5

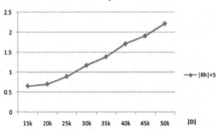

Fig. 3. Time requirement

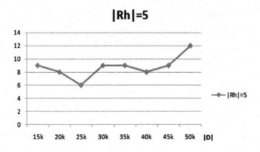

Fig. 4. Lost rules

[5,14,22=>23] and [5,14,23=>22] are very likely also sensitive rules. Consequently, the side-effect of lost rules is minimized in our architecture.

5.3 New Rules

As depicted in Fig. 5 that only one new rule appears in the 20 k dataset. The number of new rules generated during our sanitization algorithm is quite low and it tends to decrease with the increasing of dataset size. So we can say there is almost no effect of introducing new rules to the mining result during our sanitization algorithm.

Table 5. Five Rules to be Hidden

|D|	Rh	S	C	|D|	Rh	S	C
25 k	14,22,23=>5	3	50 %	40 k	25,45,48=>2	3	75 %
	5,22,23=>14	3	75 %		4,16,34=>28	3	60 %
	21,31,43=>47	3	100 %		12,39,44=>35	3	75 %
	27,43=>22	3	50 %		9,24=>36	3	50 %
	3,44=>23	4	57.143 %		26,35=>50	3	50 %
30 k	5,36=>34	3	50 %	50 k	9,27=>8	6	100 %
	12,39=>32	3	60 %		2,28,30=>46	3	50 %
	9,33,48=>43	3	75 %		24,25,45=>5	3	50 %
	13,30,31=>22	3	50 %		8,21,42=>15	3	75 %
	25,28,50=>26	3	100 %		23,24,42=>14	3	51.423 %

Table 6. Hiding Rules and Lost Rules

Rh	Lost Rules
14,22,23=>5	5,14,22=>23
5,22,23=>14	5,14,23=>22
21,31,43=>47	21,31,47=>43
	21,43,47=>31
27,43=>22	22,43=>27
3,44=>23	
	8,23=>5

Fig. 5. New rules

6 Conclusion

We proposed an architecture of privacy preserving for medical data publishing. We don't use the traditional reconstruction algorithm to reconstruct a new dataset, but direct modification in original dataset, by which can effectively reducing the cost of time.

In addition, we propose a fundamental sanitization approaches in our architecture. The approach hides a sensitive rule by reducing its r_r until either support value or confidence value of the rule below the threshold. We also put forward a concept of brother rules to reduce the execution of the algorithm.

Finally, we experiment the algorithm on seven sets of dateset. And we use three criteria to evaluate the performance of algorithm: 1. time requirement of the process. 2. number of lost rules. 3. number of new rules. Lost rules are the rules mined before the algorithm but can't be mined after that. New rules are the rules can't be mined before the algorithm but being introduced to the mining result after the process. We believe that the proposed architecture could satisfy the demands of the health department on medical data publishing.

Our future plan is to work on the privacy measurement issues. We hope to develop different hiding strategies and different arguments according to different privacy metrics, in order to adapt to different data users. Moreover, we hope to use the actual medical dataset to perform the experiment in order to get a more real mining results.

References

1. Malik, M.B., Ghazi, M.A., Ali, R.: Privacy preserving data mining techniques: current scenario and future prospects. In: 3rd IEEE International Conference on Computer Communication Technology (ICCCT), pp. 26–32 (2012)
2. Agrawal, R., Srikant, R.: Privacy preserving data mining. In: Proceedings of ACM SIGMOD Conference, pp. 439–450 (2000)
3. Fung, B.C.M., Wang, K., Chen, R., Yu, P.S.: Privacy preserving data publishing: a survey of recent developments, ACM Comput. Surv. **42**(4), art. id 14 (2010)
4. Xu, L., Jiang, C.: Information security in big data: privacy and data mining. IEEE **2**(10) (2014)
5. Matwin, S.: Privacy preserving data mining techniques: survey and challenges. In: Custers, B., Calders, T., Schermer, B., Zarsky, T. (eds.) Discrimination and Privacy in the Information Society, pp. 209–221. Springer, Berlin (2013)
6. Chen, L., Yang, J.: Privacy-preserving data publishing for free text chinese electronic medical records. In: IEEE 35th International Conference on Computer Software and Applications, pp. 567–572 (2012)
7. Chen, L., Yang, J.: A framework for privacy-preserving healthcare data sharing. In: IEEE 14th International Conference on e-Healthcare Networking, Applications and Services, pp. 341–346 (2012)
8. Hossain, A.A., Ferdous, S.M.S.: Rapid cloud data processing with healthcare information protection. In: IEEE 10th World Congress on Services, pp. 454–455 (2014)
9. Alabdulatif, A., Khalil, I.: Protection of electronic health records (EHRs) in cloud. In: 35th Annual International Conference of the IEEE EMBS Osaka, Japan, pp. 4191–4194 (2013)
10. HIPAA-General Infromation. http://www.cms.gov/HIPPAGenInfo/
11. Sweeney, L.: K-anonymity: a model for protecting privacy. Int. J. Uncertainty Fuzziness Knowl.-Based Syst. **10**(5), 557–570 (2002)
12. Machanavajjhala, A., Gehrke, J.. Kifer, D., Venkitasubramaniam, M.: l-diversity: Privacy Beyond k-anonymity. In: International Conference on Data Engineering (ICDE), pp. 24–35. IEEE Computer Society, Atlanta (2006)
13. Li, N.H., Li, T.C., Venkatasubramanian, S.: t-closeness: privacy beyond k-anonymity and l-diversity. In: 23rd IEEE International Conference on Data Engineering (ICDE), pp. 106–115. IEEE Computer Society, Istanbul (2007)
14. Gionis, A., Tassa, T.: k-anonymization with minimal loss of information. IEEE Trans. Knowl. Data Eng. **21**(2), 206–219 (2009)

15. Verykios, V.S., Bertino, E., Fovino, I.N., Provenza, L.P., Saygin, Y.: State of the art in privacy preserving data mining. ACM SIGMOD Rec. **33**(1), 50–57 (2004)
16. Sathiyapriya, K., Sadasivam, G.S.: A survey on privacy preserving association rule mining. Int. J. Data Mining Knowl. Manage. Process **3**(2), 119 (2013)
17. Zhu, J.M., Zhang, N., Li, Z.Y.: A new privacy preserving association rule mining algorithm based on hybrid partial hiding strategy. Cybern. Inf. Technol. **13**, 41–50 (2013)
18. Jain, D., Khatri, P., Soni, R., Chaurasia, B.K.: Hiding sensitive association rules without altering the support of sensitive item(s). In: Meghanathan, N., Chaki, N., Nagamalai, D. (eds.) CCSIT 2012, Part I. LNICST, vol. 84, pp. 500–509. Springer, Heidelberg (2012)
19. Le, H.Q., Arch-Int, S., Nguyen, H.X., Arch-Int, N.: Association rule hiding in risk management for retail supply chain collaboration. Comput. Ind. **64**(7), 776–784 (2013)
20. Dehkordi, M.N.: A novel association rule hiding approach in OLAP data cubes. Indian J. Sci. Technol. **6**(2), 4063–4075 (2013)
21. Bonam, J., Reddy, A.R., Kalyani, G.: Privacy preserving in association rule mining by data distortion using PSO. In: Satapathy, S.C., Avadhani, P.S., Udgata, S.K., Lakshminarayana, S. (eds.) Proceedings of the ICT Critical Infrastructure, Proceedings of 48th Annual Convention Computer Society India, vol. 2, pp. 551–558. Springer (2014)
22. Radadiya, N.R., Prajapati, N.B., Shah, K.H.: Privacy preserving in association rule mining. Int. J. Adv. Innovative Res. **2**(4), 203–213 (2013)
23. Verykios, V.S.: Association rule hiding methods. Wiley Interdiscipl. Rev. Data Mining Knowl. Discovery **3**(1), 28–36 (2013)
24. Chen, X., Orlowska, M., Li, X.: A new framework of privacy preserving data sharing. In: Proceedings of the 4th IEEE ICDM Workshop: Privacy and Security Aspects of Data Mining, pp. 47–56. IEEE Computer Society (2004)

Attribute-Based Encryption Without Key Escrow

Xing Zhang[1(✉)], Cancan Jin[2], Zilong Wen[2], Qingni Shen[2],
Yuejian Fang[2], and Zhonghai Wu[2]

[1] School of Electronics Engineering and Computer Science,
Peking University, Beijing, China
novostary@gmail.com
[2] School of Software and Microelectronics,
Peking University, Beijing, China
jincancan1992@126.com, 450275803@qq.com,
{qingnishen, fangyj, zhwu}@ss.pku.edu.cn

Abstract. Attribute-Based Encryption (ABE) is a promising cryptographic primitive for fine-grained sharing of encrypted data. However, ABE has a major shortcoming which is called the key escrow problem. Key generation center (KGC) can generate the secret key of a user with arbitrary set of attributes. Even worse, KGC can decrypt ciphertext directly using its master key. This could be a potential intimidation to data security and privacy. In this paper, we propose a novel ciphertext-policy ABE scheme without key escrow. In our construction, we use two authorities, KGC and OAA (outsourced attribute authority). Unless KGC colludes with OAA, neither KGC nor OAA can decrypt the ciphertext independently. Our scheme is proved to be selectively secure in the standard model. We give universal methods for transforming both KP-ABE and CP-ABE with a single authority to solve the problem of key escrow. Our scheme naturally supports outsourcing the decryption of ciphertexts.

Keywords: Cloud storage · Access control · Attribute-based encryption · Key escrow · Outsourcing decryption

1 Introduction

Do you think that your data storing in the online cloud storage are secure? Although cloud storage service providers, such as Dropbox, Google, Microsoft and so on, announce that they provide security mechanisms for protecting their systems, how about cloud storage service providers themselves? It is convenient for us to access our data anytime and anywhere after moving our data to the cloud. We must remain vigilant on the security and privacy of our data, especially sensitive data. It is better to encrypt sensitive data previous to uploading them to the cloud storage. Thus, even if the cloud storage is broken, the privacy of our data will not be leaked. One shortcoming of encrypting data as a whole is that it severely limits the flexibility of users to share their encrypted data at a fine-grained dimension. Assuming a user wants to grant access permission of all documents of a certain project to a project member, he either needs to

© Springer International Publishing Switzerland 2015
Z. Huang et al. (eds.): ICCCS 2015, LNCS 9483, pp. 74–87, 2015.
DOI: 10.1007/978-3-319-27051-7_7

act as an intermediary and decrypt all relevant files for this member or must give this member his secret decryption key. Neither of these options is particularly attractive. Especially, it is tough when the user wants to share different documents with different people.

Sahai and Waters [1] firstly proposed the concept of Attribute-Based Encryption (ABE) to address this issue. ABE is a cryptographic primitive for fine-grained data access control in one-to-many communication. In traditional Identity-Based Encryption (IBE) [2], the ciphertext is computed according to the targeted user's identity, and only that user himself can decrypt the ciphertext. It is one-to-one communication. As a generalization of IBE, ABE introduces an innovative idea of access structure in public key cryptosystem, making the user's secret key or ciphertext generated based on an access structure. Only the user who meets the specified conditions can decrypt the ciphertext.

Nevertheless, ABE has a major shortcoming which is called the key escrow problem. We clarify the problem as two types: (1) Type 1: key generation center (KGC) can generate a user's secret key with arbitrary access structures or set of attributes, (2) Type 2: KGC can decrypt the ciphertext directly utilizing its master key. These could be potential threats to the data confidentiality and privacy in the cloud storage, thereby affecting the extensive application in the cloud storage.

Why do we need to solve the key escrow problem? Isn't KGC trusted? Let's give an example with public key infrastructure (PKI). A PKI is an arrangement that binds public keys with respective users' identities with a certificate authority (CA). There is one point to note that PKI doesn't know users' secret keys, although PKI is trusted. However, users' secret keys are generated by KGC in ABE. Even if KGC is trusted, we still don't want it to decrypt our encrypted data.

Through our research, we give an informal conclusion that **an ABE scheme has the key escrow problem inherently if there is only one authority (KGC) in the scheme**. The secret key of a user is generated by KGC and there isn't user-specific information in the ciphertext. Otherwise, it will be contrary to the goal of ABE which is designed for fine-grained data sharing. Therefore, we pay our attention to how the cooperation between two authorities to solve the key escrow problem.

1.1   Related Work

Sahai and Waters [1] firstly presented the notion of Attribute-Based Encryption (ABE). Then, ABE comes into two flavors, key-policy ABE (KP-ABE) [3–6] and ciphertext-policy ABE (CP-ABE) [6–9]. In KP-ABE, ciphertexts are associated with sets of attributes and users' secret keys are associated with access structures. In CP-ABE, the situation is reversed, users' secret keys are labeled by attributes and ciphertexts are associated with access structures.

Hur [10, 11] solved the key escrow problem by proposing a secure two-party computation protocol. The original KGC is divided into two parts: KGC and the data storing center. The secure 2PC protocol ensures that neither of them could generate the key all alone. The KGC is accountable for authenticating the user and issues the secret key to him/her. The drawback of this approach is that it doesn't have universality and it is proved in the random oracle model. Zhang et al. [12] proposed a solution to solve key escrow problem. Zhang et al. introduced another secret key x that KGC does not know. This has some taste of our proposed scheme. However, since the user can acquire x, if the user colludes with KGC, KGC can decrypt any ciphertext. And Zhang et al. just applied this idea for FIBE.

Wang et al. [13] achieved authority accountability by combining Libert and Vergnaud's IBE scheme [14] and KP-ABE [3]. As the user's secret key contains the secret information that KGC does not know, if KGC forges secret keys in accordance with the user's identity, we can fine whether KGC or the user is dishonest according the key family number. However, KGC can still decrypt the ciphertext directly using its master key.

1.2   Our Contributions

The main contributions of our work can be summarized as follows.

(1)   We propose a scheme for solving the key escrow problem.
(2)   We prove our scheme to be selectively secure in the standard model.
(3)   We use two authorities, KGC and OAA (outsourced attribute authority) in our scheme. Our scheme can resist collusion attack from curious KGC or OAA, and even dishonest users colluding with KGC or OAA.
(4)   We give universal methods for transforming both KP-ABE and CP-ABE with a single authority to remove the problem of key escrow.
(5)   In extensions, we show that we also propose a more practical ABE scheme with outsourcing decryption.

Table 1 shows the comparisons with other related works.

1.3   Our Main Ideas

We will construct our scheme based on CP-ABE of Rouselakis and Waters [6]. There are two challenges for proposing a scheme without key escrow problem. One is how to fragment an authority into two different authorities. We must ensure that any one authority cannot decrypt the ciphertext or generate users' secret keys independently. Moreover, a protocol is necessary for the two authorities to communicate with each other to generate secret keys of users. The other is whether a universal transformation method can remove the key escrow problem from all single authority ABE schemes.

To address the first challenge, a natural idea is to make different authorities have different master keys and perform the same procedure of Key Generation. The user learning both can combine them back into the format of secret key in a single authority ABE. However, the user needs to perform additional calculations to get the final secret key in this trivial idea. If the size of a user's secret key is large, it is inefficient for a user to calculate his/her secret key. Therefore, different authorities cannot perform the same

Table 1. Comparisons with other related works

Scheme	Without Key Escrow		Security Model	Universality
	Type 1	Type 2		
[11]	✓	✓	random oracle model	✗
[13]	✓	✗	standard model	✗
Ours	✓	✓	standard model	✓

procedure of Key Generation trivially. The outsourcing decryption of ABE scheme in Green et al. [15] gives us a hint. In their scheme, decryption step is divided into two stages. Two stages means two decryption keys. Thus, can we use two authorities to generate the two decryption keys independently? We answer this question in the affirmative. However, their scheme still exists the key escrow problem.

To address the second challenge, every scheme has "α" in its master key. Changing "α" can affect the exponent of the user's secret key. The core idea is to provide a method that every authority has part of "α" and neither of them can recover "α" independently. Notice that some schemes [3, 8] use y other than α and y is equivalent to α.

1.4   Organization

The rest of this paper is arranged as follows. Section 2 introduces some cryptographic background information. Section 3 describes the formal definition of CP-ABE without key escrow (WoKE-CP-ABE) and its security model. In Sect. 4, we propose the construction of our WoKE-CP-ABE scheme. In Sect. 5, we analyze the security of our proposed scheme and compare our scheme with multi-authority attribute-based encryption. In Sect. 6, we discuss some extensions. Finally, we conclude this paper.

2   Background

2.1   Access Structure

Definition 2.1 Access Structure [16]. Let $\{P_1, P_2, \ldots, P_n\}$ be a set of parties. A collection $\mathbb{A} \subseteq 2^{\{P_1, P_2, \ldots, P_n\}}$ is monotone if $\forall B, C$: if $B \in \mathbb{A}$ and $B \subseteq C$ then $C \in \mathbb{A}$. An access structure (respectively, monotone access structure) is a collection (respectively, monotone collection) $\mathbb{A}$ of non-empty subsets of $\{P_1, P_2, \ldots, P_n\}$, i.e., $\mathbb{A} \subseteq 2^{\{P_1, P_2, \ldots, P_n\}} \setminus \{\emptyset\}$. The sets in $\mathbb{A}$ are called the authorized sets, and the sets not in $\mathbb{A}$ are called the unauthorized sets.

In our context, the role of the parties is taken by the attributes. Thus, the access structure $\mathbb{A}$ will contain the authorized sets of attributes. From now on, we focus on monotone access structures.

Definition 2.2 Linear Secret Sharing Schemes (LSSS) [16]. Let $\mathcal{K}$ be a finite field, and $\prod$ be a secret sharing scheme with domain of secrets $S \in \mathcal{K}$ realizing an access structure $\mathcal{A}$. We say that $\prod$ is a linear secret sharing scheme over $\mathcal{K}$ if:

1. The piece of each party is a vector over $\mathcal{K}$. That is, for every i there exists a constant d_i such that the piece of P_i is taken from $\mathcal{K}^{d_i}$. We denote by $\prod_{i,j}(s, r)$ the j-th coordinate in the piece of P_i (where $s \in S$ is a secret and $r \in R$ is the dealer's random input).
2. For every authorized set, the reconstruction function of the secret from the pieces is linear. That is, for every $G \in \mathcal{A}$ there exist constants $\{\alpha_{i,j} : P_i \in G, 1 \leq j \leq d_i\}$, such that for every secret $s \in S$ and every choice of random inputs $r \in R$,

$$s = \sum_{P_i \in G} \sum_{1 \leq j \leq d_i} \alpha_{i,j} \cdot \prod_{i,j}(s, r)$$

where the constants and the arithmetic are over the field $\mathcal{K}$.

The total size of the pieces in the scheme is defined as $d \triangleq \sum_{i=1}^{n} d_i$.

2.2   Bilinear Map

Definition 2.3 Bilinear Map. Let $\mathbb{G}_0$ and $\mathbb{G}_1$ be two multiplicative cyclic groups of prime order p. Let g be a generator of $\mathbb{G}_0$ and e be a bilinear map, $e : \mathbb{G}_0 \times \mathbb{G}_0 \to \mathbb{G}_1$. The bilinear map e has the following properties:

Bilinearity: for all $u, v \in \mathbb{G}_0$ and $a, b \in \mathbb{Z}_p$, we have $e\left(u^a, v^b\right) = e(u, v)^{ab}$.

Non-degeneracy: $e(g, g) \neq 1$.

Computable: there   exists   an   efficient   algorithm   for   the   bilinear   map $e : \mathbb{G}_0 \times \mathbb{G}_0 \to \mathbb{G}_1$.

Notice that the map e is symmetric since $e\left(g^a, g^b\right) = e(g, g)^{ab} = e(g^b, g^a)$.

2.3   Assumption

We state our complexity assumption below.

Definition 2.4 q-type Assumption. Initially the challenger calls the group generation algorithm with input the security parameter, picks a random group element $g \in \mathbb{G}_0$, and $q + 2$ random exponents $a, s, b_1, b_2, \ldots, b_q \in \mathbb{Z}_p$. Then he sends to the adversary the group description $(p, \mathbb{G}_0, \mathbb{G}_1, e)$ and all of the following terms:

$$g, g^s$$
$$g^{a^i}, g^{b_j}, g^{sb_j}, g^{a^i b_j}, g^{a^i b_j^2} \quad \forall (i,j) \in [q,q]$$
$$g^{a^i b_j / b_{j'}^2} \qquad \forall \left(i,j,j'\right) \in [2q, q, q] with j \neq j'$$
$$g^{a^i / b_j} \qquad \forall (i,j) \in [2q, q] with i \neq q + 1$$
$$g^{sa^i b_j / b_{j'}}, g^{sa^i b_j / b_{j'}^2} \qquad \forall \left(i,j,j'\right) \in [q, q, q] with j \neq j'$$

There is no probabilistic polynomial-time (PPT) adversary can distinguish $e(g,g)^{sa^{q+1}} \in \mathbb{G}_1$ from an element which is randomly chosen from $\mathbb{G}_1$.

3 CP-ABE Without Key Escrow

3.1 Definition

A WoKE-CP-ABE consists of five algorithms.

KGC-Setup $(1^\lambda) \rightarrow (\mathbf{PK}_{KGC}, \mathbf{MK}_{KGC})$ This is a randomized algorithm that takes a security parameter $\lambda \in \mathbb{N}$ as input. It outputs the public parameters PK_{KGC} and master key MK_{KGC}.

OAA-Setup $(\mathbf{PK}_{KGC}) \rightarrow (\mathbf{PK}_{OAA}, \mathbf{MK}_{OAA})$ This is a randomized algorithm that takes PK_{KGC} as input. It outputs the public parameters PK_{OAA} and master key MK_{OAA}. The system's public parameters PK can be viewed as $PK_{KGC} \cup PK_{OAA}$.

Key Generation This is a key issuing protocol. In this protocol, the KGC and OAA generate the user's secret key SK with a set of attributes $\mathcal{S}$ collaboratively.

Encryption $(\mathbf{PK}, \mathbf{M}, \mathcal{T}) \rightarrow \mathbf{CT}$ This is a randomized algorithm that takes as input the public parameters PK, a plaintext message M, and an access structure $\mathcal{T}$. It outputs the ciphertext CT.

Decryption $(\mathbf{CT}, \mathbf{SK}, \mathbf{PK}) \rightarrow \mathbf{M}$ This algorithm takes as input the ciphertext CT that is encrypted under an access structure $\mathcal{T}$, the decryption key SK for a set of attributes $\mathcal{S}$ and the public parameters PK. It outputs the message M if $\mathcal{T}(\mathcal{S}) = 1$.

3.2 Selective Security Model for WoKE-CP-ABE

We define a game for proving the selective security of WoKE-CP-ABE under the chosen plaintext attack.

Init The adversary $\mathcal{A}$ declares the challenge access structure $\mathcal{T}^*$ that he wishes to challenge.

Setup In this stage, the challenger $\mathcal{B}$ simulates **KGC-Setup** and **OAA-Setup** to give the public parameters PK to the adversary $\mathcal{A}$.

Phase 1 The adversary $\mathcal{A}$ issues queries for secret keys for many sets of attributes $\mathcal{S}_i$, where $\mathcal{T}^*(\mathcal{S}_i) = 0$ for all i. The challenger $\mathcal{B}$ calls Key Generation and sends SK_i to the adversary $\mathcal{A}$.

Challenge The adversary $\mathcal{A}$ submits two equal length messages M_0 and M_1. The challenger $\mathcal{B}$ flips a random coin b, and encrypts M_b with T^*. Then $\mathcal{B}$ passes the ciphertext to the adversary $\mathcal{A}$.

Phase 2 Phase 1 is repeated.

Guess The adversary $\mathcal{A}$ outputs a guess b' of b.

The advantage of an adversary $\mathcal{A}$ in this game is defined as $|\Pr[b' = b] - 1/2|$.

Definition 3.1. A ciphertext-policy attribute-based encryption scheme without key escrow is selectively secure if all PPT adversaries have at most negligible advantage in λ in the above security game.

3.3   Key Escrow Model for WoKE-CP-ABE

There are also other four types of adversaries. The adversary above (named **Type-I Adversary**) focuses on ABE scheme, and the below focus on the problem of key escrow.

Type-II Adversary. It is defined as a curious KGC. Such an adversary owns part of master key of the system and tries to extract useful information from ciphertext. However, this type adversary is restricted that he cannot collude with any user or OAA.

Type-III Adversary. It is defined as a curious OAA. This adversary is similar to type-II adversary, except the part of master key he owns. Notice that the restriction is that he cannot collude with any user or KGC.

Type-IV Adversary. It is defined as dishonest users colluding with KGC. Such an adversary owns KGC's master key and is allowed to ask for all secret keys SK of dishonest users. The goal of this adversary is to obtain useful information from ciphertext not intended for him. Notice that Type-IV adversary cannot collude with OAA.

Type-V Adversary. It is defined as dishonest users colluding with OAA. This adversary is similar to type-IV adversary except the users can collude with OAA instead of KGC. Notice that Type-V adversary cannot collude with KGC.

As we know, we suggest these four adversaries because we must show the construction is key escrow resistant. We must take type-II and type-III adversary into consideration because our scheme must prevent any key generation authority from attacking the scheme. Then type-IV adversary and type-V adversary are some kind of more "powerful" adversary, they want to gain some information about the adverse organization secret key, thus decrypting some message not intended for them.

Notice that a reasonable assumption is that KGC cannot collude with OAA. Otherwise, our scheme can be viewed as a scheme with only a single authority and this "authority" can decrypt any ciphertext according to our analysis in Sect. 1.

4   Our Construction

Let $\mathbb{G}_0$ be a bilinear group of prime order p, and let g be a generator of $\mathbb{G}_0$. In addition, let $e : \mathbb{G}_0 \times \mathbb{G}_0 \to \mathbb{G}_1$ denote the bilinear map. A security parameter λ will determine the size of the groups. For the moment we assume that attributes are elements in $\mathbb{Z}_p^*$.

Nevertheless, attributes can be any meaningful unique strings using a collision resistant hash function $H : \{0,1\}^* \rightarrow \mathbb{Z}_p^*$.

Our construction follows.

KGC-Setup $(1^\lambda) \rightarrow (PK_{KGC}, MK_{KGC})$ The algorithm calls the group generator algorithm $\mathcal{G}(1^\lambda)$ and gets the descriptions of the groups and the bilinear map $D = (p, \mathbb{G}_0, \mathbb{G}_1, e)$. Then choose the random terms $g, u, h, w, v \in \mathbb{G}_0$ and $\alpha' \in \mathbb{Z}_p$. The published public parameters PK_{KGC} are

$$\left(D, g, u, h, w, v, e(g,g)^{\alpha'} \right).$$

The master key MK_{KGC} is α'.

OAA-Setup $(PK_{KGC}) \rightarrow (PK_{OAA}, MK_{OAA})$ Choose μ uniformly at random in $\mathbb{Z}_p$. We can view α' as α/μ. The published public parameters PK_{OAA} is

$$(e(g,g)^{\alpha'})^{\mu} = e(g,g)^{\alpha}.$$

The master key MK_{OAA} is μ.

Then, the system's public parameters PK can be viewed as

$$PK = (D, g, u, h, w, v, e(g,g)^{\alpha}).$$

Key Generation KGC and OAA are involved in the user's key issuing protocol. In the protocol, KGC needs to communicate OAA to generate the user's secret key. The key issuing protocol consists of the following steps:

1. Firstly, KGC and OAA authenticate a user U with set of attributes $\mathcal{S} = \{A_1, A_2, \ldots, A_k\} \subseteq \mathbb{Z}_p$ independently.
2. KGC selects a random exponent $\theta \in_R \mathbb{Z}_p^*$ and sends it to U. θ is used to prevent OAA from obtaining U's complete secret key.
3. KGC picks $r', r_1', r_2', \ldots, r_k' \in_R \mathbb{Z}_p^*$ and computes

$$\mathcal{S}, K_0' = g^{\alpha'/\theta} w^{r'/\theta}, w^{1/\theta}, K_1' = g^{r'},$$

$$\{K_{i,2}' = g^{r_i'}, K_{i,3}' = (u^{A_i}h)^{r_i'} v^{-r'}\}_{i \in [k]}.$$

Then send it to OAA.

4. OAA chooses $r'', r_1'', r_2'', \ldots, r_k'' \in_R \mathbb{Z}_p^*$ and computes

$$\mathcal{S}, K_0'' = (K_0')^{\mu} \cdot (w^{1/\theta})^{r''}, K_1'' = (K_1')^{\mu} \cdot g^{r''},$$

$$\{K_{i,2}'' = (K_{i,2}')^{\mu} \cdot g^{r_i''}, K_{i,3}'' = (K_{i,3}')^{\mu} \cdot (u^{A_i}h)^{r_i''} v^{-r''}\}_{i \in [k]}.$$

Then send it to the user.

Notice that the role of $r'', r_1'', r_2'', \ldots, r_k''$ is to randomize the secret key. Otherwise, if a dishonest user colluded with KGC, KGC can compute $((g^{r'})^\mu)^{1/r'} = g^\mu$ and use it to decrypt any ciphertext by calculating $me(g,g)^{\alpha s}/(e(g^s, g^\mu))^{\alpha'} = m$.

5. The user obtains his/her secret key as

$$SK = (S, \theta, K_0 = K_0'' = g^{\alpha'\mu/\theta}w^{(r'\mu+r'')/\theta} = g^{\alpha/\theta}w^{r/\theta}, K_1 = K_1''$$
$$= g^{r'\mu+r''} = g^r,$$

$$\{K_{i,2} = K_{i,2}'' = g^{r_i'\mu+r_i''} = g^{r_i}, K_{i,3} = K_{i,3}'' = (u^{A_i}h)^{r_i'\mu+r_i''}v^{-(r'\mu+r'')}$$
$$= (u^{A_i}h)^{r_i}v^{-r}\}_{i\in[k]}).$$

We implicitly set $r = r'\mu + r''$, $\{r_i = r_i'\mu + r_i''\}_{i\in[k]}$.

Encryption $(PK, m, (M, \rho)) \to CT$ To encrypt a message $m \in \mathbb{G}_1$ under an access structure encoded in an LSSS policy (M, ρ). Let the dimensions of M be $l \times n$. Each row of M will be labeled by an attribute and $\rho(i)$ denotes the label of ith row $\vec{M}_i$. Choose a random vector $\vec{z} = (s, z_2, \ldots, z_n)^T$ from $\mathbb{Z}_p^n$, s is the random secret to be shared among the shares. The vector of the shares is $\vec{\lambda} = (\lambda_1, \lambda_2, \ldots, \lambda_l)^T = M\vec{z}$. It then chooses l random value $t_1, t_2, \ldots, t_l \in \mathbb{Z}_p$ and publish the ciphertext as:

$$CT = ((M, \rho), me(g,g)^{\alpha s}, C_0 = g^s,$$

$$\{C_{i,1} = w^{\lambda_i}v^{t_i}, C_{i,2} = \left(u^{\rho(i)}h\right)^{-t_i}, C_{i,3} = g^{t_i}\}_{i\in[l]}).$$

Decryption $(CT, SK, PK) \to m$ To decrypt the ciphertext CT with the decryption key SK, proceed as follows. Suppose that S satisfies the access structure and let $I = \{i : \rho(i) \in S\}$. Since the set of attributes satisfy the access structure, there exist coefficients $\omega_i \in \mathbb{Z}_p$ such that $\sum_{\rho(i)\in I} \omega_i \cdot \vec{M}_i = (1, 0, \ldots, 0)$. Then we have that $\sum_{\rho(i)\in I} \omega_i\lambda_i = s$. Now it calculates

$$\frac{me(g,g)^{\alpha s} \prod_{i\in I}(e(C_{i,1}, K_1)e(C_{i,2}, K_{i,2})e(C_{i,3}, K_{i,3}))^{\omega_i}}{(e(C_0, K_0))^\theta}$$

$$= \frac{me(g,g)^{\alpha s} \prod_{i\in I}(e(w^{\lambda_i}v^{t_i}, g^r)e((u^{\rho(i)}h)^{-t_i}, g^{r_i})e(g^{t_i}, (u^{A_i}h)^{r_i}v^{-r}))^{\omega_i}}{(e(g^s, g^{\alpha/\theta}w^{r/\theta}))^\theta}$$

$$= \frac{me(g,g)^{\alpha s}e(w,g)^{rs}}{e(g^s, g^\alpha w^r)} = m.$$

5 Analysis of Our Proposed Scheme

5.1 Selective Security Proof

In the selective security proof, we will reduce the selective security of our CP-ABE scheme to that of Rouselakis and Waters' [6] which is proved selectively secure under the q-type assumption in Sect. 2.3.

Due to space limited, we have to omit the full proof process.

5.2 Security Analysis for Problem of Key Escrow

Type-II adversary. Type-II adversary is defined as a curious KGC and restricted that he cannot collude with any user or OAA. The adversary needs to recover μ or s to decrypt ciphertext $me(g, g)^{\alpha s}$.

$$(e(g^{\alpha'}, g^s))^{\mu} \rightarrow e(g, g)^{\alpha s} \rightarrow m \text{ by using } \mu,$$

$$(e(g, g)^{\alpha})^s \rightarrow m \text{ by using } s.$$

However, it is related with discrete logarithm to compute μ or s. Since computing discrete logarithm is believed to be difficult, our scheme can resist the attack from Type-II adversary. □

Type-III adversary. This adversary is similar to type-II adversary. The adversary needs to recover α' or s to decrypt ciphertext $me(g, g)^{\alpha s}$. Since computing discrete logarithm is believed to be difficult, our scheme can resist the attack from Type-III adversary. □

Type-IV adversary. Type-IV adversary is defined as dishonest users colluding with KGC. Although this adversary can request some users' secret keys, he cannot obtain more information about μ than Type-II adversary as the users' secret keys are randomized by OAA. This adversary also needs to recover μ or s to decrypt ciphertext. Since computing discrete logarithm is believed to be difficult, our scheme can resist the attack from Type-IV adversary. □

Type-V adversary. Type-V adversary is defined as dishonest users colluding with OAA. Obviously, this adversary has less power than Type-IV adversary. The adversary needs to recover α', s or r' to decrypt ciphertext.

$$(g^{\alpha'/\theta} w^{r'/\theta})^{\theta\mu} \rightarrow g^{\alpha} w^{r'\mu}.$$

If this adversary knows r', he can calculate any set of attributes by using θ from dishonest users. r' is related with discrete logarithm problem. So our scheme can resist the attack from Type-V adversary. □

5.3   Comparing with Multi-authority Attribute-Based Encryption

In multi-authority ABE [17–20], different authorities manage different sets of attributes. Chase [17] proposed a multi-authority ABE scheme using the concepts of a trusted central authority (CA) and global identifiers (GID). However, the CA has the power to decrypt any ciphertext. Chase and Chow [18] proposed a multi-authority ABE scheme without a trusted central authority (CA). However, all attribute authorities (AAs) must communicate among each other in a secure two party key exchange protocol and each authority also needs to give non-interactive proofs of knowledge of some parameters. If the number of colluded AAs is less than $N - 1$ (N is the total number of AAs in the system), the colluded parties cannot decrypt ciphertexts which policies do not satisfy these parties' attributes. Nevertheless, an AA has absolute control over attributes belonging to itself. If an AA colludes with a dishonest user, it is equivalent that they have all the attributes keys belonging to this AA. They can decrypt more ciphertexts than this user. Our scheme can resist collusion attack from curious KGC or OAA, and even dishonest users colluding with KGC or OAA as both KGC and OAA involve in the generation of every attribute secret key. Additionally, if we apply multi-authority ABE to the scenario that users store their daily data into the public cloud, it is a problem that how to divide the sets of attributes. In a similar scenario, it will be more reasonable to adopt our scheme which enhances a single authority ABE without key escrow. When there are a lot of users, we can manage them by using a hierarchical approach [21].

6   Extensions

6.1   Universality

Our method for removing key escrow can be applicable to other ABE schemes. It is easy to transform a single authority of an ABE scheme to KGC and OAA. At setup stage, KGC performs the same Setup as the original scheme. OAA performs exponent operation on α-related part $e(g, g)^{\alpha}$.

Now we will mainly focus on key generation. We will analyze universality for CP-ABE and KP-ABE respectively.

For CP-ABE, we will describe the transformation method by analyzing our proposed scheme. The main difference between secret key of our scheme and Rouselakis and Waters' [6] is the generation of K_0. In our scheme,

$$K_0' = g^{\alpha'/\theta}w^{r'/\theta}, w^{1/\theta}, \theta \to (K_0')^{\mu} \cdot \left(w^{1/\theta}\right)^{r''} = g^{\alpha'\mu/\theta}w^{\left(r'\mu + r''\right)/\theta}$$
$$= g^{\alpha/\theta}w^{r/\theta}, \theta.$$

In Rouselakis and Waters [6], $K_0 = g^{\alpha}w^r$. When key generating, we use two more parts, $w^{1/\theta}$ and θ. We can call θ as the key-escrow-free part and $w^{1/\theta}$ as the affiliated part for randomization of secret key. Notice that OAA also needs to randomize the secret key. The reason we have analyzed in Sect. 4. By using these two parts, we have already been able to construct a scheme without key escrow.

For KP-ABE, there is a little different from CP-ABE. Let us look at an example. For KP-ABE in Rouselakis and Waters' [6], KGC also needs to generate a key-escrow-free part θ and sends it to the user. Then KGC uses the algorithm of Key Generation in [6], the only difference is replacing α with α'/θ. KGC sends it to OAA. OAA performs exponent operation with μ and randomization operation similarly with ours. Then OAA sends it to the user. From this example we can see that we only handle on exponent. It doesn't matter the format of the user's secret key in the original scheme.

The algorithm of Encryption is identical and θ is used in the algorithm of Decryption. As it is apparent, we will not analyze it any more.

6.2   A More Practical ABE Scheme with Outsourcing Decryption

One of the main performance limitations of ABE is that the size of the ciphertext and the time required to decrypt it grow with the complexity of the access structure. As computing power is limited in the mobile devices, it is unacceptable for a long decryption time. Green et al. [15] proposed a method for outsourcing the decryption of ABE ciphertexts to save the user's bandwidth and decryption time in mobile scenarios. The user has a transformation key and an ElGamal-style key. The transformation key can be given to a proxy to translate any ABE ciphertext satisfied by that user's attributes into an ElGamal-style ciphertext without revealing ciphertext's content to that proxy. Then this user can use the ElGamal-style key to decrypt that ElGamal-style ciphertext efficiently. Green et al. [15] need to perform exponential operations on every element in $\mathbb{G}_0$ of the user's secret key by using $1/z$. Although this procedure is performed by KGC in that scheme, we note that it can also be performed by the user. However, if a user wants to change his/her transformation key after using that key too much times, he/she needs to perform exponential operations on every element of his/her secret key. We are surprised to find that our scheme naturally supports outsourcing the decryption of ciphertexts. θ is already our ElGamal-style key and other parts of secret key are the transformation key. If a user wants to change θ to θ', he/she only needs to calculate $K_0^{\theta/\theta'} = (g^{\alpha/\theta}w^{r/\theta})^{\theta/\theta'} = g^{\alpha/\theta'}w^{r/\theta'}$ and updates new K_0 to the proxy. It's very practical and saves the transmission bandwidth for update.

7   Conclusion

Key escrow is quite a challenging issue in ABE. We formalize the concept of ciphertext policy attribute-based encryption without key escrow (WoKE-CP-ABE) and propose a scheme for solving the key escrow problem. In our construction, we use two authorities, KGC and OAA (outsourced attribute authority) which communicate with each other to issue secret keys for users. Unless KGC colludes with OAA, neither KGC nor OAA can decrypt the ciphertext independently. Our scheme is proved to be selectively secure in the standard model. We give universal methods for transforming both KP-ABE and CP-ABE with a single authority to solve the problem of key escrow. In addition, our scheme naturally supports outsourcing the decryption of ciphertexts. As KGC's behavior is restricted in ABE with a single authority, it will drive people to store more sensitive data into cloud and promote the application of ABE in a wider range.

Acknowledgments. This work is supported by the National High Technology Research and Development Program ("863" Program) of China under Grant No. 2015AA016009, the National Natural Science Foundation of China under Grant No. 61232005, and the Science and Technology Program of Shen Zhen, China under Grant No. JSGG2014051 6162852628.

References

1. Sahai, A., Waters, B.: Fuzzy identity-based encryption. In: Cramer, R. (ed.) EUROCRYPT 2005. LNCS, vol. 3494, pp. 457–473. Springer, Heidelberg (2005)
2. Boneh, D., Franklin, M.: Identity-based encryption from the weil pairing. In: Kilian, J. (ed.) CRYPTO 2001. LNCS, vol. 2139, pp. 213–229. Springer, Heidelberg (2001)
3. Goyal, V., Pandey, O., Sahai, A., Waters, B.: Attribute-based encryption for fine-grained access control of encrypted data. In: ACM Conference on Computer and Communications Security, pp. 89–98 (2006)
4. Ostrovsky, R., Sahai, A., Waters, B.: Attribute-based encryption with non-monotonic access structures. In: ACM Conference on Computer and Communications Security, pp. 195–203 (2007)
5. Attrapadung, N., Libert, B., de Panafieu, E.: Expressive key-policy attribute-based encryption with constant-size ciphertexts. In: Catalano, D., Fazio, N., Gennaro, R., Nicolosi, A. (eds.) PKC 2011. LNCS, vol. 6571, pp. 90–108. Springer, Heidelberg (2011)
6. Rouselakis, Y., Waters, B.: Practical constructions and new proof methods for large universe attribute-based encryption. In: ACM Conference on Computer and Communications Security, pp. 463–474 (2013)
7. Bethencourt, J., Sahai, A., Waters, B.: Ciphertext-policy attribute-based encryption. In: IEEE Symposium on Security and Privacy, pp. 321–334 (2007)
8. Cheung, L., Newport, C.: Provably secure ciphertext policy ABE. In: ACM Conference on Computer and Communications Security, pp. 456–465 (2007)
9. Waters, B.: Ciphertext-policy attribute-based encryption: an expressive, efficient, and provably secure realization. In: Catalano, D., Fazio, N., Gennaro, R., Nicolosi, A. (eds.) PKC 2011. LNCS, vol. 6571, pp. 53–70. Springer, Heidelberg (2011)
10. Hur, J., Koo, D., Hwang, S.O., Kang, K.: Removing escrow from ciphertext policy attribute-based encryption. Comput. Math Appl. **65**(9), 1310–1317 (2013)
11. Hur, J.: Improving security and efficiency in attribute-based data sharing. IEEE Trans. Knowl. Data Eng. **25**(10), 2271–2282 (2013)
12. Zhang, G., Liu, L., Liu, Y.: An attribute-based encryption scheme secure against malicious KGC. In: IEEE 11th International Conference on Trust, Security and Privacy in Computing and Communications (TrustCom), pp. 1376–1380 (2012)
13. Wang, Y., Chen, K., Long, Y., Liu, Z.: Accountable authority key policy attribute-based encryption. Sci. China Inf. Sci. **55**(7), 1631–1638 (2012)

14. Libert, B., Vergnaud, D.: Towards black-box accountable authority IBE with short ciphertexts and private keys. In: Jarecki, S., Tsudik, G. (eds.) PKC 2009. LNCS, vol. 5443, pp. 235–255. Springer, Heidelberg (2009)

15. Green, M., Hohenberger, S., Waters, B.: Outsourcing the decryption of ABE ciphertexts. In: USENIX Security Symposium (2011)

16. Beimel, A.: Secure schemes for secret sharing and key distribution. PhD thesis, Israel Institute of Technology, Technion, Haifa, Israel (1996)

17. Chase, M.: Multi-authority attribute based encryption. In: Vadhan, S.P. (ed.) TCC 2007. LNCS, vol. 4392, pp. 515–534. Springer, Heidelberg (2007)

18. Chase, M., Chow, S.S.: Improving privacy and security in multi-authority attribute-based encryption. In: ACM Conference on Computer and Communications Security, pp. 121–130 (2009)

19. Lewko, A., Waters, B.: Decentralizing attribute-based encryption. In: Paterson, K.G. (ed.) EUROCRYPT 2011. LNCS, vol. 6632, pp. 568–588. Springer, Heidelberg (2011)

20. Liu, Z., Cao, Z., Huang, Q., Wong, D.S., Yuen, T.H.: Fully secure multi-authority ciphertext-policy attribute-based encryption without random oracles. In: Atluri, V., Diaz, C. (eds.) ESORICS 2011. LNCS, vol. 6879, pp. 278–297. Springer, Heidelberg (2011)

21. Wang, G., Liu, Q., Wu, J.: Hierarchical attribute-based encryption for fine-grained access control in cloud storage services. In: Proceedings of the 17th ACM Conference on Computer and Communications Security, pp. 735–737 (2010)

An Efficient Access Control Optimizing Technique Based on Local Agency in Cryptographic Cloud Storage

Shidong Zhu[✉], Liu Jiang, and Zhenliu Zhou

College of Information, Shenyang Institute of Engineering, Shenyang, China
{sdzhu,jiangliu,zlzhou}@sie.edu.cn

Abstract. With analyzing cloud storage data security requirements, in this paper we focus on data privacy protection in cloud storage, and proposed a measure to optimize the efficiency of access control in cryptographic cloud storage. For the main users that use cloud storage services are enterprise and the community users, they have the characteristics in common that they manage their data access rights by the mode of hierarchical classification. Because of this, combined ciphertext policy attribute-based encryption (CP-ABE) algorithm and hierarchical identity-based encryption (HIBE) algorithm, we proposed to identify users by both precise identity and attribute in the process of making data access control strategy, and use hierarchy when generate keys. The advantage of this is that it can effectively protect the data privacy in cloud storage, and support precise identity and attribute access control, and fine-grained access. Furthermore, for the purpose of reducing cost of access cloud storage, we proposed an efficiency access control optimizing technique based on local agency, which can replace users to complete the ciphertext access control related operations, and cache frequently accessed data, effectively reduce the impact of using the ciphertext access control mechanisms. Experiments show that the scheme can reduce additional cost of cloud storage data protection, and suitable for using in actual scenes of cloud storage.

Keywords: Cloud storage · Ciphertext access control · Ciphertext policy Attribute-Based encryption · Data protection · Local proxy

1 Introduction

Data security is the primary factor for usage and development of cloud storage [1, 2]. Shi Xiaohong, the vice president of inc.360, said that data security is the core issue of cloud storage [3]. From the user's perspective, the ideal state is under user-controllable data protection for the need of cloud storage security. Most users, especially business users hope to obtain protection for cloud storage as local storage, when the data is stored, transmitted, shared, used and destructed in cloud [4]. Once data leak occurs, it may cause incalculable damage, because user data may contain business decisions, the core technology, trade secrets and personal privacy and other sensitive content. Therefore, the security focus of user data in cloud storage is protection of data leakage. The characteristics of cloud storage are open and shared, so the user data is vulnerable

© Springer International Publishing Switzerland 2015
Z. Huang et al. (Eds.): ICCCS 2015, LNCS 9483, pp. 88–100, 2015.
DOI: 10.1007/978-3-319-27051-7_8

to attacks and threats from networks. In addition, cloud service providers (CSP) and its staff may also leak user data actively or passively.

The most direct way to prevent leak of cloud data is to encrypt data by the user and then distribute the decryption key to control the access authority. However, it is not efficient, and greatly increases time cost to use cloud storage. A main idea for data confidentiality protection is to establish Cryptographic Cloud Storage [5] mechanism to protect the security of cloud storage sharing data with the access control policies managed by user own. In this way, even if the illegal users obtain the shared data, they can't get the plaintext.

With the target of user self-management on important data, Many researchers have proposed data protection scheme based on ciphertext access control, that is data are encrypted using symmetric algorithm by data owner, and publish both data and access policies to cloud storage, then distribute decryption keys through secure channel. Data users first fetch ciphertext from cloud storage, and decrypt ciphertext with their own private key, and obtain decryption key. This method has large amount of computation burden, and efficiency of key distribution is low.

With the development of attribute-based encryption technology, researchers have proposed ciphertext access control technology based on Ciphertext-Policy Attribute-Based Encryption (CP-ABE) [6, 7]. As access structure of CP-ABE is deployed in the ciphertext, data owners have more initiative, may decide access structure by their own. Chase resolved the bottleneck that attribute management and key distribution were managed just by a single Attribute Authority (AA) [8], and proposed to allow multiple independent AA to manage and distribute key properties. Waters presented the first access structure with full expression of CP-ABE [9].

However, using CP-ABE technology to protect data security in cloud storage still faces many problems. One is the large time cost of encryption, decryption and revocation of CP-ABE, the other is that access granularity of key distribution strategy of CP-ABE does not match the needs of most cloud storage scenarios. In this paper, we focus on solving the access efficiency and fine-grained access, and proposed a scheme of ciphertext access control based on hierarchical CP-ABE encryption algorithm, which can support fine-grained access control, and using local proxy technology to optimize the efficiency of cloud storage access.

2 Ciphertext Access Control Based on Hierarchical CP-ABE

2.1 Analysis of Cloud Storage Application Scenarios

Attribute-Based Encryption (ABE) belongs public key cryptography system, and supports fine-grained access control. In the ABE system, the user is described by a set of attributes, ciphertext are associated with attribute-based access structure, user can decrypt ciphertext only when attribute are satisfied access structure. Goyal et al. [10] divided ABE into Key-Policy Attribute-Based Encryption (KP-ABE) and CP-ABE. In access control based on KP-ABE, data users specify access control policies, this is suitable for query type applications [11]. Access structure of CP-ABE is placed in ciphertext, so that the data owner has larger initiative to decide access structure for encryption. In CP-ABE scheme, users are described by attribute set, data owner give a access tree structure, if and only if user's attribute set are satisfied access tree structure, decryption key is able to be recovered, and get plaintext.

Cloud storage users generally can be divided into three types: individual users, enterprise users and community users. The individual user refers to dependent the individual person who use cloud storage service independently, its service form are like network disk service. Individual users are less data and data shared requires, and can implement data security protection by using simple ciphertext access control mechanisms. Enterprise users are those belonging to a particular enterprise or group, which is characterized by its attributes generally associated with hierarchical structure, they usually have large data sharing requires with large amounts of data. Community users refer to the user who have a certain relationship with each other, but geographically dispersed, and have data shared requires. Consider the following scenario: teachers of ten universities in one city will use the same cloud storage service, the staff of Information Institute of A school and Information College of B school develop a research project named X. Its access control list is shown in Table 1.

Table 1. Access control list

File description	Access structure
Core Technical Documents	X Project team members, information collage dean of A, ID in {905066,307083}
Common Technical Documents	X Project team members, staff with Senior title of A information College
Teaching Materials of A School	all staff of A information College

The attribute information in this scenario relate to the organization, department, position, title, project team, precise identity, etc., and have universal representation in cloud storage applications, its characteristics are as follow:

1. Data access architecture requirements need high flexibility in size, with coarse-grained division of attributes, such as organization, department, etc., also contain precise distribution of attribute, such as employee number and position.
2. There is great difference between access structure of different files, such as the access right of teaching materials of A school may be set to: {A school} AND {Information College}; the core technical documentation will be set to: ({A School} AND {X project team members}) OR ({B School} AND {X project team members}) OR ({{A School} AND {Information College} AND {Dean}}) OR {ID: 905066} OR {ID: 307083}.
3. The right distribution of community users or enterprise users are usually associated with much attributes, and usually correspond with department structures and administrative levels.

Therefore, we need to design an access control scheme that meet demands below:

1. Flexible access control policy. Access control tree should support access control of precise identity or simple attribute access.
2. Access control structures can be represented as hierarchical structure like enterprise administrative level or departmental structure.
3. The efficiency of key distribution should be adapted to users commonly used time cost of encryption and decryption in cloud storage.

Based on HIBE system, we added precise identify attribute in access structure of CP-ABE system, and introduce domain management in access control structure of CP-ABE for generate keys and use hierarchy key distribution, as described below.

2.2 Key Generation Model Based on Hierarchical CP-ABE

Figure 1 shows the key generation model based on hierarchy CP-ABE algorithm.

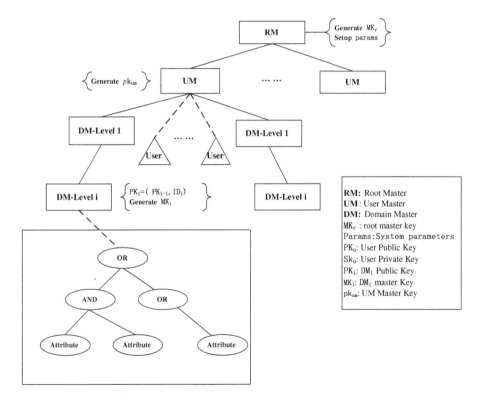

Fig. 1. Key generation model based on hierarchy CP-ABE algorithm

This model is a tree structure, consisting of a root master (RM) node and a plurality of domains, RM generates and distributes system parameters and domain keys, user master (UM) manage users, domain master (DM) is used to generate keys and attributes for the under hierarchy. RM, UM and DM node can be implemented by Local Proxy (LP) or trusted third party (TTP). Each DM and attribute has a unique ID signs, and each user has a unique ID identifier and a series of attribute flags. Ciphertext access structure comprises ID set of data user (DU) and attribute-based access structure tree T. When the data owner (DO) release access strategy, firstly, DM judge whether the ID of DU is in its precise ID set, if True, DM authorize to decrypt ciphertext without attributes judgment; otherwise, DM will analyze the attribute set in the key of DU whether satisfy the access control policies T. Access control tree T is used to represent an access control structure. Each non-leaf node x of T represents an k_x-of-num_x threshold operation: numx indicates the number of child nodes, k_x represents the threshold, $0 < k_x \leq num_x$. $k_x=1$ indicates OR operation, $k_x = num_x$ indicates an AND operation. Each leaf node x represents an attribute $att(x)$. Access control tree can describe attribute-based access control policy, to judge whether attribute set S satisfy an access control tree T is as follows:

1. Let r be the root node of T, use T_r represents T, then let T_x be the subtree that root node is x, if attribute S satisfy T_x, denoted $T_x (S) = 1$.
2. Let $x = r$, calculate $T_x (S)$: For non-leaf node x, let all child nodes of x be xc_1, ..., xc_{numx}, calculate $T_{xci}(S)(i \in [1, num_x])$, $T_x (S)$ returns 1 if and only if at least k_x number leaf nodes return 1; for the leaf node, $T_x (S)$ returns 1 if and only if $att (x) \in S$.

2.3   Key Generation Algorithm Based on Hierarchical CP-ABE

Key generation algorithm based on hierarchical CP-ABE is as follow:

Setup: RM generate master key MK_r for UM, and generate master key PK_r for UM. The process is: Select $MK_r \in \mathbb{Z}^*_q$, MK_r is master key, output system parameter $Params=<q,\mathbb{G}_1,\mathbb{G}_2,\hat{e},n,p_0,Q_0,H_1,H_2>$,($q,\mathbb{G}_1,\mathbb{G}_2,\hat{e}$) is output, n is positive integer, p_0 is generator, $Q_0=MK_r p \in \mathbb{G}_1, H_1:\{0,1\}^* \to \mathbb{G}_1$和$H_2:\mathbb{G}_2 \to \{0,1\}$, MK_r keep secret.

- **GenSK:** UM generate private key for user U using Params and MK_r. The process is: $SK_u=$ (Q-$tuple_u+mk_uP_u$), $P_u=H_1(PK_u) \in \mathbb{G}_1$.
- **GenDM:** DM manage under domain node and access control T, each DM has a unique sign. DM_i own a public key PK_i and master key MK_i, $PK_i=(PK_{i-1},ID_i)$, and generate master key for DM_{i+1}. The process is:
  Let DM_i be the parent node of DM_{i+1}, $MK_{i+1}=(mk_{i+1},Sk_{i+1},Q$-$tuple_{i+1},H_A)$;$mk_{i+1}$ is random element in

$$\mathbb{Z}^*_q;Sk_{i+1}=Sk_i+mk_iP_{i+1} \in \mathbb{G}_1,P_{i+1}=H_1(PK_{i+1}) \in \mathbb{G}_1; Q\text{-}tuple_{i+1}=(Q\text{-}$$

$$tuple_{i+1},Q_{i+1}), \text{ and } Q_{i+1}=mk_{i+1}P_0 \in \mathbb{G}_1; H_1:\{0,1\}^* \text{ is random oracle model.}$$

- **GenUser:** DM_i judges whether user U belongs its own management domain, When the condition is satisfied, DM_i generates identity key SK_{iu} of U and attribute key SAK_{iu}. The process is:

$$SK_{iu}=(Q\text{-}tuple_{i-1},mk_imk_up_0);SAK_{iu}=Sk_i+mk_imk_up_a;$$

$$mk_u=H_A(PK_u) \in \mathbb{Z}^*_q, P_a=H_1(PK_a) \in \mathbb{G}_1$$

- **Encrypt:** Let DO is the data owner, T_{do} be the access control tree of DO. Let DM_i located on the i layer to manage attribute-based access control tree T_i, for the purpose of encrypt K, DO output ciphertext $CK=$ (R,T_{do},CF), its input parameters are precise ID set $R=\{ID_{u1},...,ID_{um}\}$, attribute access control tree T_{do}, and all user public key in R and all attributes key in T_i. The paramters:

$$P_{ui}=H_1(PK_{ui}) \in G_1; \ U_{ui}=rP_{ui}; \ V=K \oplus H_2(\hat{e}(Q_0,rn_A P_u)); \ CF=[u_0,Uu_1,...,U_{um},V].$$

- **Decrypt:** Given ciphertext CK, if the precise ID set of U belongs R, then the key K can be recovered by using system parameters params and user private key SK_u. Given ciphertext CK, if the user's attributes satisfies access structure T, that means U has at least one attribute key in access control tree T, then the plaintext will be recovered by using identity key Sk_{iu} and the system parameters *params*, and user attribute secret key $\{Sk_{iu},a \mid a \in T\}$.

2.4   Ciphertext Access Control Scheme Based on Hierarchical CP-ABE

Basic process: Data will be stored in the cloud storage after encryption using symmetric encryption algorithms such as AES, which can ensure data storage security. The encryption key will be uploaded to cloud storage after encryption using CP-ABE algorithm, the data users which satisfy the access control can decrypt data by their own. Figure 2 shows the ciphertext access control process based on Hierarchical CP-ABE.

LP (or TTP) run Setup in RM, and generate system parameters *Params*, then output master key PK_r.

1. DM run GenDM and generate master key for its next DM using *Params* and its own master key. UM run GenSK and generate attribute key SK_u for the users of its domain, and pass it to each user of the domain through secure channel.
2. When sharing data, data owner DO first use symmetric encryption algorithm E to encrypt data F, and then encrypt the key K using CP-ABE algorithm, get key ciphertext $CK=$ Encypt(R,T_{do},CF), both ciphertext $EK(F)$ and key ciphertext CK will be published to cloud storage. The prrcise ID set $R=\{ID_{u1},...,ID_{um}\}$, access control tree T_{do}, and all user public key CF in R will be the parameters when decryption.
3. All users can get ciphertext from cloud storage. When data users 的 decrypt ciphertext, the first step is to judge whether the user ID belong to the corresponding domain, and if true, DM will generate user identity private key SK_{iu} and user attributes SAK_{iu}. DM first determine whether DU has precise ID that matches identity set of DM, if true, DU can obtain the decryption key by decryption CK; otherwise, continue to judge whether the attribute satisfy the access control policies T. When the above conditions are met, DU can decrypt the data using Decrypt algorithm.

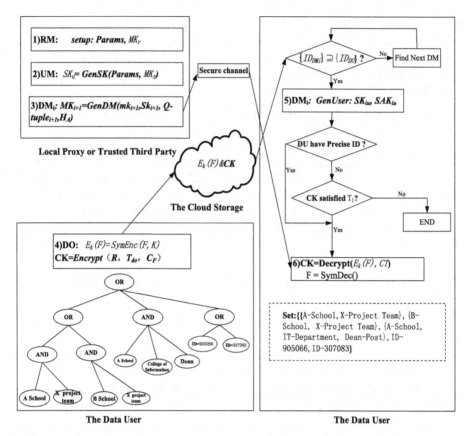

Fig. 2. Ciphertext access control process based on hierarchical CP-ABE

The safety of this scheme depends on the safety of CP-ABE algorithm and HIBE algorithm, due to space limited, we did not prove it in this paper.

3   Access Control Optimization Technology Based on Local Proxy

3.1   Time Cost of Ciphertext Access Control Scheme Based on Hierarchical CP-ABE

The mainly time cost of ciphertext access control based on hierarchical CP-ABE is as follow:

1. System initialization and key generation time cost. Setup algorithm of RM node is bilinear operation, which will be the largest calculation time cost, and followed by power operation which include once in Setup algorithm, twice in GenDM, once in GenSK and GenUser algorithm.

2. Encryption and decryption time cost. Encryption time cost include symmetric encryption algorithm and key encryption time cost using CP-ABE algorithm. As CP-ABE is asymmetric algorithm, encryption efficiency is very low, the symmetric algorithm time cost can be negligible. Decryption algorithm include decryption time cost of key ciphertext CK and decryption of ciphertext, in fact time cost of decryption is much smaller than encryption.

3. Key distribution time cost. This means the time cost that UM and DM publish all user's private keys, identity of a keys, attribute keys, this CP-ABE based keys distribution need transform access control policy to access control tree T. In general, access policies conversion is simply pretreatment, time cost is relatively small.

4. Right revocation time cost. Revocation operation is re-encryption operation of file F and key k, its process is: data owner retrieve the affected ciphertext $E_k(F)$ and CK and decryption, then use a new key k' re-encrypt the file F and figure out ciphertext $Ek'(F)$. After that, build a new access control structure T', and re-encrypt k'. The new ciphertext $Ek'(F)$ and CK' will be updated to cloud storage, and outdated ciphertext data will be deleted. The main time cost in revocation operation is data re-encryption.

The time cost of system initialization and key generation have the maximum cost for the reason of including bilinear operation and power operation. To improve the efficiency of the system, using local proxy can greatly improve the efficiency of cloud storage access, the advantages are as follows:

- Take full advantage of existing computing resources and storage resources of enterprise or community. The local proxy can be established using their existing equipment, so can save costs and avoid equipment idle.
- Protect data sharing security. Local proxy can be considered fully credible, and can achieve compulsive access control policy or implement ciphertext access control for protection of data sharing security.
- Enhance cloud storage access efficiency. Local proxy can be used to complete the operation of system initialization and key generation that take larger time cost in ciphertext access control, and cache frequently used data, reduce the frequency of cloud storage access, and improve the efficiency of cloud storage access.
- Protect sensitive data. Corporate data involves sensitive content and need to be encrypted before upload to cloud, furthermore, part of the data can be stored in local storage to avoid critical data disclosure when published to the cloud storage.

To sum up, using local proxy is an effective way to optimize the efficiency of cloud storage access.

3.2 Ciphertext Access Control Scheme Based on Local Proxy

Ciphertex access control scheme based on hierarchical CP-ABE use hierarchical structure and domain management about users and attributes. Therefore, we propose to use multi-local proxy in the scheme design, one hand, this can avoid bottleneck of single access proxy, the other is suitable the actual application scenarios of enterprise

geographically dispersed. We assume that each local proxy implement writing operation in its own exclusive space, but data can be read by other agents. The main
functions of local proxy design are as follows:

- Cloud storage access. Users interact with local proxy which replace users to
  implement encryption and decryption operations, and interact with cloud storage
  service, moreover, local proxy are also responsible for uploading encrypted files
  and download data, users no longer directly access cloud storage.
- Ciphertext access control. In our scheme, initialization operation in RM, user
  management in UM, and key generation and distribution in DM can be implemented by local proxy, and local proxy can achieve the Ciphertex access control
  policy based on hierarchical CP-ABE. This can effectively reduce the impact of
  inefficiency.
- Local data cache. Local proxy cache can set buffer which can cache high-frequency
  data, and reduce the frequency of cloud storage access.

Local proxy is mainly composed of three parts: storage interface, data processing
services and data storage services, Fig. 3 shows its basic structure below.

In Fig. 3, the object storage interface which provided by LP for data access, is up to
standard with cloud management interface CDMI [12], support PUT, GET, Delete,
FTP, NFS and other operations. In addition, we also designed a permission configure
interface to support specified data access strategy before uploading.

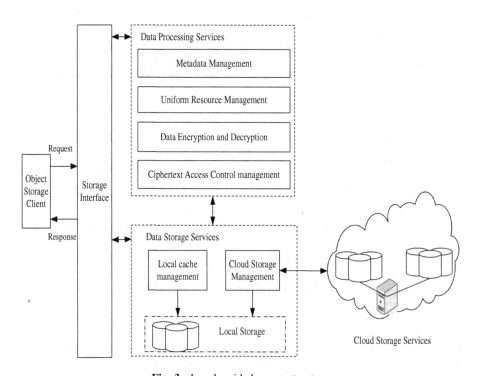

Fig. 3. Local resided proxy structure

The main function of Data Processing Services is to interact with user and receive user data, put data to the lower data storage services, and publish data to cloud. Furthermore, it receives user's instructions and gets response data from Data Storage Services, then put them to user. Data Processing Services include Metadata Management, Uniform Resource Management, Data Encryption and Decryption, Ciphertext Access Control Management and other functions.

LP generate meta data for each user data object, which include the information of data object identifier, data access policy, access time, the state of data objects, data location, key location and ciphertext location etc., also contains LP identifier which is used to distinguish released data form different proxy. URM includes resource scheduling module and duplicate management module, which is mainly responsible for the application and dispatch of resources. Data Encryption and Decryption is mainly used for data confidentiality protection, we use AES-128 algorithm in the scheme. Ciphertext Access Control Management can complete main work of access control based on hierarchical CP-ABE, including system initialization, user management, key generation, key distribution and other operations, it can take on most of overhead when users use cloud storage services, and can improve access efficiency.

Data Storage Services is responsible for manage local data cache and data storage in cloud. Local cache use LP itself storage, that to store higher frequency access data objects by using principle of the most recently used priority. Cloud Storage Management is mainly responsible for the storage of data stored in the cloud storage services, including upload/download data, optimizing data layout and other means to reduce user costs.

Let local proxy be LP_1, LP_2,..., LP_m, m represents the total number of local proxy, let $LP_j.urls$ be the data published by LP_j, let data publishing as an example, the algorithm of data processing by local proxy are shown as Algorithm 1 below.

Algorithm 1. Data Publishing algorithm by Local resided Proxy

---

INPUT: Data Owner DO, Local resided Proxy LP_j, Data Object O_i, Public parameters $Params$, Access strategy T

OUTPUT: Data location in Cloud Storage $LP_j.urls$

1. DO send O_i to LP_j, Specifies the access strategy T of O_i
2. LP_j creat Metadata
   { meta.state = creating; meta.LPID = LP.ID; meta.ID = O_i.ID; meta.T = T;
   meta.urla = urla   //urla: O_i storage Localtion
   meta.ekurl = urlb   //urlb: cipher of key storage Localtion   }
3. LP_j creat radom document key K_i
4. URM creat Replication strategy
5. LP_j run AES-128 encryption algorithm E encrypt O_i, get $E_{ki}(O_i)$
6. LP_j run Setup(), GenDM(), GenUser()
7. LP_j run Encrypt algorithm E', use T encrypt K_i, get cipher of key $E'_T(\mathbf{K_i})$
8. LP_j upload $E_{ki}(O_i)$, $E'_T(K_i)$ to cloud storage
9. LP_j return $LP_j.urls$

---

4 Experimental Results and Analysis

4.1 Experimental Data Selection

We use similar data sets to create simulation experimental data for lack of real data set using in access control based on hierarchy CP-ABE scheme. We select posting data of Netease Forum and TianYa BBS to create testing data set, among these data we select 2,854,693 posting record of Netease forum and 3,463,786 posting records in TianYa BBS from six different forums of each, all the data have filtered out pictures, video, audio etc. for testing. NetEase and TianYa BBS are used to simulate different Affiliation in the hierarchy structure, and the different forums section are used to simulate different departments, the post landlord, the post follower, the landlord's fans are used to emulate different positions, we set the user's login name as the identity ID, and area, integration, post time etc. as the attribute information.

We created each post as a data object, because the actual data objects are too large for testing, we selected data objects within 10 M. There are totally 173,598 data objects that are created, the total size of the data objects are 1329.3 GB. We set 2,618,952 data access operations in total, which include 481,248 writing operation data, about 252 GB, and 2,137,704 reading operation data objects, about 587.6 GB. We assume that each data object has 12 leaf nodes access control tree, and each read operation have been authorized.

4.2 Experimental Results and Analysis

The prototype system for testing is written in C++ running on Linux platform. The prototype system includes a local agent and a client program, local agent performs the operation of data publishing, data fetching, and ciphertext access control based on hierarchical CP-ABE etc., the client program access data through local agent. We use part of others work for reference in prototype system, which include: AES-128 and SHA256 algorithms; CP-ABE tools library [13]; The information dispersal algorithms routines in Jerasure library [14] which are used to implement the (k, n) threshold scheme. We use Hadoop distributed file system HDFS as the local cloud storage system, that are running on UBuntu platform server. Figures 4 and 5 show the time cost of publishing data and reading and writing data in different ways.

From the experimental data, we conclude that the time cost of ciphertext access control based on hierarchical CP-ABE are less than direct access control of CP-ABE, whether the operation is data publish operation or data retrieval operation, the experiment show that the access control scheme based on hierarchical CP-ABE can effectively provide access efficiency when using cloud storage service, but its time cost are greater than direct access storage cloud, the reason is to have increased the operation of ciphertext access control, which performs the protection of data privacy.

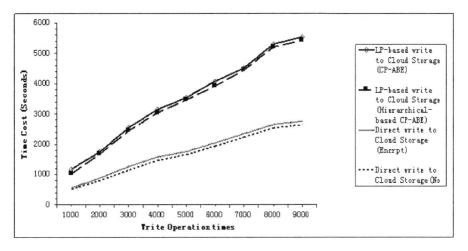

Fig. 4. Time cost comparison when publishing data in different ways

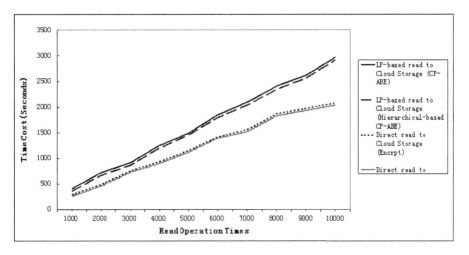

Fig. 5. Time cost comparison when retrieving data in different ways

5 Conclusion

In this paper we proposed solution about protection of data privacy when using cloud storage service from the user point of view. On the one hand, we proposed a scheme of ciphertext access control policy based on hierarchical CP-ABE which increase hierarchical structure in access right distribution and precise identity information in attribute distribution, the use of both precise identity and attributes at the same time can efficiently implement fine-grained access control, and support for key generation in hierarchy structure, this scheme can be more suitable for actual scenarios in cloud storage services. On the other hand, we proposed an efficiency access control optimizing technique based on local agency, which can implement data privacy protection. We showed the basic structure of local agents and data processing etc. experiments show that the scheme can effectively reduce the impact of using ciphertext access control mechanism and improve the access efficiency of cloud storage. Further research is the integrity protection of ciphertext, replication policy, access right revocation and optimization techniques that affect the efficiency of cloud storage access.

Acknowledgments. This research was financially supported by the Science Foundation of Education Department of Liaoning Province (No. L2014533). We thank for their support.

References

1. iResearch: China Cloud Storage Industry and User Behavior Research Report. http://report.iresearch.cn/1763.html
2. Borgmann, M., Hahn, T., Herfert, M.: On the security of cloud storage services. http://www.sit.fraunhofer.de/content/dam/sit/en/studies/Cloud-Storage-ecurity_a4.pdf
3. Shi, X.: The Core of Cloud Storage is Information Security, pp. 107–108. China Information Security, Beijing (2013)
4. Mather, T., Kumaraswamy, S., Latif, S.: Cloud Security and Privcy. O'Reilly, Media, Inc., Houston (2009)
5. Kamara, S., Lauter, K.: Cryptographic cloud storage. In: Sion, R., Curtmola, R., Dietrich, S., Kiayias, A., Miret, J.M., Sako, K., Sebé, F. (eds.) RLCPS, WECSR, and WLC 2010. LNCS, vol. 6054, pp. 136–149. Springer, Heidelberg (2010)
6. Zhang, R., Chen, P.: A dynamic cryptographic access control scheme in cloud storage services. In: Proceedings of the 8th International Conference on Computing and Networking Technology, pp. 50–55. IEEE Press, New York (2012)
7. Lv, Z., Zhang, M., Feng, D.: Cryptographic access control scheme for cloud storage. Jisuanji Kexue yu Tansuo, pp. 835–844. Computer Research and Development, Beijing (2011)
8. Chase, M.: Multi-authority attribute based encryption. In: Vadhan, S.P. (ed.) TCC 2007. LNCS, vol. 4392, pp. 515–534. Springer, Heidelberg (2007)
9. Waters, B.: Ciphertext-policy attribute-based encryption: an expressive, efficient and provably secure realization. In: Proceedings of the 14th International Conference on Practice and Theory in Public Key Cryptography, pp. 53–70. Taormina, Italy (2011)
10. Goyal, V., Pandey, O., Sahai, A.: Attribute-based encryption for fine-grained access control of encrypted data. In: Proceedings of the 13th ACM Conference on Computer and Communications Security, pp. 89–98. ACM Press, New York (2006)
11. Yu, S., Wang, C., Ren, K.: Achieving secure, scalable and fine-grained data access control in cloud computing. In: Proceedings of the IEEE INFOCOM 2010, pp. 19. IEEE Press, New York (2010)
12. SNIA: Cloud Data Management Interface (CDMI). http://snia.org/sites/default/files/CDMI%20v1.0.2.pdf
13. Bethencourt, J., Sahai, A., Waters, B.: Advanced crypto software collection ciphertext–policy attribute–based encryption. http://acsc.cs.utexas.edu/cpabe/
14. Plank, J.S., Simmerman, S., Schuman, C.D.: Jerasure: A library in C/C++ facilitating erasure coding for storage applications – version 1.2. http://web.eecs.utk.edu/∼plank/plank/papers/CS-08-627.html

Complete Separable Reversible
Data Hiding in Encrypted Image

Yin Zhaoxia[1,2], Wang Huabin[1], Zhao Haifeng[1], Luo Bin[1(✉)],
and Zhang Xinpeng[2]

[1] Key Laboratory of Intelligent Computing and Signal Processing,
Ministry of Education, Anhui University, Hefei 230601
People's Republic of China
{yinzhaoxia, wanghuabin, senith}@ahu.edu.cn,
Luobin_ahu@163.com
[2] School of Communication and Information Engineering,
Shanghai University, Shanghai 200072, People's Republic of China
xzhang@shu.edu.cn

Abstract. Reversible data hiding in encrypted image (RDHEI) is an emerging technology since it has good potential for practical applications such as encrypted image authentication, content owner identification and privacy protection. But there is one key problem of many existing published works, that the embedded data only can be extracted either before or after image decryption. In this paper, a complete separable reversible data hiding scheme in encrypted images is proposed. Additional data can be embedded into a cipher image which is encrypted by RC4 and can be extracted error-free both from the cipher domain and the plaintext domain. Moreover, the proposed method is simpler to calculate, while offering better performance. The results demonstrate that larger payload, better image quality, and error-free data extraction as well as image recovery are achieved.

Keywords: Reversible data hiding in encrypted images (RDHEI) · Privacy protection · Histogram modification

1 Introduction

Data hiding refers to technology that is used to embed additional data into multimedia and can be divided into non-reversible [1, 2] and reversible categories [3–10]. Reversible data hiding can be achieved mainly based on lossless compression [3], integer transform [4], difference expansion (DE) [5] and histogram shifting (HS) [6–8]. All of these methods have good embedding efficiency for plaintext images and can also be applied to JPEG images [9, 10].

As a typical SPED (signal processing in the encrypted domain [11]) topic, RDHEI means embedding additional data into encrypted images, and has the reversibility feature of being able to extract the additional data and recover the original image. Since there is good potential for practical applications including encrypted image authentication, content owner identification, and privacy protection, RDHEI has attracted more and more attention from many researchers [12–20].

© Springer International Publishing Switzerland 2015
Z. Huang et al. (Eds.): ICCCS 2015, LNCS 9483, pp. 101–110, 2015.
DOI: 10.1007/978-3-319-27051-7_9

In [15], an image is encrypted by a stream cipher and the data hider can embed additional data by flipping the 3 LSB (least significant bits) of pixels. Hong et al. [16] improve on this with side block matching and smoothness sorting. This year, Liao and Shu proposed an improved method [17] based on [15, 16]. A new, more precise function was presented to estimate the complexity of each image block and increase the correctness of data extraction/image recovery. However, in all of the methods mentioned above [15–17], data can only be extracted after image decryption. To overcome this problem, a separable RDHEI is proposed [18]. A legal receiver can choose 3 different options depending on the different keys held: extracting only the embedded data with the data hiding key, decrypting an image very similar to the original with the content owner key, or extracting both the embedded data and recovering the original image with both of the keys. Recently, another separable method based on pixel prediction was proposed in [19]. In the data hiding phase, a number of individual pixels are selected using a pseudo-random key, and additional bits are hidden in the two most significant bits. However, as the payload increases, the error rate also increases. Yin et al. [20] offer high payload and error-free data extraction by introducing multi-granularity permutation, which does not change the image histogram. However, leakage of the image histogram is inevitable under exhaustive attack. Moreover, in all of the methods discussed above [18–20], the embedded data can only be extracted before image decryption. That means that a legal receiver who has the data hiding key and the decrypted image cannot extract the embedded data.

To solve this problem, this paper presents a new complete separable RDHEI method based on RC4 encryption [21] and local histogram modification. Not only can the proposed method completely satisfy the definition of "separable" [18], but the embedded data can be extracted error-free both from marked encrypted images (cipher domain) and directly decrypted images (plaintext domain). However, there is a tradeoff: there should be no saturation pixels of value 0 or 255 in the image. Since saturation pixels almost are non-existent in natural images, this is a small concession. Compared with other state-of-the-art research [18, 19], the proposed method achieves higher embedding payload, better image quality and error-free image restoration.

2   Proposed Method

The framework of the proposed method is shown in Fig. 1. An image I can be encrypted to produce the encryption version I_e by using RC4 image encryption approach. This is a symmetric cipher technology and the decryption key is the same as the encryption key. Here, for simplicity, we shall call it the content owner key K_c. With the data hiding key K_d, the data hider can embed additional data A into encrypted image I_e and the marked encrypted image I'_e is generated.

On the receiver side, data extraction is completely independent from image decryption. The embedded data can be extracted from the decrypted version I' after image decryption, and also can be extracted from the cipher domain I'_e directly. With both of the keys K_c and K_d, the original image I can be reconstructed error-free. The details of image encryption, data embedding, data extraction and image recovery are

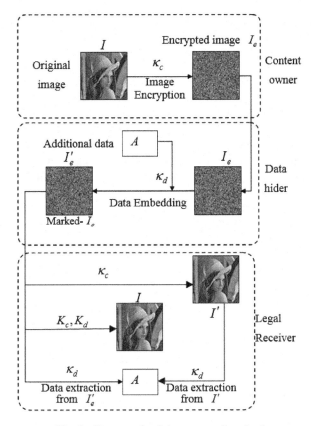

Fig. 1. Framework of the proposed method

elaborated in the following sections. First, we discuss image encryption and decryption by using RC4 [21] in Sect. 2.1.

2.1   Image Encryption and Decryption

Given a gray image $I = \{p_i\}_{i=1}^n$ sized n pixels containing no saturation pixels, p_i is the value of the i-th pixel and $p_i \in \{1, 2, \ldots, 253, 254\}$. We choose $K = \{k_j\}_{j=1}^l$, a randomly generated key-stream sized l using RC4 from a secret seed S_k. Then the image encryption is performed pixel by pixel as given in Eqs. (1) and (2) to get the encrypted image $I_e = \{q_i\}_{i=1}^n$:

$$I_e = e(I, K) \tag{1}$$

$$\begin{aligned}
e(I, K) &= (I + K) \bmod 254 + 1 \\
&= \{(p_i + k_j) \bmod 254 + 1\}_{i=1}^n \\
&= \{q_i\}_{i=1}^n
\end{aligned} \tag{2}$$

The decryption:

$$I = d(I_e, K) \tag{3}$$

$$d(I_e, K) = (I_e - 1 - K) \bmod 254 \tag{4}$$

Since the value of each grayscale pixel p_i ranges from 1 to 254, Eq. (4) has a unique solution. If the solution equals to 0, it can be revised to 254. In this paper, we divide the original image into non-overlapping blocks $I = \{B_j\}_{j=1}^l$ sized $u \times v$ at first, where $l = n/(u \times v)$. Then all the pixels in each block can be encrypted with the same k_j. Thus, each encrypted block B_j^e keeps structure redundancy to carry additional data.

2.2 Data Embedding

After image encryption, additional data can be embedded into each cipher block of $I_e = \{B_j^e\}_{j=1}^l$ to generate marked version $I_e' = \{B_j'^e\}_{j=1}^l$ based on local histogram modification, which will be described in detail in this section.

Firstly, two pixels of each block are selected randomly to use as the basis pixels, and the basis pixel values are kept unchanged during data embedding.

To carry out this process, for each image block $\{B_j^e\}_{j=1}^l$ sized $u \times v$, the two basic pixels are denoted by $\hat{q}_{j,L}$, $\hat{q}_{j,R}$ and the remaining $u \times v - 2$ pixels are denoted by $\{\bar{q}_{j,k}\}_{k=1}^{u \times v - 2}$, i.e. $B_j^e = \{\hat{q}_{j,L}, \hat{q}_{j,R}, \bar{q}_{j,k}\}_{k=1}^{u \times v - 2}$. Using the basis pixels $\hat{q}_{j,L}$, $\hat{q}_{j,R}$, two peaks in each block are determined, with $g_{j,L}$ and $g_{j,R}$ identified as Eqs. (5) and (6):

$$g_{j,L} = \min(\hat{q}_{j,L}, \hat{q}_{j,R}) \tag{5}$$

$$g_{j,R} = \max(\hat{q}_{j,L}, \hat{q}_{j,R}) \tag{6}$$

The data hider then scans the non-basic pixels $\{\{\bar{q}_{j,k}\}_{k=1}^{u \times v - 2}\}_{j=1}^l$ (i.e. excluding the two basis pixels used to determine peak values) to conceal the additional data A.

To do this, if a scanned pixel $\bar{q}_{j,k}$ is equal to the value of $g_{j,L}$ or $g_{j,R}$, a bit x extracted from A is embedded by modifying $\bar{q}_{j,k}$ to $q_{j,k}'$ according to Eq. (7).

$$q_{j,k}' = \begin{cases} \bar{q}_{j,k} - x, & \bar{q}_{j,k} = g_{j,L} \\ \bar{q}_{j,k} + x, & \bar{q}_{j,k} = g_{j,R} \end{cases} \tag{7}$$

Equation (7) shows that if a bit of value 0 is to be embedded, the value of the cover pixel remains unchanged. However, if a value of 1 is to be embedded, then depending if the value of $\bar{q}_{j,k}$ matches that of $g_{j,L}$ or $g_{j,R}$, the value is modified by $+1$. Otherwise, pixels that do not match $g_{j,L}$ or $g_{j,R}$ are either maintained or shifted by one unit using Eq. (8).

$$q'_{j,k} = \begin{cases} \bar{q}_{j,k}, & g_{j,L} < \bar{q}_{j,k} < g_{j,R} \\ \bar{q}_{j,k} - 1, & \bar{q}_{j,k} < g_{j,L} \\ \bar{q}_{j,k} + 1, & \bar{q}_{j,k} > g_{j,R} \end{cases} \tag{8}$$

In Eq. (8), it can be seen that if $\bar{q}_{j,k}$ is between the peak values, then it remains unchanged, however, if $\bar{q}_{j,k}$ is below $g_{j,L}$, then it is shifted by -1, and by $+1$ if above $g_{j,R}$. The resulting embedded blocks then make up the final embedded image $I'_e = \{B'^e_j\}^l_{j=1}$.

Please note that to make sure the embedded data can be extracted both from the cipher domain and the plaintext domain, not all of the encrypted blocks are applicable to carry data. The smoothness of an encrypted block $B^e_j = \{\hat{q}_{j,L}, \hat{q}_{j,R}, \bar{q}_{j,k}\}^{u \times v-2}_{k=1}$ is evaluated by the difference value between the minimal pixel and the maximum pixel. If it is not more than a preset threshold T, as shown in Eq. (9), the block is appropriate to embed data and accordingly a value of '1' is appended to the location map vector H. Otherwise, '0' is appended to H.

$$\max\{\hat{q}_{j,L}, \hat{q}_{j,R}, \bar{q}_{j,k}\}^{u \times v-2}_{k=1} - \min\{\hat{q}_{j,L}, \hat{q}_{j,R}, \bar{q}_{j,k}\}^{u \times v-2}_{k=1} \leq T \tag{9}$$

2.3   Data Extraction and Image Recovery

Given a marked encrypted image $I'_e = \{B'^e_j\}^l_{j=1}$ with data embedded as described in the previous section, this section describes the process of extracting embedded data and recovering the image. By this it is meant that the embedded data A can be extracted from the cipher domain I'_e before image decryption and also can be extracted from the decrypted version I' after image decryption. With both of the keys K_c and K_d, the original image I can be reconstructed error-free.

For simplicity, let $B''_j = \{\hat{q}_{j,L}, \hat{q}_{j,R}, q''_{j,k}\}^{u \times v-2}_{k=1}$ be the marked blocks with data embedded. Please note that $\{B''_j\}^l_{j=1}$ can be the cipher version I'_e and also can be the plaintext version I' decrypted from I'_e, where $K = \{k_j\}^l_{j=1}$ is a randomly generated key-stream sized l using RC4 from a secret seed S_c and the content-owner key $K_c = \{u, v, S_c\}$.

$$\begin{aligned} I' &= d(I'_e, K) \\ &= (I'_e - 1 - K) \bmod 254 \end{aligned} \tag{10}$$

To extract data from $\{B''_j\}^l_{j=1}$, we consider the non-basic pixels $\{q''_{j,k}\}^{u \times v-2}_{k=1}$ in each block. However, it is important to note that we already know the location of basic pixels by the seed S_d from $K_d = \{u, v, S_d, H\}$, and so these pixels are left untouched. The embedded data can be extracted from each block $B''_j = \{\hat{q}_{j,L}, \hat{q}_{j,R}, q''_{j,k}\}^{u \times v-2}_{k=1}$ using Eq. (11). Essentially, this means that if the value of non-basic pixel $q''_{j,k}$ is equal to either peak, then it is assumed that data is embedded, and therefore a '0' is extracted. If the value is equal to either $g_{j,L} - 1$ or $g_{j,R} + 1$, then a '1' is extracted.

$$x = \begin{cases} 0, & q''_{j,k} = g_{j,L} \text{ or } q''_{j,j} = g_{j,R} \\ 1, & q''_{j,k} = g_{j,L} - 1 \text{ or } q''_{j,k} = g_{j,R} + 1 \end{cases} \tag{11}$$

In addition to recovering the original signal, the local histogram modification process is also reversed to return the non-basic pixels $q''_{j,k}$ to their unmodified state $\bar{q}_{i,j}$. This is performed as shown in Eq. (12).

$$\bar{q}_{j,k} = \begin{cases} q''_{j,k}, & g_{j,L} < q''_{j,k} < g_{j,R} \\ q''_{j,k} + 1, & q''_{j,k} < g_{j,L} \\ q''_{j,k} - 1, & q''_{j,k} > g_{j,R} \end{cases} \tag{12}$$

3 Experiments and Results

To evaluate RDHEI, there are 4 well known and widely used key indicators: payload, quality of the directly decrypted image, number of incorrectly extracted bits and the reversibility of the original image (error rate). In this section, we conduct a number of different experiments to evaluate the performance of the proposed algorithms. We firstly show the performance of image encryption. Furthermore, the performance of the proposed RDHEI is analyzed and compared with state-of-the-art alternative approaches in terms of the payload, image quality and error rate with several commonly used standard test images.

3.1 Performance of Image Encryption

The histograms corresponding to the associated gray level pixel values before and after encryption are shown in Fig. 2, showing the original image (top row), permutation encryption by [20] (2nd row), stream cipher approach adopted by [15–19] (3rd row), and RC4 adopted in our approach with $u \times v = 2 \times 2$ (bottom row). Since the image encryption schemes introduced in [15–19] are the same, with a stream cipher adopted and applied to all bits of each pixel, the results are the same. It can be seen that, with regard to histogram distribution, leakage of the image histogram is inevitable in Ref. [20], and the image encryption method in this paper has the same uniform appearance as Refs. [15–19].

3.2 Image Quality and Payload Comparison

The payload is the number of bits embedded in each pixel and the unit of measurement is either bits or bpp (bits per pixel). The image quality is often evaluated by the PSNR (peak signal to noise ratio) between the marked and original image. As discussed previously, RDHEI is an emerging technology, but the reported small payload limits its potential for practical applications. Take Lena as an example, the maximum payload of

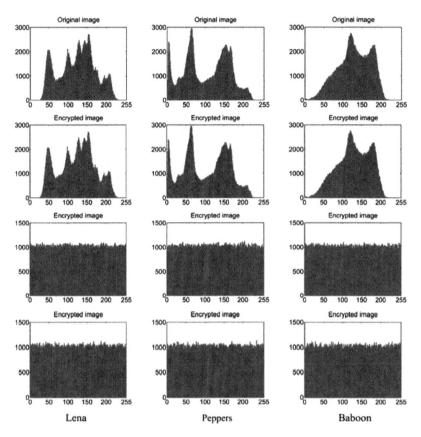

Fig. 2. Gray-level frequency histograms, showing original images (top row), permutation encryption by [20] (2nd row), stream cipher approach by [15–19] (3rd row), and RC4 adopted in our approach (bottom row).

RDHEI proposed by [18] is 8596 bits, about 0.0328 bpp. The payload of the separable method proposed by [19, 20] is much higher, but neither the image quality of [19] nor the security of [20] is satisfactory. In order to prove the value of our proposed method, Fig. 3 shows the PSNR of directly decrypted images generated by Refs. [18, 19] and the proposed method tested on Lena. All results in Fig. 3 are derived from the best parameters under a condition that the embedded data can be extracted exactly and the original image can be recovered error-free. From Fig. 3 we can see that the rate distortion performance of the proposed scheme is the best.

The final indicator, the reversibility of the original image, is the possibility of lossless recovery, and its maximum value is 1 (i.e. fully recovered). If a receiver has both keys, the original image ought to be recovered without error. However, not all images can be fully recovered in Ref [19]. Tables 1 and 2 show the error rate of image recovery in [19] and our proposed method. To get the best results, the 8-th bit of the host pixel is used to embed data in Wu's method. And we perform the experiment

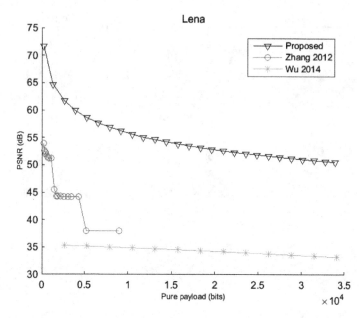

Fig. 3. Image quality and payload comparison for Lena, showing the PSNR of directly decrypted images generated by Refs. [18, 19], and the proposed method.

Table 1. Reversibility comparison on Sailboat ($T = 188$).

Methods	Payload (bpp)	PSNR (I, I')	Error rate
Proposed	0.01	58.6	0
[19]		30.63	0.1
Proposed	0.03	53.89	0
[19]		30.46	0.3
Proposed	0.04	51.29	0
[19]		30.38	0.36

Table 2. Reversibility comparison on Jet ($T = 8$).

Methods	Payload (bpp)	PSNR (I, I')	Error rate
Proposed	0.04	56.46	0
[19]		33.95	0.06
Proposed	0.08	56.07	0
[19]		33.15	0.1
Proposed	0.12	55.49	0
[19]		32.27	0.18

in each image 100 times with key from 1 to 100 to calculate the mean error rate. All experimental results show that the error rate of image in the proposed method is always 0, better than Ref. [19].

4 Conclusion

This paper proposed and evaluated a complete separable framework for reversible data hiding in encrypted images. The embedded data can be extracted error-free both from the cipher domain and the plaintext domain. However, the proposed method is not suitable for images containing saturated pixels. Future work will aim to improve this.

Acknowledgements. This research work is supported by National Natural Science Foundation of China under Grant Nos. 61502009 and 61472235, Anhui Provincial Natural Science Foundation under Grant No. 1508085SQF216, the 48th Scientific Research Staring Foundation for the Returned Overseas Chinese Scholars, Ministry of Education of China under Grant No. 1685 and the Foundation of Center of Information Support and Assurance Technology for Anhui University under Grant No. ADXXBZ201411. The authors appreciate Dr. Andrew Abel from the University of Stirling for proofreading.

References

1. Hong, W., Chen, T.S.: A novel data embedding method using adaptive pixel pair matching. IEEE Trans. Inf. Forensics Secur. **7**(1), 176–184 (2012). doi:10.1109/tifs.2011.2155062
2. Tian, H., Liu, J., Li, S.: Improving security of quantization-index-modulation steganography in low bit-rate speech streams. Multimedia Syst. **20**(2), 143–154 (2014). doi:10.1007/s00530-013-0302-8
3. Celik, M.U., Sharma, G., Tekalp, A.M., Saber, E.: Lossless generalized–LSB data embedding. IEEE Trans. Image Process. **14**(2), 253–256 (2005). doi:10.1109/TIP.2004.840686
4. Peng, F., Li, X., Yang, B.: Adaptive reversible data hiding scheme based on integer transform. Sig. Process. **92**(1), 54–62 (2012). doi:10.1016/j.sigpro.2011.06.006
5. Tian, J.: Reversible data embedding using a difference expansion. IEEE Trans. Circ. Syst. Video Technol. **13**(8), 890–896 (2003). doi:10.1109/tcsvt.2003.815962
6. Ni, Z., Shi, Y.Q., Ansari, N., Su, W.: Reversible data hiding. IEEE Trans. Circ. Syst. Video Technol. **16**(3), 354–362 (2006). doi:10.1109/tcsvt.2006.869964
7. Tai, W.L., Yeh, C.M., Chang, C.C.: Reversible data hiding based on histogram modification of pixel differences. IEEE Trans. Circ. Syst. Video Technol. **19**(6), 906–910 (2009). doi:10.1109/tcsvt.2009.2017409
8. Tsai, P., Hu, Y.C., Yeh, H.L.: Reversible image hiding scheme using predictive coding and histogram shifting. Sig. Process. **89**(6), 1129–1143 (2009). doi:10.1016/j.sigpro.2008.12.017
9. Zhang, X., Wang, S., Qian, Z., Feng, G.: Reversible fragile watermarking for locating tempered blocks in JPEG images. Sig. Process. **90**(12), 3026–3036 (2010). doi:10.1016/j.sigpro.2010.04.027
10. Qian, Z., Zhang, X.: Lossless data hiding in JPEG bitstream. J. Syst. Softw. **85**(2), 309–313 (2012). doi:10.1016/j.jss.2011.08.015
11. Erkin, Z., Piva, A., Katzenbeisser, S., Lagendijk, R.L., Shokrollahi, J., Neven, G., Barni, M.: Protection and retrieval of encrypted multimedia content: when cryptography meets signal processing. EURASIP J. Inf. Secur. **2007**, 1–20 (2007). doi:10.1155/2007/78943
12. Schmitz, R., Li, S., Grecos, C., Zhang, X.: Towards robust invariant commutative watermarking-encryption based on image histograms. Int. J. Multimedia Data Eng. Manage. **5**(4), 36–52 (2014). doi:10.4018/ijmdem.2014100103

13. Ma, K., Zhang, W., Zhao, X., Yu, N., Li, F.: Reversible data hiding in encrypted images by reserving room before encryption. IEEE Trans. Inf. Forensics Secur. **8**(3), 553–562 (2013). doi:10.1109/tifs.2013.2248725

14. Zhang, W., Ma, K., Yu, N.: Reversibility improved data hiding in encrypted images. Sig. Process. **94**, 118–127 (2014). doi:10.1016/j.sigpro.2013.06.023

15. Zhang, X.: Reversible data hiding in encrypted image. IEEE Sig. Process. Lett. **18**(4), 255–258 (2011). doi:10.1109/lsp.2011.2114651

16. Hong, W., Chen, T.S., Wu, H.Y.: An improved reversible data hiding in encrypted images using side match. IEEE Sig. Process. Lett. **19**(4), 199–202 (2012). doi:10.1109/lsp.2012.2187334

17. Liao, X., Shu, C.: Reversible data hiding in encrypted images based on absolute mean difference of multiple neighboring pixels. J. Vis. Commun. Image Represent. **28**, 21–27 (2015). doi:10.1016/j.jvcir.2014.12.007

18. Zhang, X.: Separable reversible data hiding in encrypted image. IEEE Trans. Inf. Forensics Secur. **7**(2), 826–832 (2012). doi:10.1109/tifs.2011.2176120

19. Wu, X., Sun, W.: High-capacity reversible data hiding in encrypted images by prediction error. Sig. Process. **104**, 387–400 (2014). doi:10.1016/j.sigpro.2014.04.032

20. Yin, Z., Luo, B., Hong, W.: Separable and error-free reversible data hiding in encrypted image with high payload. Sci. World J. **2014**, 1–8 (2014). doi:10.1155/2014/604876

21. Ferguson, N., Schneier, B.: Practical Cryptography. Wiley, New York (2003)

Multi-threshold Image Segmentation Through an Improved Quantum-Behaved Particle Swarm Optimization Algorithm

Wang Jiali[1(✉)], Liu Hongshen[1(✉)], and Ruan Yue[1,2,3(✉)]

[1] School of Computer Science, Anhui University of Technology,
Maanshan 243005, China
1041934179@qq.com
[2] School of Computer Science and Engineering,
Southeast University, Nanjing 210096, China
[3] Key Laboratory of Computer Network and Information Integration,
Ministry of Education, Southeast University,
Nanjing 210096, China

Abstract. Multi-threshold segmentation is a basic and widely used technique in image segmentation. The key step of accomplishing this task is to find the optimal multi-threshold value, which in essence can be reduced to multi-objective optimization problem. The quantum particle-behaved swarm algorithm (QPSO) is an effective method to resolve the problem of this class. However in practice, we found the original QPSO has imperfections, such as the excessive dropping of the diversity of the population and trapping in local optimum. In order to improve the ability of searching the global optimum and accelerate the speed of convergence, we proposed an improved quantum-behaved particle swarm algorithm (IQPSO). The experiments showed that IQPSO was superior to PSO and QPSO on the searching of multi-threshold value in image segmentation under the premise of ensuring the accuracy of solutions.

Keywords: Image segmentation · Multi-threshold segmentation · QPSO · IQPSO

1 Introduction

Image segmentation plays a critical role in the process of object recognition in digital image processing. Nowadays, the methods of image segmentation have already been proposed up to thousands [1]. Among them, threshold method is a basic and popular technique. By setting one and more thresholds based on the image histogram, we can divide the pixels in a certain threshold interval to the same object [2]. The traditional method for calculating threshold includes the maximum between-cluster variance method [3], the maximum entropy method [4], and the minimum error method [5], etc. Among them, the maximum between-cluster variance method is the most widely used method because of its simple calculation and good segmentation performance.

© Springer International Publishing Switzerland 2015
Z. Huang et al. (Eds.): ICCCS 2015, LNCS 9483, pp. 111–122, 2015.
DOI: 10.1007/978-3-319-27051-7_10

The maximum between-cluster variance method, which is also named as OTSU, is proposed in 1979 by a Japanese scholar Nobuyuki Otsu. Its basic principle is: the threshold splits the image into the target and the background. Then the average gray level of the target can be gotten as μ_1, and the proportion of the number of the pixels of the target to the whole image pixels can be gotten as ω_1. Similarly, the average gray level of the background is μ_2 and the proportion of the number of the pixels of the background to the whole image pixels is ω_2. So the maximum between-cluster variance g can be computed as formula (1).

$$g = \omega_1\omega_2(\mu_1 - \mu_2)^2 \tag{1}$$

When g obtains the maximum value under the threshold t, t is the best suitable threshold value. Extending OTSU to multi-threshold segmentation, we can get the computing formula as (2).

$$g = \sum_{k=1}^{M} \omega_k \times (\mu_k - \mu)^2 \tag{2}$$

Where M is the number of best threshold values. μ is the average gray level of the image. The variance g obtains the maximum value under the best threshold $T^* = \{t_1, t_2 \ldots t_{M-1}\}$, namely $T^* = \text{Argmax}\{g\}$.

The calculation of multi-threshold has a heavy computation burden, the time performance is low in practice. In essence, the calculation of multi-threshold (formula (2)) can be reduced to multi-objective optimization problem. So the multi-objective optimization theory and method can be used on this issue. At present, previous studies show that the quantum particle swarm optimization algorithm is an effective method to solve the problem of this class.

QPSO (quantum-behaved particle swarm optimization) algorithm is a swarm intelligence algorithm, which is proposed by Sun in 2004 from the perspective of quantum behavior [6, 7]. It is the improved version of the classical PSO (particle swarm optimization) [8]. Because the uncertainty of the quantum system determines the quantum particles could appear within the feasible region at a certain probability, QPSO algorithm has advantages of global optimization convergence compared to PSO algorithm in theory [9]. In addition, QPSO algorithm has less control parameters, simple implementation, and fast convergence speed. But in practice, for some complicated problems, it has imperfections: species diversity decreased quickly, trapping in local optimum sometimes and slow convergence speed because of defective parameters setting. Therefore, in recent years, researchers have proposed a lot of approaches to overcome these drawbacks, such as improvement of the parameters setting of contraction-expansion [10, 11], the introduction of selection and mutation operation [12], and the introduction of the strategy of multi-population co-evolution [13–15], etc.

Based on the understanding of prior works, we proposed an algorithm named as IQPSO (improved quantum-behaved particle swarm optimization) to address these imperfections. Through the application of IQPSO in multi-threshold image segmentation, the experiments results showed that IQPSO was a more effective way to solve this problem than QPSO.

2   The Basic Principle and the Analysis of QPSO

2.1   The Basic Principle

QPSO is an improvement on the PSO algorithm. PSO is a bionic algorithm simulating birds foraging behavior. In PSO algorithm, each individual in the community is called a particle i, which represents a potential solution to the problem. The motion of particles in the PSO algorithm is described by position and speed. However in quantum scenario, it is impossible to determine the position and momentum of the particle at the same time. In QPSO algorithm, we use the wave function $\Psi(X, t)$ to describe the motion of the particles, where X is the position vector of particle i at the moment t. The physical meaning of the value of the function Ψ is: its modulus square represents the probability of the appearance of particle i in position X.

QPSO algorithm assumes that the particle swarm system is a quantum particle system, each particle i moves in the Delta potential well with the centre point O. We set $X_{i,t} = (x_{1,t}, x_{2,t} ..., x_{d,t})$ as the position vector, $P_{i,t} = (p_{1,t}, p_{2,t} ..., p_{d,t})$ as the individual optimal position of particle i so far, and $P_{g,t} = (p_{1,t}, p_{2,t} ..., p_{d,t})$ as the global optimal position, where d is dimension of the problem, t is the number of iterations. So the state of the particle can be described by the wave function Ψ as Eq. (3).

$$\Psi\left(x_{i,t+1}^{j}\right) = \frac{1}{\sqrt{L_{i,t}^{j}}} \exp\left(-\frac{\left|x_{i,t}^{j} - O_{i,t}^{j}\right|}{L_{i,t}^{j}}\right) \tag{3}$$

The probability of its corresponding position is showed as Eq. (4).

$$Q\left(x_{i,t+1}^{j}\right) = \frac{1}{L_{i,t}^{j}} \exp\left(-\frac{2\left|x_{i,t}^{j} - O_{i,t}^{j}\right|}{L_{i,t}^{j}}\right) \tag{4}$$

In quantum mechanics, the final position of the particles is obtained by measurements, which will result the collapse of original quantum state to the ground state. This scenario can be simulated by the Monte Carlo stochastic simulation manner. So, the update equation of particle location is obtained as Eqs. (5–8).

$$x_{i,t+1}^{j} = O_{i,t}^{j} \pm \frac{L_{i,t}^{j}}{2} \ln\left(\frac{1}{u_{i,t+1}^{j}}\right) \tag{5}$$

$$O_{i,t}^{j} = \frac{\varphi_{1} P_{i,t}^{j} + \varphi_{2} P_{g,t}^{j}}{\varphi_{1} - \varphi_{2}} \tag{6}$$

$$L_{i,t}^{j} = 2\alpha\left|C_{t}^{j} - x_{i,t}^{j}\right| \tag{7}$$

$$C_i^j = \frac{\sum_{i=1}^{N} P_{i,t}^j}{N} \tag{8}$$

L is characteristic length of delta potential well.

u is a uniformly distributed random number in the interval [0, 1].

O is the attractive point of one particle, which can be calculated by its own previous best position $P_{i,t}$ and the swarm previous best position $P_{g,t}$ [16]. φ_1 and φ_2 are two uniformly distributed random number in the interval [0, 1].

C is the average optimal position of the history of all particles.

α is contraction-expansion coefficient, which is the only manual setup parameter of QPSO algorithm and satisfying $\alpha < 1.782$ [17]. The update of α adopts the method of line reduction with the increase of iteration times (Equation (9)).

$$\alpha = \alpha_{max} - (\alpha_{max} - \alpha_{min})\frac{t}{T} \tag{9}$$

Where T is the maximum number of iterations.

Take the Eqs. (7) and (8) into the Eq. (5), the position update formula of the particles can be rewritten as (10).

$$x_{i,t+1}^j = O_{i,t}^j \pm \alpha \left| C_t^j - x_{i,t}^j \right| \ln\left(\frac{1}{u_{i,t+1}^j}\right) \tag{10}$$

2.2   The Analysis of QPSO Algorithm

Compared with PSO algorithm, the QPSO algorithm has the following advantages:

- QPSO algorithm has merits of global convergence in theory, because the particle can be appeared in any position in the search area.
- In the QPSO algorithm, the length of a potential well is calculated by average optimal position, which makes the interaction among all the particles, and thus enhances the search ability of global optimum.
- QPSO algorithm has only position vector rather than the position and speed vectors, which leads to easier implementation.

Although QPSO has such advantages, it and its improved algorithms still have flaws: QPSO can achieve global optimization in theory, but without adaptive parameters control, the algorithm sometimes behaves not good. To the specific problem of this article, multi-threshold segmentation, the shortcomings of prematurity and slow convergence speed are obvious with the increasing number of threshold.

3   IQPSO

Aiming at the shortcomings of QPSO, we improve the algorithm performance from the following two aspects.

3.1   Avoid Prematurity—New Calculation Method of Attractive Point and Potential Well Length

In QPSO algorithm, there are two important parameters: attractive point O and potential well length L. Attractive point O, which attracts the particles in the community to converge is the center of the whole community. The potential well, whose length is defined as L, is the search space of each particle. By Eqs. (6) and (7), we can see that the attractive point O is determined by the calculation of the historical optimal location of individuals and the historical optimal location of the community. And the potential well length L is calculated by the average optimal position C.

Analyzing the calculation formulas of the two parameters, we can conclude such advantages: easy calculation and convergence, which is guaranteed by the convergence of individual optimal position and community optimal position to the attractive point O.

However, we find some disadvantages:

- In the process of searching the optimal solution, the particle adjusts its position only by the historical optimal position of its own and the historical optimal position of the community, which cause the loss of population diversity too fast. As a result, the performance of solving multi-modal function optimization problem is low.
- The attractive point O is located in the super rectangle which is formed by the vertex of the best location of individual history and community history. In the later execution phase of the search algorithm, the location of attractive point O will gradually be close to the best location of community history, which makes the algorithm premature and fall into local optimum.
- The average optimal location of community C is a relatively stable point which cannot response the searching information of the whole community in time. So the calculation of the potential well L using this parameter will lead to the reduction of global search ability of the algorithm.

Therefore, in order to increase the diversity of the population, enlarge the search scope of population, and improve the performance of QPSO algorithm to solve multimodal optimization problems, we proposed a new way to calculate attractive point O by the introduction of a disturbance vector $\Delta_{i,t}$. The formula (11) show the new calculation of the attractive point O.

$$O_{i,t}^j = \beta_{i,t} p_{i,t}^j + (1 - \beta_{i,t}) p_{a,t}^j + \Delta_{i,t}^j \tag{11}$$

$$\Delta_{i,t}^j = \frac{p_{b,t}^j - p_{c,t}^j}{2} \tag{12}$$

Combined with the new calculation of the attractive point, the potential well length L is modified as formula (13).

$$L_{i,t}^{j} = 2\alpha \left| \Delta_{i,t}^{j} \right| \tag{13}$$

$B_{i,\ t}$ is a uniformly distributed random Number in the interval $[0, 1]$.

a is a particle selected from the best q particles of $[q \cdot N]$. $q \in (0, 1]$.

b and c are two particles selected randomly from the current community satisfying $a \neq b \neq c \neq i$.

The new way of calculating the O and C results in following advantages:

(1) When some particles trapped in local optimum, the particles a, b, and c distribute in other search space, which have the opportunity to help the stagnated particles escape from local optimum.

(2) Selecting the best fitness value of q can balance the global search ability and local search ability. The larger value of q can enhance the global exploring ability, on the contrary smaller value can speed convergence. In order to balance the global search ability in earlier phase and local search ability in later phase, the value of q decreases with the increase of iteration times.

$$q = q_{max} - (q_{max} - q_{min}) \frac{t}{T} \tag{14}$$

3.2   Accelerating Convergence—Crossover Operator

Crossover operator is an important concept in genetic algorithms. It generates new individuals to expand the solution space by simulating the hybrid process of biological world. The goal of it is to make the search ability of genetic algorithm stronger. Crossover probability pc is an important parameter of crossover operators, the value of which affects the global search ability and convergence speed. Smaller crossover probability can make the individuals keep more information of their own, maintain high population diversity, and be good for global exploration. By contrast, larger crossover probability urges individuals to learn more experience and knowledge from the community, speeds up the convergence of the algorithm.

In order to increase the population diversity of the QPSO algorithm, expand the searching range of particles, and accelerate the algorithm convergence speed at the later phase, we adopt a specific crossover operator. The crossover operation is showed as follows.

Step 1: the measurement position $X_{i,t+1}$ of particle is generated by the new calculation method of attractive point O and potential well length L.

Step 2: the new measurement position $Z_{i,t+1}$ is generated by the crossover of $X_{i,t+1}$ and the historical optimal position $P_{i,t}$:

$$Z_{i,t}^j = \begin{cases} x_{i,t+1}^j, & \text{if } \text{rand}_j(0, 1) < pc \text{ or } j = j_{\text{rand}} \\ p_{i,t}^j, & \text{otherwise} \end{cases} \qquad (15)$$

Step 3: after the generation of $Z_{i,t+1}$, the historical optimal position $P_{i,t+1}$ is updated by formula (16).

$$P_{i,t+1} = \begin{cases} Z_{i,t+1}, & \text{if } f(Z_{i,t+1}) > f(P_{i,t}) \\ P_{i,t}, & \text{otherwise} \end{cases} \qquad (16)$$

$rand_j$ *(0, 1)* is a uniformly distributed random number in the interval [0, 1].
j_{rand} is a uniformly distributed random integer in [1, d].
$f(\cdot)$ is the fitness function.
pc is the crossover probability. In this article, pc is directly encoded into each particle in order to realize adaptive control. After coding, the ith particle is described as follows.

$$X_{i,t} = \left(x_{i,t}^1, x_{i,t}^2, \ldots, x_{i,t}^d, pc_{i,t} \right) \qquad (17)$$

Inspired by the adaptive method of parameter adjustment in the literature [18], we use the following rules to update crossover probability of particle i.

$$pc_{i,t+1} = \begin{cases} \text{rand}_1(0, 1), & \text{if } \text{rand}_2(0, 1) < \tau \\ pc_{i,t}, & \text{otherwise} \end{cases} \qquad (18)$$

τ is the renewal probability of the parameters. ($\tau = 0.2$ in the experiments).

4   The Application of IQPSO in Multi-threshold Image Segmentation

4.1   Implementation Steps

The steps of IQPSO doing multi-threshold image segmentation are listed as follows:

- Initialization. Set the iteration times $t = 0$. Set the size of the community N, the initial value of the crossover probability pc, the best fitness value q, the zoom factor γ, the coefficient of contraction-expansion α, and the number of thresholds M.
- In the feasible solution space, generate initial population $\{X_{1,0}, X_{2,0}, \ldots, X_{N,0}\}$ randomly, and set $P_{i,0} = X_{i,0}(i = 0, 1, \ldots, N)$.
- Select formula (2) as the fitness function. The $P_{i,\,t}$ of each particle and the $P_{g,\,t}$ is calculated according to this function.
- The attractive point O and potential well length L are calculated by formulas (11)–(13). Bring these values to formula (5) to generate the primary measurement position of the particle.

- Generate the measurement position according to the formula (15), and evaluate the value of the fitness function. According to the formula (16), update the historical optimal position $P_{i,\ t}$ and the community optimal location $P_{g,\ t}$.
- According to the formula (18), update the crossover probability.
- Check the termination conditions: if the algorithm has good fitness function value or reach the maximum number of iterations, the iteration stops. Otherwise, return to step 4).

When the algorithm is ended, $P_{g,\ t}$ is the value of optimal thresholds.

4.2   The Experimental Results and Analysis

In order to test the performance of IQPSO, we use Berkeley Segmentation Dataset [19], which contains 100 images, to do experiments. Due to limited space, we just choose the experiment results of 3 images to show the comparison.

In experiments, the performance of IQPSO algorithm is compared with OTSU; PSO and QPSO. OTSU algorithm has the best segmentation quality. PSO, QPSO and IQPSO cannot enhance the quality of segmentation because they use the OTSU as the fitness function. So the result of OTSU act the evaluation standard for the remaining three algorithms. The performance evaluation of PSO, QPSO and IQPSO is the comparison of how close are the results of these algorithms to the result of OTSU and the time consumed to get the results.

In the experiments, all the algorithms repeat 100 times. The parameters of each algorithm are set in accordance with related literature [6, 7]. The parameters of IQPSO algorithm are set as follows: the size of community $N = 20$, particle dimension $d = 2,3,4$, the largest number of iterations is 100, the coefficient α of convergence-expansion decreases from 0.7 to 0.1, the best fitness value q decrease from 0.5 to 0.1, initial crossover probability pc is 0.9, the update probability of crossover probability τ is 0.2. In order to do comparison fairly, the community size N of other algorithm are also set to 20.

The experimental environment is: Operating system: Windows 7; The processor: Intel core 2 duo P8400 processor, 2.53 GHz; Memory: 4 GB; Programming language: C#; Compiler: VS 2010.

Experiment 1: the effect of various algorithms.

The three images for testing and their gray histogram are showed as Fig. 1. For the images of Fig. 1, when the number of thresholds is 2, 3 and 4, the average fitness value and the threshold values as well as the time consumed are showed in Table 1.

When the number of thresholds is 2, 3, 4, the average time consumed of IQPSO is showed in Table 2. Tables 3 and 4 list the average fitness value (the variance values), and the corresponding thresholds of PSO, QPSO and IQPSO algorithm. The greater the value in Table 3 indicates the better performance of the algorithm.

From Tables 1 and 2, it is observed that the time consumed of IQPSO algorithm amounts to 3.6 %, 0.052 % and 0.0012 % of OTSU, when the threshold number is 2, 3 and 4. So with the increase in threshold numbers, the efficiency of IQPSO has more obvious promotion. From Tables 1, 3 and 4, it is observed that IQPSO achieve the

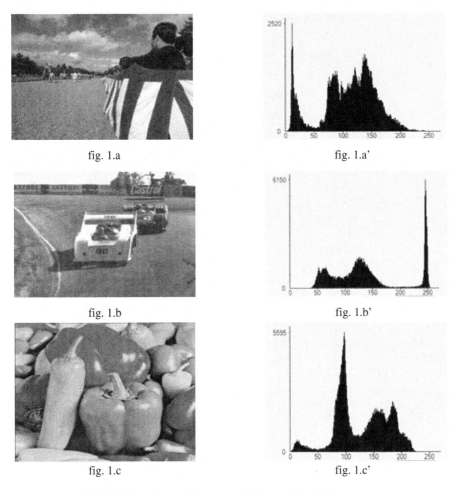

Fig. 1. Experimental images and their gray-level histograms

Table 1. The related value of OTSU

M / image	2 threshold value	fitness value	3 threshold value	fitness value	4 threshold value	fitness value
a	90,180	3054.4956	72,125,191	5608.1314	40,88,132,195	8706.0967
b	109,189	3733.8552	81,122,194	7276.9442	77,109,140,200	11879.7161
c	72,144	1254.0702	66,126,182	2528.4884	63,117,163,222	4512.9173
time (ms)	1331.0761		158305.7212		12073135.52	

Table 2. The average time of IQPSO algorithm

M	2	3	4
Time (ms)	47.3253	82.9427	139.8708

Table 3. The average fitness value (the variance values)

Image	Threshold number	Variance value		
		PSO	QPSO	IQPSO
a	2	3007.6220	3048.9612	3050.4923
	3	5390.0629	5420.7708	5587.4002
	4	8191.0253	8261.0653	8686.4310
b	2	3650.9135	3670.7367	3718.9775
	3	6612.7684	6684.3612	7266.6430
	4	8689.6185	9543.0156	11837.6126
c	2	1240.0303	1248.6809	1252.7604
	3	2455.9685	2476.8243	2523.1292
	4	3897.7765	4158.5943	4472.4178

Table 4. The corresponding thresholds

Image	Threshold number	Threshold value		
		PSO	QPSO	IQPSO
a	2	89,181	88,181	88,180
	3	71,125,194	67,121,191	68,121,190
	4	43,90,134,198	40,88,135,197	40,87,132,195
b	2	108,191	108,188	108,190
	3	72,122,198	75,121,194	81,122,194
	4	53,98,135,201	63,102,136,203	75,109,140,201
c	2	73,143	74,146	72,144
	3	65,127,190	63,127,191	65,125,186
	4	50,105,153,214	57,111,158,220	62,117,164,220

largest fitness function values, which are equal or most close to the results of OTSU algorithm. Therefore, we can draw the following two conclusions: (1) compared with OTSU algorithm, IQPSO algorithm greatly shortens the time of obtaining the threshold value. (2) Compared with the rest two optimization algorithms PSO and QPSO, the segmentation effect of IQPSO is better.

Experiment 2: the segmentation effect of OTSU algorithm and IQPSO algorithm.

When the threshold number is 4, the effect of image segmentation using IQPSO and OTSU is showed in Fig. 2. It is observed that the segmentation results of IQPSO algorithm are same as the results of OTSU method with naked eyes.

From the analysis of the above experiment results, we can draw the following conclusion: the IQPSO algorithm can improve the efficiency of multi-threshold image segmentation on the premise of achieving the accurate value.

<table>
</table>

| fig.2.a the effect of OTSU | fig.2.a' the effect of IQPSO |

| fig.2.b the effect of OTSU | fig. 2. b' the effect of IQPSO |

| fig.2.c the effect of OTSU | fig.2.c' the effect of IQPSO |

Fig. 2. The segmentation effect of OTSU algorithm and IQPSO algorithm

5 Conclusion

We proposed an improved QPSO algorithm (IQPSO) aiming at improving the efficiency of multi-threshold image segmentation. The experiments show that IQPSO is an effective method to resolve the problem. However whether IQPSO is suitable for solving other the multi-objective optimization problems or not is still an issue needed to do further study.

Acknowledgments. This work is supported by the open fund of the key laboratory in Southeast University of computer network and information integration of the ministry of education (Grant No. K93-9-2015-10C).

References

1. Xiping, L., Jiei, T.: A survey of image segmentation. Pattern Recogn. Artif. Intell. **12**(3), 300–312 (1999)
2. Pal, N.R., Pal, S.K.: A review on image segmentation techniques. Pattern Recogn. **26**(9), 1277–1294 (1993)
3. Otsu, N.: A threshold selection method from gray-level histograms. IEEE Trans. Syst. Man Cybern. **9**(1), 62–66 (1979)
4. Kapur, J.N., Sahoo, P.K., Wong, A.K.C.: A new method for gray-level picture thresholding using the entropy of the histogram. Comput. Vision Graph. Image Process. **29**(3), 273–285 (1985)
5. Kittler, J., Illingworth, J.: Minimum error thresholding. Pattern Recogn. **19**(1), 41–47 (1986)
6. Sun, J., Feng, B., Xu, W.-B.: Particle swarm optimization with particles having quantum behavior. In: Proceedings of 2004 Congress on Evolutionary Computation, pp. 325–331. Piscataway, NJ (2004)
7. Sun, J., Xu, W.-B., Feng, B.: A global search strategy of quantum-behaved particle swarm optimization. In: Proceedings of 2004 IEEE Conference on Cybernetics and Intelligent Systems, pp. 111–115. Singapore (2004)
8. Kennedy, J., Eberhart, R.C.: Particle swarm optimization. In: Proceedings of the 1995 IEEE International Conference on Neural Networks (1995)
9. Sun, J., Wu, X.J., Palade, V., Fang, W., Lai, C.-H., Xu, W.: Convergence analysis and improvements of quantum-behaved particle swarm optimization. Inf. Sci. **193**, 81–103 (2012)
10. Sun, J., Xu, W.-B., Liu, J.: Parameter selection of quantum-behaved particle swarm optimization. In: Wang, L., Chen, K., S. Ong, Y. (eds.) ICNC 2005. LNCS, vol. 3612, pp. 543–552. Springer, Heidelberg (2005)
11. Cheng, W., Chen, S.F.: QPSO with self-adapting adjustment of inertia weight. Comput. Eng. Appl. **46**(9), 46–48 (2010)
12. Gong, S.-F., Gong, X.-Y., Bi, X.-R.: Feature selection method for network intrusion based on GQPSO attribute reduction. In: International Conference on Multimedia Technology, pp. 6365–6358 (26–28 July 2011)
13. Gao, H., Xu, W.B., Gao, T.: A cooperative approach to quantum-behaved particle swarm optimization. In: Proceedings of IEEE International Symposium on Intelligent Signal Processing, IEEE, Alcala de Henares (2007)
14. Lu, S.F., Sun, C.F.: Co evolutionary quantum-behaved particle swarm optimization with hybrid cooperative search. In: Proceedings of Pacific-Asia Workshop on Computational Intelligence and Industrial Application, IEEE, Wuhan (2008)
15. Lu, S.F., Sun, C.F.: Quantum-behaved particle swarm optimization with cooperative-competitive co evolutionary. In: Proceedings of International Symposium on Knowledge Acquisition and Modeling, IEEE, Wuhan (2008)
16. Clerk, M., Kennedy, J.: The particle swarm-explosion, stability, and convergence in a multidimensional complex space. IEEE Trans. Evol. Comput. **6**(1), 58–73 (2002)
17. Sun, J., Xu, W.B., Feng, B.: Adaptive parameter control for quantum-behaved particle swarm optimization on individual level. In: Proceedings of 2005 IEEE International Conference on Systems, Man and Cybernetics, pp. 3049–3054. Piscataway (2005)
18. Brest, J., Greiner, S., Boskovic, B., et al.: Self adapting control parameters in differential evolution: a comparative study on numerical benchmark problems. IEEE Trans. Evol. Comput. **10**(6), 646–657 (2006)
19. http://www.eecs.berkeley.edu/Research/Projects/CS/vision/bsds/

Coverless Image Steganography Without Embedding

Zhili Zhou[1], Huiyu Sun[2], Rohan Harit[2], Xianyi Chen[1],
and Xingming Sun[1(✉)]

[1] School of Computer and Software, Jiangsu Engineering Center
of Network Monitoring, Nanjing University of Information Science
and Technology, Nanjing 210044, China
{zhou_zhili,0204622,sunnudt}@163.com
[2] Department of Computer Science,
New York University, New York, NY 10012, USA
{hs2879,rohan.harit}@nyu.edu

Abstract. The traditional image steganography technologies designate a cover image and embed secret data into it to form the stego-image. However, the modification traces caused by the embedding will be left in the cover image, which makes successful steganalysis possible. To fundamentally address this issue, this paper proposes a novel image steganography framework, called as coverless image steganography, which does not need to employ the designated cover image for embedding the secret data. In this framework, a series of appropriate original images which already contain the secret data are directly chosen from a constructed database, and these original images can be regarded as the stego-images. Firstly, a number of images are collected to construct the database, and these images are indexed according to their hash sequence generated by a robust hashing algorithm. Then, the secret data is transformed to a bit string and divided into a number of segments. To implement the information hiding, the images of which the hash sequences are the same as the segments are chosen from the database as the stego-images. Experimental results show that the proposed coverless image steganography framework can resist the existing steganalysis tools, and have desirable robustness to the typical image attacks such as rescaling, luminance change, and noise adding.

Keywords: Coverless image steganography · Information hiding · Without embedding · Watermarking · Digital forensics

1 Introduction

Steganography is the science of communicating secret information in a hidden manner [1]. Due to the wide use of multimedia data (digital image, audio and video) in our electronic world, the communication of secret information in a digital way is urgently required. Digital steganography, the technology utilizing multimedia data as vehicles for steganographic communication has become an important current technology in the area of information security. Different from cryptography in which communication is evident, this technology can conceal the occurrence of communication of secret information.

© Springer International Publishing Switzerland 2015
Z. Huang et al. (Eds.): ICCCS 2015, LNCS 9483, pp. 123–132, 2015.
DOI: 10.1007/978-3-319-27051-7_11

In the past two decades, many image steganography methods have been proposed in the literature [2–12]. To our knowledge, all of these steganography methods designate an appropriate cover image, and then embed secret information into it to generate the stego-image. According to reference [1], the existing image steganography methods can be roughly divided into three categories: spatial domain, frequency domain and adaptive methods. The spatial domain methods have a larger impact than the other two categories. Typical spatial domain methods include the LSB replacement [2], LSB matching [3], color palette [4] and histogram-based methods [5]. Although the modification of cover image LSB caused by the embedding mechanism of the spatial domain methods is not easily detected by human eyes, the embedded information is sensitive to image attacks. To address this issue, many frequency domain steganography methods have been proposed, such as quantization table (QT) [6], discrete Fourier transform (DFT) [7], and discrete wavelet transform (DWT) based embedding [8]. Adaptive steganography is a special case of the spatial domain and frequency domain methods. In the literature, there are many typical adaptive steganography methods, such as the locally adaptive coding-based [9], edge-based [10] and Bit Plane Complexity Segmentation (BPCS) based data embedding [11, 12].

Although the existing methods employ different technologies for image steganography, all of them have a common point. That is all of them implement the steganography by embedding the secret information into a designated cover image. Since the embedding process will modify the content of the cover image more or less, modification traces will be left in the cover image. Consequently, it is possible to successfully detect the steganography by various emerging steganalysis tools such as [13–16], all of which are based on the modification traces. If we find a novel hiding manner by which the secret information can be hidden without any modification, it will be effective to resist all of the existing steganalysis tools. How to hide the secret information without any modification? It is a challenging and exciting task.

As we know, it is a fact that any original image contains a lot of information. This information may already contain the secret data needed to be hidden with a certain probability. From Fig. 1, for the secret data $\{1, 1, 0, 1, 1, 0, 1, 0\}$, we found that the original image shown in the right of Fig. 1 already contains a pixel of which the intensity value is 218. The binary data of the intensity value 218 is $\{1, 1, 0, 1, 1, 0, 1, 0\}$, which is the same as the secret data. Therefore, if we find the appropriate original images which already contain the secret data as stego-images and communicate the

Fig. 1. The original image which already contains the secret data $\{1, 1, 0, 1, 1, 0, 1, 0\}$

secret data by transmitting these images, it can implement the steganography without any modification to these images.

Without employing the designated cover image for embedding the secret data, this paper proposes a novel image steganography framework, called coverless image steganography, to hide the secret data by finding appropriate images which already contain it. These images are regarded as stego-images, which are used for communication of the secret data. For a given secret data, the main issue of our framework lies in how to find these original images. As shown in Fig. 1, directly finding the images having the pixels of which intensity values are the same as secret data is simple, but it is not a robust manner. That is because, during communication of the secret data, these images may suffer some image attacks, which will cause the intensity values of the pixels in the images to be changed. Thus, instead of using the above manner, we find the images whose hash sequences generated by a robust hashing algorithm are the same as the secret data. In this framework, a series of appropriate original images are chosen from a constructed database by using a robust hashing algorithm. Firstly, a number of images are collected from the networks to construct a database, and these images are indexed according to their hash sequence generated by a robust hashing algorithm. Then, the secret data is transformed to a bit string and divided it into a number of segments with the equal length. To implement the information hiding, the images of which hash sequences are the same as the segments are chosen from the database as stego-images.

The main contributions of this paper are concluded as follows. Since we do not need the designated cover image for embedding secret data and thus any modification traces will not be left, the proposed coverless image steganography framework can resist all of the existing steganalysis tools. Moreover, this framework is robust to the typical image attacks, such as rescaling, luminance change, contrast enhancement, JPEG compression and noise adding, owing to the robust hashing algorithm.

The rest of this paper is organized as follows. Section 2 presents the proposed coverless image steganography framework. Section 3 analyzes the resistance to steganalysis tools and robustness of the proposed framework. Experiments are presented in Sect. 4, and conclusions are drawn in Sect. 5.

2 The Proposed Coverless Steganography Framework

The flow chart of the proposed coverless steganography framework for secret data communication is shown in Fig. 2.

In the proposed framework, an image database is first constructed by collecting a number of images from the networks. Then, for each image in the database, its hash sequence is generated by a robust hashing algorithm. Afterward, all of these images are indexed according to their hash sequences to build an inverted index structure. Note that the hashing algorithm is shared between sender and receiver.

To communicate the secret data, the sender first transforms the secret data to a bit string and divides it into a number of segments with the equal length. Then, for each segment, the image of which hash sequence is the same as the segment is found by searching in the inverted index structure. Afterward, a series of images associated to the segments, which can be regarded as stego-images, are obtained and then transmitted to the receiver. On the receiver end, the hash sequences of these received images are generated by the same hashing algorithm. Since these hash sequences are the same as the segments of the secret data, the receiver can concatenate them to recover the secret data.

According to the above, the main components of this framework for secret data communication include hash sequence generation by robust hashing algorithm, construction of the inverted index structure by image indexing, finding appropriate images by searching for the segments in the inverted index structure, and the communication of the secret data. Each component is detailed as follows.

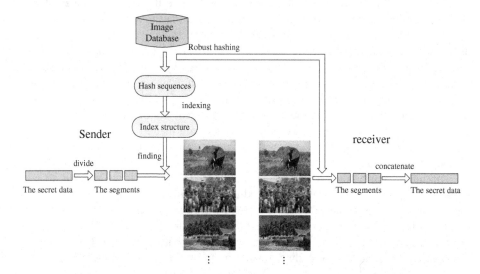

Fig. 2. The flow chart of the proposed steganography framework for secret data communication

2.1   Hash Sequence Generation by Robust Hashing Algorithm

In this subsection, we describe the robust hashing algorithm for generation of image hash sequences. As we know, during the communication, the stego-images could be manipulated by various typical attacks, such as rescaling, luminance change, contrast enhancement, JPEG compression and noise adding. Thus, the hashing algorithm should be robust to most of these attacks, so that the hash sequences of the images will not be changed during the communication. This ensures that the secret data can be reliably and correctly communicated with few losses and differences. To this end, we propose a robust hashing algorithm for generation of image hash sequences.

There are three main steps in the hashing algorithm. Firstly, for a given image, we transform the image to the gray-level image and divide the image into 3×3 non-overlapping blocks denoted as $\{b_{11}, b_{12}, \ldots, b_{ij}, \ldots, b_{33}\}$. Then, we compute the average intensity of each block, and thus obtain 9 intensity values $\{I(b_{11}), I(b_{12}), \ldots, I(b_{ij}), \ldots, I(b_{33})\}$. Finally, the intensity values are concatenated in a zig-zag order to form a vector denoted as $\{I_1, I_2, \ldots, I_9\}$, and each intensity value I_i is compared to its

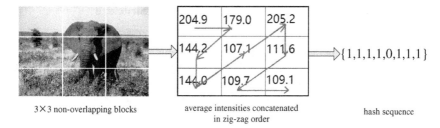

204.9	179.0	205.2
144.2	107.1	111.6
144.0	109.7	109.1

$\Rightarrow \{1,1,1,1,0,1,1,1\}$

3×3 non-overlapping blocks   average intensities concatenated in zig-zag order   hash sequence

Fig. 3. The procedure of hash sequence generation by the robust hashing algorithm

adjacent I_{i+1} by Eq. (1) to generate the hash sequence of the image $\{h_1, h_2, \ldots, h_8\}$. Figure 3 shows the procedure of the hash sequence generation by the robust hashing algorithm.

$$\begin{cases} h_i = 1, \; if \; I_i \geq I_{i+1} \\ h_i = 0, \; otherwise \end{cases}, \quad where \; 1 \leq i \leq 8 \tag{1}$$

2.2   Construction of the Inverted Index Structure by Image Indexing

Using a given 8-bit segment as the query, if we employ an exhaustive search for all of the images of which the hash sequences are the same as the query in the database, it will be very time-consuming.

To speed up the search, we first index all the images from the database according to their hash sequence. Then, we build an inverted index structure, namely lookup table T, for all the hash sequences. The lookup table T contains all possible 8 bit hash sequences as entries. Each entry points to a list storing all the IDs of the images whose hash sequence is the same as the entry. For example, suppose that the hash sequence of image A is $\{1, 1, 1, 1, 0, 1, 1, 1\}$ and its ID $ID(A)$, and it follows that $ID(A)$ falls into the list which is pointed by the entry $\{1, 1, 1, 1, 0, 1, 1, 1\}$, as shown in Fig. 4.

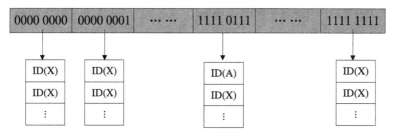

Fig. 4. The inverted index structure

It is worth noting that there should be at least one image in each list of table T. This ensures that at least one corresponding image can be found in each list of the table for any 8-bit segment, which has $2^8 = 256$ possibilities. Thus, the size of the database is no less than 256.

2.3   Finding Appropriate Images by Using the Index Structure

For a given secret data, this subsection introduces how to find a series of appropriate images which already contain the data by using the index structure.

To facilitate the communication of the secret data, the sender first transforms the secret data needed to be sent to a bit string, and then divides it into a number of segments with the equal length, namely 8-bit. Note that if the length of the bit string is not a multiple of 8 bit, several 0 s are added to the end of the string. Then, using each segment as a query, all of the images of which hash sequences are the same as the segment are obtained. It is not necessary to transmit all of them to the receiver, since each of them contains the information of the segment. Thus, only one image is randomly chosen from them for transmission. Finally, a series of images are found by searching in the inverted index structure. These images can be regarded as stego-images, since they already contain the secret data.

2.4   The Communication of Secret Data

After finding out the series of images which already contain the secret data, we will introduce how to communicate the secret data by those images in detail.

For the sender, those images are transmitted to the receiver one by one in order. For the receiver, all of the images are also received in order. The transmitting and receiving of the images in order ensures the secret data can be recovered without disorder. Once the receiver obtains all of those images, the hash sequence of each received image is generated by the same hashing algorithm used by the sender. Then, according to the order of the received images, the receiver concatenates all of their hash sequences of those images to recover the secret data. Owing to the robust hashing algorithm, the hash sequences of those images are insensitive to those image attacks mentioned in Sect. 2.1. As a result, the recovered secret data will be almost the same as the original secret data.

3   The Analysis of Reliability

This section will analyze the reliability of our steganography method in two aspects: resistance to steganalysis tools and robustness to image attacks.

3.1   The Resistance to Steganalysis Tools

As we know, an ideal image steganography method should have good resistance to various steganalysis tools.

In the literature, there are many steganography methods, which have been reviewed in Sect. 1. Unfortunately, all of them can be successfully detected by the existing steganalysis tools, which utilize the modification traces left by the embedding operations in the steganography methods. However, these steganalysis tools are not effective to detect the proposed coverless steganography method. That is because, without employing a designated cover image for embedding the secret data, our coverless steganography method directly finds appropriate original images which already contain the secret data as stego-images, and thus any modification traces will not be left in the stego-images.

3.2 The Robustness to Image Attacks

An ideal image steganography method should also be robust to various typical image attacks, so that the secret data can be accurately recovered from the stego-images when they suffer those attacks during communication.

As we know, the typical image attacks include rescaling, luminance change, contrast enhancement, JPEG compression, noise adding and so on. Since our method aims to find the appropriate original images whose hash sequences are the same as the segments of the secret data, the robustness of hashing algorithm is the basis and guarantee for dealing with these attacks. The robustness of our steganography method to each attack is analyzed as follows.

(1) Rescaling: The rescaling can change image resolution, but will not significantly change the intensity correlation between the image blocks for the following reason: the content of the 3×3 blocks is almost the same before and after rescaling, and thus the resulting hash sequence of rescaled image generated from the intensity correlation between the blocks will be quite similar to that of the original one.

(2) Luminance change and contrast enhancement: An illumination change will cause a constant to be added to each image pixel, and a contrast enhancement will cause each pixel value to be multiplied by a constant. However, the two attacks will not affect the intensity correlation between the image blocks. That is because the intensities of all pixels in each block will be added by a same value or multiplied by a same factor, and the intensity correlation between the blocks remains the same. Therefore, the hash sequence of the image attacked by luminance change or contrast enhancement is the same as its original.

(3) Noise adding, JPEG compression: These attacks can significantly change the intensity correlation between individual pixels. However, the image hash sequence is not easily affected by these attacks, since the effects can be effectively decreased by the averaging operation used in the computation of average intensities of the blocks.

4   Experiments

In this section, we will test the resistance to the steganalysis tools and the robustness to the image attacks of our method, and compare with the other steganography methods. Total of 1000 images downloaded from the networks are used to build our database. To test the performance of our method, we randomly select 200 images from our database, and then hide 8-bit secret data in each of them. Two famous steganography methods, namely LSB replacement and LSB matching, are compared with our method.

4.1   The Resistance to Steganalysis Tools

The Receiver Operating Characteristic (ROC) curve is used to test the resistance of different methods to steganalysis tools. We apply two typical steganalysis tools, namely improved standard Pairs method [13] and calibrated adjacency HCF COM [14], to detect LSB replacement and LSB matching, respectively. We use 10 % LSB steganography (i.e. 0.1 bits per pixel). Both of the two steganalysis tools are also used to deal with our steganography method.

From Fig. 5, we can see that our method has a perfect performance for resisting the typical steganalysis tools, and outperforms the two other steganography methods.

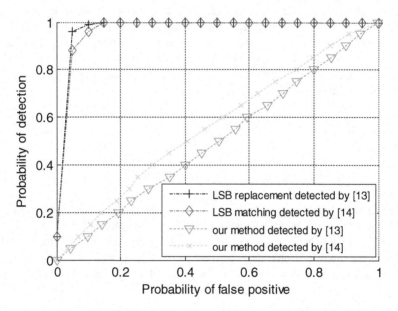

Fig. 5. The ROC curves of different methods

4.2   The Robustness to Image Attacks

To test the robustness of our method to the image attacks, we apply five typical attacks on the stego-image by Strimark [17], which is a standard benchmark employed to simulate various manipulations of digital images. These attacks are listed as follows.

(1) rescaling to 25 %,
(2) luminance change by adding the intensity of the image pixels with 10,
(3) contrast enhancement by multiplying the intensity of the image pixels with a fact of 1.2,
(4) JPEG compression with default parameters,
(5) Guassian noise adding with default parameters.

The sample error rate (SER) is employed to test the robustness of different methods to each attack. From Table 1, we can see that our method achieves the lowest SERs to

Table 1. The sample error rates (SERs) of different methods

	Rescaling	Luminance change	Contrast enhancement	JPEG compression	Guassian noise adding
LSB replacement	0.46	0.01	0.33	0.24	0.35
LSB matching	0.45	0.02	0.36	0.22	0.38
Ours	**0**	**0**	**0**	**0.03**	**0.02**

all of those attacks, compared with the other methods. That implies our method is more robust that the other methods.

5 Conclusion

In this paper, we present a coverless image steganography framework. Without employing a designated cover image for embedding the secret information, it directly finds the appropriate original images which already contain the secret data as stego-images. Since any modification traces will not be left in the stego-images, the proposed method can resist all of the existing steganalysis tools. Moreover, owing to the proposed robust hashing algorithm, our method can also be robust to various typical image attacks. However, by using our method, only 8-bit data can be hidden in each original image. Future work will focus on how to enhance the hiding capacity without degradation of the steganography performance.

Acknowledgements. This work is supported by the National Natural Science Foundation of China (NSFC) (61232016, U1405254, 61173141, 61173142, 61173136, 61373133), Jiangsu Basic Research Programs-Natural Science Foundation (SBK2015041480), Startup Foundation for Introducing Talent of Nanjing University of Information Science and Technology (2014r024), Open Fund of Demostration Base of Internet Application Innovative Open Platform of Department of Education (KJRP1406, KJRP1407), Priority Academic Program Development of Jiangsu Higher Education Institutions (PADA) Fund, Collaborative Innovation Center of Atmospheric Environment and Equipment Technology (CICAEET) Fund, National Ministry of Science and Technology Special Project Research GYHY201301030, 2013DFG12860, BC2013012.

References

1. Cheddad, A., Condell, J., Curran, K., Mc Kevitt, P.: Digital image steganography: survey and analysis of current methods. Sig. Process. **90**(3), 727–752 (2010)
2. Wu, H.C., Wu, N., Tsai, C.S., Hwang, M.S.: Image steganographic scheme based on pixel-value differencing and LSB replacement methods. In: Proceedings-Vision Image and Signal Processing, vol. 152, pp. 611–615 (2005)
3. Mielikainen, J.: LSB matching revisited. IEEE Sig. Process. Lett. **13**(5), 285–287 (2006)
4. Johnson, N.F., Jajodia, S.: Exploring steganography: seeing the unscen. IEEE Comput. **31**(2), 26–34 (1998)

5. Li, Z., Chen, X., Pan, X., Zheng, X.: Lossless data hiding scheme based on adjacent pixel difference. In: Proceedings of the International Conference on Computer Engineering and Technology, pp. 588–592 (2009)
6. Li, X., Wang, J.: A steganographic method based upon JPEG and particle swarm optimization algorithm. Inf. Sci. **177**(15), 3099–3109 (2007)
7. McKeon, R.T.: Strange Fourier steganography in movies. In: Proceedings of the IEEE International Conference on Electrio/information Technology (EIT), pp. 178–182 (2007)
8. Chen, W.Y.: Color image steganography scheme using set partitioning in hierarchical trees coding, digital Fourier transform and adaptive phase modulation. Appl. Math. Comput. **185**(1), 432–448 (2007)
9. Chang, C.C., Kieu, T.D., Chou, Y.C.: Reversible information hiding for VQ indices based on locally adaptive coding. J. Vis. Commun. Image Represent. **20**(1), 57–64 (2009)
10. Luo, W., Huang, F., Huang, J.: Edge adaptive image steganography based on LSB matching revisited. IEEE Trans. Inf. Forensics Secur. **5**(2), 201–214 (2010)
11. Kawaguchi, E.: BPCS-steganography – principle and applications. In: Khosla, R., Howlett, R.J., Jain, L.C. (eds.) KES 2005. LNCS (LNAI), vol. 3684, pp. 289–299. Springer, Heidelberg (2005)
12. Hioki, H.: A data embedding method using BPCS principle with new complexity measures. In: Proceedings of Pacific Rim Workshop on Digital Steganography, pp. 30–47 (2002)
13. Ker, A.D.: Improved detection of LSB steganography in grayscale images. In: Fridrich, J. (ed.) IH 2004. LNCS, vol. 3200, pp. 97–115. Springer, Heidelberg (2004)
14. Ker, A.: Steganalysis of LSB matching in grayscale images. IEEE Sig. Process. Lett. **12**(6), 441–444 (2005)
15. Xia, Z.H., Wang, X.H., Sun, X.M., Liu, Q.S., Xiong, N.X.: Steganalysis of LSB matching using differences between nonadjacent pixels. Multimedia Tools Appl. (2014). doi:10.1007/s11042-014-2381-8
16. Xia, Z.H., Wang, X.H., Sun, X.M., Wang, B.W.: Steganalysis of least significant bit matching using multi-order differences. Secur. Commun. Netw. **7**(8), 1283–1291 (2014)
17. Petitcolas, F.: Watermarking schemes evaluation. IEEE Sig. Process. Mag. **17**(5), 58–64 (2000)

Coverless Information Hiding Method Based on the Chinese Mathematical Expression

Xianyi Chen[1], Huiyu Sun[2], Yoshito Tobe[3], Zhili Zhou[1], and Xingming Sun[1(✉)]

[1] School of Computer and Software and Jiangsu Engineering Center of Network Monitoring, Nanjing University of Information Science and Technology, Nanjing 210044, Jiangsu, China
{0204622,zhou_zhili,sunnudt}@163.com
[2] Department of Computer Science, New York University, New York NY 10012, USA
hs2879@nyu.edu
[3] Aoyama Gakuin University, Kanagawa 252-5258, Japan
yoshito-tobe@rcl-aoyama.jp

Abstract. Recently, many fruitful results have been presented in text information hiding such as text format-based, text image-based method and so on. However, existing information hiding approaches so far have been very difficult to resist the detecting techniques in steganalysis based on statistical analysis. Based on the Chinese mathematical expression, an efficient method of coverless text information hiding is presented, which is a brand-new method for information hiding. The proposed algorithm directly generates a stego-vector from the hidden information at first. Then based on text big data, a normal text that includes the stego-vector will be retrieved, which means that the secret messages can be send to the receiver without any modification for the stego-text. Therefore, this method is robust for any current steganalysis algorithm, and it has a great value in theory and practical significance.

Keywords: Coverless text information hiding · Chinese mathematical expression · Generation method · Steganography

1 Introduction

Information hiding is an ancient but also young and challenging subject. Utilizing the insensitivity of human sensory organs, as well as the redundancy of the digital signal itself, the secret information is hidden in a host signal, which does not affect the effect on sensory and value in use of the host signal. The host here covers all kinds of digital carriers such as the image, text, video and audio [1]. Since the text is the most frequently used and extensive information carrier, its research has attracted many scholars' interest, and has obtained many results.

There are four main types of text information hiding technologies: the text format-based, text image-based, generating method-based and embedding method-based natural language information hiding.

© Springer International Publishing Switzerland 2015
Z. Huang et al. (Eds.): ICCCS 2015, LNCS 9483, pp. 133–143, 2015.
DOI: 10.1007/978-3-319-27051-7_12

Text format based information hiding method mainly achieves the hiding of secret information by changing the character spacing, inserting invisible characters (spaces, tabs, special spaces, etc.) and modifying the format of documents (PDF, HTML, Office). For example, the [2, 3] hided data via changing the characters such as the row spacing, word spacing, character height and character width. The [4–8] embedded data that utilized the programming language to modify certain properties of the Office document (including NoProofing attribute values, character color attributes, font size, font type, font underline, Range object, object's Kerning property, color properties, etc.). Based on the format information of disk volume, Blass et al. proposed a robust hidden volume encryption in [9, 10]. The hiding capacity of information hiding methods based on text format is large, but most of them can't resist the attack of re-composing and OCR. They can't resist the steganography detection based on statistical analysis ([11, 12]).

The main idea of **information hiding method based on text image** is to regard a text as a kind of binary image. Then it combines the features of binary images with texts to hide data. For example, [13] embedded information by utilizing the parity of the numbers of black and white pixels in the block, in [14, 15], information was embedded by modifying the proportion of black-white pixels in a block and the pixel values of the outer edge, respectively. The embedding of secret information is realized by the rotation of the strokes of the Chinese characters in [16]. In addition, based on hierarchical coding, Daraee et al. [17] presented an information hiding method. Satir et al. [18] designed a text information hiding algorithm based on the compression method, which improved the embedding capacity. The biggest problem of text image based information hiding method is that it can't resist re-composing and OCR attacks. After re-composing the characters of the hidden information into a non-formatted text, the hidden information hiding would completely disappear.

Generation method based natural language information hiding method utilizes the natural language processing (NLP) technologies to carry secret information by generating the similar natural text content. It can be divided into two types: the primary text generation mechanism and the advanced text generation mechanism. The former is based on probability statistics, which is coded by utilizing the random dictionary or the occurrence frequency of the letter combinations, and then the generated text meets the natural language of statistical characteristics. The latter is based on the linguistic approach. Based on linguistic rules, it carries the secret data by using the imitation natural language text without specific content [19]. In these methods, due to the lack of artificial intelligence for the automatic generation of arbitrary text, the generation text always contains the idiomatic mistakes or common sense errors, or sentences without complete meaning. Moreover, it may cause incoherent semantic context and poor text readability, which is easily to be recognized by human eyes [20, 21].

Embedding method based natural language information hiding method embeds the secret information by using different granularity of modification of the text [22, 23]. According to the scope of the modified text data, the embedding method can be divided into lexical level information hiding and sentence level information hiding. The former method hides the messages by means of substitution of similar characters [24], substitution of spelling mistakes [25], substitution of abbreviations/acronyms and words in complete form [26], etc. Based on the understanding of the sentence structure and its semantics, the latter method changes the sentence structure to hide information, and then utilizes the syntactic transformation and restatement technology in the same situation of its meaning and style [27–30]. Embedding method is the focus and hotspot of text information hiding in current research. However, this method needs the support of natural language processing technology, such as syntactic parsing, disambiguation, automatic generation, etc., so that the information embedded into the text meets rationality of words, collocation accuracy, syntactic structure, and the statistical characteristics of language [31]. Because of the limitation of the existing NLP technology, it is hard to realize the hiding algorithm. In addition, there are still some deviation and distortion in the statistic and linguistics [32].

From the above we can see that the text information hiding has made many research results, but there are still some problems such as weak ability in anti-statistical analysis, bad text rationality and so on. Furthermore, theoretically as long as the carrier is modified, the secret message will certainly be detected. As long as the secret information exists in the cover, it can hardly escape from steganalysis. Thus, the existing steganography technology is facing a huge security challenge, and its development has encountered a bottleneck.

The proposed method firstly carries on syntactic parsing about the information to be hidden and divides it into independent keywords, then uses the Chinese mathematical expression [33] to create a locating tags. After that, utilizing the cloud search services-multi-keyword ranked search [34, 35], a normal text containing the secret information can be retrieved, which achieves the direct transmission of the secret information. It doesn't require any other carriers and modifications, while it can resist all kinds of existing steganalysis methods. This research has an important positive significance for the development of information hiding technology.

2 Related Works

The Chinese character mathematics expression was proposed by Sun et al. in 2002 [33]. The basic idea is to express the Chinese characters as a mathematical expression so that the operands are components of Chinese characters and the operators are six spatial relations of components. Some definitions are given below.

Definition 1. A basic component is composed of several strokes, and it may be a Chinese character or a part of a Chinese character.

Definition 2. An operator is the location relation between the components. Let A,B be two components, A lr B, A ud B, A ld B, A lu B, A ru B and A we B represent that A and B have the spatial relation of left-right, up-down, left-down, left-upper, right-upper, and whole enclosed respectively. An intuitive explanation of the six operators is shown in Fig. 1.

Definition 3. The priority of the six operators defined in Definition 3 is as follows: (1). () is the highest; (2). we, lu, ld, ru are in the middle; (3). lr, ud are the lowest; the operating direction is from left to right.

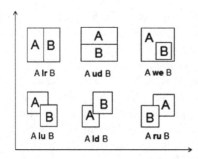

Fig. 1. Intuitive explanation of the defined operators

Using the selected 600 basic components and the six operators in Fig. 1, we can express all the 20902CJK Chinese characters in UNICODE 3.0 by utilizing the mathematical expressions. It is very nature and has a simple structure, and every character can be processed by certain operational rules as general mathematical expressions. After the expression of Chinese characters into the mathematical symbols, many processing of the Chinese information will become simpler than before.

According to the Chinese mathematical expression, we can see that if the appropriate components are selected as the location label of the secret message, it is better than that of the word or phrase being selected directly as the index in terms of many indicators such as randomness, distinguishability and universalness.

3   Proposed Method

Instead of conventional information hiding that needs to search an embedded carrier for the secret information, coverless information hiding requires no other carriers. It is driven by the secret information to generate an encryption vector, and then a normal text containing the encrypted vector can be retrieved from the big data of text, so the secret message can be embedded directly without any modification.

From the above analysis, there are three characteristics of the coverless information hiding algorithm: The first one is "no embedding", that is, a carrier can't embed secret information by modifying it. The second is "no additional message need to be transmitted except an original text", that is, other than the original agreement, there should not be any other carriers additionally used to send auxiliary information, such as the details or parameters of the embedding or extraction. The third is "anti-detection", which can resist all kinds of the existing detection algorithms. Based on the above characteristics together with the related theory of the Chinese mathematical expression, this paper presents a text-based coverless information hiding algorithm.

3.1   Information Hiding

For the coverless information hiding based on text, we first segment the secret data into words, then convert the Chinese words on a word-to-word basis, design the locating tags, generate the keywords that contain the converted secret data and the locating tags. Furthermore, we search the texts that contain the keywords in the database so as to achieve the information hiding with zero modification.

Let m be a Chinese character, and $\mathcal{T}$ be a set of the 20902CJK Chinese characters in UNICODE 3.0. Suppose the secret message is $M = m_1 m_2 \ldots m_n$, the conversion and location process of its secret information can be summarized as in Fig. 2. The details can be introduced as the following:

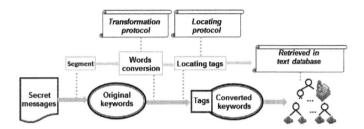

Fig. 2. Secret information conversion and positioning process

(1) *Information segmentation.* Based on the interdependence of the syntactic parsing, M is segmented into $\mathcal{N}$ non-overlapping keywords $w_i(i = 1, 2, \cdots \mathcal{N})$, where $||w_i|| \leq \ell$ and ℓ is a predetermined threshold for controlling the length of the keywords. The greater the ℓ, the higher the security, but the extraction of the secret information is more difficult. From the research of the Chinese information entropy, the choice of ℓ is often no more than three.

(2) *Words conversion.* Segment the text database retrieved into keywords according to the rules of information segmentation in step (1), and then calculate the frequency of every keywords in the text database, finally sort the words in descending order according to the frequency of occurrence $\mathcal{P} = \{p_1, p_2, \ldots, p_t\}$. So the word transformation protocol can be designed as follows:

$$p_i' = \mathcal{F}_c(p_i, \mathrm{k}), i = 1, 2, \cdots, s;$$

Where $\mathcal{F}_c(p_i, \cdot)$ is the transformation function used for the statistic and analysis of the text database, this function is open for all users, and $\cdot$ is the private keys of the information receiver, such as the k of the above formula, and s is the number of keywords of the text database. Where the difference between the quantities of p_i and p_i' is not too much, if not, a commonly-used word will be converted into a rarely-used word, which will greatly decrease the retrieval efficiency of stego-text. Therefore, using the $\mathcal{F}_c$, the converted keyword $w \cdot_i$ of w_i can be calculated, we can obtain the converted secret message $\mathcal{W} \cdot = w \cdot_1 w \cdot_2 \ldots w \cdot_{\mathcal{N}}$.

(3) *Get the locating tags.* For the text database retrieved, divide the Chinese characters into various components by using the Chinese mathematical expression first, and then calculate the frequency of every component, finally sort the components in descending order according to the frequencies of occurrence. Select the component whose appearance time is in the top 50 and then determine the locating

sequence according to the user's key. For $i = 1, 2, \cdots \mathcal{N}$, suppose b_i is the corresponding component of the located keyword w_i', when $\mathcal{N} > 50$, the keywords have the same located tags every 50 numbers.

For many components, the corresponding Chinese characters are often not unique. In order to find the stego-text that contains the secret information, we first calculate the r characters with the biggest numbers of appearance $m_i^j (j = 1, 2, \ldots, r)$ for every component b_i, combine every m_i^j with the keyword w_i' and research them from the text database, then sort m_j^i according to the number of occurrences. Utilizing the user's key, select the alternative character from the top 5 Chinese characters, so the location tags $\mathcal{L}_i (i = 1, 2, \cdots \mathcal{N})$ are calculated.

(4) Combining $\mathcal{L}_i$ with w_i' and obtain $\mathcal{D}_i (i = 1, 2, \cdots \mathcal{N})$, where $\mathcal{D}_i$ is the keyword retrieved in the text database.

In order to find the normal text that contains the keywords retrieved $\mathcal{D} = \{\mathcal{D}_i | i = 1, 2, \cdots \mathcal{N}\}$, the creation of large-scale text database plays a crucial role. It not only emphasizes of "high speed, wide range, great quantity", but also follows the principle of "quality, standardization and accuracy". Moreover, in order to improve the anti-detection performance, the quality of the text needs to be controlled from two aspects: One is to ensure that the text is normal with no secret information; the second is to ensure that the text is standardized in line with the language specification.

Based on the above text database, the keyword indexing technology is applied to find every $\mathcal{D}_i (i = 1, 2, \cdots \mathcal{N})$ in the database and built the reverse file index $\mathcal{ID}_i$, then search for a text that contains the secret information. If the search-string is found, then send it to the receiver; otherwise, divide it into two segments and re-retrieve it again until the right text is found. In order to avoid the suspicion, text classification can be used to the retrieval process, such as emotional and situational classification methods, which can avoid the retrieved results having non-relevant texts being grouped together.

It is worth mentioning that, from the above information hiding process we can see, the word conversion protocol is essentially a data encryption and the locating protocol is essentially a mapping. The two together realize the purpose of enhancing security and determining the location of the secret information. This idea isn't presented from nothing, but has a profound historical heritage. When choosing poetries as a text database, the keywords do not convert and the first word of each sentence is selected as the location tags, which is the ancient acrostic poem.

This skill is used in the peasant uprising famous novel "outlaws of the marsh" chapter sixty, which is about Chinese Northern Song Dynasty (1119-1121), such as Fig. 3. The normal reading order is from left to right, and its meaning is praising the general Lu Junyi. However, combine the initial letter in each line, we will get 卢俊义反, whose meaning is that "卢 will defect to the enemy"(卢 and 芦 is a homonym), thus achieving the purpose of hiding information in public document.

3.2 Information Extraction

In the conventional text information hiding, the stego-text is normal for a stranger but is abnormal for the receiver, so the receiver can extract the secret information by analyzing

Fig. 3. Left is the acrostic and right is the picture of Lu Junyi.

the abnormalities. However, in the coverless information hiding, the stego-text is actually an open and normal text, and the receiver can't extract the secret information by finding the abnormal place. Let the stego-text be $\mathbb{S}$, and k is the private key, then the process of extraction is showed as Fig. 4. The details can be introduced as follows.

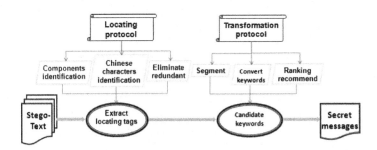

Fig. 4. The flowchart of the information extraction

(1) *Extraction preprocessing.* Because the text database is open to all users, they are also available as public information of the 50 Chinese components for marking and the corresponding Chinese characters, denoted $b = \{b_i | i = 1, \ldots, 50\}$ and $m_i = \{m_i^j | j = 1, \ldots\}$ respectively. Therefore, utilizing the user's private key, we can get the located component and its order of appearance. Moreover, based on the statistical results, it is also easy to get the Chinese characters $\mathcal{L} = \{\mathcal{L}_i | i = 1, 2, \cdots, \mathcal{N}\}$ in the database.

(2) *The extraction of candidate keywords.* Sequentially scan the stego-text $\mathbb{S}$, then extract the candidate locating tags $\mathcal{CL} = \{\mathcal{CL}_i | i = 1, 2, \cdots \mathcal{N}'\}$ and the candidate keywords $\mathcal{S}' = \{\mathcal{S}_i' | i = 1, 2, \cdots \mathcal{N}'\}$ according to the user location components set, where $\mathcal{N}' \geq \mathcal{N}$.

When $\mathcal{N}' = \mathcal{N}$, then $\mathcal{CL}$ is the locating tags of the secret information, skip step (3) to step (4); When $\mathcal{N}' > N$, there exist the non-locating components that are contained in $\mathcal{CL}$, they should be eliminated from $\mathcal{CL}$ with step (3).

(3) *Eliminate the redundant tags.* The procedure is introduced as follows:

(a) Compare $\mathcal{CL}_i$ with $\mathcal{L}_i$ from $i = 1$, if $\mathcal{CL}_i = \mathcal{L}_i$, update $i = i + 1$ and execute the step (a) again, otherwise skip to step (b);

(b) If $\mathcal{CL}_{i-1} \neq \mathcal{CL}_i$, but both of them have the same components, then $\mathcal{CL}_i$ is not a location tag, delete it and skip to step (a). If $\mathcal{CL}_{i-1} \neq \mathcal{CL}_i$ and they have the different components, then compare the quantity sorting of the two Chinese characters in text database, and the Chinese character that doesn't meet the keys of receiver isn't the locating tag, then delete it from $\mathcal{CL}$; otherwise skip to step c);

(c) If $\mathcal{CL}_{i-1} = \mathcal{CL}_i$, then at least one character isn't the locating tag between $\mathcal{CL}_{i-1}$ and $\mathcal{CL}_i$, so combine $\mathcal{CL}_{i-1}$ and $\mathcal{CL}_i$ with its subsequent keywords to generate the keyword retrieved $\mathcal{D}_i$, delete the one with smaller number and skip to the step (a);

When the correct tags are calculated, locate it in $\mathbb{S}$, and then extract the character strings $\mathcal{S}_i(i = 1, 2, \cdots, \mathcal{N})$ after the locating points, where $\|\mathcal{S}_i\| = \ell$;

(4) Since each keyword is divided by the dependency syntax before the hiding, the length of every keyword ℓ_{wi} may not be exactly the same, where $1 \leq \ell_{wi} \leq \ell$. Moreover, because of the words conversion, the keywords cannot be accurately extracted. Therefore, when using the inverse transform of word conversion $\mathcal{F}_c^{-1}(p_i, k)$ to restore the string $\mathcal{S}_i$, the obtained candidate keywords set $\mathbb{K}_i = \left\{ \mathbb{K}_i^j | 1 \leq j \leq \ell \right\}$ is not unique;

(5) Select a keyword from every $\mathbb{K}_i(i = 1, 2, \cdots \mathcal{N})$, and generate the candidate secret messages by researching the language feature and the word segmentation based on user background, then measure the confidence of the candidate secret information by analyzing the edit distance and similarity of the keywords, a rank can then be recommended to the receiver;

(6) Utilize the sorted recommended information, then combine the language analysis with Chinese grammar features, we can access the secret information M = $m_1 m_2 ... m_n$.

4 Example Verification

In order to clearly describe the above information hiding process, we explain it by a simple example. For example, let the secret information M be 无载体信息隐藏好, then the procedure of the hiding is shown in Fig. 5.

Firstly, segment M into $w_1 = $ 无, $w_2 = $ 载体, $w_3 = $ 信息, $w_4 = $ 隐藏, $w_5 = $ 好, then design the words conversion protocol $\mathcal{F}_c(p_i, k)$, where $\mathcal{F}_c(p_i, k)$ can be set to: "无→息, 载体→一门, 信息→古老, 隐藏→充满, 好→的"..

Secondly, analyze the text database and calculate the statistic values, then choose the suitable component for the locating, where we set the components of the Chinese characters as "$\mathcal{b}_1 = $亻, $\mathcal{b}_2 = $日, $\mathcal{b}_3 = $无, $\mathcal{b}_4 = $勹, $\mathcal{b}_5 = $戈".

Thirdly, select the locating tags from the candidate Chinese characters, where we obtain the locating tags $\mathcal{L}$: "$\mathcal{L}_1 = $信、$\mathcal{L}_2 = $是、$\mathcal{L}_3 = $既、$\mathcal{L}_4 = $的、$\mathcal{L}_5 = $战", and the keywords set retrieved is $\mathcal{D} = \{$"信息", "是一门", "既古老", "的充满", "战的"$\}$.

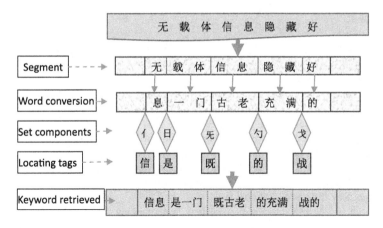

Fig. 5. Example results of the information hidding procedure

Finally, retrieve the text database to find a stego-text which contains the locating tags and keywords, where using the rules of the above, 信息隐藏是一门既古老又年轻的充满挑战的学科 is a stego-text with the retrieved secret information 无载体信息隐藏好.

In the case of the recipient's encrypted text information 信息隐藏是一门既古老又年轻的充满挑战的学科, because of the absence of redundant components, the extraction process is the inverse process of the embedding process. The realization is relatively simple, so we will not repeat them now.

5   Conclusions

This paper presented a text information hiding method, which is based on Chinese mathematical expression. Instead of the conventional information hiding method that needs to find an embedding carrier for the secret message, the proposed method requires no other carriers. First, an encryption vector is generated by the secret information, and then a normal text containing the encrypted vector is retrieved from the text database, which realizes embedding directly without any modification of the secret data. Therefore, the proposed method can resist all kinds of existing steganalysis methods. This research has an important positive significance for the development of information hiding technology.

Acknowledgments. This work is supported by the National Natural Science Foundation of China (NSFC) (61232016, U1405254, 61502242, 61173141, 61173142, 61173136, 61373133), Jiangsu Basic Research Programs-Natural Science Foundation (SBK2015041480), Startup Foundation for Introducing Talent of Nanjing University of Information Science and Technology (S8113084001), Open Fund of Demonstration Base of Internet Application Innovative Open Platform of Department of Education (KJRP1402), Priority Academic Program Development of Jiangsu Higher Education Institutions (PADA) Fund, Collaborative Innovation Center of Atmospheric Environment and Equipment Technology (CICAEET) Fund, National Ministry of Science and Technology Special Project Research GYHY201301030, 2013DFG12860, BC2013012.

References

1. Cox, I.J., Miller, M.L.: The first 50 years of electronic watermarking. J. Appl. Signal Process. **2**, 126–132 (2002)
2. Low, S.H., Maxemchuk, N.F., Lapone, A.M.: Document identification for copyright protection using centroid detection. IEEE Trans. Commun. **46**(3), 372–383 (1998)
3. Brassil, J.T., Low, S.H., Maxemchuk, N.F.: Copyright protection for the electronic distribution of text documents. Proc. IEEE **87**(7), 1181–1196 (1999)
4. Ffencode for DOS (2015). http://www.burks.de/stegano/ffencode.html
5. WbStego4.2 (2015). http://home.tele2.at/wbailer/wbstego/
6. Kwan M. Snow (2015). http://www.darkside.com.au/snow/index.html
7. Koluguri, A., Gouse, S., Reddy, P.B.: Text steganography methods and its tools. Int. J. Adv. Sci. Tech. Res. **2**(4), 888–902 (2014)
8. Qi, X., Qi, J.: A desynchronization resilient watermarking scheme. In: Shi, Y.Q. (ed.) Transactions on Data Hiding and Multimedia Security IV. LNCS, vol. 5510, pp. 29–48. Springer, Heidelberg (2009)
9. Blass, E.O., Mayberry, T., Noubir, G., Onarlioglu, K.: Toward robust hidden volumes using write-only oblivious RAM. In: Proceedings of the 2014 ACM Conference on Computer and Communications Security (CCS 2014), pp. 203–214 (2014)
10. Mayberry, T., Blass, E.O., Chan, A.H.: Efficient Private file retrieval by combining ORAM and PIR. In: Proceedings of 20th Annual Network & Distributed System Security Symposium (NDSS 2014), pp. 1–11 (2014)
11. Goyal, L., Raman, M., Diwan, P.: A robust method for integrity protection of digital data in text document watermarking. Int. J. Sci. Res. Dev. **1**(6), 14–18 (2014)
12. Kwon, H., Kim, Y., Lee, S.: A tool for the detection of hidden data in microsoft compound document file format. In: 2008 International Conference on Information Science and Security, pp. 141–146 (2008)
13. Wu, M., Liu, B.: Data hiding in binary images for authentication and annotation. IEEE Trans. Multimedia **6**(4), 528–538 (2004)
14. Zhao, J., Koch, E.: Embedding robust labels into images for copyright protection. In: Proceedings of the International Congress on Intellectual Property Rights for Specialized Information, Knowledge and New Technologies, Australia, pp. 242–251 (1995)
15. Xia, Z.H., Wang, S.H., Sun, X.M., Wang, J.: Print-scan resilient watermarking for the Chinese text image. Int. J. Grid Distrib. Comput. **6**(6), 51–62 (2013)
16. Tan, L.N., Sun, X.M., Sun, G.: Print-scan resilient text image watermarking based on stroke direction modulation for Chinese document authentication. Radioengineering **21**(1), 170–181 (2012)
17. Daraee, F., Mozaffari, S.: Watermarking in binary document images using fractal codes. Pattern Recogn. Lett. **35**, 120–129 (2014)
18. Satir, E., Isik, H.: A compression-based text steganography method. J. Syst. Softw. **85**(10), 2385–2394 (2012)
19. Wayner, P.: Disappearing Cryptography: Information Hiding: Steganography & Watermarking, 2nd edn. Morgan Kaufmann, San Francisco (2009)
20. Taskiran, C.M., Topkara, U., Topkara, M.: Attacks on lexical natural language steganography systems. In: Proceedings of the SPIE, Security, Steganography and Watermarking of Multimedia Contents VIII, San Jose, USA, pp. 97–105 (2006)
21. Meng, P., Huang, L.S, Yang, W.: Attacks on translation based steganography. In: 2009 IEEE Youth Conference on Information, Computing and Telecommunication, Beijing, China, pp. 227–230 (2009)

22. Nematollahi, M.A., Al-Haddad, S.A.R.: An overview of digital speech watermarking. Int. J. Speech Technol. **16**(4), 471–488 (2013)

23. Mali, M.L., Patil, N.N., Patil, J.B.: Implementation of text watermarking technique using natural language. In: IEEE International Conference on Communication Systems and Network Technologies, pp. 482–486 (2013)

24. Xiangrong, X., Xingming, S.: Design and implementation of content-based English text watermarking algorithm. Comput. Eng. **31**(22), 29–31 (2005)

25. Topkara, M., Topkara, U., Atallah, M.J.: Information hiding through errors: a confusing approach. In: Proceedings of the SPIE International Conference on Security, Steganography, and Watermarking of Multimedia Contents, San Jose, 6505 V (2007)

26. Rafat, K.F.: Enhanced text steganography in SMS. In: 2009 2nd International Conference on Computer, Control and Communication, Karachi, pp. 1–6 (2009)

27. Meral, H.M., Sankur, B., Ozsoy, A.S.: Natural language watermarking via morphosyntactic alterations. Comput. Speech Lang. **23**(1), 107–125 (2009)

28. Liu, Y., Sun, X., Wu, Y.: A natural language watermarking based on chinese syntax. In: Wang, L., Chen, K., Ong, Y.S. (eds.) ICNC 2005. LNCS, vol. 3612, pp. 958–961. Springer, Heidelberg (2005)

29. Kim, M.Y., Zaiane, O.R., Goebel, R.: Natural language watermarking based on syntactic displacement and morphological division. In: 2010 IEEE 34th Annual Computer Software and Applications Conference Workshops, Seoul, Korea, pp. 164–169 (2010)

30. Dai, Z.X., Hong, F.: Watermarking text documents based on entropy of part of speech string. J. Inf. Comput. Sci. **4**(1), 21–25 (2007)

31. Gang, L., Xingming, S., Lingyun, X., Yuling, L., Can, G.: Steganalysis on synonym substitution steganography. J. Comput. Res. Dev. **45**(10), 1696–1703 (2008)

32. Peng, M., Liu-sheng, H., Zhi-li, C., Wei, Y., Ming, Y.: Analysis and detection of translation based steganography. ACTA Electronica Sinica **38**(8), 1748–1752 (2010)

33. Sun, X.M., Chen, H.W., Yang, L.H., Tang, Y.Y.: Mathematical representation of a chinese character and its applications. Int. J. Pattern Recogn. Artif. Intell. **16**(8), 735–747 (2002)

34. Xia, Z., Wang, X., Sun, X., Wang, Q.: A secure and dynamic multi-keyword ranked search scheme over encrypted cloud data. IEEE Trans. Parallel Distrib. Syst. **99** (2015). doi: 10.1109/TPDS.2015.2401003

35. Fu, Z., Sun, X., Liu, Q., Zhou, L., Shu, J.: Achieving efficient cloud search services: multi-keyword ranked search over encrypted cloud data supporting parallel computing. IEICE Trans. Commun. **98**, 190–200 (2015)

System Security

Network Information Security Challenges
and Relevant Strategic Thinking
as Highlighted by "PRISM"

Jing Li[(✉)]

Intellectual Property Research Institute of Xiamen University,
Xiamen, China
Lijinglaw@xmu.edu.cn

Abstract. The emergence of cloud computing, big data and other technologies has ushered us in a new age of information-based lifestyle and is profoundly changing the global economic ecology. It follows that network security risk has also become one of the most severe economic and national security challenges confronted by various countries in the 21st Century. The recent "PRISM" event has exposed the weakness of the Chinese network information security. Given the huge risks, it is high time that China reconsiders network information security strategy so as to ensure citizen rights, network information security and national security while making the most of new technologies to improve economic efficiency. As such, this paper attempts to analyze the challenges confronted by China in terms of network information security in the context of the "PRISM" event, with a view to constructing the Chinese network information security strategy from the perspective of law.

Keywords: Personal data and privacy · Cyber governance · Network information security · Chinese network information security strategy

1 Introduction

The emergence of cloud computing, big data and other technologies has ushered us in a new age of information-based lifestyle and is profoundly changing the global economic ecology. It follows that network security risk has also become one of the most severe economic and national security challenges confronted by various countries in the 21st Century. The recent "PRISM" event, which is a secret surveillance program under which the United States National Security Agency (NSA) collects internet communications from at least nine major US internet companies, has exposed the weakness of the Chinese network information security. Given the huge risks, it is high time that China reconsiders network information security strategy so as to ensure citizen rights, network information security and national security while making the most of new technologies to improve economic efficiency. As such, this paper attempts to analyze the challenges confronted by China in terms of network information security in the context of the "PRISM" event, with a view to constructing the Chinese network information security strategy from the perspective of law.

© Springer International Publishing Switzerland 2015
Z. Huang et al. (Eds.): ICCCS 2015, LNCS 9483, pp. 147–156, 2015.
DOI: 10.1007/978-3-319-27051-7_13

2 Huge Challenges Confronted by China in Terms of Network Information Security as Highlighted by "PRISM"

2.1 Abuse of Emerging Technologies Increases Network Security Vulnerability

Melvin Kranzberg, a famous American technology history expert, pointed out that "Technology is neither good nor bad, nor is it neutral. Technological progress tends to impose influence on environment, society and people to an extent that exceeds the direct purpose of technological equipment and technology itself, and this is just about interaction between technology and social ecology." [1] Technology itself will not threaten network security. The root of network security risks is abuse of technology. The American government and the network giants involved in the "PRISM" event took advantage of the features, i.e. cross-region, invisibility, large-scale destruction and uncertainty, of new technologies and increased global network security vulnerability. Learning about the influence of new technologies on Chinese network security is a necessary precondition for the construction of the Chinese network security strategy.

"Cloud" technology amplifies data risks. "Cloud computing" refers to the remote digital information storage technology which enables users to access documents stored in the internet via any device connected to the internet [2]. The cloud computing technology has both advantages and disadvantages. For one thing, users have easy access to data sharing and backup thanks to this technology, but for another, it is likely to give rise to new technical risks and social conflicts.

First of all, a cloud computing service provider may "legally infringe upon" individual privacy and security of Chinese users based on regulatory arbitrage, which means that in the internet context, certain multi-national enterprises evade unfavorable regulation by means of choosing to apply laws in their favor [3]. The cloud computing servers may be located in different countries. As different regulations on data security obligation, data loss liability, privacy protection, data disclosure policies, etc. are applicable in different countries, the discrepancy in regulatory laws make it possible for cloud service providers to take advantage of regulatory arbitrage. Take Google Company, which was involved in the "PRISM", for instance. In spite that Google provides network service to Chinese users, its server is located in California, the United States. By subscribing to its Google Drive service, users have to agree that Google may "use the user's data according to Google's privacy policy". However, Google reserves the right to change its privacy policy at any time. Google's up-to-date privacy policy provides as follows: "We will share personal information of users with companies, organizations or individuals outside of Google if we have a good-faith belief that access, use, preservation or disclosure of the information is reasonably necessary to meet any applicable law, regulation, legal process or enforceable governmental request." As such, Google is entitled and obliged to conform to the request of the National Security Agency (NSA) of the United States where its server is located by providing NSA with the data stored by users. As the inevitable digital intermediary of internet users for the purpose of information transmission and storage, it is "legal" in the United States for cloud computing service providers to disclose user information to the American government. However, it severely damages individual information privacy and security of users in another country and may even influence the national security of another country.

Secondly, the mode of "separated data owner and controller" of cloud computing makes it even harder to realize physical regulation and accountability of network information. In a tradition mode, data stored in local technical facilities is controllable logically and physically, and hence the risk is also controllable. In a cloud computing mode, user data is not stored in local computers but stored in a centralized manner in remote servers outside the firewall. As a result, the traditional information security safeguarding method relying on machines or physical network boundaries cannot function any more. When an information security event occurs, the log records may be scattered in multiple hosts and data centers located in different countries. Therefore, even applications and hosting service deployed by the same cloud service provider may impose difficulty in record tracing, which no doubt makes it harder to collect evidence and keep data confidential [4].

Big data technology shakes basic principle of data protection. Big data refers to a more powerful data mining method applied by various organizations by relying on mass data, faster computer and new analytical skills for the purpose of mining concealed and valuable relevant data [5]. All internet giants involved in the "PRISM", including Google, Microsoft, Facebook and Yahoo, utilize the big data technology in different forms and make data their main assets and value source.

Firstly, big data may shake the footstone of data protection regulations. EU data protection instructions, EU general data protection draft regulations and data protection laws of other countries in the world mostly rely on the requirement of "transparency" and "consent" so as to ensure that users can share personal information on a known basis [6]. However, the nature of big data is to seek unexpected connection and create results difficult to predict through data mining and analysis [7]. Users are not sufficiently aware of the object and purpose they have consented to. What's more, the company itself which utilizes data mining technology cannot predict what will be discovered through the big data technology. As such, it is very difficult to realize "consent" in a substantial sense.

Secondly, huge commercial profit brought by the big data technology may induce service providers to disregard users' privacy and then threaten data security. In the context of the internet, on the one hand, multiple network information media have access to users' big data, and owing to the big data technology, such information media can easily obtain and process such information at extremely low costs; on the other hand, big data can generate astounding commercial profit: According to the report of McKinsey & Company, big data contributes USD 300 billion to the health industry in the United State and EUR 250 billion to the public administration industry in Europe on an annual basis [8]. As a result, network media with access to customers' huge data are mobilized enough to take advantage of their customers' big data in ways unimaginable and often undetectable for users. More and more commercial organizations start to see potential commercial opportunities in reselling collected data and begin to make a profit in this way. Large-scale financial institutions start to market data relating to payment cards of their customers (e.g. frequented stores and purchased commodities); in Holland, a GPS positioning service provider sells its customers' mobile geocoding to governmental agencies including police service, while such data have been originally designed to make planning for optimal installation of automatic transmission radar traps. In the face of huge profit temptation with nobody knowing and supervising, it is likely that information media will utilize information in a manner deviating from the original intention, thereby exposing users' information to great risks.

2.2 Information Asymmetry in Chinese Network Information Security Market Leads to Market Failure

Due to the cost of and technical obstacle in disclosing network security risks as well as the lack of network information security legislation in China, the Chinese network information security market suffers from information asymmetry. Due to the lack of information truthfully reflecting network security risks, the industry cannot accurately decide the quantity of network security products to be supplied. Such market failure makes network information security risks inevitable.

Technical obstacle in and cost of disclosing network security risks result in inherent information deficiency in network information security market. Owing to the invisibility, complexity and mobility of network information security risks, relevant information of network security risks is inherently deficient. Meanwhile, since the announcement of network security risk events is likely to damage market share, reputation and customer base, private companies often lack incentives to disclose network security risk events. Research shows that for each security hole made public, the share price of the distributor will drop by around 0.6 % on the average. In other words, each time a hole is disclosed, market value amounting to approximately USD 860 million will be lost [9]. Network security risk information asymmetry does not mean non-investment or overcapitalization in network security. On the contrary, it means that "correct preventive measures are not invested at an ideal percentage." [10] Due to the lack of correct cognition of threat and precaution, users and enterprises tend to invest in Jack-of-all-trade solutions. In the meantime, security enterprises will not be pressed enough to bring new technologies into the market so as to defend against material threat.

Lack of network information security legislation in China intensifies market failure. With respect to citizen network information security, China has not promulgated any specialized law. In 2009, China instituted the crime of infringing upon citizens' personal information in the Criminal Law, but such provision only applies to "staff of national organs or financial, telecom, transportation, education and medical treatment institutions". Network service providers processing citizens' personal information in the network space are not included. Meanwhile, such provision has been criticized as "lacking operability" due to its unclear definition of accountable circumstances and lack of explicit punishment standards [11]. Cases of liabilities being investigated based on such provision have been rare to be seen so far. Current network security legislation appears in a scattered manner in administrative regulations, departmental regulations and local governmental regulations with relatively low effect levels or applies to specific industries or specific information objects exclusively. As such, even though certain enterprises are suspected of infringing upon the Chinese citizens' network information security as exposed by the "PRISM", owing to the lack of network information security legislation in China, China is confronted with the awkward situation of "incapable of liability investigation with no laws applicable to such events." Due to the lack of legislative regulations, enterprises are not legally obliged to ensure network security and announce network disclosure events. Worse still, the announcement of data disclosure events may attract more attention from regulators, thereby increasing operating costs for the enterprises and even the whole industry. It follows that enterprises lack incentives to disclose information security risks and hence information asymmetry is intensified.

3 Developing the Chinese Network Information Security Protection Strategies

The "PRISM" event sounded the alarm for network information security in China. It is both necessary and urgent to actively develop the Chinese network information security protection strategies from the perspective of law. With respect to the network information security protection strategies, it is a precondition to define the obligations and liabilities of network service providers at the core of improving network users' right of remedies. In the meantime, it is also important to safeguard legal rights on a global basis and promote the international negotiations in favor of China. Reflections in this thesis are undertaken from the domestic and international perspectives.

3.1 The Domestic Perspectives

For the purpose of developing the network information security protection strategies, foremost efforts shall be made to improve the regulation and accountability mechanism of network information processing behaviors, correct market failure and realize the maximal efficacy of policies in terms of ensuring network security and promoting technical development and application.

Specialized legislation shall be promulgated to define obligations and liabilities of network service providers. Currently, the Chinese network information security sector is highly chaotic, largely because existing laws do not sufficiently provide for legal obligations and liabilities of network service providers in terms of network information security, which means that settlement of user information security issues and information security disputes in reality often relies on the license agreements between network service providers and users. Network service providers tend to use their own advantageous positions to avoid relevant risk issues in the service agreements as much as possible and disclaim legal liabilities for customer personal data loss, data disclosure, data destruction, etc. which will inevitably damage information security of extensive network users. At the same time, in the context of such emerging technologies as cloud computing and big data, the features, i.e. cross-region, invisibility, large-scale destruction and uncertainty, of network information security risks have raised higher requirements for the Chinese network information security legislation objectively. As such, it is advisable to define the obligations and liabilities of network service providers from the following aspects:

The obligation of continuous data security protection of network service providers should be established. It means that all business subjects or organizations involved in data processing must implement and maintain reasonable and suitable security procedures and practices, so as to protect personal information against illegal access, loss, destruction, use, revision or disclosure. Due to rapid technical innovation, network risk sources and forms keep changing, which decides that the data security protection obligation is not once-for-all but a continual process. Specifically, "reasonable and suitable security measures" require companies to undertake continual and uninterrupted processes to regularly assess risks, identify risks and take suitable security measures against the risks, monitor and verify effective implementation of security measures and ensure continual adjustment and update of security measures based on technical development. The specific security measures to be taken are subject to the discretional decisions of companies.

The obligation of data disclosure warning should be established so as to ensure users' right to know. Due to the invisibility, immediateness and joint nature of network security risks, users may not know about information disclosure or loss until serious criminal results have occurred. As such, in order to prevent that information disclosure results in users' suffering from derivative consequences which are even more severe, network service providers' obligation of announcing data disclosure must be defined. In other words, all enterprises and institutions processing sensitive personal information must, after such information is disclosed in an unintended manner, send notices and warning to affected users within certain time limit. What is noteworthy is that the scope of sensitive information should be defined with respect to such obligation, which includes without limitation ID Card No., financial institution accounts or credit card numbers. The notification should be made via electronic means or traditional media with national influence so as to ensure notification coverage and timeliness, and that notification circumstances should be loss, revision, destruction or unpermitted access of individual users' data.

The liabilities of network service providers should be defined. Network service providers failing to perform the data protection obligation should assume liabilities at different levels, including such administrative punishments as being issued the violation notification by the competent department, being instructed to correct, administrative penalty and revocation of operation qualification. Meanwhile, users whose personal data has been damaged should be entitled to claim civil compensation for damages against network service providers. From the criminal level, network service providers should be included into the subject scope of the crime of infringing upon citizens' personal information and the specific affirmation standard for "grave circumstances" should be defined.

It is advisable to introduce the EU "long-arm" provision for the purpose of restraining cross-border information flow. The "long-arm" provision is a data protection principle characteristic of EU which is designed to ensure that EU citizens transmitting personal data outside EU can enjoy data protection similar to that enjoyed within EU by restraining cross-border data transfer by data processers located outside EU and within multinational corporate groups, particularly third-country data processors in the context of cloud computing. As a result, such a principle has "long-arm" effect applicable in a cross-domain manner. This principle realizes restraint over subjects outside EU mainly through three mechanisms: (1) The country-specific protection level assessment mechanism, i.e. EU has the right to assess whether a third country has provided sufficient data security protection. If a third country fails to provide sufficient protection upon assessment, EU will forbid transmission of personal data to such third country and will negotiate with such third country. (2) The Binding Corporate Rules (BCR), i.e. corporate internal policies restraining personal data transfer to organizations established by corporate groups in countries not providing sufficient data protection (including privacy principles relating to data security, quality and transparency, validity-related tools such as audit, training and complaint handling systems, and elements proving that BCR is binding). The Draft provides that a multinational enterprise may perform the obligation of sufficient protection by formulating BCR according to the requirement of the Draft and then submitting the BRC to the main data protection regulator for approval. (3) Standard data protection provisions or permitted contractual provisions, i.e. besides BCR, a multinational enterprise may also perform the obligation of sufficient protection by applying standard data protection provisions adopted by EU. Where it is necessary to apply contractual provisions reached through independent negotiation, such provisions shall be subject to prior approval from the regulator [12]. The cloud computing technology allows the storage or processing of a country's data in another country. Therefore, network risks may break away from the restriction of time and place and the source place and consequential place of risks may be totally isolated, which has made it difficult for the Chinese regulator to control network security, collect evidence and implement accountability. Considering actual needs arising from the development of new technologies, it is advisable to introduce the EU "long-arm" provision and explicitly stipulate that the Chinese laws regarding network security apply to companies or organizations established outside China, provided that such subjects process Chinese users' information or provide outsourcing service. The specific restraint mechanism includes supervision over such subjects' operation entities in China. If no operation entity is set up in China, Chinese enterprises should be required to perform the network security protection obligation stipulated by Chinese laws jointly with such subjects in a contractual manner.

Improving network user right safeguard mechanism at the core of the right of remedy. Without remedy, right is unguaranteed. In the face of increasing security risks in the network space, it is highly urgent to improve the right of remedy of users.

The burden of proof in favor of users should be established. In the network service relationship, once a user selects a certain service provider, such service provider will gain control power over the user's data and may access the user's trade secret and individual private information by inspecting the user's records. As such, the user is placed in a relatively disadvantaged position in terms of acquisition of and negotiation over technology and information. To this end, in order to prevent network service providers from misusing their advantageous positions in the network service relationship, and taking into account the difficulty confronted by individual users in obtaining evidence from the network, it should be regulated that with respect to user loss resulted by network secret disclosure, network service providers should mainly assume the burden of proof while performing relevant obligations of data security protection.

A one-stop competent authority should be established. Network information security involves multiple social administration links, including individual privacy, commercial order, telecommunication facility security, financial security, public security and national security. Competent authorities of each link are involved in part of the network supervision functions, but the multiple administration system where everybody doing things in his own way has increased the uncertainty and cost of corporate compliance and made it more difficult for citizens to safeguard their legal rights. It is thus advisable to set up a network information security competent authority covering all industries. Considering the strategic significance of network security, such competent authority should be directly under the State Council, and its responsibilities should include the followings: develop network information security policies and strategies; supervise whole-industry network security compliance with corresponding administrative enforcement power, serve as a reception portal processing user complaints concerning network information security, and facilitate the settlement of user disputes regarding network security in a low-cost, high-efficiency and one-stop manner.

Multi-level remedy procedures should be provided. Besides traditional judicial procedures, it is advisable to introduce mediation and arbitration procedures specific to the features of network data protection disputes, i.e. extensive involvement, strong technicality and time sensitivity, as well as to set up an arbitration commission under the network competent authority dedicated to the processing of personal information disputes. Consisting of supervisory government officials, network security technicians, consumer representatives, internet service provider representatives, scholars, etc., the arbitration commission should propose a mediation plan within the given time limit for the reference of various parties. If the plan is accepted by various parties, it should be implemented as a binding document; if not, judicial procedures should be started. On the other hand, as data disclosure involves a great number of people, and the internet industry, as an emerging industry, will suffer from huge cost if time-consuming independent action is resorted to, it is advised that the procedure of data protection class action/arbitration be stipulated, the effect and procedure linkage between action and arbitration be defined and guidance be provided to settle disputes quickly and conveniently through class action or arbitration.

3.2 The International Perspectives

With respect to the development of the Chinese network information security protection strategy, not only the domestic legislation and law enforcement system should be perfected but also efforts should be made to exert influence on the tendency of future negotiation and international cooperation in terms of network security international standards.

Today, network security has become a common challenge confronted by the international community. It is no longer possible to realize prevention against network security risks in the closed domestic law system exclusively, but rather cooperation and settlement should be sought after in the international law framework. Under many circumstances, the network security issue is no longer a country's internal judicial issue but rather a judicial issue involving multiple countries. Particularly, information leakage events with extensive influence and involving parties in multiple countries such as the "PRISM" will inevitably involve practical difficulties in terms of cross-border evidence collection, coordination of dispute jurisdiction and definition of law application [13]. Currently, many international organizations, including the United Nation (UN), Organization for Economic Co-operation and Development (OECD), Asia Pacific Economic Cooperation (APEC), European Union (EU), North Atlantic Treaty Organization (NATO), Group of Eight, International Telecommunication Union (ITU) and International Organization for Standardization (ISO), are addressing the issue of information and communication infrastructure. Some newly established organizations have started to consider the development of network security policies and standards, and existing organizations also actively seek to expand their functions to this field [14]. Such organizations' agreements, standards or practices will generate global influence. Meanwhile, following the "PRISM" event, various countries start to adjust their existing network security strategies successively. It is foreseeable that the coming several years will be a crucial period propelling the establishment of the network security international cooperation framework. As the leading network security victim and the largest developing country, on the one hand, China should conduct relevant research to systematically learn about the features and tendencies of various countries' network security strategies, particularly evidence of certain countries infringing upon another country's citizen network information security, so as provide backup to China in safeguarding legal rights in the international battlefield; on the other hand, it is necessary that China takes the initiative to participate in the development of network security international conventions and standards so as to fully express China's reasonable appeal for interest and actively strive for China's benefit in the network space through close cooperation with various countries and by virtue of various international platforms.

4 Conclusions

Network information technology is like a double-edged sword which can either vigorously facilitates a country's economic development or monopolizes global information. What is disclosed by the "PRISM" event is only a tip of the iceberg of the network information security risks confronted by China. As such, it is highly urgent to thoroughly explore the roots of network information security risks and develop national network security strategies conforming to the industrial development and security benefit of China. The current idea of the Chinese network information security strategies is as follows: for one thing, the domestic legislation and remedy system should be developed on the precondition of defining obligations and liabilities of network service providers at the core of improving the right of remedy of network users so as to correct market failure and realize the maximal efficacy of policies in terms of ensuring network security and promoting technical development and application; for another, legal rights should be safeguarded on a global basis and international negotiations should be promoted in favor of China so as to safeguard China's interest in the network space. China can overcome the current obstacles and prevent against potential risks only by closely centering on chains and cruxes handicapping Chinese network information security.

References

1. Boyd, D., Crawford, K.:Six Provocations for Big Data, http://softwarestudies.com/cultural_analytics/Six_Provocations_for_Big_Data.pdf
2. Simmons, J.L.: Buying you: the Government's use of fourth-parties to launder data about 'The People'. Columbia Bus. Law Rev. **3**, 956 (2009)
3. Froomkin, A.M.: The internet as a source of regulatory arbitrage. In: Kahin, B., Nesson, C.: Borders in Cyberspace: Information Policy and the Global Information Structure, p. 129. MIT Press, Massachusetts (1997)
4. Dupont, B.: The Cyber Security Environment to 2022: Trends, Drivers and Implications. http://papers.ssrn.com/sol3/papers.cfm?abstract_id=2208548
5. Rubinstein, I.: Big data: the end of privacy or a new beginning? Int. Data Priv. Law **3**(2), 74 (2013)
6. Kuner, C., Cate, F.H., Millard, C., Svantesson, D.J.B.: The challenge of 'Big Data' for data protection. Int. Data Priv. Law **2**(2), 47–49 (2012)
7. Tene, O., Polonetsky, J.: Big data for all: privacy and user control in the age of analytics. Northwest. J. Technol. Intellect. Property **5**, 261 (2013)
8. McKinsey Global Institute: Big Data: The Next Frontier for Innovation, Competition, and Productivity. http://www.mckinsey.com/insights/business_technology/big_data_the_next_frontier_for_innovation
9. Telang, R., Wattal, S.: impact of software vulnerability announcements on the market value of software vendors-an empirical investigation. IEEE Trans. Softw. Eng. **33**, 8 (2007)
10. Moore, T.: The economics of cybersecurity: principles and policy options. Int. J. Crit. Infrastruct. Prot. **3**(3–4), 110 (2010)
11. Lieyang, Q.: It is Essential to clarify the standard of punishment of infringing personal privacy, PSB Newspaper. http://www.mps.gov.cn/n16/n1237/n1342/n803715/3221182.html
12. European Union: How will the EU's data protection reform make international cooperation easier? http://ec.europa.eu/justice/data-protection/document/review2012/factsheets/5_en.pdf
13. Yan, Z., Xinhe, H.: Cyber security risk and its legal regulation. Study Dialectics Nat. **28**(10), 62 (2012)
14. THE WHITE HOUSE: Cyberspace Policy Review: Assuring a Trusted and Resilient Information and Communications Infrastructure. http://www.whitehouse.gov/assets/documents/Cyberspace_Policy_Review_final.pdf

A Lightweight and Dependable Trust Model for Clustered Wireless Sensor Networks

Nannan Shao[✉], Zhiping Zhou, and Ziwen Sun

School of Internet of Things Engineering,
Jiangnan Universtiy, Wuxi, China
snnjiangnan@sina.com

Abstract. The resource efficiency and dependability are the most basic requirements for a trust model in any wireless sensor network. However, owing to high cost and low reliability, the existing trust models for wireless sensor networks can not satisfy these requirements. To take into account the issues, a lightweight and dependable trust model for clustered wireless sensor network is proposed in this paper, in which the fuzzy degree of nearness is adopted to evaluate the reliability of the recommended trust values from the third party nodes. Moreover, the definition of a self-adapted weighted method for trust aggregation at CH level surpasses the limitations of the subjective definition of weights in traditional weighted method. Theoretical analysis and simulation results show, compared with other typical trust models, the proposed scheme requires less memory and communication overhead and has good fault tolerance and robustness, which can effectively guarantee the security of wireless sensor network.

Keywords: Wireless sensor networks · Trust model · Clustered wireless sensor network · Fuzzy degree of nearness · Self-adapted weighted method

1 Introduction

As an effective complement to encryption and authentication, trust mechanism which can effectively resist malicious attacks from the internal network, has caused widespread concerns [1–3] from researchers in recent years. Although researches of trust model for wireless sensor networks (WSN) are in its early stages, researchers have made many achievements [4–7]. However, these models are subject to lots of different conditions, such as limited resources. More specifically, they are unable to meet the requirements of large-scale sensor networks. At present, there are few trust models for clustered WSN, such as ATRM [8], GTMS [9], HTMP [10] and LDTS [11].

For a clustered wireless sensor network [12–14], clustering algorithm can improve the throughput and scalability of the network effectively. Establishing trust relationship in the cluster environment can effectively ensure the safety and reliability of the network [15]. Undoubtedly, the dependability and resource efficiency of a trust model are the most basic requirements for any wireless sensor network which includes clustered wireless sensor networks. However, due to their high cost and low reliability, the

© Springer International Publishing Switzerland 2015
Z. Huang et al. (Eds.): ICCCS 2015, LNCS 9483, pp. 157–168, 2015.
DOI: 10.1007/978-3-319-27051-7_14

existing trust models for clustered WSN can not meet the above requirements. There is still a lack of trust models for clustered WSN which meet the requirements of both the resource efficiency and trust reliability.

In order to solve the above problem, a lightweight and dependable trust model is proposed in this paper for clustered wireless sensor network, in which a lightweight trust decision-making scheme is used. Fuzzy degree of nearness is adopted to evaluate the reliability of the recommended trust values from the third party nodes and then assign weights to them based on the reliability, which can greatly weaken the effect of malicious nodes to trust evaluation. In addition, we define the adaptive weight approach for trust fusion at the cluster head levels, which can surpass the limitations of the subjective definition of weights in traditional weighting methods. What is more, it can resist collusion attack in a certain extent.

2   Description of the Proposed Trust Model

2.1   Network Model

In WSNs, in order to optimize the transmission route and achieve the purpose of saving the network energy, the topological structure of clustered network is adopted. In clustered wireless sensor networks, except the base station, nodes are generally divided into two types: ordinary sensor nodes (CM) and cluster head node (CH), which is shown in Fig. 1.

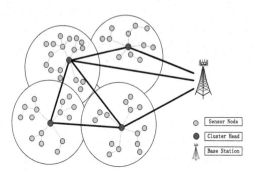

Fig. 1. Model of clustered wireless sensor network

The trust model proposed in this paper constructs on the clustered wireless sensor network topology for node trust evaluation. Sensor nodes monitor and record communication behaviors of its neighbor nodes in a test cycle Δt and its monitoring events include successful interactive behaviors and unsuccessful interactive behaviors of the monitoring nodes. If the monitoring results achieve the expectation, the monitoring event is defined as a successful interaction, otherwise, an unsuccessful interaction. In this paper, all sensor nodes in the network are assumed to have a unique identity identified with a triple < location, node type, node subtype > [11]. According to the different roles of nodes in the clustered WSN, the proposed trust model evaluates trust relationship in two levels: intra-cluster trust evaluation as well as inter-cluster trust evaluation.

2.2   Trust Evaluation at Intra-cluster Level

CM-to-CM Direct Trust Calculation. We define the direct trust evaluation method of CMs within the cluster as follows:

$$T_{i,j}(\Delta t) = \left\lceil \frac{10 \times \alpha_{i,j}(\Delta t)}{\alpha_{i,j}(\Delta t) + \beta_{i,j}(\Delta t)} \left(\frac{1}{\sqrt{\beta_{i,j}(\Delta t)}} \right) \right\rceil \tag{1}$$

In which Δt is the time window whose size can be set by the specific scenario. Thus, with the passage of time, the time window will forget old observations and add new observations. $\lceil \cdot \rceil$ is the nearest integer function, such as $\lceil 4.56 \rceil = 5$. $\alpha_{i,j}(\Delta t)$ and $\beta_{i,j}(\Delta t)$ respectively present the total numbers of successful and unsuccessful interactions of node i with node j during the time Δt. Under special circumstances, if $\alpha_{i,j}(\Delta t) \neq 0$ and $\beta_{i,j}(\Delta t) = 0$, set $T_{i,j}(\Delta t) = 10$. If $\alpha_{i,j}(\Delta t) + \beta_{i,j}(\Delta t) = 0$, which means there is no interactions during the time Δt, set $T_{i,j}(\Delta t) = \Re_{ch,j}(\Delta t)$ (as shown in formula (5)). $\Re_{ch,j}(\Delta t)$ is the feedback trust towards node j from the cluster head ch. Thus, it can be seen that a CM evaluates its neighbor nodes' trust value based on $T_{i,j}(\Delta t)$ and $\Re\pi_{ch,j}(\Delta t)$.

Given that there is no need to consider the feedback trust between CMs, namely the direct trust value towards the evaluated nodes from the third parties, the proposed mechanism can save lots of network resources. Besides, we can see from the formula (1) that, along with the number of interactive failure increasing, the expression $1 \Big/ \sqrt{\beta_{i,j}(\Delta t)}$ rapidly tends to 0 which means that the proposed scheme has the characteristics of strict punishment for the failure interactions. The characteristics of strict punishment can prevent suddenly attacks from those malicious nodes with high trust degree effectively.

CH-to-CM Feedback Trust Calculation. We assume that except the cluster head, there exists N-1 CMs within a cluster. The cluster head ch periodically broadcasts a trust request packet within the cluster. And all CMs will forward the trust values towards other CMs to ch as a response and then a matrix Φ is formed to maintain the trust values, which is shown as following:

$$\Phi = \begin{bmatrix} T_{1,1} & T_{1,2} & \cdots & T_{1,N-1} \\ T_{2,1} & T_{2,2} & \cdots & T_{2,N-1} \\ & & \ddots & \\ T_{N-1,1} & T_{N-1,2} & \cdots & T_{N-1,N-1} \end{bmatrix} \tag{2}$$

Where $T_{i,j}(i \in [1, N-1] \ j \in [1, N-1],)$ represents the direct trust value of node i towards node j. When $i = j$, $T_{i,j}$ means a node's rating towards itself. In order to avoid advocating, cluster head ch will drop this value in the fusion of feedback trusts.

From formula (1), we can see that $T_{i,j}$ is the monitoring results of different nodes towards the same property (trust value) of the same node during the same time period. Thus, generally speaking, these data has a great similarity and tends to a central value.

If malicious nodes slander other nodes, its trust value on the target object will deviate significantly from the normal ones and be recognized. According to the above idea, the concept of the fuzzy degree of nearness in fuzzy mathematics is introduced. Using the maximum and minimum nearness degree theory [16], we can measure the reliability of each node's trust values towards the node j during the same monitoring period.

During a monitoring period, the nearness of trust values of node k and node l towards node j is defined as follows:

$$\sigma_{k,l} = \min\{T_{k,j}, T_{l,j}\} / \max\{T_{k,j}, T_{l,j}\} \tag{3}$$

Furthermore, we can obtain the nearness degree matrix S of all nodes about node j, shown as follows:

$$S = \begin{bmatrix} \sigma_{1,1} & \sigma_{1,2} & \cdots & \sigma_{1,N-2} \\ \sigma_{2,1} & \sigma_{2,2} & \cdots & \sigma_{2,N-2} \\ & & \ddots & \\ \sigma_{N-2,1} & \sigma_{N-2,2} & \cdots & \sigma_{N-2,N-2} \end{bmatrix} \tag{4}$$

It can been seen that, for the elements in any line k in the matrix S, if the value of $\sum_{l=1}^{N-2} \sigma_{k,l}$ is relatively large, the trust value of node k towards node j is close to the trust values of the other nodes towards node j, which means a high reliability. On the contrary, if the value of $\sum_{l=1}^{N-2} \sigma_{k,l}$ is smaller, it means that the trust value of k towards j deviates significantly from the center value of the recommended trust values, namely, the reliability of the trust value of node k towards node j is low.

In order to ensure the objectivity and accuracy of trust evaluation, node j' trust value is obtained by the fusion of other nodes' trust values towards it within the cluster. ω_k is the weight assigned to different recommendations during the fusion process, and $\Re_{ch,j}(\Delta t)$ represents the fusion of the recommended trust values, shown as follows:

$$\Re_{ch,j}(\Delta t) = \sum_{k=1}^{N-2} \omega_k T_{k,j} \tag{5}$$

Where ω_k satisfies $\sum_{k=1}^{N-2} \omega_k = 1$ ($0 \le \omega_k \le 1$). According to the above content, ω_k depends on the reliability of each node's trust value towards node j. That means it is related to the nearness of trust values. Thus, it should contain all the information of the nearness of trust values of node k and other nodes, which should be defined as follows:

$$\omega_k = \sum_{l=1}^{N-2} \sigma_{k,l} \left/ \sum_{k=1}^{N-2} \sum_{l=1}^{N-2} \sigma_{k,l} \right. \tag{6}$$

In summary, the trust decision-making rules at intra-cluster level are as follows: whenever node i needs to interact with node j, it will check whether there is any interactions with node j within a certain time interval. If there is, then makes decisions directly, otherwise, node i will request its CH for feedback trust.

2.3   Trust Evaluation at Inter-cluster Level

According to the features of clustered sensor networks, CHs and CMs both have the resource-constrained limitation, while the base station has stronger capacity of computing and storage, and there is neither the resource-constrained problem. Therefore, saving energy is still a basic requirement of CHs during the process of calculating trust values.

CH-to-CH Direct Trust Calculation. During the process of interactions between clusters, a CH records the interactions with other CHs. We define the direct trust evaluation method of a CH i towards a CH j as follows:

$$Y_{i,j}(\Delta t) = \left\lceil \frac{10 \times \mu_{i,j}(\Delta t)}{\mu_{i,j}(\Delta t) + v_{i,j}(\Delta t)} \left(\frac{1}{\sqrt{v_{i,j}(\Delta t)}} \right) \right\rceil \tag{7}$$

Where $\mu_{i,j}(\Delta t)$ and $v_{i,j}(\Delta t)$ respectively present the total number of successful and unsuccessful interactions of CH i and CH j during the time Δt. Under special circumstances, if $\mu_{i,j}(\Delta t) \neq 0, v_{i,j}(\Delta t) = 0$, then we set $Y_{i,j}(\Delta t) = 10$.

BS-to-CH Feedback Trust Calculation. We assume there are M CHs in the whole network, which means the whole network is divided into M clusters. The base station bs broadcasts a trust request packet periodically across the whole network. And all CHs will forward the trust values towards other CHs to bs and then a matrix Ψ is formed to maintain the trust values, which can be seen as follows:

$$\Psi = \begin{bmatrix} Y_{1,1} & Y_{1,2} & \cdots & Y_{1,M} \\ Y_{2,1} & Y_{2,2} & \cdots & Y_{2,M} \\ & & \ddots & \\ Y_{M,1} & Y_{M,2} & \cdots & Y_{M,M} \end{bmatrix} \tag{8}$$

According to the same method in Sect. 2.2, CH j's feedback trust value at the base station bs is as follows:

$$\Im_{bs,j}(\Delta t) = \sum_{k=1}^{M-1} W_k Y_{k,j} \tag{9}$$

Where W_k is the weight assigned to different recommendations from other CHs towards CH j during the fusion process.

Self-adaptive Comprehensive Trust Calculation at CHs. In clustered sensor networks, CHs form the virtual skeleton of inter-cluster routing. CHs are responsible for forwarding the data fusion through other CHs to the base station. Therefore, the cluster head selection is a crucial step for reliable communication. For the purpose of the reliable communication of the whole network, the objectivity and accuracy of cluster head's trust value is very important. Here we use the thought of most trust researches, namely, calculating the comprehensive trust value of CHs, mainly including two parts: first-hand trust information $Y_{i,j}(\Delta t)$ and the second-hand trust information $\Im_{bs,j}(\Delta t)$. Therefore, the comprehensive trust of CHs is calculated as follows:

$$O_{i,j}(\Delta t) = \lceil 10 \times ((1 - W) \times Y_{i,j}(\Delta t) + W \times \Im_{bs,j}(\Delta t)) \rceil \qquad (10)$$

In which W is defined as follows:

$$W = \begin{cases} \omega_l & Y_{i,j} \leq \theta \\ \omega_h & Y_{i,j} > \theta \end{cases} \qquad (11)$$

Where $0 < \omega_l < 0.5 < \omega_h < 1$, θ is the default trust threshold. When the trust value of CH i towards CH j is below the default trust threshold θ, which indicates CH j performs malicious behavior, the value of W is small. That means the trust value evaluation is mainly dependent on the judgment of CH i itself, which can prevent other cluster heads to implement collusion attacks to boost CH j. When the trust value of CH i towards CH j is above the default trust threshold θ, the value of W is big, which indicates the trust value evaluation is mainly dependent on the other cluster heads' judgments. In this way, we can prevent malicious nodes from rapidly accumulating a high trust value, which may cause the difficulty to detect malicious nodes.

In summary, at inter-cluster level, we define the trust decision-making rules as follows: when CH i needs to interact with CH j, it will compute $Y_{i,j}(\Delta t)$ based on the history interactions between CH i and CH j. And at the same time, i will request the base station for feedback trust. Then the two trust sources are fused to get a comprehensive trust value, based on which CH i makes its decision.

3 Model Analysis and Performance Comparison

3.1 Security Analysis

In clustered WSN trust model, malicious attacks caused by model's vulnerability mainly include the following types: garnished attack, bad-mouthing attack and collusion attack.

In order to resist the above malicious attacks, in this paper, we set up three corresponding safety line. First of all, in the calculation of direct trust, expression $1 / \sqrt{\beta_{i,j}\Delta t}(1 / \sqrt{v_{i,j}\Delta t})$ rapidly approaches zero along with the number of unsuccessful interactions increasing. This means that the proposed scheme has the characteristics of severe punishment for the unsuccessful interactions, which can effectively prevent malicious nodes with a high trust degree from implementing attack. This is the first kind of safe defense. Secondly, in the calculation of feedback trust, the theory of fuzzy nearness degree is introduced. Based on the node's reliability, we assign weights to the recommendations in the fusion of recommendation trust from the third-party. That means if malicious nodes launch slandering/boosting attacks, their trust values on the target object will deviate significantly from the normal ones for recognition. Accordingly, assign a smaller weight to the recommendations, which will reduce the effect from malicious nodes on target node's trust value, namely effectively resisting bad-mouthing attacks. This is the second kind of safe defense. In the calculation of trust at inter-cluster level, we propose a self-adaptive weight factor, which adaptively select weights according to the specific circumstances of the evaluated nodes. That is to say, when the trust value of CH j is below a preset threshold, the trust value calculation mainly depends on the judgment of CH i itself, which can prevent other CHs implementing collusion attacks to boost the trust value of CH j. When the trust value of CH j is above a preset threshold, the trust value calculation is mainly dependent on the recommendations from other CHs, which can prevent malicious nodes rapidly accumulating high trust value, resulting in the difficulty to detect malicious nodes, and finally harms network security. This is the third kind of safe defense.

3.2   The Analysis and Comparison of Communication Overheads

In order to estimate the communication overhead under the full-load condition, similar to the literature [8], we assume a worst case, that is to say, each CM needs to interact with all the other CMs in the cluster, and each CH needs to interact with all the other CHs in the whole network. Meanwhile, every CH will collect the feedback trust from all the intra-cluster CMs, and BS will collect the feedback trust from all the CHs in the network. Suppose that in the network there is M clusters whose average size is N. That means there are N nodes including the cluster head in a cluster.

In the trust evaluation at the intra-cluster level, when node i needs to interact with node j, it will send a feedback trust request to its CH at most. Accordingly, a trust reply will be received by node i. If node i needs to communicate with all the other intra-cluster nodes, then the maximum communication cost will be $2(N–2)$. If all the nodes want to interact with each other, the maximum communication cost will be $2(N–2)(N–1)$. Similarly, in order to collect all the feedback trust from its $(N–1)$ intra-cluster nodes, a CH needs to send $(N–1)$ trust requests and in response receive $(N–1)$ trust replies. Therefore, the whole communication overhead is $2(N–1)$. Finally, we get the maximum intra-cluster communication cost $C_{intra} = 2(N - 2)(N - 1) + 2(N - 1)$

In the trust evaluation at the inter-cluster level, when CH i needs to communicate with CH j, it will send a feedback trust request at most. Therefore, the maximum communication cost is two data packets. When CH i needs to interact with all the other CHs in the whole network, the maximum communication cost is $2(M–1)$. Once all the CHs need to interact with each other, the maximum communication cost is $2(M–1)M$. In order to collect all the feedback trust from all CHs, the BS will send M trust requests and in response receive M trust replies. Thus, the whole communication cost is $2M$. Therefore, the maximum inter-cluster communication cost is $C_{inter} = 2(M - 1)M + 2M$.

Table 1. Communication overheads

	Communication overheads
The proposed scheme	$2M[(N-2)(N-1)+(N-1)]+2M(M-1)+2M$
LDTS	$2M[(N-2)(N-1)+N]+2(M-1)^2+2M$
GTMS	$2M[(N-2)(N-1)N]+2M(M-1)$
ATRM	$4M[(N-1)N]+4M(M-1)$

Therefore, the maximum communication overhead in the network introduced by our proposed scheme is $C_{max} = m \times C_{intra} + C_{inter}$. Table 1 gives the communication overheads of three different schemes under the worst case.

Figure 2 gives the communication costs of four different trust models for a large-scale clustered wireless sensor network, in which the number of nodes is 10000. From Fig. 2 it can be seen that, the communication overhead of our proposed scheme is similar to LDTS, but significantly better than ATRM and GTMS. In the former part of the curve, less communication cost is needed in the proposed scheme, ATRM and LDTS. With the increase of the clusters in the network, the proposed scheme, GTMS and LDTS need less communication cost and the proposed one and LDTS is significantly lower than that of GTMS. Therefore, in the aspect of communication overhead, the proposed scheme is suitable for clustered wireless sensor networks of all sizes.

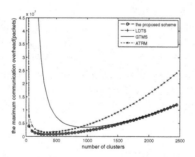

Fig. 2. Communication costs with 10,000 nodes

3.3 The Analysis and Comparison of Storage Costs

As shown in Table 2, there is a small trust database at each CM. Each record occupies 7-byte storage space, thus, the storage cost of each CM will be $7(N-2)$. And the size of the trust database is mainly determined by the average size of the cluster. Every CH keeps two tables, one for storing feedback trust matrix (see Eq. (2)), which will result in

Table 2. Storage costs of the trust database at CM

Node ID	Number of interactions		CM-to-CM direct trust	CH-to-CH feedback trust
	$\alpha_{i,j}$	$\beta_{i,j}$		
2 bytes	2 bytes	2 bytes	0.5 bytes	0.5 bytes

a storage cost of $0.5M(N-1)^2$. And in the other table, CH keeps a trust database similar to that of CM whose size of each record is also the same as that of CM, resulting in a storage cost of $7(M\text{-}1)$. Therefore, the storage cost for each CH is $7(M-1)+0.5M(N-1)^2$. The storage costs of the various trust models are given in Table 3, where N is the average size of each cluster, M is the number of clusters, Δt is the time window defined in GTMS, and K is the number of trust contexts defined in ATRM.

Table 3. Analysis and comparison of storage requirements

	CH	CM
The proposed scheme	$7(N-2)$	$7(M-1)+0.5M(N-1)^2$
LDTS	$7(N-1)$	$7(M-1)+0.5M(N-1)^2$
GTMS	$(N-1)(4+4\Delta t)$	$(M+N-2)(4+4\Delta t)$
ATRM	$30N+8(K-1)$	$30(M+N)+2(4K-19)$

Figure 3(a) and (b) give a comparison of storage overheads of four various trust models for a large-scale clustered wireless sensor network. From Fig. 3(a), we can see that the storage overhead of the proposed scheme is slightly lower than LDTS, but obviously lower than the other two schemes, which indicates that the scheme needs less storage overheads than the other three ones at the CM level. It can been from Fig. 3(b) that with the number of the clusters increasing, compared with GTMS and ATRM, this proposed scheme needs less storage overheads, which means this scheme is more suitable for large-scale wireless sensor networks with a smaller cluster size.

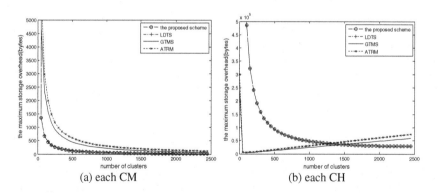

(a) each CM   (b) each CH

Fig. 3. Storage overhead with 10,000 nodes

4   Simulation Experiments and Analysis

In our simulation experiments, there exist three kinds of sensor nodes, namely CM, CH and BS. A CM and a CH can exist in two forms, either a cooperator or a rater. As a cooperator, a CM can be divided into two categories: good CM (GCM) and bad CM

(BCM) based on its behavior. GCM will provide successful communication behaviors according to the network protocol and BCM will cause the failure of communication behaviors. Accordingly, as a rater, a CM can also be classified into two categories: honest CM (HCM) and malicious CM (MCM) according to its behavior. HCM always provide a reasonable evaluation for other CMs while MCM gives arbitrary evaluation towards other CMs between 0 and 10. Similarly, CH can also be divided into GCM, BCM, HCM and MCM. Simulation scenario is set in the area of 1000 m*1000 m in which 1000 sensor nodes (namely $m \times n = 1000$) are randomly distributed. We analyze the models by setting different clusters.

In order to reflect the reliability of the trust management system, we analyze the data packet delivery ratio (PSDR). The higher a PSDR is, the higher the reliability is. We assume in the network, most of the CMs and CHs perform well, where BCM, BCH respectively comprise 10 %. This assumption is close to the real scene.

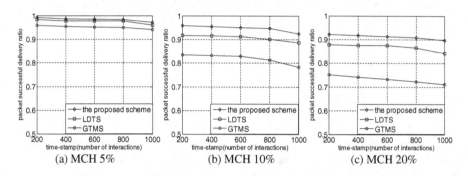

(a) MCH 5%   (b) MCH 10%   (c) MCH 20%

Fig. 4. PSDR comparison of various trust models

Figure 4 shows the comparison of PDSR of three various trust models with different percentages of MCHs. In the experiments, we assume that there are 95 % honest CMs, and the remaining 5 % CMs are malicious. Then set the percentage of MCHs as 5 %, 10 % and 20 %, respectively meaning an honest sensor network environment, a relatively honest one and a dishonest one. From (a), we can see that under the honest network environment, PDSR of the three schemes are very high. However, compared with (a), (b) and (c) have big differences. With the percentage of MCHs increasing, performances of the three schemes are significantly decreased. Relatively speaking, the performance of the proposed scheme is relatively stable, significantly better than the other two schemes, with strong robustness. This is because in the presence of malicious attacks, the proposed scheme uses the concept of fuzzy nearness degree for recommendation trust fusion, which improves the accuracy of trust calculation. At the same time, in order to reduce the risk of trust evaluation, we define a self-adaptive weight factor for the fusion of direct trust and feedback trust, which ensures the objectivity of the trust and contributes to the effective recognition of malicious nodes, thus improving the reliability and security of the whole network.

Figure 5 gives the comparison of PDSR of three various trust models with different percentages of MCMs. It can be seen from the figure, compared with the other two

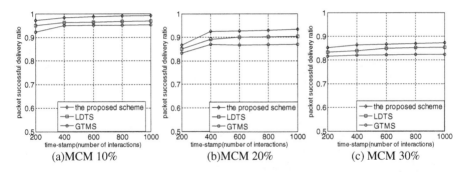

Fig. 5. PSDR comparison of various trust models

schemes, our scheme has a higher reliability. (a) gives the simulation results in an honest network environment, where there are 10 % MCMs as well as 10 % MCHs. We can see that the performances of the three schemes are relatively stable. (b) and (c) shows the experimental results under the relatively honest and dishonest network environments, from which we can see that, with the increase of percentage of MCMs, the performances of the three schemes have decline of different degrees. But the proposed scheme still outperforms LDTS and GTMS, indicating that the reliability of the proposed scheme is higher and it is more applicable to clustered WSN.

5 Conclusions

The resource efficiency and dependability are the basic requirements for a trust model in any wireless sensor network. However, owing to high cost and low reliability, the existing trust models for wireless sensor networks can not satisfy these requirements. In view of the above problems, a lightweight and dependability trust model is proposed in this paper. By the introduction of the nearness of fuzzy in fuzzy theory, we measure the reliability of the third-party recommended trust to improve the accuracy and objectivity of the calculation of trust, which contributes to detect malicious nodes. Moreover, the definition of a self-adapted weighted method for trust aggregation at CH level surpasses the limitations of the subjective definition of weights in traditional weighted method. Theoretical analysis and simulation results show that, compared with the other classical WSN trust models, the proposed scheme requires less memory and communication overheads. Besides, it can effectively resist the garnished attack, bad-mouthing attack and collusion attack. With a high reliability, the proposed model can effectively guarantee the security and normal operation of the whole network.

Acknowledgement. The paper is supported by the Nature Science Foundation of Jiangsu Province (No. BK20131107).

References

1. Khalid, O., Khan, S.U., Madani, S.A., et al.: Comparative study of trust and reputation systems for wireless sensor networks. Secur. Commun. Netw. **6**, 669–688 (2013)
2. Kant, K.: Systematic design of trust management systems for wireless sensor networks: a review. In: 4th IEEE International Conference on Advanced Computing and Communication Technologies (ACCT), pp. 208–215 (2014)
3. Ishmanov, F., Malik, A.S., Kim, S.W., et al.: Trust management system in wireless sensor networks: design considerations and research challenges. Trans. Emerg. Telecommun. Technol. **26**, 107–130 (2015)
4. Ganeriwal, S., Balzano, L.K., Srivastava, M.B.: Reputation-based framework for high integrity sensor networks. ACM Trans. Sensor Netw. (TOSN) **4**, 15 (2008)
5. Yao, L., Wang, D., Liang, X., et al.: Research on multi-level fuzzy trust model for wireless sensor networks. Chin. J. Sci. Instru. **35**, 1606–1613 (2014)
6. Duan, J., Gao, D., Yang, D., et al.: An energy-aware trust derivation scheme with game theoretic approach in wireless sensor networks for IoT applications. IEEE Internet Things J. **1**, 58–69 (2014)
7. Zhang, M., Xu, C., Guan, J., et al.: A novel bio-inspired trusted routing protocol for mobile wireless sensor networks. KSII Trans. Internet Inf. Syst. (TIIS). **8**, 74–90 (2014)
8. Boukerche, A., Xu, L., EL-Khatib, K.: Trust-based Security for wireless Ad Hoc and sensor networks. Comput. Commun. **30**, 2413–2427 (2007)
9. Shaikh, R.A., Jameel, H., d'Auriol, B.J., et al.: Group-based trust management scheme for clustered wireless sensor networks. IEEE Trans. Parallel Distrib. Syst. **20**, 1698–1712 (2009)
10. Bao, F., Chen, R., Chang, M.J., et al.: Hierarchical trust management for wireless sensor networks and its applications to rrust-based routing and intrusion detection. IEEE Trans. Netw. Serv. Manage. **9**, 169–183 (2012)
11. Li, X., Zhou, F., Du, J.: LDTS: a lightweight and dependable trust system for clustered wireless sensor networks. IEEE Trans. Inf. Forensics Secur. **8**, 924–935 (2013)
12. Younis, O., Fahmy, S.: HEED: a hybrid, energy-efficient, distributed clustering approach for ad-hoc sensor networks. IEEE Trans. Mob. Comput. **3**, 366–379 (2004)
13. Wei, D., Jin, Y., Vural, S., et al.: An energy-efficient clustering solution for wireless sensor networks. IEEE Trans. Wireless Commun. **10**, 3973–3983 (2011)
14. Javaid, N., Qureshi, T.N., Khan, A.H., et al.: EDDEEC: enhanced developed distributed energy-efficient clustering for heterogeneous wireless sensor networks. Procedia Comput. Sci. **19**, 914–919 (2013)
15. Han, G., Jiang, J., Shu, L., et al.: Management and applications of trust in wireless sensor networks: a survey. J. Comput. Syst. Sci. **80**, 602–617 (2014)
16. Yang, J., Gong, F.: Consistent and reliable fusion method of multi-sensor based on degree of nearness. Chin. J. Sens. Actuators **23**, 984–988 (2010)

The Optimization Model of Trust
for White-Washing

Zhidan Wang[1,3]([⊠]), Jian Wang[1], and Yanfei Zhao[2]

[1] College of Computer Science and Technology,
Nanjing University of Aeronautics and Astronautics, Nanjing 210016, China
zhd_wang@163.com, wangjian@nuaa.edu.cn
[2] School of Technology, Nanjing Audit University, Nanjing 211815, China
nuaafei@nau.edu.cn
[3] Information Technology Research Base of Civil Aviation Administration
of China, Civil Aviation University of China, Tianjin 300300, China

Abstract. With the increase of trust recommendation in the network services
and applications, a large number of corresponding attacks including white-
washing attacks have emerged. This paper proposes a trust optimization model
in recommendation system to counter the white-washing attacks. The proposed
model first separates the white-washing nodes from other nodes by dividing the
nodes into different groups. The grouping will limit the dubious white-washing
nodes in the proposed model so as to take these nodes much more cost to
become a normal node. Meanwhile, the normal interactions are not affected. Our
experimental results show that the proposed model can insulate suspicious
white-washing nodes effectively, and ensures the normal interaction activities
among normal nodes at the same time. Thus, the proposed model can resist the
white-washing attacks effectively.

Keywords: Trustworthy recommendation · White-washing prevention · Nodes
guarantee

1 Introduction and Related Work

Nowadays, more and more services rely on the network. As the openness and anonymity
of the network, there are often huge risks behind these services. Based on the research of
twitter user's behavior, Bilge [1] pointed out that users will click the message sent by
attackers unconsciously after attackers gets their trust which would bring losses to them.
Jagatic [2] expressed that the stolen specific information of users got a higher success
rate on phishing. As the enormous increase of social network users, many kinds of
malicious behaviors and related malicious nodes have appeared which consume network
resources, damage the interests of others and endanger the safety of the public network.
There are different kinds of trust models [3–8] which can help users select the desirable
services in huge network system, but they usually neglect the white-washing behavior.
When the trust of malicious node in the system is low, the node can withdraw and
re-enter into the system with a new identity. In this way, the node can have a higher
initial trust, and thus it is able to continue its malicious behavior.

© Springer International Publishing Switzerland 2015
Z. Huang et al. (Eds.): ICCCS 2015, LNCS 9483, pp. 169–180, 2015.
DOI: 10.1007/978-3-319-27051-7_15

The prime factors for white-washing are as follows: (a) The cost of the new user registration is low, so it is easy for a user to get a new identity. (b) A new user often has higher initial trust. (c) Most trust models do not consider nodes' history dwell time (the time from the user register to right now) in the system. As the network is openness, it's impossible to increase the cost of user registration. So in order to resist white-washing, it's a must to take dwell time and appropriate initial trust into account.

Huang [9] has taken dwell time into consideration, which split all the services in the same domain into the mature service queue and the novice service queue so that the new services only compete with new ones until they grow matured. However, it is unfair to the mature services those are in the back of the mature queue for that they may be better than top services in the novice queue. So it needs a better way to select service between two queues. Some bind presenter and presentee together with feedback method [10, 11], but they dampen the enthusiasm of nodes to join system because the new nodes do not have a large number of interaction, as a result, they cannot recommend or be recommended effectively. It doesn't conform to the demand of network. Barra [12] resists the entry of malicious nodes by increasing the system sensitivity, i.e., when a malicious node in the system is found, the system will increase its standards for a period of time, thus shielding the malicious nodes. But this method is appropriate for live streaming system instead of the network.

In this paper, all nodes in the system will be divided into two different groups: safe group and dubious group, and nodes in different group have different right: safe nodes can recommend directly, while dubious nodes can recommend only when there is a safe node providing guarantee for it. Hence the major contributions of this paper can be summarized as follows:

- A trustworthy recommendation model is proposed, which contains grouping process and guaranteed process.
- The experiments show that the model can resist the white-washing attacks effectively, and ensure normal interaction activities of the other nodes at the same time.

The remainder of this paper is organized as follows. Section 2 presents the trustworthy recommendation model. Section 3 shows the experimental result. Section 4 concludes the paper.

2   Trustworthy Recommendation Mechanism

2.1   Brief Description

Consulting the method of defining trust in real society, the existing models always define trust with direct trust, indirect trust and recommendation trust, which are expressed as $DT(x,y)$, $IT(x,y)$ and $RT(x,y)$ and they are all one-way trust. In this paper, the recommendation trust is divided in two parts: self-recommendations and recommendations of others (hereinafter, they are referred to as SR and OR). Additionally, we use GT_x to express the global trust in this paper which is a comprehensive evaluation of node x and the specific calculation is:

$$GT_x = \frac{1}{n}\sum_{i=1}^{n} DT(i,x) \tag{1}$$

The model proposed in the paper is made up of four parts: nodes grouping, TOPSIS-based nodes guarantee, trust attenuation and trust updating. To describe the model better, we define the following tuples:

Resource Demand Application (RDA) = (Demander_ID, ServiceContents, TimeStamp)

Here, Demander_ID refers to the node who requests resource; ServiceContents refers to the requested resource; TimeStamp refers to the time of sending RDA.

Resource Recommend Message (RRM) = (Recommend_ID, ServiceContents, Response_Time, Recommend_Oneself_bool, Guarantor_ID)

Here, Recommend_ID refers to the node who provides the recommendation; ServiceContents refers to the recommended resource; Response_Time refers to the time of sending RRM; Recommend_Oneself_bool refers to the node is SR or OR; Guarantor_ID refers to the node who make a guarantee.

Figure 1 is the graph of the main network structure.

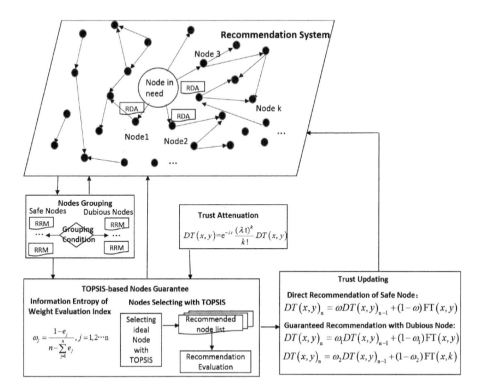

Fig. 1. Recommendatory network structure and frame of trust value computing

2.2   Nodes Grouping

As the prime behavior of malicious nodes is malicious evaluation, so the malicious nodes' evaluations will have distinct difference with the other nodes. Here defines departure degree of evaluation behavior as follows:

Departure Degree of Evaluation Behavior(DD_x)

DD_{xy} refers to the departure degree of evaluation behavior from node x to node y compared with the behavior from other nodes to node y, which is calculated by the difference value of variance before and after the evaluation of node x joining the group of evaluation values.

$$DD_{xy} = \left| SD_y - SD_{y-x} \right| \tag{2}$$

Where SD_y refers to the variance of the nodes group that have direct interaction with y; SD_{y-x} also refers to the variance of the nodes group that have direct interaction with y, but without x.

Then the departure degree of x can be expressed as;

$$DD_x = 1 - \frac{1}{n} \sum_{i=1}^{n} DD_{xi} \tag{3}$$

Here, DD_x is made with the trend to cooperate with the date below, i.e., the smaller DD_x is, the lower departure degree of x is.

When a node has white-washed, it has a higher initial trust value, a low dwell time, and the trading record is null. So here uses dwell time, number of trading, global trust and departure degree to divide the nodes into two groups: safe group and dubious group.

Defining tuple $<T, N, GT, DD>$ T, N, GT, DD refer to dwell time, number of trading, global trust and departure degree in turn. And Th, Nh, GTh, DDh refer to critical value of the four indexes above separately. Then the grouping rule is:

Only $T_i \geq Th, N_i \geq Nh, GT_i \geq GTh, DD_i \geq DDh$, node can be assigned to safe group, otherwise, it will be assigned to dubious group.

Defining critical coefficient γ $(0 \leq \gamma \leq 1)$, here γ means to eliminate the last γ nodes after sorting. i.e. If the critical coefficient of dwell time is 0.3, it will eliminate the last 30 % nodes after sorting by dwell time, then the critical dwell time is the minimum number of the remaining 70 % nodes. The critical coefficient is higher, the grouping conditions are stricter, and the nodes in safe group are more credible. When the critical coefficient is 0, the model degrades into a traditional model.

2.3   TOPSIS-Based Nodes Guarantee

In the recommendation system, to ensure the credibility of recommendation, only the nodes in safe group can recommend resource to the nodes in need directly; to ensure the fairness of recommendation, the nodes in dubious group can recommend resource with the guarantee of safe nodes. Here, the system evaluates each index with the information entropy, and then selecting the recommended resource with TOPSIS.

Information Entropy Weight of Evaluation Index. Information entropy is a measurement index of uncertainty in information theory, i.e., the more information an index carries and transmits, the smaller the remaining uncertainties and the residual entropy are, i.e., this index is more useful than others on decision. Here, the weight of information entropy is used to reflect the importance of each index in decision-making.

Supposing there are m nodes, each node contains n assessment indexes. Making the evaluation matrix $X = (x_{ij})_{m \times n}$, x_{ij} represents the jth evaluation index of the ith node. Here, data is standardized as each dimension of index is different:

$$sx_{ij} = \frac{x_{ij}}{\sqrt{\sum_{i=1}^{m} x_{ij}^2}}, \quad i = 1, 2 \ldots m; j = 1, 2 \ldots n \tag{4}$$

The information entropy of jth evaluation index can be expressed as follows:

$$e_j = -\frac{1}{\ln m} \sum sx_{ij} \ln sx_{ij}, \quad j = 1, 2 \ldots n \quad 0 \le e_j \le 1 \tag{5}$$

As the information entropy of evaluation index is higher, the weight of the index should be smaller. Then, the weight of information entropy of each index is:

$$\omega_j = \frac{1 - e_j}{n - \sum_{j=1}^{n} e_j}, \quad j = 1, 2 \ldots n \tag{6}$$

Only if $sx_{i1} = sx_{i1} = \ldots = sx_{in}$ is satisfied, can e_j reach the maximum value, meanwhile, $\omega_j = 0$, that is to say the jth index provides no useful information.

Nodes Selecting with TOPSIS. After the nodes in need send RDAs in the system, there will be two cases:

Direct Recommendation of Safe Node:.

In this circumstances, there is no limit on the recommendation, safe nodes can provide their SRs to the requirement node directly. And the node in need will calculate the recommendation trust value with the direct/indirect trust and global trust as follows:

$$RT(x, y) = \begin{cases} \alpha DT(x, y) + (1 - \alpha)GT_y & x \text{ has direct interaction with } y \\ \beta IT(x, y) + (1 - \beta)GT_y & x \text{ has no direct interaction with } y \end{cases} \tag{7}$$

Where α, β are the regulatory factors.

Guaranteed Recommendation for Dubious Node. The safe node has no required resource, however some dubious nodes have. So the safe node can select a dubious node which has the resource and guarantee for its resource, then recommend it to the node in need. The interaction diagram is: (Fig. 2)

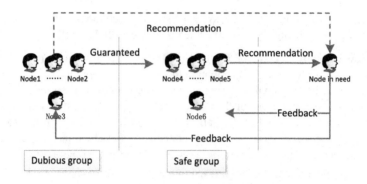

Fig. 2. Interaction diagram

When a safe node is ready to provide a guarantee, it may receive more than one request of dubious nodes, therefore there should be a method to help safe nodes select dubious nodes. Here, we use the method of TOPSIS which is short for Technique for Order Preference by Similarity to an Ideal Solution. The idea of TOPSIS is sorting the nodes according to the close degree to the ideal target. If the node closest to the best solution and farthest away the worst solution, it will be the optimal node. Otherwise, it will be the worst. In this paper, the TOPSIS is simplified, only profitability index is taken into account.

Supposing there are m nodes, each node contains n assessment indexes. Making the evaluation matrix $X = (x_{ij})_{m \times n}$, then the weighted decision matrix is $Y = (y_{ij})_{m \times n}$ where $y_{ij} = \omega_j \times sx_{ij} (i = 1, 2 \ldots m; j = 1, 2 \ldots n)$.

The set of best value Y^+ and the set of worst value Y^- are:

$$Y^+ = \{y_1^+, y_2^+ \ldots y_n^+\} = \{\max y_{ij} | j \in J_e\}, i = 1, 2 \ldots n$$
$$Y^- = \{y_1^-, y_2^- \ldots y_n^-\} = \{\min y_{ij} | j \in J_e\}, i = 1, 2 \ldots n \tag{8}$$

Where J_e refers to profitability index. Then the distance between evaluation value and best/worst value is:

$$df_i^+ = \sqrt{\sum_{j=1}^{n} \left(y_{ij} - y_j^+\right)^2}, i = 1, 2 \ldots m \tag{9}$$

$$df_i^- = \sqrt{\sum_{j=1}^{n} \left(y_{ij} - y_j^-\right)^2}, i = 1, 2 \ldots m \tag{10}$$

Then, the close degree of the dubious node to ideal node is:

$$cd_i = \frac{df_i^-}{df_i^+ + df_i^-}, i = 1, 2 \ldots m \tag{11}$$

Apparently, $0 < cd_i \le 1$, and the cd_i is bigger, the degree of dubious node to ideal node is closer.

Then the node in need will calculate the recommendation trust value among safe node, dubious node and itself similar to direct recommendation of safe node,.

$$RT(x,y) = \begin{cases} \alpha_1 DT(x,k) + (1-\alpha_1)(\delta GT_y + (1-\delta)GT_k) \\ \quad x \text{ has direct interaction with } k \\ \alpha_2 IT(x,k) + (1-\alpha_2)(\delta GT_y + (1-\delta)GT_k) \\ \quad x \text{ has no direct interaction with } k \end{cases} \qquad (12)$$

Where x is the node in need, y is the dubious node and k is the safe node, α_1, α_2, δ are the regulatory factors.

2.4 Trust Attenuation

Social network is dynamic, real-time and the user behavior is also changing. Therefore, trust value should have the characteristics of attenuation as time grows. Assuming that to time t, the happened trading number is $N(t)$, the relationship between trading number and time conforms to Poisson Distribution according to [13]:

$$f(N(t)) = P\{N(t+s) - N(s) = k\} = e^{-\lambda t}\frac{(\lambda t)^k}{k!}, k = 0, 1, 2\ldots \qquad (13)$$

Where k is the trading number and λ is the trading number for unit time.

So, at time t, the direct trust of x to y is:

$$DT(x,y) = e^{-\lambda t}\frac{(\lambda t)^k}{k!}DT(x,y) \qquad (14)$$

2.5 Trust Updating

After interaction, the nodes in need should provide the corresponding feedback trust to the nodes who provide recommendation, then update previous trust. At this time, there are still two cases:

Feedback in Direct Recommendation of Safe Node. Assuming that the feedback of x to y is $FT(x,y)$, then the direct trust of x to y is updated to:

$$DT(x,y)_n = \omega DT(x,y)_{n-1} + (1-\omega)FT(x,y) \qquad (15)$$

Feedback in Guaranteed Recommendation for Dubious Node Assuming that the feedback of x to y's guarantee is $FT(x, y)$, the feedback of x to k's recommendation is $FT(x, k)$, then the direct trust of x to y and x to k are updated to:

$$DT(x, y)_n = \omega_1 DT(x, y)_{n-1} + (1 - \omega_1)FT(x, y) \tag{16}$$

$$DT(x, y)_n = \omega_2 DT(x, y)_{n-1} + (1 - \omega_2)FT(x, k) \tag{17}$$

Where $\omega_1, \omega_2, \omega_3$ are regulatory factors of feedback,$DT(x, y)_n$ refers to the trust value after updating, $DT(x, y)_{n-1}$ refers to the trust value before updating.

As the number of users is enormous, frequently updating the groups is needless and impossible. So it sets a rate here, only recently increased interactions in the system up to the rate of update, it can update all the system parameters include grouping.

3   Experiments and Analysis

The experiments simulate the trust recommendation model and verify the model's property of resisting white-washing. Meanwhile, through the comparison with Peer-Trust model [14], it can be verified that this paper's model can resist malicious nodes well (Table 1).

Table 1. Parameter setting

Parameters	Setting
Number of nodes	1000
Kinds of resource	1000(Each node contains 20 kinds of resources in average)
Critical coefficient γ	0.3(optimistic)0.5 (ordinary) 0.7(negative)
Initial global trust	0.5
Regulatory factors of evaluation α 、 β 、 α_1 、 α_2 、 δ	$\alpha = 0.6$ $\beta = 0.5$ $\alpha_1 = 0.6$ $\alpha_2 = 0.5$ $\delta = 0.5$
Regulatory factors of feedback ω 、 ω_1 、 ω_2	$\omega = 0.5$ $\omega_1 = 0.4$ $\omega_2 = 0.6$

The experiment is composed by several trading cycles and every safe node has once interaction in a cycle. Experiments based on Matlab2014b, running environment is CPU 2.6 GHz, 8 G memory.

Experiment 1. The Analysis of White-washing Resistance. The existing white-washing resistant models are always applied to resource sharing system, which usually use the number of available resources to measure the effectiveness of the models. However, our model is used in recommendation system, of which the effectiveness can only be measured by the interval of the recommendation made by malicious nodes before and after white-washing, as the trust change can not decide whether the recommendation is accepted. So the experiment which shows the trading cycles with and without our model does not make comparisons between our white-washing models and other same models, but between our model and the traditional recommendation trust model.

With our model whether the malicious node is white-washed or not, the malicious node can only stay in the dubious group which cannot recommend resource to others directly from beginning to end. When the white-washed node re-enter the system, it has the lowest dwell time among all nodes in the system. So if the white-wash node wants to be transferred into the safe group, it will cost more time then before.

The figure below shows the average number of trading cycles the malicious nodes cost with and without our model when the malicious nodes want to be transferred into the safe group, here $\gamma=0.3$. Without our model, the nodes cost about 25 trading cycles to enter into the safe group, but it will cost about 50 trading cycles with our model. Obviously, the malicious nodes will cost more time to be transferred into the safe group from the dubious group with our model (Fig. 3).

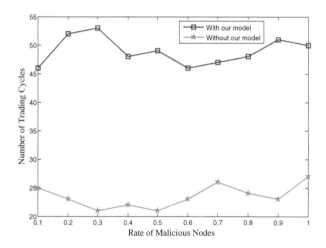

Fig. 3. Average cost of trading cycles with and without our model

In oder to ensure the positivity of common nodes, this model give a high initial global trust value to new nodes. So the white-washed node's close degree may higher then itself before. However, as the white-washed node's dwell time is the lowest and the record of transaction is null, its close degree may be still not high enough to be selected by safe nodes even though it is higher then before. Thus the white-washed nodes can not profit more with this model, the behavior of white-washing is meaningless.

Experiment 2. The Analysis of Malicious Behavior Resistance. In the experiment, we select four kinds of nodes from the system, there are one malicious node with a high global trust value, one malicious node with a low global trust value, one normal node with a high global trust value and one normal node with a low global trust value. The figure below shows the change of these four nodes'global trust in 40 trading cycles. As the the malicious nodes make a malicious behavior in the system, their global trust

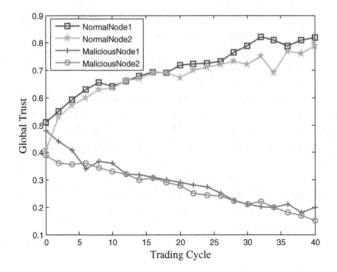

Fig. 4. The change of nodes along with the trading cycle increase

dropped rapidly and reach a stable level about 0.2. On the contrary, the normal nodes'global trust go up steadily and reach a stable level about 0.8. Above all, this model can distinguish the malicious node and normal node well (Fig. 4).

Experiment 3. The Analysis of Malicious Nodes in Different Scale. In this experiment, the critical coefficient of index are 0.3,0.5,0.7 for respectively which is designed for three different system strategy: optimistic, ordinary and negative, and compare them with PeerTrust model. The rate of successful interaction in our model is always higher than PeerTrust model, especially when $\gamma=0.7$, the rate is much higher than others.

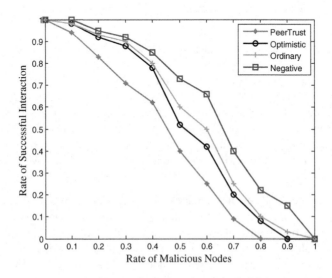

Fig. 5. The rate of successful interaction when the rate of malicious nodes is changing

But the number of safe nodes is reduced enormously with this negative system strategy, it will decrease the positivity of nodes in the system. So we only suggest using negative system strategy when there are too many malicious node (Fig. 5).

4 Conclusion

Currently, the research of white-washing resistance mainly aims at the free-riding problem in P2P. However, the white-washing can also be taken as a method for malicious nodes to make malicious behavior continuously. This paper grouped the nodes in the recommendation system into two groups: safe group and dubious group. For different group, system made up different rules when interacting: nodes in safe group could provide recommendation to the nodes in need directly; nodes in dubious group could only provide recommendation to the nodes in need with the guarantee of safe nodes. The model restricted the nodes that had white-washed well and distinguished the malicious node and normal node well, meanwhile, it performed better than PeerTrust with different rate of malicious nodes.

In the future, we will further work on a variety of different attack behaviors in trust system, such as intermittent malicious behavior, strategic cheating and so on. Additionally, we should improve the model in this paper through the comprehensive consideration of various factors, and conduct an experiment based on actual environmental.

Acknowledgement. This work is partly support by the Fundamental Research Funds for the Central Universities(No.NZ2015108), and the China Postdoctoral Science Foundation funded project(2015M571752), and the Jiangsu Planned Projects for Postdoctoral Research Funds (1402033C),and Open Project Foundation of Information Technology Research Base of Civil Aviation Administration of China(NO.CAAC-ITRB-201405).

References

1. Bilge, L., Strufe, T., Balzarotti, D., Kirda, E.: All your contacts are belong to us: automated identity theft attacks on social networks. In: Proceedings of the 18th international conference on World wide web, pp. 551–560. ACM (2009)
2. Jagatic, T.N., Johnson, N.A., Jakobsson, M., Menczer, F.: Social phishing. Commun. ACM **50**, 94–100 (2007)
3. Wang, X., Liu, L., Su, J.: Rlm: a general model for trust representation and aggregation. IEEE Trans. Serv. Comput. **5**, 131–143 (2012)
4. Malik, Z., Akbar, I., Bouguettaya, A.: Web services reputation assessment using a hidden markov model. In: Baresi, L., Chi, C.-H., Suzuki, J. (eds.) ICSOC-ServiceWave 2009. LNCS, vol. 5900, pp. 576–591. Springer, Heidelberg (2009)
5. Yahyaoui, H.: A trust-based game theoretical model for Web services collaboration. Knowl.-Based Syst. **27**, 162–169 (2012)
6. Huang, K., Yao, J., Fan, Y., Tan, W., Nepal, S., Ni, Y., Chen, S.: Mirror, mirror, on the web, which is the most reputable service of them all? In: Basu, S., Pautasso, C., Zhang, L., Fu, X. (eds.) ICSOC 2013. LNCS, vol. 8274, pp. 343–357. Springer, Heidelberg (2013)

7. Malik, Z., Bouguettaya, A.: Rateweb: reputation assessment for trust establishment among web services. VLDB J. Int. J. Very Large Data Bases **18**, 885–911 (2009)
8. Yahyaoui, H., Zhioua, S.: Bootstrapping trust of Web services based on trust patterns and Hidden Markov Models. Knowl. Inf. Syst. **37**, 389–416 (2013)
9. Huang, K., Liu, Y., Nepal, S., Fan, Y., Chen, S., Tan, W.: A novel equitable trustworthy mechanism for service recommendation in the evolving service ecosystem. In: Franch, X., Ghose, A.K., Lewis, G.A., Bhiri, S. (eds.) ICSOC 2014. LNCS, vol. 8831, pp. 510–517. Springer, Heidelberg (2014)
10. Kudtarkar, A.M., Umamaheswari, S.: Avoiding white washing in P2P networks. In: First International Communication Systems and Networks and Workshops, 2009, COMSNETS 2009, pp. 1–4. IEEE (2009)
11. Chen, J., Lu, H., Bruda, S.D.: Analysis of feedbacks and ratings on trust merit for peer-to-peer systems. In: International Conference on E-Business and Information System Security, 2009, EBISS'09, pp. 1–5. IEEE (2009)
12. de Almeida, R.B., Natif, M., Augusto, J., da Silva, A.P.B., Vieira, A.B.: Pollution and whitewashing attacks in a P2P live streaming system: analysis and counter-attack. In: 2013 IEEE International Conference on Communications (ICC), pp. 2006–2010. IEEE (2013)
13. Wang, G., Gui, X.-L.: Selecting and trust computing for transaction nodes in online social networks. Jisuanji Xuebao (Chin. J. Comput.) **36**, 368–383 (2013)
14. Xiong, L., Liu, L.: Peertrust: supporting reputation-based trust for peer-to-peer electronic communities. IEEE Trans. Knowl. Data Eng. **16**, 843–857 (2004)

Malware Clustering Based on SNN Density Using System Calls

Wang Shuwei[1], Wang Baosheng[2], Yong Tang[2(✉)], and Yu Bo[2]

[1] National University of Defense Technology, Changsha 400073, Hunan, China
[2] Institute of Network and Information Security, National University of Defense Technology, Changsha 400073, Hunan, China
ytang@nudt.edu.cn

Abstract. Clustering is an important part of the malware analysis. The malware clustering algorithms commonly used at present have gradually can not adapt to the growing number of malware. In order to improve the malware clustering algorithm, this paper uses the clustering algorithm based on *Shared Nearest Neighbor (SNN)*, and uses frequencies of the system calls as the features for input. This algorithm combined with the *DBSCAN* which is traditional density-based clustering algorithm in data mining. This makes it is a better application in the process of clustering of malware. The results of clusters demonstrate that the effect of the algorithm of clustering is good. And the algorithm is simple to implement and easy to complete automated analysis. It can be applied to actual automated analysis of malware.

Keywords: Malware · Clustering · SNN · System calls

1 Introduction

The number of malware of the world current continue to exponential growth. The current samples' size store in Sample Library is gradually approaching one hundred million, the everyday average number of new samples is about 200000. Malware still is the most main threat to information security. Due to limited resources, in order to use the limited resources against huge malware more effective, find out new families have research value is the most important tasks of automatic analysis. In order to complete this goal, the malware clustering is indispensable work. The effective of clustering has a close relationship with whether we can quickly find out new families. In the academic research and practical application in the past, the malware clustering algorithm often used mainly including simple k - means clustering. But in the case of navigating, families' sizes are extreme imbalance. For example, the number of Trojans named Zbot reached 350000 in Antiy's sample library, while the Flame only has 57 samples. Find out new families are composed of very small amounts of samples in large database through clustering, is also a challenge to the traditional malware clustering algorithm.

The work was supported the project supported by the National Natural Science Foundation of China (Grant No. 61472437).

Z. Huang et al. (Eds.): ICCCS 2015, LNCS 9483, pp. 181–191, 2015.
DOI: 10.1007/978-3-319-27051-7_16

2 Related Work

Academia conducted research around malware clustering. Horng-Tzer Wang [1] provides a system based on structural sequence comparison and probabilistic similarity measures for detecting variants of malware. The system uses system calls sequences generated from sandbox represented by Markov chains, and uses the classical k-means clustering algorithm. Xin Hu [2] proposes the system called MutantX-S, which extracts the opcode form the system memory mirroring of the malware through shelling process, and converts the high-dimensional feature vectors to low-dimensional space. The system adopts with prototype-based close-to-linear clustering algorithm. Orestis Kostakis [3] uses the edit distance graphs (GED) as the basis for measuring the similarity of graphs. They use the simulated annealing algorithm (SA) and the lower bound of graph edit distance calculated GED to improve the accuracy and efficiency of calculation of similarity between the graphs of entire system. Battista Biggio [4] studied how the behavior of toxic pollution clustering algorithm, they explained the process of poisoning the single-linkage hierarchical clustering. In the process, they use Bridge-based attacks which repeated bridging the two neighboring families to make the algorithm failed. Yanfang Ye [5] puts forward to establish a system of AMCS which uses the frequency of opcode and operation code sequence as the feature. The system uses hierarchical clustering and k-medoids hybrid hierarchical clustering method, this system has been used commercially. Roberto Perdisci [6] and others establish the system VAMO which is an evaluation system to assess the effectiveness of the clustering algorithm is proposed. Bayer U [7] converts the dynamic analysis of malware to the record file of behavior, uses LSH to avoid calculating the distances between samples which below the threshold, they use the results of a hierarchical clustering of LSH to cluster. Kazuki Iwamoto [8] proposes a automatic malware classification method, which extracts features by conducting the static analysis of malware and the structure of source code of malware. In this paper an API sequence's graph is created. Guanhua Yan [9] explores the efficiency of several classification methods commonly used for different characteristic vectors. Silvio Cesare [10, 11] designs Malwise system, the system is based on the analysis of the information entropy to complete the process of shelling of malware. It can automatically extract the control flows of samples, by generating K-Subgraph features and Q-gram characteristics to complete pre filtering, then using precise and approximate matching algorithm for malware. Shi, Hongbo [12] uses the frequencies of call DLLs as characteristic vectors, uses the GHSOM(growing hierarchical self-organizing map) of neural network for malware. Jae wook-Jang [13] obtains social network of system calls. They generate the completely system calls' graphs by recording behaviors of the system calls of samples and the social networks between calls.

It is rarely used clustering algorithms based on density in the study of the early stage of malware clustering. But in the field of data mining, the clustering algorithms based on density for high-dimensional data clustering has a good effect. So we will use the clustering algorithms based on density of malware for the further research. And clustering algorithms using different features in the prophase study, and I think using system calls as the features have a good effect. So I will choose system calls as the features of cluster research.

3 Methodology

3.1 Feature Extract

Pack for malware is an important factor to interference with the analysis of malware, and has a huge influence on the results of static analysis especially. In order to reduce the interference caused by packing, we extract the system calls of malware from dynamic analysis as features. For extracting feature, we get the system calls called in the process of execution. But different malware from different families may call the same system calls during execution. To solve this problem, this paper uses the frequencies of the system calls called by malware.

In the process of feature extraction, we first run malware for getting the system calls' sequences. Store all the system calls called into the database, and determine unique ID for each system calls said its position in the feature vectors. Then for each malware, we statistic all the times of system calls called. Then we place frequencies of the system calls in the corresponding position of feature vector. Finally, the fixed feature vectors generated for each malware. According to the preliminary analysis, the system calls often called by malware are only a small part of all system calls. So the length of feature vectors generated by this method will be not too long. Figure 1 depicts the process of feature extraction.

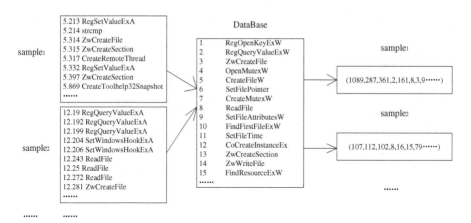

Fig. 1. The process of feature extraction

3.2 Calculate Similarity

Because of the extracted feature vectors are fixed, so we can use the distances between feature vectors to measure the similarity of malware. Euclidean distance is a frequently used definition. This paper uses the frequencies of the system calls called by malware as characteristics, in this case, we want the importance of each system calls are same. This way of distance calculation let the importance of every position in the vectors are same. This also means that the importance of each system calls are same. The results of Euclidean distance calculation are the real distance between feature vectors in space.

For example, there are two vectors $\vec{x} = (x1, x2, \ldots, xn)$ and $\vec{y} = (y1, y2, \ldots, yn)$ in n dimensions and the Euclidean distance calculation formula is:

$$distance = \sqrt{\sum_{i=1}^{n} (xi - yi)^2}. \tag{1}$$

After Euclidean distance calculation, the distances between the samples are partial. So sample points are relatively loose. In order to reduce the errors caused by the loose of samples, we use the *Shared Nearest Neighbor (SNN)* to define and quantify the similarities between samples. In order to further calculate each *SNN* similarities of malware, we need to calculate the values of *kNN* for each malware. The definition of *kNN* given by *Definition 1*. In simple terms, the sample *p's kNN* contains the *k* nearest feature vectors corresponding to the samples to the feature vector of sample *p*. As shown in Fig. 2 is the *1NN, 4NN and 5NN* of sample *p*.

Definition 1. *k nearest neighbors (kNN)* : set *p* is a sample of data set, and define the distance between *p* and the kth nearest neighbor as *k-distance(p)*. The *kNN* of *p* contains all of the samples whose distance to *p* is less then *k-distance(p)*. Formula is:

$$N_{kNN}(p) = \{q \in D \setminus \{p\} | d(p, q) \le k - distance(p)\}. \tag{2}$$

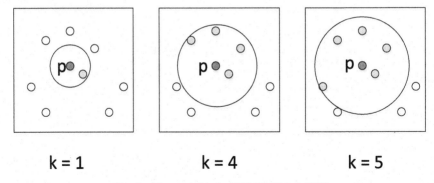

Fig. 2. The sample p's 1NN, 4NN and 5NN

In essence, as long as the two samples are in each other's nearest neighbor list, *SNN* similarity is the number of their shared adjacent. Its definition is given in *Definition 2*.

Definition 2. *SNN* similarity: if *p* and *q* are two samples. If *NN(p)* and *NN(q)* on behalf of the set of the nearest neighbor of *p* and *q*. the calculation of degree of similarity between them using the following equation:

$$similarity(p, q) = size(NN(p) \cap NN(q)). \tag{3}$$

The computing algorithm of *SNN* similarity is given in Algorithm 1. Graphical explanation are given in Fig. 3. The two samples (black) each have eight nearest neighbors and contain each other. A total of four (gray) nearest neighbors are shared. So the *SNN* similarity between the two samples is 4.

Algorithm 1. SNN similarity computing algorithm

---

1. Find out k - nearest neighbors of all points.
2. If two points x and y are not in the k - nearest neighbors of each other then
3.　　Similarity (x,y) ← 0
4. Else
5.　　Similarity (x,y) ← The number of shared nearest neighbors
6.End If

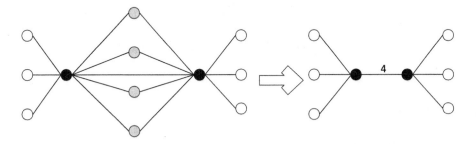

Fig. 3. *SNN* similarity calculation

Because *SNN* similarity reflect the local structure of points of the sample space, so they are relatively insensitive to the change of density and spatial dimensions. The definition of *SNN* density given in *Definition 3*. *SNN* density measure the extent a sample is surrounded by similar points.

Definition 3. *SNN* density. Sample *p's* density of *SNN* is the number of samples determined by given similarity threshold *SIM* according to the data set of *D*. Formula is:

$$N(p) = \{q \in D\backslash\{p\}|similarity(p,q) \leq SIM\}. \tag{4}$$

3.3　Clustering Algorithm Based on SNN Density

In this paper, we use the clustering algorithm based on *SNN* density, this algorithm combines the *SNN* density and *DBSCAN* algorithm. Firstly *SNN* similarity between each samples should be calculated. Then with the parameters of the *Eps* and *MinPts* determined by user as input, we use *DBSCAN*. The algorithm automatically determines the number of clusters for samples. But not all of the points were clustering. Abandoned points including noise and outliers. Based on *SNN* density clustering algorithm to produce such clusters, points of one cluster are strongly related to each other.

Using clustering of malware based on *SNN* density is mainly divided into the following steps: (1) the first step is calculating the *SNN* density of each samples; To complete this step, we should determine a specified threshold *Eps* to find out all samples whose *SNN* similarity are greater than or equal to *Eps*. (2) then find out core samples; In this step, we use a specified threshold *MinPts*, find out all samples whose *SNN* density greater than *MinPts*, marked as core samples. (3) generate clusters from core samples; If the two core samples' similarity is greater than or equal to *Eps*, it is combined into a cluster. (4) then let samples whose similarities with the core samples are greater than or equal to *Eps* belong to the clusters composition with the nearest core samples, and mark the samples whose similarities with the core samples are less than *Eps* as noise.

4   Experiments and Results

4.1   Generate Feature Vectors

Experimental data sets are 8910 samples of malware from 113 families. These malware named by the *MD5* and *CRC32*. *MD5 (CRC32)* is name format. These samples provided by Antiy. At the same time they provide the dynamic and static information these samples produced in the process of automatic analysis. The information include system calls, registry operation, file create, delete, and so on. In order to improve the information of the 8910 samples, we will offer more detailed information for each samples. Including opcode, mnemonic and function calls. With the dynamic and static information provided by Antiy, we will release the data set is composed of 8910 samples in August.

In our experiment, we extract the information of the system calls from information documents from Antiy. Said in a document, the system calls information are shown in Fig. 4. The attribute *'type'* in node *<ACTION_CLUSTER>* said the corresponding system call. This node contains all time points and detailed information of the corresponding system call. In the process of feature extraction, according to the node information extract the system calls' sequences of each malware firstly. In this process, some malware have problems such as document formats, failed to extract system calls' sequences. Only 8793 samples complete this process.

After successfully extracted system calls' sequences from malware. We iterate through all the system calls' sequences, and store system calls into a database. We use

```
<ACTION_CLUSTER type="RegEnumValueW">
  <ACTION time="2014-04-07 01:40:41:966 +0800">
    <RETURN>0x00000000</RETURN>
    <MODULE>0x004747F0@0A6296CB4B719B3B714042591E4A36CD.0DA42060</MODULE>
    <REPEATED>0</REPEATED>
    <DETAILS>{"hKey": "0x000001C8", "dwIndex": "0x00000000", "cValueName": "0x00000013", "dwType":
    <TID>1300</TID>
    <RESULT>0</RESULT>
  </ACTION>
  <ACTION time="2014-04-07 01:40:41:967 +0800">
    <RETURN>0x00000000</RETURN>
    <MODULE>0x004747F0@0A6296CB4B719B3B714042591E4A36CD.0DA42060</MODULE>
    <REPEATED>0</REPEATED>
    <DETAILS>{"hKey": "0x000001C8", "dwIndex": "0x00000001", "cValueName": "0x00000006", "dwType":
    <TID>1300</TID>
    <RESULT>0</RESULT>
  </ACTION>
```

Fig. 4. The information of malware system calls

the order of the system calls stored in the database to determine each system calls' unique ID. Because of the operations of the database are simple, and emphasis on efficiency. So we adopt SQLite. The 8793 malware call a total of 152 system calls. Therefore, every malware produces a feature vector length of 152. Each system calls' corresponding ID is its location in the feature vectors. Then statistics the times of malware called for each system calls. Then generate feature vectors. For example, *RegOpenKeyExA* corresponding ID to 18. If sample *p* calls *RegOpenKeyExA* 100 times, the feature vector of *p*'s value is 100 in location 18.

4.2   SNN

First of all, according to the malware corresponding fixed-length feature vectors, using the Euclidean distance formula to calculate the distances between the malwares. Because the limit of laboratory equipment performance, so we have to save the distances calculated in texts. We create files for each malware to keep distances with all other malware. So each samples need to compute the distance twice to store in the different samples' corresponding text. To induce the time for writing texts, we only store the top ten nearest distances for each samples.

According to the calculated distances between all malware obtain each corresponding *kNN*. This paper obtains the *kNN* of malware when k = 10 and k = 20. Similarly, the files' name and the corresponding distances of *kNN* are stored in files. Then, calculate SNN similarity between any malware according to each malware's *kNN* files. On the basis of Algorithm 1, if both malware in each other's *kNN* list, statistics the number of malwares' shared adjacent. Finally create files for each malware which are used to store the malware *SNN* similarity with all samples.

SNN similarity between all malware are calculated, according to the different *Eps* we can identify malware's *SNN* density. In order to better display the effects of different *Eps*, in the case of k = 10 we take *Eps* = 1, 2,…, 10 to respectively calculated *SNN* density. The same for k = 20, we take *Eps* = 5, 6,…, 15 to respectively calculated *SNN* density. For each *Eps* produces *SNN* density, we set up *MinPts* value in the same way in order to select the core samples. Given in Table 1 is under the condition of k = 10, different number of core samples determined by different *Eps* and *MinPts*.

4.3   Clustering Results

The number of clusters from different *Eps* and *MinPts* are given in. When the Eps and *MinPts* rather smaller, clustering effect is poor. *Eps* = 1 and *MinPts* = 3 as an example, the largest cluster get from the proceeds of clustering contains nearly 1800 samples. And the smallest cluster only contains single-digit samples. When the *Eps* and *MinPts* are larger, the clustering effect is good. But good results based on the expense of a large number of samples. The final samples from clusters are only a few of all samples. An extreme example, when the *Eps* = 10 and *MinPts* = 10, the clustering makes four clusters, each clusters' accuracy reached 100 %. But the four clusters contains only 40 samples (Table 2).

Table 1. The core samples size with different Eps and MinPts in 10NN

MinPts Eps	1	2	3	4	5	6	7	8	9	10
1	8095	7431	6807	6142	5424	4715	3942	3206	2392	1611
2	8017	7338	6747	6079	5363	4663	3894	3158	2355	1571
3	7914	7196	6533	5910	5210	4521	3783	3036	2231	1485
4	7729	6907	6235	5596	4954	4300	3551	2800	2017	1294
5	7449	6460	5773	5163	4535	3864	3156	2406	1710	1055
6	6945	5880	5138	4498	3800	3171	2566	1900	1308	739
7	6149	4986	4201	3508	2888	2342	1811	1350	903	503
8	4977	3700	2853	2198	1705	1352	1051	792	542	305
9	2905	1758	1222	873	661	508	371	272	212	123
10	227	179	145	115	103	83	65	58	58	40

Table 2. The number of clusters with different Eps and MinPts in 10NN

MinPts Eps	1	2	3	4	5	6	7	8	9	10
1	451	316	284	274	266	271	282	275	275	254
2	475	328	306	280	280	291	293	278	275	252
3	534	376	337	321	316	316	309	294	287	255
4	652	462	408	385	360	353	340	315	282	227
5	834	574	475	435	414	393	361	307	257	189
6	976	650	541	485	446	386	334	271	204	130
7	1075	692	553	467	388	324	250	189	130	81
8	1164	693	495	356	257	188	134	95	71	38
9	975	401	219	129	86	61	41	28	21	12
10	92	44	27	17	14	10	7	6	6	4

We detailed statistics for $k = 20$, *Eps* = 5 and *MinPts* = 5, through clustering produced 414 clusters, of which about 50 % clusters whose samples belong to one families with a 90 % probability, nearly half of which whose samples belong to one families with 100 % probability. But according to the number of clusters and the number of real families provided by data set, each family's samples are assigned to at least one cluster. And if a cluster contains 100 % of the samples belonging to one family, the family effect is still good in the other clusters. This kind of situation is shown in Fig. 6.

```
Cluster No.6
24DA5767222658DADBDF885924078017(25878F10)  Backdoor.Win32.LolBot
23D3F31D9F4A552502F16632F82FCA38(C77887BA)  Backdoor.Win32.LolBot
2847E095F7B28C4B158615CC163DE8C9(443C4343)  Backdoor.Win32.LolBot
07F03ED7840704A0AE140B47A33CEC30(77FE0F1E)  Backdoor.Win32.LolBot
330C358F728F05D0C5AE7948A497F2D9(C6AF120E)  Backdoor.Win32.LolBot
8C97700AF03229F8F4DA48002A01FDAF(45DBA6E7)  Backdoor.Win32.LolBot
238CF69958629245B8BF6062D3B89A00(3A9019F5)  Backdoor.Win32.LolBot
27BE316C8C5E6767B0EDA650E5B6B631(F499A621)  Backdoor.Win32.LolBot
6A27730AE2553C29108AC129F101C602(8849ABA5)  Backdoor.Win32.LolBot
2C733E1429CB8C0859265063DCF881DE(43D3E8E1)  Backdoor.Win32.LolBot
2814FF8642E2E3FB1497064014E35478(9336F023)  Backdoor.Win32.LolBot
B5C72D6B765E59BCF53C6C2055BC2CFA(747880B6)  Backdoor.Win32.LolBot
270FFE4A41B006B888B8214A9100F582(C986CC6E)  Backdoor.Win32.LolBot
2EAB5879BE3777A824EE411EAAFFAEB6(C82CE96C)  Backdoor.Win32.LolBot


Cluster No.27
EB214A47FA7937246A9577AD984D052B(445A524F)  Backdoor.Win32.LolBot
00D5C9DFA6C249C9CE0537B70D58A27B(E2623D12)  Backdoor.Win32.LolBot
1118AAA97520DB1DF88229D7F331DA24(CE26EF7F)  Backdoor.Win32.LolBot
11E20C29153712AEB92AC7B5C435C784(D462B83C)  Backdoor.Win32.LolBot
B87F62FC683E332AA2D7BF3FC055AE76(97680C0C)  Backdoor.Win32.LolBot
8F3C660011ECCF39B6522FBB0FF4FD9E(E698C75C)  Backdoor.Win32.LolBot
B82B5E974E92AB43A08CD86EA8624E32(909DF7F0)  Backdoor.Win32.LolBot
933E889927D816143245BFD2E96F641C(10BE3A1E)  Backdoor.Win32.LolBot
D209BE7E75E57B2417D3B2530141E531(3A23F757)  Backdoor.Win32.LolBot
B24D01324F122F8F74C5F589AE177623(C39C7CEB)  Backdoor.Win32.LolBot
3A7293FC86FA441B2F8379EEB0D38BAF(CBEB21FF)  Backdoor.Win32.LolBot
D14599E3A7C1D952C74F9A0D0529775F(7B2E6743)  Backdoor.Win32.LolBot
```

Fig. 6. Backdoor.Win32.LolBot's samples in different clusters

5 Evaluation and Discuss

Based on SNN density clustering algorithm effect is good for sparse samples. And extracting system calls as feature vectors has high efficiency, simple algorithm. Using the system calls' frequencies can not only reflect to the different samples call the same system calls, but also there are simple to calculate, and can be done through simple statistical work. Due to the limited number of system calls, the amount of system calls often called by malware are more limited. So using system calls frequencies can generate fixed vectors. Usually the length of the vectors will not be too long, thus it can reduce the work to reduce the dimension from the high dimensional vectors and save the time. For incremental samples, it is unnecessary to clustering each time. We can quickly determine their families by looking for the nearest core samples' families. To sum up, after improving the algorithm, it can be used in the clustering analysis of malware in real environment.

According to the number of clusters the generated by clustering, we can find that the samples of a family are usually together into one or more clusters. Found by looking at the clusters generated by clustering, the algorithm effect is not ideal in the edge of the families. One obvious phenomenon is a small number of clusters mixed samples from two families. Reasons for this phenomenon may have (1) separately use system calls' frequencies. Do not rule out the possibility of different function with the same frequencies of system calls. (2) clustering algorithm based on SNN density on the boundary treatment effect is not very ideal. Two families closely may be connected by some intermediate samples, so it is difficult to divide the boundary.

Found in statistical accuracy, the families' names of samples provided by Antiy is not common. Families whose clustering effect relatively good less than half part of all families. And these families' samples labeled by Kaspersky and Microsoft on VT are belonging to the same families. And other families whose clustering effect are not very good labeled by Kaspersky and Microsoft on the VT determine the parts of samples of family does not belong to the family truely. So, in order to further determine the accuracy of clustering algorithm, it is needed to further screening of samples.

An in-depth analysis for the experimental results to determine *Eps* and *MinPts* is ours future work. And we will do other similar works to compare with this paper's work.

6   Conclusion

Malware clustering analysis is one of the important part of the current automatic analysis of malware. Fixed-length feature vectors formed by the system calls' frequencies are easy to obtain. It also makes the algorithm can be better applied to the actual. In this paper, through the calculation of Euclidean distance to determine actual distance of the samples. Then according to the distance of samples to calculate the kNN. Determined SNN similarity between any two samples by each samples' kNN. Finally by determining the appropriate parameters to product the core samples, boundary samples and noise samples. The algorithm improved the accuracy of the clustering of the malware. Laid a good foundation for the further malware automatic analysis.

References

1. Wang, H.-T., Mao, C.-H., Wei, T.-E., Lee, H.-M.: Clustering of similar malware behavior via structural host-sequence comparison. In: IEEE 37th Annual Computer Software and Applications Conference (2013)
2. Hu, X., Bhatkar, S., Griffin, K., Kang, G.: MutantX-S: scalable malware clustering based on static features. In: Proceedings of the 2013 USENIX Conference on Annual Technical Conference (2013)
3. Kostakis, O.: Classy: fast clustering streams of call-graphs. Data Min. Knowl. Dis. **28**, 1554–1585 (2014)
4. Biggio, B., Rieck, K., Ariu, D., Wressnegger, C., Corona, I., Giacinto, G., Rol, F.: Poisoning behavioral malware clustering. In: Proceedings of the 2014 Workshop on Artificial Intelligent and Security Workshop (2014)

5. Ye, Y., Li, T., Chen, Y., Jiang, Q.: Automatic malware cate-gorization using cluster ensemble. In: Proceedings of the 16th ACM SIGKDD International Conference on Knowledge Discovery and Data Mining, pp. 95–104(2010)
6. Perdisci, R., ManChon, U.: VAMO: towards a fully automated malware clustering validity analysis. In: Proceedings of the 28th Annual Computer Security Applications Conference (2012)
7. Bayer, U., Comparetti, P.M., Hlauscheck, C., et al.: Scalable, behavior-based malware clustering. In: 16th Symposium on Network and Distributed System Security (NDSS) (2009)
8. Iwamoto, K., Wasaki, K.: Malware classification based on extracted API sequences using static analysis. In: Proceedings of the Asian Internet Engineeering Conference (2012)
9. Yan, G., Brown, N., Kong, D.: Exploring discriminatory features for automated malware classification. In: Rieck, K., Stewin, P., Seifert, J.-P. (eds.) DIMVA 2013. LNCS, vol. 7967, pp. 41–61. Springer, Heidelberg (2013)
10. Cesare, S., Xiang, Y., Zhou, W.: Malwise: an effective and efficient classification system for Packed and Polymorphic Malware. IEEE Trans. Comput. 62, 1193–1206 (2013)
11. Cesare, S., Xiang, Y., Zhou, W.: Control flow-based malware variant detection. IEEE Trans. Dependable Secure Comput. 11, 304–317 (2014)
12. Hongbo, S., Tomoki, H., Katsunari, Y.: Structural classification and similarity measurement of malware. IEEJ Trans. Electr. Electron. Eng. 9, 621–632 (2014)
13. Jang, J.-W., Woo, J., Yun, J., Kim, H.K.: Mal-netminer: malware classification based on social network analysis of call graph. In: Proceedings of the Companion Publication of the 23rd International Conference on World Wide Web Companion (2014)

Analyzing Eventual Leader Election Protocols for Dynamic Systems by Probabilistic Model Checking

Jiayi Gu[1], Yu Zhou[1,2($\boxtimes$)], Weigang Wu[3], and Taolue Chen[4]

[1] College of Computer Science and Technology,
Nanjing University of Aeronautics and Astronautics, Nanjing 210016, China
{gujiayi,zhouyu}@nuaa.edu.cn
[2] State Key Laboratory for Novel Software Technology,
Nanjing University, Nanjing 210023, China
[3] Department of Computer Science, Sun Yat-sen University,
Guangzhou 510006, China
wuweig@mail.sysu.edu.cn
[4] Department of Computer Science, Middlesex University, London, UK
t.chen@mdx.ac.uk

Abstract. Leader election protocols have been intensively studied in distributed computing, mostly in the static setting. However, it remains a challenge to design and analyze these protocols in the dynamic setting, due to its high uncertainty, where typical properties include the average steps of electing a leader eventually, the scalability etc. In this paper, we propose a novel model-based approach for analyzing leader election protocols of dynamic systems based on probabilistic model checking. In particular, we employ a leading probabilistic model checker, PRISM, to simulate representative protocol executions. We also relax the assumptions of the original model to cover unreliable channels which requires the introduction of probability to our model. The experiments confirm the feasibility of our approach.

Keywords: Dynamic systems · Verification · Leader election · Probabilistic model checking

1 Introduction

Recent years have witnessed an increasingly booming interest in dynamic systems [1–4] since they have been widely applied in many fields such as distributed systems [5, 6], neural networks [4] etc. Accordingly, problems which have been studied in the traditional distribution computing are revisited in this new setting. For example, eventual leader election protocols have gradually become a focus in the dynamic system. However, to the best of our knowledge, most existing works related to leader election protocol design are based on static systems. Indeed, it is very difficult to design such a protocol/algorithm and analyze its properties with the presence of uncertainty in the context of dynamic systems.

© Springer International Publishing Switzerland 2015
Z. Huang et al. (Eds.): ICCCS 2015, LNCS 9483, pp. 192–205, 2015.
DOI: 10.1007/978-3-319-27051-7_17

Model checking is a traditional approach to verifying a design artifact against certain specification. Because the verification is conducted automatically, and a counter-example can be generated if the specification is unsatisfied to reveal potential mistakes in the design, model checking has gained wide popularity and thus become the mainstream verification technique [7, 8]. To cope with the underlying uncertainty, probabilistic model checking has been proposed. Generally here the transitions are extended with probabilities. It provides a rigorous methodology for the modeling and analysis of a wide uncertainty [7, 9].

Motivated by the above considerations, we adopt probabilistic model checking to analyze some properties, such as scalability and efficiency related issues, of leader election protocols for dynamic systems featuring a high degree of uncertainty. PRISM [10], a leading open-source-probabilistic model checker, is used to construct models of various categories of systems and analyze their random or probabilistic features. It can be applied in many fields, such as communication protocols, distributed algorithms or any other systems of specific subjects like biology. PRISM provides a simulator to generate sample paths through a designed model. Via simulator, one can clearly observe the executions of the model and the exact time of achieving the target designed at the beginning of experiment. Such mechanism is very useful for our experiments which will be introduced in the subsequent part of this paper.

The main contributions of this paper are as follows. Firstly, we construct a model based on the existing protocol [2]. Through the PRISM simulator, we can analyze the average cost of steps of electing a leader. Moreover, we also give a scalability analysis for the protocol which has not been discussed in the original work. Secondly, we extend the assumptions of the original protocol and consider the unreliable message transmitting in channels. Particularly, we add the probability to verify the hypothesis that the value of this probability is related to the efficiency of leader election.

The rest of the paper is structured as follows. In Sect. 2, we briefly describe related concepts of dynamic systems and give an introduction to the processes in the system and the way of communication in such systems. In Sect. 3, we propose a modified eventual leader election algorithm for dynamic systems based on the work proposed in [2]. Section 4 presents model design and two relevant experiments. We discuss related work in Sect. 5 and finally conclude the paper in Sect. 6.

2 Dynamic System and Assumptions

The concept of the dynamic systems is described, in a nutshell, as a kind of distributed system with processes entering and leaving the systems dynamically [3]. Many systems can be regarded as a particular instance of dynamic systems, for example, peer-2-peer systems [11], wireless ad hoc networks [12] and etc. In addition, as mentioned in [2], it is obvious that there are certain similarities between traditional static systems and the dynamic ones. Hence it is not uncommon that some researchers have been attempting to adapt the protocol designed for the static system for the dynamic system rather than to design it from the scratch. In brief, a dynamic system model can be extended from its static counterpart and the work needs to be done is to provide an adaptation of the protocol designed for the static model.

2.1 Processes in a Dynamic System

As defined in [2], the dynamic system consists of infinitely many processes, but the number of processes of each run is finite. In other words, no matter what the integer value n is, there are more than n processes for all runs. In contrast, for each run, there is always a bound on the number of processes. However, despite the bound in each run, a protocol has no access to that bound since it changes over runs. Because of this, there is no existing protocol designed for the model with an upper bound on the amount of processes which can be demonstrated in [5, 13].

Each process has its own unique identity. For example, a process denoted p_i means a process with its identity i. However, a process will be assigned with a new identity as a new process when it re-enters the system. Below we use some notations as follows:

$up(t)$: at time $t \in N$, the set of processes existing in the system. These processes have joined the system before time t and they have not crashed or left before time t.

$$STABLE = \left\{ i | \exists t : \forall t' \geq t, p_i \in up(t') \right\}.$$

$STABLE$ is the set of processes which will never crash or leave since enter the system. We note that this set is similar to its counterpart in the static model, i.e., the set of *correct* processes. Recall that in the static model, if a process does not crash during a run, it is considered to be a correct one; otherwise, it is considered as faulty. Moreover, in the static model, there is an integer n-f which denotes the number of correct processes and guarantees these processes not to be blocked forever. Similarly, in the dynamic model, a value α is proposed to define the number of static process and prevent processes from blocking forever. Therefore, we have the following correspondence between the static model and the dynamic model, i.e., n-f corresponds to α, and p_i corresponds to $i \in STABLE$.

2.2 Communication in the Dynamic System

All the processes in the dynamic system communicate with each other via the query-response primitive. Based on the existing work on the leader election in dynamic systems [2, 3], we describe such query-response primitive as follows:

(1) Once a process broadcasts a query message, then all the live processes in the system (including the sending process itself) can receive it.
(2) The process which has sent a query message will keep waiting until it has received "enough" messages from the other processes. It should be underscored that "enough" means a specific number α mentioned before.

More specifically, each process broadcasts a query message within the system. To avoid the condition that process blocks forever, only α responses are waited for the process which has sent the query message. (The number of α is defined previously.) During this period, we define a response that arrives among α responses p_i is waiting for as winning response, and similarly, the set of processes from which p_i has received a winning process to its last query terminated before or at time t is considered as $winning_i(t)$.

In light of the above considerations, the assumption regarding the query response pattern can be formulated $MP_{ds\psi}$:

In the dynamic system, there are time t, process p_i that $i \in STABLE$, and set Q of processes such that $\forall t' \geq t$, we have:

(1) $Q \subseteq up(t')$;
(2) $i \in \bigcap_{j \in Q} winning_j(t')$; and
(3) $\forall x \in up(t') : Q \cap winning_x(t') \neq null$.

Intuitively, after time t, there exist a subset Q of a universal set $up(t')$ of the dynamic system, and a stable process denoted by p_i. For every process in Q, p_i always belongs to the intersection of their $winning_j(t')$. And simultaneously, for every process existing in $up(t')$, the intersection of Q and $winning_x(t')$ is always not empty.

3 The Eventual Leader Protocol and PRISM Model Design

The leader election protocol is based on the existing work [2]. In our paper, we borrow the idea from the software engineering community and re-examine the protocol model through probabilistic model checking. Particularly, we utilize PRISM model checker to conduct the analysis which is lacking in [2]. Such an analysis allows us to investigate the protocol from a different perspective. More importantly, we extend the model by relaxing crucial assumptions previously made on the environment (i.e., the communication is reliable), and perform a considerably more detailed quantitative analysis.

3.1 Algorithm Introduction

Generally, the original protocol consists of four tasks. For details, we refer interested readers to [2]. In this subsection, we give a very brief introduction to these four tasks.

The key function of task1 is to diminish the size of the set of candidate leader denoted by *trust*. In task2, it reveals that when the process has received a *QUERY* message from other processes (besides itself), it will send a *RESPONSE* message immediately. In the original protocol [2], the paper posed a very strong assumption that the underlying channel is reliable, i.e., no message loss is allowed. However, in many cases, this is an unrealistic assumption as the underlying network could usually only provide best-effort delivery. Whether or not the *RESPONSE* message can reach its destination (the process which sends a *QUERY* message) cannot be determined in advance. Here we use the concept of probability to address this issue. Namely, we introduce a parameter named *ratio_suc* to evaluate the probability of sending a *RESPONSE* message and making it successfully reach to its destination. In addition, the responsibility of task3 is to update the *trust* set by comparing the *log_date* when a certain process receives a *TRUST* message from other processes. And it also supervises its *trust* set to ensure it is not empty. On top of it, the duty of task4 is to modify the value of leader according to its *trust* set.

To be more specific, a process p_i is always keeping such working cycle as follows.

---

while(true)
    broadcast $QUERY$ (i) to the whole system;
    wait until $RESPONSE(j, rec\ from_j)$ received from α processes;
    $RECFROM_i$ = the union of rec_from of those senders;
    $trust_i = trust_i \cap RECFROM_i$;
    rec_from_i = the set of the senders which send $RESPONSE$;
    if $trust_i$ is modified
        broadcast $TRUST(trust_i, log\_date_i)$ to the whole system;
    endif
endwhile

Algorithm 1. task1

---

upon $QUERY$ (i) is received from p_i
    $ratio\_suc$: send $RESPONSE(j, rec\_from_j)$ to p_i;

Algorithm 2. task2

Firstly, it sends a $QUERY$ message and then it keeps waiting until α $RESPONSE$ messages have been received. Next it updates $RECFROM_i$ by computing the union of the rec_from_i of all the processes sending $RESPONSE$. Afterwards the $trust_i$ should be modified by set intersection. Moreover, it updates its rec_from_i set based on the ids of those processes which have sent $RESPONSE$ messages. If this value has been changed, then process p_i should broadcast another message named $TRUST$ to the system so as that all processes in the system can adjust their leader accordingly as shown in Algorithm 3.

The operation of every process is the same as the way of p_i introduced above. After some time, a unique leader will be eventually elected once all trust sets keep stable (unchanged) and the identity of leader of all processes point to the same value.

In addition, each component of data structure of a process is introduced as below and its value should be initialized. We use the data structure of process p_i as an example.

Among all variables, rec_from_i is the set of processes where p_i receives $RESPONSE$ messages. $RECFROM_i$ is the union set of rec_from. And $trust_i$ is the set of candidate-leaders. Besides, log_date_i is a logical time defining the age of $trust_i$. Moreover, $leader_i$ is the leader of p_i.

All variables should be initialized as follows.

$$log\ date_i= 0\ ;$$
$$trust_i= \pi;$$
$$leader_i= i\ ;$$
$$RECFROM_i= \pi\ ;$$

```
upon TRUST(trust_i,log_date_i) is received from p_i
    if log_date_i == log_date_j
        trust_j = trust_j ∩ trust_i;
    else if log_date_i > log_date_j
        trust_j = trust_i;
        log_date_j = log_date_i;
    endif
    if trust_j == null
        trust_j = π;
        log_date_j = log_date_i;
    endif
```

Algorithm 3. task3

```
if trust_i == null or trust_i == π
    leader_i=i;
else
    leader_i=min(trust_i);
endif
```

Algorithm 4. task4

3.2   PRISM Model

Following the above descriptions, we model the protocol in PRISM. In order to demonstrate the procedure clearly, we assume that the system consists of four processes and the value of α is set to be three.

Data Structure The data structure in the model consists of global variables and local variables. For the former, we use four reply counters and a signal counter. Every reply counter corresponds to a process and its target is to count the number of received *RESPONSE* messages. And for the whole system, there is a signal counter aiming to monitor whether or not the leader has been elected. All variables should be initialized to be 0.

$$global\ reply\_i :\ [0..\alpha]\ init\ 0;$$

$$global\ signal :\ [0..1]\ init\ 0;$$

For the latter, the local variables of every process are classified into three categories. In the first category (shown in Listing 1.1), each variable ranges over from 0 to N and is initialized to be N. It should be noticed that N here is equal to $(2^n - 1)$ where n is the number of the processes in the system. Actually in our example, its value is set to 15 $(2^4 - 1)$. The reason will be made clear later. In the second category (shown in Listing 1.2), each variable is of Boolean value and the role is to classify whether or not the required messages have been received. In the third category (shown in Listing 1.3), every variable is a counter which is used to increase the values of execution steps or any other similar information. Therefore, $process_i$ in the system has its data structure as below.

Listing 1.1. First category

```
rec_from_i     :  [0..15] init 15;
RECFROM_i   :  [0..15] init 15;
trust_i          :  [0..15] init 15;
new_trust_i   :  [0..15] init 15;
num_i           :  [0..15] init 15;
a_i               :  [0..15];
b_i               :  [0..15];
c_i               :  [0..15];
```

Listing 1.2. Second category

```
query_i          :  [0..1]  init  0;
response_i1    :  [0..1]  init  0;
response_i2    :  [0..1]  init  0;
response_i3    :  [0..1]  init  0;
response_i4    :  [0..1]  init  0;
```

Listing 1.3. Third category

```
sign_i1          :  [0..1]  init  0;
sign_i1          :  [0..1]  init  0;
sign_i1          :  [0..1]  init  0;
sign_i1          :  [0..1]  init  0;
s_i               :  [0..6]  init 0;
log_date_i      :  [0..m] init 0;
leader_i         :  [1..4]  init i;
```

In the first category (shown in Listing 1.1), rec_from_i is a decimal number which in fact should be converted to a binary string. This string represents a set of processes sending *RESPONSE* messages. And similarly, *RECFROM_i* is the union of *rec_from* of the processes in rec_from_i, $trust\_i$ is a candidate leader set and new_trust_i is a temporary *trust_i*. Moreover, *a_i*, *b_i* and *c_i* are also temporary variables which store the variables participating in the AND and OR operations.

In the second category (shown in Listing 1.2), *query_i* denotes whether or not *process_i* has sent *QUERY* message. And *response_ij* represents whether *process_i* has sent the *RESPONSE* message to *process_j*.

In the third category (shown in Listing 1.3), *sign_ij* is used to record the steps, despite the fact that it has only two choices. *s_i* is the same as *sign_ij* which records the execution steps of every process. And *log_date_i* is a log variable used to note the logical time of *trust_i*. And obviously *leader_i* is the leader belonging to *process_i*.

Key Procedures. According to the given algorithm, we design PRISM modules for every process. The algorithm is shown in Sect. 3.1. It should be noticed that we assume that α here is equal to three for illustration.

We note that since there are no APIs or relevant methods supporting the set operations in PRISM, we translate two sets to binary strings and then use these two strings to complete the AND and OR operations. Evidently they are equivalent to the intersection and union operations of sets respectively.

Listing 1.4. calculating *rec_from_i*

```
[ ] (signal=0)&(reply_i=3)&(s_i=1)
->(rec_from_i'=(response_1i=1?1:0)+...+(response_4i =1?8:0))
&(a_i'=(response_1i=1? rec_from_1 : rec_from_2))
&(b_i'=(response_1i=1&response_2i=1)? rec_from_2 : rec_from_3)
&(c_i'=(response_1i=1&response_2i=1&response_3i=1)? rec_from_3 : rec_from_4 )&(s_i'=2);
```

In brief, Listing 1.4 demonstrates the procedure of calculating *rec_from_i*. Once the guard is satisfied, *rec_from_i* will change its value by means of given formula. The guard consists of three conditions: (1) whether or not the leader has been elected (denoted by *signal* = 0); (2) whether or not *reply_i* equals to three (denoted by *reply_i* = 3); (3) *process_i* keeps state1 (denoted by *s_i* = 1), and then *rec_from_i* calculates its value. For example, if *process_i* has received *RESPONSE* messages from *process_1*, *process_3* and *process_4*, then *rec_from_i* will change its value to 13 since *response_1i* is 1, *response_3i* is 4 and *response_4i* is 8 and consequently the sum of them is 13. Simultaneously, *a_i* will change to *rec_from_1*, *b_i* will adjust to *rec_from_3* and *c_i* will be modified by *rec_from_4*.

Listing 1.5. calculating *RECFROM_i*

```
[ ] (signal=0)&( s_i =2)
->(RECFROM_i'=max(max(mod( a_i ,2) ,mod( b_i ,2)) ,mod( c_i ,2))
+max(max(mod( floor (a_i /2) ,2) ,mod( floor (b_i/2) ,2)) ,mod( floor (c_i/2) ,2))*2
+max(max(mod( floor (a_i /4) ,2) ,mod( floor (b_i/4) ,2)) ,mod( floor (c_i/2) ,2))*4
+max(max( floor (a_i/8) , floor (b_i/8)) , floor (c_i/ 8))*8)&( s_i'=3);
```

The information modification regarding to *RECFROM_i* is demonstrated in Listing 1.5. It should be pointed that *RECFROM_i* compares with every digit of a_i, b_i and c_i, and then select the maximum of them as the digit. After that, it multiplies the weight of every digit and sums them. The variable *trust_i* has the similar solution.

Listing 1.6. broadcasting *TRUST*

```
[ syn ] (signal =0)&( s_i =4)&( new_trust_i != trust_i) &( log_date_j=log_date_i)-> solution1 ;
[ syn ] (signal =0)&( s_i =4)&( new_trust_i != trust_i ) &(log_date_j>log_date_i)-> solution2 ;
[ syn ] (signal =0)&( s_i =4)&( new_trust_i != trust_i ) &(log_date_j<log_date_i)-> solution3 ;
```

The algorithm regarding to *TRUST* has three branches (shown in Listing 1.6). Each time, one of them must be executed. Considering this trait, we use a synchronization sign to tackle this issue. The above demonstration can successfully fulfill the mission.

Listing 1.7. getting *leader_i*

```
[ ] (signal=0)&((CH1=CH2)&(CH2=CH3)&(CH3=CH4))->(signal '=1);
[done] (s_i !=6)&((CH1=CH2)&(CH2=CH3)&(CH3=CH4) ) | (signal =1) -> (s_i'=6);
```

The unique leader of the system will be elected once all leader_i points to the same objects (shown in Listing 1.7). And the time after the unique leader has been elected, it always keeps the status that "elected". Therefore, we design the solution above.

4   Model Design and Experiments

Usually, users are interested in whether or not the protocol can elect a unique leader in the dynamic system as fast as possible, so the efficiency is a crucial concern. Considering the characteristic of the system and analyzing several possible factors, we make assumptions that the time of electing a unique leader of the system is related to the number of processes in the system and also the channel reliability of processes among the whole system communicating with each other via sending query-response primitive messages.

4.1   Scalability of the System

Various factors may influence the efficiency of election one of which is the number of processes in the system. To verify this hypothesis, we attempt to design an experiment of three systems each of which with different number of processes. Besides, for each system, any other variables should be fixed, such as the probability of successfully sending messages.

In our experiments, we consider three systems with three, four and five processes respectively. For each of them, we repeat the simulation 100 times and then compute

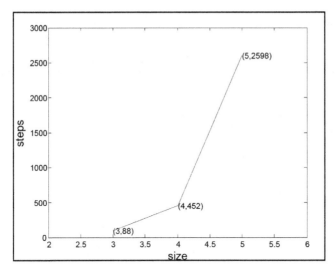

Fig. 1. Average steps of execution

the average steps of execution they spent on electing a leader. We set that the probability of sending *RESPONSE* messages is 1.0 because this time we only concentrate on the influence of the size of system rather than other factors. Based on the above setup, we record the results of each system as follows:

In Fig. 1, apparently with the system size increasing, the average number of execution steps that system spends on electing a leader grows rapidly. From the first experiment regarding the system consisting of three processes, the number of steps is around 88 on average. While adding a new process to the system, the average number grows to 452. When we continue to add another process, the result reaches 2598, approximately 5 times of the former one. In Fig. 2, we use a box plot to illustrate that with the increasing size of the system, the variance of the number of execution steps grows rapidly as well. Therefore we conclude that the size of the system must be controlled well. Otherwise, leader election in the dynamic system will be too costly to be affordable.

4.2 Unreliable Channels

As mentioned earlier, processes communicate with each other by query-response messages, and the probabilities of successfully sending messages, especially sending *RESPONSE* messages, are related to the efficiency of electing a leader in the dynamic system. In order to verify this assumption, we vary our model with three different probabilities capturing the channel reliability, i.e., the ratio of successfully sending *RESPONSE* messages among different processes.

Recall that the probabilities are introduced in task2. And the parameter denoted by *ratio_suc* means the ratio of successfully sending messages. We adopt three different values of *ratio_suc* - 0.5, 0.7, 0.9 - respectively to demonstrate the fact that the efficiency

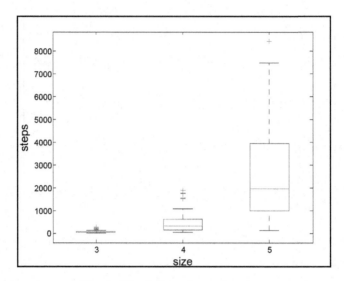

Fig. 2. Distribution of execution steps

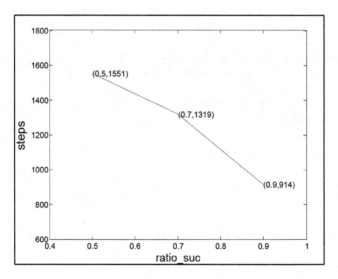

Fig. 3. Average steps of execution

of electing a leader is influenced by the probability of sending messages. This fact can be revealed by the number of execution steps, and the result is illustrated by Figs. 3 and 4.

In Fig. 3, it is obvious that the average steps of execution decrease smoothly with the increasing of probability of successfully sending *RESPONSE* messages. When the probability is 0.5, the cost of average execution steps equals to 1551 steps. And once the probability increases to 0.9, the cost diminishes to 914 steps.

In Fig. 4, we can clearly observe that the variance of execution steps decreases with the rising probability of successfully sending messages. Simultaneously the number of outliers also reduces with this rising. Because of the conditions demonstrated above, we can conclude that the ratio of sending *RESPONSE* messages successfully plays a vital role in the efficiency of leader election in the dynamic system and thus we should guarantee the stability of the communication channels in the system in order to improve the efficiency.

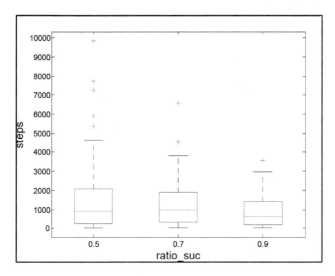

Fig. 4. Distribution of execution steps

5 Related Work

Most existing leader election algorithms are based on static systems [14–16], while in contrast, their counterparts relied on dynamic systems have attracted less attention. However, currently various applications are based on the dynamic system and thus the status of the dynamic system cannot be neglected any longer. The importance of leader election, which is one the fundamental building blocks of distributed computing, should be highlighted in the dynamic system.

Mostefaoui et al. [2] adapted an existing eventual leader election protocol designed for the static model and then translated it to a similar model suiting in the dynamic systems by means of comparing those two models' traits and adapting some specific features. In the paper, it was also theoretically proved that the resulting protocol was correct within the proposed dynamic model.

In [3], we also proposed a hierarchy-based eventual leader election model for dynamic systems. The proposed model was divided into two layers. The main idea in the lower part was to elect cluster-heads of every cluster while the target in the upper one was to elect global leader of the whole system from these existing cluster-heads. The concept of the model was to distinguish the important processes from all processes and then paid more attention to those selected ones in order to diminish the size of concerns and then improve the efficiency.

In addition, Larrea et al. [17] has pointed out the details and the keys to elect an eventual leader. In other words, to achieve the goal of electing an eventual leader, there are some significant conditions which must be satisfied, such as stability and synchrony condition-a leader should be elected under the circumstance of no more processes joining in or leaving out the system. The proposed algorithm relies on entering time stamp comparing.

Meanwhile, there is another line of work with regard to applying formal methods to protocol verification, for example [18, 19]. In [18], Havelund et al. employed the real-time verification tool UPPAAL [20] to perform a formal and automatic verification of a protocol existing in reality in order to demonstrate how model checking had an influence on practical software development. Although it is unrelated with eventual leader election, it demonstrates the feasibility of applying such technique to real world protocols. In [19], Yue et al. used PRISM to present an analysis of a randomized leader election where some quantitative properties had been checked and verified by PRISM. However, the work did not cover the issues for dynamic systems, which is the main focus of the current paper.

6   Conclusions and Future Work

In this paper, we have investigated and analyzed properties of eventual leader election protocols for dynamic systems from a formal perspective. Particularly, we employ PRISM to model an existing protocol, and illustrate the average election round and its scalability via simulation. Moreover, we relax the assumptions made by the original protocol and utilize probability to model the reliability of message channel. We also illustrate relationships between the reliability and the efficiency of election rounds taken by the revised protocol based on probabilistic model checking. In the future, we plan to extend our model and cover more performance measure such as the energy assumption to give a more comprehensive analysis framework.

Acknowledgements. The work was partially funded by the NSF of China under grant No.61202002, No.61379157 and the Collaborative Innovation Center of Novel Software Technology and Industrialization.

References

1. Yang, Z.W., Wu, W.G., Chen, Y.S., Zhang, J.: Efficient information dissemination in dynamic networks. In: 2013 42nd International Conference on Parallel Processing, pp. 603–610 (2013)
2. Mostefaoui, A., Raynal, M., Travers, C., Patterson, S., Agrawal, D., Abbadi, A.E.: From static distributed systems to dynamic systems. In: Proceedings of the 24th Symposium on Reliable Distributed Systems (SRDS05), IEEE Computer, pp. 109–118 (2005)

3. Li, H., Wu, W., Zhou, Yu.: Hierarchical eventual leader election for dynamic systems. In: Sun, X.-h., Qu, W., et al. (eds.) ICA3PP 2014, Part I. LNCS, vol. 8630, pp. 338–351. Springer, Heidelberg (2014)
4. Chen, S., Billings, S.A.: Neural networks for nonlinear dynamic system modelling and identification. Int. J. Control 56(2), 319–346 (1992)
5. Merritt, M., Taubenfeld, G.: Computing with infinitely many processes. In: Herlihy, M.P. (ed.) DISC 2000. LNCS, vol. 1914, pp. 164–178. Springer, Heidelberg (2000)
6. Guerraoui, R., Hurfin, M., Mostéfaoui, A., Oliveira, R., Raynal, M., Schiper, A.: Consensus in asynchronous distributed systems: a concise guided tour. In: Krakowiak, S., Shrivastava, S.K. (eds.) BROADCAST 1999. LNCS, vol. 1752, pp. 33–47. Springer, Heidelberg (2000)
7. Jha, S.K., Clarke, E.M., Langmead, C.J., Legay, A., Platzer, A., Zuliani, P.: A bayesian approach to model checking biological systems. In: Degano, P., Gorrieri, R. (eds.) CMSB 2009. LNCS, vol. 5688, pp. 218–234. Springer, Heidelberg (2009)
8. Bradley, A.R.: SAT-based model checking without unrolling. In: Jhala, R., Schmidt, D. (eds.) VMCAI 2011. LNCS, vol. 6538, pp. 70–87. Springer, Heidelberg (2011)
9. Kwiatkowska, M., Norman, G., Parker, D.: PRISM: probabilistic symbolic model checker. In: Field, T., Harrison, P.G., Bradley, J., Harder, U. (eds.) TOOLS 2002. LNCS, vol. 2324, pp. 200–204. Springer, Heidelberg (2002)
10. Kwiatkowska, M., Norman, G., Parker, D.: PRISM 4.0: verification of probabilistic real-time systems. In: Gopalakrishnan, G., Qadeer, S. (eds.) CAV 2011. LNCS, vol. 6806, pp. 585–591. Springer, Heidelberg (2011)
11. Zhou, R.F., Hwang, K.: Powertrust: A robust and scalable reputation system for trusted peer-to-peer computing. IEEE Trans. Parallel Distrib. Syst. 18(4), 460–473 (2007)
12. Vaze, R., Heath, R.W.: Transmission capacity of ad-hoc networks with multiple antennas using transmit stream adaptation and interference cancellation. IEEE Trans. Inf. Theory 58(2), 780–792 (2012)
13. Aguilera, M.K.: A pleasant stroll through the land of infinitely many creatures. ACM Sigact News 2, 36–59 (2004)
14. Gupta, I., van Renesse, R., Birman, K.P.: A probabilistically correct leader election protocol for large groups. In: Herlihy, M.P. (ed.) DISC 2000. LNCS, vol. 1914, pp. 89–103. Springer, Heidelberg (2000)
15. Mostefaoui, A., Raynal, M., Travers, C.: Crash-resilient time-free eventual leadership. In: Proceedings of the 23rd IEEE International Symposium on Reliable Distributed Systems, 2004, pp.208–217. IEEE (2004)
16. Bordim, J.L., Ito, Y., Nakano, K.: Randomized leader election protocols in noisy radio networks with a single transceiver. In: Guo, M., Yang, L.T., Di Martino, B., Zima, H.P., Dongarra, J., Tang, F. (eds.) ISPA 2006. LNCS, vol. 4330, pp. 246–256. Springer, Heidelberg (2006)
17. Larrea, M., Raynal, M.: Specifying and implementing an eventual leader service for dynamic systems. In: 2011 14th International Conference on Network-Based Information Systems (NBiS), pp. 243–249 (2011)
18. Havelund, K., Skou, A., Larsen, K.G., Lund, K.: Formal modeling and analysis of an audio/video protocol: an industrial case study using uppaal. In: IEEE 18th Real-Time Systems Symposium, 2p (1997)
19. Yue, H., Katoen, J.-P.: Leader election in anonymous radio networks: model checking energy consumption. In: Al-Begain, K., Fiems, D., Knottenbelt, W.J. (eds.) ASMTA 2010. LNCS, vol. 6148, pp. 247–261. Springer, Heidelberg (2010)
20. Behrmann, G., David, A., Larsen, K.G.: A tutorial on UPPAAL. In: Bernardo, M., Corradini, F. (eds.) SFM-RT 2004. LNCS, vol. 3185, pp. 200–236. Springer, Heidelberg (2004)

A Dynamic Resource Allocation Model for Guaranteeing Quality of Service in Software Defined Networking Based Cloud Computing Environment

Chenhui Xu[1]($\boxtimes$), Bing Chen[1], Ping Fu[2], and Hongyan Qian[1]

[1] Institute of Computer Science and Technology,
Nanjing University of Aeronautics and Astronautics, Jiangsu 210016, China
{xuchenhui_cd, cb_china, qhy98}@nuaa.edu.cn
[2] Central Washington University, Ellensburg, WA, USA
pingfu@cwu.edu

Abstract. Software Defined Network (SDN) has emerged as a promising network architecture that enables flexible management and global vision for network resource. The centralized control and programmability provide a novel approach to realize resource management for supporting end-to-end quality of service (QoS) guarantee. For real-time computing system and applications, cloud computing provider has to consider QoS metrics when they provide services for cloud user. In this paper, we propose an end-to-end QoS management framework in SDN-based cloud computing architecture. Depending on the characteristic of control plan separates from data plan in SDN, we present a QoS guaranteed approach with allocate resource dynamically for all cloud users by route optimization algorithm. Besides, we combine the queue technology to ensure high priority users request when there no candidate path calculating by routing algorithm. Numerical experiment results show that our propose framework can provide QoS guaranteed for cloud users' requirement.

Keywords: Software defined networking · Cloud computing · Quality of service · Queue

1 Introduction

Cloud computing is a model for enabling ubiquitous, convenient, on-demand network access to a shared pool of configurable computing resources (e.g., networks, servers, storage, applications, and services) that can be rapidly provisioned and released with minimal management effort or service provider interaction [1]. It is parallel and distributed system that provides services dynamically depending on service level agreement (SLA) of cloud computing provider and user. There are three fundamental service models offered by cloud computing provider that are Software as a Service (SaaS), Platform as a Service (PaaS) and Infrastructure as a Service (IaaS). The objective of cloud computing is provide high available, high reliable and elastic service that supported by data center management, virtualization, ability of massive data processing,

© Springer International Publishing Switzerland 2015
Z. Huang et al. (Eds.): ICCCS 2015, LNCS 9483, pp. 206–217, 2015.
DOI: 10.1007/978-3-319-27051-7_18

security etc. And virtualization technology is the core of cloud computing that allows user to access network resources by renting virtual machines (VMs) [2].

There are various network data on cloud as the result of Internet users have increased tremendously over the past few years. Some applications, such as multimedia, video conferencing and voice over IP (VoIP) need high bandwidth resource and computer power, for example throughput for real-time multimedia services, low latency (delay) for VoIP, or online gaming with low jitter. Cloud providers encounter several challenges when they provide services for many cloud users simultaneously [3]. One of the most important is satisfy QoS requirement for each multimedia user or each application user. In the IP network, a variety of techniques have been proposed to achieve preferable quality of service including overprovisioning, buffering, traffic shaping, the bucket algorithm, resource reservation etc. Over the past decade, the Internet Engineering Task Force (IETF) has explored several QoS (quality of service) architectures, but none has been truly successful and globally implemented.

Software Defined Networking (SDN) is a novel network paradigm that decouples the forwarding plane and control plane [4]. The most significant feature of SDN is to provide centralized control and global view of the network. Then it can realize fine-grained control for network flows and allocate the resource reasonably. It enables network as a programmable component of the larger cloud infrastructure and provides virtualization of the underlying network [5]. However, SDN has not been used extensively as the cloud computing provider. Therefore, we present a QoS management framework in SDN-based cloud computing environment, which take full advantage of centrality and programmability of SDN. And the network controller serves as service manager in cloud computing architecture, which offers resource reservation and on-demand bandwidth. OpenFlow is the communication interface between the controller and forwarding layers of SDN architecture. The forwarding layer can be composed of abundant virtual machines (VMs) acting as cloud providers. Our work is focus on SDN controller to implement bandwidth allocation and resource management for the requirement of cloud users.

We classify cloud user service traffic flows into QoS flow and best-effort flow which following shortest path originally. The QoS flow means that it needs more network resource and QoS parameters, such as bandwidth, packet loss, jitter, delay, throughput, must be guaranteed. The controller will run dynamically routing algorithms to calculate available route when the current link load exceed the load threshold. Depending on the requirement of users or application feature, we differentiate traffic flows into different level priority and combine the queue technique to guarantee the transmission of the high priority flow. Some numerical results are provided and analyzed to show that our framework can guarantee the QoS and satisfy the quality of experience (QoE) for cloud users.

The rest of this paper is organized as follows. Section 2 reviews the main work for QoS provisioning in cloud computing environment. Section 3 discusses the QoS implement framework we proposed in this paper and optimization scheme for route calculate. Section 4 presents the experiments verification for bandwidth allocation and resource reservation for cloud users. Finally, Sect. 5 concludes the research work.

2   Related Work

Internet users have shared amount of data such as multimedia data and real-time data on the cloud. Therefore, QoS is one of the essential characteristic to be achieved in the field of cloud computing and SDN. Service Level Agreements (SLAs) are established and managed between cloud service provider and cloud user to negotiate the resource allocation and service requirement [6]. However, SALs are mostly plain written documents from lawyers, which are static and published on the providers' web sites. It is restrict to achieve service satisfaction between network service provider and user dynamically.

Reference [6] presents an automated negotiation and creation of SLAs for network services through combining WS-agreement standard with OpenFlow standard, which deliver QoS guarantees for VMs in the cloud. Their approach allows customers to query and book available network routes between their hosts including a guaranteed bandwidth. Reference [7] proposes a unified optimal provisioning algorithm that places VMs and network bandwidth to minimize users' costs. They have accounted for uncertain demand by formulation and solving a two-stage stochastic optimization problem to optimally reserve VMs and bandwidth. Akella [8] proposes a QoS-guaranteed approach for bandwidth allocation by introducing queue techniques for different priority users in SDN based cloud computing environment. The flow controller selects the new path by using greedy algorithm. However, their approach is implemented in OpenVswitch [9] and they have not employed the SDN controller. Then their scheme lacks of centralized control and programmability. Besides, they will contribute much work in OpenVswitch to meet their design.

In order to implement QoS control, there are many innovation approaches have been researched in SDN. Reference [10] describes an adaptive measurement framework that dynamically adjusts the resources devoted to each measurement task, while ensuring a user specified level of accuracy. To efficiently use TCAM resources, [11] proposes a rule multiplexing scheme, which study the rule placement problem with the objective of minimizing rule space occupation for multiple unicast sessions under QoS constraints. Reference [12] proposed CheetahFlow that a novel scheme to predict frequent communication pairs via support vector machine and detect the elephant flows and rerouted to the non-congestion path to avoid congestion.

Some routing algorithms have been used to realize dynamical management of network resource. Reference [13] describes the two algorithms that are randomized discretization algorithm (RDA) and path discretization algorithm (PDA) to solve the -approximation of delay constrained least-cost routing (DCLC). Their simulations show that RDA and PDA run much faster than other route algorithm on average. Reference [14] described the distributed QoS architectures for multimedia streaming over SDN. They consider an optimization model to meet the multimedia streaming requirements in the inter-domain. However, they only employing dynamic routing to minimize the adverse effects of QoS provisioning on best-effort flows. It is possible that there are no enough available paths to be rerouted for QoS flows which will lead to poor performance for transmission of QoS flow in complex network. In this research, we select available path by routing algorithm when the current link cannot meet the users' requirement.

Particularly, we combine the queue technique to satisfy the requirement of high priority flow when there no candidate paths calculated by routing algorithm.

3 The Propose QoS Controller Architecture

The proposed QoS architecture is designed in SDN controller which provides reservation and on-demand bandwidth service. We send statistics request to forwarding devices by using OpenFlow protocol to acquire state information such as network load, delay, jitter, and available bandwidth of link, which are indispensable element to implement QoS control [15]. In order to mitigate the overload of communication between controller and switches, we create the address resolution protocol (ARP) proxy to learn MAC address. OpenFlow standard, which enables remote programming of the forwarding plan, is first SDN standard and a vital element of an open software defined network architecture. Therefore, our framework can run multiple routing algorithms simultaneously to allocate network resource dynamically in SDN controller. The design principle is that our architecture must be compatible with current OpenFlow specification which need not extra modification for switch hardware, OpenFlow protocol and end hosts. This approach ensures that our solution is practical with little extra effort to upgrade.

3.1 System Modules

The QoS framework our proposed in SDN-based cloud computing environment is shown in Fig. 1. It includes six modules to implement QoS control in SDN controller.

1. State Collector: Controller will send state request instruction periodically to OpenFlow enabled switches to collect the resource state. There are several state messages supported by OpenFlow protocol including port message, flow entry message, queue message etc.
2. State Manager: This function will process the resource statistics received from state collector. It will analysis the state massage and determine whether the link load exceeds the threshold or trigger reroute module to calculate new path.
3. Topology Finder: This module is responsible for discovering the forwarding devices and maintaining the connectivity through data received from switches. It will real-time update the topology structure when the network elements have changed.
4. Flow Classifier: This module will differentiate the traffic flow type depending on type of service (ToS) field in IPv4 header or source IP address when they get to controller. We classify traffic flows into QoS flow and best-effort flow. Furthermore, all traffic flows will be set different priority depending on cloud users' level.
5. Routing Calculation: This function run two routing algorithms in parallel depending on the performance requirements and objective of different flows. It will select the shortest path by Dijkstra algorithm for raw traffic and calculate feasible path for high priority flow according to routing optimization algorithm when their service request cannot be satisfied.

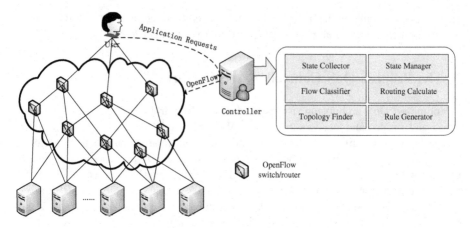

Fig. 1. System Framework

6. Rule Generator: This function will package the route and control information into flow entry and send it to forwarder devices.

In addition to this, we combine queue technique to guarantee high priority flow when there no candidate path calculated by routing optimization algorithm, which will lead to heavy congestion and packet loss. We will configure the multiple queues on forwarders to support resource reservation when the topology starts up.

To implement QoS control in SDN, we ignore the communication overhead produced between controller and forwarder devices and the extra cost from routing optimization algorithm. We assume that there exists multipath in the topology so that the rerouting module can select the candidate path. Our framework resolves three challenge problems. Firstly, we send the stats request message which supported by OpenFlow specification to the OpenFlow-enable switch to acquire the statistics that will be analyzed to determine resource scheduling. Secondly, In order to improve the efficiency of controller, we delete the original flow entry to update flow entry generated by route calculation algorithm instead of modifying the original flow entry directly. Finally, we map different level flow marked by flow classifier module into corresponding queue that had configured by OVSDB protocol. The workflow of our framework is described below:

- We will configure different level queues on each port of OpenFlow switches by using the OVSDB protocol. It is performed when the controller establishes an OpenFlow session with OpenFlow switches.
- When the new flow gets to network, the controller will choose the shortest path depending on Dijkstra algorithm supported by routing calculation module.
- Flow and port statistics are collected from the switches periodically through OpenFlow protocol. They are analyzed in state manager module to estimate the network condition.

- In order to mitigate the impact on best-effort flow, routing calculate function reroutes the feasible path for QoS flow when the state manager module detects the congestion or packet loss. The initial flow entry will be deleted before the new flow entry is installed.
- The QoS flow and best-effort flow are mapped into the different level queues configured in the step 1 when they fight the common path which cannot provide enough bandwidth for all flows.

3.2 Route Optimization

We will reroute the available path for QoS flow by using route optimization algorithm when there exist congestion on shortest path shared by QoS flow and best-effort flow. We consider the route optimization as a Constrained Shortest Path (CSP) Problem, which is the important part in select a cost metric and constrains where they both characterize the network conditions and support the QoS requirements. There are many QoS parameters such as packet loss, delay, delay variation (jitter), bandwidth and throughput to measure the performance of network. Hilmi et al. [14] described that some QoS indicators may differ depending on the type of the application. For example, multimedia applications that have sensitive requirement for total delay and video streaming are based on delay variation to guarantee the quality of experience. Therefore, in this paper we employ the packet loss and delay variations that are universal QoS indicators for a lot of service requirement as the constrained parameters.

We regard a network as a directed simple graph G (N, A), where N indicates the set of node s and A is the set of links. $R_{s,t}$ represents a set of all routes between source node s and destination node t. For any route $r \in R_{s,t}$ we define cost $f_C(r)$ and $f_D(r)$ delay variation as,

$$f_C(r) = \sum_{(i,j) \in r} c_{ij}, f_D(r) = \sum_{(i,j) \in r} d_{ij}. \tag{1}$$

Where $c_{i,j}$ and $d_{i,j}$ are cost and delay variation coefficients for the arc (i,j), respectively. The CSP problem is to minimize path cost function $f_C(r)$ of routing path r subject to a given constraint D_{max} as below,

$$\min\{f_C(r) | r \in R(s,t), f_D(r) < D_{\max}\} \tag{2}$$

We select the cost metric as follows,

$$c_{ij} = (1 - \beta)d_{ij} + \beta p_{ij} \text{ for } 0 \le \beta \le 1, \forall (i,j) \in A. \tag{3}$$

The variable $d_{i,j}$ indicates the delay variation for traffic on link (i,j), $p_{i,j}$ is the packet loss measure, and β is the scale factor.

We employ the LARAC (Lagrange Relaxation based Aggregated Cost) algorithm to resolve CSP problem, which follows Hilmis scheme [16, 17]. Firstly, it will find the shortest path r_C by Dijkstra algorithm depending on path cost c. If the shortest path r_C satisfies the constrain condition D_{max}, it will be the feasible path; otherwise, it will calculate the shortest path r_D constrained by delay variation. If this path does not satisfy the delay variation constrain D_{max}, there will no feasible path in the current network and the algorithm will stop; otherwise, it will call circulation iteratively until finding the feasible path that satisfies constraint.

It is shown that LARAC is a polynomial time algorithm that efficiently finds a good route in $O\ ([n + mlogm]^2)$, where n and m are the number of nodes and link, respectively. LARAC also provides a lower bound for the theoretical optimal solution, which leads us to evaluate the quality of the result. Moreover, by further relaxing the optimality of paths, an easy way is provided to control the trade-off between the running time of the algorithm and the quality of the found paths.

3.3   Queue Technique and Policy

There exist multiple types of cloud users on the Internet, which have different needs for network resource. Then we classify the traffic flows into two types implemented by flow classifier module that are QoS flow and best-effort flow. There are many methods to differentiate the type of flows such as the type of service, application type and IP address. We will allocate priority for different level cloud users by above method which will be mapped into corresponding queues. Furthermore, QoS flow was classified as two subtypes in this research, QoS flow-1, QoS flow-2 that represent different level priority. Similarly, it also can be divided into more subtypes depending on the real situation. The QoS flows having higher level than best-effort flow will enter the higher priority queue to acquire sufficient bandwidth resource.

For every router or switch, QoS configurations are assigned to queues, which are related to ports. Each port has a number of queues that have been divided into different levels, assigned to it (The number is about 8). Packets which are going to be forwarded are first assigned to one of these queues, and then getting forwarded from that port. Different QoS parameters, such as maximum and minimum bandwidth cap are configured to these queues. Combining the queue technique in QoS control approach, it can dispose the troublesome situation that there is no candidate path calculated by routing optimization algorithm and have to satisfy the requirement of QoS flow.

4   Experiment Validation

In this section, we introduce the prototype implementation and validation for our approach presented in Sect. 3. We test the emulation experiment in Mininet 2.2.0 [18] environment that will construct the network topology. The hosts created by Mininet can be regard as cloud provider and cloud user. The SDN controller is responsible for resource management and control by connecting the Mininet environment.

Our scheme is implemented in RYU controller 3.15 [19] which is a component based software defined networking framework and it provides software components with well-defined API that make it easy for developers to create new network management and control applications. The experiment topology is shown in Fig. 2.

It consists of eight OpenFlow enabled switches to build prototype network. In this test scenario, we use OpenVswitch 2.3.1 which is a production quality multi-layer virtual switch as forwarding devices and OpenFlow 1.3 as communication protocol between controller and forwarder. We define the H1 as cloud user and H2, H3, H4 is cloud provider that will provide service for H1. We will observe the performance of our QoS control approach by measure the bandwidth, packet loss and delay variation.

In order to simulate the actual cloud user application requirement, we customize iperf network test tool to generate traffic flows [20]. In this test scheme, we employ three test flows shown in the Table 1 as cloud users' application requirement. QoS flow 1 need more network resource then it is given highest priority among the network. The best-effort traffic is the background flow to change the congestion degree in test network. To observe the direct effect of QoS control on the flow performance, we use UDP to set specified bandwidth for two QoS flows and best-effort traffic.

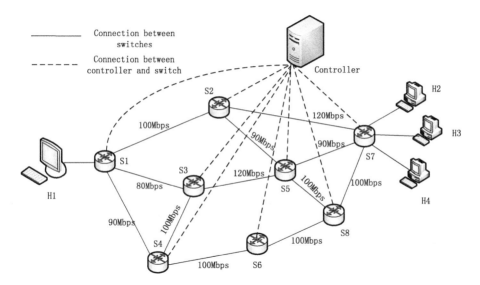

Fig. 2. Network Topology

Tab.1. Network Experiment Flows

Src	Dst	FlowType	Rate
H1	H2	QoS Flow1	50Mbps
H1	H3	QoS Flow2	40Mbps
H1	H4	Best-Effort	80Mbps

For QoS flow1, QoS flow 2 and best-effort traffic, they have different level priority and bandwidth requirement. For the purpose of achieving to congestion, we set specified bandwidth constraint for all links in test network. Firstly, H1 send the QoS flow 1 and QoS flow 2 to the corresponding destination hosts H2 and H3 while background flow started at 20 s. Initially, the controller will calculate shortest path for new flow by Dijkstra algorithm and install flow entries into OpenFlow switches. The total bandwidth of three traffic flows will exceed the link threshold when the best-effort traffic gets to network at 20 s. Then it will be congestion condition on shortest path and cannot guarantee the requirement of services without QoS control. However, our QoS control framework will reallocate the network resource for traffic flows to avoid the congestion problem occurred on shared path.

In the Fig. 3, we present a comparison of our experiment results by using the proposed approach with the ones without a use of the proposed approach. We implement our QoS control scheme at 40 s and observe the change of throughput. The throughput of two QoS flows and best-effort have increased and trended to steady state quickly. The routing algorithm calculates an available route for QoS flow1. Then QoS flow 1 can be guaranteed by selecting another lowest load path. Experiment shows that routing algorithm has not found appropriate route for QoS flow 2 because of the constraint of cost and delay. However, QoS flow 2 has higher priority than best-effort so it can be guaranteed by mapping into high priority queue. In general, our scheme ensures highest priority traffic firstly and tries to mitigate the effect on best-effort traffic.

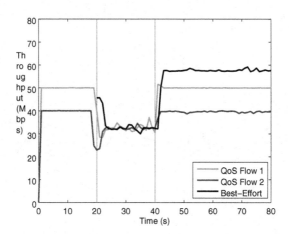

Fig. 3. Throughput for Two QoS Flows and Best-effort

The delay variation of three test flows is shown in Fig. 4. The QoS flow 1 and QoS flow 2 have suffered from great fluctuation when best-effort gets to network at 20 s. Three test flows keep jittering between 20 s and 40 s because of without our QoS control scheme. The delay variation of QoS flow 1 and QoS flow 2 has decreased after we turn on QoS control at 40 s. Although QoS flow 2 still exist fluctuation that influenced by best-effort. It is acceptable for many applications to satisfy the quality of transmission. The background traffic is limited to provide available bandwidth for QoS flow. We also evaluate the packet loss ratio among the implement for our proposed scheme in Fig. 5. Similarly, the phenomenon of packet loss has disappeared when QoS flow 1 reroute another path and best-effort is mapped into low priority queue.

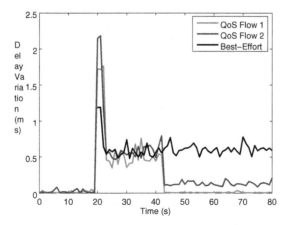

Fig. 4. Delay Variation for Two QoS Flows and Best-effort

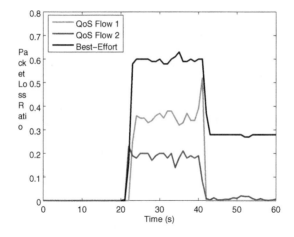

Fig. 5. Packet Loss Ratio for Two QoS Flows and Best-effort

5   Conclusion

We have studied a QoS-guaranteed approach in software defined networking (SDN) based cloud computing environment. SDN provides grate benefit for cloud computing provider to make the network easy to manage and customize. The cloud services usually need to be distinguished according to their services priority and requirement. In this paper, we differentiate the traffic flows into QoS flow and best-effort traffic for different service level. We propose the routing optimization algorithm to reroute feasible path for high priority flow when their service requirement cannot be guaranteed. Furthermore, we combine the queue technique to allocate suf-ficient bandwidth for high priority flow when the routing algorithm cannot find the available path. We have implemented and tested our approach in Mininet based on

OpenVswitch. Experimental results have shown that our approach can provide an end-to-end QoS guarantees for cloud user. In the future work, we will validate our QoS framework by OpenFlow physical switch in the large-scale network.

Acknowledgements. We thank the reviewer for their valuable feedback. This work was supported by the Industry-University-Research Combination Innovation Foundation of Jiangsu Province (No. BY2013003-03) and the Industry-University-Research Combination Innovation Foundation of Jiangsu Province (No. BY2013095-2-10).

References

1. Mell, P., Grance, T.: The NIST definition of cloud computing (v15). Technical report, National Institute of Standards and Technology (2011)
2. Wood, T., Ramakrishnan, K.K. Shenoy, P., Merwe, J.: Cloudnet: Dynamic pooling of cloud resources by live wan migration of virtual machines. In: 7th ACM SIGPLAN/SIGOPS international conference on virtual Execution Environments, pp. 121–132. ACM Press (2011)
3. Hoefer, C.N. Karagiannis, G.: Taxonomy of Cloud Computing Services. In: IEEEGLOBECOM Workshops, pp. 1345–1350 (2010)
4. McKeown, N., Anderson, T. Balakrishman, H., Parulkar, G., Peterson, L., Rexford, J., Shenker, S., Turner, J.: Openflow: enabling innovation in campus networks. In: ACM SIGCOMM Computer Communication Review, pp. 69–74. ACM Press (2008)
5. Tootoonchian, A., Gorbunov, S. Ganjali, Y. Casado, M. Sherwood, R.: On controller performance in software-defined networks. In: USENIX workshop on Hot Topics in Management of Internet, Cloud, and Enterprise Networks and services (Hot-ICE), pp. 893–898. IEEE Press (2014)
6. Korner, M., Stanik, A. Kao, O.: Applying QoS in software defined networks by using WS-Agreement. In: 6th IEEE International Conference on Cloud Computing Technology and Science, pp. 893–898. IEEE Press (2014)
7. Chase, J., Kaewpuang, R. Wen, Y.G. Niyato, D.: Joint virtual machine and bandwidth allocation in software defined network (SDN) and cloud computing environments. In: IEEE International Conference on Communications (ICC), pp. 2969–2974. IEEE Press (2014)
8. Akella, A.V., Xiong, K.Q.: Quality of Service (QoS) guaranteed network resource allocation via software defined networking (SDN). In: 12th IEEE International Conference on Dependable, Autonomic and Secure Computing, pp. 7–13. IEEE Press (2014)
9. OpenvSwitch: A production quality, multilayer virtual switch. http://openvswitch.github.io/
10. Moshref, M., Yu, M.L., Govindan, R., Vahdat, A.: DREAM: dynamic resource allocation for software-defined measurement. In: ACM SIGCOMM Computer Communication Review, pp. 419–430. ACM Press (2014)
11. Huang, H., Guo, S., Li, P., Ye, B.L., Stojmenovic, I.: Joint optimization of rule placement and traffic engineering for QoS provisioning in software defined network. In: IEEE Transactions on Computers. IEEE Press (2014)
12. Su, Z., Wang, T., Xia, Y., Hamdi, M.: CheetahFlow: towards low latency software defined network. In: IEEE International Conference on Communications, pp. 3076–3081. IEEE Press (2014)
13. Chen, S., Song, M., Sahni, S.: Two techniques for fast computation of constrained shortest paths. In: IEEE Transactions on Networking, pp. 1348–1352. IEEE Press (2008)

14. Egilmez, H.E., Tekalp, M.: Distributed QoS architectures for multimedia streaming over software defined networks. In: IEEE Transactions on Multimedia, pp. 1597–1609 IEEE Press (2014)
15. Kim, H., Feamster, N.: Improving network management with software defined networking. In: IEEE Communications Magazine, pp. 114–119. IEEE Press (2013)
16. Juttner, A., Szviatovski, B., Mecs, I., Rajko, Z.: Lagrange relaxation based method for the QoS routing problem. In: 20th Annual Joint Conference of the IEEE Computer and Communications Societies, pp. 859–868. IEEE Press (2001)
17. Egilmez, H.E. Civanlar, S. Tekalp, A. M.: An Optimization Framework for QoS Enabled Adaptive Video Streaming Over OpenFlow Networks. In IEEE Transactions on Multimedia, pp. 710–715. IEEE Press (2013)
18. Mininet: Network Emulator. http://yuba.stanford.edu/foswiki/bin/view/OpenFlow/Mininet
19. RYU: Component-based Software defined Networking Framework. http://osrggithub.io/ryu/index.htmlMininet
20. Iperf: TCP/UDP Bandwidth Measurement Tool. https://iperf.fr/

Research and Development of Trust Mechanism in Cloud Computing

Jun Xu[1(✉)], Feng Xu[1], Wenna Chang[2], and Haiguang Lai[3]

[1] Nanjing University of Aeronautics and Astronautics, Nanjing, China
Xuj023@126.com
[2] Yancheng Teachers University, Yancheng, China
nuanxin@syyz.com
[3] PLA University of Science and Technology, Nanjing, China
lite@263.net

Abstract. As a flexible security mechanism, trust mechanism is widely used in various complex application scenarios. The research on trust and its spread mechanism has become a new hotspot in the fields of E-commerce, Internet of things and Cloud computing. In this paper, we first deeply analyzed the relationship between trust mechanism and cloud computing security, and pointed out the existing problems of current models. We then surveyed some typical trust mechanism according to different mathematic theories of trust computation. We also summarized the latest research achievements of trust model and trust calculation method in cloud computing environment. Based on these studies, we forecasted the direction of further research on trust mechanism.

Keywords: Cloud computing · Trust mechanism · Trust calculation · Reputation · Cloud computing security

1 Introduction

Cloud computing is a new kind of computing model, which takes resource rent, application hosting and outsourcing as the core. Cloud computing has become a hotspot of computer technology quickly, and enhance greatly the ability of processing resources. However, the security challenges of cloud computing should not be overlooked. Only in 2014 occurredpan-European automated real-time gross settlement system 70 million user information was leaked. Home Depot company's payment systems suffered cyber attacks and nearly 56 million credit card users' information was in danger. Sony Pictures was attacked by hackers. Therefore, to make companies organize large-scale application of cloud computing technology and platform, we must thoroughly analyze and solve the security problems in cloud computing.

There is ubiquitous latent danger about data security and privacy because of cloud computing's dynamic nature, randomness, complexity and openness. The main security issues of the current cloud computing are how to implement a mechanism to distinguish and isolate bad users to refrain users from potential safety threat. Meanwhile, services and the quality of service providers in the cloud computing environment are uneven, and the service provider is not sure to provide authentic, high-quality content

© Springer International Publishing Switzerland 2015
Z. Huang et al. (Eds.): ICCCS 2015, LNCS 9483, pp. 218–229, 2015.
DOI: 10.1007/978-3-319-27051-7_19

and services. Therefore, it is essential to confirm the quality of cloud services and cloud services provider.

Current research to solve the above problems are concentrated on the study of trust and the mechanism of reputation aspect, whose basic idea is to allow trading participants to evaluate each other after the transaction, and according to all the evaluation information to each participant to calculate this participant's credibility to provide references about choosing trade object to the other trading partners in network in the future.

This paper is based on the key issues of trust mechanism to introduce its latest research achievements. Section 2 of this paper introduced the concepts of cloud computing. Section 3 analyzed relationship between the trust mechanism and cloud computing security deeply. Section 4 selected the latest and typical trust model to classify and review based on different methods of mathematics calculation. Section 5 to review separately based on trust mechanism's application situation of security problems in cloud computing layers. Section 6 analyzes current problems and prospects new research opportunities.

2 Cloud Computing

At present, although there are many versions of the definition of cloud computing, the most comprehensively accepted is the definition of the National Institute of Standards and Technology [1], they believe cloud computing has five indispensable characteristics: On-demand self-service, Broad network access, Resource pooling, Rapid elasticity, Measured service, and the cloud services are divided into 3 levels: IaaS, PaaS, SaaS. In order to achieve localization of computing resources, now Microsoft, IBM and other companies can be considered to provide a new service model of server container leasing services, which is called Hardware as a Service, HaaS [2].

HaaS, IaaS, PaaS, and SaaS are different in the functional scope and focus. HaaS only meets the needs of tenants hardware resources, including storage space, computing power, network bandwidth and so on, focusing on the performance of the hardware resources and reliability. IaaS provides pay-as, measurable resource pools function in heterogeneous resources environment, taking the full use of hardware resources and users' requirements into account; not only the integration of the underlying hardware resources does PaaS concern about, but also provides users with customizable applications services by deploying one or more application software environments. SaaS not only achieves the full advantage of the underlying resources required, it must also provide users with customizable application services through the deployment of one or more application software environment. Paper [3] summarizes a cloud service delivery model according to various embodiment ways of various service models, which is shown in Fig. 1:

Cloud computing is essentially a methodological innovation in infrastructure design, which has shared pool of IT resources composed by a large number of computer resources. Cloud computing model has significant advantages in information processing, information storage and information sharing, making dynamical creation of highly visualized application services and data resources available to users.

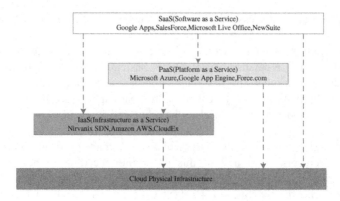

Fig. 1. Cloud service delivery model

3   Trust Mechanism and Cloud Computing Security

In the complex network environment, threats to security may be in the form of various ways. But generally speaking, the network security is intended to provide a protective mechanism, to avoid being vulnerable to malicious attacks and illegal operations. Basically all security mechanisms have adopted some trust mechanism to guard against security attacks. But the development of any mechanism is accompanied by the game between user and mechanism builder. With the understanding of the trust mechanism, a variety of attacks to trust mechanism have emerged.

The key issues included in trust mechanism are trust modeling and data management. The tasks of trust modeling are to design scientific trust model, describing and reflecting the trust relationship in the system accurately by using appropriate metrics. Data management relates to safety, efficient storage, access trust and their distribution in a distributed environment which is in the absence of centralized control.

Security and privacy are the most concerned issues of cloud computing users. With the emergence of more and more security risks, industry and academia have put forward appropriate security mechanisms and management methods. Its main purposes are to prevent cloud service providers from malicious leak or sell privacy information of user, collecting and analyzing user data. Paper [4] summarized security problems faced by cloud computing of specific services from technical perspective for the layers. Paper [5] proposed a Framework including Cloud Computing Security Service System and Cloud Computing Security Evaluation System.

Trust modeling and study of credibility management in cloud computing are still in their infancy. Study of Trust Management in the current includes the establishment and management of trust between service providers and their trust with users. Its main information security ideas can be summarized as the three-dimensional defense and defense in depth, forming a whole life cycle of the safety management whose main feature are warning, attack protection, response and recovery.

4   Trust Model

For different application scenes, many scholars used different mathematical methods and tools to build various models of trust relationship. This section will introduce common trust modes from the perspective of mathematical methods such as weighted average, probability theory, fuzzy logic, gray reasoning, machine learning, statistical analysis and analyze specific trust calculation.

4.1   Trust Model Based on Weighted Average

Trust model based on weighted average is the trust value to be formed by the weighted average, forming the trust evaluation from comprehensive views of different aspects, which may be divided into global trust model and local trust model. EigenTrust model [6] is the most representative incalculation model study of global trust model. Eigen-Trust obtain global trust value of each peer by iteration based on the reputation of peers' transaction history by using a similar Page Rank algorithm, as shown in Eq. (1):

$$\vec{t}^{(k+1)} = (1-a)C^T\vec{t}^{(k)} + a\vec{p} \tag{1}$$

Where, C represents a global trust value vector which is a normalized local trust value matrix $[c_{ij}]$, $\vec{t}^{(k)}$ is the trust value vector afterK iterations, $\vec{p}$ is global trust value vector of the pre-trusted peers ($p_i = 1/|P|$ if $i \in P$, otherwise $p_i = 0$), P is pre-trusted peer set.

PowerTrust algorithm [7] has improved algorithm EigenTrust mainly from three aspects: (1) confirm trusted peers collection reasonably. By mathematical reasoning, proved the existence of the power-law relationship among peers evaluation, namely there is a few Power peers, which formed credible set of peers by PowerTrust. (2) speed up the convergence of the iteration process. PowerTrust put forward the strategy of Look-ahead Random Walk (LRW), which made trust value polymerization rate improved greatly. (3) establish a dynamic applicable mechanism. Its disadvantages include: (1) It calculated the trust value without considering about the volume of transaction, which allow malicious users to accumulate trust by small transactions and deceive on large transactions easily. (2) there is no penalty to malicious behaviors.

PeerTrust [8] gives a local trust model, the trust value of peers is calculated only by the peers who have had dealings with them, without the entire network iteration, the mathematical description of the model is shown as Eq. (2):

$$T(u) = \alpha \sum_{i=1}^{I(u)} S(u,i) * Cr(p(u,i)) * TF(u,i) + \beta * CF(u) \tag{2}$$

Where $p(u,i)$ is the set of peers which trade with peer μ in the i-th transaction, and the credibility of peer v is $Cr(v)$, $TF(u,i)$ is the trust factor produced by the transaction with peer μ, α and β are weight parameter of standardized trustvalues, and $\alpha + \beta = 1$.

PeerTrust's advantages are: (1) the evaluation factors are normalized so that malicious peers can't submit too high or too low rating. (2) proposed a trust evaluation polymerization method PSM based on personal similarity to resist malicious peers' collusion attack. (3) established a trust calculation method by using adaptive time window to inhibit dynamic swing behavior of peers.

DyTrust model [9] presented a dynamic trust model based on the time frame, which takes the impact of time on the trust calculations into account, the authors also introduced four trust parameters in computing trustworthiness of peers, namely, short time trust, long time trust, misusing trust accumulation and feedback credibility. Paper [10] refined trust algorithm by introducing the experience factor, improving the expansibility of feedback reliability algorithms in Dytrust model. Paper [11] further improved the Dytrust model and enhanced the aggregation ability of feedback informationby introducing risk factor and time factor.

4.2 Trust Model Based on Probability

In the probabilistic trust model mainly use the maximum likelihood estimation, Bayesian and other mathematical methods to calculate the value of the trust.

Maximum Likelihood Estimation (MLE) is a method of probability-based trust reasoning, mainly for the probability model and beliefs model. In the circumstance of probability distribution of trust is known and the parameters of the probability distribution are unknown.

Despotovic et al. [12] presented a way of calculating the peers trust by using MLE, the algorithm thought: Supposing θ_j is peer j's honest interaction probability, $p_1, p_2,$ $\ldots, p_n$ is the peer has history interaction with peer j, after the interaction, $l_1, l_2, \ldots$ $l_k, \ldots, l_n$ is the probability that $p_1, p_2, \ldots, p_n$'s dishonest feedback evaluation to peer j, $P[Y_k = y_k]$ presents the probability of observing report y_k from peer p_k, it was expressed as follow:

$$P[Y_k = y_k] = \begin{cases} l_k(1 - \theta_j) + (1 - l_k)\theta_j \ if \ y_k = 1 \\ l_k\theta_j + (1 - l_k)(1 - \theta_j) \ if \ y_k = 0 \end{cases} \tag{3}$$

The likelihood function can be expressed as:

$$L(\theta_j) = P[Y_k = y_k]P[Y_2 = y_2]\ldots P[Y_n = y_n] \tag{4}$$

Where, $y_1, y_2, \ldots, y_n$ are independent reports of each other. Their experiment showed that good calculations can be accomplished even with 10–20 reports recovered. In order to improve the accuracy of the estimate, the author introduced the concept of peers liedegree, but not giving calculation of the peers liedegree, and estimate value got by this method is either 0 or 1, which is difficult to accurately portray the credibility of peers.

Bayesian approach is posterior probability estimate based on the outcome, which is suitable for the probability model and the belief model. The difference with the MLE is that it specifies the prior probability distribution for presumed parameters, and then according to the transaction results, using Bayes' rule to speculate posterior probability of parameters.

In Bayesian methods, Dirichlet prior probability distribution is assuming there are k kinds of results, the prior probability distribution of each result appears uniform distribution, i.e., the probability of each occurrence is 1/k. There is a total of n transactions, and each transaction gives the evaluation, wherein the number of appearance of i $(i = 1, 2, ..., k)$ evaluation is $m_i(\sum m_i = n)$. The posterior distribution of parameter p to be estimated is:

$$f(p, m, k) = \frac{1}{\int_0^1 \prod_{i=1}^{k} x^{(m_i + C/k - 1)} dx} \prod_{i=1}^{k} p_i^{(m_i + C/k - 1)} \tag{5}$$

Wherein, C is a preset constant. The bigger is C, the smaller is evaluation results 'expectation value to the parameters p. C is generally chosen as k. Bayes estimate expected value of the i-th evaluation results' appearance probability is:

$$E(p_i) = \frac{m_i + C/k}{C + \sum_{i=1}^{k} m_i} \tag{6}$$

Paper [13] proposed trust algorithm based on Dirichlet distribution. Using probabilistic expectations to express confidence reflect the uncertainty of confidence. Introducing time decay factor in the calculation process, it can suppress partially malicious users' malicious transactions after accumulating certain confidence value. But it didn't give too much consideration to the ability of the algorithm's resistance to malicious acts or to the recommendation trust and transaction volume.

4.3 Trust Model Based on Fuzzy Logic

Membership in the fuzzy theory can be regarded as the extent that body belonging to a trusted collection. After fuzzy evaluation of data, according to fuzzy rules based on these fuzzy data, trusted system inferthe trustworthiness degree of the body. Fuzzy reasoning process can be divided into three procedures: fuzzification, fuzzy inference and defuzzification (Fig. 2).

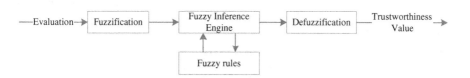

Fig. 2. Fuzzy inference framework

Paper [14] proposed a method of Fuzzy-based Trust Evaluation FTE, based on fuzzy reasoning, which has three input parameters in the fuzzy process: Weighted Trustworthiness Value (WTV), Opinion Weight (OW) and Agent Credibility (AC). When calculating WTV, consider two aspects of the data, direct transaction record and recommended transaction record. Supposing S is the amount of transactions, t_{val} was trading evaluation, n is the current time, and m is the evaluation time, calculation formula of WTV is shown as (7).

$$WTV = \frac{\sum_{s=1}^{S} \left[e^{-(n-m)/D} * \left((t_{val} - t_{\min})/(t_{\max} - t_{\min}) \right) * 5 \right]}{S} \tag{7}$$

D is the time decay function, fuzzy membership function value triangular fuzzy reasoning fuzzy when trust. After defuzzification, numerical trust value can be obtained. FTE algorithm enhanced the ability to resist against malicious behavior by adjusting WTV, OW and AC three input parameters. The downside is that: (1) There is no calculation or assessment of OW. (2) It can be challenging to choose the membership function with high efficiency. (3) There is no demonstration of the model's convergence.

FuzzyTrust [15] use the fuzzy logic inference rules to compute peers' global reputation. It has a high detection rate of malicious peers, however, the model did not consider the trust factors that affect the quality of the evaluation, and the authors did not demonstrate the convergence of the model. FRTrust [16] uses the fuzzy theory to calculate the peer trust level, reducing the complexity of the trust computation, and improves the trust ranking precision. Paper [17] puts forward the ETFT model by the combination of the evidence theory and fuzzy logic, which improves the adaptation ability of the model in the dynamic environment, and the aggregation speed of the recommendation trustis accelerated.

4.4   Trust Model Based on Statistical Analysis

It's based on statistical analysis method, depending on different application context by integrating multiple dimensions associated with the trust, such as historical information, contextual information, and reputation information to predict the trust relationship of high accuracy.

UgurKuter et al. [18] proposed an inference trust relationship based on probability network, and proposed trust reasoning algorithm SUNNY to calculate the trust value of social network. Jie et al. [19] presented presumed framework of social relationships by learning various networks, which synthesized social theory as a factor graph model, and validly improved the accuracy of reasoning the category of social relations in the target network. Rettinger et al. [20] resolved the problem of trust reasoning based on past observations and contextual information and proposed trust model IHRTM, which uses statistical relationship learning to obtain context sensitive information, including trustee's individual characteristics and situational state. However, the model due to lacking of adaptive learning strategy that it has some limitations in practical applications.

Khiabani et al. [21] propose to build trust model UTM by the integration of history, recommendations, and other contextual information to calculate the scores between individuals, which can be efficiently used for low-interaction environments.

4.5 Trust Model Based on Machine Learning

Methods based on machine learning can be divided into two categories: forecasting methods of supervision trusts and unsupervised trusts forecasting methods. The main idea is to use machine to learn methods to dynamically generate rules, then combining fuzzy reasoning and rule-based reasoning to obtain the trust level of the entity.

Supervision Trusts prediction method first extracts features from the source data, and then based on these features of the training binary classifier. Liu et al. [22] presented a classification method to deal with the trust prediction problem. However, the results of the assessment are absolute, that is, trust and not, and the uncertainty of trust is ignored. Zolfagharet al. [23] proposed the formation of trust incentive framework, and use data mining and classification method for the formation of the trust, the trust proposed framework consists of knowledge, association, similarity, self-confidence and other factors.

Unsupervised trust prediction methods are mostly based on trust evolution, which depends on the trust relationship already existed in the user; but when the trust relationship is very sparse, trust evolution may fail. Tang et al. [24] research trust prediction through exploration homogeneous effect, and build trust forecasting model hTrustby using low- rank matrix factorization technique. Ref. [25] take the impact of sociological theory on the trust relationship predict into account, through the study of social class theory and homogeneity theory to obtain the development law of trust relationship, and then build a trust relationship prediction model to solve the data sparseness problem, increasing the precision of trust relationship forecast.

5 Trust Model in Cloud Computing

Cruz et al. [26] have summed up the security problem in cloud computing, which includes the infrastructure security, data security, communication security and access control. Trust management has become the bridge of interaction entities in cloud computing. This section describes the application of trust model in the aspects of virtual machine security, user security, application reliability and service quality.

5.1 Trust Model in Virtual Machine

In the cloud infrastructure, the virtual machine is widely used as the carrier of the user data, and how to guarantee the credibility of the virtual machine becomes the key means to ensure the cloud computing security. Because of the trust evidence sources of cloud computing nodes are usually insufficient, and during the attestation process sensitive information of the involved nodes is easily exposed. [27] presented a trust-based trustworthiness attestation model (TBTAM) for virtual machine, when calculate the trustworthiness of virtual machine, TBTAM considers both direct trustworthiness and feedback trustworthiness, and then uses the group-signature method for proof protection, which protects the privacy of nodes and reduces the attack possibilities. Their experimental results indicate that the model can validly identify spiteful peers and protect privacy of virtual machine peers during the running process.

5.2   Trusted Service Mechanism for Cloud Computing

Due the uncertainty and the reliability of the application in cloud computing. Tan et al. [28] presented a cloud workflow trust model TWFS service-oriented scheduling to meet the requirements of ES integration. They proposed balance strategies to help users to balance different requirements, including trust evaluation, execution time, execution cost of fuzzy multi-objective problem. The key idea of the TWFS algorithm is to find the optimum solution with the deadline constraint by adjusting the weights of time and cost.

When assign the weight of recommendation trust, the similarity between users a and i was computed by the Pearson correlation coefficient (PCC) as follows:

$$\omega_{ai} = \frac{\sum_{j \in S} (v_{aj} - \overline{v_a})(v_{ij} - \overline{v_i})}{\sqrt{\sum_{j \in S} (v_{aj} - \overline{v_a})^2 + (v_{ij} - \overline{v_i})^2}} \tag{8}$$

where $avg(v_i)$ is the average rating by user i.

Using max-min as the operator, when calculate the trust evaluation of the service. The calculation of the execution time and the execution price is similar to that of this.

TWFS can form an optimum workflow application while meeting different constraints from users. Meanwhile, it puts a general trust metric scheduling algorithm to consider direct trust and recommendation trust. However, TWFS does not consider the dynamic of the cloud environment, and be vulnerable to malicious attacks.

5.3   Services Quality Evaluation

Jagpreet et al. [29] proposed a trust model to estimate service providers to help users choose the most dependable service provider and service, the model based on feedback trust by introducing three different types of trust (namely, interaction-based trust, compliance-based trust and recommendation-based trust.), According to its priority assigned different weights, in order to calculate the trust service providers. However, their paper didn't introduce how the weight is distributed, and the model is lack of dynamic.

For cloud computing environment dynamic presence of trust issues, paper [30] proposed a trust model based on double excitation and detection of deception (CCIDTM). The model proposes a set of cloud computing services property evaluation, and used the service attribute weight factor to measure the service attribute relative service evaluation of the important degree. This model introduced a dynamic trust mechanism trust decay with time, the establishment of the service provider service user behavior and evaluate the behavior of a double incentive. It presents a conspiracy to deceive detection algorithm to improve dynamic adaptability and comprehensive evaluation model. Compared with the existing trust model, the model assessment results closer to service provider of real service behavior, can effectively resist all kinds of malicious conduct attacks, showed good robustness, but the model does not consider the quality of composite services in cloud computing environment.

5.4 User Trust Evaluation

In order to distinguish user behavior from cloud computing environment, the paper [31] proposed a cloud computing trust model based on user behavior called Fuzzy ART. To ensure the identity and behavior of users in the system, a softcomputing technique is proposed which an unsupervised learning technique to classify the virtual clients based on their behavior.

To ensure cloud security in complex and dynamic environment, LVet al. [32] effectively confirmed the untrusted cloud terminal users and correctly analyzing their abnormal behavior. This paper adopted the method of fuzzy analytic network process (FANP) based on triangular fuzzy numbers, which can reflect the fuzziness of expert evaluation through using fuzzy numbers, and weaken the subjectivity of simply using ANP. However, the node trust value of the model has a large time complexity, and is not suitable for large-scale distributed environment, and the algorithm is not effective and the lack of convincing.

To solve the increasingly prominent security issues during the process of multi-tenants visit in cloud computing, the paper [33] proposed a security access control model based on user behavior trust. The model obtained the user's behavior evidence through real-time monitoring of massive users' access behavior in the cloud. The comprehensive evaluation of user's behavior trust based on fuzzy consistent matrix effectively improves the operation efficiency of the model, eliminating the complex judgment matrix adjustment process. It established the dynamic allocation mechanism of user service level based on behavior trust level, not only can effectively control the users' non security access behavior, protecting the important resource in the cloud, but also establish long-term trust mechanism between the users and the cloud service by the real-time feedback of user behavior trust status.

6 Summary and Prospect

The research of trust management system is from centralized trust to distributed trust relationship, from static to dynamic trust model, from single to multiple input factor model, from evidence theory model to a variety of mathematical model. It can be said that the study of trust relationship is a very active direction.

However, through summary we can see that the research on the trust mechanism has the following problems in the theory and the realization: (1) The current study of trust mechanism is lack of risk mechanism and performance evaluation criteria of the unified trust model. (2) In the existing research, the performances of the trust model are mostly evaluated by the method of simulating experiment, and there is no real performance evaluation.

Through this paper, we can see that in the cloud computing and other new computing environment, various security requirements and application mode have put forward new challenges to the trust mechanism. With the emergence of new computing models and computing environments, such as cloud computing, internet of things and so on, refining scientific problems under the new situation of trust mechanism and carrying on the research have more urgent significance.

At the same time, it should also continue to explore new models suitable for describing the dynamic trust relationship, combining knowledge of other subjects, such as machine learning, artificial intelligence, etc.

Acknowledgments. This work is supported by the China Aviation Science Foundation (NO. 20101952021) and the Fundamental Research Funds for the Central Universities (NO. NZ2013306).

References

1. Mell, P., Grance, T.: The NIST definition of cloud computing. Nat. Inst. Stand. Technol. **53**, 50 (2009)
2. Chuang, L., Wen-Bo, S.: Cloud Computing Security: Architecture, Mechanism and Modeling. Chin. J. Comput. **36**, 1765–1784 (2013) (in Chinese)
3. Almorsy, M., Grundy, J., Müller, I.: An analysis of the cloud computing security problem. In: Proceedings of APSEC 2010 Cloud Workshop, Sydney, Australia, 30 November 2010
4. Subashini, S., Kavitha, V.: A survey on security issues in service delivery models of cloud computing. J. Netw. Comput. Appl. **34**, 1–11 (2011)
5. Feng, D.G., Zhang, M., Zhang, Y., Zhen, X.U.: Study on cloud computing security. J. Softw. **22**, 71–83 (2011)
6. Kamvar, S.D., Schlosser, M.T., Garcia-Molina, H.: The Eigentrust algorithm for reputation management in P2P networks. In: Proceedings of the 12th International World Wide Web Conference, WWW 2003 (2003)
7. Kai, H., Zhou, R.: PowerTrust: a robust and scalable reputation system for trusted peer-to-peer computing. IEEE Trans. Parallel Distrib. Syst. **18**, 460–473 (2007)
8. Li, X.: Liu, L.: PeerTrust: supporting reputation-based trust for peer-to-peer electronic communities. IEEE Trans. Knowl. Data Eng. **16**, 843–857 (2004)
9. Jun-Sheng, C., Huai-Ming, W.: DyTrust: A time-frame based dynamic trust model for P2P systems. Chin. J. Comput. **29**, 1301–1307 (2006) (in Chinese)
10. Shao-Jie. W., Hong-Song, C.: An improved DyTrust trust model. J. Univ. Sci. Technol. Beijing, **30**, 685–689 (2008) (in Chinese)
11. Zhi-Guo, Z., Qiong, C., Min-Sheng, T.: Trust model based on improved DyTrust in P2P network. Comput. Technol. Dev. 174–177 (2014) (in Chinese)
12. Despotovic, Z., Aberer, K.: Maximum likelihood estimation of peers; performance in P2P networks. In: The Second Workshop on the Economics of Peer-to-Peer Systems (2004)
13. Haller, J., Josang, A.: Dirichlet reputation systems. In: 2012 Seventh International Conference on Availability, Reliability and Security, 112–119 (2007)
14. Schmidt, S., Steele, R., Dillon, T.S., Chang, E.: Fuzzy trust evaluation and credibility development in multi-agent systems. Appl. Soft Comput. **7**, 492–505 (2007)
15. Song, S., Kai, H., Zhou, R., Kwok, Y.K.: Trusted P2P transactions with fuzzy reputation aggregation. IEEE Internet Comput. **2005**, 24–34 (2005)

16. Javanmardi, S., Shojafar, M., Shariatmadari, S., Ahrabi, S.S.: FRTRUST: a fuzzy reputation based model for trust management in semantic P2p grids. Int. J. Grid Util. Comput. **6**, (2014)
17. Tian, C., Yang, B.: A D-S evidence theory based fuzzy trust model in file-sharing P2P networks. Peer Peer Netw. Appl. **7**, 332–345 (2014)
18. Kuter, U.: Using probabilistic confidence models for trust inference in web-based social networks. ACM Trans. Int. Technol. Toit Homepage **10**, 890–895 (2010)
19. Tang, J., Lou, T., Kleinberg, J.: Inferring social ties across heterogeneous networks. In: WSDM 2012, 743–752 (2012)
20. Rettinger, A., Nickles, M., Tresp, V.: Statistical relational learning of trust. Mach. Learn. **82**, 191–209 (2011)
21. Khiabani, H., Idris, N.B., Manan, J.L.A.: A Unified trust model for pervasive environments – simulation and analysis. KSII Trans. Int. Inf. Syst. (TIIS) **7**, 1569–1584 (2013)
22. Liu, H., Lim, E.P., Lauw, H.W., Le, M.T., Sun, A., Srivastava, J., Kim, Y.A.: Predicting trusts among users of online communities: an epinions case study. In: Ec 2008 Proceedings of ACM Conference on Electronic Commerce, pp. 310–319 (2008)
23. Zolfaghar, K., Aghaie, A.: A syntactical approach for interpersonal trust prediction in social web applications: Combining contextual and structural data. Knowl. Based Syst. **26**, 93–102 (2012)
24. Tang, J., Gao, H., Hu, X.: Exploiting homophily effect for trust prediction. In: Proceedings of the Sixth ACM International Conference on Web Search and Data Mining, 53–62 (2013)
25. Ying, Wang, Xin, Wang, Wan-Li, Zuo: Trust prediction modeling based on social theories. J. Softw. **12**, 2893–2904 (2014). (in Chinese)
26. Cruz, Z.B., Fernández-Alemán, J.L., Toval, A.: Security in cloud computing: a mapping study. Comput. Sci. Inf. Syst. **12**, 161–184 (2015)
27. Zheng-Ji, Z., Li-Fa, W., Zheng, H.: Trust based trustworthiness attestation model of virtual machines for cloud computing. J. Southeast Univ. (Nat. Sci. Ed.) **45**(1), 31–35 (2015) (in Chinese)
28. Tan, W., Sun, Y., Li, L.X., Lu, G.Z., Wang, T.: A trust service-oriented scheduling model for workflow applications in cloud computing. IEEE Syst. J. **8**, 868–878 (2014)
29. Sidhu, J., Singh, S.: Peers feedback and compliance based trust computation for cloud computing. In: Mauri, J.L., Thampi, S.M., Rawat, D.B., Jin, B. (eds.) Security in Computing and Communications, vol. 467, pp. 68–80. Springer, Heidelberg (2014)
30. Xiao-Lan, X., Liang, L., Peng, Z.: Trust model based on double incentive and deception detection for cloud computing. J. Electron. Inf. Technol. **34**(4), 812–817 (2012) (in Chinese)
31. Jaiganesh, M., Aarthi, M., Kumar, A.V.A.: Fuzzy ART-based user behavior trust in cloud computing. In: Suresh, L.P., Dash, S.S., Panigrahi, B.K. (eds.) Artificial Intelligence and Evolutionary Algorithms in Engineering Systems, vol. 324, pp. 341–348. Springer, India (2015)
32. Yan-Xia, L., Li-Qin, T., Shan-Shan, S.: Trust evaluation and control analysis of FANP-based user behavior in cloud computing environment. Comput. Sci. **40**, 132–135 (2013) (in Chinese)
33. Guo-Feng, S., Chang-Yong, L.: A security access control model based on user behavior trust under cloud environment. Chin. J. Manag. Sci. **52**, 669–676 (2013) (in Chinese)

Analysis of Advanced Cyber Attacks
with Quantified ESM

Blaž Ivanc[1,2(✉)] and Tomaž Klobučar[1]

[1] Jozef Stefan Institute, Ljubljana, Slovenia
blaz.ivanc@ijs.si, tomaz@e5.ijs.si
[2] Jozef Stefan International Postgraduate School,
Ljubljana, Slovenia

Abstract. Advanced cyber attacks represent a serious threat to a critical infrastructure. Attack modeling is a way to timely recognize weaknesses and potential threat performances, which in practice want to be avoided. In order to improve attack modeling we defined an attack tree-based model named the Enhanced structured model (ESM). The ESM enables better understanding of attack implementation, which results in improved identification of security weaknesses and analysis of the existing security policy. The ESM is also very suitable as a tool to impart knowledge in the field of advanced cyber security in terms of offensive security. To enable analysts more credible basis for decision support and even more effective transfer of knowledge and new insights into the educational process we present in this paper a quantification of the ESM.

Keywords: Attack vector · Enhanced structural model · Expert assessment · Malicious software code · Vulnerability

1 Introduction

Critical infrastructure with many intertwining technologies represents a big area of possible implementations of the attacks. Because of its importance, it is interesting for many different attackers whose motives vary widely. The components of availability and integrity are essential in cyber security of critical infrastructure. The design and maintenance of adequate cyber security are thus crucial. Considering all of the above we establish that the advanced cyber attacks represent a serious, persistent and real threat to a critical infrastructure.

Attack modeling is essential in security design and assessments in critical infrastructure. It is a way to timely recognize weaknesses and potential threat performances, which in practice want to be avoided. Attack modeling techniques can be divided into static or structural and dynamic or behavioral models [1]. Based on previous categorization, models can be divided into attack tree models which are the structural type of models and petri-nets [2].

In order to improve attack modeling in the critical infrastructure we defined an attack tree-based model named the Enhanced structured model (ESM) [3, 4]. The model enables better understanding of attack implementation, which results in improved

© Springer International Publishing Switzerland 2015
Z. Huang et al. (Eds.): ICCCS 2015, LNCS 9483, pp. 230–243, 2015.
DOI: 10.1007/978-3-319-27051-7_20

identification of security weaknesses and analysis of the existing security policy. The objective of the model was to offer analysts an efficient tool for attack modeling. The ESM is also very suitable as a tool to impart knowledge in the field of advanced information security in terms of offensive security.

To enable analysts more credible basis for decision support and even more effective transfer of knowledge and new insights into the educational process we present in this paper a quantification of the ESM.

The sections in the paper are further organized as follows: Sect. 2 is the background, inter alia, introducing attack modeling, the ESM model and CVSS framework. Section 3 presents the quantification of the ESM model with an additional explanation of the rules for applying the attribute values and the purpose of quantification. The validation and an example of the use of the ESM can be found in Sect. 4. In Sect. 5 an overview of recent attack trees as a basic structural technique for attack modeling is given. Section 6 is a discussion followed by a conclusion in the last section.

2 Background

This section briefly presents the basis for further understanding. Thus, first of all, we introduce the purpose of attack modeling followed by the brief presentation of the ESM model and CVSS standard.

2.1 The Purpose of Attack Modeling

Attack modeling is one of the most important methods for detecting weak points of information systems and networks. It raises security awareness and helps us to prepare for possible scenarios which we would like to avoid in practice. If we prepare ourselves for potential security incidents, we can adequately protect corporate environment and make sure the incidents do not occur.

Yan et al. state that the flaw hypothesis and the attack trees are two main approaches in security testing and engineering [5]. In the attack modeling field, two approaches have been developed, e.g. attack trees and stochastic models [6]. The attack tree is a formal structured method for attack modeling [7].The attack tree is the basis for some other models, such as the protection tree [8] and the defense tree [9].

2.2 Enhanced Structural Model

In an effort to improve attack modeling in a critical infrastructure and remedy certain weaknesses of the existing models, we developed a model called the Enhanced Structural Model (ESM) [4]. The models, such as ESM, are based on a modular approach which allows the expert analysts of different disciplines to work on the development of the model at the same time. The model eliminates certain limitations that are present in the attack modeling for example high abstract demonstration of the attacks and low flexibility of the course of the operation to a particular target.

Figure 1 displays an example of ESM. The main differences in comparison to the basic attack tree model are:

- two additional Khand nodes,
- demonstration of exploited vulnerabilities,
- integrated information about attack vectors,
- integrated information about countermeasures,
- segmentation of the attack tree.

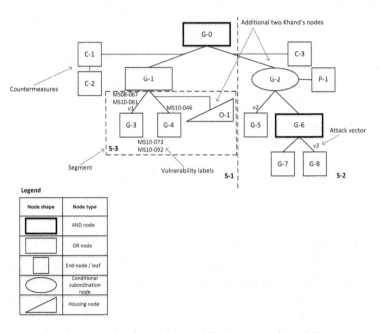

Fig. 1. Example of ESM intended for cyber attack modeling.

2.3   CVSS Standard

CVSS (Common Vulnerability Scoring System) is an open framework for communicating the characteristics and severity of software vulnerabilities [10]. It is used by manufacturers of software applications and security engineers in user organizations. It is also present in search systems, vulnerability management, security management and with researchers.

The framework consists of three metric groups: base, temporal and environmental metric group. Base metric group represents the basic characteristics of vulnerability that do not change over time or with user's environment. Temporal metric group and environmental metric group do not affect published CVSS scores of individual vulnerabilities in the public databases. The treatment and use of the CVSS standard in the papers is thus based on the base metric group, which consists of a total of six metric groups. In order to calculate the CVSS vulnerability assessments all the metrics in this section are needed.

Hereinafter we will be interested in the values of the access complexity attribute and the overall effect which results in three separate attributes. The access complexity indicates the complexity of the attack in order to exploit already discovered vulnerability; that is when the attacker already has an access to the system. Possible stock values are: high, medium and low. The impact attribute consists of three related metrics (confidentiality, integrity and availability impact) which measure how the exploited vulnerability immediately affects assets in terms of loss of confidentiality. The same stock values apply, i.e.: none, partial and complete.

3   Quantification of the Enhanced Structural Model

For deliberate security decisions we need metrics that allow us to know the effect on the system in a successfully implemented individual attack. In the analysis of the attack models the qualities of different attributes are taken into consideration. A set of attributes is broad and often includes various attributes of probabilities, risks, the effects of the attacks, the expenses– particularly in terms of security systems [11].

Our selection of attributes intentionally avoids the use of probability and those attributes with probability as one of the factors. The ESM model is in first place intended for modeling sophisticated cyber attacks on critical infrastructure, the characteristics of which are a clear target and desired objective of the attack. That is why our set of attributes of the model is the following:

- Cost: It expresses the financial value of an individual attack in the operation. Most often this is an accounting value and it is not generally identifiable, because the value of the same attack techniques often varies.
- Complexity: It displays the complexity of a particular attack technique. The score can be based on the value that can be understood from the scoring systems, such as CVSS.
- Impact: It represents numerically expressed impact on the system caused by an individual attack. As in the complexity section, the value here is given analytically or with the help of the scoring systems.

In Table 1 the rules relate to the use of the presented attributes. Attribute values are applied only to the end-node, the values of intermediate and root nodes are calculated according to the rules.

Table 1. Rules overview: the use of the attributes in the ESM

	AND node	OR node
Cost	$\sum_{i=1}^{n} cost_i$	$Min_{i=1}^{n} cost_i$
Complexity	$Max_{i=1}^{n} complexity_i$	$Min_{i=1}^{n} complexity_i$
Impact [8]	$\dfrac{10^n - \prod_{i=1}^{n}(10 - impact_i)}{10^{(n-1)}}$	$Max_{i=1}^{n} impact_i$

Individual values for the end node attributes are set by analysts. The cost of the attack can be supported by traditional financial calculation. The values for the complexity attribute can result from different frameworks for communicating characteristics and impacts of vulnerability. Among the utilities for the selection of the value, we can also classify other tools to detect vulnerability, intrusion detection systems and tools to manage security updates systems in the event of an established laboratory environment or otherwise acquired capacities. The values for the impact attribute can be defined after a preliminary analytical preparation, which creates a mapping of numerical value into a descriptive definition of the value. Such mapping is shown in Table 2, summarized in the display [8]:

Table 2. The mapping of numerical value of the impact into a descriptive definition.

Numerical Range	Impact Definition
1-3	Minor impact to system.
4-6	Moderate impact to system.
7-9	Severe impact to system.
10	System completely compromised, inoperable, or destroyed.

Justification for the rules selection:

- Cost: In calculating the cost of the AND node it is clear that we calculate the sum value of the subnodes - the offspring of the node for which in a given moment the cost is calculated. For OR node we choose the lowest value of the available values in the subnodes. This is based on the assumption that we choose those steps in the attack that cause least expenses.
- Complexity: In calculating the value of the complexity attribute, we choose the highest value in the AND node, especially if the attribute can be interpreted as the complexity of the given action. The AND node does not have the possibility to select between different subnodes. In case of the OR node we select the lowest value of complexity (e.g., "low"), because we want to perform the operation with minimal effort.
- Impact: Here, it is worth mentioning how to apply the rate [8] where the AND node has a greater attribute value than the impact in the individual subnode. This is justified by the fact that the invader caused additional damage with each attack in an individual subnode. The maximum value for the attribute of the subnodes is selected in the OR node.

3.1   Application of Rules on Additional Nodes in the Enhanced Structural Model

The Enhanced structural model uses two additional nodes that Khand proposes in his set of nodes [12]. It is important to note that the decisions within these two nodes are of situational nature. That means that decision-making is based on the rules of secondary character, since the purpose of the additional subnodes is to enable the development and the analysis of the scenarios dependent on time-dependent operating states of target systems, the presence of insiders and others. Table 3 presents the rules for attributes for one of the nodes – conditional subordination node (CSUB). In this attribute, the $value_i$ presents the value of individual attribute by the AND operation of nodes that are descendants of the CSUB node. $Value_p$ represents the value of the attribute in the actuator node which is attached to the CSUB node. It should also be noted that unlike in the CSUB node, the housing (second) node in the ESM is not classified as an intermediate node, but has a function of the end-node.

Table 3. Rules for the set of attributes in the ESM in the CSUB node

	Conditional subordination node
Cost	If $\sum_{i=1}^{n} cost_i < cost_p$ then $\sum_{i=1}^{n} cost_i$ else $cost_p$
Complexity	If $Max_{i=1}^{n} complexity_i < complexity_p$ then $\sum_{i=1}^{n} complexity_i$ else $complexity_p$
Impact	If $\dfrac{10^n - \prod_{i=1}^{n}(10 - impact_i)}{10^{(n-1)}} > impact_p$ then $\dfrac{10^n - \prod_{i=1}^{n}(10 - impact_i)}{10^{(n-1)}}$ else $impact_p$

It is considered for the CSUB that the objective has been achieved when all subgoals in nodes-offspring reach a target. It can also be that a node-initiator is selected to reach the objective (Figure P-1). This node can therefore be written as follows: G-0 = P-1 or (G-1 and G-2).

3.2   The Objective of the Proposed Quantification of the ESM Model

The use of relatively simple quantification of the ESM model has three main goals:

1. The proposed use and the application of the attributes allow analysts an identification of the most favorable values for individual and mutually independent attributes. It further allows the identification of:

   • The minimum possible cost to carry out an attack.
   • The minimum level of complexity that still allows the performance of the attack.
   • The maximum impact that can be achieved with an attack.

2. In intermediate nodes, those are partial objectives of the attack, a support for decision-making is provided in the selection of individual subtree structure given the preferred attribute (i.e. cost, complexity or impact).
3. Improving the existing ESM model that with its set of qualities summarizes the capacity of attack modeling with structural models. At the same time it does not require an extensive basic knowledge of attack modeling. This is especially suitable for the use of tools in higher education programs, mainly in social sciences.

4   Presentation of the Use with a Practical Example

This section is intended to illustrate an example and is composed as follows: first comes a presentation of computer-network operation with the ESM model, which is equipped with all five properties belonging to it. In line with this model, there are four standard tables that allow mapping codes (nodes, attack vectors, exploited vulnerabilities and segments) in understandable descriptions. This is followed by the reading of the model. The detailed methodology of the use of the ESM model can be found in [4].

Furthermore, the section presents the application of attributes. There is a table displaying the assignment of attribute values to the end-node in the model and calculations of the values in the root of the tree structure and intermediate nodes.

4.1   Presentation of the Operation with ESM

Figure 2 shows the operation described by the ESM model. It is followed by corresponding Tables 4, 5, 6, 7, and 8 with a description of the individual parameters in the model.

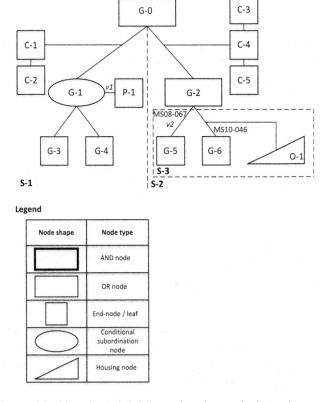

Fig. 2. ESM model with main goal G-0 "eavesdropping on the internal communications".

Table 4. Description of nodes for the enhanced structural model in Fig. 2.

Node	Description
G-0	Eavesdropping on the internal communications
G-1	Capturing traffic data with a physical presence
G-2	Remote use of a malicious software code
G-3	Access to local network
G-4	ARP poisoning
G-5	Spreading through the network
G-6	Spreading through removable media
P-1	Eavesdropping on the optical fiber
O-1	Spreading through project files

Table 5. Description of the attack vectors labelled in the enhanced structural model in Fig. 2.

Vector	Description
v1	Optical Splitting Technique (e.g. FGB – Fiber Bragg Gratings)
v2	DLL Hijacking

Table 6. Description of segments labelled in the enhanced structural model in Fig. 2.

Segment	Description
S-1	Physical presence of an operational worker
S-2	The use of malicious software code
S-3	Structure of malicious code spreading

Table 7. Description of vulnerabilities exploited

Vulnerability label	Description
MS08-067	Windows Server Service Vulnerability
MS10-046	Windows Shell LNK Vulnerability

Table 8. Description of security countermeasures labelled in the enhanced structural model in Fig. 2.

Countermeasure	Description
C-1	Valid end-to-end encryption mechanisms
C-2	Static ARP tables
C-3	Network-isolated systems
C-4	Control over the events in computer resources
C-5	Network system for intrusion detection

Model reading: The main objective of the attack described by the model presents a node G-O "eavesdropping on the internal communications". The node is of OR type and that means we can decide between nodes G-1 or G-2, so-called partial objectives, to carry out an attack.

The node G-1 is Conditional subordination node (CSUB). In order to achieve the objective of this node, i.e. "capture traffic data with the physical presence", we need to carry out such an activity in the G-3 node as well as an activity envisaged by the G-4 node. In implementing G-4 node there is an additional information item present, represented by the attack vector (v1) that prescribes a specific offensive method. Due to the properties of the CSUB node, the objective can also be achieved with an alternative implementation of the actuator node P-1. Here we also encounter the prescribed offensive method presented with the parameter v2.

The G-2 node is a classic OR type of the node. To achieve the objective of this node we can choose between the activities in the nodes G-5 and G-6 as well as in the housing node O-1. In line with the rules of the OR logic expressions, both activities in nodes G-5 and G-6 can be carried out. However, if we choose an activity with an O-1 node, then we certainly did not finish the G-6 activity, because there is a XOR operation between the nodes. This part of the tree structure is equipped with codes of exploited vulnerability. The codes direct us to the proper selection of certain attribute values in individual nodes when used as standards to assess vulnerability.

4.2   Value Application

Table 9 shows attribute values for all end-nodes in the model. These values have different sources: an expert assessment, the accounting value and the value of parameters according to the CVSS standard. Nodes G-5 and G-6 offer an additional information item; that is vulnerability. As shown in the table, in our case, the value application can be assigned from the CVSS standard. For the "complexity" attribute, we chose the value of the attribute "access complexity" in the CVSS for the selected vulnerability. For "impact" attribute, we selected a value of the overall effect within the base metric score of the CVSS standard for the selected vulnerability.

Below is the calculation of the value for all the attributes in the main objective of the model, i.e. G-0. Results show that the operation with the aim of "eavesdropping on

Table 9. Application of attribute values to the end-node

End-node	Attribute values*	Source
G-3	Cost: 1500€	Accounting value
	Complexity: MEDIUM	Expert assessment
	Impact: 5	Expert assessment
G-4	Cost: 100€	Accounting value
	Complexity: LOW	Expert assessment
	Impact: 7	Expert assessment
G-5	Cost: 700€	Estimation
	Complexity: LOW	CVSS
	Impact: 10	CVSS
G-6	Cost: 1000€	Estimation
	Complexity: MEDIUM	CVSS
	Impact: 10	CVSS

(*Continued*)

Table 9. (*Continued*)

End-node	Attribute values*	Source
P-1	Cost: 500€	Accounting value
	Complexity: MEDIUM	Expert assessment
	Impact: 5	Expert assessment
O-1	Cost: 2000€	Estimation
	Complexity: HIGH	Expert assessment
	Impact: 8	Expert assessment

Values are only an example of the application of the
attribute value. They are set according to the selected
target, its environment and the complexity of the
operation and that is why values for the same operation
or attack can vary.

the internal communications" can be achieved for at least 500€. Furthermore, it is
possible to carry out the operation with non-complex techniques. A set of scenarios for
the operation enables carrying out the attack with maximum effect. It should be noted
that attributes are mutually exclusive. In our case the attack for 500€ is thus not least
demanding or has maximum impact. The quantification with a set of attributes is
merely a support for decision-making, but the task of the analysts is to decide themselves which attributes they prefer.

- **Attribute value for the operation described by the model:**
    - Cost: 500€
    - Complexity: LOW
    - Impact: 10

Below are the attribute values in partial objectives, i.e. nodes G-1 and G-2. The
values of the partial objectives allow analysts to decide whether to carry out an attack
on the left or right subtree structure. The decision is based on secondary information
not shown in the model (e.g. the characteristics of target systems).

- **Value of intermediate objectives:**
    - G-1: Capturing traffic data
        Cost: 500€
        Complexity: MEDIUM
        Impact: 8,5
    - G-2: Remote use of a malicious software code
        Cost: 700€
        Complexity: LOW
        Impact: 10

We can see that the value of the cost of an attack, the minimum value required to
reach the target, originates from the left subtree structure with the main objective G-1.
Values for the complexity and impact originate from subtree structure with the main
objective G-2.

5 Review of the Use of the Attributes in the Attack Tree Model and Its Extensions

Authors in [13] present a case study using an extended attack tree called attack defense tree. Their model consists of defense nodes and a set of different attributes. Case study consists of four phases: creation of the model, attribute decoration, preparation of attribute value and at the end calculation. Different attributes are used for the case study (costs, detectability, difficulty, impact, penalty, profit, probability, special skill and time), which are presented in the table below, including a description and stock values.

In a feasibility study author [14] solves the problem of the construction of big attack trees and their maintenance. In his work, thus, he proposes an approach to automatize the construction of such models. He states that the automatic construction of a model for a specific threat is to some extent feasible. Further handmade manufacture is thus required in lower parts of the model. In order to support the automatic construction of the model, it is necessary to have different inputs, architecturally as well as tools for making risk assessments and a set of security knowledge.

The authors [15] present the foundations of the expanded tree attack model which increases the expressiveness of the model using the operator that allows the modeling of ordered events. Their model, named SAND attack tree, thus includes sequential conjunctive operator – SAND. In the paper the model is semantically defined, the semantics is based on the series-parallel (SP) graphs. With the work on attributes within their model, authors also allow a quantitative analysis of the attacks using the bottom-up algorithm.

The author [16] states that present information systems are becoming more dynamic and comprehensive, that is why the security models face the problem of scalability. Furthermore, he says that the existing security models do not allow for the capture and analysis of unforeseen scenarios resulting from unknown attacks. In the dissertation, the author thus states methods appropriate for security modeling in large systems and developing methods for the efficient treatment of countermeasures. On the basis of the above, inter alia, he presents a hierarchical security model and methods of assessments and thus reaches pre-set goals.

The authors [17] use the attack tree for the systematic presentation of possible attacks in the proposal of a new quantitative approach to security analysis of the computer system. The authors [18] focus on the treatment of defense against malicious attacks that system administrators have to deal with. In the analysis, they use attack tree to optimize the security function. The attack tree deals with attributes that are relevant when facing attacks and counter-measure settings. They thus provide better support for decision-making and a choice among possible solutions.

The authors [19] use the attack tree model as a basis to identify malicious code on the Android systems. The expanded version of the model allows new, flexible way of organization and the usage of rules. Furthermore, a combination of static and dynamic analysis enables better accuracy and performance. The authors [20] want to demonstrate with their contribution that the attacker profiling can be a part of already existing quantitative tools for security assessment. This provides a more precise assessment of item changes during changes of subordinate components and allows greater analytical flexibility in terms of foresight, prioritization and prevention of attacks.

6 Discussion

Structural models for attack modeling, such as attack tree, face various complaints. Some say that in the attack tree modeling it is difficult to reuse or divide certain attack trees [21]. Others point to the insufficient accuracy in the presentation of the attack in the model analysis [22]. That is why we introduced our ESM model with features that enable a more realistic view of the attacks. The main objective of the first design of the ESM model was a contribution to a better understanding of the attack implementation and identification of security weaknesses.

When discussing a set of related techniques in the field of attack trees, we found the quantification of security, particularly with bottom-up algorithms, a very active area. The quantification of the ESM model presented in the paper provides support in attack analysis by the presence of three mutually independent attributes. Such support is mostly useful when the model offers an alternative way of the implementation of the attack and a need for a more tangible basis for the selection of the attack. The model does not offer friendly options to find the best way of carrying out complete attack given the selected attribute. Also, individual values of the root structures can come from different branches. This means that, for example, the model with the value of the cost attribute in the main goal (G-0) shows the lowest price for carrying out the attack, but does not allow the achievement of the impact that is displayed by this attribute in the same node.

As mentioned in the paper, the allocation of the initial value of the attribute in the final attributes is based on various sources. The accounting value as well as the impact of the attack are merely an illustration in the validation. The objectivity of values is achieved only when we have sufficient information about target systems which enable the design of the ESM model, as well as secondary information which can vary in different targets of the same attack. An additional source of input for the allocation of the attribute value is the CVSS standard, but this scoring does not address the economic impact in case of exploited vulnerability. Besides, basic metrics of the CVSS standard and the scoring itself can be differently interpreted.

7 Conclusion

Modeling sophisticated cyber attacks plays an important role in information security. Attack modeling tools provide effective support for the analysis and identification of system weaknesses in different phases of its life cycle. Based on the evaluation of the ESM model mentioned in the paper, we conclude that our model presents numerous advantages, particularly in terms of education.

The ESM model in its first form has been presented on the basis of the analysis of known malicious code. Nevertheless, the model did not consist of clear set of attributes, rules for calculating the attributes, and resources to allocate input values of the attributes. Also, the question of treating additional nodes besides AND/OR remained open. We reached one of our goals, the quantification of the model. CVSS standards were selected for the input values of individual attributes. The standard so far proved to be up-to-date and informative.

In the future, we plan to test the Quantified ESM on a wider set of complex examples. It would be reasonable to integrate a database with known vulnerabilities and other associated attributes and create a catalogue with the implemented threats and their analyses.

References

1. Pietre-Cambacedes, L., Bouissou, M.: Beyond attack trees: dynamic security modeling with Boolean logic Driven Markov Processes (BDMP). In: European Dependable Computing Conference, pp. 199–208 (2010)
2. Fovino, I.N., Masera, M., De Cian, A.: Integrating cyber attacks within fault trees. Reliab. Eng. Syst. Saf. **9**, 1394–1402 (2009)
3. Ivanc, B., Klobucar, T.: Attack modeling in the critical infrastructure. J. Electr. Eng. Comput. Sci. **81**(5), 285–292 (2014)
4. Ivanc, B., Klobučar, T.: Modelling of information attacks on critical infrastructure by using an enhanced structural model, Jozef Stefan International Postgraduate School (2013)
5. Yan, J., He, M., Li, T.: A Petri-net model of network security testing. In: IEEE International Conference on Computer Science and Automation Engineering, pp. 188–192 (2011)
6. Ten, C.W., Manimaran, G., Liu, C.C.: Cybersecurity for critical infrastructures: attack and defense modeling. IEEE Trans. Syst. Man Cybern. Part A: Syst. Humans **4**, 853–865 (2010)
7. Camtepe, A., Bulent, Y.: Modeling and detection of complex attacks. In: Third International Conference on Security and Privacy in Communications Networks and the Workshops, pp. 234–243 (2007)
8. Edge, K., Raines, R., Grimaila, M., Baldwin, R., Bennington, R., Reuter, C.: The use of attack and protection trees to analyze security for an online banking system. In: Proceedings of the 40th Hawaii International Conference on System Sciences, p. 144b (2007)
9. Bistarelli, S., Fioravanti, F., Peretti, P.: Defense trees for economic evaluation of security investments. In: The First International Conference on Availability, Reliability and Security, pp. 416–423 (2006)
10. Mell, P., Scarfone, K., Romanosky, S.: A Complete Guide to the Common Vulnerability Scoring System Version 2.0. (2007)
11. Kordy, B., Pietre-Cambacedes, L., Schweitzer, P.: DAG-based attack and defense modeling: Don't miss the forest for the attack trees. Comput. Sci. Rev. **13–14**, 1–38 (2014)
12. Khand, P.A.: System level security modeling using attack trees. In: 2nd International Conference on Computer, Control and Communication, pp. 1–7 (2009)
13. Bagnato, A., Kordy, B., Meland, P.H., Schweitzer, P.: Attribute decoration of attack-defense trees. Int. J. Secure Softw. Eng. **3**(2), 1–35 (2012)
14. Paul, S.: Towards automating the construction & maintenance of attack trees: a feasibility study. In: Proceedings of the 1st International Workshop on Graphical Models for Security, pp. 31–46 (2014)
15. Jhawar, R., Kordy, B., Mauw, S., Radomirović, S., Trujillo-Rasua, R.: Attack trees with sequential conjunction. In: Federrath, H., Gollmann, D. (eds.) SEC 2015. IFIP AICT, vol. 455, pp. 339–353. Springer, Heidelberg (2015)
16. Hong, J.B.: Scalable and Adaptable Security Modelling and Analysis, PhD Thesis. University of Canterbury (2015)
17. Almasizadeh, J., Azgomi, M.A.: Mean privacy: a metric for security of computer systems. Comput. Commun. **52**, 47–59 (2014)

18. Dewri, R., Ray, I., Poolsappasit, N., Whitley, D.: Optimal security hardening on attack tree models of networks: a cost-benefit analysis. Int. J. Inf. Secur. **11**(3), 167–188 (2012)

19. Zhao, S., Li, X., Xu, G., Zhang, L., Feng, Z.: Attack tree based android malware detection with hybrid analysis. In: IEEE 13th International Conference on Trust, Security and Privacy in Computing and Communications, pp. 1–8 (2014)

20. Lenin, A., Willemson, J., Sari, D.P.: Attacker profiling in quantitative security assessment based on attack trees. In: Bernsmed, K., Fischer-Hübner, S. (eds.) NordSec 2014. LNCS, vol. 8788, pp. 199–212. Springer, Heidelberg (2014)

21. Dalton, G.C., Mills, R.F., Colombi, J.M., Raines, R.A.: Analyzing attack trees using generalized stochastic Petri nets. In: Information Assurance Workshop, pp. 116–123 (2006)

22. Pudar, S., Manimaran, G., Liu, C.C.: PENET: a practical method and tool for integrated modeling of security attacks and countermeasures. Comput. Secur. **28**(8), 754–771 (2009)

A Web Security Testing Method
Based on Web Application Structure

Xueyong Yu$^{(\boxtimes)}$ and Guohua Jiang

Nanjing University of Aeronautics and Astronautics, Nanjing, China
yongyu_good@126.com, jgh@nuaa.edu.cn

Abstract. Description model of Web application structure can be used to depict the Structure of a Web application, it can also provide testing guidance for ordinary testing of Web application. In this paper, we proposed an improved description model named Web Relation Graph on the basis of Page Navigation Graph, which can describe the complex relationships in Web application. Web Relation Graph can provide guidance for Web ordinary testing, it also can provide assistance for security testing for Web application. And we used vulnerability-related paths to describe the security of the Web applications on the Web Relation Graph. We also proposed a new security testing framework on the basis of vulnerability-related paths. The framework contained two parts, client-side testing and server-side testing. Client-side testing is for testing the client entities in the paths with the methods of static analysis and penetration testing. Server-side testing is for testing the server entities with the methods of tainted-analysis and dynamic testing.

Keywords: Web security testing · Web application architecture · Web relation graph · Testing framework · Tainted analysis

1 Introduction

Web security testing is an important research direction of software testing. Web security testing is for testing the vulnerabilities in Web applications, like SQL Injection, Cross-Site script, CSRF etc. The previous researches about Web security testing focused on the vulnerabilities themselves. There are many studies in the researches using penetration testing, which has been a necessary part in Web application testing. Almost all Web system would take penetration testing before releasing. The research in [1] used the penetration testing [2] on the basis of summarizing the attack mode of XSS and SQL Injection. The research in [3] used petri nets to build penetration testing. There is also research about building penetration model based on network attack graph [4]. The method of static tainted analysis[5, 6] can be used to test the Web vulnerabilities based tainted data. The research in [7] used the method of abnormal behavior monitoring to make sure whether there were vulnerabilities in JavaScript program. The method also was used to test SQL injection and cross-site script of Web applications [8]. However, these methods tested the application from the perspective of the Web vulnerabilities.

© Springer International Publishing Switzerland 2015
Z. Huang et al. (Eds.): ICCCS 2015, LNCS 9483, pp. 244–258, 2015.
DOI: 10.1007/978-3-319-27051-7_21

In the traditional Web application testing, Web application structure descriptions models can provide guidance for the traditional Web application testing, such as the Web page navigation graph [9] proposed by Filippo. The later researchers improved this model, the improved model proposed in [10] can be used to describe the Web applications with frame. The models in [11–13] could be used to depict the Web applications developed with the technology of dynamic pages. These models could only provide testing guidance for the traditional testing, can not be used for security testing. The existing research about Web security testing is not based on the analysis of the structure of Web application.

In this paper, we propose a improved model named Web relation graph on the basis of page navigation graph. We use vulnerability related path to describe the security information of the Web application on the basis of Web relation graph. Vulnerability related path provides testing guidance for SQL injection and cross-site script. We also propose a security testing framework on the basis of vulnerability related path to test these two types of vulnerabilities.

2 Web Application Structure Analysis

The purpose of structure analysis is to describe the Web application. In this section, we propose a new model named *Web relation graph* (WRG) and introduce several types of paths in WRG which can describe the security of Web application.

2.1 Web Relation Graph

Web relation graph (*WRG*) is an improved model of *PNG*. In *WRG*, we make a more detailed classification for the types of Web elements. WRG can not only be used to describe the diverse types of elements in Web applications, but also can depict the complex relationships between these elements.

Define 2.1. *WRG* = (*NP*, *NS*, *NSP*, *NDB*, *EN*, *ED*, *EG*), WRG is a directed graph. *NP*, *NS*, *NSP*, *NDB* are the four different types of nodes, *EN*, *ED*, *EG* are the three different types of edges. Figure 1 shows the model graph.

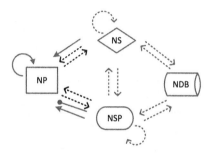

Fig. 1. WRG model

(1) nodes $N = NP \cup NS \cup NSP \cup NDB$.

NP represents the static pages. The static pages in the Web applications. In Web applications, static pages are displayed in the client browser, provides interactive features for users; *NS* represents Web services. Web services are running in the server of the Web application, which can receive and process the request of the client; *NSP* represents Web dynamic service pages, which can not only receive and handle the client requests, but also generate new static pages; *NDB* represents database.

(2) edges $E = EN \cup ED \cup EG$;

EN for navigation edge, represent the navigation relationship between two elements. $EN = \{(n_1, n_2) | n_1 \in NP \cup NS \cup NSP, n_2 \in NP\}$. There are two types of navigate edge, hyperlinks and redirection; *ED* for data edge, represent the data transfer relationship of two elements, $ED = \{(n_1, n_2) | (n_1 \in NS \cup NSP, n_2 \in NS \cup NSP) \vee (n_1 \in NS \cup NSP, n_2 \in NP \cup NDB) \vee (n_1 \in NP \cup NDB, n_2 \in NS \cup NSP)\}$. Data submitted is a phenomenon of *ED*; *EG* for generating edge, indicating one Web element is constructed by another Web element by spacial execution logic, $EG = \{(n_1, n_2) | n_1 \in NSP, n_2 \in NP\}$. *EG* only exists between *NSP* and *NP*.

Define 2.2. When a data edge e $(e \in ED)$ exist between two Web elements, there exit data transfer phenomena Web entities exist between these two elements, then the collection of the data pass through e is $Data_e$.

A simple scene of user login described by WRG is shown in Fig. 2. User submit the personal information to the server by n_1. Verification process take place in n_2 and n_7. If the validation is successful, entered personal center. In WRG, personal center n_4 is constructed by dynamic service page n_3. Different users will enter different personal center. When the users log out from the personal center n_4, the service n_5 will clear the personal information from the session, then user can enter the start page n_1. Otherwise, enter the wrong tips page n_6, can user redirect to n_1 from n_6.

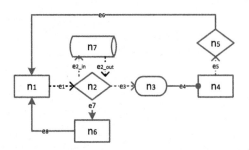

Fig. 2. WRG of login scene

2.2   Classification of WRG Elements

In *WRG*, we classify the elements into to two categories according to the elements distribution. The first one is the client element, which exist in the client side and provides interactive features for users. The second is server elements, which exist in the server side, and provide data access and processing functions. The detail is presented in Table 1.

Table 1. Classification of WRG elements

Element type	Node type	Description
Client element	NP	Display in the client browser, provide interactive feature
Server element	NDB, NS, NSP	Running on the server, provide services of data accessing and handling

2.3   Paths in WRG

A path in *WRG* represents one execution of Web application, testers need to calculate the paths and test them. In the actual situation of using Web application, one execution perform a redirecting from one static page to another static page from the user's perspective. In *WRG*, we treat the paths from the perspective of application actual execution. So we add a construction to the paths in *WRG*.

Constraint 2.1. WRG path needs to meet the following constraints: Start node and end node of a complete *WRG* path must be *NP* type; And other nodes in the path can not be *NP* type.

We will discuss several special types of paths in *WRG* based on this constraint.

Definition 2.3. There exists path p in WRG, if all the edges of p are the data edge (*ED*), this path is called the *data relation path*.

Figure 3 depict a sample of data relation path. $\bigcap\limits_{i=1}^{n} Dataeki \bigcup\limits_{k=1}^{n} Di,j,k$

Fig. 3. Data relation path

Definition 2.4. n_i and n_j are Web elements in WRG, $D_{i,j}$ is the collection of the data transferred from n_i to n_j. If there exist a *data relation path* p_k between n_i and n_j, $D_{i,j,k}$ is the collection of the data transferred by p_k. If there are sevarial paths Ek between n_i and n_j, $Ek = \{ek_1, ek_2,.., ek_n\}$, $D_{i,j,k} = $, $D_{i,j} = $ 。

In addition to the *data relation path*, there are two other special types of paths which have relations with Cross-Site Script and SQL injection. These two types of paths can describe the security properties of Web applications.

SQL injection is a type of vulnerability associated with the database scripts. In the case of SQL injection being triggered, malicious users filled the input controllers with malicious SQL scripts, then submit the information to the server via the network. Server received, process the data, generate SQL statements and injected the statements into the database to complete a malicious database operations.

In WRG, the malicious data was submitted to *Web Service (NS)* or *Dynamic Service Page (NSP)* from *static page (NP)* through *data edge (ED)*. These two types of elements integrate the malicious data to SQL statement and inject data into database. The detail data transfer mode as shown in Fig. 4. In *WRG*, SQL injection only exist in the *SQL injection related path*. The detail depiction as shown in Definition 2.5.

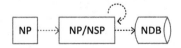

Fig. 4. Data transaction of SQL injection

Definition 2.5. In WRG, *SQL injection related path P* needs to satisfy the following conditions.

(1) There exist a path segment p' in P, the start node of p' is static page (*NP*), and the end node of p' is database node(*NDB*).
(2) p' is *data relation path (DRP)*, if n_s is the start node, and n_e is the end node of p', $D_{s,e} \neq \emptyset$;

Cross-site script is a type of vulnerability which is associated with the *Javascript, actionscript* and so on. There are two types of Cross-Site script, reflection type and storage type. The differences of these two types is whether the data will be transferred to the database. When XSS is exploited, malicious data is filled in the client, and submitted to the server. After the server received the data, these data will be used to generate new pages, or be passed directly to the static pages with Ajax. When the users receive these data, Web browser will execute the script in data.

So, there are two cases in *WRG*. In the first case, data is transferred with Ajax technology. In the second case, data will be to re-transferred to users via constructing static pages. The detail data transfer mode as shown in Fig. 5. In *WRG*, cross-site script only exists in the *XSS related path*. The detail depiction of the *XSS related path* as shown in Definition 2.6.

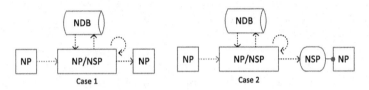

Fig. 5. Data transaction of XSS

Definition 2.6. In *WRG*, *XSS related path P* needs to satisfy any one of the following conditions. *P*'s start node n_s and *P*'s end node n_e are both static pages (*NP*).

(1) *P* is a *data relation path* (DRP), and $D_{s,e} \neq \emptyset$;
(2) The last edge of *P* is a generation edge (*EG*), others are data edge (*DE*), and the last but one node is n_c, and $D_{s,c} \neq \emptyset$;

SQL injection related path and *XSS related path* are called *vulnerability related path* (VRP), vulnerabilities only exist in these paths.

Here, we discuss the scene depicted in Fig. 6, the data transfer situation as follow: $Data_{e1} = \{username, password\}$, $Data_{e2\_in} = \{username, password\}$, $Data_{e2\_out} = \{id, age, username\}$, $Data_{e3} = \{username, id, age\}$, $Data_{e5} = \{log\_out\}$. In Fig. 6, there are four complete *WRG* paths. In these four paths, the path 1 meets the Definitions 2.5 and 6, path 3 meets the Definition 2.5, and the other paths are normal *WRG* paths.

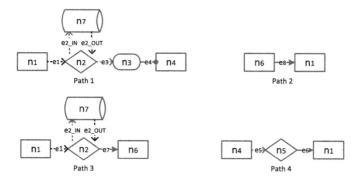

Fig. 6. Paths in scene

Tester need to test the vulnerabilities in the paths which meet the conditions of *vulnerability related path*. The specific security testing method for the *vulnerability related path* is discussed in Sect. 3.

3   Web Security Testing Framework

We can use *WRG* to describe Web application, and describe the security properties of Web application with *vulnerability related paths*. *WRG* can provide guidance for security testing. In this section, we propose a security testing framework on the basis of *vulnerability related path*. This framework contains client side testing and server side testing. The framework as shown in Fig. 7.

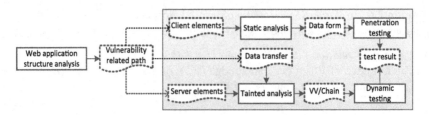

Fig. 7. Security test framework

3.1   Client Side Testing

Client side testing is for testing the client side of *vulnerability related path*, the purpose is to find the flaws in client side. There are two main parts in client side testing processing, static analysis and penetration testing. In the static analysis testing processing, we propose a model named *data form* to describe the main information in client elements.

3.1.1   Client Element Static Analysis

NP is the client element in *vulnerability related path*, can provide interactive features for users, and provide conditions for attack. The attackers exploit the SQL injection and cross-site script via the client elements. HTML and XHTML, the static page encoding language, provide the main functions to collect users' information. So the main task in static analysis is to extract these controls from the client elements.

These controls are named *injection point*. The main types of *injection points* are shown in Table 2. In this paper, we only care about two types of *injection points*. The first one is the type which can provide input functions for users, this type is called *input injection point*, *INPUTS* is the set of *input injection point*. The second one is the type which can trigger the submit event. This one is called *event injection points*, *BUTTONS* for the set of *event injection points*. When the users trigger the submit event of an *event injection point*, the data in *Inputs Injection Points* can be submitted to the server.

Table 2. Injection points

Injection points	Attributes
Document	cookies, domain, forms, links, titles, URL
Form	action, method, id
Input	Name, id, type, value
Button	name, id, type, value

3.1.2   Data Form

There is some relations between *input injection points* and *event injection points*, we propose a model named *data form* to describe the relations. The detail definition of *data form* is shown in Definition 3.1.

Definition 3.1. Data form DF = (INPUTS, BUTTONS, dfs), INPUTS for set of *input injection points*; *BUTTONS for set of event injection points*; *dfs* = {*<vars, button >* | *vars* $\subseteq$ *INPUTS, button*$\in$*BUTTONS*}, < *vars, button* > needs to meet the follow conditions: the trigger of *button*'s event can produce *request*, and *vars* are the part of the *request*.

Algorithm 3.1
inputs: the DOM model of a static page: *document*; **Outputs**: *dfs*;
Step1. Iterate the elements in *document*, add the *input injection point* to *INPUTS*, add the *event injection point* to *BUTTONS*, Jump to Step2;
Step2. Fill all the elements in *INPUTS* with normal data, and jump to Step3;
Step3. Iterate the elements in *BUTTONS*, the current element is *BT*, trigger the submit event of *BT*. If the state of *document* changes, jump to Step4; Otherwise go on the Step3 until there is no more elements in *BUTTONS*;
Step4. Create *df* = *<vars, button>*, crawl current *request* from *document*, analyze the variables in *request*, and add the variables which exist in *INPUTS* into the *vars*, set *button=BT*, *dfs=dfs* $\cup${*df*}, jump to Step5;
Step5. Reset the state of the *document* and jump to Step3;

Algorithm 3.1 is used to create the *data form* model of a static page. In Fig. 8, we gave a example. Firstly, fill the *input injection points* normal data, and trigger the submit events of *event injection points*, and analyze the *Request*.

Segment of html code:
```
1 <form id="f₁" action="u₁" method="post">
2    <input type="text" name="v₁" id="UN"/>
3    <input type="password" name="v₂" id="PWD"/> </form>
5 <button onclick="document.getElementById("f₁").submit();" id = "b₁"/>
6 <form id="f₂" action="u₂" method="get">
7    <input type="text" name="v₃" id="CS"/>
8 <input type="submit" id="b₂" value="confirm" /> </form>
```
Analysis:
1). *INPUTS*={v_1, v_2, v_3}; *BUTTONS*={b_1, b_2};
2).Trigger b_1's submit event, *Request*="v_1=xx&v_2=xx", *df1*=<{v_1,v_2},b_1>, *dfs*={*df₁*};
3). Trigger b_2's submit event, *Request*="v_3=xx", *df₂*=<{v_3},b_2>, *dfs*={*df₁*,*df₂*};

Fig. 8. Segment of HTML

3.1.3   Penetration Testing

The main function of security mechanism in client elements is to validate the data from users. The penetration testing is based on *Data Form*. Each penetration test with a < *vars, button* > in *dfs*, tester need to inject the test cases into *vars*, and trigger the submit event of the *button*, then crawl and analyze the HTTP request.

3.1.4   Data Transfer

In a *vulnerability related path*, there may exist data transfer between client elements and server elements. And data will transfer by a data edge $e(e \in ED)$, $Data_e$ present the data transfer via e. Considering the XSS related path p in Fig. 9. Data edge e_1 exist between n_1 and n_3, and $Data_{e1} = \{v_1, v_2\}$, data edge e_2 exist between n_2 and n_3, and $Data_{e2} = \{v_1\}$. In path p, n_2 will only receive and handle the data in $Data_{e1}$, and these data come from n_1. When we test the server element n_2, we only focus on the security mechanism for the data in $Data_{e1}$.

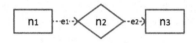

Fig. 9. WRG path

In Web application, a server element n_i will match with a processing module $class_i$.
$\bigcup_{i=1}^{n} DTEi\ DTE_i$ presents the data transfer to n_i ($ni \in NS$), $DTE_i = \{< var, class_i > \mid e$'s end point is n_i ($e \in ED$), $var \in Data_e$, $class_i$ presents the n_i's processing module}. DT presents the data transfer in a *vulnerability related path*, $DT = $.

3.2   Server Side Testing

There are two parts in server side testing, static analysis and dynamic testing. In static analysis, we analyze the code of *server elements* with the method of static taint analysis, consider the security of Web application from the perspective of vulnerability variables, We propose *vulnerability variable analysis model* to describe the service elements and extract the appropriate security mechanism from the *server elements*. *Vulnerability variable analysis model* combines the features of taint analysis model and information flow model, and the algorithm is proposed on the basis on the model for calculating the variables and the corresponding mechanism. Dynamic testing is the final step in the server side testing, the purpose of this step is to test the security mechanism extracted in the static analysis. The result of dynamic testing is the testing result of server side testing.

3.2.1   Vulnerability Variable

From the perspective of tainted analysis, the data from outside of the system will be considered to be unreliable, and the variable with these data is called *tainted variables*. In Web application, *tainted variables* almost come from client, and most of the them come from users. In the server side testing, the variables comes from client and users are called *candidate variables*. Definition 3.2 gives a detail depiction of the *candidate variables*. After *candidate variables* been received and handled, part of these variables may be delivered to other users or injected into database, application will be attacked. These variables will be called *vulnerability variables*.

Definition 3.2. TV is the set of *tainted variable*, *CV* presents the set of *candidate variable*, and satisfy the following conditions.

(1) $CV \subseteq TV$, *CV* is the child set of *TV*;
(2) $\forall v \in CV$, variable *v* transfers from client to server, and the data in *v* come from users' inputs.

Definition 3.3. VV presents the set of *vulnerability variable*, and *VV* should satisfy the following conditions.

(1) $VV \subseteq CV$, *VV* is a child set of *CV*;
(2) $\forall v \in VV$, variable *v* transfer from server to client or to database;
(3) $\forall v_i \in VV$, there are several validation functions for v_i, $f_1...f_n$. The set of these function named $Chain_i$. $Chain_i$ is the security mechanism of server side, the object of static analysis is to find *VV* and the corresponding *Chain*. The dynamic testing is to test the functions in *Chain*, the result is the final result of server side testing.

3.2.2   Server Element Analysis

We propose a static analysis model named *vulnerability variable analysis model (VVAM)* to describe and analysis the server elements. Definition 3.4 gives detail depiction of vulnerability *variable analysis Model*.

Definition 3.4. VVAM = (Vars, States, Ops, f, IFS), *Vars* present the set of variables and constants; *States* presents the set of variables states, *States = {Nor, Candi, Vur, PCandi}*, *Nor* is the normal variable state, *Candi* is the *candidate variable* state, *Vur* is the *vulnerability variable* state, *PCandi* is *suspected candidate variable* state; *Ops* is the set of data operation, there are four types of data operations. *N* is normal operation, *M* is make operation (receive the data from outside, spread the tainted data etc.), *C* is clean operation (security mechanism), *V* is expose operation (trigger the vulnerability), several examples for these operations are shown in Table 3.

Table 3. Operation and examples

Symbol	Example of operation
N	Definition: *string str = new String("");*
M	Request: *string str = request.getParameter ("username");*
C	Replace: *username = username.replace("script", "");*
V	Data query: *set set = statement.executeQuery();*
	Page construction: < *%=session.getObject("username")%>*

f: States × *Ops* → *States* is variable state transition map, shown in Fig. 10.

In Fig. 10, when a variable is defined, it's state is *Nor*. *M* operation leads to tainted information transferring, the state of a variable will change to *Candi* with *M* operation. When the state of variable is *Candi*, the variable is a candidate variable which contains tainted information. *C* operation is clean operation, security mechanism. In the

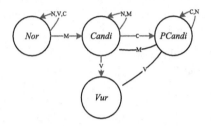

Fig. 10. Variable state transition

traditional tainted analysis, the state of a variable will change to Nor. However, the security mechanism may not always be effective. So there will be two types of transform, changed to *Nor* or maintain. So we increase a new state *PCandi* which is a uncertain state in the transition. *V* is exposing operation, the vulnerability will be exposed when operating the variable under *Candi* with *V*.

IFS presents information flow, $IFS = \{< num, src, dest, func > | src, dest \in Vars, func \in Ops\}$. *num* for the number of a flow; *src* for the source variable; *dest* for the destination variable, the information is flowing to the destination variable from the source variable in a information flow; *func* for the function in a flow. *IFS* is used to depict the data transferring in server elements and analysis the vulnerability. The detail construction rules according to [4].

VVAM can describe the information of the *server element*. We can extract *VV* and *Chain* from *VVAM* with the Algorithm 3.2.

Algorithm 3.2

input: Data Transfer *DT*; *output*: Chain, VV;

Step1. create sets: *Chain*, *VV*, *CV*, and set them blank;

Step2. iterate *DT*, current element $dt_i=<v_i,c_i>$,jump to Step3; When iteration end, terminate algorithm;

Step3. $dt_i=<v_i,c_i>$, resolve the entrance method of c_i, and get the *Path*, the set of paths in c_i, *i* increase;

Step4. iterate *Path*, the current path is p_j, and generate the information flow of p_j, get IFS_j and jump to Step 5; If the set *Path* is empty, jump to Step 2;

Step5. iterate IFS_j, search the element $r_n=<n, v_k, v_m, f_n>$　$v_k=v_i$ and f_n is *M* type operation, if find this element, add v_k and v_m into CV and jump to step6; or jump to Step 4;

Step6. create validation chain $Chain_i$, and temporary vulnerability variables set VV_i. Iterate the elements after r_n, $r_{n+1}=<n+1, v_t, v_l, f_{n+1}>$, *n* increase;

    Step6.1. if $v_t \in CV$, and f_{n+1} is *M* type operation, then $CV = CV \cup \{v_t\}$;

    Step6.2. if $v_t \in CV$, and f_{n+1} is *C* type operation, then $Chain_i = Chain_i \cup \{f_{n+1}\}$;

    Step6.3. if $v_t \in CV$, and f_{n+1} is *V* type operation, then $VV_i = VV_i \cup \{v_t\}$;

    if IFS_i iterate end, then $Chain=Chain \cup Chain_i$; if $VV_i = \emptyset$, then $VV=VV \cup \{v_i\}$, reset *CV* and jump to Step4;

3.2.3   Dynamic Testing

After the analysis, we need test the functions in the validation chain with traditional testing methods. In dynamic testing, test cases were designed with the data mutation method in [15]. The server side testing result of a *vulnerability related path* perform that weather the security mechanism for the vulnerability variables is perfect. The testing result in this section as the final test result of server side testing.

3.3   Judgment Criterion

The framework propose in Sect. 3 is for the security testing to *vulnerability related path*. The presence of the vulnerabilities in a *vulnerability related path* depend on the result of client side testing and the result of server side testing. Table 4 shows the judgment criterion of the whole path.

Table 4. Judgment criterion

Client side	Server side	Whole path
Exist	Exist	Exist
Exist	Non-existent	Non-existent
Non-existent	Exist	Non-existent
Non-existent	Non-existent	Non-existent

In the judgment criterion, there is no vulnerabilities in the whole path as long as any side of the path make defense perfectly before the vulnerabilities being triggered.

4   Implementation and Experiment Analysis

4.1   Tool Implementation

We implement a tool named WebTester with the method in Sect. 3. The tool contains two parts, client side module and server side module. Client side module for testing the client elements, and server side module for testing the server elements.

Client side module is based on WebBrowser, a controls with the function of Web browser. The analysis result of the module is *DT* and the security cases of client elements. There are four child modules in this client side module, DOM analysis module, Data Form analysis module, Automatic test module and Relationship analysis module. Figure 11 describe the structure of these modules.

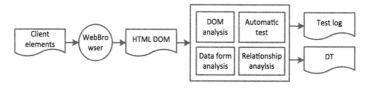

Fig. 11. Structure of client side module

The server side module is based on JTB [16], a syntax tree generation tool. The analysis result is the vulnerability variables and security mechanism in the server elements. Server side module contains three child modules, syntax tree and program structure analysis module, information flow generation module, and tainted analysis module. Figure 12 shows the structure of server side module.

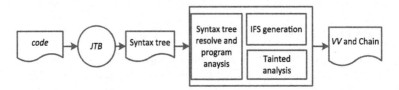

Fig. 12. Structure of server side testing tool

4.2   Experiment Analysis

With the security testing method in this paper, we analyze and test an actual Web application named AccountMSystem. AccountMSystem is a Web application used for managing projects fund of *Nanjing University of Aeronautics and Astronautics*. We construct the WRG as shown in Fig. 13, and we extract the three types of WRG paths from the diagram.

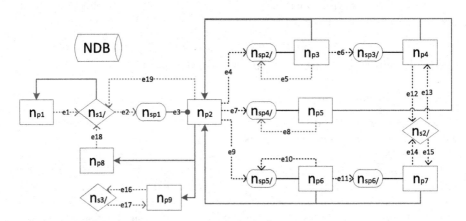

Fig. 13. WRG of AccountMSystem

The basic information of the application is shown in Table 5.

Table 5. Basic information of the application

Lines of code	NP	NSP	NS	NDB
13779	9	6	3	1

We analyze and test this application with WebTester, the results are shown in Table 6. There are 10 *SQL related paths*, 11 *XSS related paths* and 9 other paths in the WRG. The results show that the SQL injection vulnerabilities only exist in *SQL related paths*, and cross-site script vulnerabilities only exist *XSS related paths*.

Table 6. Test result

	SQL related	XSS related	NON
Numbers of paths	10	11	9
Numbers of paths with vulnerabilities	3	6	0

5 Conclusion

In this paper, we consider the Web security from the perspective of the structure of the Web application. We propose WRG to describe the structure and security properties of Web application. At the same time, we classify the elements of the WRG into two types, client elements and server elements, and propose a security testing framework on the basis of *vulnerability related path*. The testing framework contains client side testing and server side testing. The test results of these two parts determine whether there are vulnerabilities in a *vulnerability related path*. The client side testing is to test the security mechanism in the client elements. In this part we propose the model named data form to describe the information of the client elements and use the method of penetration testing on basis of data form. The server side testing is to test the security mechanism in the server side elements. In this part, use the method of static taint analysis to extract the security mechanism in the server side elements. In the last part of the sever side testing, we need to test the security mechanism with dynamic testing. In the end of this paper, we implement a testing tool named WebTester with the method described in Sect. 3. WebTester can make some assist for tester in Web security test. In the future work, we will improve *Web relation graph* model and hope to describe more types of Web vulnerabilities with *Web relation graph*.

References

1. Mookhey, K.K., Burghate, N.: Detection of SQL injection and cross-site scripting attacks (2004). http://www.securityfocus.com/infocus/1768
2. McGraw, Gary: Software security. IEEE Secur. Priv. **2**(2), 80–83 (2004)
3. MeDermott, J.P.: Attack net penetration testing. In: Proceedings of the 2000 Workshop on New Security Paradigms (NSPW2000), pp. 15–21. Bellybutton, Ireland (2000)
4. Jiye, Z., Xiao-quan, X.: Penetration testing model based on attack graph. Comput. Eng. Des. **26**(6), 1516–1518 (2005)
5. Huang, Q., Zeng, Q.-K.: Taint propagation analysis and dynamic verification with information flow policy. J. Softw. **22**(9), 2036–2048 (2011)
6. Lam, M.S., Martin, M.C., Livshits, V.B., Whaley, J.: Securing Web applications with static and dynamic information flow tracking. In: Proceedings of the 2008. ACM (2008)

7. Hallaraker, O., Vigna, G.: Detecting malicious javascript code in mozilla. In: Proceeding of 10th IEEE International Conference on Engineering of Complex Computer Systems (ICECCS 2005), pp. 85–94. IEEE, Shanghai, China, CS (2005)

8. Huang, Y.W., Huang, S.K., Lin, T.P.: Web application security assessment by fault injection and behavior monitoring. In: Proceedings of the 12th International Conference on World Wild Web, WWW 2003, pp. 148–159 (2003)

9. Ricca, F., Tonella, P.: Analysis and testing of web applications. In: Proceedings of the 23rd International Conference on Software Engineering, pp. 25–34 (2001)

10. Ricca, F., Tonella, P.: Web site analysis: structure and evolution. In: Proceeding of International Conference on Software Maintenance, pp. 76–86 (2000)

11. Tonella, P., Ricca, F.: A 2-layer model for the white-box. In: Proceeding of 26th Annual International Telecommunications Energy Conference on 2004, pp. 11–19 (2004)

12. Ricca, F., Tonella, P.: Using clustering to support the migration from static to dynamic web pages. In: Proceeding of the 11th IEEE International Workshop on Program Comprehension, pp. 207–216 (2003)

13. Ricca, F.: Dynamic model extraction and statistical analysis of web application. In: Proceeding of 4th International workshop on Web Site Evolution, pp. 43–52 (2002)

14. Ricca, F., et al.: Understanding and restructuring web sites with ReWeb. IEEE MultiMedia Cent. Sci. Technol. Res. **8**, 40–51 (2001)

15. Chen, J.F., Wang, Y.D., Zhang, Y.Q.: Automatic generation of attack vectors for stored-XSS. J. Grad. Univ. Chin. Acad. Sci. **29**(6), 815–820 (2012)

16. JTB: the java tree builder homepage [EB/OL] (2000). http://compilers.cs.ucla.edu/jtb/jtb-2003

An Improved Data Cleaning Algorithm Based on SNM

Miao Li, Qiang Xie[(⊠)], and Qiulin Ding

College of Computer Science and Technology,
Nanjing University of Aeronautics and Astronautics,
Nanjing 210016, China
limsunny@126.com, 7878414@qq.com,
qlding@nuaa.edu.com

Abstract. The basic sorted-neighborhood method (SNM) is a classic algorithm to detect approximately duplicate records in data cleaning, but the drawback is that the size of sliding window is hard to select and the attribute matching is too frequent so the detection efficiency is unfavorable. An optimized algorithm is proposed based on SNM By setting the size and speed of the sliding window variable to avoid missing record comparisons and reduce unnecessary ones, also it uses cosine similarity algorithm in attribute matching to improve precision of detection, and the Top-k effective weight filtering algorithm is proposed to reduce the number of attribute matching and improve the detection efficiency. The experiment results show that the improved algorithm is better than SNM in recall rate, precision rate and execution time efficiency.

Keywords: Data cleaning · Approximately duplicate records · SNM · Top-k

1 Introduction

With the rapid development of social information technology, more and more enterprises built its own data warehouse, but the enterprise system databases have inevitably dirty data problem because of data entry errors, spelling errors, missing fields and other factors, many areas involve data cleaning technology such as text mining, search engine, government agency, enterprise data warehouse and so on. Data cleaning aims to improve data quality by removing data errors and approximately duplicate records from the original data, approximately duplicate records mean the records that have semantic differences but actually imply the same entity, it's a waste of storage space and will affect the real distribution of the data if the database contains too many approximately duplicate records, so the detection and elimination of approximately duplicate records is one of the most critical issues in data cleaning.

The critical point of detection and elimination of approximately duplicate records is the match/merge problem, of which the most complicated step is to determine whether two records are similar, however, due to errors from various reasons or different representations for the same entity in different data sources, detecting whether two records are equal is not a simple arithmetic calculation. So far the common recognition algorithms are Field matching algorithm, N-gram matching algorithm, Clustering

© Springer International Publishing Switzerland 2015
Z. Huang et al. (Eds.): ICCCS 2015, LNCS 9483, pp. 259–269, 2015.
DOI: 10.1007/978-3-319-27051-7_22

algorithm and Edit distance algorithm and so on. The most simple way is to traverse all the records in database and compare each pair of them, but the algorithm's time complexity is $O(n^2)$ and that time consumption is not appropriate for the large database system. Sort/merge method is the standard algorithm to detect approximately duplicate records in database, its basic idea is to sort the data set first and then compare the adjacent records. Reference [1] assigned each record a N-gram value, then sorted the records according to the value and used the priority queues to cluster these records. Reference [2] raised the concept of variable sliding window and proposed to reduce missing match and improve the efficiency by adjusting the window's size promptly according to the result of comparison between the similarity value and the threshold. Reference [3] proposed the concept of filtering mechanism,attributes were divided into sort set R_k and mode set R_m, the algorithm sorted all the records many times according to the attributes in R_k, after each sort, called the detection function, repeated the process until all the approximately duplicate records were figured out. Reference [4] adopted the clustering algorithm to gather all the probably similar records in a cluster and then make pair-wise comparisons of these records. Reference [5] used the dependence graph concept to calculate the key attributes in the data table, then divided the record set into several small record sets according to the value of the key attribute and detected approximately duplicate records in each small record set. When merging the duplicate records, a master record was kept and the information of other duplicate records was merged into the main record, then deleted these records. This method can be applied to the duplicate record detection of big data quantity and can improve the detection efficiency and accuracy. Reference [6] proposed to use the ranking method to assign every attribute a appropriate weight based on the approximately duplicate records detection algorithm, the detection accuracy was improved by the influence of weight on the similarity calculation between two attributes during the process of record comparison.

All the related work above is based on the sort/merge idea and aims to improve the algorithm's efficiency by reducing the number of records for comparison. But in large data era, the reduced records are far from enough compared to the whole data set, the effect is not very remarkable to the detection and the real-time efficiency in data cleaning through this method. Therefore, considering that each pair of records is compared through one to one matching of the corresponding attribute, it's adoptable to improve the efficiency by reducing unnecessary attribute matching, so this paper proposes an improved data cleaning algorithm, which uses sliding window with variable size and speed in order to avoid missing record comparisons and reduce unnecessary ones, the cosine similarity algorithm is adopted to do the attribute matching to improve the matching accuracy. We also raise the Top-k effective weight filtering algorithm, firstly we select Top-k attributes with higher weights to start the matching, then calculate the sum of the k similarity values combined with weights and decide whether to match the remain attributes according to the result of comparison between the sum and the threshold, if the sum is less than the threshold set previously, we continue to do the comparison, otherwise we consider the two records are not approximately duplicate and finish the comparison in advance. By reducing the number of attribute comparisons, the real-time efficiency of record detection is greatly improved.

2 SNM Algorithm

The basic sorted-neighborhood method (SNM) is a typical algorithm based on the sort/merge idea, the key idea of SNM is to create a sorting keyword first, then sort the data set according to the keyword and make similar records to a neighboring region as much as possible, then slide a fixed size window on the sorted data set and each record in the data set is compared only with the records in the range of the sliding window. Assuming that there are w records in the sliding window, when the window moves, the original first record in the window is removed, and the new coming record is going to be compared with the original $W-1$ records to detect whether they're approximately duplicate records or not. SNM algorithm reduces the number of comparisons and improves the matching efficiency by applying the sliding window, the algorithm's time complexity is O $(w*n)$. There are two main drawbacks of the SNM, the first one is that the size of the sliding window is hard to set, it will lead to unnecessary record comparisons if the window is too big, however it will cause missing matching and reduce the detection accuracy if the window is too small. The second one is that the attribute matching is too frequent, though the application of sliding window has limited the times of the record matching, it's still huge time-consuming work for the entire data set and this is very unfavorable for some industries which have strict requirements for real-time efficiency in data cleaning. Considering the drawbacks above of SNM we present the idea of sliding window with variable size and speed and apply the cosine similarity algorithm to calculate similarity of attributes, also we propose the Top-k effective weight filtering algorithm during attribute matching and finally combine the similarity values and weights of attributes to calculate record similarity.

3 The Design of Improved SNM Algorithm

3.1 The Sliding Window with Variable Size and Speed

For the problem that the window size is too hard to set of SNM algorithm, the improved algorithm we propose uses a variable sliding window, we set the window size between a maximum value and a minimum value, the size and moving speed of the window is flexibly adjusted according to the result of comparison between the record similarity value and the threshold. The improved algorithm sets 3 parameters, the maximum window size w_{max}, the minimum window size w_{min} and the minimum threshold *lowthreshold*, we also set 3 variables, the current window size w_i, the moving speed v_i and the number of approximately duplicate records *Sim_num*, we record the similarity between R_l and Rn as $Sim(R_l, Rn)$. The initial value of the window size w_i equals w_{min}, firstly compare the record R_l with other records in the window, when it comes to the record Rw_{min} and $Sim(R_l, Rw_{min})$ is more than *lowthreshold*, then enlarge the window size w_i and continue to compare R_l with the next record until $Sim(R_l, Rn)$ is less than *lowthreshold* or w_i exceeds w_{max}, at the same time we adjust the moving speed of the window during the process of record comparison in order to improve matching efficiency, the current moving speed is calculated as follows:

$$V_i = Int(Wi - \frac{Sim\_num}{Wi}(Wi - 1)) \tag{1}$$

According to the descriptions above we can see that v_i complies with linear changes, the value of *Sim_num* is between 0 and w_i, When *Sim_num* = w_i, the moving speed v_i equals 1, when *Sim_num* = 0, the moving speed is v_i.

3.2 Attribute Matching Algorithm

Considering the drawbacks of SNM, we calculate attribute similarity by applying the cosine similarity algorithm which is used to calculating text similarity, a good method to calculate the similarity between different texts or short text messages is to map these words in the texts to vector space so we get the mapping relationship of the words and vector data, and then we get the text similarity value by calculating the degree of the difference between several or more different vectors, that's the key idea of the cosine similarity algorithm. The improved algorithm of SNM proposes to use the cosine similarity algorithm in detection of approximately duplicate records, we represent each attribute value as a vector by segmenting the value into words, and then get the similarity value between two attributes by calculating the cosine of the angle between inner product space of two vectors. The cosine of angle 0 is 1 and the cosine of any other angles is less than 1, the minimum value of cosine is -1, so we can make sure whether two vectors have approximately same direction according to the cosine of the angle between them. Usually we calculate the cosine only when the angle between two vectors is less than 90 degree so the cosine is always between 0 and 1. In the triangle constituted by vectors, we assume that vector a is (x_1, y_1), vector b is (x_2, y_2), so we calculate the cosine as follows:

$$\cos(\phi) = \frac{x_1 x_2 + y_1 y_2}{\sqrt{x_1^2 + y_1^2} \times \sqrt{x_2^2 + y_2^2}} \tag{2}$$

we extend the formula to multidimensional space, assuming that A and B are two multidimensional vectors, $A = (A_1, A_2, ..., An)$, $B = (B_1, B_2, ..., Bn)$, so the cosine between A and B is as follows:

$$\cos(\phi) = \frac{\sum_1^n (A_i \times B_i)}{\sqrt{\sum_1^n A_i^2} \times \sqrt{\sum_1^n B_i^2}} \tag{3}$$

The comparison between the records depends on the comparison between the attributes in detection of approximately duplicate records, so it has an important influence on the algorithm efficiency to segment the value of attributes into strings, we apply the cosine similarity algorithm in the detection because of its small time complexity and strong recognition ability. So we record the similarity between R_1 and R_2 as $Sim(R_1,R_2)$, segment the attribute into strings and sort the strings in alphabetical order, represent the strings as a vector with weights, so we get the similarity value between two attributes by calculating the cosine of the angle between inner product space of two vectors and then combine the sum of attribute similarity values with the weights we can get the value of $Sim(R_1,R_2)$. Assuming that R_1 and R_2 represent two records with each attribute given a special weight W_i and there are n attributes participating in comparison, $Sim(R_1,R_2)$ means record similarity and $Sim(R1_i,R2_i)$ means attribute similarity, so the records' similarity can be computed as follows:

$$Sim(R1,R2) = \frac{\sum_{i=1}^{n} Valid[i] \times W_i \times Sim(R1_i, R2_i)}{\sum_{i=1}^{n} Valid[i] \times W_i} \tag{4}$$

3.3   Top-k Effective Weight Filtering Algorithm

Typically, the number of approximately duplicate records in the entire data set is very small and some unnecessary comparisons waste a lot of time, so it'll greatly improve the detection efficiency if we exclude the records which seem not to be duplicate records high probability. The main time consumption of record similarity detection lies in the calculation of attribute similarity, so we can assign different weights W_i to different attributes according to their contribution to the record, the greater the contribution, the larger the value of weight. The key idea of the improved algorithm of SNM is to choose Top-k attributes with higher weights to do comparisons first, then add the similarity values of k attributes combined with weights to get the sum value, which we record as *KSimilar*, if *KSimilar* is more than W_2 which represents the minimum threshold we set previously, we consider that the two records are not approximately duplicate and finish the attribute comparison, otherwise continue the comparison. The Top-k effective weight filtering algorithm can shorten the detection time to a large extent and avoid losing data records, from the descriptions above we can know that the duplicated records to be merged after detection are all matched through all the attributes, the records only matched through k attributes are left in the data set, so we can detect most of the similar records in relatively short time and avoid missing potential data information.

The pseudo code is as follows:

Input: R1 and R2 represent two records, W1 represents
the threshold of attribute similarity, W2 represents the
threshold of the sum of top-k attribute similarity
values,LowThreshold represents the threshold of record
similarity.

```
Output:True/False
1.For i=1 to n do begin
2.If ((R1.Field[i]==null&&R2.Field[i]!=null)//
        (R1.Field[i]!=null&&R2.Field[i]==null))
3.Valid[i]=0;
4.Else
5.Valid[i]=1;
6.End;
7.For i=1 to n Do
8.For j=1 to i Do
9.If (W_j<W_{j+1})
10.Swap(Field[j],Field[j+1]);
11.End ;
12.End ;
13.For i=1 to k Do
14.MinFieldSimilar=MAX;
15.FieldSimilar =Sim(R1.Field[i],R2.Field[i]);
16.If (FieldSimilar<MinFieldSimilar) then
        MinFieldSimilar=FieldSimilar;
17.End ;
18.If (MinFieldSimilar>W1) then return False;
19.Else KSimilar=KSimilar+Valid[i]*W_i*FieldSimilar;
20.End;
21.If (KSimilar<=W2)then RSimilar=KSimilar
22.For i=k+1 to n Do
23.FieldSimilar =Sim(R1.Field[i],R2.Field[i]);
24.If (FieldSimilar<MinFieldSimilar) then
        MinFieldSimilar=FieldSimilar;
25.End ;
26.IF (MinFieldSimilar>W_1) then return False;
27.Else RSimilar=RSimilar+Valid[i]*W_i*FieldSimilar;
28.End;
29.If (RSimilar<=LowThreshold)then return True
30.Else return False;
31.Else return False;
```

Only when both records are not null or null at the same time for the attribute i, the
comparison result for that attribute can be counted and Valid[i] is set to 1, otherwise
Valid[i] is set to 0. From line 1 to 6, the function fills the array Valid to ensure the null
attributes will affect the result of comparisons. From line 7 to 12, the function ranks the
attributes in descending order according to their weights. From line 13 to 20, the
function calculates the similarity value of R1 and R2 as the formula shows. During the
comparing, the function firstly selects the Top-k attributes with higher weights to do
comparisons because they more representative in the similarity of records. From
line 21 to 31, the function compares the value *KSimilar* with the threshold W2, if
KSimilar is less than W2, then continue to calculate the similarity of remain attributes
to get the record similarity, otherwise we finish the progress.

4   The Evaluation Criteria of Data Cleaning Algorithm

There are two evaluation criteria for the approximately duplicate records cleaning algorithm, the recall rate and the precision rate.

4.1   Recall Rate

Recall rate refers to the percentage that approximately duplicate records correctly identified by the algorithm accounts for the actual approximately duplicate records contained in the data set. Assuming that A1, A2, A3, B1, B2, B3 and C1 represent 6 records, among which {A1, A2, A3} and {B1, B2, B3} are respectively duplicate records of A and B, if we identified {A1, A2, C1} and {B1, B2} are duplicate records through a data cleaning process, then Recall = 4/6*100 % = 66.67 %.

4.2   Precision Rate

Precision rate refers to the percentage that approximately duplicate records correctly identified by the algorithm accounts for all the approximately duplicate records identified by the algorithm. Precision rate aims at detecting whether the duplicate records which have been identified belong to the same entity, that is the detection of the existence of false identification. In the above example Precision = 4/5*100 % = 80 %.

5   Experiment

We compare the improved algorithm with the SNM algorithm in the same operating environment according to three aspects, the recall rate, the precision rate and execution time. The experimental operating environment is Inter CPU 2.93 GHz and the memory is 2 GB, the software environment is as follows: the operating system is Windows7 Ultimate Microsoft, the experimental program is written in Java and the development environment is Visual Studio Microsoft 2010. The data set for test comes from the daily monitoring data of a ship management system, due to the condition that the value of the threshold in SNM algorithm is less than 1 we set *LowThreshold* to 0.63, during the running process of the algorithm the window size ranges from 10 to 100.

5.1   The Effect of Different Window Sizes on the Experimental Results

In this experiment, we choose 1000, 5000, 10000 records separately to make several experiments to detect the effect of different window sizes on the experimental results, under the premise of a fixed value of *LowThreshold* as 0.63, we adjust the window size according to the result of the record matching and record the numerical changes of the recall rate and execution time at the same time.

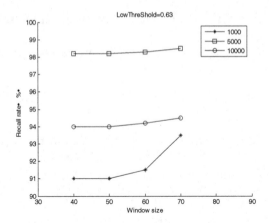

Fig. 1. Recall rate with different window size

Figure 1 shows different recall rates with different window sizes and the value of *LowThreshold* is 0.63. We can see that the recall rate increases with the increase of the window size, so the algorithm can identify more duplicate records and improve the efficiency of the detection.

Figure 2 shows different execution time with different window sizes and the value of *LowThreshold* is 0.63. We can see that the execution time's growth rate is comparatively gentle and the algorithm's performance is stable.

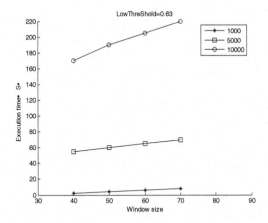

Fig. 2. Execution time with different window size

5.2 The Comparison Between SNM and the Improved SNM

We made comparisons of the two algorithms in recall rate, precision rate and execution time and the result is as follows (Figs. 3, 4 and 5):

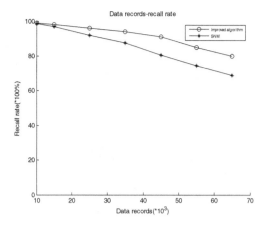

Fig. 3. Data records and recall rate

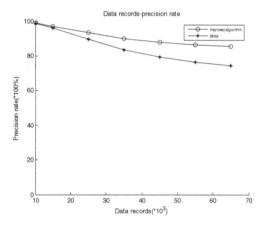

Fig. 4. Data records and precision rate

From the results above we can see in the improved SNM data cleaning algorithm, the preprocessing procedure of the attributes during the sort of the data set and the application of the cosine similarity algorithm plus the Top-k effective weight filtering algorithm during the calculation of attribute similarity have remarkably improved the recall rate and precision rate compared with the SNM algorithm, and also the usage of the sliding window with variable size and speed during record comparison has obvious improvement on the execution time.

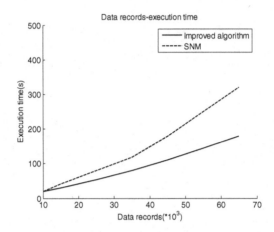

Fig. 5. Data records and execution time

6 Conclusion

The detection and elimination of approximately duplicate records is a complicated job in data cleaning, most of all the detection part greatly effect the time efficiency, this paper introduces an improved algorithm based on SNM, the improved algorithm proposes to use the sliding window of variable size and speed during record matching, apply the cosine similarity algorithm and the Top-k effective weight filtering algorithm during the calculation of attribute similarity. The experiment results show that the improved algorithm improves recall rate and precision rate, reduces the false identification and optimizes the time efficiency. Further work still needs to be researched on reducing the number of attribute comparisons, for example we can cluster the records first, and then select one record as a representation of each cluster to participate in the comparison and in this way we can improve the time efficiency of the duplicate records detection effectively.

References

1. Hylton, J.A.: Identifying and merging related bibliographic records. M S dissertation, MIT Laboratory for Computer Science Technical Report, MIT, p. 678 (1996)
2. Li, J.: Improvement on the algorithm of data cleaning based on SNM. Comput. Appl. Softw. (2008)
3. He, L., Zhang, Z., Tan, Y., Liao, M.: An efficient data cleaning algorithm based on attributes selection. In: 2011 6th International Conference on Computer Sciences and Convergence Information Technology (ICCIT), pp. 375–379. IEEE (2011)
4. Madnick, S.E., Wang, R.Y., Lee, Y.W., Zhu, H.W.: Overview and framework for data and information quality research. ACM J. Data Inf. Qual. **1**, 2 (2009)
5. Omar, B., Hector, G., David, M., Jennifer, W., Steven, E., Su, Q.: Swoosh: a generic approach to entity resolution. VLDB J. **18**, 255–276 (2009)

6. Sotomayor, B.: The globus toolkit 3 programmer's tutorial, 2004, pp. 81–88, Zugriffsdatum (2005). http://gdp.globus.org/gt3-tutorial/multiplehtml/
7. Monge, A., Elkan, C.: The field matching problem: algorithms and applications. In: Proceedings of the 2nd International Conference of Knowledge Discovery and Data Mining (1996)
8. Krishnamoorthy, R., Kumar, S.S., Neelagund, B.: A new approach for data cleaning process. In: Recent Advances and Innovations in Engineering (ICRAIE), pp. 1–5. IEEE (2014)
9. Chen, H.Q., Ku, W.S., Wang, H.X., Sun, M.T.: Leveraging spatio-temporal redundancy for RFID data cleansing. In: Proceedings of the 2010 ACM SIGMOD International Conference on Management of Data, pp. 51–62 (2010)
10. Zhang, F., Xue, H.F., Xu, D.S., Zhang, Y.H., You, F.: Big data cleaning algorithms in cloud computing. Int. J. Interact. Mobile Technol. (2013)
11. Arora, R., Pahwa, P., Bansal, S.: Alliance rules for data warehouse cleansing. In: International Conference on Signal Processing Systems, pp. 743–747. IEEE (2009)
12. Ali, K., Warraich, M.: A framework to implement data cleaning in enterprise data warehouse for robust data quality. In: 2010 International Conference on Information and Emerging Technologies (ICIET), pp. 1–6. IEEE (2010). 978-1-4244-8003-6/10
13. Li, J., Zheng, N.: An improved algorithm based on SNM data cleaning algorithm. Comput. Appl. Softw. 25(2), 245–247 (2008). doi:10.3969/j.issn.1000-386X.2008.02.089
14. Luo, Q., Wang, X.F.: Analysis of data cleaning technology in data warehouse. Comput. Program. Skills Maintenance 2 (2015)
15. Dai, J.W., Wu, Z.L., Zhu, M.D.: Data Engineering Theory and Technology, pp. 148–155. National Defense Industry Press, Beijing (2010)
16. Zhang, J.Z., Fang, Z., Xiong, Y.J.: Data cleaning algorithm optimization based on SNM. J. Central South Univ. (Nat. Sci. Ed.) 41(6), 2240–2245 (2010)
17. Wang, L., Xu, L.D., Bi, Z.M., Xu, Y.C.: Data cleaning for RFID and WSN integration. Ind. Inf. IEEE Trans. 10(1), 408–418 (2014)
18. Tong, Y.X., Cao, C.C., Zhang, C.J., Li, Y.T., Lei, C.: CrowdCleaner: data cleaning for multi-version data on the web via crowd sourcing. In: 2014 IEEE 30th International Conference on Data Engineering (ICDE), pp. 182–1185. IEEE Computer Society (2014)
19. Volkovs, M., Fei, C., Szlichta, J., Miller, R.J.: Continuous data cleaning. In: 2014 IEEE 30th International Conference on Data Engineering (ICDE), pp. 244–255. IEEE (2014)
20. Dallachiesa, M., Ebaid, A., Eldawy, A., Elmagarmid, A., Ilyas, I.F., Quzzani, M., Tang, N.: NADEEF: a commodity data cleaning system. In: Proceedings of the 2013 ACM SIGMOD International Conference on Management of Data. ACM (2013)
21. Ebaid, A., Elmagarmid, A., Ilyas, I.F., Quzzani, M., Yin, S., Tang, N.: NADEEF: a generalized data cleaning system. Proc. VLDB Endowment 6, 1218–1221 (2013)
22. Broeck, J.V.D., Fadnes, L.T.: Data cleaning. Epidemiol. Principles Pract. Guidel. 66 (2013)

Enhancing Security of IaaS Cloud with Fraternal Security Cooperation Between Cloud Platform and Virtual Platform

Jie Yang[✉], Zhiqiang Zhu, Lei Sun, Jingci Zhang, and Xianwei Zhu

Zhengzhou Information Science and Technology Institute, Zhengzhou, China
{1105118750,1056670972}@qq.com,
{xdjs_zzq,zjcsdhr}@163.com, sll02@sina.com

Abstract. IaaS cloud provides customers on-demand computational resources such as mass storage, virtual machine and network. However, it also raises some security problems that may hold back its widespread adoption. Since IaaS leverages many technologies, it inherits their security issues. For example, to provision and manage these computing resources, cloud platform and virtual platform are indispensable, but their security issues don't disappear, and even bring in some new security issues. What's more, their protection mechanisms are mutually independent and don't exploit each other's security advantages. That leaves security blind spots between them and can't guarantee the security of whole IaaS cloud. In this paper, we introduce security cooperation between cloud platform and virtual platform to address privacy and security issues of IaaS, and build secure IaaS cloud based on OpenNebula and Xen. Our approach leverages each component's security advantages and unites them into secure IaaS cloud, and experiments show it just incurs little performance overhead.

Keywords: Network separation · Security cooperation · Cloud computing security · Flow control protocol · Attack surface · Virtual platform

1 Introduction

Cloud computing [1–3] is a way to offer on-demand computational resources over the network in an easy and transparent manner. Thanks to the increasing demand for Internet services and communication, the extent and importance of cloud computing are rapidly increasing and obtaining a huge attention in the industrial and scientific communities. Cloud computing comprised of three service models and four deployment models. These service models are Software as a Service (SaaS), Platform as a Service (PaaS), and Infrastructure as a Service (IaaS). And, the four deployment models are the private, community, public and hybrid cloud, that refer to the location of the cloud infrastructure.

IaaS provides virtual and physical hardware as a service and entire infrastructure is delivered over the Internet. And it is the most offered cloud service layer by public cloud providers and also the most used by customers. There are numerous open source cloud platform that offers building IaaS over Internet, such as OpenStack [4], OpenNebula [5], Eucalyptus [6], CloudStack [7] and so on. However, plenty of vulnerabilities have been

© Springer International Publishing Switzerland 2015
Z. Huang et al. (Eds.): ICCCS 2015, LNCS 9483, pp. 270–282, 2015.
DOI: 10.1007/978-3-319-27051-7_23

ascertained in many services they provided, ranging from denial of service to authentication bypass to abortive input-validation to malicious insiders. The cloud platform appears to assume complete trust among services that is why these vulnerabilities are particularly problematic. Thus, no matter which one service is compromised may impact the security of other cloud services. Further, compromised cloud services can launch masses of programs as privileged processes, qualifying adversaries to do everything he wanted on cloud service hosts.

What's more, there is an obvious vulnerability that cloud platform executes management command directly in privileged VM of virtual platform with bare-metal Hypervisor, such as Xen [8], Hyper-V [9], VMware ESXi [10] and so on. Cloud customers can straight access the cloud service hosts when they obtain cloud service (virtual machine, for example), in some service deploy architecture. That is because cloud platform vendors want to free management server from huge access pressure. Clearly, this vulnerability exposes the privileged VM to both legitimate users and adversaries who can access the network. As we all know, once privileged VM is compromised by adversaries, that means the virtual platform and all the virtual machines running on this virtual platform are compromised.

While the cloud platform vendors take countermeasures to protect the host running could services from attack. But practices have proven current approaches are incomplete. For example, OpenStack requires that forwarding requests to services must be authorized firstly. But, request is turned into several interface calls among services, and the safety of invoking method call is not validated. Also, Researchers have done a lot of work to protect virtual platform from internal or external attacking. For instance, HyperSafe [11] and HyperSentry [12] both address to enhance the security of the hypervisor by either enforcing control-flow integrity or measuring its integrity dynamically. NOVA [13] is a micro-kernel based hypervisor [14, 15] that disaggregates the traditional monolithic hypervisor into a system with different purpose components, and improves its security by enforcing capability-based access control for different components in hypervisor. Murray, Milos and Hand propose a way to improve the security of the management software in Xen by moving the domain building utilities into a separate domain. Further, In Xoar [16], the functionality of Dom0 has been separated into nine classes of single-purpose service VMs, each of which contains a piece of functionality logic that has been decoupled from the monolithic Dom0. But, the safety protection measures of cloud platform and virtual platform are independent from each other and have no consistent security goals. Therefore, it's hard to guarantee the security of IaaS cloud.

In this paper, we propose a substitutable approach, called SCIaaS, which introduces security cooperation between cloud platform and virtual platform to address privacy and security issues in IaaS. Our approach uses both security features of virtual platform and cloud platform to isolate privileged VM from the open network environment, and isolate management network from Internet. Also, it protects user's privacy from attacks launched by malicious insiders. In conclusion, this paper makes the following contributions.

- The case of using virtual machine isolation to isolate privileged VM from NetVM, which is the network components separated from privileged VM and building flow channel between privileged VM and NetVM to fine-grained control the control flow from cloud platform. That significantly reduces the attack surface [17] of privileged VM and isolates the management network from Internet.

- A set of protection techniques that provide users' privacy protection against adversaries who are even malicious insiders.
- A prototype implementation of our approach that leverages OpenNebula and Xen, which is demonstrated with a little performance overhead.

In this paper, the IaaS cloud architecture we discussed is based on OpenNebula and Xen, and the remainder of this paper proceeds as follows. Section 2 identifies threats to IaaS cloud and describes the threat model. Section 3 firstly discusses our design goals, and then describes our approaches and the overall architecture of security enhanced IaaS cloud. Section 4 describes how to securely control the information flow between privileged VM and the network VM. Section 5 discusses the virtual machine images protection. The prototype and performance evaluation results are discussed in Sect. 6. We then conclude this paper and possible future work in Sect. 7.

2 Motivation and Threat Model

This section first describes the attack surface of IaaS cloud built with OpenNebula and Xen, and then talks over the threat model of SCIaaS.

2.1 The Attack Surface of IaaS Cloud

IaaS provides a pool of resources such as storage, networks, servers, and other computing resources in the form of virtualized systems, and customers access them through the Internet. With IaaS cloud, cloud users have better control over the security compared to the other service models if there is no security hole in hypervisor. Cloud users control the software running in their virtual machines, and they are also responsible for configuring security policies correctly. However, the underlying network, storage and computing infrastructures are controlled by cloud providers. IaaS providers must undertake a substantial effort to secure their systems in order to minimize these threats resulted from communication, monitoring, creation, mobility, and modification.

Figure 1 depicts the typical architecture of IaaS cloud and its attack surface. In IaaS cloud, cloud platform manages virtual machines or hosts usually by executing management command directly in privileged VM of virtual platform with bare-metal hypervisor over network. As Guest VMs are usually managed through the management tools via privileged interfaces to the hypervisor, they could be arbitrarily inspected and tampered with by not only the hypervisor but also the management tools in privileged VM. That leads to compromising Guest VMs easily by malicious cloud operators or users who can access privileged VM (i.e., attack surface 4). In principle, cloud operators and cloud users should be granted with the least privilege and will not be able to compromise Guest VMs. In practice, cloud operators or cloud users are usually granted with higher privilege more than they should have, as it is usually difficult to define the proper privilege precisely for them (i.e., attack surface 3). For example, a cloud operator may leverage over-powerful privileged interface to compromising privileged VM, and a cloud user might attack privileged VM through compromising network service of privileged VM.

What's more, in IaaS environments, a VM image is a prepackaged software template, which contains virtual machine configurations files that are used to create VMs. Thus, these images are essential for the security of the cloud. Malicious users can compromise other users or even the cloud system by storing images containing malicious code into public repositories. Furthermore, cloud operators might dump a VM's memory image for offline analysis, stealthily migrate or clone a VM to a shadow place for replaying via the internal maintenance interface, or even copy away all VM's virtual disks (i.e., attack surface 1). And the vulnerabilities of identity and access management may lead to the attack that cloud users or operators leverage services of cloud platform to compromising privileged VM and further compromising Guest VM or hypervisor.

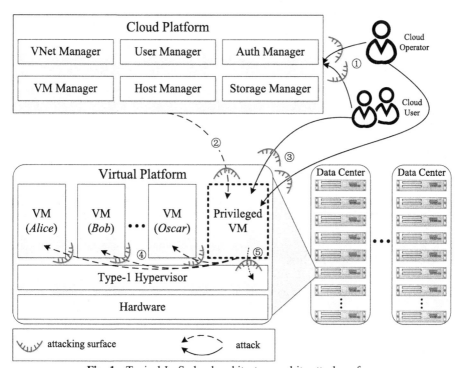

Fig. 1. Typical IaaS cloud architecture and its attack surface.

2.2   Assumptions and Threat Models

Adversaries: Considering that there are several attack surfaces in IaaS cloud, we consider both remote adversaries (malicious cloud users) and local adversaries (malicious cloud operators) and assume that they have full control over the host management stack of cloud platform or VM management stack. An adversary may leverage the powerful management interfaces of cloud platform to dump a Guest VM's memory, inject malicious code to the VM, or even steal the VM's virtual disks.

Assumptions: We assume the IaaS cloud providers themselves don't propose to be malicious or with the goal of compromising or stealing its customers' sensitive information. And, we assume there will be no internal physical attacks such as placing probes into the buses and freezing all main memory. Actually, typical data centers usually have strict control of physical accesses, and there are surveillance cameras to log and monitor such accesses. While, as cloud operators might leverage the VM management interfaces or even physical maintenance to access the disk storage easily, we assume that the external disk storage is not trustworthy. Furthermore, we assume that the hypervisor of virtual platform is trusted for its smaller TCB. We also assume that the code instantiating the functionality of the privileged VM containing bugs that are a potential source of compromise. Consider that in the case of a monolithic privileged VM, a successful attack on any one of its numerous interfaces can lead to numberless exploits against guest VMs. The virtual platform has a hug attack surface. So it's a good idea that isolating privileged VM from the source of compromise. Therefore, we assume that the isolated privileged VM is trusted.

Security Guarantees: The purpose of SCIaaS is to prevent the malicious VM management stack and host management stack of cloud platform from compromising a Guest VM, thus providing both secrecy and integrity to a VM's states. SCIaaS guarantees that all accesses to a VM, such as VM management, VM loginning and memory dumping, can only be done when the access's subject is authorized by privileged VM. A malicious cloud operator cannot issue arbitrary control flow transfers from the cloud platform to privileged VM. Instead, all control flow transfers between the cloud platform and privileged VM can only be done through a well-defined protocol. What's more, SCIaaS guarantees that VM's virtual disks can only be accessed by the VM or privileged VM, and the others can only see the encrypted version of those virtual disks.

3   Goals and Approaches

This section first depicts the design goals of SCIaaS, and then describes approaches to achieving these goals. Finally, we present the overall architecture of SCIaaS.

3.1   Design Consideration

The primary goal of SCIaaS is to provide security protection to IaaS cloud by security cooperation between cloud platform and virtual platform.

   Attack Surface Reduction: As we all can see, the attack surfaces of IaaS mostly focus on privileged VM of virtual platform, that is to say that privileged VM is a critical component of IaaS from a security perspective. What's more, the privileged VM also houses smorgasbord of functionality such as device system boot, emulation and multiplexing, administrative toolstack, etc. Each of them is presented to multiple Guest VMs over different functionality-specific interfaces. And a successful attack on any of them places the overall virtual platform in danger. Hence, reducing the attack surface of privileged VM is import to reduce security risks of virtual platform and further enhance IaaS security.

Every Action with Authentication: It is import to guarantee that each action of cloud users and cloud operator must be authenticated. Therefore, not only cloud platform should authenticate users and operators but also virtual platform. And it's necessary that virtual platform is fully aware of the high-level information about visitor. Furthermore, the root of authentication is not provided by IaaS cloud provider, it should be the trusted third party.

Privacy Protection: Clearly, privacy is one of the most relevant inconveniences for fastening the widespread adoption of the cloud for many business-critical computations, that is because that the underlying network, storage, and computing infrastructure is controlled by cloud providers. Hence, privacy protection is an important part of security-enhancing IaaS cloud.

Security Cooperation: As cloud platform and virtual platform are located in different layers of IaaS cloud, they also own different security attributes in IaaS cloud, therefore, it is a flawed trust assumption that virtual platform is trusted for cloud platform and only cloud platform influences the security of IaaS. Apparently, just enhance security of them separately can not guarantee security assurance of IaaS cloud. Accordingly, we firmly believe that the goal can be achieved by integrating the security mechanism of cloud platform and virtual platform.

3.2   Approach Overview

Our approach is based on security cooperation between cloud platform and virtual platform. SCIaaS takes full advantage of security attribute of virtualization, and combines the higher level security knowledge of cloud platform for enhancing security of IaaS cloud.

Attack surface reduction using virtualization separation: We strongly in favor of the view that one approach to improving the security of a system or software is to reduce its attack surface. And the basic countermeasures of attack surface reduction are to reduce entry points available to untrusted users, reduce the amount of code running, and eliminate services requested by relatively few users[1]. What's more, the mainly attack surface comes from the network, as mostly adversaries access the virtual platform only through network. Hence, we separate the network functionality from the privileged VM, and reduce entry points of privileged VM available to cloud users and operators through control the control flow between privileged VM and NetVM. Furthermore, we just only allow cloud operators or users to request services via NetVM.

Access control through identity authentication: In computer security, there are many general access control mechanisms, such as authentication, authorization, access approval, and audit. A system that is supposed to be used only by those authorized must attempt to detect and exclude the unauthorized. Access to it is therefore usually controlled

---

[1] https://en.wikipedia.org/wiki/Attack_surface.

by insisting on an authentication procedure to establish with some degree of confidence the identity of the user, granting privileges established for that identity. One such procedure allows virtual platform and cloud platform to identify user, control activity of users in the IaaS cloud, generate reports by username and set user based policies.

Image protection with cryptography: IaaS cloud is revolutionizing how information technology services and resources are managed and used, but the revolution comes with new security problems. One of the security problems is how to securely manage the virtual machine images, which encapsulate each application of the cloud. The initial state of every virtual machine in the cloud is determined by some image. That is why the image with high integrity is so essential. Hence, we encrypt or encrypt cloud user's images in privileged VM, and the key is managed by cloud user.

3.3   The SCIaaS Architecture

Figure 2 shows the overall architecture of SCIaaS, which is a typical architecture of security cooperation in IaaS cloud. SCIaaS separates network functionality from the privileged VM of virtual platform, and uses an independent virtual machine (called NetVM) to undertake the separated network functionality. There are two NetVM (internal NetVM and external NetVM) for virtual platform in SCIaaS. The external NetVM is responsible for providing network service for Guest VM, and cloud users access their virtual machine also via NetVM. The internal NetVM just only to handle the control flows from cloud platform and the data flow of virtual disks, and transmit

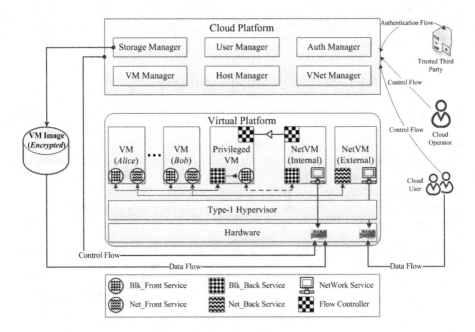

Fig. 2. Overall architecture of SCIaaS

the control flow to privileged VM through the control flow protocol. What's more, the internal NetVM and external NetVM are in different network segments that isolates IaaS cloud from Internet very well.

Furthermore, SCIaaS uses the trusted third party to provide authentication service for IaaS cloud and distributes the authentication to virtual platform, where the accessed resources located in. Cloud platform and virtual platform utilize each of their security advantages, existing knowledge and access control decisions to enhance their own security and further enhance security of IaaS cloud. Also, SCIaaS keeps virtual machine images always be encrypted when it out of the runtime environment of privileged VM, hypervisor and the virtual machine.

4 Securing Control Flow

As the cloud operators manage virtual platform via that cloud platform sends control command to privileged VM of virtual platform over network, and SCIaaS separates network functionality from privileged VM. Hence, we build the flow channel between privileged VM and NetVM to transmit control flow.

4.1 The Secure Flow Channel Architecture

Figure 3 depicts the architecture of secure flow channel. It is mainly comprised of *flow controller client* located in NetVM, *flow controller server* located in privileged VM and *secure flow control protocol*. *Flow controller client* encapsulates the control flow from cloud platform, according to the *secure flow control protocol*, and sends the encapsulated flow to *flow controller server*. Also, *flow controller server* parses the encapsulated flow from *flow controller client*, based on the *secure flow control protocol*, and executes the control command in privileged VM. The *secure flow control protocol* defines interaction between *flow controller server* and *flow controller client*, and what control flow can be transmitted between NetVM and privileged VM. What's more, the hypervisor guarantees that the secure flow channel is trusted and the secure flow channel only can be built between privileged VM and NetVM.

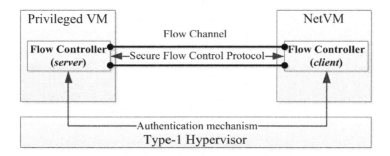

Fig. 3. The secure flow channel architecture

4.2   The Secure Flow Control Protocol

The *secure flow control protocol* (*SFCP*) control the flow between privileged VM and NetVM. It can protect privileged VM from malicious flow by filtering the undefined control flow, and exposes very narrow interface to cloud platform. This protocol is message-based, and all flow share a common header followed by an optional data packet. The optional data packet stands specific control flow. In *SFCP*, *flow controller client* denoted by *FCC* and flow controller server denoted by *FCS*. The details of *SFCP* as follows:

1. The privileged VM setups *FCS*, and initializes the runtime environment of *FCS*;
2. When the NetVM is instantiated, NetVM setups *FCC* and also initializes the run-time environment of *FCC*, then connects to *FCS*;
3. *FCC* sends its supported version of *SFCP* to *FCS* when their connection is established;
4. *FCS* reply with its own supported version of *SFCP* to *FCC*, if protocol versions don't mach, the connection is closed, then they finish the handshake stage;
5. *FCC* receives control command from cloud platform, and encapsulates the control command and parameters to protocol messages, then sends to *FCS*;
6. *FCS* parses the protocol messages, if the parsed control command is not defined, *FCS* sends error-message to *FCC*, otherwise, *FCS* executes the control command and sends the execution results to *FCC*;
7. FCS parses the reply messages, and returns it to cloud platform;
8. Looping the step 6 and 7.

5   Virtual Machine Image Protection

Figure 4 illustrates the architecture of virtual machine image encryption. In SCIaaS, virtual platform accesses storages through *nfs/nas* [18, 19] over network, and stores virtual machine images in the form of chipper text in RAID [20, 21]. What's more, both cloud platform and virtual platform can't decrypt the encrypted virtual machine images

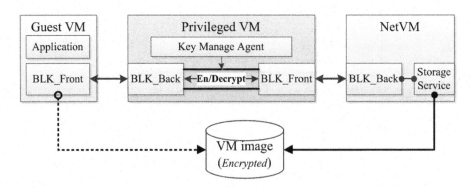

Fig. 4. The architecture of virtual machine image encryption

as they don't have the decryption key, but virtual platform can do that with the help of cloud user who own that virtual machine. And the encryption and decryption all occur in privileged VM of virtual platform, the key agreement also happened in privileged VM. That is because we believe the privileged VM is trusted after network separation. The virtual machine protection in the lifecycle of virtual machine as follows.

1. **Instantiating virtual machine:** Firstly, the privileged VM obtain the encrypted virtual machine image through NetVM (file access between privileged VM and NetVM via BLK_Front and BLK_Back). Secondly, the key manage agent gets key from the virtual machine owner through key agreement protocol. Finally, privileged VM decrypt the image, and the virtual machine builder instantiate virtual machine.
2. **Virtual machine running:** If virtual machine reads file from image, the privileged VM decrypt the related file, otherwise, the privileged VM encrypt the related file.
3. **Destroying virtual machine:** When cloud user destroys his or her virtual machine, the privileged VM encrypts the virtual machine's states and the plaintext part of image, and then destroys the key.

6 Prototype and Performance Evaluation

We implement SCIaaS based on OpenNebula-4.8 and Xen-4.4, the network topology of SCIaaS depicted as Fig. 5, and the prototype illustrated as Fig. 6. Table 1 shows the hardware and software configuration of SCIaaS.

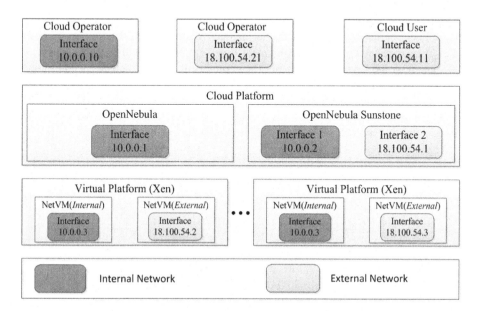

Fig. 5. The network topology of SCIaaS

Fig. 6. The prototype of SCIaaS

Table 1. The hardware and software configuration of SCIaaS

Configuration	Cloud platform	Virtual platform
CPU	Xenon-E5-2680, 2.8 GHz	Xenon-E5-2680, 2.8 GHz
Memory	64G	64G
Disk	6T	1T
Host OS	CentOS 6.5	Fedora 20

We present a quantitative comparison of SCIaaS and OpenNebula&Xen to prove that SCIaaS is efficient. We focused into the deployment as well as clean-up times of VMs. We experiment with the deployment time of 5 VMs (the five VMs with same VM image) on the same physical host. The deployment process includes pending time and the transition time of a VM between the active and the running state. And this two IaaS cloud have same hardware and software configuration illustrated as Table 1. The pending time and time from active to running state depicted in Figs. 7 and 8, and the results show that SCIaaS just incurs little performance overhead.

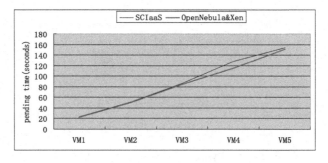

Fig. 7. Concurrent at-once pending time of deploy

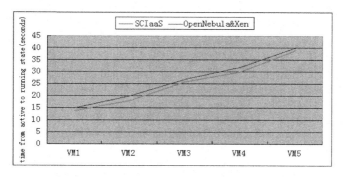

Fig. 8. The time from active to running state

7 Conclusion and Future Work

Cloud computing offers great potential to improve productivity and reduce costs. It also poses many new security risks. In this paper, we explore these risks in depth from the join between cloud platform and virtual platform in IaaS cloud. In particular, we analyze the attack surface of IaaS cloud, and find that the privileged VM of virtual platform is the focus. We present an approach (called SCIaaS) that addresses those vulnerabilities and argue that our approach is implementable and efficient. In our approach, we propose that utilizing security cooperation between cloud platform and virtual platform to enhance the security of IaaS cloud. In specifically, we separate network functionality from privileged VM and build secure flow control channel for control command transmitted between cloud platform and virtual platform. Also, we protect the virtual machine images from malicious attack via cryptographic. At last, we implement the prototype of SCIaaS based on OpenNebula4.8 and Xen4.4, and experiments show that the prototype system just incurs little performance overhead.

In our approach, security cooperation between cloud platform and virtual platform just stays in some security mechanisms, and doesn't think about it with the security requirement of the whole system. We expect that bringing security policy into both cloud platform and virtual platform with unified standard in the future.

References

1. Armbrust, M., Fox, A., Griffith, R., Joseph, A.D., Katz, R., Konwinski, A., et al.: A view of cloud computing. Commun. ACM **53**(4), 50–58 (2010)
2. NIST, NIST: The NIST definition of cloud computing. Commun. ACM **53**(6), 50–50 (2011)
3. Wei, L., Zhu, H., Cao, Z., Dong, X., Jia, W., Chen, Y., et al.: Security and privacy for storage and computation in cloud computing. Inf. Sci. **258**(3), 371–386 (2014)
4. Corradi, A., Fanelli, M., Foschini, L.: VM consolidation: a real case based on openstack cloud. Future Gener. Comput. Syst. **32**(2), 118–127 (2014)
5. Milojičić, D., Llorente, I.M., Montero, R.S.: Opennebula: a cloud management tool. IEEE Internet Comput. **15**(2), 11–14 (2011)

6. Sempolinski, P., Thain, D.: A comparison and critique of eucalyptus, OpenNebula and Nimbus. In: 2010 IEEE Second International Conference on Cloud Computing Technology and Science (CloudCom), pp. 417–426. IEEE (2010)
7. Paradowski, A., Liu, L., Yuan, B.: Benchmarking the performance of OpenStack and CloudStack. In: 2014 IEEE 17th International Symposium on Object/Component/Service-Oriented Real-Time Distributed Computing (ISORC), pp. 405–412. IEEE Computer Society (2014)
8. Barham, P., Dragovic, B., Fraser, K., Hand, S., Harris, T., Ho, A., et al.: Xen and the art of virtualization. In: Proceedings of SOSP-03: The Nineteenth ACM Symposium on Operating Systems Principles, vol. 19, pp. 164–177. ACM, New York, NY (2003)
9. Leinenbach, D., Santen, T.: Verifying the Microsoft hyper-V hypervisor with VCC. In: Cavalcanti, A., Dams, D.R. (eds.) FM 2009. LNCS, vol. 5850, pp. 806–809. Springer, Heidelberg (2009)
10. Tian, J.W., Liu, X.X., Xi, L.I., Wen-Hui, Q.I.: Application on VMware Esxi virtualization technique in server resource integration. Hunan Electr. Power **6**, 004 (2012)
11. Wang, Z., Jiang, X.: HyperSafe: a lightweight approach to provide lifetime hypervisor control-flow integrity. In: Proceedings of S&P, Oakland, pp. 380–395 (2010)
12. Azab, A.M., Ning, P., Wang, Z., Jiang, X., Zhang, X., Skalsky, N.C.: HyperSentry: enabling stealthy in-context measurement of hypervisor integrity 65. In: Proceedings of the 17th ACM Conference on Computer and Communications Security, pp. 38–49. ACM (2010)
13. Steinberg, U., Kauer, B.: NOVA: a microhypervisor-based secure virtualization architecture. In: Proceedings of the European Conference on Computer Systems, pp. 209–222 (2010)
14. Dall, C., Nieh, J.: KVM/ARM: the design and implementation of the Linux arm hypervisor. In: Proceedings of International Conference on Architectural Support for Programming Languages and Operating Systems, vol. 42, pp. 333–348 (2014)
15. Seshadri, A., Luk, M., Qu, N., Perrig, A.: SecVisor: a tiny hypervisor to provide lifetime kernel code integrity for commodity oses. SOSP **41**(6), 335–350 (2007)
16. Colp, P., Nanavati, M., Zhu, J., Aiello, W., Coker, G., Deegan, T., et al.: Breaking up is hard to do: security and functionality in a commodity hypervisor. In: Proceedings of ACM Symposium on Operating Systems Principles, pp. 189–202 (2011)
17. Manadhata, P.K., Wing, J.M.: An attack surface metric. IEEE Trans. Softw. Eng. **37**(3), 371–386 (2011)
18. Shepler, S., Callaghan, B., Robinson, D., Thurlow, R., Beame, C., & Eisler, M., et al. (2000). Nfs version 4 protocol. *Ousterhout*, "Caching in the Sprite Network File System," ACM Transactions on Computer Systems 6(1)
19. Hitz, D., Lau, J., Malcolm, M.: File system design for an NFS file server appliance. In: USENIX Technical Conference, vol. 1 (1994)
20. Wada, K.: Redundant arrays of independent disks. In: Liu, L., Özsu, T. (eds.) Encyclopaedia of Database Systems. Springer, New York (2009)
21. Savage, S., Wilkes, J.: AFRAID - a frequently redundant array of independent disks. Parity **2**, 5 (1996)

Cloud Platform

Cluster Analysis by Variance Ratio Criterion and Quantum-Behaved PSO

Shuihua Wang[1,2(✉)], Xingxing Zhou[1], Guangshuai Zhang[1],
Genlin Ji[1,2], Jiquan Yang[1,2], Zheng Zhang[3], Zeyuan Lu[4],
and Yudong Zhang[1,2(✉)]

[1] School of Computer Science and Technology, Nanjing Normal University,
Nanjing 210023, Jiangsu, China
{wangshuihua,zhangyudong}@njnu.edu.cn
[2] Jiangsu Key Laboratory of 3D Printing Equipment and Manufacturing,
Nanjing 210042, Jiangsu, China
[3] Viterbi School of Engineering, University of Southern California,
Los Angeles, CA 90089, USA
[4] Center of Medical Physics and Technology, Hefei Institutes
of Physical Science, Chinese Academy of Sciences, Hefei 230031, China

Abstract. (**Aim**) A novel and efficient method based on the quantum-behaved particle swarm was proposed to solve the cluster analysis problem. (**Methods**) The QPSO was utilized to detect the optimal point of the VAriance RAtio Criterion (VARAC), which was created by us as fitness function in the optimization model. The experimental dataset had 4 groups (400 data in total) with three various degrees of overlapping: non-overlapping, partial overlapping, and intensely overlapping. The proposed QPSO was compared with traditional global optimization algorithms: genetic algorithm (GA), combinatorial particle swarm optimization (CPSO), and firefly algorithm (FA) via running 20 times. (**Results**) The results demonstrated that QPSO could locate the best VARAC values with the least time among the four algorithms. (**Conclusions**) We can find that QPSO performs effectively and fast for the problem of cluster analysis.

Keywords: VAriance RAtio Criterion (VARAC) · Cluster analysis · Particle swarm optimization (PSO) · Quantum-behaved PSO

1 Introduction

The aim of cluster analysis is grouping a set of objects in the principle that objects in one cluster are more familiar with each other, than those in other clusters. Cluster analysis belongs to unsupervised learning, and it is a popular technique used for statistical analysis for data in following applications, such as case-based reasoning [1], prediction [2], commerce and finance [3], identification, quantitative description [4], and pattern recognition [5].

So far, there have been a number of experts and scholars made research and exploration on the cluster analysis, and generated a lot of efficient algorithms [6]:

(i) Connectivity-based Clustering: They are founded on the thought of objects being more similar with nearby objects than objects farther away. (ii) Center based

© Springer International Publishing Switzerland 2015
Z. Huang et al. (Eds.): ICCCS 2015, LNCS 9483, pp. 285–293, 2015.
DOI: 10.1007/978-3-319-27051-7_24

Clustering: Central vector can express clusters. The famous k-means clustering transform the problem to a minimization problem [7]: search the n cluster centers, and classify the instance to the closest cluster center. (iii) Distribution-based Clustering: All the objects belong to the same distribution presumably which called clusters. This kind of method approximately represents that sampling random objects generate artificial datasets from a distribution. (iv) Density-based Clustering: We define the area with higher density than the remainder of the dataset as the clusters. For the objects in the sparse areas, we suppose them as noise and border points, such as DBSCAN.

In this paper, we concentrate our mind on center-based methods. This method includes two typical algorithms: (1) fuzzy c-means clustering (FCM), and (2) k-means clustering. The algorithm gets the solution via iterating which depends on the initial partition. If an improper initial partition was selected, the result could be trapped to a local minimum, and therefore could not obtain the global minimal point.

To solve above problem, the bound and branch algorithm was used to find the global optimum clustering [8]. However, the cost of computation time is high, which impedes its usage. In the last decade, researchers proposed the evolutionary algorithms for clustering, considering they are insensitive to initial settings and they are capable of jumping out of local minimal areas. Take as instances, the clustering approach based on the combinatorial particle swarm algorithm was proposed by Jarboui et al. [9]. Cross-cultural research in point and applied multi-algorithm voting (MAV) method for cluster analysis was proposed by Gelbard et al. [10]. Considering that the k-means algorithm closely depended on the initial population and converged to local optimum areas, Niknam and Amiri [11] presented a new hybrid evolutionary algorithm named FAPSO-ACO-K,which consisted of ant colony optimization (ACO), k-means algorithms, and fuzzy adaptive particle swarm optimization (FAPSO). Zhang et al. [12] proposed a chaotic artificial bee colony (CABC) to find the solution of the partition clustering problem. Abul Hasan and Ramakrishnan [13] believed that optimize robust and flexible techniques must produce good consequence for clustering data. They provided an investigation of combined evolutionary algorithms for cluster analysis. A new Dynamic Clustering approach based on Particle swarm optimization and Genetic algorithm (DCPG) algorithm was proposed by Kuo et al. [14]. Then, Zhang and Li [15] employed firefly algorithm (FA) and tested 400 data of 4 groups. Yang et al. [16] proposed and explored the idea of exemplar-based clustering analysis optimized by genetic algorithms (GA). Wan [17] once used the method of combination of k-means clustering analysis (K) and particle swarm optimization (PSO) named KPSO to solve the problems of building landslide susceptibility maps. A multi-objective optimization (MOO) method combined with cluster analysis was proposed by Palaparthi et al. [18] to study the relation of the form-function with vocal folds. NSGA-II (An evolutionary algorithm) was utilized to integrate MOO with the laryngeal sound source (a finite element model). Zhang et al. [19] proposed the weighted k-means clustering based on improved GA. Ozturk et al. [20] proposed a dynamic clustering method with improved binary artificial bee colony algorithm.

However, above algorithms have following shortcomings. The speed of convergence is too slow, or even trapped to local minima points that can cause a wrong solution. In this paper, we presented the quantum-behaved PSO (QPSO) algorithm for optimization.

The remainder of this article is made up of the following content. Section 2 defines the clustering model, and meanwhile, the encoding strategy and clustering criterion are provided. Section 3 introduces the mechanisms of QPSO. Section 4 introduces the experiments, which have three categories of data generated manually with different overlapping degrees. Finally, Sect. 5 is about some conclusions and offers future works.

2   Model Definition

We will depict the problem of partitional clustering in this section. It is supposed that there are n samples $B = \{b_1, b_2, \ldots, b_n\}$ in the d-D metric space. We divide the samples into k groups. Each $b_i \in R^d$ is a feature vector with d real valued measures of the given objects. The clusters can be depicted in the form of $U = \{u_1, u_2, \ldots, u_k\}$, then those clusters should comply with the principles as follows:

$$
\begin{aligned}
&u_m \neq \phi \ (m = 1, 2, 3, \ldots, k) \\
&u_m \cap u_v = \phi \ (m \neq v) \\
&\cup u_m = \{1, 2, 3, \ldots, k\}
\end{aligned}
\tag{1}
$$

The problem of optimization model lies in finding out the minimal partition U^*, which performs the best among all solutions. In order to translate the cluster analysis task to an optimization problem, two related issues need to be solved: (1) the encoding strategy; (2) the criterion function.

2.1   Encoding Strategy

The encoding strategy is in an n-Dimensional space because the dataset contains n objects. In this study, each dimension stands for an object. The individual $X = \{x_1, x_2, \ldots, x_n\}$ is related to the clustering style of n objects. Note that x_j lies in the range of $\{1, 2, 3, \ldots, k\}$, in which, j represents the index of object.

We set n to 9 and k to 3. Suppose the 1st, 5th, and 7th object belong to the first cluster, and 2nd, 6th, and 8th object belong to the second, and the 3rd, 4th, and 9th object belong to the third cluster. The solution of encoding is illustrated in Fig. 1.

Cluster	Object
One	(1,5,7)
Two	(2,6,8)
Three	(3,4,9)

	x_1	x_2	x_3	x_4	x_5	x_6	x_7	x_8	x_9
X	1	2	3	3	1	2	1	2	3

Fig. 1. Illustration of encoding strategy used in this study

2.2   Criterion Function

Given a data set, we can choose several criteria to measure the adequacy. The "VAriance RAtio Criterion (VARAC) [12]" was the most common strategy of partitional clustering, while the definition is

$$VARAC = \frac{X_2}{X_1} \times \frac{n-k}{k-1} \tag{2}$$

Here X_1 stands for the in-cluster and X_2 denotes between-cluster variations. They are defined as:

$$X_1 = \sum_{j=1}^{k} \sum_{i=1}^{n_j} \left(b_j^i - \bar{b}_j \right)^T \left(b_j^i - \bar{b}_j \right) \tag{3}$$

$$X_2 = \sum_{j=1}^{k} n_j \left(\bar{o}_j - \bar{o} \right)^T \left(\bar{o}_j - \bar{o} \right) \tag{4}$$

in which n_j denotes the cardinal of the cluster c_j, b_j^i denotes the i-th object assigned to the cluster c_j, $\bar{b}_j$ stands for sample means of n-dimensional size, which belongs to j-th cluster (cluster center), and $\bar{b}$ stands for the n-dimensional vector of overall sample means (data center). $(n-k)$ stands for the freedom degree of the in-cluster variations, and $(k-1)$ stands for the freedom degree of the between-cluster variations.

So, compact clusters are desired to have small values of X_1 and separated clusters are desired to be with big values of X_2. Hence, the desired data partition leads to a larger value of VARAC. In order to make VARAC as an maximization criterion, we use the normalization term of $(n-k)$ divided by $(k-1)$, so that preventing the ratio from increasing monotonically with cluster number.

3   Optimization Algorithm

3.1   PSO

PSO use a group of particles, updating over iterations, to performs searching [21]. For seeking the optimal solution, each particle keeps track of two types of best positions: (1) the previously best (p_b) position; (2) the global best (g_b) position in the swarm [22].

$$p_b(i, t) = \arg \min_{k=1,\ldots,t} [f(P_i(k))], i \in \{1, 2, 3, \ldots, N\} \tag{5}$$

$$g_b(t) = \underset{\substack{i = 1, \ldots N \\ k = 1, \ldots t}}{\arg \min} [f(P_i(k))] \tag{6}$$

in which, i stands for the index of the particle among the population from 1 to N, which denotes the size of the population, i.e., the number of all particles. t is the index number of present iteration, f the fitness function, i.e., the objective function of the optimization problem, and P the position of the particle. It uses two equations of both (7) and (8) to renew the two characteristics of the particles: the velocity (T) and the position (P) of all particles.

$$T_i(t+1) \leftarrow \omega T_i(t) + c_1 q_1 (p_b(i,t) - P_i(t)) + c_2 q_2 (g_b(t) - P_i(t)) \tag{7}$$

$$P_i(t+1) \leftarrow T_i(t+1) + P_i(t) \tag{8}$$

here ω stands for the inertia value, which was employed to make proper balance between the global exploration and local exploitation of the fitness function. q_1 and q_2 are randomly distributed variables in the range of [0, 1]. c_1 and c_2 are acceleration coefficients, which are positive constant parameters.

It is necessary to set an upper value for the velocity (T). We used the technique of velocity clamping [23] to prevent particles from going out of the solution space. This can help improve the divergence degree of particles within the solution space [24].

3.2   QPSO

The main shortage of PSO is that it has a tendency to fall into local optima, although its excellent performance in convergence [25]. Inspired by trajectory analysis and quantum mechanics, the quantum-behaved PSO (QPSO) is developed.

The PSO works as a quantum-like system, among which each single particle of the system is supposed spinless and acts a quantum behavior based on the wave function (WF) without taking account of the interference from other particles. Further, assume each individual particle moves towards a potentially better delta of the search space. van den Bergh and Engelbrecht [26] yielded each particle converges to its local attractor a_i defined as

$$a_i = \frac{c_1 \times pbest(i) + c_2 \times gbest}{c_1 + c_2} \tag{9}$$

In QPSO, the search space and solution space have different quality. Without offering any details about the particle position, which is important to measure the fitness value, WF or probability function of the particle position, which describes the particle state in the quantized search space. Therefore, it is necessary to perform state transformation among two spaces [27].

Collapse, which is used to evaluate the particle position, denotes the transformation from quantum state to classical state. Based on the Monte Carlo method, the particles position is expressed as:

$$P_i(t+1) = \begin{cases} a_i(t) + \frac{L_i(t)}{2}\ln(\frac{1}{z_1}) & z_2 > 0.5 \\ a_i(t) - \frac{L_i(t)}{2}\ln(\frac{1}{z_1}) & \text{otherwise} \end{cases} \tag{10}$$

here z_1 and z_2 are random numbers generated by the uniform probability distribution function, varying between 0 and 1. L is closely related to energy intension of the potential well, specifying the search range of a particle named as the creativity or imagination of the particle. Its formulation can be given by

$$L_i = 2\vartheta|m_b - P_i| \tag{11}$$

where ϑ is called the creativity coefficient (or contraction-expansion coefficient), and m_b denotes the mean best of the population (or Mainstream Thought). The definition of the average of the p_b positions of all particles is expressed as

$$m_b(t) = \frac{\sum_{i=1}^{N} p_{b,i}(t)}{N} \tag{12}$$

Formula (12) serves as the iterative function of the particle positions of the QPSO [28].

4   Experiments and Discussions

The simulations were run on the platform of a HP laptop with 3.2 GHz processor and 16 GB RAM, with Windows 8 operating system. The program codes were in-house developed based on the 64bit Matlab 2015a (The Mathworks ©), which is a high-level numerical computing environment and 4th generation programming language.

4.1   Artificial Data

Suppose $n = 400$, k is assigned with a value of 4, d is assigned with a value of 2, we used a multivariate Gaussian distribution to randomly generate three kinds of artificial data: (1) Non-overlapping (NO), (2) partially overlapping (PO), (3) intensely overlapping (IO). Figure 2 shows distributions of the data generated manually.

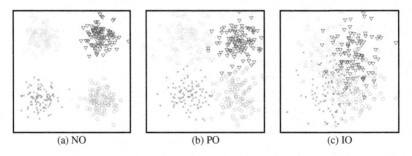

(a) NO   (b) PO   (c) IO

Fig. 2. Artificial data to three different overlapping degrees

4.2   Algorithm Comparison

Tests concerning comparison in the QPSO,the GA [16], CPSO [9], and FA [15] were taken. The results, derived from 20 times running to eliminate the randomness in each algorithm, are listed in Table 1.

Table 1. Simulation results for four-hundred artificial data based on twenty runs

Overlapping degree	VARAC	GA [16]	CPSO [9]	FA [15]	QPSO (Proposed)
NO	Best	**1683.2**	**1683.2**	**1683.2**	**1683.2**
	Mean	1321.3	1534.6	**1683.2**	**1683.2**
	Worst	451.0	1023.9	**1683.2**	**1683.2**
PO	Best	**620.5**	**620.5**	**620.5**	**620.5**
	Mean	594.4	607.9	618.2	**618.7**
	Worst	512.8	574.1	573.3	**589.1**
IO	Best	**275.6**	**275.6**	**275.6**	**275.6**
	Mean	184.1	203.8	221.5	**238.7**
	Worst	129.0	143.5	133.9	**151.2**

From Table 1, we found that for NO instances, the four algorithms find the optimal VARAC of 1683.2 at least for one time. Additional to it, both FA and QPSO succeeds for all 20 runs.

For the PO data, all the four algorithms: GA, CPSO, FA, and QPSO can get the optimal VARAC of 620.5 by 20 runs. The average values of VARACs by those algorithms are 594.4, 607.9, 618.2, and 618.7, respectively. The worst values of VARACs are 512.8, 574.1, 573.3 and 589.1. This suggested that the QPSO performs better than GA, CPSO, and FA.

For the IO data, the GA, CPSO, FA, and QPSO can find the best VARAC of 275.6. Again, the average and worst VARACs of QPSO are 238.7 and 151.2, which are better than those of GA (184.1 and 129.0), CPSO (203.8 and 143.5), and FA (221.5 and 133.9). This further validated the effectiveness of QPSO.

5   Conclusion and Future Work

We proposed a novel clustering method combining of VARAC and QPSO in this paper. From experiments on three types (NO, PO, IO) of artificial data, we can conclude that the QPSO was superior to GA, CPSO, and FA under different overlapping degrees.

Our future work will focus on following aspects: (1) Develop a method that can automatically determine the number of clusters; (2) Use more benchmark data to test the proposed method; and (3) Apply the proposed to practical clustering problems, such as disease detection [29, 30] and others.

Acknowledgment. This paper was supported by NSFC (610011024, 61273243, 51407095), Program of Natural Science Research of Jiangsu Higher Education Institutions (13KJB460011, 14KJB520021), Jiangsu Key Laboratory of 3D Printing Equipment and Manufacturing (BM2013006), Key Supporting Science and Technology Program (Industry) of Jiangsu Province (BE2012201, BE2014009-3, BE2013012-2), Special Funds for Scientific and Technological Achievement Transformation Project in Jiangsu Province (BA2013058), Nanjing Normal University Research Foundation for Talented Scholars (2013119XGQ0061, 2014119XGQ0080), and Science Research Foundation of Hunan Provincial Education Department (12B023).

Conflict of interest

We have no conflicts of interest to disclose with regard to the subject matter of this paper.

References

1. Zhu, G.N., Hu, J., Qi, J., Ma, J., Peng, Y.H.: An integrated feature selection and cluster analysis techniques for case-based reasoning. Eng. Appl. Artif. Intell. **39**, 14–22 (2015)
2. Amirian, E., Leung, J.Y., Zanon, S., Dzurman, P.: Integrated cluster analysis and artificial neural network modeling for steam-assisted gravity drainage performance prediction in heterogeneous reservoirs. Expert Syst. Appl. **42**, 723–740 (2015)
3. Tsai, C.F.: Combining cluster analysis with classifier ensembles to predict financial distress. Inf. Fusion **16**, 46–58 (2014)
4. Klepaczko, A., Kocinski, M., Materka, A.: Quantitative description of 3D vascularity images: texture-based approach and its verification through cluster analysis. Pattern Anal. Appl. **14**, 415–424 (2011)
5. Illarionov, E., Sokoloff, D., Arlt, R., Khlystova, A.: Cluster analysis for pattern recognition in solar butterfly diagrams. Astro. Nachr. **332**, 590–596 (2011)
6. Wang, S., Ji, G., Dong, Z., Zhang, Y.: An improved quality guided phase unwrapping method and its applications to MRI. Prog. Electromagnet. Res. **145**, 273–286 (2014)
7. Ayech, M.W., Ziou, D.: Segmentation of Terahertz imaging using k-means clustering based on ranked set sampling. Expert Syst. Appl. **42**, 2959–2974 (2015)
8. Trespalacios, F., Grossmann, I.E.: Algorithmic approach for improved mixed-integer reformulations of convex generalized disjunctive programs. INFORMS J. Comput. **27**, 59–74 (2015)
9. Jarboui, B., Cheikh, M., Siarry, P., Rebai, A.: Combinatorial particle swarm optimization (CPSO) for partitional clustering problem. Appl. Math. Comput. **192**, 337–345 (2007)
10. Gelbard, R., Carmeli, A., Bittmann, R.M., Ronen, S.: Cluster analysis using multi-algorithm voting in cross-cultural studies. Expert Syst. Appl. **36**, 10438–10446 (2009)
11. Niknam, T., Amiri, B.: An efficient hybrid approach based on PSO, ACO and k-means for cluster analysis. Appl. Soft Comput. **10**, 183–197 (2010)
12. Zhang, Y., Wu, L., Wang, S., Huo, Y.: Chaotic artificial bee colony used for cluster analysis. In: Chen, R. (ed.) ICICIS 2011 Part I. CCIS, vol. 134, pp. 205–211. Springer, Heidelberg (2011)
13. Abul Hasan, M.J., Ramakrishnan, S.: A survey: hybrid evolutionary algorithms for cluster analysis. Artif. Intell. Rev. **36**, 179–204 (2011)
14. Kuo, R.J., Syu, Y.J., Chen, Z.Y., Tien, F.C.: Integration of particle swarm optimization and genetic algorithm for dynamic clustering. Inf. Sci. **195**, 124–140 (2012)
15. Zhang, Y., Li, D.: Cluster analysis by variance ratio criterion and firefly algorithm. JDCTA: Int. J. Digit. Content Technol. Appl. **7**, 689–697 (2013)

16. Yang, Z., Wang, L.T., Fan, K.F., Lai, Y.X.: Exemplar-based clustering analysis optimized by genetic algorithm. Chin. J. Electron. **22**, 735–740 (2013)
17. Wan, S.A.: Entropy-based particle swarm optimization with clustering analysis on landslide susceptibility mapping. Environ. Earth Sci. **68**, 1349–1366 (2013)
18. Palaparthi, A., Riede, T., Titze, I.R.: Combining multiobjective optimization and cluster analysis to study vocal fold functional morphology. IEEE Trans. Biomed. Eng. **61**, 2199–2208 (2014)
19. Zhang, T.J., Cao, Y., Mu, X.W.: Weighted k-means clustering analysis based on improved genetic algorithm. Sens. Mechatron. Autom. **511–512**, 904–908 (2014)
20. Ozturk, C., Hancer, E., Karaboga, D.: Dynamic clustering with improved binary artificial bee colony algorithm. Appl. Soft Comput. **28**, 69–80 (2015)
21. Ghamisi, P., Benediktsson, J.A.: Feature selection based on hybridization of genetic algorithm and particle swarm optimization. IEEE Geosci. Remote Sens. Lett. **12**, 309–313 (2015)
22. Zhang, Y., Wang, S., Phillips, P., Ji, G.: Binary PSO with mutation operator for feature selection using decision tree applied to spam detection. Knowl.-Based Syst. **64**, 22–31 (2014)
23. Wang, S., Dong, Z.: Classification of Alzheimer disease based on structural magnetic resonance imaging by kernel support vector machine decision tree. Prog. Electromag. Res. **144**, 171–184 (2014)
24. Wang, S., Zhang, Y., Dong, Z., Du, S., Ji, G., Yan, J., Yang, J., Wang, Q., Feng, C., Phillips, P.: Feed-forward neural network optimized by hybridization of PSO and ABC for abnormal brain detection. Int. J. Imaging Syst. Technol. **25**, 153–164 (2015)
25. Lin, L., Guo, F., Xie, X.L., Luo, B.: Novel adaptive hybrid rule network based on TS fuzzy rules using an improved quantum-behaved particle swarm optimization. Neurocomputing **149**, 1003–1013 (2015)
26. van den Bergh, F., Engelbrecht, A.P.: A study of particle swarm optimization particle trajectories. Inf. Sci. **176**, 937–971 (2006)
27. Davoodi, E., Hagh, M.T., Zadeh, S.G.: A hybrid improved quantum-behaved particle swarm optimization-simplex method (IQPSOS) to solve power system load flow problems. Appl. Soft Comput. **21**, 171–179 (2014)
28. Fu, X., Liu, W.S., Zhang, B., Deng, H.: Quantum behaved particle swarm optimization with neighborhood search for numerical optimization. Math. Prob. Eng. **2013**, 10 (2013). doi:10.1155/2013/469723
29. Zhang, Y., Dong, Z., Wang, S., Ji, G., Yang, J.: Preclinical diagnosis of magnetic resonance (MR) brain images via discrete wavelet packet transform with tsallis entropy and generalized eigenvalue proximal support vector machine (GEPSVM). Entropy **17**, 1795–1813 (2015)
30. Zhang, Y., Wang, S., Phillips, P., Dong, Z., Ji, G., Yang, J.: Detection of Alzheimer's disease and mild cognitive impairment based on structural volumetric MR images using 3D-DWT and WTA-KSVM trained by PSOTVAC. Biomed. Signal Process. Control **21**, 58–73 (2015)

Failure Modes and Effects Analysis Using Multi-factors Comprehensive Weighted Fuzzy TOPSIS

Wenjun Zhang[✉] and Fenglin Zhang

College of Economics and Management, Nanjing University
of Aeronautics and Astronautics, Nanjing, Jiangsu, China
1032523256@qq.com, zflnuaa@163.com

Abstract. An improved comprehensive weighted fuzzy TOPSIS method is proposed for ranking because of the multiple evaluating sources of risk factors weights. In order to reduce the inaccuracy of failure assessment, subjective weight of expert's assessment and objective weights of system are taken into account. Focus is each experts of the FMEA team is respectively given different weights due to the different research fields of experts. The obtained comprehensive weight reflects multi-factors simultaneously and the relative closeness degree is more accurate. At the same time, the ranking of failure modes are closer to the actual situation. Finally, the feasibility and effectiveness of the proposed method is illustrated by the example of the metro door system.

Keywords: Failure modes and effects analysis · Multi-factors integrated-weights · Fuzzy TOPSIS · The metro door system

1 Introduction

Failure mode and effect analysis (FMEA) technique has become an indispensable tool in the safety and reliability analysis of product or process. The literature [1] integrated the FMEA and FAHP method, combining with the experts' evaluation date, to calculate the risk level of construction and rank the failure modes. FMEA and AHP are used in the detection and maintenance of large crane for evaluating each component's importance and determining the priority in literature [2]. The traditional FMEA method is used to sort all of the failure modes based on the risk priority number (RPN). The RPN calculation method evaluates the risk factors occurrence (O), severity (S) and detection (D) of a failure mode through different intermediary scores according to the real application situations in different companies and industries. However, the risk factors in real world are difficult to be precisely estimated and the traditional FMEA has many defects in evaluate standard, computation method of RPN, the weights of risk factors, etc.

In view of above defects, some methods have been put forward to conquer the traditional FMEA's setbacks. The literature [3] had carried on the analysis to the failure mode from the angle of multi attributes. The literature [4] used Fuzzy rule interpolation and reduction technology to establish the fuzzy FMEA model. Considering the flexible evaluation structure of TOPSIS, Sachdeva et al. [5] applied crisp TOPSIS into FMEA

© Springer International Publishing Switzerland 2015
Z. Huang et al. (Eds.): ICCCS 2015, LNCS 9483, pp. 294–305, 2015.
DOI: 10.1007/978-3-319-27051-7_25

approach and only use the Shannon's entropy concept to assign objective weights for the risk factors. Sachdeva et al. [6] also applied this method on a digester of paper mill. In fact, the crisp TOPSIS is not proper to FMEA approaches although it has reasonable and flexible structure, because risk factors in practice are difficult to be precisely estimated. Also, objective weights based on Shannon's entropy only cannot fully reflect the importance of the risk factors because it ignores the experts' knowledge. In view of these defects, many scholars consider to use fuzzy TOPSIS instead of precise TOPSIS analysis. The literature [7] provides a two-phase framework consisting of fuzzy entropy and fuzzy TOPSIS to improve the decision quality of FMEA risk analysis. But the fuzzy entropy-based weights could also not well reflect the experts' knowledge and experience. Literatures [8, 9] are the application of TOPSIS in the performance and risk evaluation.

We put forward a more reasonable, more accurate and more flexible FMEA method based on fuzzy TOPSIS and comprehensive weighted method. The fuzzy weighted TOPSIS approach not only benefits from experts' knowledge and experience but also makes full use of intrinsic information in the evaluating process. In addition, it also give experts assigned a certain weight according to the expert's research area.

The Sect. 2 of this paper introduces a new FMEA based on fuzzy TOPSIS. A case of metro door system components' failure is presented in Sect. 3 to illustrate the feasibility of the proposed method. The fourth part summarizes the thesis and illustrates the advantages and limitations of the method proposed in this paper.

2 Basic Concepts of Fuzzy Weighted TOPSIS

The fuzzy TOPSIS model is established by Chen and Hwang [10]. Subsequently, Chen [11] defines the Euclidean distance between two fuzzy numbers. It has laid a good foundation for the application of fuzzy TOPSIS in the field of FMEA. The principal line of this paper is fuzzy TOPSIS method. The structural framework of new FMEA method is shown in Fig. 1.

2.1 Weight Determination for Risk Factors

Assume that choose S (Severity), O (Occurrence) and D (Detectability) of failure and their weights are unequal. The steps of determining the weights are as follows:

Step 1: construct evaluation matrix

Assume there are m failure modes (FMs) to be evaluated against n risk factors (RFs). The selected experts use linguistic variables to evaluate the ratings of FMs. Table 1 gives the linguistic scale for evaluation of the FMs. The ratings of all FMs related to each RF can be calculated with Eq. (1). The expression is as follows:

$$\tilde{x}_{ij} = \frac{1}{k} \left[\tilde{x}_{ij}^1 + \tilde{x}_{ij}^2 + \cdots + \tilde{x}_{ij}^k \right] \tag{1}$$

Where $\tilde{x}_{ij}^k$ is the rating of the ith FM related to the jth RF from kth expert.

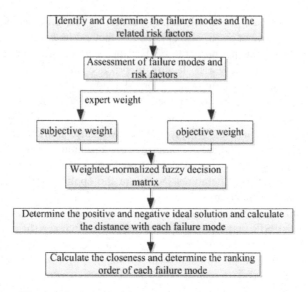

Fig. 1. The structural framework of new FMEA method

Table 1. Linguistic terms for failure modes

Linguistic variables	Fuzzy values
Very Low (VL)	(0,0,1,2)
Low (L)	(1,2,3,4)
Medium (M)	(3,4,6,7)
High (H)	(6,7,8,9)
Very High (VH)	(8,9,10,10)

The form of the initial evaluation matrix D is expressed as follows:

$$D = \begin{array}{c} FM_1 \\ FM_2 \\ \vdots \\ FM_m \end{array} \begin{bmatrix} \tilde{x}_{11} & \tilde{x}_{12} & \cdots & \tilde{x}_{1n} \\ \tilde{x}_{21} & \tilde{x}_{22} & \cdots & \tilde{x}_{2n} \\ \vdots & \vdots & \vdots & \vdots \\ \tilde{x}_{m1} & \tilde{x}_{m2} & \cdots & \tilde{x}_{mn} \end{bmatrix} \tag{2}$$

Then, all the linguistic variables are converted into trapezoidal fuzzy numbers according to Table 1. Then, the defuzzifier method proposed by Chen and Klien [12] is used to get the specific value; the formula is shown as follows:

$$P_{ij} = \frac{\sum_{i=0}^{n}(b_i - c)}{\sum_{i=0}^{n}(b_i - c) - \sum_{i=0}^{n}(a_i - d)} \tag{3}$$

The values of c and d always remain the same.

Step 2: determine subjective and objective weights for RFs

In order to reflect the knowledge of the experts and the inherent information of the system, consider the subjective and objective method to determine the weight of each RF. In addition, experts are assigned different weights according to the differences.

(1) Determine subjective weights for RFs

It is assumed that there are k experts and j RFs in assessment, the evaluation terms will be transformed into triangular fuzzy number based on Table 2. Use the form $a^l_{jk}(a^1_{jk}, a^2_{jk}, a^3_{jk})$ to express. Each expert is assigned a weight to be represented by λ_k, and the estimated information of each FM is integrated into the average value.

$$\tilde{w}_j = \frac{1}{k}\left[\tilde{w}^1_j + \tilde{w}^2_j + \cdots + \tilde{w}^k_j\right] \tag{4}$$

$$w^k_j = \lambda_k a^l_{jk}, l = 1, 2, \ldots, s \tag{5}$$

Where w^k_j represents the importance of the jth risk factor from the kth experts' evaluation. L represents the number of fuzzy numbers (for example, the triangular fuzzy number is 3, and the trapezoidal fuzzy number is composed of 4 values).

According to Eqs. (4, 5), the fuzzy subjective weight is converted into crisp value w_{sj}. Assuming triangular fuzzy number is M = (m_1, m_2, m_3), then the solution of the fuzzy equation is expressed as:

Table 2. Fuzzy ratings for the weights of risk factors

Ratings	Fuzzy numbers
Very Low (VL)	(0,0,0.25)
Low (L)	(0,0.25,0.5)
Moderate (M)	(0.25,0.5,0.75)
High (H)	(0.5,0.75,1)
Very High (VH)	(0.75,1,1)

$$P(\tilde{M}) = \frac{m_1 + 4m_2 + m_3}{6} \tag{6}$$

(2) Determine objective weights for risk factors

The entropy weight method is used to calculate the objective weights, the steps are:

① Normalize the evaluation matrix. In this paper, the formula of Deng et al. [13] is used to carry out the standardization of each element. Following is the expression.

$$r_{ij} = \frac{x_{ij}}{\sum\limits_{i=1}^{m} x_{ij}} \tag{7}$$

② Calculate the entropy values of each risk factor using entropy weight method. Let e_j denote the entropy of the jth factor.

$$e_j = -\frac{1}{\ln m} \sum_{i=1}^{m} r_{ij} \ln r_{ij} \tag{8}$$

Where k is a constant and makes the value of e_j in the range of 0 to 1.

③ The objective weight of each criterion is obtained by the following formula:

$$w_{oj} = \frac{1 - e_j}{\sum_{j=1}^{n} (1 - e_j)} \tag{9}$$

In the formula, the greater $(1 - e_j)$ is, the more important jth risk factor will be.

Step 3: Integration of risk factor weight

To amplify the difference between weights of RFs, the multiplicative combination weighting method is adopted. That is, multiply the objective weight and subjective weight first and then normalize the product to obtain the comprehensive weight.

$$w_j = \frac{w_{sj} \times w_{oj}}{\sum\limits_{j=1}^{n} w_{sj} \times w_{oj}} \tag{10}$$

Where w_{sj} represents the subjective weight, w_{oj} is the objective weight and w_j is the combinational weight.

2.2   Failure Modes Evaluation

Apply Chen's fuzzy TOPSIS method in the evaluation. In this paper, the trapezoidal fuzzy number instead of triangular fuzzy number was introduced and used for calculation the distance. The ranges of numbers in evaluation matrix D belong to [0, 1].

Assuming that B and C represent the set of benefit criteria and the cost criterion set, the normalized fuzzy decision matrix method is as follows:

$$\tilde{r}_{ij} = \left(\frac{a_{ij0}}{b_{j0}^+}, \frac{a_{ij1}}{b_{j0}^+}, \frac{b_{ij1}}{b_{j0}^+}, \frac{b_{ij0}}{b_{j0}^+} \right), j \in B; \tag{11}$$

$$\tilde{r}_{ij} = \left(\frac{a_{j0}^-}{b_{ij0}}, \frac{a_{j0}^-}{b_{ij1}}, \frac{a_{j0}^-}{a_{ij1}}, \frac{a_{j0}^-}{a_{ij0}} \right), j \in C. \tag{12}$$

$b_{j0}^+ = \max_i b_{ij0}$, $j \in B$; $a_{j0}^- = \min_i a_{ij0}$, $j \in C$. Therefore, the normalized fuzzy decision matrix $\tilde{R} = [\tilde{r}_{ij}]_{m \times n}$ can be obtained. Given the relative importance of risk factors, construct the weighted normalized fuzzy decision matrix $\tilde{V} = [\tilde{v}_{ij}]_{m \times n}$.

$$\tilde{v}_{ij} = \tilde{r}_{ij} \cdot w_j \tag{13}$$

Then, the fuzzy positive/negative ideal solutions are defined as follows:

$$A^+ = (\tilde{v}_1^+, \tilde{v}_2^+, \ldots, \tilde{v}_n^+) \tag{14}$$

$$A^- = (\tilde{v}_1^-, \tilde{v}_2^-, \ldots, \tilde{v}_n^-) \tag{15}$$

Where $\tilde{v}_j^+ = (\max(\tilde{v}_{i1}^+), \ldots, \max(\tilde{v}_{in}^+))$, $\tilde{v}_j^- = (\min(\tilde{v}_{i1}^-), \ldots, \min(\tilde{v}_{in}^-))$.
The distance between failure mode and A^+/A^- can be obtained as follows:

$$d_i^+ = \sum_{j=1}^n d(\tilde{v}_{ij}, \tilde{v}_j^+) \tag{16}$$

$$d_i^- = \sum_{j=1}^n d(\tilde{v}_{ij}, \tilde{v}_j^-) \tag{17}$$

The distance of two fuzzy numbers will be calculated with the following formula:

$$d(\tilde{p}, \tilde{q}) = \sqrt{\frac{1}{4}\left[(p_1 - q_1)^2 + (p_2 - q_2)^2 + (p_3 - q_3)^2 + (p_4 - q_4)^2\right]} \tag{18}$$

Where $\tilde{p} = (p_1, p_2, p_3, p_4)$, $\tilde{q} = (q_1, q_2, q_3, q_4)$ are two trapezoidal fuzzy numbers. The closeness coefficients of all failure modes for ranking order are obtained as follows:

$$C_i = \frac{d_i^-}{d_i^+ + d_i^-} \tag{19}$$

The closer to the positive ideal solution and farther from the negative ideal solution the FM is, the closer to 1 the C_i is. Therefore, the managers can select the FM with greatest risk based on the closeness coefficient for arranging improvement resources.

3   Case Analysis

The paper uses the example-reliability analysis of metro door system failure mode in literature [14] to illustrate the improved fuzzy TOPSIS method.

3.1   Background

With the rapid growth of urban population, the subway is playing a more and more important role in people's life. The reliability of door system is related to the passengers' personal safety and the metro trains' normal operation. So it is very important to carry out the risk and reliability analysis for the subway door system in order to find out the weak link in the process of design and maintenance.

The door system is mainly composed of electrical control components, guiding device, foundation bearing device and locking device driver subsystem. The operating principle of the metro door system is shown in Fig. 2.

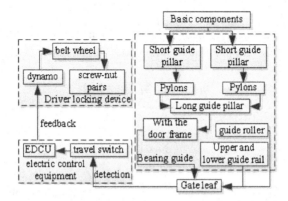

Fig. 2. The operating principle of the metro door system

3.2   Practical Analysis

A metro company's door failure information during a period time is used for statistical analysis. Select seven common failure modes of the door components to analyze and research, details are shown in Table 3.

Table 3. The common failure modes of metro door

No.	Failure modes
FM1	Roller loose
FM2	rolling wheel wear
FM3	Long guide pillar bad lubrication
FM4	EDCU function failure
FM5	Off-travel switch S1 damaged
FM6	Nut component damage
FM7	Nut components loosening

Assuming that the FMEA analysis team consists of 5 experts from different departments and the 5 members are given different relative weights. The steps of FMEA analysis using the comprehensive weighted fuzzy TOPSIS are as follows:

(1) Construct evaluation matrix.

The experts use the linguistic terms (shown in Table 1) to evaluate the ratings of failure modes with respect to risk factors and present them in Table 4. These linguistic evaluations are transformed into trapezoidal fuzzy numbers. Then, the fuzzy failure modes evaluation matrix will be constructed, as shown in Table 5.

Table 4. Evaluation information for failure modes

No.	Severity	Occurrence	Detection
FM1	L,L,M,L,L	L,L,M,L,M	M,L,L,M,M
FM2	L,M,L,M,M	L,M,L,L,L	L,M,L,L,M
FM3	L,M,L,L,L	L,L,L,M,M	M,M,H,M,M
FM4	H,VH,H,VH,H	M,H,M,M,M	H,M,H,L,M
FM5	H,M,H,H,H	M,M,M,M,M	M,M,H,M,M
FM6	H,M,H,H,M	M,M,M,M,H	M,L,M,M,M
FM7	L,M,M,M,H	VL,L,L,VL,L	M,L,M,M,M

Table 5. The fuzzy failure modes evaluation matrix

No.	S	O	D
FM1	(1.4,2.4,3.6,4.6)	(1.8,2.8,4.2,5.2)	(2.2,3.2,4.8,5.8)
FM2	(2.2,3.2,4.8,5.8)	(1.4,2.4,3.6,4.6)	(1.8,2.8,4.2,5.2)
FM3	(1.4,2.4,3.6,4.6)	(1.8,2.8,4.2,5.2)	(3.6,4.6,6.4,7.4)
FM4	(6.8,7.8,8.8,9.4)	(3.6,4.6,6.4,7.4)	(3.8,4.8,6.2,7.2)
FM5	(5.4,6.4,7.6,8.6)	(3,4,6,7)	(3.6,4.6,6.4,7.4)
FM6	(4.8,5.8,7.2,8.2)	(3.6,4.6,6.4,7.4)	(2.6,3.6,5.4,6.4)
FM7	(3.2,4.2,5.8,6.8)	(0.6,1.2,2.2,3.2)	(2.6,3.6,5.4,6.4)

(2) Determine subjective and objective weights of each risk factor.

① Subjective weight. Experts evaluate the importance of risk factors by using the weighted variables (shown in Table 2), and use the formulas (4–6) to convert the fuzzy subjective weights to concrete values, the results are shown in Table 6.

Table 6. Evaluation information for importance of S, O and D

Risk factors	S	O	D
Experts weights	(0.15,0.2,0.3,0.25,0.1)	(0.15,0.2,0.3,0.25,0.1)	(0.15,0.2,0.3,0.25,0.1)
Linguistic	H,H,VH,VH,M	M,H,M,M,VH	M,L,L,M,L
w_{sj}	0.470	0.333	0.196

② Objective weight. Using formula (7) normalizes the fuzzy failure mode evaluation matrix; the standard value r_{ij} of each failure mode is obtained (shown in Table 7). Then, the entropy e_j and the objective weight w_{oj} are calculated by using the formulas (8–9) (shown in Table 8).

Table 7. The normalized matrix of failure modes

No.	S	O	D
FM1	0.092	0.130	0.125
FM2	0.115	0.115	0.113
FM3	0.092	0.130	0.161
FM4	0.211	0.185	0.161
FM5	0.182	0.172	0.161
FM6	0.170	0.185	0.138
FM7	0.137	0.078	0.138

Table 8. The e_j, $1-e_j$ and objective entropy weight of risk factors

	S	O	D
e_j	0.863	0.845	0.861
$1-e_j$	0.136	0.154	0.138
w_{oj}	0.317	0.360	0.321

(3) Integration of risk factor weight

The comprehensive weight (shown in Table 9) for each risk factor is calculated by combining subjective weight and objective weight based on Eq. (10).

Table 9. The fuzzy normalized evaluation matrix and comprehensive weight for S, O and D

No.	S	O	D
	$w_s = 0.448$	$w_o = 0.362$	$w_d = 0.189$
FM1	(0.148,0.255,0.383,0.489)	(0.243,0.378,0.567,0.702)	(0.297,0.432,0.648,0.783)
FM2	(0.234,0.34,0.51,0.617)	(0.189,0.324,0.486,0.621)	(0.243,0.378,0.567,0.702)
FM3	(0.148,0.255,0.383,0.489)	(0.243,0.378,0.567,0.702)	(0.486,0.621,0.864,1)
FM4	(0.723,0.829,0.936,1)	(0.486,0.621,0.864,1)	(0.513,0.648,0.837,0.973)
FM5	(0.574,0.68,0.808,0.914)	(0.405,0.54,0.81,0.945)	(0.486,0.621,0.864,1)
FM6	(0.51,0.617,0.766,0.872)	(0.486,0.621,0.864,1)	(0.351,0.486,0.729,0.864)
FM7	(0.34,0.446,0.617,0.723)	(0.081,0.162,0.297,0.432)	(0.351,0.486,0.729,0.864)

(4) Failure modes evaluation by fuzzy weighted TOPSIS

On the basis of normalized fuzzy decision matrix (Table 9), construct the weighted fuzzy decision matrix (Table 10) by using the formulas (11–13). FPIS and FNIS are determined as follows:

$$A^* = [(1;1;1;1);(1;1;1;1);(1;1;1;1)], \ A^- = [(0;0;0;0);(0;0;0;0);(0;0;0;0)].$$

Then, the distance d_i^+, d_i^- are calculated according to Eqs. (16)–(18), as shown in Table 11. The closeness coefficients calculated by the fuzzy TOPSIS are the basis for ranking order of each FM. The closeness coefficient of each FM based on Eq. (19) and the rank of all FMs are also determined in Table 11.

The approach based on comprehensive weighted fuzzy TOPSIS is used to rank for FMs. In Table 11, the ranking order of seven common FMs in door system is as follows: FM4 > FM5 > FM6 > FM3 > FM7 > FM2 > FM1. That FM4 (EDCU function failure) is the most important and has the highest priority, followed by FM5 (off-travel switch S1 damaged), 6 (nut components damage), 3 (long guide pillar bad lubrication), 7 (nut components loosening), 2 (rolling wheel wear) and 1 (roller loose).

Table 10. The weighted normalized fuzzy decision matrix

No.	S	O	D
FM1	(0.066,0.114,0.171,0.219)	(0.088,0.137,0.205,0.254)	(0.056,0.082,0.123,0.148)
FM2	(0.104,0.152,0.228,0.276)	(0.068,0.117,0.176,0.225)	(0.046,0.071,0.107,0.133)
FM3	(0.066,0.114,0.171,0.219)	(0.088,0.137,0.205,0.254)	(0.092,0.117,0.164,0.189)
FM4	(0.324,0.372,0.419,0.448)	(0.176,0.225,0.313,0.362)	(0.097,0.123,0.158,0.184)
FM5	(0.257,0.305,0.362,0.41)	(0.146,0.195,0.293,0.342)	(0.092,0.117,0.164,0.189)
FM6	(0.228,0.276,0.343,0.391)	(0.176,0.225,0.313,0.362)	(0.066,0.092,0.138,0.164)
FM7	(0.152,0.2,0.276,0.324)	(0.029,0.058,0.107,0.156)	(0.066,0.092,0.138,0.164)

Table 11. The closeness coefficient and ranking order of each failure mode

No.	d_i^+	d_i^-	C_i	Ranking
FM1	2.588	0.445	0.146	7
FM2	2.578	0.455	0.150	6
FM3	2.549	0.482	0.159	4
FM4	2.205	0.817	0.270	1
FM5	2.287	0.741	0.244	2
FM6	2.312	0.716	0.236	3
FM7	2.563	0.469	0.154	5

3.3 Results Comparison and Discussion

According to Table 11, the priority order of the 7 failure modes of the metro door system is obtained. The results obtained in this paper are compared with the results of literature [14] and the details are shown in Table 12.

As can be seen from the results of two method's comparative analysis in Table 12 that the gray correlation degrees of FM4 (EDCU function failure), FM5 (travel switch S1 breakage) and FM6 (nut component damage) are much less than the other four FMs in

Table 12. Comparison of two methods

No.	Fuzzy evidential reasoning and grey relation		Comprehensive weighted fuzzy TOPSIS	
	Grey relational degree	Ranking	Relative closeness	Ranking
FM1	0.890	7	0.146	7
FM2	0.872	5	0.150	6
FM3	0.876	6	0.159	4
FM4	0.652	1	0.270	1
FM5	0.691	2	0.244	2
FM6	0.691	2	0.236	3
FM7	0.831	4	0.154	5

literature [14]. These three FMs should be regarded as the key to affect the normal work of the door system and we should focus on the design and improvement. Similarly, the ranking is obtained by using the comprehensive weighted fuzzy TOPSIS. The relative closeness degrees of FM4, FM5 and FM6 are significantly higher than the other 4 FMs with high priority in design improvement and maintenance. The three FMs of the former are FM4 > FM5/FM6, while the latter is FM4 > FM5 > FM6. The FM5 and FM6 get the same gray correlation degree in former, but from the fuzzy assessments in Table 4 we can see clearly: the values of two FMs are different, so be fully consistent with the results indicates that the method has some disadvantages. The results obtained by the latter have little difference and prove the feasibility and applicability of the synthetic weighted fuzzy TOPSIS method. In the two methods, the lowest priority is FM1 (roller loose), which means that the importance of roller loose is the lowest in the door system.

In addition, the former does not take the weight of experts into account; each expert's weight is also taken into consideration in the latter method. Because these experts do not specialize in all professional, in order to get more consistent results with the actual situation, the experts' weights are considered in the research. This is also an innovation of the comprehensive weighted fuzzy TOPSIS method.

4   Conclusions

Although the application of fuzzy TOPSIS in the field of FMEA is relatively less, the results of the research have proved the feasibility and validity of this method. This paper mainly studies the method of multi-factor comprehensive weighted fuzzy TOPSIS and its application. Specifically, on the basis of the original method, synthetically consider the subjective and objective factors and assess the differences between experts with given relative weights, and make the results obtained more accurate and closer to the actual situation. The advantages of the new FMEA are as follows:

(1) Do not multiply the value of three risk factors directly and eliminate the existent questions in the simple multiplication.

(2) The comprehensive weight is composed of subjective weight from expert evaluation and objective weight from internal system, combined with the relative weights of experts, making the results more accurate, more persuasive.

(3) Linguistic terms are used in the new FMEA.

(4) The proposed method is applicable to a variety of risk factors.

Of course, in order to improve the quality of products or services, reduce the risk of operation and maintenance, it is necessary to test the effective and practical of the proposed method. In the future research, the FMEA method can be integrated with other tools to research the failure risk and reliability of the system.

References

1. Hong, Z., Yang, L.: Application of metro project risk evaluation based on FMEA combined with FAHP and frequency analysis. J. Eng. Manag. **29**(1), 53–58 (2015)
2. Shuzhong, Z., Qinda, Z.: Components importance degree evaluation of large crane based FMEA and variable weight AHP. J. Chongqing Univ. Technol. Nat. Sci. **28**(5), 34–38 (2014)
3. Braglia, M.: MAFMA: multi- attribute failure mode analysis. Int. J. Qual. Reliab. Manag. **17**(9), 1017–1033 (2000)
4. Taya, K.M., Lim, C.P.: Enhancing the failure mode and effect analysis methodology with fuzzy inference technique. J. Intell. Fuzzy Syst. **21**(1–2), 135–146 (2010)
5. Sachdeva, A., Kumar, D., Kumar, P.: Maintenance criticality analysis using TOPSIS. In: Proceedings of the IEEE International Conference on Industrial Engineering and Engineering Management (IEEM 2009), Hong Kong, pp. 199–203. IEEE Press, Piscataway (8–11 December 2009)
6. Sachdeva, A., Kumar, D., Kumar, P.: Multi-factor failure mode criticality analysis using TOPSIS. J. Ind. Eng. Int. **5**(8), 1–9 (2009)
7. Wang, C.H.: A novel approach to conduct risk analysis of FMEA for PCB fabrication process. In: Proceedings of the IEEE International Conference on Industrial Engineering and Engineering Management (IEEM 2011), Singapore, pp. 1275–1278. IEEE Press, Piscataway (6–9 December 2011)
8. Xionglin, Z., Caiyun, Z.: Service performance evaluation of TPL suppliers based on triangular fuzzy TOPSIS. Techn. Methods **34**(2), 176–179 (2015)
9. Can, L., Fengrong, Z., et al.: Evaluation and correlation analysis of land use performance based on entropy-weight TOPSIS method. Trans. Chin. Soc. Agric. Eng. (Trans. CSAE) **29**(5), 217–227 (2013)
10. Chen, S.J., Hwang, C.L.: Fuzzy Multi Attribute Decision Making, vol. 375. Springer, New York (1992)
11. Chen, C.T.: Extension of the TOPSIS for group decision-making under fuzzy environment. Fuzzy Sets Syst. **114**(1), 1–9 (2000)
12. Chen, C.B., Klien, C.M.: A simple approach to ranking a group of aggregated fuzzy utilities. IEEE Trans. Syst. Man Cybern. Part B **27**(1), 26–35 (1997)
13. Deng, H., Yeh, C., Willis, R.J.: Intercompany comparison using modified TOPSIS with objective weights. Comput. Oper. Res. **27**, 963–973 (2000)
14. Jun, X., Xiang, G.: Failure mode criticality analysis of metro door system. Modular Mach. Tool Autom. Manuf. Tech. **3**, 49–52 (2014)

Efficient Query Algorithm
of Coallocation-Parallel-Hash-Join
in the Cloud Data Center

Yao Shen[1(✉)], Ping Lu[2], Xiaolin Qin[1], Yuming Qian[2],
and Sheng Wang[1]

[1] Department of Computer Science and Technology, Nanjing University
of Aeronautics and Astronautics, Nanjing 210016, China
{shenycs,qinxcs}@nuaa.edu.cn, ssxbily@163.com
[2] ZTE Corporation, Nanjing Research and Development Center,
Nanjing 210012, China
{lu.ping,qianyuming}@zte.com.cn

Abstract. In the hybrid architecture of cloud data center, the data division is an important factor that affects the performance of query. For the costly join operations which applies the way of hybrid mapreduce, the overhead of network transmission and I/O is huge that requires large-scale transmission of data across the nodes. In order to reduce the data traffic and improve the efficiency of join queries, this paper proposes an efficient algorithm of Coallocation Parallel Hash Join (CPHJ). First, CPHJ designs a consistent multi-redundant hashing algorithm that distributes the table with join relationship in the cluster according to its join properties, which improves the data locality in the join query processing, but also ensures the availability of the data. Then, On the basis of consistent multi-redundant hashing algorithm, parallel algorithm of join query called ParallelHashJoin is proposed that effectively improves the efficiency of join queries. The CPHJ method applies in the data warehouse system of Alibaba and experimental results indicate that the workpiece ratio of CPHJ in that query is nearly five times more likely than the hive system.

Keywords: Mapreduce · Big data · Join query · Coallocation · Hadoop

1 Introduction

Along with the fast development of Internet applications, researchers will face a tough challenge towards storing and processing massive data. Traditional database technology cannot meet the needs of massive data management due to the weakness of scalability and the limitation of high cost. In recent years, Google has put forward many mainstream technologies for storing and analyzing mass data, such as a distributed file system GFS [1], and a parallel programming framework MapReduce [2–4].

Based on the design philosophy of GFS and MapReduce, the Hadoop project under the open source community Apache implemented Hadoop-DFS and Hadoop-MapReduce, the former is a distributed file system and the latter can be understood as a parallel programming framework. Currently, Hadoop has been widely applied to

© Springer International Publishing Switzerland 2015
Z. Huang et al. (Eds.): ICCCS 2015, LNCS 9483, pp. 306–320, 2015.
DOI: 10.1007/978-3-319-27051-7_26

Yahoo, Facebook and other Internet companies to deal with storage and analysis of mass data. Due to MapReduce programming model at a low level, developers need to write different MapReduce applications to handle different tasks for data analysis, which led to a problem that programs may be difficult to maintain and reuse. In order to facilitate the development of the upper application, Hive [5–7], Pig [8] and other techniques have been proposed to encapsulate MapReduce programming framework, providing call interface of SQL for the upper application which makes things easier.

In the query of statistical analysis, JOIN is one of the main operations. Hive uses a sort merge algorithm when dealing with JOIN operation (SortMergeReduceJoin, hereinafter referred to as Reduce Join). The implementation of the algorithm is cut into Map and Reduce two stages: In the Map phase, sort the Join properties of the two tables that to be connected; In the Reduce stage, merge and connect the sorted results that generated in every map stages and then output the query results. But there are two problems with this algorithm: (1) a large number of intermediate results generated in map stage needs to be transmitted to the Reduce side through the network, which consume a lot of bandwidth and bring negative influence to the efficiency of the algorithm; (2) Multiple merge and sort operations are required, which lead to greater cost and longer execution time.

In response to these problems, we propose parallel join query processing algorithm based on the consistency of multi-redundant in mapreduce environment (Co-Location Parallel HashJoin, hereinafter referred to as CPHJ). The basic idea of CPHJ algorithm is hash the value of the connection properties in the two tables which often make Join operations, in dealing with Join queries, CPHJ algorithm can obtain the results by performing HashJoin algorithm only in the Map stage. So it reduces the time overhead of a query processing without performing Reduce stage. The proposed algorithm has been applied in the Alibaba data warehouse (Alibaba distributed data warehouse, referred to as ADW). The results show that when apply CPHJ to deal with Join queries on partition properties, the execution time is only about 20 % of the ReduceJoin algorithm used in Hive. Ideas presented in this paper still apply to the query of Groupby.

The second section describes related work; then the main idea of the CPHJ algorithm introduced in the third section, also with the analysis of the performance of the algorithm; in Sect. 4 gives the experimental results and analysis; the last section is the conclusion and prospect.

2 Related Work

In the storage and processing of massive data, driven by a large number of research institutes and companies, the development of cutting-edge technology is very quickly. Google, Amazon, IBM and Microsoft and other companies have invested heavily in this area of scientific research, proposed variety of innovative management technology about massive data. These studies focused on three levels: the storage, computing of massive data and user interface.

The storage layer provides reliable storage and efficient access service of file about massive data. The main techniques include Google's distributed file system GFS,

Hadoop's HDFS, KFS [9, 10], Amazon's S3 [11, 12] and so on. Computing layer provides parallel computing services for massive data and use API that provided by the storage layer to read the data. In the process of implementing, the computing layer will return the real-time status of the job to the interface layer and feedback the final execution results until the end of the job. Parallel computing technology towards processing massive data includes Google's MapReduce, Hadoop and Microsoft's Dryad [13], etc. The function of interface layer is to provide programming API, interactive shell and web GUI interface. It also makes syntax analysis, semantic analysis and query optimization to the SQL sentence that users submit to the system (Or other query languages).Finally, it is converted to one or more jobs to perform by the computing layer. Currently, the main research work on interface layer includes Hive, Pig, Scope [14], DryadLINQ [15], Sawzall [16] and so on.

Hive is a representative work on the interface layer that mainly used in Facebook's analysis work of massive data. It provide call interface of SQL similar sentence to upper applications with the Hadoop DFS as the storage engine and Hadoop MapReduce as the computational engine. When processing join queries, Hive mainly adopts the algorithm of ReduceJoin.

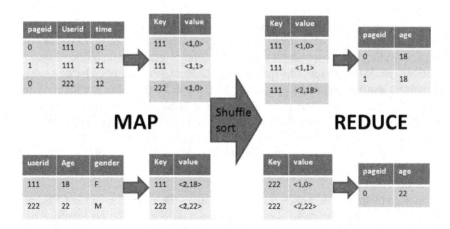

Fig. 1. The process of ReduceJoin

As shown in Fig. 1, the algorithm of ReduceJoin is divided into 3 stages: Map, shuffle/Sort and Reduce. In the stage of Map, each map task deal with one data block and the temporary results exported by Map task partition by the primary key value and write to the local as <key, value> pairs: the value of the join attribute as the 'key', and in the 'value' inject the label of the table so as to indicate the source of the data. In Shuffle/Sort stage the provisional results exported by Map task transfer to the corresponding Reduce task in accordance with the value of the 'key'. The reduce task aggregate several data from more than one partition that produced in the map task and perform multiple Sort/Merge operations. Then, it output the final results of join queries with the reduce function connected by merging and sorting partition data.

During the execution of ReduceJoin, the Reduce stage only performs after the completion of all the Map phases. It will bring a lot of network traffic and makes less efficient that Reduce tasks need to pull the intermediate results produced by the map side. Meanwhile, Reduce task should perform multiple operations of Sort/Merge which requires a lot of calculations and results in lower efficiency of the algorithm.

3   CPHJ Algorithm of Parallel Join Processing

Aiming at the problem of low efficiency in performing ReduceJoin, we propose the techniques of CPHJ to make join queries based on the localization of data. The technology consists of two parts: strategy of data distribution (Coallocation) and algorithm of parallel join processing (Parallel HashJoin).

As a result of applying hash technology to distribute the data tables on the clusters, the algorithms of parallel join make partitions as processing unit and only need to execute Map tasks to perform join queries until the final work is completed, which avoid the huge cost of time that Reduce brings and significantly enhance the efficiency of the join query.

3.1   Strategy of Data Distribution

The distribution strategy of data is a key problem in the issue of parallel queries which directly affects the efficiency of the query. Currently, there are a lot of research works on the distribution strategy of data, and many effective parallel distribution methods of data are proposed, such as Round-Robin, Hash, Range-Partition [17], CMD [18] and many other methods of data distribution based on clustering and consistent hashing [19].

CPHJ applies hashing techniques to distribute the data and divides the data into the corresponding partition according to the hash value which calculated from some property of a table. As far as the join query is concerned, it can be converted to a calculation only carried in the Map phase by hash partitioning and to further optimize the utilization of computing resources, we can control the number of hash partitions in order to adjust the granularity of join queries. Hash partitioning just logically realize the aggregation of related data, on the physical level, one partition often contains multiple files and each file consists of a plurality of data blocks which distributed on different nodes. The purpose of the strategy of hashing data distribution is to centrally store the related data on the same physical node. Meanwhile, the strategy of data distribution also provides support for column storage, with regard to which, different columns of the same tuple can be stored aggregately on the same node, which take further advantage of column storage.

CPHJ take distributed file system of hadoop DFS as the underlying storage mechanism, but in HadoopDFS application-aware data distribution method is not supported. We add the strategy of hash data distribution on the basis of HadoopDFS. We propose a consistent multi-redundant hashing algorithm to support localized calculation of data and ensure the fault tolerance of modified HadoopDFS unchanged.

The consistent multi-redundant hashing algorithm based on the consistent hashing algorithm which is thought mainly to solve the problem of hotspot on network [20]. In the light of multiple copies are not considered in the consistent hashing algorithm which only take single data into consideration, consistent multi-redundant hashing algorithm amend and expand the consensus hashing algorithm, which support the storage of multiple redundant copies so as to achieve the same effect of aggregate the related data from multi-redundant copies. The proposed algorithm is also in favor of the concept of virtual nodes proposed by Dynamo [21] that one real node can be mapped into multiple virtual nodes, and a hash ring is needed in the algorithm that the configuration is shown in Fig. 2.

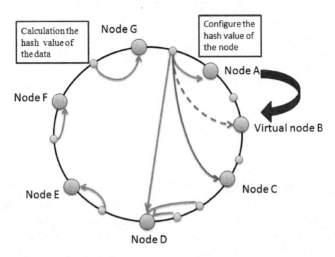

Fig. 2. Example of hash ring in the algorithm of consistent multi-redundant hashing

The proposed algorithm of consistent multi-redundant hashing is as follows:

Step one: first calculate the hash value of the data node and then configure it to a ring of hash.

Step two: calculate the hash value of data and also map it into the ring of hash. In terms of hash partition, the value of it is the hash value of data; for column or clustered column storage file which is non-hash partition, the hash value is hashing the pathname in the storage file system which removes the labels of the column.

Step three: map the data to the nearest node clockwise. In respect of multiple copies of the data, then continue to select a new node along the ring until enough copies are stored. The mapped node should store the data.

Step four: If the selected node is a virtual node and the actual node that represented by the virtual node has already kept a copy, and if the disk of the node is full or abnormal situation occurs then skip the node and continue to find next one.

Consistent multi-redundant hashing algorithm can keep nodes from joining or quitting frequently and prevent huge overhead presented by changing the original mapping relationship. While avoiding the data belongs to the same hash partition or the files of different column from the same table are mapped to different nodes, relevant data can achieve aggregation on physical level so as to enhance the performance of queries.

3.2 Algorithm of Parallel Hash Join

Parallel Hash Join (PHJ) is an algorithm of parallel join query which performs only in Map side. The main idea is in the light of join query submitted by users, judge that the query can be processed by the algorithm of PHJ by determining whether the multiple data tables involved in the calculation are carried out hash partition and with the same number. The query processing engine makes the appropriate analysis of lexical and syntax to the SQL statement submitted by user and generates the optimized task of Mapreduce. The optimized map task uses hash partition as the unit and the appropriate number of join query tasks are generated according to the number of hash partition. The PHJ algorithm only runs in Map stage and the results of query output directly from the Map side while the Reduce phase is not considered.

As shown in Fig. 3, the same hash partition of Hash-XXX which is in data table A and B will make join query by the same Map task. The proper result of query comes from gathering all the calculations in the hash partition, and there isn't any interaction between each task. Take advantage of the consistent multi-redundant hashing, the data from relevant hash partition is stored on the same physical node which can save network bandwidth and computing resources.

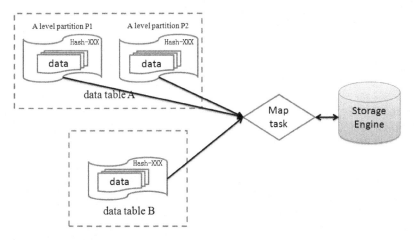

Fig. 3. ParallelHashJoin query between two tables

3.3 Analysis the Performance of the Algorithm

The main purpose of the CPHJ algorithm is to take advantage of the locality of the data so as to avoid network traffic during querying and enhance the efficiency of join query. The following analyses the performance of ParallelHashJoin when distributing data without using the consistent multi-redundant hashing algorithm. Assuming the number of nodes in cluster is M, B_j as the total number of data blocks used in task j, and $b_i (0 \leq i < M)$ on behalf of the number of data blocks used in tasks runs on node i, then $B_j = \sum_{i=0}^{M-1} b_i$; C represents the number of hash partition, and D stands for the quantity of data, so the average amount of data in each data block is $\frac{D}{B_j}$; the average number of data blocks calculated in the same partition of task j is $\frac{B_j}{C}$. In map stage partition works as processing unit, and the scheduling algorithm will try to ensure the locality of every data blocks, so the remaining number of data blocks in every map is $\frac{B_j}{C} - 1$, and the local probability of data in each map is $\left(\frac{1}{M}\right)^{\left|\frac{B_j}{C}-1\right|}$. Suppose there are R copies, which probability will be $\left(\frac{R}{M}\right)^{\left|\frac{B_j}{C}-1\right|}$, so the local probability of total data is $\left(\frac{R}{M}\right)^{\left|\frac{B_j}{C}-1\right| \times C}$. In the execution of the ParallelHashJoin algorithm, since the task scheduler will try to ensure the locality of a data block, the amount of data that needs to be pulled by every map task is:

$$\left|\frac{B_j}{C} - 1\right| \times \left[\left(1 - \frac{R}{M}\right) \times \frac{D}{B_j}\right] = \left|\frac{B_j}{C} - 1\right| \times \left[\left(1 - \frac{R}{M}\right) \times \frac{D}{\sum_{i=0}^{M-1} b_i}\right]$$

So, the total amount of data being pulled is:

$$P = \left|\frac{B_j}{C} - 1\right| \times \left[\left(1 - \frac{R}{M}\right) \times \frac{D}{\sum_{i=0}^{M-1} b_i}\right] \times C \tag{1}$$

Assuming the amount of data D need to be processed by the task of ParallelHashJoin is 3 TB, the number of hash partition C is 500, the total number of data blocks used in task j is 10000, that is B_j equals 10000. So in the algorithm of PHJ, the average amount of data blocks $\frac{B_j}{C}$ processed by every map is 20, and the range of the numbers of machines is [3,200], the obtained results are shown in Fig. 4.

Figure 4 shows that first, the network is heavily loaded and the amount of data is increasing monotonically as the expansion of the number of nodes, which leads to poorer locality of data and worse the performance of the algorithm. Secondly, the numbers of copies also affect the amount of data pulled by map. When the number of nodes in the cluster is in a smaller range, the quantity of copies greatly affects the amount of data to be pulled, but the differences become smaller as the growing number of machines.

When the number of nodes in cluster is very small, such as 3, and the number of data copies also is 3, then each node has a complete copy of all data. It can be seen from Fig. 4, it does not need to pull data from the network. When then number of copies is 1 and 2, 1.9 TB and 0.95 TB data need to be pulled respectively. As the number of nodes

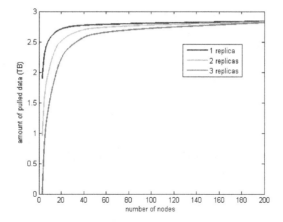

Fig. 4. Traffic of different number of copies

in cluster reaches a certain size, such as 50 machines, and the amount of data need to be pulled are 2.79 TB, 2.736 TB and 2.679 TB when the number of copies respectively are 1, 2 and 3, respectively accounting for 93 %, 91.2 % and 89.3 % of the total amount of calculations. When the nodes in the cluster reach a larger scale, such as the number of 250, the amount of data to be pulled are 2.839 TB, 2.8272 TB and 2.816 TB, the proportion of which stand at 94.6 %, 94.3 % and 93.7 % respectively in the total amount of calculations。

Thus, in case of not using coallocation, only a very small amount of data is able to achieve locality. The locality of data is very poor that large amount of data need to be transferred across the network.

Due to the storage layer stores file by dividing blocks, in the same amount of data to be processed, we adjust the size of the data blocks. Supposing the average numbers of data blocks to be processed respectively are 10, 20 and 30, the number of copies are all 3 and the remaining parameters unchanged; Fig. 5 shows the results obtained.

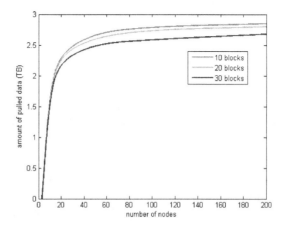

Fig. 5. Traffic of different block size of data

As can be seen from Fig. 5, the size of data blocks also have certain effects on the amount of data to be pulled in the situation of the total data to be processed unchanged. Configure larger data blocks can reduce the amount of data pulled across the network to a certain extent which improve the locality of the data. But on the whole, the amount of data which should be pulled is still great.

In summary, in the case of not using consistent multi-redundant hashing algorithm to distribute data, the locality of data is comparatively poorer when performing ParallelHashJoin. Even in the case of a smaller number of clusters, there is only very small amounts of data can achieve locality. The network load is very heavy that most of the data are transmitted through the network. If adopting consistent multi-redundant hashing algorithm to distribute data, then the relevant data are gathered on the same physical node which make the locality of data reach 100 % by scheduling the tasks to the physical nodes that store data aggregately. The network load in the cluster can be significantly reduced and the performance of join query is able to be improved greatly.

4   Analysis of Experimental Results

4.1   The Experimental Environment and Data

In order to test the performance of CPHJ algorithm, we compare it with the join query processing algorithm of SortMergeReduceJoin(Reduce Join) which used in the Hive system. The experimental environment is 30 servers in Alibaba, each server is configured as follow: eight processing cores, 16 GB of memory, 12 hard drives and the capacity of each disk is 1 TB. Among them, one node as the master node, a node as client, the other 28 nodes as storage and compute nodes, in tests using only one disk in each node. The data tables used in the experiment are stored according to the number attribute of AliWangWang which is divided into 500 copies of hash partitioning. The size of data area is set to 128 MB, every host exclusively occupies the network bandwidth of 100 Mb, and assign 6 map computing slots and 2 reduce computing slots in each computing node. Two large real datasets used in Alibaba are applied in the experiment, the detailed information of datasets are shown in Table 1.

Table 1. Experimental data

Table	Replication	Information		Record number (Billion)
		Size (GB)	Occupied size (GB)	
Profiles	3	15.4	46.2	0.6
Alifriend	3	520	1560	12.7

4.2   Experiment and Analysis

We compare the ReduceJoin used in Hive system with ParallelHashJoin and CPHJ, and then make comparative analysis and performance testing. Specific results are as follows:

4.2.1 Performance Comparison Test of Join Query in the Entire Table

Experiment 1 makes a comparative analysis of the performance of join query in entire table. Query statements used in the experiment are shown in Table 2. Among them, ReduceJoin applies H-SQL, while ParallelHashJoin and CPHJ use the query language of T-SQL which is applied in the data warehouse of Alibaba. The semantics of these query language are consistent.

Table 2. SQL statements used in the Experiment 1

Join query	SQL sentence
Reduce join	insert Cover table ctp select a. MONTH, b.ali1, a.AGE, a.SEX, b.ali2 from profiles alifriend b on ali_AMU = b.ali1
ParallelHashJoin	insert Cover table ctp select /* + ParallelHashJoin(a)*/ a. MONTH, b.ali1, a.AGE, a.SEX, b.ali2 from profiles alifriend b on a. ali _AMU = b.ali1
CPHJ	insert Cover table ctp select /* + ParallelHashJoin(a)*/ a. MONTH, b.ali1, a.AGE, a.SEX, b.ali2 from profiles a join alifriend b on a.ali_AMU = b.ali1

The results are illustrated in Fig. 6 that the performance of ParallelHashJoin is far better than ReduceJoin used in hive, in short, the execution time of the former is only 49.8 % of the latter one. The big part of the results comes from: (1) the start-up cost of reduce task is great; (2) Map and Reduce tasks need to pull data from the network, which involves not only the network overhead and the frequent I/O of the disk. The CPHJ that consider locality of data improves the performance further compared with ReduceJoin and ParallelHashJoin, the execution time of which only accounts for 26 % of ReduceJoin used in hive system and the speedup ratio is 3.76.

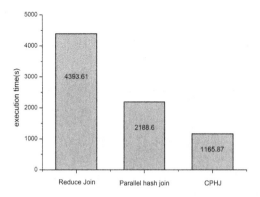

Fig. 6. Comparison of execution time of Reduce Join, ParallelHashJoin and CPHJ

4.2.2   Performance Comparison Test of Join Query with the Range

The experiment 2 tests the performance of join query with the range. The condition of selective query is the number of AliWangWang is less than 200000000; ReduceJoin uses the expression of H-SQL, while ParallelHashJoin and CPHJ apply T-SQL. Query statements are shown in Table 3.

Table 3. SQL statements used in the Experiment 2

Join query	SQL sentence
Reduce join	insert Cover table ctp select a. MONTH, b.ali1, a.AGE, a.SEX, b.ali2 from profiles alifriend b on ali_AMU = b.ali1 where a. ALI_Amu < 200000000
ParallelHashJoin	insert Cover table ctp select /* + ParallelHashJoin(a)*/ a. MONTH, b.ali1, a.AGE, a.SEX, b.ali2 from profiles alifriend b on ali_AMU = b.ali1 where a. ALI_Amu < 200000000
CPHJ	insert Cover table ctp select /* + ParallelHashJoin(a)*/ a. MONTH, b.ali1, a.AGE, a.SEX, b.ali2 from profiles alifriend b on ali_AMU = b.ali1 where a. ALI_Amu < 200000000

As demonstrated in Fig. 7, the speed-up ratio of ParallelHashJoin compares with ReduceJoin is 2.06, and CPHJ compares with ReduceJoin is 4.63. Compared with CPHJ of join query in entire table, CPHJ of join query with the range make fewer output and less constrained by network conditions so as to obtain greater speedup ratio.

4.2.3   Performance Comparison Test of Join Query with Low Selectivity

Experiment 3 verifies the performance of each algorithm with the join query of low selectivity. In Experiment 3, the query condition with low selectivity is a.ALI_-Num = 226357. ReduceJoin uses the expression of H-SQL, while ParallelHashJoin and CPHJ apply T-SQL. Query statements are shown in Table 4.

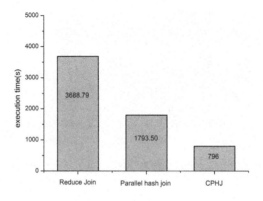

Fig. 7. Comparison of execution time of Reduce Join, ParallelHashJoin and CPHJ

Table 4. SQL statements used in the Experiment 3

Join query	SQL sentence
Reduce join	insert Cover table ctp select a. MONTH, b.ali1, a.AGE, a.SEX, b.ali2 from profiles alifriend b on ali_AMU = b.ali1 where a. ALI_Amu = 226357
ParallelHashJoin	insert Cover table ctp select /* + ParallelHashJoin(a)*/ a. MONTH, b.ali1, a.AGE, a.SEX, b.ali2 from profiles alifriend b on ali_AMU = b.ali1 where a. ALI_Amu = 226357
CPHJ	insert Cover table ctp select /* + ParallelHashJoin(a)*/ a. MONTH, b.ali1, a.AGE, a.SEX, b.ali2 from profiles alifriend b on ali_AMU = b.ali1 where a. ALI_Amu = 226357

As demonstrated in Fig. 8, the speed-up ratio of ParallelHashJoin compares with ReduceJoin is 2.49. The execution time of CPHJ only accounts for 19.2 % of ReduceJoin, and the speedup ratio is 5.2. The experimental results show that, the performance of CPHJ algorithm is much better than Hive's ReduceJoin. With respect to join query in full table, experiment 3 is characterized by a large number of data entry and very little data output. In terms of CPHJ algorithm, the data are from the local and the impact of the network is ultimately minimal that very few of results need to be transmitted, all of which obtain the maximum speedup ratio and more significant advantages of performance.

4.2.4 Load Balancing Experiments

The experiment 4 tests the effect of localized data distribution strategy on the load balance of data, and compared with rack-aware distribution strategy which applied in hadoop. In the experiment, we adopt 28 servers as storage nodes, the data tables are divided by the number of AliWangWang, and the number of hash partition is 500. The experimental results are depicted in Fig. 9.

As shown in Fig. 9, the load condition is linear which apply the strategy of data locality to store data, while the load status is serrated under the distribution strategy of rack-aware. As the number of copies is 3, according to consistent multi-redundant hashing algorithm, the number of hash partition stored in 6 nodes is less than that in the remaining 22.

From $\overline{X} = \frac{1}{n}\sum_{i=1}^{n} X_i$, we can obtain the average value of the load and use the sample variance to measure the volatility of the load. Based on the quantitative analysis, we obtain that the sample variance which applies the strategy of data locality is 0.00064, and the sample variance of the distribution strategy of rack-aware is 40.59. That means, the load fluctuation of the former one is much smaller than the latter one. With respect to the distribution strategy of rack-aware which result in imbalance of the data load by selecting storage nodes randomly, the strategy of data locality can improve the distribution of the load in the cluster.

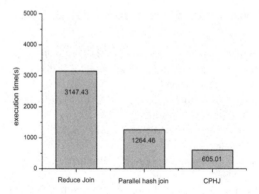

Fig. 8. Comparison of execution time of Reduce Join, ParallelHashJoin and CPHJ

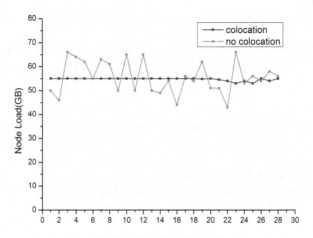

Fig. 9. Cluster nodes load

5 Conclusion

This paper presents an efficient parallel algorithm of join query which is called CPHJ for short. CPHJ designs a consistent multi-redundant hashing algorithm that distributes the table with join relationship in the cluster according to its join properties, which improves the data locality in the join query processing, but also ensures the availability of the data. On the basis of consistent multi-redundant hashing algorithm, parallel algorithm of join query called ParallelHashJoin is proposed that effectively improves the processing efficiency of join queries. The CPHJ method applies in the data warehouse system of Alibaba and experimental results indicate that the workpiece ratio of CPHJ in that query is nearly five times more likely than the hive system.

Acknowledgments. Project supported by National Natural Science Foundation of China (61373015, 61300052), the National High Technology Research and Development Program of

China (863 Program) (No. 2007AA01Z404), Research Fund for the Doctoral Program of High Education of China (No. 20103218110017), a project funded by the Priority Academic Program Development of Jiangsu Higher Education Institutions (PAPD), the Fundamental Research Funds for the Central Universities, NUAA (No. NP2013307), Funding of Jiangsu Innovation Program for Graduate Education KYLX_0287, the Fundamental Research Funds for the Central Universities.

References

1. Ghemawat, S., Gobioff, H., Leung, S.T.: The Google file system. In: Proceedings of the SOSP 2003, pp. 20–43 (2003)
2. Dean, J., Ghemawat, S.: MapReduce: simplified data processing on large clusters. Commun. ACM **51**(1), 107–113 (2003)
3. Yang, H., Dasdan, A., Hsiao, R.L., et al.: Map-reduce-merge: simplified relational data processing on large clusters. In: Proceedings of the 2007 ACM SIGMOD International Conference on Management of Data. ACM, pp. 1029–1040 (2007)
4. Lämmel, R.: Google's MapReduce programming model –Revisited. Sci. Comput. Program. **70**(1), 1–30 (2008)
5. Apache Hive. http://hadoop.apache.org/hive/
6. Thusoo, A., Sarma, J.S., Jain, N., et al.: Hive: a warehousing solution over a map-reduce framework. Proc. VLDB Endowment **2**(2), 1626–1629 (2009)
7. Thusoo, A., Sarma, J.S., Jain, N., et al.: Hive-a petabyte scale data warehouse using hadoop. In: 2010 IEEE 26th International Conference on Data Engineering (ICDE), pp. 996–1005. IEEE (2010)
8. Olston, C., Reed, B., Srivastava, U., et al.: Pig latin: a not-so-foreign language for data processing. In: Proceedings of the 2008 ACM SIGMOD International Conference on Management of Data, pp. 1099–1110. ACM (2008)
9. White, T.: Hadoop: the Definitive Guide. O'Reilly, Sebastopol, CA (2012)
10. Apache Hadoop. http://hadoop.apache.org
11. Murty, J.: Programming Amazon Web Services: S3, EC2, SQS, FPS, and SimpleDB. O'Reilly Media Inc., Sebastopol, CA (2009)
12. Patten, S.: The S3 Sookbook: Get Cooking with Amazon's Simple Storage Service. Sopobo (2009)
13. Isard, M., Budiu, M., Yu, Y., et al.: Dryad: distributed data-parallel programs from sequential building blocks. ACM SIGOPS Operating Syst. Rev. **41**(3), 59–72 (2007)
14. Chaiken, R., Jenkins, B., Larson, P.Å., et al.: SCOPE: easy and efficient parallel processing of massive data sets. Proc. VLDB Endowment **1**(2), 1265–1276 (2008)
15. Yu, Y., Isard, M., Fetterly, D., et al.: DryadLINQ: a system for general-purpose distributed data-parallel computing using a high-level language. In: OSDI, vol. 8, pp. 1–14 (2008)
16. Pike, R., Dorward, S., Griesemer, R., et al.: Interpreting the data: parallel analysis with Sawzall. Sci. Programm. **13**(4), 277–298 (2005)
17. DeWitt, D.J., Gerber, R.H., Graefe, G., et al.: A High Performance Dataflow Database Machine. Computer Science Department, University of Wisconsin (1986)
18. Li, J., Srivastava, J., Rotem, D.: CMD: a multidimensional declustering method for parallel database systems. In: Proceedings of the 18th VLDB Conference, pp. 3–14 (1992)
19. Chen, T., Xiao, N., Liu, F., et al.: Clustering-based and consistent hashing-aware data placement algorithm. J. Softw. **21**(12), 3175–3185 (2010)

20. Karger, D., Lehman, E., Leighton, T., et al.: Consistent hashing and random trees: distributed caching protocols for relieving hot spots on the World Wide Web. In: Proceedings of the Twenty-Ninth Annual ACM Symposium on Theory of Computing. ACM, pp. 654–663(1997)
21. DeCandia, G., Hastorun, D., Jampani, M., et al.: Dynamo: Amazon's highly available key-value store. In: SOSP, vol. 7, pp. 205–220 (2007)

Dynamic Data Driven Particle Filter for Agent-Based Traffic State Estimation

Xiang-wen Feng[1]($\boxtimes$), Xue-feng Yan[1], and Xiao-lin Hu[2]

[1] College of Computer Science and Technology, Nanjing University
of Aeronautics and Astronautics, Nanjing, China
897649107@qq.com, byxf@nuaa.edu.cn
[2] Department of Computer Science, Georgia State University,
Atlanta, GA 30303, USA
cxhu@cs.gsu.edu

Abstract. Particle filter is a good algorithm to deal with non-linear and non-Gaussian problem, but it undergoes high computational complexity and particle degradation problem, and there are few researches in the field of agent-based traffic state estimation. In this paper, a dynamic data driven particle filter is proposed to estimate the traffic states by assimilating real-time data from limited sensors. As the simulation run, the proposed particle filter method can optimize its execution strategies based on the simulation result; furthermore, the real-time data injected into the method can be adjusted dynamically. The agent-based simulation model can display the results in detail, and the traffic state on all roads can be estimated when the particle filter execute to certain precision. Experimental results indicate the framework can estimate the traffic state effectively and the improved particle filter algorithm poses a high accuracy with faster speed.

Keywords: Particle filter · Particle degradation · Agent-based simulation · Traffic state estimate

1 Introduction

Traffic state estimation has become a research hotspot due to the increasingly serious traffic congestion problems. It is difficult to evaluate traffic flow only by static data due to its' features of nonlinear, non-Gaussian and high dimension random [1]; The rapid development of static and dynamic sensors on real road network allows us to get real-time data that can reflect the critical nature of traffic flow, such as the vehicles' average speed and density. The rational use of dynamic sensor data turns into the key to improve the accuracy of traffic state estimation [2]. Bi Chang and Fan in [3] proposed a particle filter based approach to estimate freeway traffic state using a macroscopic traffic flow model, traffic flow's speed and density collected by the measurement detectors were assimilated into the model, experiment results proved that particle filter had an encouraging estimation performance.

Particle filter (PF) is a data assimilation method used to solve the recursive state estimation problem. Unlike Kalman Filter and its' optimized algorithm, PF does not

© Springer International Publishing Switzerland 2015
Z. Huang et al. (Eds.): ICCCS 2015, LNCS 9483, pp. 321–331, 2015.
DOI: 10.1007/978-3-319-27051-7_27

depend on the assumption of linear or Gaussian noise, and is able to be applied for various systems even with non-linear and non-Gaussian noise [7–9]. In PF algorithm, weighted particles are used to describe the posterior distribution of system state, but particle degradation usually happens after several iterations. Normally, the degradation can be overcome by particle resampling, nevertheless it may result in particle enervation which means particles with bigger weights being selected time after time, and makes the particles lose diversity [6]. So how to prevent particle degradation and keep particle diversity turns into the key to apply particle filter.

Agent-based modeling (ABM) is a relatively new approach to modelling system composed of autonomous, interacting agents, and a way to model the dynamics of complex adaptive systems [4]. In [5] an agent-based microscopic pedestrian flow simulation model was presented, the comparison between simulation results and empirical study results reveals that the model can approach the density-speed fundamental diagrams and the empirical flow rates at bottlenecks within acceptable system dimensions. Considering the similarities between pedestrian flow and vehicle flow, it is reasonable to model the traffic flow using agent-based method.

In this paper, we apply particle filter to agent-based traffic simulation model which attracts few focus but the same important as the macro ones. The particle degradation and enervation problems are solved based on the thought of dynamic data driven application system (DDDAS). The traffic state on all roads can be estimated based on the simulation states.

The rest of this paper is organized as follows. The general information about particle filter is introduced in Sect. 2. Section 3 shows the agent-based traffic simulation model. Section 4 describes the dynamic data driven particle filter in detail, the experiments and results are presented in Sect. 5. Conclusions are drawn in the last section.

2 Related Work

2.1 Fundamental of Particle Filtering

Dynamic system can be defined as dynamic discrete state-space model as shown below, Eq. (1) shows the system transition model and Eq. (2) shows the measurement model. In the equations, s_t is the state variable, m_t is the measurement variable; $f(.)$ is the evolution function of state variable; $g(.)$ is the mapping function from state variable to measurement variable; γ_t and ω_t are independent random variables. The estimate of s_t is based on the set of $m_{1:t} = \{m_i, i = 1, 2, \ldots, t\}$.

$$s_{t+1} = f(s_t, t) + \gamma_t. \tag{1}$$

$$m_t = g(s_t, t) + \omega_t. \tag{2}$$

The core algorithm of the particle filter is sequential importance sampling (SIS). In SIS, the algorithm undergoes plenty of iterations. Each iteration, the observation m_t and the previous state of the system S_{t-1} are received, the sample set $s_{t-1}^{(i)} \in S_{t-1}$ can be got from the proposal density $q(s_t^{(i)}|s_{t-1}^{(i)}, m_t)$ to predict the next state, and then the weight of each particle will be updated as $w_n^i = \{w_n^i, i = 1, 2, \ldots n\}$. The SIS method suffers a serious drawback: after a few iteration steps, most of the normalized weights are very close to zero, and the degeneracy phenomenon is unavoidable. Liu et al. in [10] introduced an approximate method to measure particle degradation as shown in Eq. (3).

$$\hat{N}_{eff} = [\sum_{i=1}^{N} (w_n^i)^2]^{-1} \tag{3}$$

In order to solve the degradation problem, the resample algorithm is added after weight normalization. In the resampling step, samples drawn with a probability proportional based on the normalized sample weights are used to update the system state. To sum up, the basic particle filter can be summarized as below.

Step 1. Particle generation: sample N particles from the predictive distribution.

Step 2. Weight computation: assume the N particles' states at time step t are $s_t^i, i = 1, \ldots, N$, compute the importance weights $w_t^i, i = 1, \ldots, N$. Normalize the weights according to $\hat{w}_t^i \propto w_t^i [\sum_{i=1}^{N} w_t^i]^{-1}$.

Step 3. Resampling: based on the resampling algorithm, discard the low weight particles in the particle set $[\{s_t^i, w_t^i\}_{i=1}^{N}]$. Continue the estimation based on the new particle set $[\{s_t^i, w_t^i\}_{i=1}^{N}]'$ for a time step. Set $t = t+1$, return to *Step 1*.

2.2 Agent-Based Traffic Model

An agent-based model normally has three elements [4]: agents' attributes and behaviors; agents' relationships and methods of interaction; agents' environment. In this paper, vehicles are the basic agents; they have attributes like initial speed, ideal speed et al. Vehicles travelling on the road network and behave according to the car-following model and lane-changing model. We use MovSim to describe the agents' environment, which is a microscopic lane-based traffic simulation platform, initiated and contributed by Arne Kesting, Martin Budden, Ralph Germ, and Martin Treiber respectively. MovSim uses a self-defined gradational structure file to describe and construct the topological relation of the road network accurately.

The vehicles' behaviors and interaction are following the Intelligent Driver Model (IDM) [11]. IDM is discretized in space, and the traffic flow can be divided into several road segments. The vehicle's acceleration and deceleration depends on its speed and the vehicles before or after it, while when the vehicle need to change its' traveling route, all vehicles around it should be taken into consideration. IDM can be described as in Eqs. (4) and (5); this expression combines the free-road acceleration strategy $\dot{v}_{free}(v) = a[1 - (v/v_0)^\delta]$ and deceleration strategy $-a(s^*/s)^2$.

$$\frac{dv}{dt} = a \left[1 - \left(\frac{v}{v_0} \right)^\delta \right] - a \left[\frac{s^*(v, \Delta v)}{s} \right]^2 \tag{4}$$

$$s^*(v, \Delta v) = s_0 + \max\left[0, \left(vT + \frac{v\Delta v}{2\sqrt{ab}}\right)\right] \tag{5}$$

3 Improved Adaptive Particle Filter in Traffic Flow Estimation

3.1 Traffic Flow State-Space Conversion Model

To simulate the real traffic scene using agent-based method, we describe the system model below. Assume the road is composed of N road segments, the data that can represent the traffic flow states of each road segment at $t - 1$ is $RN(t-1) = \{fData_{t-1}[1], fData_{t-1}[2]...fData_{t-1}[N]\}$. To evaluate the status of vehicles, the measurement model (MM) is needed to transform RN(t − 1) to compare with the real-time data. Assume k sensors are deployed in the predefined locations on the road network, the states of the real road can be descried as $RRN(t-1) = \{rData_{t-1}[1], rData_{t-1}[2]...rData_{t-1}[k]\}$. We use MM method in Eq. (6) to extract k group of data from the simulation system to compare with the real-time data RRN(t − 1).

$$SRN(t-1) = \{sData_{t-1}[1], sData_{t-1}[2]...sData_{t-1}[k]\} = MM(RN(t-1)) \tag{6}$$

The dynamic state-space model is defined in Eq. (7), $RN(t-1)$ and $RN(t)$ are the statuses of traffic flow at time $t - 1$ and t respectively; *EnMovSim* is the improved system model based on MovSim; *PF* is the assimilation model; $RRN(t-1)$ is the sensor data which can represents the real roads' states. $\gamma(t)$ is the state noises.

$$RN(t) = EnMovSim(PF(MM(RN(t-1)), RRN(t-1)) + \gamma(t)) \tag{7}$$

3.2 Traffic Simulation Framework Based on DDDAS

DDDAS is a combination of simulation and the real world [12]; it is a good way to deal with real-time systems like traffic simulation. Data assimilation is an essential algorithm in DDDAS; its main function is to improve the accuracy of the simulation system by dealing with real-time data. The existing data assimilation rarely works on agent-based traffic simulation models. More importantly, the lack of analytical structures of agent-based model makes it difficult to apply traditional assimilation methods. Thanks to the thought of DDDAS, data from real road system can be continually assimilated into the agent-based model to improve the simulation results. The simulation model and the type of assimilated data can be adjusted by analyzing the simulation states.

The traffic state estimation framework is shown in Fig. 1. The "Sensor data management" module can collect real-time traffic data from different type of sensors distributed on the road network; it can provide certain traffic data to the "Computing Center" by dealing with these sensor data. The "Computing Center" can initialize plenty of simulation particles according to the basic information about the road network and vehicles, the deviation between the simulation result and the real scene can be narrowed by assimilate real-time data from "Sensor data management". The data assimilation method can optimize its' parameters and execution strategy based on the simulation result, the type and frequency of sensor data from "Sensor data management" can be adjusted similarly. As the particle filter execute to certain precision, the concerned traffic state can be estimated and the simulated agent-based traffic scene can be displayed.

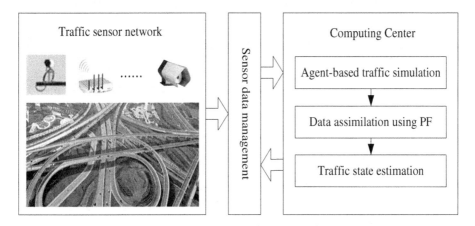

Fig. 1. Dynamic data driven traffic state estimation framework

3.3   Methods Taken to Solve Particle Degradation

PF has the ability to overcome rapid changes in dynamic systems. Yet, it undergoes particle degradation after a few iterations. Customarily, particle degeneracy problem can be solved by implement a huge amount of particles; however it is always impractical due to the computational complexity. In this paper, we mainly use two ways to deal with this problem: firstly, the random model is introduced after the resampling step; secondly, strengthen the dynamic relationship between the simulation model and the real-time data. Figure 2 shows the proposed PF. The following will be described respectively.

Probability distribution has important applications in Traffic Simulation. For example, negative exponential distribution can simulate the randomly arrival of multi-channel vehicles, Normal distribution is able to describe the random speed distribution or probability distribution of some random events. In this paper, random data is added into the vehicles' basic parameters (speed, position, acceleration, etc.) based on proper probability distribution after the resampling step, so that different particles, even particles overlapped in the resampling step, will have certain differences, thus relieve the particle enervation problem caused by resample algorithm.

DDDAS intended to constitute a mutual cooperation system between the simulation and the real scene. Firstly, in the initial simulation, simple real-time data is injected to

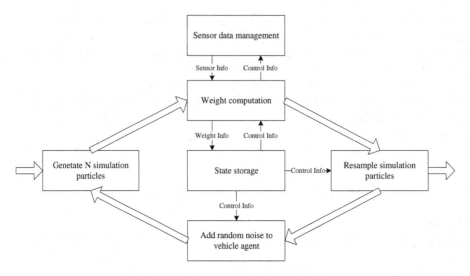

Fig. 2. Dynamic data driven particle filter

accelerate the simulation process. When the simulation results reach a certain precision, the assimilation data will be changed into comprehensive ones. Secondly, the scope of the random value has a negative relationship with the average weight of the current particle set. In other words, at the beginning of the simulation, there may have a big difference between the simulation and the real scene, the simulation can be speed up by adding relatively large random variables. During the process of the simulation approaching to the real state, the random variables should be decreased to ensure the stability of the simulation results. Lastly, if the particle set satisfies the diversity requirement, which can be judged by $\hat{N}_{eff}$, the resampling step will be ignored. Otherwise, the resample will be executed based on the recalculated normalized weight with $\hat{N}_{eff}$. The detailed steps are described in the next section.

3.4 Dynamic Data Driven Particle Filter in Traffic Data Assimilation

The dynamic data driven particle filter (DPF) used in traffic state estimation can be summarized into the following steps. We use *step1* to initialize N simulation threads; the loop of step 2 to 7 achieves continuous traffic flow state-space conversion.

Step 1. Initialize N simulation thread in EnMovSim based on the real traffic scene. Each thread is independent of each other and can be synchronized to simulate the next time's traffic states based on the specified road network and travel model.

Step 2. Generate N particles from the predictive distribution.

Step 3. Weight computation: compute the N particles' weight by comparing the sensor data with the simulation data. The weight of particle i at time t can be calculated using Eq. (8), a is the penalty factor that shown in Eq. (9), $senD_{[1-k]}(t)$ is the density of traffic flow get from the "Sensor data management". $simD_{[1-k]}(i,t)$ is the density get from the measurement model. Equation (11) shows the compute method of *sum*.

At the beginning of the simulation, set $b = 1$, when PF execute to certain precision, set b as in Eq. (10). $senS_{[1-k]}(t)$ is the real average speed. $simS_{[1-k]}(t)$ is the speed got from the measurement model. If the value of a, b, or sum is 0, we values it as 0.1. The weights are normalized as in Eq. (12).

$$w(i,t) = 1/(\lceil a \rceil * \lceil b \rceil * \lceil sum \rceil) \tag{8}$$

$$a = \left| max\left(senD_{[1-k]}(t)\right) - max\left(simD_{[1-k]}(i,t)\right) \right| \tag{9}$$

$$b = \left| max\left(senS_{[1-k]}(t)\right) - max\left(simS_{[1-k]}(i,t)\right) \right|/k \tag{10}$$

$$sum = \sum_{i=1}^{K} \left| simD_{[i]}(i,t) - senD_{[i]}(t) \right| \tag{11}$$

$$\tilde{w}(i,t) = w(i,t)/\sum_{j=1}^{N} w(j,t) \tag{12}$$

Step 4. Calculate the effective number of particles in Eq. (13) and the average weight in Eq. (14), if $\hat{N}_{eff} > 0.4*N$, go to *Step 6*, otherwise continue to *Step 5*.

$$\hat{N}_{eff} = [\sum_{i=1}^{N} (\tilde{w}(i,t))^2]^{-1} \tag{13}$$

$$\bar{w}(t) = \sum_{i=1}^{N} w(i,t)/N \tag{14}$$

Step 5. Resample: to solve the particle enervation problem, the normalized weight should be recalculated as in Eq. (15). In [13], it has been proved that if $0 < \hat{N}_{eff}^{-c} < 1$, then $\tilde{\tilde{w}}(i,t) > \tilde{w}(i,t)$, which means the little weight of particle is increased, and thus relieves the enervation problem. It can be proved that $0 < \hat{N}_{eff}^{-c} < 1$ in Eq. (16), and from the equation we can conclude that the more diverse the particles are, the fewer particles will be copied, thus keep the particles' diversity. The replication sequence which saves the particle number to be copied will be calculated in Eq. (17). Update the states of particles based on the replication sequence.

$$\tilde{\tilde{w}}(i,t) = [\tilde{w}(i,t)]^{\hat{N}_{eff}^{-c}} / \sum_{j=1}^{N} [\tilde{w}(j,t)]^{\hat{N}_{eff}^{-c}}, (0 < c < 1) \tag{15}$$

$$\hat{N}_{eff}^{-c} = [\sum_{i=1}^{N} (\tilde{w}(i,t))^2]^c, \sum_{i=1}^{N} \tilde{w}(i,t) = 1, 0 < c < 1 \Rightarrow 0 < \hat{N}_{eff}^{-c} < 1 \tag{16}$$

$$\sum_{j=1}^{m-1} \tilde{w}(j,t) < u_i \le \sum_{j=1}^{m} \tilde{w}(j,t), u_i \sim (\frac{1}{n}, \frac{2}{n}, \frac{3}{n} \ldots \frac{n-1}{n}, \frac{n}{n}) \qquad (17)$$

Step 6. The proper random factors added in vehicles' parameters are shown in Eq. (18). Where $rand(1, -1)$ means -1 or 1 randomly, $N(\mu, \sigma^2)$ is a normal distribution whose mean is μ and variance is σ.

$$P'(t, i) = P(t, i) + f(\bar{w}(t)) * rand(1, -1) * N(\mu, \sigma^2) \qquad (18)$$

Step 7. Set $t = t + 1$, return to *step 2* or end the algorithm.

4   Experiments and Discussion

In order to evaluate the effectiveness of the dynamic data driven PF in agent-based traffic state estimation. The experiment is carried out based on the main road from the Ming Palace to Zhongshan Gate in Nanjing (the left of Fig. 3). The real road network is simplified based on fieldwork and Google Map, the final road network defined in MovSim is shown in the right of Fig. 3. There are 10 vehicle entrances, vehicles from R71, R34, R7 and R23 can affect the traffic flow on the marked road directly. Assume there are 4 kinds of vehicles traveling on the road network which are shown in Table 1, *Len* is vehicle's length, *InitS* is the initial speed, *IdealS* is ideal speed, *MinI* is the minimum interval between vehicles, *Acc* is acceleration and *Dec* is deceleration. Table 2 shows the inflow of each entrance. Assume a number of sensors are deployed on the road network based on a uniform distribution, and the marked road has 4 sensors at the position of 200 m, 400 m, 600 m and 800 m respectively.

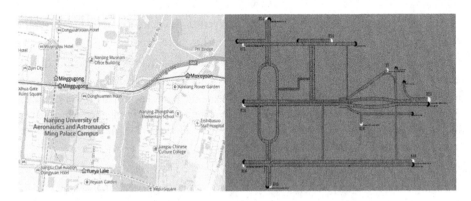

Fig. 3. Road network from the Ming Palace to Zhongshan Gate in Nanjing

Initialize a single-thread simulation based on the road network and vehicle information, set a breakdown point at a random position of the marked road. The congestion will occur due to the breakdown of the lane. Run the simulation for 300 s, all the

Table 1. Vehicles' basic parameters of different type

Name	Model	Len	InitS	IdealS	MinI	Acc	Dec
Car	IDM	4.0 m	25 km/h	50 km/h	2 m	2.5 m/s^2	4.0 m/s^2
Small bus	IDM	7 m	15 km/h	45 km/h	3 m	2.5 m/s^2	4.0 m/s^2
Medium bus	IDM	10 m	10 km/h	40 km/h	4 m	2.0 m/s^2	3.5 m/s^2
Large bus	IDM	12 m	10 km/h	35 km/h	5 m	2.0 m/s^2	3.0 m/s^2

Table 2. Inflow of each entrance

Entrance Id	Inflow (veh/h)	Entrance Id	Inflow (veh/h)
R7	100	R45	500
R18	200	R66	100
R23	1200	R70	800
R34	500	R71	500
R44	100	R74	800

vehicles' parameters at each time will be recorded to act as the "real" sensor data. Remove the breakdown point and restart the simulation with 100 simulation threads. In this paper, SIS, UPF [14] and DPF are used to assimilate the "real" data respectively, and the related results are shown below.

The $\hat{N}_{eff}$ in each algorithm are shown in Fig. 4, it can be concluded that SIS suffers particle degradation problem, and the particles lose diversity in PF after the iteration of resampling; UPF and DPF can keep the particles' diversity within an appropriate range, while DPF can reduce a lot of resampling operation. Figures 5 and 6 show the vehicles' density and average speed among the marked road at 180 s, respectively, we can see that the traffic simulation using DPF is the most close to real scene. The performance of different particle filter algorithms is displayed in Table 3; it is obviously that DPF can simulate the traffic flow accurately with faster speed, which indicate that the dynamic

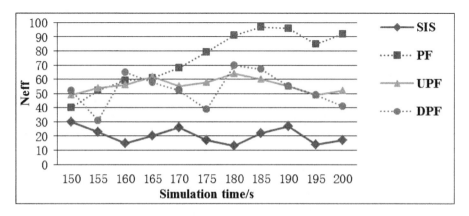

Fig. 4. Effective particle numbers in different particle filter algorithm

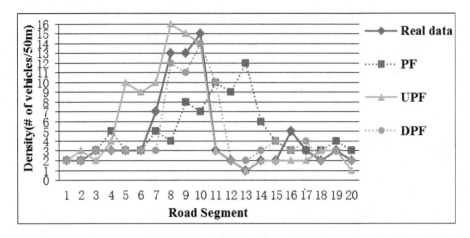

Fig. 5. Vehicles' density at 180 s

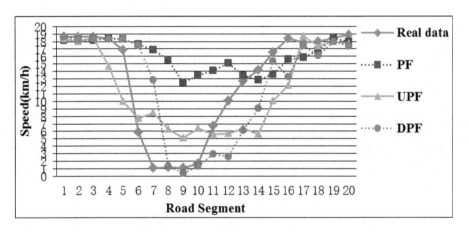

Fig. 6. Vehicles' average speed at 180 s

Table 3. Performance of different particle filter algorithms

Algorithm	RMSE-density	RMSE-speed	Runtime/s
PF	9.523	6.231	215
UPF	4.112	4.210	200
DPF	4.231	3.486	180

data driven methods used in weight computation, resample and random model really work to solve the particle degradation and enervation problem as well as speed up the execution time.

5   Conclusions

In this paper, the dynamic data driven PF for traffic state estimation is presented, the agent-based traffic model and dynamic data driven application are described in detail. We solved the particle degradation and enervation problem by optimizing the execute strategy of particle filter in weight computation, resample, and random model dynamically. A road network from the Ming Palace to Zhongshan Gate in Nanjing is used as an experimental object, the experiment indicates the proposed particle filter can keep the diversity of the simulation particles, and the proposed framework can estimate traffic state effectively with faster speed.

References

1. Zhang, G., Huang, D.: Short-term network traffic prediction with ACD and particle filter. In: 2013 5th International Conference on Intelligent Networking and Collaborative Systems (INCoS), pp. 189–191 (2013)
2. Herrera, J.C., Bayen, A.M.: Traffic flow reconstruction using mobile sensors and loop detector data. University of California Transportation Center Working Papers (2007)
3. Corporation, H.P.: Particle filter for estimating freeway traffic state in Beijing. Math. Probl. Eng. **70**, 717–718 (2013)
4. Macal, C.M., North, M.J.: Tutorial on agent-based modelling and simulation. J. Simul. **4** (112), 151–162 (2010)
5. Liu, S., Lo, S., Ma, J., Wang, W.: An agent-based microscopic pedestrian flow simulation model for pedestrian traffic problems. IEEE Trans. Intell. Transp. Syst. **15**, 992–1001 (2014)
6. Wang, Z., Liu, Z., Liu, W.Q., Kong, Y.: Particle filter algorithm based on adaptive resampling strategy. In: 2011 International Conference on Electronic and Mechanical Engineering and Information Technology (EMEIT), pp. 3138–3141 (2011)
7. Arulampalam, S., Maskel, S., Gordon, N., Clapp, T., Arulampalam, S., Maskel, S., Gordon, N., Clapp, T.: A tutorial on PFs for on-line non-linear/non-gaussian bayesian tracking. Sci. Program. **50**, v2 (2002)
8. Chowdhury, S.R., Roy, D., Vasu, R.M.: Variance-reduced particle filters for structural system identification problems. J. Eng. Mech. **139**, 210–218 (2014)
9. Ruslan, F.A., Zain, Z.M., Adnan, R., Samad, A.M.: Flood water level prediction and tracking using particle filter algorithm. In: 2012 IEEE 8th International Colloquium on Signal Processing and its Applications (CSPA), pp. 431–435 (2012)
10. Liu, J.S.: Metropolized independent sampling with comparisons to rejection sampling and importance sampling. Stat. Comput. **6**, 113–119 (1996)
11. Kesting, A., Treiber, M., Helbing, D.: Enhanced intelligent driver model to access the impact of driving strategies on traffic capacity. Philos. Trans. R. Soc. **368**, 4585–4605 (2009)
12. Darema, F.: Dynamic data driven applications systems: a new paradigm for application simulations and measurements. In: Bubak, M., van Albada, G.D., Dongarra, J., Sloot, P.M.A. (eds.) ICCS 2008, Part III. LNCS, vol. 3038, pp. 662–669. Springer, Berlin, Heidelberg (2004)
13. Zhu, J., Wang, X., Fang, Q.: The improved particle filter algorithm based on weight optimization. In: 2013 International Conference on Information Science and Cloud Computing Companion (ISCC-C), pp. 351–356 (2013)
14. Merwe, R.V.D., Doucet, A., Freitas, N.D., Wan, E.A.: The unscented particle filter. In: Nips, pp. 584–590 (2000)

An Improved Dynamic Spectrum Access Scheme in Cognitive Networks

Qingwei Du[✉] and Yinmeng Wang

College of Computer Science and Technology,
Nanjing University of Aeronautics and Astronautics,
Nanjing, China
duqingwei@nuaa.edu.cn, wangyinmeng1112@163.com

Abstract. Dynamic spectrum Access is the key technology in cognitive networks. And spectrum auction has been considered as an effective way for dynamic spectrum Access. In this paper, we propose a spectrum allocation scheme with the goal to maximize the revenue of primary user (PU) and then try to minimize the interference among secondary users (SUs). There are two steps during the scheme: auction and allocation. During the auction phase, winner determination problem (WDP) is modelled as a knapsack problem, and then Genetic Algorithm is selected to solve it in polynomial time. After that, a payoff function is proposed to ensure that all the SUs can get non-negative utilities only with their truthful information. During the allocation phase, we try to minimize the interference while allocating the released channels to all the winners. Finally, simulation experiments show that the proposed auction mechanism has a better performance in solving the problem of WDP.

Keywords: Dynamic spectrum access · Spectrum auction · Genetic algorithms · Truthful

1 Introduction

The spectrum has become a scarce resource and cognitive technology as a prospective approach has been proposed to overcome the trouble by achieving dynamic spectrum access [1]. In a cognitive network, the owners of spectrums are called primary users (PUs) and the users that have to apply spectrums from PUs are secondary users (SUs). Literatures introduced the sharing spectrum between PUs and SUs [2–4].

Recently, solving dynamic spectrum access problem by economical tools has become more and more popular [5]. There is a non-profit controller called spectrum broker who hosts the auction activities [6]. Tao et al. discussed the online auction based on the relay selection scheme [7]. H. Ahmadi et al. tried to put learning strategy into the auction mechanism to get satisfactory results [8], but its algorithms complexity is high and we can only get a better one at last. Wei et al. considered various strategies is selected by different SUs and this can bring better revenue as well as longer delay time [9]. Peng wanted to maximize the trading volume by a price system [10], when the spectrum PU leased more than SUs needed, he try to cut the price and vice versa, obviously, it's too completed. Qinhui took the location factors into auction activity and

© Springer International Publishing Switzerland 2015
Z. Huang et al. (Eds.): ICCCS 2015, LNCS 9483, pp. 332–343, 2015.
DOI: 10.1007/978-3-319-27051-7_28

began to care about the QoS [11]. The situation taken into account by Mohammad, the real environment has many malicious users and they designed a real game between SUs in the auction process [12], but it is difficult to reach the Nash equilibrium. Dejun et al. also studied the truth about SUs' biddings information and clustering management SUs to give the mechanism a better scalability [13]. Xinyun broke the time and frequency into several littler cells and SUs bidded for the amount of the cells and proposed a scheme named Norm-based Greedy Scheme [14]. Joseph et al. tried to put the dynamic spectrum allocation as knapsack problems and aimed at maximizing spectrum usage while lowering management overhead [15]. Based on this, Changyan ameliorated the idea in three ways: rearrangement, interchange and replacement [16]. But none of those papers have taken the location factor into account, using genetic algorithms to solve it in polynomial time and trying to minimize the interference during the allocation part.

In this paper, we model dynamic spectrum access as a knapsack problem. For all the SUs who bid the spectrum from PU have only two statues: 1 denotes a winner for the spectrum and 0 denotes the opposite. When SUs bid for the spectrum, they also send their private information like location to the spectrum broker, and then the broker determines all the winners. A payment rule is proposed to assure that every SU can win the spectrum only by a truthful bid. Next step is allocating all the free channels to the winners.

The main contributions of this paper are as follows:

- The dynamic spectrum access problems have been modelled as knapsack problems. Then Genetic Algorithms are selected to solve it in polynomial time. Modified Genetic Algorithms make it more suitable for solving knapsack problems.
- Adopt Second-price scheme to determine the payment prices of winners.
- Allocation the free channels to all the winners, trying to minimize the interference according to the location information.

The rest of this paper is organized as follows. In Sect. 2, we propose the system model. In Sect. 3, we illustrate the details of the spectrum access scheme and prove the optimize payment rule can assure the networks' truth. Section 4 presents the simulation results and Sect. 5 concludes our paper.

2   System Model

For simplicity we consider a cognitive network with only one PU, multiple SUs and a central entity named spectrum broker. PU allows SUs access to idle channels for the extra profit. In an auction, the number of auctioned channels provided from PU is denoted as m, maybe the bandwidths of channels are various but, for the sake of simplicity, we assume they are the same. We denote the SUs by $N = \{1, 2, 3, \ldots, n\}$ and the spectrum broker is non-profit. SUs have different demands for spectrums and calculates the value themselves for their needed spectrum, denoted by $V = \{v_1, v_2, \ldots, v_n\}$. Their bidding prices can be denoted by $B = \{b_1, b_2, \ldots, b_n\}$, and their demands can be denoted by $D = \{d_1, d_2, \ldots, d_n\}$. We call the network is truth when $v_i = b_i$. For conveniences, the SUs can only get all their requirements or nothing.

At the start of the auction, PU and SUs submit their own information to the spectrum broker. The spectrum broker collects all these information and determines an optimal allocation scheme. After all, the broker figures out the payments and payoff for SUs and PU.

3   Dynamic Spectrum Access

In this section, the improved truthful spectrum access scheme with a novel spectrum auction and allocation mechanism is discussed in detail. We first formulate the winner determination problem (WDP) as a knapsack problem and use genetic algorithms to solve it. Also we modified the genetic algorithms to adapt to the spectrum auction we proposed. After that, a pricing scheme like Second-Price Auction is designed to ensure that all SUs can have a non-negative utility only by their real information. Of course, we do a simple proof later. Finally, we try to allocate the freed channels to all the winners in a way with lower interference as possible.

3.1   Winner Determination Problem

The improved spectrum auction is made up of one PU and multiple SUs. Define the PU has m channels to free, wherein m can be calculated by $m = \lfloor t/w \rfloor$, t represents the total quantity of spectrum PU leases and w means the bandwidth of a channels. Similarly we define n as the number of SUs. Each su_i has a different channels demand d_i and a private valuation v_i for their demand. v_i equals the monetary value of Shannon capacity that su_i could gain from d_i demand channels as

$$v_i = \sigma_i d_i \log_2(1 + \eta_i) \tag{1}$$

Here σ_i is the currency weight and η_i means the signal-to-noise ratio (SNR). Both of them are constants for every su_i [17]. Before the auction, PU reports its information to the spectrum broker. SUs send their bids also, which can be denoted as Bid_i, $i = 1, 2, \ldots, n$. Each bid Bid_i is specified as a 2-tuple (b_i, d_i), where

- d_i is the number of channels su_i demands: $d_i = \lceil k_i/w \rceil$, where k_i is the spectrum demand of the bidder su_i and w is the bandwidth of each channel.
- b_i indicates the payment su_i is willing to pay for its demand d_i.

After obtaining the complete information, the spectrum broker formulates an optimization problem to determine the winners to maximize the social welfare, which means maximize the total payment price from all winning SUs. The formulated optimization problem is

$$\max_{\{x_i, \forall i \in n\}} \sum_{i=1}^{n} q_i * x_i \tag{2}$$

$$(1) \quad \sum_{i=1}^{n} q_i x_i \leq m$$

$$(2) \quad x_i \in \{0, 1\}$$

Where $x_i = 1$ means su_i win the spectrum leased by PU in the auction and $x_i = 0$, otherwise. The first constraint means that the total amount of channels SUs obtain cannot exceed the quantity leased from PU. When the winner determination problem has been solved, a novel payment function was designed. In simple words, the winners' payment is a function depend on the second highest price, so the computational method of q_i is

$$q_i = \sqrt{d_i} * \max_{k \in B_{i^-}} \left(\frac{b_k}{\sqrt{d_k}} \right) \tag{3}$$

And we will introduce it in details later in the payment rule part. B_{i^-} is a subset of SUs whose $b_i / \sqrt{d_i}$ values are no bigger than SU_i. Nevertheless the winner determination problem is difficult to solve, so in the next subsections, we will introduce how to use Genetic Algorithms to solve it.

It is such a challenge to solve the problem shows in formula (2) in polynomial time. In this paper, the puzzle has been modelled as knapsack problems and the Genetic Algorithms is selected as the near-optimal solution. It has been proved that the Genetic Algorithms have a better performance in solving knapsack problems. And we can get a solution not worse than the traditional Greedy Algorithm.

3.2 Genetic Algorithms

The winner determination problem (WDP) can be regarded as knapsack problems, but there are no algorithms could guarantee to run out the problem in polynomial time [18]. Genetic Algorithms have been proved to be well the suited for optimal solutions to such knapsack problems and they can find out the optimal solutions of optimization problems efficiently [19].

Genetic Algorithms has been improved in many aspects. Here we decided to use hybrid genetic algorithms [20] - a combination of greedy algorithms and genetic algorithms - to solve the winner determination problem. First of all, we can get one initial chromosome by greedy algorithms to guarantee that genetic algorithms can convergence to a better value at lease. But it has many insufficient if we just use the existing algorithm without any modification to solve the spectrum allocation problem in cognitive networks.

3.3 Improved Genetic Algorithms

The proposed algorithm improved the performance of this algorithm in the following several aspects:

- If one chromosome is not a solution, drop the bidder from the one with minimum $b_i/\sqrt{d_i}$ value, which means search the states of SU from the tail of the inequation (4).
- Do not allow the same chromosome in one population, which can prevent convergence to the current highest fitness chromosomes.
- Modify fitness function to make it more suitable for the new payment rule.

And then, the principal steps of improved Genetic Algorithms are listed:

(a) *Start*: Initialize the first generation of population.
  (i) Get one chromosome by Greedy Algorithm.
      Sort the bidders according to the under standard, inequality (4).

$$\frac{b_1}{\sqrt{d_1}} \geq \frac{b_2}{\sqrt{d_2}} \geq \cdots \geq \frac{b_i}{\sqrt{d_i}} \geq \cdots \geq \frac{b_n}{\sqrt{d_n}} \tag{4}$$

  (ii) Randomly generate all the other chromosomes in the first generation.
(b) *Inspection*: Check every chromosome in the population whether is a real solution. If the SUs' total demand is bigger than the pack size, then drop bidders from the tail of the inequation (4).
(c) *Fitness*: Calculate the fitness value of each chromosome in the population. The fitness function of *ith* chromosome in the population can be got by

$$fitness(i) = \sum_{l=1}^{n} (x_l * \sqrt{d_l} * \max_{k \in B_{l-}}(\frac{b_k}{\sqrt{d_k}})) \tag{5}$$

(d) *Generate a new population:*
  (i) Selection: Choose the highest fitness two chromosomes based on the values obtained from the step Fitness, if the top two chromosomes are the same, delete and remain chromosomes until the top two are different.
  (ii) Crossover: The only difference with the traditional Genetic Algorithm is paying attention to the question: don't allow the same chromosomes.
  (iii) Mutation: The mutation operation has no different with the traditional Genetic Algorithm.
(e) *Replace*: Replacing the current population with the new population.
(f) *Judge*: Judging whether the end condition is satisfied. If cases, stop the algorithm or return to step 2 on the contrary.

Here we will introduce the improved genetic algorithms in detail with the help of pseudo-code. Table 1 lists some important notations used in our paper.

Spectrum broker collected all the bidding information from SUs and PU, and it initializes the first generation of population. First get one chromosome by Greedy Algorithm and get others randomly.

Table 1. Information notations in this paper

Symbol	Meaning
pop	The population of genetic information
pop_size	The population's chromosomes number
chromo_size	The length of a chromosome, equals n
fitness_value	The fitness value of each chromosome
top_two	The highest fitness two chromosomes

In step Inspection, checking all the chromosomes in the population whether they are really solutions should be the first. If the total demand of a chromosome is bigger than m, search the states of SU from the tail of the inequation (4), if the state is 1, change it to 0 until the total demand does not exceed m.

```
Algorithm 1          Inspection
for i=1:pop_size do
     sum=0;
     for j=1:chromo_size do
         if pop(i,j)==1 then
              sum+=bid(2,j);
         end
     end
     if sum>m then
         change the states from 1 to 0 by the tail of the
     inequation (4) until sum<=m
     end
end.
```

The next step is calculating the fitness. Different from the traditional simple summation, we create a new formula for a better reasonability with the newly payment rule. We use the sum of the payoff function ($\sum_{i \in winners} q(i)$) as the chromosome's fitness value instead of the biddings' ($\sum_{i \in winners} v_i$). $q(i)$ can be computed out by Eq. (3). The fitness values of chromosomes are the basis of the next step Selection.

In the Selection part, we traverse the current population and choose the different top two high fitness chromosomes to be used for generating the new solutions.

Not a simple crossover operation like the traditional Genetic Algorithm, we select different strategies to generate a new population. Firstly, or operation between the top two chromosomes can bring one new solution. Secondly, crossover operation between the top two can bring another two chromosomes. Finally, choice chromosomes in the current population according to the fitness value descending to join the new population. It is worth noting that during this step, the same chromosome is not allowed in the new population. In order to facilitate understanding, we give the code.

Algorithm 2   Crossover

```
pop_old=pop;      pop=zeros(pop_size,chromo_size);
//or operation between the top two
for i=1:chromo_size do
    pop(1,i)=top_two(1,i)|top_two(2,i);
end
num=2;
//crossover operation between the top two
for i=1:chromo_size do
    if i%2==1 then
        pop(2,i)=top_two(1,i);    pop(3,i)=top_two(2,i);
    else
        pop(2,i)=top_two(2,i);    pop(3,i)=top_two(1,i);
    end
end
if pop(2) is not exist in pop then
    num++;
end
if pop(3) is not exist in pop then
    num++;
end
//choose the best chromosomes to produce new population
while num<=pop_size do
    if pop_old(max) is not exist in pop then
        pop(num)=pop_old(max);    num++;
    else
        delete pop_old(max) from pop_old
    end
end.
```

The Mutation process is simple and easy to implementation, and we do nothing to improve this part, so we no longer explain it in detail. By now a new generation population comes into being. If the ending condition is not satisfied, return to the step Check or get the best solution.

3.4 Payment Rule

In this part, we mainly introduce the payment rule after all the winners are determined. We adopt the idea of Second Price Auction to form a new payment function in order to better adapt to our auction. The payment of each winner should be defined by the maximize value in a set of whose values are no larger than it. Based on this, we can calculate the payment of each winning su_j by distinguishing two cases:

- If su_j loses the auction (i.e., $B_{j^-} = \emptyset$), then its payment is 0.

- If su_j wins the auction, and its demand is d_j and $B_{j^-} \neq \emptyset$, the payment q_j can be represented as

$$q_j = \sqrt{d_j} * \max_{k \in B_{j^-}} \left(\frac{b_k}{\sqrt{d_k}} \right) \tag{6}$$

Since that the auction scheme can guarantee the network's truthful, we will do a simple proof for it. That is to say that the spectrum auction scheme could maximize the social welfare on the basis of two basic constraints: incentive compatibility and individual rationality.

The auction scheme has incentive compatibility, which means each SU can get a non-negative only by truthful bidding. We only need to consider the following two cases.

(a) su_j takes part in the auction by its truthful bidding $(v_j = b_j)$ can get the utility $u_j \geq 0$. i.e., (i) su_j loses the auction and its utility $u_j = 0$; (ii) su_j wins the auction and gets the utility:

$$u'_j = v_j - q_j = v_j - \sqrt{d_j} * \max_{k \in B_{j^-}} \left(\frac{b_k}{\sqrt{d_k}} \right) \geq 0 \tag{7}$$

(b) su_j takes part in the auction untruthfully $(i.e., v_j \neq b_j)$, and its utility would be affected only if its bidding price is larger than the real value. If su_j loses the auction, we define its utility is $u_j = 0$, otherwise, the only condition su_j may have the chance to win is $b_j / \sqrt{d_j} \geq \max_{k \in B_{j^-}} (b_k / \sqrt{d_k}) \geq v_j / \sqrt{d_j}$. In this case, its utility can be prove to be non-positive as

$$u'_j = v_j - q'_j = v_j - \sqrt{d_j} * \max_{k \in B_{j^-}} \left(\frac{b_k}{\sqrt{d_k}} \right) < v_j - \sqrt{d_j} * \frac{b_j}{\sqrt{d_j}} < 0 \tag{8}$$

In conclusion, su_j can't increase its utility by an untruthful bidding no matter how much bigger it is.

The auction scheme has individually rational, that is to say our scheme should guarantee each truthful SU would have a non-negative utility. If su_j loses the auction, its utility is zero. Otherwise, su_j wins and its utility can be calculated as:

$$u_j = v_j - q_j = b_j - \sqrt{d_j} * \max_{k \in B_{j^-}} \left(\frac{b_k}{\sqrt{d_k}} \right) = \left[\frac{b_j}{\sqrt{d_j}} - \max_{k \in B_{j^-}} \left(\frac{b_k}{\sqrt{d_k}} \right) \right] * \sqrt{d_j} \geq 0 \tag{9}$$

The above non-equality would happen when su_j participates in the auction process truthfully and wins. End here, the payment rule can obtain the biggest social welfare on the basis of two basic: incentive compatibility and individual rationality.

3.5   Allocation Channels

In this part, a new channels allocation strategy is put forward to reduce the disturbance among winners. First of all, the winners are divided into several part of mutually disjoint by their location information and communication ranges. After dividing the winners, we allocate the channels across different part because the interference in the same part is much bigger than that in different. Below is a simple example (Fig. 1).

4   Numerical Results

In this part, we do some simulations to evaluate the improved genetic algorithm in the

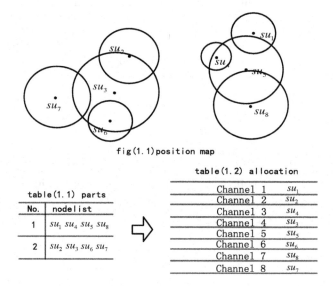

fig(1.1)position map

table(1.2) allocation

table(1.1) parts

No.	node list
1	su_1 su_4 su_5 su_8
2	su_2 su_3 su_6 su_7

Channel 1	su_1
Channel 2	su_2
Channel 3	su_4
Channel 4	su_3
Channel 5	su_5
Channel 6	su_6
Channel 7	su_8
Channel 8	su_7

Fig. 1. Divide the winners

auction step. For comparison purpose, the greed algorithm is simulated as a benchmark.

The considered cognitive radio network consists of 20 SUs and one PU. For the PU, the number of auctioned channels it offers is randomly selected in [20, 50] Chs. For each SU $i, \forall i \in N$, its spectrum requirement is randomly in [5, 50], while its SNR γ_i is random in [50, 100]. All the results are based on average over 1000 runs.

Figure 2 shows the social welfare with different solutions to WDP. It shows that the improved genetic algorithms can improve the initial population by greedy algorithms. Which means that genetic algorithms could not worse than greedy. Moreover, the improved genetic algorithms did a better job as we see from the figure.

Figure 3 shows the SUs' satisfaction ratio of the improved genetic algorithms, genetic algorithms and greedy algorithms. From the figure, we can know that a higher

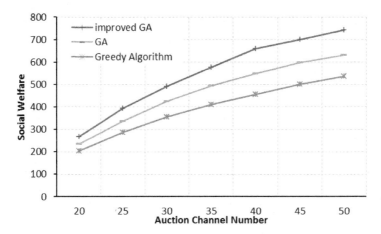

Fig. 2. Performance of the improved GA on WDP

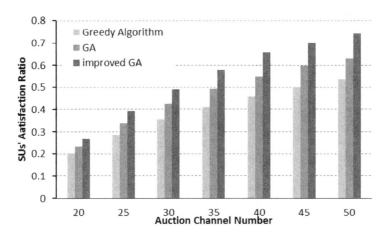

Fig. 3. Comparison on SUs' satisfaction ratio

SUs' satisfaction ratio could be gotten by the improved genetic algorithms. In other words, more SUs' could get spectrum.

5 Conclusion

In this paper, we proposed a truthful spectrums auction between one PU and multiple SUs. The auction processes are regarded as a knapsack problem, and the genetic algorithm is marked to solve it. In order to improve the efficiency of the genetic algorithms, we did the improvement in four aspects. By now, all the winners can be determined with a higher income. We designed a payment rule to ensure the authenticity of the auction. A simple proof has also been given for the truthful and economically robust. Numerical results show that the auction algorithm has a good performance in solving the winner determination problem. In our paper, there are many aspects that can be improved such as the hidden-node problem mentioned in [21]. In the future study, a more comprehensive consideration should be taken into the auction framework to have a higher practicability.

References

1. Haykin, S.: Cognitive radio: brain-empowered wireless communications. IEEE J **23**, 201–220 (2005)
2. Liang, W., Xin, S., Hanzo, L.: Cooperative communication between cognitive and primary users. Inst. Eng. Technol. **7**, 1982–1992 (2012)
3. Zhai, C., Zhang, W., Mao, G.: Cooperative spectrum sharing between cellular and ad-hoc networks. IEEE Trans. Wirel. Commun. (2014)
4. Ng, S.X., Feng, J., Liang, W., Hanzo, L.: Pragmatic distributed algorithm for spectral access in cooperative cognitive radio networks. IEEE Trans. Commun. (2014)
5. Rui Wang, Hong Ji, Xi Li.: A novel multi-relay selection and power allocation scheme for cooperation in cognitive radio ad hoc networks based on principle-agent game. Inf. Commun. Technol. (2013)
6. Song, M., Xin, C., Zhao, Y., Cheng, X.: Dynamic spectrum access: from cognitive radio to network radio. IEEE Wirel. Commun. **19**(1), 23–29 (2012)
7. Xu, H., Jin, J., Li, B.: A secondary market for spectrum. IEEE Infocom (2010)
8. Jing, T., Zhang, F., Cheng, W., Huo, Y., Cheng, X.: Online auction based relay selection for cooperative communications in CR networks. In: Cai, Z., Wang, C., Cheng, S., Wang, H., Gao, H. (eds.) WASA 2014. LNCS, vol. 8491, pp. 482–493. Springer, Heidelberg (2014)
9. Ahmadi, H., Chew, Y.H., Reyhani, N., Chai, C.C., DaSilva, L.A.: Learning solutions for auction-based dynamic spectrum access in multicarrier systems. Comput. Netw. 60–73 (2014)
10. Zhong, W., Xu, Y., Wang, J., Li, D., Tianfield, H.: Adaptive mechanism design and game theoretic analysis of auction-driven dynamic spectrum access in cognitive radio networks. EURASIP J. Wirel. Commun. Networking (2014)
11. Lin, P., Zhang, Q.: Dynamic spectrum sharing with multiple primary and secondary users. IEEE Trans. Veh. Technol. (2011)
12. Wang, Q., Ye, B., Lu, S., Gao, S.: A truthful QoS-aware spectrum auction with spatial reuse for large-scale networks. IEEE Trans. Parallel Distrib. Syst. **25**(10), 2499–2508 (2014)
13. Alavijeh, M.A., Maham, B., Han, Z., Nader-Esfahani, S.: Efficient anti-jamming truthful spectrum auction among secondary users in cognitive radio networks. In: IEEE ICC-Cognitive Radio and Networks Symposium (2013)
14. Yang, D., Xue, G., Zhang, X.: Truthful group buying-based auction design for cognitive radio networks. In: IEEE ICC-Mobile and Wireless Networking Symposium (2014)
15. Wang, X., Sun, G., Yin, J., Wang, Y., Tian, X., Wang, X.: Near-optimal spectrum allocation for cognitive radio: a frequency-time auction perspective. In: GLOBECOM-Wireless Communication Symposium (2012)
16. Mwangoka, J.W., Marques, P., Rodriguez, J.: Broker based secondary spectrum trading. In: 6th International ICST Conference on Cognitive Radio Oriented Wireless Networks and Communications (2011)

17. Yi, C., Cai, J.: Combinatorial spectrum auction with multiple heterogeneous sellers in cognitive radio networks. In: IEEE ICC-Cognitive Radio and Networks Symposium (2014)
18. Gao, L., Xu, Y., Wang, X.: MAP: Multiauctioneer progressive auction for dynamic spectrum access. IEEE Trans. Mob. Comput. **10**(8), 1144–1161 (2011)
19. Mochon, A., Saez, Y., Isasi, P..: Testing bidding strategies in the clock-proxy auction for selling radio spectrum: a genetic algorithm approach. In: IEEE Evolutionary Computation (2009)
20. Sachdeva, C, Goel, S.: An improved approach for solving 0/1 Knapsack Problem in polynomial time using genetic algorithms. In: IEEE International Conference on Recent Advances and Innovations in Engineering (2014)
21. Liu, L., Li, Z., Zhou, C.: Backpropagation-based cooperative location of primary user for avoiding hidden-node problem in cognitive networks. In: International Journal of Digital Multimedia Broadcasting, Hindawi Publishing Corporation (2010)

The Design and Implementation of a Dynamic Verification System of Z

Jun Wang, Yi Zhuang$^{(\boxtimes)}$, and Siru Ni

College of Computer Science and Technology, Nanjing University
of Aeronautics and Astronautics, Nanjing, Jiangsu, People's Republic of China
nuaa_wangj@163.com, {zy16,nisr}@nuaa.edu.cn

Abstract. Z notation can accurately describe static structures and operation specifications of software. Predicate calculus is used to perform validation and verification of Z models. The existing validation tools of Z are aimed to check the expected behavior of software model, while they cannot automatically verify the correctness and safety of the software. This paper proposes a software model named ZA (Z-Automata) to describe the behavior and data constraints of software, by combining the elements of Z notation and FA (Finite Automata). An extended temporal logic is defined, and a model checking algorithm ZAMC (Z-Automata Model Checking) is designed to perform the verification of ZA's expected properties. For the practical usage of our ZA model and ZAMC algorithm, we implement a prototype of Z Dynamic Verification System (ZDVS), which can be used as a modeling and verification tool for Z models. The illustration of the modeling and verification process of a case study shows that our ZA model can describe data constraints within the software behavior, and can automatically verify the expected properties of the Z model.

Keywords: Z notation · Finite automata · Model checking · Temporal logic

1 Introduction

Software, as carrier of information technology, bears the mission of interactions between human and computers. It has been widely used in people's daily life, as well as in industrial production, aviation, spaceflight and so on. The growing demand for software has led to its greater complexity and larger scale. At the same time, ensuring dependability of software is becoming a strong requirement in many fields. As a result, the software designers face with new challenges at the stages of design, implementation and maintenance of software development these years.

Z [1–5] is a formal specification language used for describing computer programs and computer-based systems in general. Theorem proving [6–8] and animation [9–11] are two main categories of analysis methods for Z notation. The former usually uses predicate logic reasoning to prove the static properties of a Z model. The latter employs a query approach to confirm the expected system behavior by accepting or denying the manually input operations. The decisions are made depending on whether there is any inconsistency between the specification of the operation input and the global constraints

© Springer International Publishing Switzerland 2015
Z. Huang et al. (Eds.): ICCCS 2015, LNCS 9483, pp. 344–355, 2015.
DOI: 10.1007/978-3-319-27051-7_29

of the Z model. These two categories of analysis methods are both unable to automatically verify the temporal properties of a given Z model.

Model checking [12], or property checking, is a technology dealing with the following problem: given a model of a state transition system, exhaustively and automatically check whether this model meets a given formula. Usually, the formula describes temporal properties such as safety and liveness [13]. Because of its conciseness and efficiency, model checking technology has been widely adopted to verify temporal properties of hardware and software systems for over three decades.

Because Z lacks the ability of describing system temporal behavior, building a proper state transition system is the primary step to study the model checking method on Z. A state transition system based on FA (Finite Automata) can describe the run-time behavior of software, but it is insufficient in describing data constraints, comparing with Z's syntax based on set theory and first-order logic. Some of the current studies on model checking Z are based on transforming Z to a middle language that can be model checked by existing tools [14]. Other related works use new structures such as ZIA [15, 16], which is a combination model of Z notation and interface automata targeted at component based systems. By combining Z and state transition structures, we can establish a more comprehensive system model, and study its model checking method accordingly. However, the existing researches have not implemented automatic model transformation between Z and those hybrid models, which is insufficient for industrial usage.

In this paper, we design and implement a prototype system ZDVS. Firstly, we define a formal model ZA (Z-Automata) combining Z and FA (Finite Automata). The generation algorithm from the basic structures of Z to ZA is studied to enhance the practical usage of our hybrid model. Further on, a model checking algorithm ZAMC is proposed to automatically verify the temporal/data constraints within the structure and behavior specified by ZA. Finally, a case study is used to illustrate the correctness and feasibility of ZDVS.

2   ZA Model

To verify dynamic temporal behavior of a system, we take the advantages of the predicate logic description ability of Z notation and the temporal description ability of FA. In this section, we give the formal definition of ZA model and design a generation algorithm to transform Z static model to ZA.

2.1   Formal Definition of ZA

In order to facilitate the study of model checking Z, and to establish a formal relationship between Z specification and ZA model, we present a formal definition of ZA. First of all, we define some useful notations in Definition 1, to help the definition of ZA. Secondly, we define a simplified structure of Z models as ZA_{static} in Definition 2, to delineate the element set we need to map to FA.

Definition 1. Assume that a Z schema declaresas $x_1, \ldots, x_n$ its variables, the invariants in the schema can be seen as an n-ary predicate. We use the form S_{p_n} to state the n-ary prediction. In particular, we denote the pre-conditions of an operation schema Op as pre_{Op}, and the post-conditions as $post_{Op}$.

Definition 2. A ZA Static Model

$$ZAstatic = (State, Operation) \tag{1}$$

consists of the following elements:

- *State* is a finite set of state spaces. Its elements correspond to the state schemas in a Z specification.
- *Operation* is a finite set of operations. Its elements correspond to the operation schemas in a Z specification.

We has designed and implemented a Z notation parser as a crucial component of ZDVS, to analyze an input Z model and transform it to a ZA_{static} model written by C++. The formal definition of ZA is given as follows.

Definition 3. A ZA Model

$$ZA = (S, S_0, \Sigma, \delta, F, M) \tag{2}$$

consists of the following elements:

- S is a finite set of states.
- $S_0 \subseteq S$ is a finite set of initial states.
- Σ is a finite set of operations.
- $\delta \subseteq (S \times \Sigma \times S)$ is a finite set of state transitions. A state transition $(s, a, s') \in \delta$ represents that system transits from state s to s'.
- F is a finite set of end states.
- M denotes a binary relationship between S, Σ and the elements in ZA_{static}, such that $M = (F_s, F_\Sigma)$. The definitions of its tuples are as follows:
  F_s is a mapping from S to *State*, i.e.,

$$F_s(s) = state, \text{ where } s \in S, state \in State \tag{3}$$

F_Σ is a mapping from Σ to *Operation*, i.e.,

$$F_\Sigma(a) = op, \text{ where } a \in \Sigma, op \in Operation \tag{4}$$

According to Definition 3, the prerequisite of a state transition $(s, a, s') \in \delta$ is that state s meets the pre-conditions, and s' meets the post-conditions of operation a, that is, $s| = pre_{F_\Sigma(a)}$ and $s'| = post_{F_\Sigma(a)}$ hold.

2.2   The Generation of ZA Model

After the formal definition of ZA model, we propose a generation algorithm which builds a ZA model from the ZA_{static} model. The input of the algorithm is ZA_{static} = (*State, Operation*), and the output is a ZA model.

The procedure of the generation is described as follows:

- *Step 1.* Initialization phase. Initialize s_0 and a stack St;
- *Step 2.* Add s_0 to S_0 and S. Build the one-to-one relationship between *Operation* and Σ, and the relationship between *State* and S.;
- *Step 3.* Push s_0 onto St;
- *Step 4.* Get the top element s of St, while St is not empty;
- *Step 5.* For each operation a_i in Σ, if $s| = pre_{F_\Sigma(a_i)}$ is true, perform a_i on s and get a new state s';
- *Step 6.* If $s'| = post_{F_\Sigma(a)}$ is true and it meets the global constrains, add (s, a_i, s') to δ;
- *Step 7.* If s' doesn't exist, add s' to S and push it onto St. If it's an end state, add it to F;
- *Step 8.* Go to *step 5*, until all operations in Σ are considered;
- *Step 9.* Go to *step 4*, until St is empty;
- *Step 10.* Output the ZA model.

Figure 1 gives the pseudo code of ZA model generation algorithm according to the above procedure.

3   Model Checking ZA

In this section, we define a set of temporal logic formulas called ZATL (Z-Automata Temporal Logic) to describe the expected temporal properties of the system. Further on, a model checking algorithm called ZAMC (Z-Automata Model Checking) is proposed to perform the verification towards such properties.

3.1   Temporal Logic Formula Towards ZA

First of all, we define some useful notations in Definition 4, to help the definition of ZATL.

Definition 4. A finite state sequence $\pi = (s_0, s_1, \ldots, s_n)$ is used to describe a state transition path in a ZA model, where $s_i \in S$ and $(s_i, a, s_{i+1}) \in \delta (i \in N, i < n)$. We define that π and each state s_i in π satisfy the relation $\pi[i] = s_i$. We denote $\Pi(s)$ as a set of paths starting from s, that is, $\prod(s) = \{\pi | \pi[0] = s\}$. By $[[\varphi]]_s$ we denote a set of states where formula φ holds. By $[[\varphi]]_\pi$ we denote a set of paths in which all states satisfy φ.

ZATL compliances with the following elements:

- $\square$ is the always operator. $\square\varphi$ means that φ is always true.
- $\diamond$ is the sometimes operator. $\diamond\varphi$ means that φ is sometimes true.

```
input: ZM_analyzed=(State,Operation) , InitialInfo
output : ZA = (S, S_0, Σ, δ, F, M)
Initialize ZAModel s_0←InitialInfo; S, S_0, Σ, δ, F← φ; InitStack <Stack>St;
S_0 ← {s_0} ,S ← S ∪ {s_0}
for each op_i ∈ Operation
        Define F_Σ(a_i) = op_i; Σ ← Σ ∪ {a_i}
end for
<Stack>St← s_0
while ! StackEmpty(St)
        <Stack>St → s
        for each a_i ∈ Σ do
                if s| = pre_{F_Σ(a_i)}
                s'← a_i(s)
                if s'| = post_{F_Σ(a_i)} ∧ s'| = F_S(s')_{p_n}
                    δ ← δ ∪ {(s,a_i,s')}
                                    if '∉ S S ← S ∪ {s'}; <Stack>St ←s';
                                    end if
                                    if s' is final state thenF ← F ∪ [s'];
                                    end if
                            end if
                    end if
        end for
end while
```

Fig. 1. The pseudo code of ZA model generation algorithm

- **A** is the all quantifier.
- **E** is the exist quantifier.

Definition 5. The syntax of ZATL is defined as follows:

- The atomic proposition φ_{p_n} is a ZATL formula.
- If φ and ψ are ZATL formulas, so are $\neg\varphi$, $\varphi \wedge \psi$, $\varphi \vee \psi$.
- If φ is a ZATL formula, so are A $\square$ φ, E $\square$ φ, A $\diamond$ φ, E $\diamond$ φ.
- If and only if the above rules are used for limited times, we get a ZATL formula.

Definition 6. The semantics of ZATL is defined as follows:

- $[[\varphi_{p_n}]]_s = \left\{ s | \varphi| = F_S(s)_{q_m} \right\}$, where p and q are predicates, $n, m \in N$;
- $[[\neg\varphi]]_s = S - [[\varphi]]_s$;

- $[[\varphi_1 \wedge \varphi_2]]_s = [[\varphi_1]]_s \cap [[\varphi_2]]_s;$
- $[[\varphi_1 \vee \varphi_2]]_s = [[\varphi_1]]_s \cup [[\varphi_2]]_s;$
- $[[\mathbf{A} \ \square \ \varphi]]_\pi = \{\pi | \forall \pi \in \prod(s_0) \cdot (\forall s \in \pi \cdot (s_{p_n}| = \varphi))\}$
- $[[\mathbf{A} \diamond \varphi]]_\pi = \{\pi | \forall \pi \in \prod(s_0) \cdot (\exists s \in \pi \cdot (s_{p_n}| = \varphi))\};$
- $[[\mathbf{E} \ \square \ \varphi]]_\pi = \{\pi | \exists \pi \in \prod(s_0) \cdot (\forall s \in \pi \cdot (s_{p_n}| = \varphi))\}$
- $[[\mathbf{E} \diamond \varphi]]_\pi = \{\pi | \exists \pi \in \prod(s_0) \cdot (\exists s \in \pi \cdot (s_{p_n}| = \varphi))\}.$

The first four formulas represent the composition mode of φ. The last four formulas are temporal logic formulas used to describe properties of system.

$\mathbf{A} \ \square \ \phi$ denotes that all the states in the system satisfy φ. $\mathbf{A} \diamond \varphi$ denotes that there is at least one state satisfying φ in every path of the system. $\mathbf{E} \ \square \ \varphi$ denotes that there is at least one path in which all the states satisfy φ. And $\mathbf{E} \diamond \varphi$ denotes that there is at least one state in the system satisfying φ. These formulas can be used to describe the dependability properties of system such as liveness and safety.

3.2 ZAMC Algorithm

In order to verify whether the given system satisfies the property described by a ZATL formula, we propose a model checking algorithm based on counterexample searching strategy. For each formula we design different searching strategies depending on its semantics.

(1) Input formula 1: $\varphi' = \mathbf{A} \ \square \ \varphi$.

Formula 1 denotes that formula φ holds for all the states in the system. If the given ZA model meets this condition, the system satisfies formula φ'. Otherwise, the system doesn't satisfy φ'. The counterexample of formula 1 is a state on which formula φ doesn't hold. The verification procedure of formula 1 is as follows.

> *Step 1.1.* Get an unprocessed element s in set S;
> *Step 1.2.* If s doesn't satisfy φ, the system doesn't satisfy φ'. Output current state s as a counterexample, and the verification ends up with *false*;
> *Step 1.3.* If s satisfies φ, go to *Step 1.1*;
> *Step 1.4.* Output *true* of this verification.

(2) Input formula 2: $\varphi' = \mathbf{A} \diamond \varphi$.

Formula 2 denotes that there is at least one state satisfying φ in every path of the system. If the given ZA model meets this condition, the system satisfies formula φ'. Otherwise, the system doesn't satisfy φ'. The counterexample of formula 2 is a path in which none of the states satisfies φ. The verification procedure of formula 2 is as follows.

Step 2.1. If initial state s_0 satisfies φ, the system satisfies formula φ'. Verification process ends, and output *true*;

Step 2.2. Otherwise, put s_0 into queue Q;

Step 2.3. While Q is not empty, get state s from Q;

Step 2.4. If s doesn't satisfy φ, update current searching path. If $s \in F$, we find a counterexample. So the verification ends up with *false*;

Step 2.5. If s satisfies φ, put all unprocessed successor states of s into Q;

Step 2.6. Go to *Step 2.3*, until Q is empty;

Step 2.7. If we find a counterexample, output the counterexample according to searching path. Otherwise, output *true*.

(3) Input formula 3: $\varphi' = \mathbf{E} \,\square\, \varphi$.

Formula 3 denotes that there is at least one path in which all the states satisfy φ. If the given ZA model meets this condition, the system satisfies formula φ'. Otherwise, the system doesn't satisfy φ', that is, in every path of the system there is at least one state that doesn't satisfy φ. As a result, we can formalize it as $\mathbf{A} \,\diamond\, \neg\varphi$, thus the verification of formula 3 can use the verification procedure of formula 2. Firstly, we verify whether the system satisfy formula $\mathbf{A} \,\diamond\, \neg\varphi$. Then, invert the result as output.

(4) Input formula 4: $\varphi' = \mathbf{E} \,\diamond\, \varphi$.

Formula 4 denotes that there is at least one state in the system satisfying φ. If the given ZA model meets this condition, the system satisfies formula φ'. Otherwise, the system doesn't satisfy φ', that is, none of the states satisfies φ. The verification procedure of formula 4 is as follows.

Step 4.1. Get an unprocessed element s in set S;

Step 4.2. If s satisfies φ, the system satisfy φ'. And the verification ends up with *true;*

Step 4.3. If s doesn't satisfy φ, go to *Step 4.1*;

Step 4.4. Output *false* of this verification. Any state can be used as a counterexample.

Figure 2 gives the procedure of ZAMC.

4 Design and Application of ZDVS

Based on the ZA model and the ZAMC algorithm, we realize a prototype system called ZDVS (Z Dynamic Verification System). In this section, we present its framework and procedure. A case study is used to illustrate the correctness and effectiveness of our method.

input : ZA = $(S, S_0, \Sigma, \delta, F, M)$, where M = (F_S, F_δ), $\varphi' \in$ ZATL
output: ZA| = φ'?
Initialize *checkpath* $\leftarrow \phi$
for each $\varphi' \in Sub(\varphi)$ do
   case $\varphi' = \mathbf{A} \,\square\, \varphi$
      for each $s \in S$
           if $s| = \varphi$ continue;
           else *result* $\leftarrow$ 0; output s; break;
      end for
     result $\leftarrow$ 1;
   case $\varphi' = \mathbf{A} \,\diamondsuit\, \varphi$
     if $s_0| = \varphi$ *result* $\leftarrow$ 1; break;
     else   *result* $\leftarrow$ -1
          \<queue\>Q $\leftarrow s_0$
          while !*QueueEmpty*(Q)
               \<queue\>Q $\rightarrow s$
               if ! $(s| = \varphi)$ then
                    if $s \in F$ *result* $\leftarrow$ 0; output any $\pi \in \prod(s_0)$; break;
                  for each s' $(s, a, s') \in \delta$ if s' *is not visited* then
             \<queue\>Q $\leftarrow s'$
          end while
      end if
     if $(result = -1)$ *result* $\leftarrow$ 1
   case $\varphi' = \mathbf{E} \,\square\, \varphi$
     if ! $(s_0| = \varphi)$ then *result* $\leftarrow$ 0; output any $\pi \in \prod(s_0)$; break;
     else *result* $\leftarrow$ -1
          \<queue\>Q $\leftarrow s_0$; update *checkpath*
          while !*QueueEmpty*(Q)
               \<queue\>Q $\rightarrow s$
          if $s| = \varphi$ then
               if $s \in F$ *result* $\leftarrow$ 1; break;
             for each s' $(s, a, s') \in \delta$
                  if s' *is not visited* then \<queue\>Q $\leftarrow s'$; update
        checkpath
          end while
      end if
     if $(result = -1)$ *result* $\leftarrow$ 0; output a *counterexample* according to
checkpath
    case $\varphi' = \mathbf{E} \,\diamondsuit\, \varphi$
       for each $s \in S$
            if $s| = \varphi$ *result* $\leftarrow$ 1; break;
            else continue;
      result $\leftarrow$ 0; output any $s \in S$
  return *result*;

Fig. 2. The procedure of ZAMC

4.1   Framework of ZDVS

ZDVS has three main modules, including the modeling module, the verification module and the user interface module. Figure 3 gives the flow diagram of ZDVS.

Firstly, we transform Z specification to ZA_{static} model by implementing a parser in the modeling module, to analyze Z notation and transform it to ZA_{static} model written by C++. Then, we implement the ZA model generation algorithm in the modeling module to build the corresponding ZA model.

In the verification module, we design a command parser to obtain the input ZATL formulas (through the user interface module), and implement the ZAMC algorithm to verify the ZA model.

The user interface module provides the necessary interaction between user and system, such as the input of ZATL formulas, and the display of the counterexamples if the verification ends up with *false*.

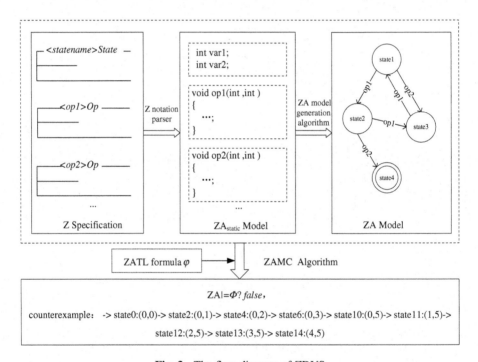

Fig. 3. The flow diagram of ZDVS

4.2   A Case Study

In this section, we describe the modeling and analysis procedure of a case study to illustrate the correctness and effectiveness of ZDVS. The inputs of ZDVS are Z specification represented by LaTeX and ZATL formula φ, while the output is the result of model checking. If the result is *false*, it also gives a counterexample.

The case study contains 4 schemas as shown in Fig. 4, including a state schema and 3 operation schemas. The corresponding ZA model generated by ZDVS contains 30 states and 3 actions.

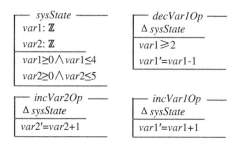

Fig. 4. Z specification of the instance

We use 4 temporal logic formulas as inputs of the model checking process, which are listed as follows.

A $\square$ var1 $\leq$ 3, denotes that var1 in all the states of the system is equal or greater than 3.
A $\diamond$ var1 $>$ 4, denotes that for every path of the system there is at least one state in which var1 is greater than 4.
E $\square$ var1 $\geq$ var2, denotes that there is at least one path in which all the states satisfy var1 $\geq$ var2.
A$\diamond$ var1 $\geq$ var2 && var2 $>$ 2, denotes that there is at least one state in the system satisfying var1 $\geq$ var2 && var2 $>$ 2.

Figure 5 shows the verification result of formula **A**$\diamond$ var1 $>$ 4. Since the result is *false*, the system outputs a counterexample.

Illustration on the case study shows that the proposed ZA model can enhance the descriptive power by combining Z notation and FA. The prototype system ZDVS is able to correctly parse the input Z specification and generate the corresponding ZA model, accept and analyze the input ZATL formulas, and verify the system temporal properties automatically and effectively.

5   Discussion and Conclusion

In order to verify the temporal properties of Z model, this paper designs and implements a prototype system ZDVS to perform the model transformation and model checking on a proposed hybrid software model ZA. Our main contributions are as follows:

1. A formal software model called ZA is defined by combining Z notation and FA. The proposed ZA model can specify not only static structure and operation specifications, but also temporal constraints of the targeted system. A generation algorithm is designed to build ZA model from ZA_{static}, a simplified structure of Z specification.

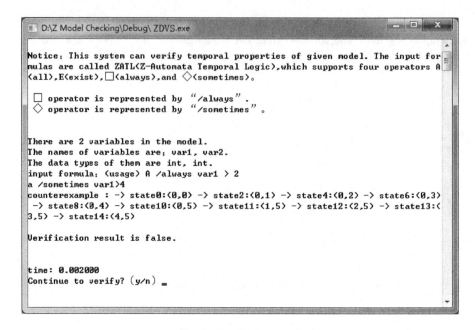

Fig. 5. Verification result

2. A model checking algorithm towards the ZA model is proposed. Firstly, a temporal logic called ZATL is defined to describe the temporal properties of the ZA model. Then, we propose a model checking algorithm called ZAMC to verify the ZATL formulas.

3. A prototype system called ZDVS is realized to perform our proposed methods. A case study is used to illustrate the correctness and effectiveness of ZDVS.

Future work of this paper includes further study on hybrid software models and their temporal logic, and the performance enhancement of their model checking algorithms.

References

1. ISO I. IEC 13568: 2002: Information technology–Z formal specification notation–Syntax, type system and semantics. ISO (International Organization for Standardization), Geneva, Switzerland (2002)
2. SPIVEY J M. The Z notation: a reference manual. In: International Series in Computer Science. Prentice-Hall, New York, NY (1992)
3. Wordsworth, J.B.: Software Development with Z: A Practical Approach to Formal Methods in Software Engineering. Addison-Wesley Longman Publishing Co. Inc, Reading (1992)
4. Ince, D.C., Ince, D.: Introduction to Discrete Mathematics, Formal System Specification, and Z. Oxford University Press, Oxford (1993)

5. Abrial, J.-R., Schuman, S.A., Meyer, B.: Specification language. In: McKeag, R.M., Macnaghten, A.M. (eds.) On the Construction of Programs: An Advanced Course. Cambridge University Press, Cambridge (1980)
6. Z/EVES Homepage (2015). http://z-eves.updatestar.com/
7. ProofPower Homepage (2015). http://www.lemma-one.com/ProofPower/index/
8. Martin, A.P.: Relating Z and first-order logic. Formal Aspects Comput. **12**(3), 199–209 (2000)
9. ProB Homepage (2015). http://www.stups.uni-duesseldorf.de/ProB/index.php5/Main_Page
10. Jaza Homepage (2005). http://www.cs.waikato.ac.nz/∼marku/jaza/
11. Zlive Homepage (2015). http://czt.sourceforge.net/zlive/
12. Clarke, E.M., Grumberg, O., Peled, D.: Model Checking. MIT Press, Cambridge (1999)
13. Alpern, B., Schneider, F.B.: Recognizing safety and liveness. Distrib. Comput. **2**(3), 117–126 (1987)
14. Smith, G.P., Wildman, L.: Model checking Z specifications using SAL. In: Treharne, H., King, S., Henson, M.C., Schneider, Steve (eds.) ZB 2005. LNCS, vol. 3455, pp. 85–103. Springer, Heidelberg (2005)
15. Cao, Z., Wang, H.: Extending interface automata with Z notation. In: Arbab, F., Sirjani, M. (eds.) FSEN 2011. LNCS, vol. 7141, pp. 359–367. Springer, Heidelberg (2012)
16. Cao, Z.: Temporal logics and model checking algorithms for ZIAs. In: 2010 2nd International Conference on Proceedings of the Software Engineering and Data Mining (SEDM). IEEE (2010)

Maximizing Positive Influence in Signed Social Networks

Huanhuan Wang$^{(\boxtimes)}$, Qun Yang, Lei Fang, and Weihua Lei

Institute of Computer Science and Technology,
Nanjing University of Aeronautics and Astronautics, Nanjing, China
HuanhuanWang_nuaa@126.com, qun.yang@nuaa.edu.cn,
{18205099730,leiweihuaba0}@163.com

Abstract. Influence maximization problem focuses on finding a certain number of influential people to make their influence maximized in social networks. As positive influence has more practical significance in the viral marketing, we propose Positive Influence Maximization (PIM) problem and apply it in signed social networks. Considering the attitude of users to products, we propose a new propagation model named Linear Threshold model with Attitude (LT-A). In the model, each node has a new parameter η which denotes the attitude of node, and each edge has a new parameter ρ which denotes the relationships between nodes. We prove the PIM problem is NP-hard and the influence spread function is monotonous and submodular. Therefore, we use a greedy algorithm to obtain a solution with an approximation ratio of (1 − 1/e). Extensive experiments are conducted on two real-world network datasets and experimental results show that we can achieve higher influence spread than other existing approaches by using our model.

Keywords: Influence maximization · Propagation model · Attitude · Signed social networks

1 Introduction

Recently, online social networks have developed rapidly. They are becoming epidemic platforms of interaction and communication in our daily life. Due to their information spreading capability, the social networks are widely applied to viral marketing. In viral marketing, the merchants usually select a certain number of influential users and other people could be influenced by them because of the word-of-mouth effect in the social networks. The Influence Maximization (IM) problem is how to find those influential users to maximize the influenced users in social networks.

Usually, a social network is denoted as a graph $G = (V, E)$, each node in V represents a user and each edge in E represents relationships between users. IM problem aims to find K nodes as a seed set so that the number of nodes reached by influence spread is maximized under a propagation model. IC (Independent Cascade) model and LT (Linear Threshold) model are two classical propagation models, which are proposed by Kempe et al. [1]. IM problem is considered as a discrete optimization problem [1] and has proved to be a NP-hard problem. It can achieve an approximate optimal

© Springer International Publishing Switzerland 2015
Z. Huang et al. (Eds.): ICCCS 2015, LNCS 9483, pp. 356–367, 2015.
DOI: 10.1007/978-3-319-27051-7_30

solution within $(1 - 1/e)$ ratio by using greedy algorithm as the influence function is monotonous and submodular. Nevertheless, the greedy algorithm is inefficient and has serious scalability problem. To improve the efficiency and scalability, a lot of improved greedy or heuristic algorithms have been proposed in [6–9, 13, 19, 20].

Although many works have been done on IM problem, mostly of them only consider whether the nodes are activated or not, paying no attention to the opinions of nodes. However, as the users can hold positive or negative opinion, the activated users can also be activated with positive or negative opinion, which makes different in viral marketing. Thus, the opinions of nodes should be considered. Meanwhile, as the relationship between the users is different, the impact a user's opinion can have on others is also different. Therefore, the relationship between nodes should be measured to determine whether an activated node will hold positive or negative opinion.

In view of the above problems, we define the PIM problem in signed social networks and extend the influence propagation model. The signed social network is a network in which edge weight can denote relationship between nodes. In signed social networks, the relationships between nodes can be positive, which denotes trust, or negative, which denotes distrust [13]. In signed social network, if a node trusts another node, it will hold the same opinion with the other node, and if a node distrusts another node, it will hold the opposite opinion with the other node.

In this paper, the contributions that we made as follows:

- We propose a Linear Threshold with Attitude (LT-A) model for PIM problem in signed social networks, defining an attitude function to calculate the attitude weight of the node.
- We demonstrate that PIM problem under LT-A model is NP-hard. We also prove the influence function of PIM problem under the LT-A model is monotonous and submodular, this allows a greedy algorithm to get an approximation optimal solution within $(1 - 1/e)$ ratio.
- We conduct experiments on two real signed social network datasets, Epinions and Slashdot.

The rest of this paper is organized in the following. In Sect. 2, we discuss related work. In Sect. 3, we propose our influence propagation model, LT-A. And then, we prove the influence function is monotonous and submodular. In Sect. 4, we first give the definition for the PIM problem in signed social networks, and then prove it is a NP-hard problem. After that, we give the greedy algorithm. In Sect. 5, we present our experiments and give the analysis and result of our experiments. In Sect. 6, we give our conclusions.

2 Related Work

Influence maximization problem is first studied by Domingos and Richardson [2, 3], they model the problem with a probabilistic framework and use Markov random fields method to solve it. Kempe et al. [1] further formulate the problem as a discrete optimization problem. They prove that the problem is NP-hard and propose two basic models: IC model and LT model. They also present a greedy algorithm to get the approximate optimal solution. But the efficiency of the algorithm is low and its scalability is not good. To solve these problems, a lot of effective algorithms are proposed.

Leskovec et al. [4] put forward Cost Effective Lazy Forward (CELF) algorithm which significantly shorten the execution time by 700 times. Goyal et al. [5] further improve the original CELF algorithm to CELF++. In addition, [6–9] also shorten the execution time by improving the efficiency of the greedy algorithm or proposing heuristic algorithms.

However, most works on PIM problem make the assumption that all users hold positive attitude, but in reality some users may hold negative attitude, For example, some people will buy iPhone 6 because they like its appearance, but others will hold negative attitude because iPhone 6 is found vulnerable to bend, they may not buy them. If the negative relationships are ignored, the result of influence maximization will be over-estimated. Therefore, negative attitude should also be taken into account in PIM problem. Chen et al. [10] first extend IC model to IC-N, adding a parameter called quality factor to reflect negative opinions of users. There are several deficiencies in their model. Firstly, in their model, the activated node holds the same opinion with the node which activates it. But in real life, a user may not trust another user, so when a node is activated by the other nodes, it may not hold the same opinion as the node activating it. Secondly, in [10], they assume that each node holds the same opinion all the time, but users may change their opinions when they are affected by others. Thirdly, in [10], they ignore individual preference. Actually, when considering individual preference, the degree that people affected by others is different as people may have their own opinion towards a product.

In [11], the personal preference is taken into account. The model in [11] is on the basis of that the opinions users can have are positive, neutral and negative. They propose a two-phase influence propagation model, OC model (opinion-based cascading model).

In [12], considering the opinion modification problem, they proposed an extended LT model with instant opinions. Besides, to express the different influence between users, they define a trust threshold in the model to justify whether a node follows or opposes the attitude from its neighbors. However, the trust threshold they defined is equivalent for each edge in the graph, while actually different neighbors will give different influence.

Considering the above problems, Li et al. study the IM problem in signed social networks [13]. In signed social networks, instead of comparing the influence weight with trust threshold to determine if two nodes hold trust or distrust relationship, there is a weight on each edge, 1 and −1, 1 denotes one node trust the other node, and -1 denotes distrust [14]. By using signed social networks, Li et al. [13] propose an extended model based on IC model, Polarity-related Independent Cascade (IC-P) model. They considered polarity related influence maximization problem. In this paper, we will focus on positive influence maximization problem as in viral marketing positive influence maximization is more important.

3   Linear Threshold Model with Attitude

In this section, we represent how to formulate a signed social network as a graph, and then propose the Linear Threshold model with Attitude (LT-A).

3.1   Formulating Signed Social Networks

An unsigned social network is denoted as a directed graph $G = (V, E, \omega)$, where V is a node set, and E is an edge set. Nodes represent users in social networks and edges represent relationships between them. ω is the edge weight on E, which changes in $[0, 1]$. $\omega_{(u,v)}$ is regarded as the influence from u to v.

A signed social network is denoted as a directed and signed graph $G = (V, E, \omega, \rho)$, where ρ represents the sign of each edge, its value can be 1 or -1, 1 means the positive (trust) relationship, -1 means the negative (distrust) relationship. P is a matrix of ρ on all edges. As shown in Fig. 1, the relationships between nodes show the asymmetry. i.e. $\omega_{(u,v)} \neq \omega_{(v,u)}$ and $\rho_{(u,v)} \neq \rho_{(v,u)}$.

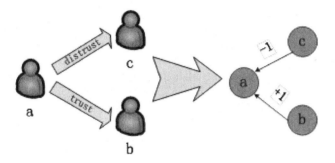

Fig. 1. An instance of modeling a signed social network

3.2   Linear Threshold Model with Attitude

The classical Linear Threshold (LT) model for influence maximization in social networks is first introduced in [3]. In the LT model, each node is active or inactive. The state of a node can be changed from inactive to active, but not vice versa. Besides, each node has a threshold θ_v range between 0 and 1. If $\sum_{v \in A_u^t} \omega(v, u) \geq \theta_u, (v, u) \in E$, where A_u^t is the neighbors of u which have been activated at time t, u will become active at time $t + 1$. At time $t = 0$, the seed set S is set active while other nodes are inactive, nodes in S try to activate their inactive neighbors, if the activation condition is satisfied, the activation will succeed, the process will go on until no nodes can be activated. Once a node is activated, its state will never be changed.

In the viral marketing, different users can hold different attitude to the product, and the attitude can be changed by the influence from their friends. However, the classical propagation model, LT model, does not take the attitude factor into account.

So we propose the LT-A model based on LT model. We define a parameter named attitude weight η which represent the real attitude to product in virtual marketing. We add the parameter to each node in the model. As the attitude maybe positive or negative, we make the attitude weight range between -1 and 1 to distinguish the different attitude. $\eta_v < 0$ denotes the attitude of v is negative, $\eta_v > 0$ denotes the attitude of v is positive. If η = 0, it denotes the node holds negative attitude because of negative dominance rule. The rule reflects the negativity bias phenomenon which has been studied in the social psychology [15–18], and has been applied in [6, 10]. The value of η can be calculated by a formulation which will be described in the following section.

The propagation process of the LT-A model is as follows. At time t = 0, there is a certain seed set S ∈ V in which each node is active and holds positive attitude, that is $\eta_v = 1$, $v \in S$ (η_v is set to 1 to achieve maximal benefit), $\eta_u = 0$, $u \in (V - S)$. At time t > 0, node $v \in (V - S)$ is activated when the total weights of its activated in-neighbors reach its threshold, and its attitude weight η_v will be changed and the attitude weight will not change later. The process ends when no more activation happens.

3.3 Concepts of the Model

We now present the model in detail. Notations used in this paper are summarized in Table 1. Each node has two parameters, θ denotes threshold and η denotes attitude weight. Every edge in the signed social networks also has two parameters. One is influence weight ω, which denotes the influence between nodes. The other is relationship weight ρ, which denotes the relationships between nodes. In the LT-A model, the following criteria should be satisfied.

Given v ∈ V,ω(u,v)ϵ[0, 1], , where

$$\sum_{u \in V/v} \omega(u, v) \leq 1 \tag{1}$$

Value of $\rho_{(u,v)}$ is 1 or −1, $\rho_{(u,v)} = 1$ denotes the node v will follow the attitude of node u, $\rho_{(u,v)} = -1$ denotes the node v will against the attitude of node u. θ_v denotes threshold, $\theta_v \in [0, 1]$, η_v denotes the attitude weight, $\eta_v \in [-1, 1]$.

In the propagation process, v can be activated if $\sum_{u \in A_v^t} \omega(u, v) \geq \theta_v$, η can be calculated by

$$\eta_v^t = \sum_{u \in A_v^t} \eta_u * \rho_{(u,v)} * \omega(v, u) \tag{2}$$

The attitude weight will be updated once the node is activated and it will be never changed. Intuitively, the nodes in the LT-A model have three states: active with positive attitude, active with negative attitude and inactive.

Table 1. Notation table

Notation	Descriptions
ω	The influence weight of edge
ρ	The relationship weight of edge
η	The attitude weight of one node
θ	The threshold of one node
S	Seed set
k	The number of seed set
A_v^t	The set of activated neighbors of node v at step t

4   Properties of the Model

Definition   1. *(Monotonous)* $G = (V, E, \omega, \rho)$ $f : 2^U \rightarrow R^+$ is   monotonous   if $f(S) \leq f(t)$ *for all* $S \subseteq T \subseteq V$.

Definition 2. *(Submodular) A function in a signed graph is submodular if* $f(S \cup \{u\}) - f(S) \geq f(T \cup \{u\}) - f(T))$ *for all* $S \subseteq T, u \in V \backslash T$.

Theorem 1. *For any influence graph* $G = (V, E, \omega, \rho)$, *the influence spread function* $\delta_G(S)$ *on S is monotonous.*

Proof 1. Let $S \subseteq T \subseteq V$, so the number of nodes in T is larger than those in S. Then the neighbors of nodes in T contain neighbors in S. Therefore, nodes in T can positively activated more nodes than nodes in S unless the superfluous relationship weights between nodes in T\S and their neighbors are negative. Consequently, $\delta_G(S) \leq \delta_G(T)$. Thus, $\delta_G(S)$ on S is monotonous.

Theorem 2. *For any social network graph* $G = (V, E, \omega, \rho)$, *the function* $\delta_G(S)$ *on S is submodular.*

Proof 2. Suppose $S \subseteq T \subseteq V$ and $u \in V \backslash T$. In the graph, influence propagation on all edge is a random event, so we can obtain a subgraph named G'. Let $\varphi(G)$ denote the set of all the subgraphs, that is, $G' \in \varphi(G)$. Let $Pro(G')$ is the probability that G' can be got. We can achieve

$$\delta_G(S) = \sum\nolimits_{G' \in \varphi(G)} Pro(G') \delta_{G'}(S) \tag{3}$$

We give the $\delta_G(S)$ a similar transformation as follows:

$$\delta_G(S) = \sum\nolimits_{u \in S} \sum\nolimits_{v \in Y_u} \eta_u * \prod\nolimits_{(i,j) \in \gamma^G(u,v)} \omega(i,j) * \rho(i,j) \tag{4}$$

Let $\gamma^G(u, v)$ denotes the set of the shortest path from u to v, let Y_u denotes the set of all neighbors influenced by node u.

According to formulas (2) and (3) we can achieve:

$$\delta_G(S) = \sum_{G' \in \varphi(G)} \sum_{u \in S} \sum_{v \in D_u} Pro(G') * \eta_u * \prod_{(i,j) \in \gamma^{G'}(u,v)} \omega(i,j) * \rho(i,j) \quad (5)$$

Let $\gamma^G(S, v)$ denotes the shortest path from the node in set S to node v in subgraph G'. $d^{G'}(S, v)$ denotes the length of the shortest path. Then we can get $d^{G'}(S, v) \geq d^{G'}(T, v)$. If $d^{G'}(u, v) \geq d^{G'}(S, v)$, we have $\delta_{G'}(S \cup \{u\}) - \delta_{G'}(S) = \delta_{G'}(T \cup \{u\}) - \delta_{G'}(T)$. If $d^{G'}(u, v) \leq d^{G'}(T, v)$, we have $\delta_{G'}(S \cup \{u\}) - \delta_{G'}(S) \geq \delta_{G'}(T \cup \{u\}) - \delta_{G'}(T)$ as $\delta_{G'}(S)$ is monotonically decreasing. If $d^{G'}(T, v) < d^{G'}(u, v) < d^{G'}(S, v)$, we get $\delta_{G'}(S \cup \{u\}) - \delta_{G'}(S) > 0 = \delta_{G'}(T \cup \{u\}) - \delta_{G'}(T)$. Therefore, $\delta_G(S)$ on S is submodular.

5 Positive Influence Maximization Problem

5.1 PIM Problem

We give the definition of the PIM based on LT-A model.

Definition 3. *(PIM problem) Given a positive integer k, which is the number of the seed set with positive attitude, and a social network graph G = (V, E, ω,), in which the state of each node in the graph can be active with positive attitude, active with negative attitude and inactive., PIM problem is to find a k-size seed set which can be used to maximize the number of the influenced nodes with positive attitude in the social networks.*

$\delta()$ denotes the influence spread function. Given a seed set S, the value of $\delta(S)$ represents the expected number of nodes which are active with positive attitude by S under the LT-A propagation model.

PIM problem is to find a seed node set which can make the positive influence maximized, it can be formalized as:

$$S = \max_{S \in V, |S| = k} \delta(S) \quad (6)$$

When solving the PIM problem, it is assumed that when the node is selected as a seed node, the value of its attitude weight η is 1. And, we only choose the positive node as a seed set.

Theorem 3. *For any social network graph $G = (V, E, \omega, \rho)$, the problem of finding the seed set S which makes $\delta(S)$ maximized is NP-hard.*

Proof 3. To prove this, firstly, a special instance under the LT-A model is considered. As an unsigned social network can be regarded as a special signed social network, the relationship weight of each node ρ is 1 and only positive influence is propagated under LT model in the signed networks. As IM problem in the social network is NP-hard, in the theory of NP-hardness, if a problem is NP-hard on a restricted class of problem instances, then it is also NP-hard [11]. As we have argued that IM problem is a special case of PIM problem, thus PIM problem is NP-hard. It can be concluded that the PIM problem is NP-hard.

5.2   LT-A Greedy Algorithm for PIM

Based on Theorems 1, 2 and 3, PIM problem under LT-A model can be solved by a greedy algorithm which can achieve a $(1 - 1/e)$ approximation ratio. In view of the efficiency problem, we use CELF optimization to reduce the execution time. The LT-A Greedy algorithm we propose is as follows.

In the LT-A Greedy algorithm, firstly, the initialization of S is null, we select the first seed node by the following process. We set the attitude weight of each node is 1, and then respectively calculate their positive influence spread according the propagation process of LT-A model. We choose the node which has the maximum positive influence spread add in the seed set S. Secondly, the attitude weight of node in S is set1, and then we select a node in V/S add in S to calculate the influence spread based on LT-A model. In the final, we add the node which has the maximum positive influence spread in S as the second seed node. In similar approach, we select the other seed nodes until the size of seed set S is k.

```
Algorithm 1. LT-A Greedy algorithm
Input: Graph G=( V,E,ω,ρ) ,k ∈ N,  θ, η
Output: A seed set S of size k , v ∈ S, η_v > 0
1: Initialize S=∅
2: for i=1 to k do
3:    for  any v ∈ (V/S)& η_v > 0 do
4:       if i =1,set  η_v = 1
5:           m=0
6:         for j=1 to R do
7:             m=m+ (δ(S ∪ v)-δ(S))
8:         end for
9:           m=m/R
10:   end for
11: v=max v ∈ (S\V){m}
12: S=S ∪{v},  η_s = 1
13: end for
14: Return S
```

6   Experiments

6.1   Datasets

We use two datasets: Epinions and Slashdot. In both datasets, the relationships between users are explicitly labeled. We can get the two network datasets from Stanford Large Network Dataset Collection in [21, 22]. The statistics of the two datasets is showed in Table 2.

- **Epinions.** An online product review site where users determine to trust or distrust others by seeing their product reviews and ratings.
- **Slashdot.** A technology-related news website where users can submit and evaluate current primarily technology oriented news. Friend and foe links between the users are contained in this network.

Table 2. Statistics of the datasets

Dataset	Node	Edge
Epinions (original)	131828	841372
Epinions (subgraph)	12000	53750
Slashdot (original)	82144	549202
Slashdot (subgraph)	12000	56312

6.2   Algorithm

We conduct experiments on above-mentioned two datasets by using our LT-A greedy algorithm and other algorithms. Then we evaluate their experimental results. The other algorithms are the greedy algorithm based LT model [4] (LT Greedy algorithm), Positive Out-Degree algorithm [13] and Random algorithm [1]. The LT Greedy algorithm is a general greedy algorithm with CELF optimization on LT model. The Positive Out-Degree algorithm is an algorithm that we select top k largest positive out-degree nodes as the seed set. The Random algorithm is an algorithm that we randomly select k nodes as a seed set. The two heuristic algorithms are based on our new model, LT-A.

The parameters in the experiments are set as follows. For each node, the value of threshold θ can be a random value between 0 and 1, as stated in Sect. 3, the attitude η of seed nodes is set to 1, and the rest of node attitude can be computed by the formula (2). For each edge, the value of influence weight ω can also be a random value between 0 and 1, which must be satisfied $\omega(u, v)\epsilon[01]$ and criteria (1). The value of relationship weight ρ can be achieved from the real-world datasets, Epinions and Slashdot. As too large number of seed nodes can bring into long execution time and previous works are always set k = 50, we set the number of seed nodes k to be 50, we compare make comparisons of the positive influence spread in different sizes of seed set.

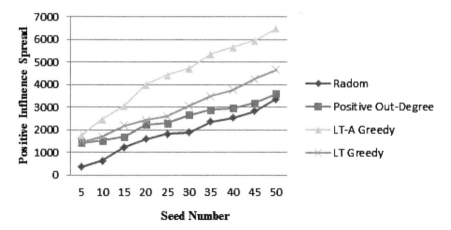

Fig. 2. Positive influence spread for Epinions

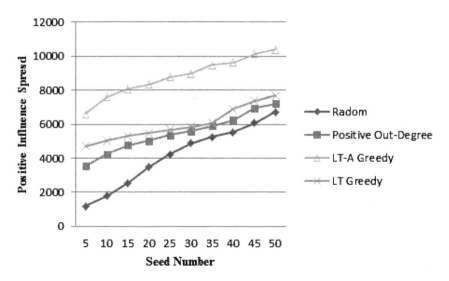

Fig. 3. Positive influence spread for Slashdot

6.3 Experiment Results

Figures 2 and 3 respectively show the positive influence spread in real-world datasets, Epinions and Slashdot. From Fig. 2, we can get that the positive influence calculated by LT-A Greedy is higher than other algorithms, when the number of seed set is 50, positive influence by LT-A Greedy is 39.2 % higher than by LT Greedy. In Fig. 3, the trend is more obvious. As we add two practical parameters, attitude weight and relationship weight into our model and make it closer to the actual, the result is as expected. Therefore, we conclude that the LT-A greedy algorithm outperforms LT greedy and other heuristics in terms of positive influence spread.

7 Conclusions

We study positive influence maximization in the signed social networks. Considering that different users have different attitudes (positive or negative) toward a product, and users may hold different attitudes because of the users who affect them, we propose a new model named LT-A. The PIM problem in the signed social networks aims to maximize positive influence in these networks. Since in the viral marketing, positive influence better promote product sales, we focus on maximizing positive influence. We prove that PIM problem under the LT-A model is NP-hard, and the influence function has monotone and submodularity properties. Based on the above works, we propose a greedy algorithm named LT-A greedy algorithm to get the solution. We conduct experiments on two real-world datasets, Epinions and Slashdot. From the experimental results, we conclude that our model can achieve higher influence spread and is suitable for maximizing the positive influence in viral marketing.

References

1. Kempe, D., Kleinberg, J., Kleinber, J.: Maximizing the spread of influence through a social network. In: Knowledge Discovery and Data Mining (KDD), pp. 137–146 (2003)
2. Domingos, P., Richardson, M.: Mining the network value of customers. In: Knowledge Discovery and Data Mining (KDD), pp. 57–66 (2001)
3. Richardson, M., Domingos, P.: Mining knowledge-sharing sites for viral marketing. In: Knowledge Discovery and Data Mining (KDD), pp. 61–70 (2002)
4. Leskovec, J., Krause, A., Guestrin, C., Faloutsos, C., VanBriesen, J., Glance, N.: Cost-effective outbreak detection in networks. In: Knowledge Discovery and Data Mining (KDD), pp. 420–429 (2007)
5. Goyal, A., Lu, W., Lakshmanan, L.V.S.: CELF++: optimizing the greedy algorithm for influence maximization in social networks. In: International Conference Companion on World Wide Web (WWW), pp. 47–48 (2011)
6. Chen, W., Wang, C., Wang, Y.: Scalable influence maximization for prevalent viral marketing in large scale social networks. In: Knowledge Discovery and Data Mining (KDD), pp. 1029–1038 (2010)
7. Chen, W., Yuan, Y., Zhang, L.: Scalable influence maximization in social networks under the linear threshold model. In: International Conference on Data Mining (ICDM), pp. 88–97 (2010)
8. Lu, W., Lakshmanan, L.V.S.: Simpath: an efficient algorithm for influence maximization under the linear threshold model. In: International Conference on Data Mining (ICDM), pp. 211–220 (2011)
9. Lu, Z., Fan, L., Wu, W., Thuraisingham, B., Yang, K.: Efficient influence spread estimation for influence maximization under the linear threshold model. Comput. Soc. Netw. 1(1), 1–19 (2014)
10. Chen, W., Collins, A., Cummings, R., Ke, T., Liu, Z., Rincon, D., Yuan, Y.: Influence maximization in social networks when negative opinions may emerge and propagate. In: SDM vol. 11, pp. 379–390 (2011)

11. Zhang, H., Dinh, T.N., Thai, M.T.: Maximizing the spread of positive influence in online social networks. In: Distributed Computing Systems (ICDCS), pp. 317–326. IEEE Press (2013)
12. Li, S., Zhu, Y., Li, D., Kim, D., Ma, H., Huang, H.: Influence maximization in social networks with user attitude modification. In: International Conference on Communications (ICC), pp. 3913–3918. IEEE Press (2014)
13. Li, D., Xu, Z.M., Chakraborty, N., Gupta, A., Sycara, K., Li, S.: Polarity related influence maximization in signed social networks. PLoS ONE 9(7), e102199 (2014)
14. Hassan, A., Abu-Jbara, A., Radev, D.: Extracting signed social networks from text. In: Association for Computational Linguistics Workshop Proceedings of TextGraphs-7 on Graph-based Methods for Natural Language Processing, pp. 6–14 (2012)
15. Rozin, P., Royzman, E.B.: Negativity bias, negativity dominance, and contagion. Pers. Soc. Psychol. Rev. 5(4), 296–320 (2001)
16. Baumeister, R.F., Bratslavsky, E., Finkenauer, C.: Bad is stronger than good. Rev. Gen. Psychol. 5(4), 323–370 (2001)
17. Peeters, G., Czapinski, J.: Positive-negative asymmetry in evaluations: the distinction between affective and informational negativity effects. Eur. Rev. Soc. Psychol. 1, 33–60 (1990)
18. Taylor, S.E.: Asymmetrical effects of positive and negative events: the mobilization-minimization hypothesis. Psychol. Bull. 110(1), 67–85 (1991)
19. Li, Y., Chen, W., Wang, Y., Zhang, Z.L.: Influence diffusion dynamics and influence maximization in social networks with friend and foe relationships. In: International Conference on Web Search and Data Mining (WSDM), pp. 657–666 (2013)
20. Bhagat, S., Goyal, A., Lakshmanan, L.V.: Maximizing product adoption in social networks. In: International Conference on Web Search and Data Mining (WSDM), pp. 603–612 (2012)
21. Epinions social network. http://snap.stanford.edu/data/soc-Epinions1.html
22. Slashdot social network. http://snap.stanford.edu/data/soc-Slashdot0811.html

OpenFlow-Based Load Balancing for Wireless Mesh Network

Hanjie Yang[1(✉)], Bing Chen[1], and Ping Fu[2]

[1] Institute of Computer Science and Technology,
Nanjing University of Aeronautics and Astronautics, Nanjing, Jiangsu, China
jane09-01@hotmail.com, cb_china@nuaa.edu.cn
[2] Central Washington University, Washington, USA
pingfu@cwu.edu

Abstract. Wireless mesh network (WMN), an emerging network which is the pivotal technology for the next generation networks, is intended to provide reliable data transmission at low cost and high throughput. Load balancing is an essential problem, which affects the performance of the network. OpenFlow, an emerging technology, can effectively monitor and manage the network topology as well as network traffic, via the separation of the data layer and the control layer. This paper proposed an OpenFlow-based WMN and a channel related solution to solve the load balance. Control of each node dynamically changes while the network traffic changes, and the channel allocation along with the establishing of data paths will be promptly adjusted. We have built our WMN testbed with OpenFlow-based wireless mesh nodes. We carried out some experiments to evaluate our solution. Our experiments confirm that OpenFlow sets a good technology to solve wireless mesh network load imbalance.

Keywords: Wireless mesh network · OpenFlow · SDN · Load balancing

1 Introduction

Wireless mesh networks are intended for the last mile broadband Internet access to extend or enhance Internet connectivity for mobile clients, which can provide high network throughput, as well as optimal load balancing. In a typical mesh network, mesh routers collect information from local mesh nodes, and the routing algorithm decides the forwarding paths according to these information. Traditional wireless mesh routing algorithms are usually distributed, so that the solution of the network is usually deployed on each mesh nodes. It is difficult to increase the routing algorithm, and then achieve the higher network throughput.

In wireless mesh networks, load balancing is critical. Load imbalance makes some nodes become bottleneck nodes. Because the forwarding traffic of these nodes are too much, the network performance will decline throughout the network. How to build optimal mesh networks with load balancing has been studied theoretically. A variety of routing algorithms have been put forward to solve the load balancing problem in mesh networks. However, these algorithms can't dynamically adapt to current network topology and dataflow changes, avoid the bottleneck node, and select the most stable link to establish a route.

© Springer International Publishing Switzerland 2015
Z. Huang et al. (Eds.): ICCCS 2015, LNCS 9483, pp. 368–379, 2015.
DOI: 10.1007/978-3-319-27051-7_31

OpenFlow is a new kind of protocol created initially for communication in a programmable network, via the separation of the data layer and control layer. Using OpenFlow in a wireless network has been put forward [1]. Hence, we are considering that we can develop a wireless mesh network based-on OpenFlow to acquire information from the whole network, then the controller decides the best data path, which can ensure high throughput data transfer. In this paper, we propose an OpenFlow-based wireless mesh network architecture. The object of our work is to present our OpenFlow-based network design and the load balancing performance under practical application scenarios.

In the following sections, we present related works about the solutions for load balancing in wireless mesh networks in Sect. 2. Section 3 describes the background of OpenFlow-based Mesh nodes, as well as our design of the OpenFlow-enabled mesh nodes and controller. In Sect. 4, we describe something about the experimental environment, how we implement our testbed. Section 5 describes the detailed setup of our experiments. We considered several scenarios and the solution to solve the load imbalance and the analyzing of the results.

2 Related Work

There has been significant prior works on load balancing strategies based on traditional wireless mesh networks. Most prior works focus on distributed algorithms, where the mesh nodes communicate only with their neighborhood [3, 4]. Routing protocols for mesh networks can generally be divided into proactive routing, reactive routing, and hybrid routing strategies [2]. Nevertheless, most of these protocols do not provide load balancing strategy. Because of the put forwarding of OpenFlow, a centralized algorithm in WMN is possible.

In the [5], the combination of the OpenFlow and the WMN has been proposed for the first time. In that paper, OpenFlow and a distributed routing protocols (OLSR) are combined in a Wireless Mesh Software Defined Network (wmSDN). Load balancing using both wireless mesh network protocols and OpenFlow is discussed in [6]. The experiments in the paper demonstrate the improved performance of OpenFlow over traditional mesh routing protocols. As it shows that the OpenFlow controller is able to make centralized decisions on how to optimally route traffic so that the computational burden at each node is minimized. However, the study does not consider the link quality between the mesh nodes and the topology of the network does not contain the gateway nodes. In the [9], the author proposed a prototype mesh infrastructure where flows from a source node can take multiple paths through the network based on OpenFlow to solve the load balancing for wireless mesh network. However, the study doesn't adequately consider the multi radio interfaces of the mesh nodes. Therefore, considering the characteristics of the wireless mesh network, we proposed a solution for multi-interfaces wireless mesh networks. We also have implemented the OpenFlow-enabled mesh network testbed which each node in the testbed has two radio interfaces.

3   The Wireless Mesh Network Based on OpenFlow

3.1   Wireless Mesh Network

A wireless mesh network (WMN) is a kind of ad hoc network, however it communicates in multi-hop fashion instead of communicating in one-hop fashion in typical ad hoc network. All the links between the wireless mesh nodes are established by radio. Akyildiz et al. [8] describes the wireless mesh network as dynamically selforganized and selfconfigured networks, with the mesh nodes automatically establishing an ad hoc network and maintaining the mesh connectivity.

Instead of being another type of ad hoc networking, WMNs diversify the capabilities of ad hoc networks with many advantages such as low up-front cost, easy network maintenance, robustness and reliable service coverage, etc. Nowadays, the WMNs are undergoing rapid commercialization in many application scenarios such as broadband home networks, community networks and high-speed metropolitan area networks, etc. WMNs consist of two types of nodes: mesh router and mesh client. Mesh routers conform the wireless backbone of the network, while the mesh clients are connected to the network through them. Further, there are some mesh routers with a gateway (GW) capabilities, which are connected to other communication networks (including the Internet) through wired links.

In a general way, there are three types of the wireless mesh network, which is classified through architecture: infrastructure WMN/Backbone WMNs, client WMNs and hybrid WMNs. In the infrastructure WMN/Backbone WMNs, mesh routers form a mesh of self-configuring, self-healing links among themselves, providing a backbone for mesh clients. Client WMN is a kind of peer-to-peer network among clients. Thus, a Client WMN is actually the same as a conventional ad hoc network. Hybrid WMN is the combination of infrastructure and client WMNs. Hybrid WMNs offer the best coverage area, as mesh clients can access to the network through mesh routers as well as directly meshing with other mesh clients.

3.2   Software-Defined Networking

Software-defined networking (SDN) is a new kind of network architecture to enable people build programmable networks as a way to reduce the complexity of network configuration and management. It can facilitate the provisioning of network services in a deterministic, dynamic, and scalable manner. SDN currently refers to approaches for networking in which the control plane and the data plane are decoupled and is governed by a logically centralized controller. This characteristic reduces the complexity in the network, managing the network as one entity. There will be an interface provided by the controller in order to configure networks and the controller is responsible for directing the configuration to the network. In this case, network operators are able to dynamically adjust the network's traffic flows to meet the changing needs while optimizing the network resource usage.

However, under the circumstances of wireless mesh networks, SDN still faces several challenges. Firstly, the centralized controller will cause a single point of failure:

if a WMR loses communication with the controller, the new flows fail transmitting; if the SDN controller fails, the whole network breaks down. Furthermore, centralized control for WMN would require transferring a considerable amount of status information and configuration commands between WMN nodes and the centralized control entity, which will cause the longer delays. To deploy an appropriate SDN strategy, we can make better use of SDN technologies.

3.3 OpenFlow

OpenFlow was originally designed for providing a real experiment platform to campus network researchers designing innovation network architecture, then McKeown et al. [10] started promoting SDN concept, and the concept aroused wide attention of academia and industry. It is a new switching protocol based on the concept of software defined networking(SDN).

OpenFlow-enabled switches move packet forwarding intelligence to the OpenFlow controller, while keeping the switches simple. In legacy switch structures, there is a control domain and a forwarding domain. As there is no control domain residing at an OpenFlow-based switch, the forwarding domain can be kept simple, and they do the forwarding function based on the flow tables. The functionality of the control domain is now moved to the control network, which was referred to as at least one OpenFlow controller or more. The controller is connected to every switch by a secure channel, using the OpenFlow protocol. OpenFlow makes packet forwarding and routing more intelligent than legacy routing solutions, making it possible to develop more complex routing protocols that further improve network performance. In our implementation, we utilize the protocol OpenFlow 1.3 [7] to construct our OpenFlow-based wireless mesh node.

3.4 OpenFlow-Based Wireless Mesh Node

In a typical mesh-based wireless network, there are generally three components: mesh clients, mesh routers and Internet gateways. In this paper, each mesh node (including Internet gateway) is based on OpenFlow and responsible for mesh connectivity and traffic routing. Because of the OpenFlow, each node is divided into two virtual planes, a data plane and a control plane. The control plane of the traditional mesh node resides on the switch. Thus, the OpenFlow Based mesh node's resides on the network-wide controller. The data plane consists of a set of rules, which the flow tables are sent by the controller. As shown in Fig. 1(a), we install OpenvSwitch for each device. The control and the data interfaces of each mesh node are two different physical interfaces.

The OpenFlow defines a secure channel between the data plane and the controller plane using a set of rules, properties, an expiration time and a list of actions. The properties specify packet source, original header values, and switch ports. When a new packet arrives at the switch network interface, while there is no match rule in the switch, the switch will ask the controller and the controller will decide whether the packet is dropped or forwarded.

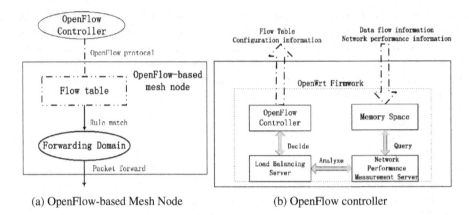

(a) OpenFlow-based Mesh Node   (b) OpenFlow controller

Fig. 1. Architecture of mesh node and controller

3.5 OpenFlow Controller

In our hypothesis, the OpenFlow controller does not only have the function of distributed flow table, also can change some of the configuration to the OpenFlow-based switches. On this occasion, we have modified the POX controller, making the system can identify the IP addresses of the connecting nodes, also can log on these mesh nodes and configure them.

We consider the architecture of the OpenFlow controller is like the Fig. 1(b). The controller consists of memory space, network performance measurement server, load balancing server, and OpenFlow controller. The performance server queries information from the OpenFlow-based switches/Internet Gateway and builds a data store used to support the load balancing server. Network topology changes are sent to this controller, then the controller will update the information including the channel usage based on the new network graphs. The main purpose of the OpenFlow controller is to perform basic load balancing tasks. The processing of the task is described as followed: (1) the controller achieves the source and destination addresses by searching the keyword of packet_in message from the source node, (2) the performance server may do the strategic analysis according to the information from memory space, (3) load balancing server firstly calculates a set of alternate paths using OLSR algorithm, and selects a optimal path from them in accordance with the strategics, (4) OpenFlow controller will send flow table and configuration information to ensure the data transmit correctly.

There has been some simple strategics: Each data flow can be assigned to a separate path and the assignments can change dynamically based on network state; High priority traffic will get better service while the best effort traffic suffers most of the damage; The 'fat' non-realtime traffic flows can be split to multiple paths as long as the paths end at the same gateway etc.

4 Testbed and Implementation

Our testbed was a small scale wireless mesh network consisted of at least four wireless routers which was placed as depicted in Fig. 2. The experiments were conducted inside our lab building.

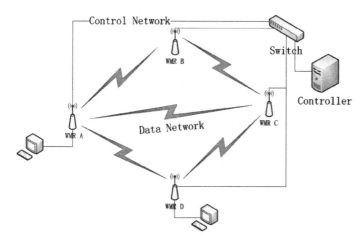

Fig. 2. WMN testbed with OpenFlow controller

All the wireless routers in our testbed are the PC Engines ALIX series of system boards, alix2d2, and their features shown in Table 1. We use the Linux-based x86 platform due to the extensible memory, radio adaptability via miniPCI cards, low power consumption, and low cost. Wireless routers have 2 Ethernet channels, 2 miniPCI slots which can use 802.11 a/n or 802.11 g/b wireless cards as wireless interfaces. The firmware of the wireless routers was replaced with the custom OpenWRT firmware [11], a system can be described as a very well-known embedded Linux distribution.

For the firmware we used the OpenWRT trunk r43753, which is based on Linux kernel version 3.14.26. This version of OpenWRT supports the OpenvSwitch 2.3. In these experiments, we use a custom POX controller, which is a controller based on NOX for rapid deployments of SDNs using Python as our OpenFlow controller. Because the interface of the wireless radio is limited, we use out-of-band control network with a wired connection.

5 Solution and Experiment

In this section we present our solution for load balancing in OpenFlow-based wireless mesh network, and the results of our experiment are implemented in our testbed. We make use of network measurement tool-iPerf for throughput and bandwidth measurements.

Table 1. Features of the system boards

	Hardware features
Interface	2 10/100/1000 Mbps LAN Ports
	2 USB 2.0 Port
	2 miniPCI wireless interface
	Wireless features
WLM200N2-26	2.4–2.4835 GHz
	23 dBm output power(per chain)/26 dBm(aggregate)
	802.11 b/g
WLM200N5-23 ESD	5.150–5.975 GHz
	23 dBm output power(per chain)/26 dBm(aggregate)
	802.11 a/n

We proposed a simple idea to solve the load imbalance problem in OpenFlow-based wireless mesh network in our paper. The setting of the wireless link of each mesh node is focused on in our solution. Figure 3 shows the basic topology of our network, including the basic elements of the wireless, wireless mesh nodes, and gateway nodes. Followed, we consider two load balancing scenarios: (1) the basic setup of the data flow paths, (2) data flow path redirection between links. The goal of this section is to provide load balancing configurations sample under different scenarios. Also, experiments are conducted to evaluate our OpenFlow-based wireless mesh network.

5.1   Basic Setup of the Data Flow Paths

Basic setup of the data flow paths is the first step before the load balancing. OpenFlow provides such a capability by sending flow table to establish the data path. Also, our controller will remotely connect to the switches, so that the controller can change the configuration in realtime. Figure 4 shows the schematic for setting up a data flow path.

Experimental Description. As shown in Fig. 4, both node a and node b are mesh nodes, and node g is a gateway with a connection to the Internet or another network.

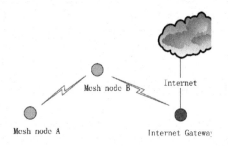

Fig. 3. Basic topology of WMN

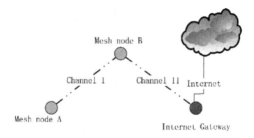

Fig. 4. Basic setup of data flow paths

All kinds of data servers are deployed in the Internet, from where the mesh networks request data. To setup a connection between node *a* and node *b* is our goal in this section. Assume node *b* already has a connection to node *g*. Now consider a scenario where a new node *a* joins the network. It needs to find its next-hop neighbor so that node *a* can communicate with the Internet. In this scenario, node *b* is the neighbor, and a wireless link using channel 1 represents the added flow path.

Experimental Procedure. To implement this scenario, traditional solutions require relatively high local computation capability. We show how to add the data path using OpenFlow controller in this section. As shown in Table 2, controller addressed this by sending flow tables and configuration instructions to mesh nodes, and no further action is required at local mesh routers. This setup servers as the foundation for the flow redirection.

When node *a* want to connect with node *b*, the controller will firstly establish an available wireless link by sending configuration instructions to them, setting the same channel and mesh_id. Thereafter, for node *a*, we identify the virtual OpenFlow switch as *id_node_a*, and the ingress port where data packets origination from node *a* labeled as *port_node_a*. When the OpenFlow switch receives data flow matching flow rules, the header of the packet will be manipulated in case of following the flow actions. In our scenario, the destination of node *a*'s packets is node *b*. Hence, packets form node *a* must modify their destination IP and MAC addresses. The *set_dst_ip* and *set_dst_-mac* fields are used to rewrite packet headers, so the *node_b_ip* and *node_b_mac* are the IP and MAC addresses of node *b*, respectively. The modified packets must be output through the wireless radio interface, defined as *node_a_port*. The node *b*'s configuration is similar to node *a*, except the destination. According to the appropriate rules, the gateway will forward the packets which the IP of the destination is out of this network segment.

Flow tables are pushed by the controller, and after that the data path between node *a* and gateway *g* is established. In this scenario, the host communicates with the Internet with two hops link. The iPerf measurement tool shows the TCP throughput averaging at 4.04 Mbits between node *a* and the Internet. The measurement was maintained for 10 min and repeated five times.

Table 2. Flow tables and configuration instructions(basic setup of the data flow paths)

	Node A	Node B
Configuration Instructions	mesh channel: 1 meshid: MeshTrain	mesh channel: 1 meshid: MeshTrain
Flow rule	switch: id_node_a port: port_node_a	switch: id_node_b port: port_node_b
Flow actions (forward)	set-dst-ip: node_b_ip set-dst-mac: node_b_mac output: node_a_port	set-dst-ip: destination_ip set-dst-mac: destination_mac output: node_b_port

5.2   Data Flow Path Redirection Between Links

Redirecting data traffic between links is an essential way for implementing network load balancing. Figure 5 shows the schematic.

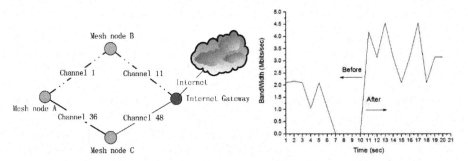

Fig. 5. Data flow path redirection between links

Fig. 6. Throughput before and after path redirection

Experimental Description. Node *a*, *b* and *c* are mesh nodes, and node *g* is an Internet gateway with a connection to the Internet. Assume a link is already established from node *a* and to gateway *g* via node *b*, as described in last section. The target of this section is to redirect data flows from node *a* to node *c* while node *b* experiences unexpected conditions or a new data packet arrives. This is a simple sample for load balancing.

Experimental Procedure. Flow tables and configuration instructions for this scenario are shown in Table 3. When we want to redirect a new data path, we must remove the old one. For node *a*, we remove the flow actions for *a-b* link, and send a new flow table for *a-c* by modified the destination IP and MAC addresses with node *c*'s(*node_c_ip* and *node_c_mac*). Node *c* modifies the packet headers to the destination.

In our experiment, node *a* sends data to gateway *g* via node *b* before data flow redirection. Due to the reduction of the node *b*'s signal, the system decides to adjust the data link. The new path offers higher average throughput because we use the 802.11 a/n wireless radio card while the former uses 802.11 b/g wireless radio card. Figure 6 shows the TCP throughput performance results measured by iPerf before and after redirection. It can be seen that throughput increases after flows are redirected to the new path with stable wireless channels.

Table 3. Flow tables and configuration instructions(data flow path redirection between links)

	Node A	Node C
Configuration instructions	mesh channel: 36	mesh channel: 36
	meshid: MeshTrain	meshid: MeshTrain
Flow rules	switch: id_node_a	switch: id_node_c
	port: port_node_a	port: port_node_c
Flow actions (remove)	set-dst-ip: node_b_ip	
	set-dst-mac: node_b_mac	
	output:node_a_port	
Flow actions (forward)	set-dst-ip: node_c_ip	set-dst-ip: destination_ip
	set-dst-mac: node_c_mac	set-dst-mac: destination_mac
	output: node_a_port	output: node_c_port

5.3   Some Results Analysis

Since we use the OpenFlow controller change the connecting channel dynamically before the data transmitted. We need to consider the influence of the data path establishment. We measured the response time at each hop at least 100 times in the experiment. We compared the performance based-on our testbed with the traditional mesh network. It can be seen that the response time increase along with the increase of hops. As the Fig. 7(a) shown, there is only little difference between traditional networks and our OpenFlow-based networks. Figure 7(b) shows the TCP performance measured by iPerf at each hop. It can be seen that the throughput is about half of the prior hop's throughput. After three hops, traditional network averages at 4.26 Mbps throughput and the network with OpenFlow averages at 3.21 Mbps. Nowadays, people have not taken full advantage of the network bandwidth, we think the bandwidth consumption using centralization OpenFlow control is only a small amount of. Instead, the network performance will be improved, as well as improving the network bandwidth utilization. The communication among the control plane has influenced the throughput of the data plane. From the above, we confirmed that using OpenFlow in a wireless mesh network is reasonable and feasible.

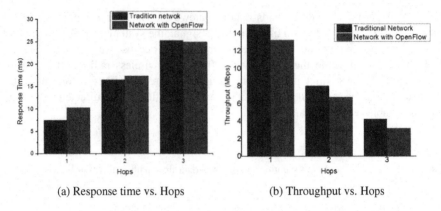

(a) Response time vs. Hops   (b) Throughput vs. Hops

Fig. 7. Performance results comparison

6 Conclusion and Future Work

In this paper, we described an OpenFlow-based wireless mesh network, which allows flexible control of OpenFlow-based switches, to solve the load balancing problem. Regarding the network characteristics, the traditional solutions in a typical wireless mesh network which requires compute-intensive routing algorithms running at each mesh node are abandoned. The architecture of the network presented in our paper combines a centralized OpenFlow controller and several OpenFlow-based mesh nodes (or the Internet gateway). When the monitor server in the controller finds the congestion over the network or a new arriving of the data flow, the controller will set up the data path including the channel of each link if necessary. Our experiments confirm that OpenFlow is an available technique to wireless mesh networks. As future work, we plan to develop an adaptive load-aware routing algorithm for multi-interface wireless mesh networks based-on OpenFlow, and plan to experimentally evaluate the approach.

Acknowledgment. This work was supported in part by the Industry-University-Research Combination Innovation Foundation of Jiangsu Province (No. BY2013003-03) and the Industry-University-Research Combination Innovation Foundation of Jiangsu Province (No. BY2013095-2-10).

References

1. Jagadeesan, N.A., Krishnamachari, B: Software-defined networking paradigms in wireless networks: a survey. ACM Comput. Surv. **47**(2), 11 p. (2014). Article 27, doi:10.1145/2655690
2. Alotaibi, E., Mukherjee, B.: A survey on routing algorithms for wireless ad-hoc and mesh networks. Comput. Netw. **56**(2), 940–965 (2012)
3. Hu, Y., Li, X.-Y., Chen, H.-M., Jia, X.-H.: Distributed call admission protocol for multi-channel multi-radio wireless networks. In: Global Telecommunications Conference, 2007, GLOBECOM 2007, pp. 2509–2513. IEEE 26–30 November 2007

4. Brzezinski, A., Zussman, G., Modiano, E.: Distributed throughput maximization in wireless mesh networks via pre-partitioning. IEEE/ACM Trans. Networking **16**(6), 1406–1419 (2008)
5. Detti, A., Pisa, C., Salsano, S., Blefari-Melazzi, N.: Wireless mesh software defined networks (wmSDN). In: 2013 IEEE 9th International Conference on Wireless and Mobile Computing, Networking and Communications (WiMob), vol. 6983, pp. 89–95. IEEE (2013)
6. Chung, J., Gonzalez, G., Armuelles, I., Robles, T., Alcarria, R., Morales, A.: Characterizing the multimedia service capacity of wireless mesh networks for rural communities. In: 2012 IEEE 8th International Conference on Wireless and Mobile Computing, Networking and Communications (WiMob), pp. 628–635. IEEE (2012)
7. Open Networking Foundation. https://www.opennetworking.org/
8. Akyildiz, I.F., Wang, X.: A survey on wireless mesh networks. IEEE Commun. Mag. **43**(9), S23–S30 (2005)
9. Yang, F., Gondi, V., Hallstrom, J.O., Wang, K.C., Eidson, G.: OpenFlow-based load balancing for wireless mesh infrastructure. 2014 IEEE 11th Consumer Communications and Networking Conference (CCNC), pp. 444–449. IEEE (2014)
10. Parulkar, G.M., Rexford, J., Turner, J.S., Mckeown, N., Anderson, T., Balakrishnan, H., et al.: Openflow: enabling innovation in campus networks. ACM SIGCOMM Comput. Commun. Rev. **38**(2), 69–74 (2008)
11. OpenWrt. https://openwrt.org/

SPEMS: A Stealthy and Practical Execution Monitoring System Based on VMI

Jiangyong Shi[✉], Yuexiang Yang, Chengye Li, and Xiaolei Wang

School of Computer, National University of Defense Technology,
Changsha, China
{shijiangyong,yyx,lichengye,xiaoleiwang}@nudt.edu.cn

Abstract. Dynamic analyzing has been proposed for over decades to tracing the execution of programs. However, most of them need an agent installed inside the execution environment, which is easy to be detected and bypassed. To solve the problem, we proposed a system named SPEMS which utilized virtual machine introspection (VMI) technology to stealthily monitor the execution of programs inside virtual machines. SPEMS integrates and improves multiple open-source software tools. By inspecting the whole process of sample preparation, execution tracing and analysis, it is able to be applied in large scale program monitoring, malware analyzing and memory forensics. Experiments results show our system has remarkable performance improvement compared with former works.

Keywords: Dynamic analysis · VMI · Cloud security · Execution monitoring

1 Introduction

Dynamic analysis based on behaviors provides a new perspective to analyze malware. Different from static code analysis, it runs malware in a controlled environment called sandbox and gets the behaviors triggered by malware upon the operation system. With this technique, we can perform the malware analysis automatically at a large scale. Several systems have been implemented, such as CWSandbox [1], Anubis [2], Cuckoo [3] etc. Among them, Cuckoo is a well-developed sandbox and active in malware analysis and forensics for its open source and module style design. However, Cuckoo uses an agent in guest virtual machine (VM) to communicate with the host, which would be easily detected by and under attack of malware.

The problem met by Cuckoo can be solved by a technique named virtual machine introspection (VMI). VMI has been developed for over decade since Garfinkel first proposed the concept in [4]. It is defined as a way to extract VM information from out of VM, thus has advantages of isolation, interpretation and interposition. VMI has been widely used in security areas such as malware analysis [5], IDS [6], memory forensics [7]. By implementing security tools out of virtual machine, it can keep stealthy while in the same time monitoring the context of virtual machines, which is a combination of isolation and interpretation. As these two features have been widely utilized to deploy new security tools, the feature of interposition has not been broadly researched. In this paper, we analyzed the interposition feature of VMI and its potential usage in program execution monitoring.

© Springer International Publishing Switzerland 2015
Z. Huang et al. (Eds.): ICCCS 2015, LNCS 9483, pp. 380–389, 2015.
DOI: 10.1007/978-3-319-27051-7_32

Although VMI is suitable for stealthy monitoring, these solutions are either performance costing or only usable under strictly limited condition, which makes them unpractical in large scale of malware analyzing as Cuckoo does. To make VMI practically usable, we inspected the entire process of malware analyzing, including virtual environment preparation, execution tracing and result analyzing. We utilized some of the open-source works and improved them to make it practical usable. Our main contribution is an integrated VMI-based program execution monitoring system, namely SPEMS, which includes VM snapshotting, out-of-box file injecting, process injecting and execution tracing. Our system can also be used in forensic and intrusion detection.

The rest of the paper is organized as follows: The second part discussed the development of VMI technique and related works. The main job and implementation is discussed in the third part. Related experiments and results are discussed in fourth part. Finally, a conclusion is drawn in the last part.

2 Related Works

VMI is divided into two kinds in [5], namely in-band VMI and out-of-band VMI. Lares [13] is a typical in-band VMI which is designed for protecting in-guest security tools and transfer information to hypervisor. While in-band VMI has advantages of easy to implement and low performance cost, it is easy to be detected by malware. So we mainly discuss out-of-band VMI which is also the main trend of VMI developing.

LibVMI [8], formerly called XenAccess, is a C library with Python bindings that makes it easy to monitor the low-level details of a running virtual machine by viewing its memory, trapping on hardware events, and accessing the vCPU registers. Works related with LibVMI include include VMwall [6], VMI-Honeymon [9] and RTKDSM [10]. They are more focus on obtaining guest information passively rather than active trigger the VM to get what we need, which limit their usage in monitoring. Some solutions like NICKLE [11], SecVisor [12], Lares [13] deal with protection of the guest OS' code or data structures, but none could deal with the user-space program execution tracing.

Recent works like SPIDER [14], DRAKVUF [15], Virtuoso [16] and VMST [17, 18] actively inspect a VM's state, which used in VM configuration and intrusion defense. SPIDER is a VMI-based debugging and instrumentation using instruction-level trapping based on invisible breakpoint and hardware virtualization. Spider hides the existence of invisible breakpoint in the guest memory by utilizing the Extended Page Table (EPT) to split the code and data view seen by the guest, and handles invisible breakpoint at the hypervisor level to avoid any unexpected in-guest execution.

All of the above tools or projects cannot provide practical usage in large-scale malware analysis either for performance reasons or for automation reasons. DRAKVUF use #BP injection technique of SPIDER to initiate the execution of malware samples and monitor kernel internal functions and heap allocations. Then it use LibVMI to intercept Xen events and mapping guest memory to host. Although DRAKVUF reduces resources cost via copy-on-write memory and disk, the CPU cost is still very high. And it is only capable of starting existing malware samples, not able to inject samples. What's more, DRAKVUF cannot monitor user-level function calls. To make DRAK-VUF practically usable, we improved it by adding support of monitoring function calls of specified process and module, including user-level function calls. And we proposed an out-of-band based injection method to submit malware samples into VM.

3   Implementation

The main framwork of our system SPEMS is shown in Fig. 1. It is consisted with three parts: sample preparation, execution tracing and system calls analysis. The sample preparation part is for preparing the execution environment for malware samples. Considered the increasing amount of malware samples, we designed a workflow for snapshots taking, virtual machine clone and sample injecting to increase the reusability and productivity. The execution tracing part is the core part of our system, which utilized open-source tools such as LibVMI and Rekall to parse the guest OS symbol and translate guest memory to accessible. Moreover, we improved DRAKVUF in some aspects to reduce the CPU cost and refine the result. The system calls analysis part is used to further analyzing the results obtained from execution tracing. The actual analysis method can be adjustable and various according to actual demand. In order to keep the generosity, we are not going to discuss the detailed implementation of this part. But to who may concern, please referred to our former works [21, 22] for details of using system calls sequence to further analyzing the behavior of malware.

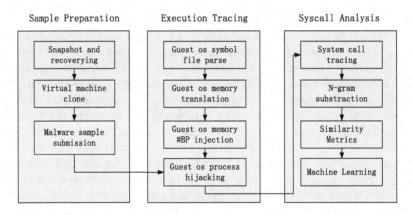

Fig. 1. Framework of SPEMS

3.1   Sample Preparation

To analyze malware samples, we should first put the samples into the guest VM and run it. As our goal is to build an automatic system to monitor large amounts of malware samples, it is not an option to do it manually. Although we can copy samples into VM using network protocols such as SSH, NFS and SMB, it will leave traces on system and break the isolation between guest and host. That's why we use out-of-box injection techniques which directly modify the VM disk to put samples on it. Sample injection can be divided into volume based and file based. Share folders such as vmtools and xentools are file based. Hot-plug block devices and live modification of VM disk are volume based. Even though commercial products such as VMware ESX and Citrix XenServer both can share file between the host and the VM by tools like vmtool and xentool, it is not available to open-source virtualization software such as KVM and Xen. Besides, it is also a risk of VM escape attack as reported earlier [19]. To avoid the use of network connection and ensure the isolation between host and VM, we utilize guestfish [20] to inject malware samples into the VM. Guestfish is a shell and command-line tool which uses libguestfs and exposes all of the functionality of the libguestfs API. Guestfish provided api to copy file into and out of VM, which we used to copy samples into VM.

While it's easy to take snapshot and recovery VMs for XenServer and ESX, even KVM provides snapshot mechanism, it is not officially done to Xen. But there have been a lot of unofficial solutions to this, such as byte-by-byte snapshot using xm and dd, logical volume manager (LVM) incremental method, rsync based, and ZFS based. Among them, LVM's copy-on-write (cow) disk capability and Xen's native cow memory interface is very suitable to backup Xen VM state and recovery it in a short period of time. We implement it with a script as follows. The total time of snapshotting is less than 10 s of 1 GB memory and 1 GB backend logical volumn VM disk in our test. And the recovery stage costs less than 5 s. The time cost of injection stage is related with the sample file size. In our test, it is almost the same speed as local disk write operation, except that the mounting of guest disk to host costs additional 20 s more or less. Combined LVM with guestfish, it is able to inject malware samples into VM disk without leaving traces and quickly recovery disk to a clean state after the analysis is completed. The code of these processes is listed below.

```
------------------- take a snapshot or the original vm
xl save win7 win7.sav //save the memory state
------------------- clone a new vm for sample analysis
lvcreate -s -L 1G -n win7-snap01 /dev/vg/win7 //create a
backend of the original disk volume
xl create win7-snap01
------------------- inject samples into clone vm
guestfish -rw -a /dev/vg/win7-snap01 --mount /dev/sda2 /
copy-in samples-in-host /directory/of/vm
Exit
------------------- remove the clone vm after VMI
lvremove /dev/vg/win7-snap01 //remove the backend lv of
the vm
xl destroy win7-snap01
------------------- recovery the original vm
xl restore win7.sav
```

3.2   Execution Tracing

To trace the execution of guest VM execution, we used and improved DRAKVUF. DRAKVUF is a novel tool for exacting virtual machine behaviors and injecting samples into existing process. It use #BP injection to trap kernel functions of VM. First, it parses pdb files of windows system to get the relative virtual address (RVA). Then by looking into FS and GS registers we can get the virtual address (VA) of _KPCR structure. By subtracting the RVA from RA we can get the kernel base address. With kernel base address, we can locate any functions or structures of interest and inject an INT3 (0xCC) breakpoint into that place. After injecting breakpoint, any write or read to the place will cause break event which will be delivered to callback functions for further processing, such as print or save the register contents, which contain function names and arguments.

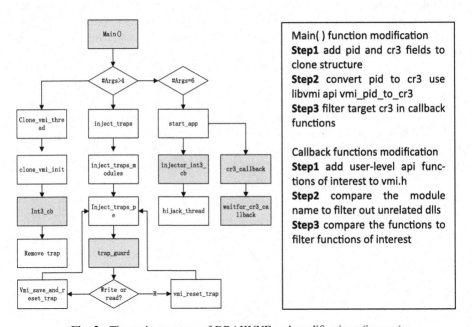

Fig. 2. The main structure of DRAKVUF and modifications (in gray)

It uses technology such as cow disk and cow memory to reduce the resource cost. Besides, it uses vlan to separate the cloned vms. For these reasons, DRAKVUF is very suitable in analyzing malware samples. The main structure of DRAKVUF is shown in Fig. 2.

However, the CPU cost of DRAKVUF is heavy to as much as 100 % in our test. The reasons for this are DRAKVUF traps all kernel functions and intercept all heap allocations and file operations. Besides, DRAKVUF only traps kernel functions. Even though kernel functions are more important and can be used to detect rootkit, it doesn't represent the general behavior of malware. To reduce the CPU cost and make

DRAKVUF more applicative to normal malware analysis, we add a mechanism to filter unrelated kernel functions and add traps to user-level sensitive function calls which may indicate malicious behaviors, such as those exported by dynamic loaded libraries of kernel32, advapi32, wininet, ws2_32, and so on. By doing so, we can obtain comprehensive malware behavior report consists of both the kernel-level and user-level behavior. The functions that we trap are listed in Table 1. These functions are chosen from Cuckoo, a well-known open-source sandbox, such that we can get a similar result as Cuckoo does to user-level malware while in the same time is capable of detecting kernel-level rootkits by kernel trapping. We modified the four callback functions to add support to trap user-level functions and filter unrelated kernel functions. And we modified the main function to specify the process to trap and monitor so as to refine the results. The details are shown in Fig. 2.

Table 1. Added functions to be trapped

Modules	#	Examples
Ntdll.dll	62	NtCallbackReturn, LdrLoadDll, NtWriteFile
Kernel32.dll	24	CreateDirectoryW, CopyFileA, CreateThread
Ws2_32.dll	32	Getaddrinfo, socket, WSARecv
Advapi.dll	32	RegOpenKeyExA, RegSetValueExA, OpenServiceA
Wininet.dll	13	InternetOpenA, InternetOpenUrlA, InternetWriteFile

After the modification, we can get the user-level function calls information of the given malware process, which will be further processed in next stage of function calls analyzing. For details of the analyzing process, please refer to our former works [21, 22].

4   Evaluation

To test the effect of our system, we designed several experiments. The hardware configuration of our experiments is a Dell PowerEdge R730xd server with Intel Xeon E5-2603 v3 CPU, 2 TB disk and 32 GB memory. The virtualization environment is Xen 4.4.1 with network configured by openvswitch.

The first experiment is to evaluate the snapshot method for Xen. As shown in Fig. 3, the time of a 20 GB LVM disk creation is less than 1 s which can be ignored. The memory saving operation costs 7 s, 10 s, 14 s respectively for saving memory size of 1 GB, 2 GB and 4 GB. The major costing is injecting samples, this is because the injection needs to mount guest disk. But the time increases slowly with the size of the disk, as shown Fig. 3. The time of memory saving and recovering increase linearly with the size of memory, but are all less than 15 s. The clone of VMs mainly consists of LVM disk creation which costs less than one second and can be ignored. Overall, the total process of sample preparation costs less than one minute, which is acceptable in practical use, especially when running multiple cloned VMs concurrently.

The second experiment is to compare SPEMS with DRAKVUF. The CPU cost of SPEMS drops critically compared with DRAKVUF during the test, from nearly 100 %

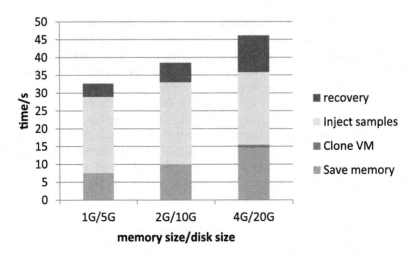

Fig. 3. Time cost of sample preparation under different memory and disk size

to about 10 %. This difference causes the programs' execution time differs greatly as shown in Table 2. While DRAKVUF runs, it is almost impossible to do other operations on VM and the execution is slow as a snail's pace, which is abnormal and would lead to the disclosure of monitoring existence. SPEMS are 13 times faster than DRAKVUF in average. We attribute this improvement to the use of filter mechanism. This improvement, combined with the snapshot and clone mechanism, makes our system more stealthy and practical usable. Even though SPEMS dramatically reduced the time cost of DRAKVUF, there is still time gap between the origin execution and the VMI-based execution. This time is hard to vanish as the trapping and dealing of breakpoints will cost time. However, as long as we can keep the normal execution of user programs, it is possible to utilize active VMI as shown in [23] to modifying the time value returned by relative function calls to deceive user-level applications.

Table 2. Time cost of operations

	WINZIP	IExporer	RegBak
Original	14 s	7 s	3 s
DRAKVUF	11 min 21 s	4 min 6 s	3 min 42 s
SPEMS	50 s	18 s	6 s

Besides, the top 5 extracted function calls of different applications during 5 min compared with the original DRAKVUF is shown in Table 3. We selected three typical applications to respectively represent the operation on file, network, and registry. File operation is simulated by uncompressing a collection of 700 malware samples. Network operation is simulated by accessing one of the most famous web portals (www. msn.cn). Registry operation is simulated by RegBak (a famous registry backup and restore tool). From Table 3 we can see that the top 5 trapped functions of SPEMS are totally different with DRAKVUF because we added a lot of user-level function calls while DRAKVUF only traps kernel-level functions. Even though we filtered out many less sensitive kernel functions, the important information is clearer, rather than missed. Take the WINZIP program as an example, DRAKVUF traces large amounts of kernel functions such as ExAllocatePoolWithTag and NtCallbackReturn, which cannot represent the general behavior of uncompressing. While SPEMS successfully traced the function calls of loading libraries related with uncompressing.

Table 3. TOP 5 function calls (The gray rows are the result of DRAKVUF while the white ones are the result of SPEMS, figures behind the function names are the number of calls of this function. Functions in bold represent the most related behavior to the program.)

	1	2	3	4	5
WIN ZIP	ExAllocateP oolWithTag 1232937	NtCallbackRe turn 199069	NtOpenP rocess 68089	NtQueryInfor mationProcess 66156	NtClose 41946
	LdrGetDllHa ndle 25329	LdrGetProce dureAddress 10595	GetSyste mMetrics 6431	GetCursorPos 131	**LdrLoadDll** **24**
IExpl orer	ExAllocateP oolWithTag 318447	NtWaitForSin gleObject 32359	NtReleas eMutant 26506	NtOpenProces s 23568	NtClose 16584
	RegQueryVa lueExW 12834	RegOpenKey ExW 12367	RegEnum KeyExW 11451	RegEnumKeyW 11415	**recv** **2873**
Reg Bak	ExAllocateP oolWithTag 417097	NtOpenProce ss 39852	NtClose 29031	NtCallbackRet urn 21560	NtWaitForSi ngleObject 17169
	GetSystem Metrics 2693	LdrGetProce dureAddress 198	CreateDir ectoryW 51	**RegOpenKeyE** **xW** **51**	LdrLoadDll 41

5   Conclusions

Dynamic analyzing of malware behaviors have been developed for decades and VMI technic has also been proposed for over last decade. Combining the two to accomplish stealthy and automatic malware analyzing has been the pursuing of security researching field. However, due to high performance cost and limited application area, past works are not really practical. To improve this, we inspected the whole process of malware analyzing, including virtual environment preparation, execution tracing and result analyzing. Our main contribution is an integrated VMI-based malware execution monitoring system, namely SPEMS, which includes Xen VM snapshotting, out-of-box file injecting, process injecting and execution tracing. Experiments show that the performance improved a lot compared with former works and is acceptable in practical malware analysis. Combined with machine learning methods, SPEMS can be further extended to use in forensic and intrusion detection. Besides analyzing program using VMI, the data security of VM should also be noticed. Related works such as [24, 25] will be our future research direction.

References

1. Willems, G., Holz, T., Freiling, F.: Toward automated dynamic malware analysis using CWSandbox. IEEE Secur. Priv. **5**, 32–39 (2007)
2. Bayer, U., Moser, A., Kruegel, C., Kirda, E.: Dynamic analysis of malicious code. J. Comput. Virol. **2**, 67–77 (2006)
3. Cuckoobox. http://www.cuckoosandbox.org/
4. Garfinkel, T., Rosenblum, M.: A virtual machine introspection based architecture for intrusion detection. In: NDSS, pp. 191–206 (2003)
5. Jiang, X., Wang, X., Xu, D.: Stealthy malware detection through vmm-based out-of-the-box semantic view reconstruction. In: Proceedings of the 14th ACM Conference on Computer and Communications Security, pp. 128–138 (2007)
6. Srivastava, A., Giffin, J.T.: Tamper-resistant, application-aware blocking of malicious network connections. In: Lippmann, R., Kirda, E., Trachtenberg, A. (eds.) RAID 2008. LNCS, vol. 5230, pp. 39–58. Springer, Heidelberg (2008)
7. Nance, K., Bishop, M., Hay, B.: Investigating the implications of virtual machine introspection for digital forensics. In: ARES 2009 International Conference on Availability, Reliability and Security, 2009, pp. 1024–1029 (2009)
8. Payne, B.D.: Simplifying virtual machine introspection using libvmi. Sandia report (2012)
9. Lengyel, T.K., Neumann, J., Maresca, S., Payne, B.D., Kiayias, A.: Virtual machine introspection in a hybrid honeypot architecture. In: CSET (2012)
10. Hizver, J., Chiueh, T.C.: Real-time deep virtual machine introspection and its applications. In: Proceedings of the 10th ACM SIGPLAN/SIGOPS International Conference on Virtual Execution Environments, VEE 2014, pp. 3–14. ACM, New York (2014)
11. Riley, R., Jiang, X., Xu, D.: Guest-transparent prevention of kernel rootkits with VMM-based memory shadowing. In: Lippmann, R., Kirda, E., Trachtenberg, A. (eds.) RAID 2008. LNCS, vol. 5230, pp. 1–20. Springer, Heidelberg (2008)
12. Seshadri, A., Luk, M., Qu, N., Perrig, A.: SecVisor: a tiny hypervisor to provide lifetime kernel code integrity for commodity OSes. In: Proceedings of Twenty-First ACM SIGOPS Symposium on Operating Systems Principles, SOSP 2007, vol. 41, pp. 335–350. ACM, New York (2007)
13. Payne, B.D., Carbone,M., Sharif,M., Lee, W.: Lares: an architecture for secure active monitoring using virtualization. In: Proceedings of the 2008 IEEE Symposium on Security and Privacy, SP 2008, pp. 233–247. IEEE Computer Society, Washington, DC (2008)
14. Deng, Z., Zhang, X., Xu, D.: Spider: stealthy binary program instrumentation and debugging via hardware virtualization. In: Proceedings of the 29th Annual Computer Security Applications Conference, pp. 289–298 (2013)

15. Lengyel, T.K., Maresca, S., Payne, B.D., Webster, G.D., Vogl, S., Kiayias, A.: Scalability, fidelity and stealth in the drakvuf dynamic malware analysis system. In: Proceedings of the 30th Annual Computer Security Applications Conference, pp. 386–395 (2014)
16. Dolan-Gavitt, B., Leek, T., Zhivich, M., Giffin, J., Lee, W.: Virtuoso: narrowing the semantic gap in virtual machine introspection. In: IEEE Symposium on Security and Privacy (SP), pp. 297–312. IEEE, New York (2011)
17. Fu, Y., Lin, Z.: Space traveling across VM: automatically bridging the semantic gap in virtual machine introspection via online Kernel data redirection. In: Proceedings of the 2012 IEEE Symposium on Security and Privacy, SP 2012, pp. 586–600. IEEE Computer Society, Washington, DC (2012)
18. Fu, Y., Lin, Z.: Bridging the semantic gap in virtual machine introspection via online Kernel data redirection. ACM Trans. Inf. Syst. Secur. 16(2) (2013)
19. VM escape. https://cve.mitre.org/cgi-bin/cvename.cgi?name=CVE-2008-0923
20. Guestfish. http://libguestfs.org/guestfish.1.html
21. Qiao, Y., Yang, Y., He, J., Tang, C., Liu, Z.: CBM: free, automatic malware analysis framework using API call sequences. Adv. Intell. Syst. Comput. 214, 225–236 (2014)
22. Qiao, Y., Yang, Y., Ji, L., He, J.: Analyzing malware by abstracting the frequent itemsets in API call sequences. In: Proceedings of the 12th IEEE International Conference Trust Security Privacy Computing and Communications (TrustCom), 2013, pp. 265–270 (2013)
23. Dinaburg, A., Royal, P., Sharif, M., Lee, W.: Ether: malware analysis via hardware virtualization extensions. In: Proceedings of the 15th ACM Conference on Computer and Communications Security, pp. 51–62 (2008)
24. Mei, S., Wang, Z., Cheng, Y., Ren, J., Wu, J., Zhou, J.: Trusted bytecode virtual machine module: a novel method for dynamic remote attestation in cloud computing. Int. J. Comput. Intell. Syst. 5, 924–932 (2012)
25. Shuang, T., Lin, T., Xiaoling, L., Yan, J.: An efficient method for checking the integrity of data in the cloud. China Commun. 11, 68–81 (2014)

A Total Power Control Cooperative MAC Protocol for Wireless Sensor Networks

Xiongli Rui[1,2]([✉]), Xuehong Cao[1], and Jie Yang[2]

[1] College of Telecommunications and Information Engineering,
Nanjing University of Posts and Telecommunications, Nanjing 210003, China
ruixiongli@njit.edu.cn, caoxh@njupt.edu.cn
[2] Department of Communication Engineering,
Nanjing Institute of Technology, Nanjing 211167, China
yangjie@njit.edu.cn

Abstract. Energy conservation is a key design issue for a battery-limited wireless sensor network (WSN). Compared with non-cooperative communication, cooperative communication can significantly reduce the total transmit power, because of the introducing space diversity. First, theoretical analysis for the total transmission power of non-cooperative communication and cooperative communication under the bit error rate (BER) constraint of the destiny node is presented. Then, the relay selection strategy aiming to select the best relay node, which leads to the minimal total transmit power, is discussed. On the base of these works, we propose a distributed cooperative MAC protocol to lengthen the network lifetime. The channel state informations (CSIs) are estimated according to the strength of control packets. In this protocol, a helper ready to send (HTS) packet is introduced and the packet format of clear to send (CTS) is extended. Simulations show that the new MAC protocol can effectively save the energy and lengthen the network lifetime.

Keywords: Wireless sensor network · Cooperative MAC · Energy conservation

1 Introduction

Wireless sensor networks (WSNs) are envisioned as consisting of a large number of tiny, battery-limited, multifunctional sensor nodes that are deployed nearly every area, such as building automation, environmental monitoring, target tracking, and industrial process controlling. Because of the constrained energy resources, the sensor nodes need to guarantee the lifetime of the battery for a few months or more than a year to overcome the difficulty of recharging or replacing a discharged battery. Effective management of energy consumption and design of a low-power network have been the important issues, which have led to repeated research in media access control (MAC) protocols.

Cooperative communication is considered to be a good technique for energy consumption. The conception of cooperative communication is originated in Multiple-Input Multiple-Output (MIMO) technology. To reduce the multi-path fading

© Springer International Publishing Switzerland 2015
Z. Huang et al. (Eds.): ICCCS 2015, LNCS 9483, pp. 390–403, 2015.
DOI: 10.1007/978-3-319-27051-7_33

and obtain spatial diversity gain, it exploits the distributed antennas to form a virtual MIMO system, which overcomes the difficulties such as implementing more than one antenna to a small signal node. Most of the earlier cooperative communication works mainly focus on the physical layer aspects [1, 2] while recent works examine the cooperative technology considering the MAC layer [3–11] and network layer [12–14]. In recent years, interest in cross-layer cooperation has increased because of its significant influence in both the theory and the practice of networks.

The MAC layer plays an essential role in data transmissions with complex constraints, which controls multi-user access through common wireless channels and provides relative transparent data transmission services to upper layer. CoopMAC [3] is the early cooperative MAC proposed by Pei Liu. Every node in CoopMAC needs to maintain a cooperative node list recording the neighbors' rate and time of the last packet. When the source node needs to transmit a packet, it chooses a best relay node according to the end-to-end minimal transmission time. CoopMAC improves the reliability and throughput but costs more memory. The opportunistic cooperative MAC protocol proposed in [4] is based on cross-layer technology and is designed to improve the throughput by selecting the relay node which has the best channel. References [5, 6] select the best relay by inter-group and intra-group competitions. The grouping and competing method improves the throughput, but also costs additional energy in corresponding control packets overhead. To maintain the fairness and reduce the loss rate of control frame, [7] proposed RCMAC. RCMAC transmits clear to send (CTS) packets and acknowledge (ACK) packets through by the relay, which has the fastest transmit rate. Based on 802.11, ECCMAC [8] improves the throughput by choosing the relay which has the shortest transmit time and uses network coding. To improve the throughput, STiCMAC [9] employs multiple relays and combines with the distributed space-time coding.

As mentioned above, most of the proposed cooperative MACs are designed to improve the throughput while relatively little works focus on reducing energy consumption. But for energy constrained wireless networks, such as WSN, energy conservation is particular important. Motivated by this, we propose the total power control MAC (TPC-MAC) protocol. The major contributions of this paper can be summarized as follows:

– A distributed cooperative MAC protocol is proposed, which can introduce space diversity to mitigate the multi-path fading.
– A relay selection strategy is discussed, which can lead to the minimal network total transmit power and prolong the lifetime of the network.

The rest of this paper is structured as follows. In Sect. 2, System models for a cooperative network and a non-cooperative network are presented. The theoretical total transmission power for these two network models is analyzed. Section 3 shows the details of the proposed protocol. Section 4 shows the numerical results. Finally, Sect. 5 concludes the paper.

2   System Models and Power Analysis

Consider a WSN with N nodes randomly distributed in a circular area as shown in Fig. 1. The destiny node locates in the center of the circle. Let S, D, R denote the source node, the destiny node and the relay node. Then, a typical three-node cooperative communication model is presented. h_{sd}, h_{sr} and h_{rd} are the channel gains of S-D, S-R and R-D, which are circularly symmetric complex Gaussian random variable with zero mean and the variance σ^2, i.e. $(0, \sigma^2)$.

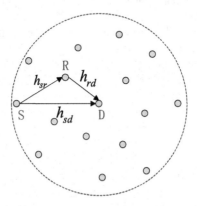

Fig. 1. WSN with N nodes randomly distributed

The follow paragraph analyzes the total transmit power of non-cooperative model and cooperative model in decode and forward (DF).

2.1   Non-cooperative Model

Each sensor node in a non-cooperative model only transmits its own data packet to the destiny node. When a packet is transmitting, other nodes in the sensing range keep silence. Let $x(n)$ denote the signal to be transmitted from S to D. The signal $x(n)$ can be the data of other nodes that S routes through the destiny node, or it can be the data of S itself. The data received at D can be expressed as:

$$y_{sd} = \sqrt{P_{S_{Non-coop}}} h_{sd} x(n) + n_{sd} \tag{1}$$

where $P_{S_{Non-coop}}$ is the transmit power of S, n_{sd} is the AWGN with zero mean and the variance N_0, i.e. CN(0, N_0). The channel variance σ_{sd}^2 of h_{sd} is modeled as:

$$\sigma_{sd}^2 = \eta D_{sd}^{-\alpha} \tag{2}$$

where η is a constant determined by the propagation environment, D_{sd} denotes the distance between S and D, and α is the path loss factor ($\alpha = 2$ for free space and $3 < \alpha < 4$ for urban environment). Considering M-PSK modulation and using a BER formulation in [15], the average BER upper bound can be expressed as:

$$BER \leq \frac{AN_0}{bP_{S_{Non-coop}}\sigma_{sd}^2 log_2^M} \tag{3}$$

where $b = sin^2(\pi/M)$, $A = (M-1)/2M + sin(2\pi/M)/4\pi$. Take (2) into (3) and consider the constraint of performance requirement $BER \leq \varepsilon$, where ε denotes the maximum allowable BER, the minimal total transmit power of S is given by:

$$P_{S_{Non-coop}} = \frac{AN_0 D_{sd}^\alpha}{b\varepsilon\eta log_2^M} \tag{4}$$

Under the constraint of ε, when S is nearer to D, the transmit power requirement $P_{S_{Non-coop}}$ is lower.

2.2 Cooperative Model

Each sensor node in a cooperative wireless sensor network can act as a source node or a relay node. DF protocol is used as the cooperative strategy, which includes two transmission phases. Let's consider a typical three node cooperative model shown in Fig. 1. During transmission phase 1, the source node S transmits signal $x(n)$ using power $P_{S_{coop}}$. The signal is appended with redundancy check (CRC) before transmission. The signal received at the relay node R and destiny node D can be expressed as (5) and (6), respectively.

$$y_{sr} = \sqrt{P_{S_{coop}}}h_{sr}x(n) + n_{sr} \tag{5}$$

$$y_{sd} = \sqrt{P_{S_{coop}}}h_{sd}x(n) + n_{sd} \tag{6}$$

where $P_{S_{coop}}$ is the transmit power of S in a cooperative model, h_{sd}, h_{sr}, n_{sr} and n_{sd} are modeled as $CN(0, \sigma_{sd}^2)$, $CN(0, \sigma_{sr}^2)$, $CN(0, N_0)$ and $CN(0, N_0)$, respectively. During transmission phase 2, if the relay node R correctly decodes the signal received from the source node S, it helps forward the signal. If R decodes the signal incorrectly, it discards the signal. The signal received at the destiny node D can be expressed as:

$$y_{rd} = \sqrt{P_R}h_{rd}x(n) + n_{rd} \tag{7}$$

where P_R denotes the transmit power at the relay node R, h_{rd} is modeled as $CN(0, \sigma_{rd}^2)$ and n_{rd} is modeled as $CN(0, N_0)$. After transmission phase 1 and phase 2, the destiny node D combines the signals y_{sd} and y_{rd} using maximum ratio combing (MRC).

So, when the relay node participates in the communication between the source node and the destiny node, the total transmit power can be expressed as:

$$P_{Sum} = P_{S_{coop}} + P_R \tag{8}$$

If all channel links are available, considering the results of incorrectly decoding and correctly decoding at the relay node R, averaging the conditional BER over the Rayleigh distributed random variables, the upper bound of average BER with M-PSK modulation can be expressed as [15]:

$$BER \leq \frac{A^2 N_0^2}{b^2 P_{S_{coop}}^2 \sigma_{sd}^2 \sigma_{sr}^2 log_2 M} + \frac{B^2 N_0^2}{b^2 P_{S_{coop}} P_R \sigma_{sd}^2 \sigma_{rd}^2 log_2 M} \tag{9}$$

where $B = 3(M-1)/8M + sin(2\pi/M)/4\pi - sin(4\pi/M)32\pi$. To obtain the minimum of total transmit power, considering the constraint of performance requirement $BER \leq \varepsilon$, where ε denotes the maximum allowable BER, (8) can be expressed as:

$$\varepsilon = \frac{A^2 N_0^2}{b^2 P_{S_{coop}}^2 \sigma_{sd}^2 \sigma_{sr}^2 log_2 M} + \frac{B^2 N_0^2}{b^2 P_{S_{coop}} P_R \sigma_{sd}^2 \sigma_{rd}^2 log_2 M} \tag{10}$$

By expressing power P_R in term of $P_{S_{coop}}$, the total transmit power minimization problem can be expressed as:

$$\begin{aligned} min \quad & P_{sum} = P_{S_{coop}} + P_R \\ s.t. \quad & P_R = f(P_{S_{coop}}) \\ & P_{S_{coop}} > 0, P_R > 0 \end{aligned} \tag{11}$$

By setting the derivative to be zero, the values of $P_{S_{coop}}$ and P_R leading to the minimum P_{Sum} can be expressed as:

$$P_{S_{coop}} = \sqrt{E/2C} \tag{12}$$

$$P_R = \sqrt{2E/C}\Big/(E - 2D) \tag{13}$$

where, $C = (b^2 \varepsilon \sigma_{sd}^2 \sigma_{sr}^2 log_2 M)/BN_0^2$, $D = A^2 \sigma_{rd}^2/B\sigma_{sr}^2$, $E = (2D + 1 + \sqrt{8D+1})/2$. When BPSK is applied, $A = 1/4, B = 3/16, b = 1$.

So, if we select a relay which can lead to $P_{Sum} < P_{S_{Non-coop}}$, the transmit power can be reduced. But an unsuitable relay results in more energy consumption than direct transmission. To show this, we make a simulation comparing the values of P_{Sum} and $P_{S_{Non-coop}}$, because the formula comparison is very complicated. Figure 2 is the results. The distance between S and D is 30 m. The parameters are shown in Table 1. In the figure, the bigger two circles define the transmission range of S and D according the max transmit power constraint P_{max}. All nodes in the intersection of the two circles can hear either S or D and have the capacity to act as a relay. But only those nodes located in the dotted circle, such as R1, can lead to $P_{Sum} < P_{S_{Non-coop}}$. Nodes outside the dotted circle, such as R2, lead to $P_{Sum} > P_{S_{Non-coop}}$. When the control packets are considered, the suitable relay range becomes smaller.

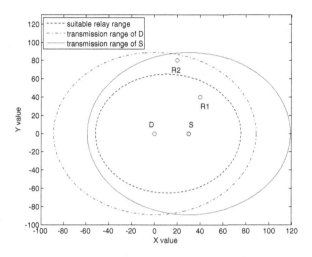

Fig. 2. Suitable relay range

3 Proposed Cooperative MAC Protocol: TPC-MAC

This section presents an overview of 802.11, discusses the basic idea of TPC-MAC protocol, and introduces the details of the protocol.

3.1 Overview of IEEE 802.11 MAC

Most of the works on cooperative MAC are based on the RTS/CTS/ACK mechanism of 802.11 DCF. The source node which needs to transmit a packet detects the channel by sensing. If the channel is detected idle for distributed inter-frame space (DIFS) duration, it backs off for a random time period and then transmits a request-to-send (RTS) packet. If the destiny node correctly received the RTS packet, it transmits a CTS packet after a short inter-frame space (SIFS) time to acknowledge the channel reservation and ready to receive the data packet. During the packets exchange of RTS and CTS, communication between the source node and the destiny node is established and parameters are initialized. The neighbor nodes in the communication range of the source node and the destiny node update their NAV durations by extracting the duration fields in RTS and CTS packets. Once the reservation of channel is completed, the data packet is transmitted by the source node after SIFS duration. Then, the source node waits for an ACK packet from the destiny node. Figure 3 shows the handshake mechanism timing of 802.11 RTS/CTS/ACK.

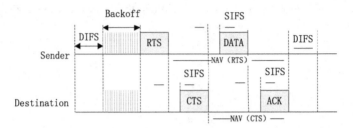

Fig. 3. Handshake mechanism timing of RTS/CTS/ACK

3.2   Basic Idea of TPC-MAC

Although the mechanism of 802.11 RTS/CTS/ACK showed in Fig. 3 solves the problem of hide node, it is not suitable for cooperative communication because of the absence of a relay node. The modifications can be cataloged into two kinds: (1) extending the packet format of RTS and adding a filed for a selected relay node address. Thus, the selected relay can be invited to help the source transmitting packets. (2) Adding a helper ready to send (HTS) packet, which is transmitted by an opportunistic relay developed in some competition with some parameter constraints. The relay transmits the HTS packet to declare to participate in cooperative communication. Nodes in (1) need additional storage overhead to maintain a table containing some parameters, such as relay ID, relay rate and last transmission time. And for a scenario where wireless nodes move fast, the table should be updated frequently, or the selected relay node may be out of the communication range. We propose the TPC-MAC using the second kind of modifications.

TPC-MAC focuses on reducing the total transmit power of a network. A good relay selection strategy is the key point of a cooperative MAC design. Most of the proposed relay selection strategies are based on the instantaneous or average channel state information, transmission rate, throughput, interrupt probability, bit error rate, energy constraint, etc. Based on the perspective of energy balance, reference [11] selects the maximum residual energy node as the relay node. But from the aspects of the node location, the channel state and the network's total energy consumption, this selected relay node may not be the best relay node. A relay node far away from the source node and destination node needs more transmit power than that of a near one under the same parameter constraints. So energy waste cannot be avoided in [11].

To minimize the total energy consumption of the network, we select the best relay under the constraint of destination node's BER. Different relay leads to different total transmit power because of the different values of $P_{S_{coop}}$ and P_R. The best relay node will leads to the minimal total transmit power, which can be expressed as:

$$P_{sum}^k = min\{P_{sum}^i, i = 1, 2, 3, \ldots N\} \tag{14}$$

Where k is the best relay, i denotes the candidate relay node, P_{sum}^k, P_{sum}^i denote the total transmit power of the network with the respectively relay node k, i. N is the number of candidate relay nodes.

3.3 TPC-MAC Protocol Details

TPC-MAC protocol is based on the RTS/CTS/ACK mechanism. We extend the packet format of CTS by adding a power field, which indicates the minimal transmit power for the source node in non-cooperative model. A HTS packet piggybacked $P_{S_{coop}}$ is used to complete the relay competition. All control packets are transmitted with the max power and all data packets are transmitted with the optimal calculated power. In this section, the detail TPC-MAC protocol is explained as follow.

Source Node. When a source node has to transmit a packet, it detects whether the channel is idle. If the channel keeps idling for a DIFS duration, the source node starts a random back off duration. When the back off counter counts down to zero, the source node transmits a RTS packet(at 1 Mb/s) to the destiny node. Then, the source node waits for the CTS packet and the HTS packet respectively from the destiny node and the best relay node. If both the CTS packet and the HTS packet are received in sequence, the source node extracts $P_{S_{coop}}$ from the HTS packet and transmits the data packet after a SIFS duration of receiving the HTS packet. If the source node does not receive any HTS packet in 2 SIFS duration after receiving a CTS packet, it extracts $P_{S_{Non-coop}}$ from the CTS packet and then transmits the data packet. After that, the source waits for the ACK packet from the destiny node. Once the ACK packet is received, the source node will handle the next data packet in its queue; otherwise, it will perform random back off and restart the handshake mechanism.

Destiny Node. If the destiny node receives a RTS packet from the source node, it measures the channel state information (CSI) between the source node and itself, then calculates the transmit power $P_{S_{Non-coop}}$ and attaches the $P_{S_{Non-coop}}$ to the CTS packet. After a SIFS time, the destiny node transmits the CTS packet and waits for the HTS packet from the neighbor nodes. If any HTS packet is not received in 2SIFS duration after it transmits the CTS packet, the destiny node prepares to receive the unique data packet transmitted by the source node. That means the communication between the source node and the destiny node will be in the non-cooperative model, because there is no suitable relay node. If a HTS packet is received, the destiny node waits for two data packets respectively from the source node and the best relay node. MRC is used to process these two data packets. Whether it is in a non-cooperative model or in a cooperative model, the destiny node transmits an ACK packet to the source node after the data packet is correctly received and processed.

Candidate Relay Node. Each relay candidate node that has heard both the RTS packet and the CTS packet estimates the CSI between the source node and itself, the destiny node and itself, and calculates σ_{sr}^2 and σ_{rd}^2 according the strength of the RTS packet and the CTS packet. σ_{sd}^2 can be calculated out according to the non-cooperative model transmit power of the source node $P_{S_{Non-coop}}$ extracted in the CTS packet. Then, using formulas (12) and (13), the relay candidate node calculates the cooperative transmit power $P_{S_{coop}}$, P_R and P_{Sum}. If $P_{S_{Non-coop}}$ is larger than P_{Sum}, the relay candidate node set its countdown timer according the value of P_{Sum}. When the timer reaches zero and the channel is idle, it transmits a HTS packet attached by $P_{S_{coop}}$. If $P_{S_{Non-coop}}$ isn't larger than P_{Sum} or a HTS packet is already overheard transmitting, the relay candidate node keeps silence. Thus, the best relay node, which leads to the minimum total transmit power of the network is selected.

Relay Node. After successfully transmitting the HTS packet, the relay node waits for the data packet transmitted by the source node. If the received data packet can be decoded correctly, the relay forwards it to the destiny node using the calculated transmit power P_R.

The exchange of control packets in TPC-MAC and the corresponding NAV setting are shown in Fig. 4. To notify the transmit power, we extend the CTS packet format and add a 2bytes power field for $P_{S_{Non-coop}}$. The HTS packet format is designed as the same of the CTS packet, and the 2bytes power field is used for $P_{S_{coop}}$. Figure 5 shows the formats of a CTS packet and a HTS packet.

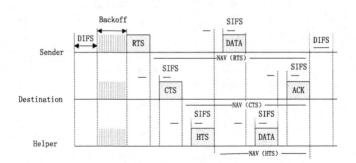

Fig. 4. TPC-MAC timing

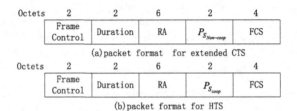

Fig. 5. Packet format

4   Simulation Results

In this section, we demonstrate the performance advantages of the proposed TPC-MAC protocol via some numerical simulations. The WSN we considered is shown in Fig. 1. The range radius is set equal to the transmission range, which is calculated as 89 m. Assuming there are 100 sensor nodes randomly distributed in the circular area. The destiny node is located in the center of the area. The wireless channels are assumed as the Rayleigh flat fading with variance incorporating the position information and not to change during one packet transmission period. Table 1 defines the related parameters, where the energy consumption and some MAC parameters are quoted from [11]. We compare TPC-MAC protocol with MMRE [16] and WcoopMAC [11] in the same environment. MMRE is a direct transmission scheme using energy balance algorithm. WcoopMAC is a cooperative transmission scheme picking the largest residual energy node as the best relay node. MMRE and WcoopMAC are both for the purpose of reducing the energy consumption and extending the network life. Three kinds of lifetime definition are used in most of the proposed cooperative MAC. One is defined as the time when the first sensor node dies. The second is defined as the time when a certain ratio sensor nodes die. The third kind network lifetime is defined as the total data packets received at the destiny node when the network cannot transmit any data packet to the destiny node. For simplicity, neglecting the energy consumption of every node in the sensing or sleeping state, we define the network lifetime as the third kind definition.

Table 1. Parameter setting

Parameter	Value	Parameter	Value
f_c	2.4 GHz	η	1
ε	10^{-3}	α	2
E_{init}	1 J	N_0	40 dBm
E_{es}	0.0001 J	P_{max}	0.2 W
E_p	0.005 J	Data rate	10 KB
E_c	0.01 J	Packet size	8192 bits
E_{cs}	0.0002 J	Transmission range	89 m

NOTE: E_{init}: initial energy per node; E_{es}: energy consumed to receive and calculate a data packet; E_p: energy consumed at the relay node for data processing; E_c: energy consumed by the circuit for a data packet transmitting; E_{cs}: energy consumed for one control packet.

Performances with BER constraint under BPSK modulation over different sensor numbers are compared in Fig. 6. We note that, the lifetime performance is improved as the sensor node number increases, because the total network energy is increased.

MMRE performs the worst, even if it uses both the residual energy information (REI) and CSI. This is because of the absence of cooperation communication mechanism. WcoopMAC employing a cooperative communication scheme and picking the maximum residual energy node as the relay node performs much better than MMRE. TPC-MAC performs the best performance. This is because the relay selection strategy presented in Sect. 3.2 can reduce more energy consumption of the total network.

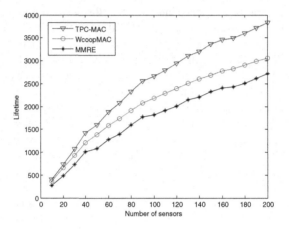

Fig. 6. Network lifetime comparison under different sensor numbers

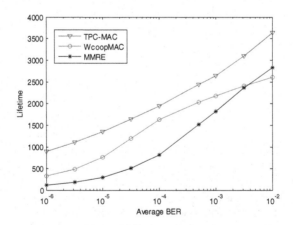

Fig. 7. Lifetime under different BER constraints

Figure 7 considers the network lifetime under the different BER constraints. The number of sensor node is 100. In order to see the performance with high BER requirement, the max transmission power limit is not considered. According to formula (4) or (10), when the BER requirement becomes higher, the transmit power becomes larger because of the smaller BER value. So, we can see in Fig. 7, the network lifetimes of the compared three kinds MAC increase all when the BER value increases. The lifetime of TPC-MAC can remain at about twice as the lifetime of WcoopMAC when the BER value is smaller than 10^{-5}. When the BER requirement is low, the transmission energy saved by power optimization in WcoopMAC can't make up the extra energy consumption of the control packets. Thus, the performance of MMRE is better than WcoopMAC when the BER requirement is low. In TPC-MAC, the candidate relay node compares the total transmission power of cooperative and non-cooperative scheme. If the total transmission power of cooperative scheme is larger than the non-cooperative scheme, the candidate relay keeps silence. So the lifetime of TPC-MAC in Fig. 7 is longer than WcoopMAC and MMRE.

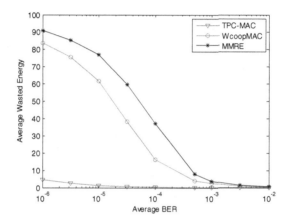

Fig. 8. Average wasted energy comparison under different average BER

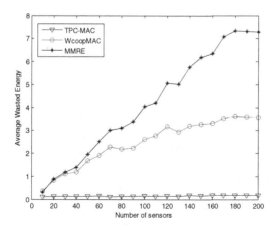

Fig. 9. Average wasted energy comparison under different sensor numbers

We compared the average wasted energy under different BER value with 100 sensor nodes in the network. Figure 8 shows the total network residual energy when the network is dead. When the BER value is smaller than 10^{-4}, TPC-MAC is much more efficient than WcoopMAC and MMRE in terms of energy savings.

Figure 9 considers the network average wasted energy with different sensor node numbers under the constraint of BER value 10^{-3}. The average wasted energy in WcoopMAC and MMRE almost present the linear growth as the number of sensor node increases. The change of sensor node number does not have much impact on TPC-MAC. This is because the TPC-MAC adaptively chooses the cooperative or non-cooperative communication scheme and picks the best relay node which leads to the minimal total transmit power.

5   Conclusion

In this paper, a distributed cooperative MAC protocol named TPC-MAC is proposed to extern the lifetime of distributed WSNs. In this protocol, both total transmission power of the network and CSI are considered to select the best relay node. Under the constraint of average BER value at the destiny node, the transmit power of the source node and the relay node are optimized to achieve the minimal total transmit power. Simulation results demonstrate that TPC-MAC can effectively reduce the energy consumption and improve the network lifetime compared with MMRE and WcoopMAC, especially in a high BER requirement network.

Acknowledgement. This work was supported by Innovation Project of SCI&Tec for College Graduates of Jiangsu Province (CXZZ12_0475) and Innovation Project of Nanjing Institute of Technology (QKJA201304).

References

1. Laneman, J.N., Tse, D.N.C., Wornell, G.W.: Cooperative diversity in wireless networks: efficient protocols and outage behavior. IEEE Trans. Inf. Theor. **50**(12), 3062–3080 (2004)
2. Hunter, T.E., Nosratinia, A.: Diversity through coded cooperation. IEEE Trans. Wirel. Commun. **5**(2), 283–289 (2006)
3. Liu, P., Tao, Z., Narayanan, S., Korakis, T., Panwar, S.S.: Coopmac: a cooperative mac for wireless LANs. IEEE J. Sel. Areas Commun. **25**(2), 340–354 (2007)
4. Yuan, Y., Zheng, B., Lin, W., Dai, C.: An opportunistic cooperative MAC protocol based on cross-layer design. In: International Symposium on Intelligent Signal Processing and Communication Systems, ISPACS 2007, pp. 714–717. IEEE (2007)
5. Zhou, Y., Liu, J., Zheng, L., Zhai, C., Chen, H.: Link-utility-based cooperative MAC protocol for wireless multi-hop networks. IEEE Trans. Wirel. Commun. **10**(3), 995–1005 (2011)
6. Shan, H., Cheng, H.T., Zhuang, W.: Cross-layer cooperative mac protocol in distributed wireless networks. IEEE Trans. Wirel. Commun. **10**(8), 2603–2615 (2011)

7. Kim, D.W., Lim, W.S., Suh, Y.J.: A robust and cooperative MAC protocol for IEEE 802.11a wireless networks. Wirel. Pers. Commun. **67**(3), 689–705 (2012)
8. An, D., Woo, H., Yoo, H., et al.: Enhanced cooperative communication MAC for mobile wireless networks. Comput. Netw. **57**(1), 99–116 (2013)
9. Liu, P., Nie, C., Korakis, T., Erkip, E., Panwar, S., Verde, F., et al.: STicMAC: a MAC protocol for robust space-time coding in cooperative wireless LANs. IEEE Trans. Wirel. Commun. **11**(4), 1358–1369 (2011)
10. Himsoon, T., Siriwongpairat, W.P., Han, Z., Liu, K.J.R.: Lifetime maximization via cooperative nodes and relay deployment in wireless networks. IEEE J. Sel. Areas Commun. **25**(2), 306–317 (2007)
11. Zhai, C., Liu, J., Zheng, L., Xu, H.: Lifetime maximization via a new cooperative MAC protocol in wireless sensor networks. In: IEEE Global Telecommunications Conference, GLOBECOM 2009, Hawaii, USA, pp. 1–6, 30 November–4 December 2009
12. Ibrahim, A., Han, Z., Liu, K.: Distributed energy-efficient cooperative routing in wireless networks. IEEE Trans. Wirel. Commun. **7**(10), 3930–3941 (2008)
13. Razzaque, M.A., Ahmed, M.H.U., Hong, C.S., Lee, S.: QoS-aware distributed adaptive cooperative routing in wireless sensor networks. Ad Hoc Netw. **19**(8), 28–42 (2014)
14. Chen, S., Li, Y., Huang, M., Zhu, Y., Wang, Y.: Energy-balanced cooperative routing in multihop wireless networks. Wirel. Netw. **19**(6), 1087–1099 (2013)
15. Su, W., Sadek, A.K., Liu, K.J.R.: SER performance analysis and optimum power allocation for decode-and-forward cooperation protocol in wireless networks. In: Proceedings of IEEE Wireless Communications and Networking Conference, WCNC 2005, New Orleans, LA, vol. 2, pp. 984–989 (2005)
16. Chen, Y., Zhao, Q.: Maximizing the lifetime of sensor network using local information on channel state and residual energy. In: Proceedings of the Conference on Information Science and Systems, CISS 2005. The Johns Hopkins University, March 2005

Parallel Processing of SAR Imaging Algorithms for Large Areas Using Multi-GPU

Xue Wang[✉], Jiabin Yuan, and Xingfang Zhao

College of Computer Science and Technology, Nanjing University of Aeronautics and Astronautics, Nanjing, China
snow@nuaa.edu.cn

Abstract. The procedure of Synthetic Aperture Radar (SAR) data processing is extraordinarily time-consuming. The traditional processing modes are hard to satisfy the demand for real-time which are based on CPU. There have been some implementations on singe GPU owing to its excellent ability of parallel processing. But there is no implementation on multi-GPU for larger areas. A multi-GPU parallel processing method is proposed including task partitioning and communication hiding in this paper. Furthermore, a detailed comparison of implementation effect among Range Doppler algorithm (RDA), Chirp Scaling algorithm (CSA) and ωK algorithm (ωKA) has been shown in this paper by implementing them on multi-GPU. Experimental results show ωKA has the longest execution time and the highest speedup compared to RDA and CSA. All the algorithms satisfy real-time demand on multi-GPU. Researches can select the most suitable algorithm according to our conclusions. The parallel method can be extended to more GPU and GPU clusters.

Keywords: SAR imaging · Multi-GPU · Parallelization · RDA · CSA · ωKA

1 Introduction

Synthetic Aperture Radar (SAR) is a kind of active microwave imaging radar, which can generate similar images to optical imaging in the condition of low visibility. Due to its capability of all-day, all-weather, SAR technique has been currently a hot topic in the area of Photogrammetry and Remote Sensing. It has huge potential in military, agricultural, forestry, ocean and other fields [1–3]. However, the high resolution SAR system has heavy computation since it receives a huge amount of data and needs complex computation to generate the final images. Some applications have high real-time requirements that lead to higher request to SAR system.

At present, the post processing of SAR image use workstations or giant servers which are based on Central Processing Units (CPU) and is rather time-consuming. Many real-time SAR systems are designed with special DSP and FPGA [4–7]. All of the above need complex programming and expensive hardware devices. At the same time, the increased resolution request of SAR system which causes the rapid growth of computational time.

Graphics Processing Unit (GPU), which was once a highly specialized device designed exclusively for manipulating image data but has grown into a powerful

© Springer International Publishing Switzerland 2015
Z. Huang et al. (Eds.): ICCCS 2015, LNCS 9483, pp. 404–416, 2015.
DOI: 10.1007/978-3-319-27051-7_34

general purpose stream processor–capable of high computational performance on tasks exhibiting sufficient data parallelism. Compute Unified Device Architecture (CUDA), which is an expansion of C, greatly encourages the development of GPU in the field of High Performance Computing (HPC) [9]. The excellent float-point performance and high memory bandwidth available in modern GPU makes them very attractive for SAR data processing.

Up to now, RDA, CSA and ωKA all have been implemented on GPU, especially on a single GPU. An optimal choice is processing the whole data on GPU one-time when the SAR data size doesn't exceed the GPU global memory. The entire processes are on GPU without communication between CPU and GPU. Most of GPU parallel methods adopt this approach [11–14]. References [15, 16] designs a multi-GPU parallel method using RDA and ωKA respectively. In their methods the data size assigned to each GPU is smaller than GPU global memory and the computation are independent on each GPU. All of the approaches above are very restricted when the SAR data size becoming larger than the GPU global memory. Compared to the research above, the work of [10] is very intensive that both asynchronous execution and CUDA stream are considering in their design. While there are still no completely detailed multi-GPU parallel methods of SAR data processing and no researches on the comparison of the three algorithms implemented on GPU.

Inspired by [10], this paper proposes an elaborately-designed parallel method for large scales SAR imaging processing on single-CPU/multi-GPU architecture. SAR data task is divided into sub-task and then be send to each GPU. Then the sub-task is further divided into smaller ones and CUDA steam is created to process them in each GPU. Moreover, CUDA asynchronous execution functions are called to overlap the communication between CPU and GPU.

RDA, CSA and ωKA are all implemented using this new parallel method. Detailed analysis of experimental results is in Sect. 4 including execution time, speed up ratio and parallel efficiency (2 or 4 GPUs are used). A detailed comparison result of the three algorithms is showed in Sect. 5 and researchers can get a few practical proposals when choosing the most suitable algorithms in special occasions. The parallel method is also can be extended to more GPU and GPU clusters.

The rest of paper is organized as follows. Section 2 briefly introduces RDA, CSA, ωKA and GPU features. Section 3 presents the multi-GPU method of SAR imaging algorithms. Then the experimental results and analysis are discussed in Sect. 4. Finally, conclusions are drawn in Sect. 5.

2   Back Ground

2.1   SAR Imaging Algorithms

There are three main high resolution SAR imaging algorithms: RDA, CSA and ωKA. They are all widely used in practical application, so the research on speeding up the SAR imaging procedure is essential and significant. The advantages and disadvantages of these three algorithms have been discussed in detail [8].

Regard raw SAR data as a complex matrix that the rows represent range direction and the columns represents azimuth direction. The principal operations of range direction include vector multiplication, Fast Fourier Transform (FFT)/Inverse Fast Fourier Transform (IFFT) and interpolation. Azimuth direction operations are primarily FFT/IFFT. Normalization operation is needed after each IFFT. Both operations in range and azimuth direction have high parallelism. Each direction can be divided into small data block at rows or columns level (Fig. 1). The datum blocks with low coupling can be processed in parallel on GPU.

Fig. 1. For azimuth processing and for range processing

In the design of this paper, we assume that the raw SAR data are always stored in range direction in host memory and the final images are also stored in range direction. Owing to the conversion between range direction and azimuth direction during the imaging processing procedure, multiple transposed operations (4 times in this paper) are needed. When processing in range direction, cudaMemcpy()/cudaMemcpy Async() is called to transmit data between the CPU and GPU. CudaMemcpy2D()/cudaMemcpy2DAsync() is called in the relative condition.

Figure 2 shows the procedure of the three algorithms. They have much the same algorithm structure roughly and the parallel method is universal when deployed on GPU.

2.2 GPU Features– Asynchronous Concurrent Technology and CUDA Stream

As the outstanding performance of GPU parallel processing, the general-purpose computation on GPU (GPGPU) technology has been playing an important role in massively parallel computing. The architecture of GPGPU is organized into an array of highly threaded stream multiprocessors (SMs). It has numbers of stream processors (SPs) that share control logic and instruction cache [9]. The GPU has evolved into a highly parallel, multithreaded, many-core processor with tremendous computational horsepower and high bandwidth compared to a traditional CPU. It also has a few excellent features such as Asynchronous Concurrent Technology and CUDA stream which make it more efficient for applications with low data coupling.

In order to facilitate concurrent execution between host and device, some function calls are asynchronous: Control is returned to the host thread before the device has completed the requested task. CUDA applications manage concurrency through streams. A stream is a sequence of commands that execute in order. Different streams may execute their commands out of order with respect to one another or concurrently. CUDA stream and Asynchronous Concurrent Technology are used cooperatively. Some devices of compute capability 1.1 [9] or higher can perform copies between page-locked host memory and device memory concurrently with kernel execution.

Benefiting from these two features, the data transfer time and kernel execution time are successfully overlapped in our implementation.

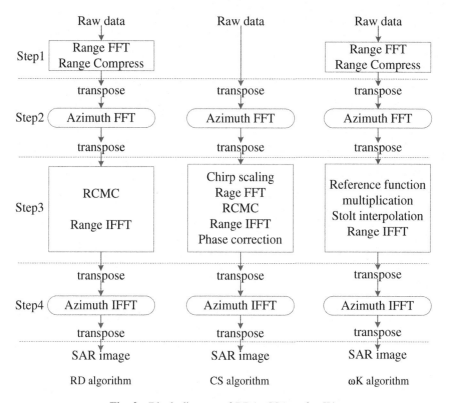

Fig. 2. Block diagram of RDA, CSA and ωKA

3 SAR Algorithm Design on Multi-GPU

3.1 SAR Data Partitioning on Multi-GPU

Each computation step has high parallelism in SAR imaging algorithms. The core idea of the multi-GPU parallel method is dividing the raw SAR data into sub-data equally by range/azimuth direction and then sending to each GPU. In each GPU the sub-data is further divided into smaller ones by range/azimuth direction, which we call cell-data here. Multiple CUDA streams (3 in this paper) are created to process the cell-data. Combing with Asynchronous Concurrent Technology, the transmission time between CPU and GPU is fully overlapped and the effect graph is shown is Sect. 4 (Figs. 5 and 6). Figure 3 shows the cell-data processing on each stream.

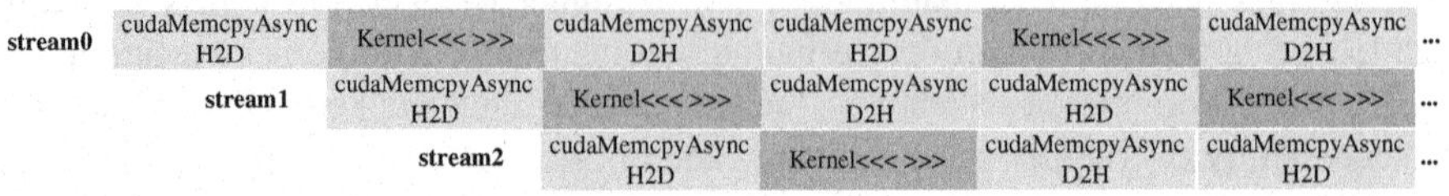

Fig. 3. Data partitioning and asynchronous processing on GPU

3.2   Memory Allocation on CPU and GPU

Double precision floating type is adopted both in design and implementation of this paper. Assume the size of raw SAR data is $Na \times Nr$ (Na represents the number of pulses in azimuth and Nr represent the number of sampling points in range). Page-locked host memory is used and the size is $Na \times Nr$.

Assume the size of cell-data is M_c. Three streams are created on each GPU and three pieces of cell-data are processed simultaneously. The Stolt interpolation operation in ωKA needs two part of space with same size, so it needs six part of storage space in the size of M_c on each GPU. In addition, cufftPlan1d() create plan to allocate space on each stream. The total size of storage space on one GPU is no more than the global memory. All memory spaces are freed after processing.

When processing in azimuth direction, the number of pluses about cell-data is

$$cr = \frac{M_c}{16 \times Na}.$$

When processing in range direction, the number of sampling points in cell-data is

$$ca = \frac{M_c}{16 \times Nr}.$$

3.3   Kernel Design on GPU

In this paper, CUFFT library is utilized to realize FFT/IFFT. Other kernels are self-designed such as Stolt interpolation, fftshift, normalization, vector multiplication et al. In order to improve the execution efficiency both fftshift and transposition adopt the modes of out-place operations. FFTW is supported on CPU implementation.

3.4   Flow Chart of Parallel Method

Figure 4 is the flow chart of parallel method. CSA is used as an example to clearly describe the parallel method using multi-GPU. The parallel method is adapted to all the three kinds of algorithms.

The raw SAR data in CPU memory is stored in range direction in the whole processing procedure. Assume there are 4 GPU (0, 1, 2, 3) and 4 threads are issued to control them by the host side.

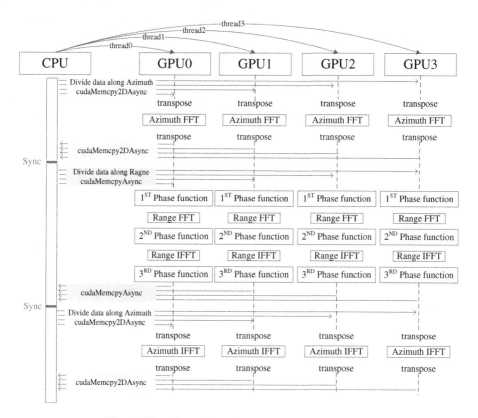

Fig. 4. Flow chart of parallel processing on multi-GPU

(1) Divide the raw SAR data into 4 pieces in azimuth direction. Each one is labelled as *subDataNa$_i$* (*i* represents the number of GPU). Then sending the starting address of *subDataNa$_i$* to *GPU$_i$*.

(2) *subDataNa$_i$* is further divided into cell-data in *thread$_i$*. Each cell-data is labeled as *cell$_j$* (*j* = 0, 1, 2, 3... according to the order of storage in memory). The function of cuadMemcpy2DAsync() is called to transmit cell-data to *GPU$_i$* by 3 streams. *cell$_j$* belongs to *stream$_l$*(l = *j*%3). Then azimuth FFT and transposition are

performed on each stream. The results are sending to CPU by cuadMem-cpy2DAsync().

(3) Synchronous operation is necessary before next data partitioning to guarantee all the GPU have finished (2) on the host side.
(4) Divided the raw SAR data into 4 pieces in range direction. Each one is labelled as $subDataNr_i$(i represents the number of GPU). Then sending the starting address of $subDataNr_i$ to GPU_i.
(5) $subDataNr_i$ is further divided into cell-data in $thread_i$ and each cell-data is labeled as $cell_j$. The cuadMemcpyAsync() is called to transmit cell-data to GPU_i by 3 streams (the same to (2)). Then three times phase multiplication and range FFT/IFFT is performed on each stream. The results are sending to CPU by cuadMemcpyAsync().
(6) Synchronous operation.
(7) The same as (1).
(8) The same as (2) but replace azimuth FFT with azimuth IFFT.
(9) Wait all threads finish their work and the final image matrix is stored in range direction.

In this paper, Pthread is used to issue multiple CPU threads and handle multiple GPUs. The synchronize operation on CPU side adopted mutex lock mechanism.

4 Experiments and Analysis

This paper implements RDA, CSA and ωKA on CPU, single GPU, 2 and 4 GPU respectively. All the implementations adopt double precision floating point type and have the same processing accuracy. The size of SAR simulation data is 1G (8192 × 8192), 2G (16384 × 8192), 4G (32768 × 8192), 8G (32768 × 16384) respectively. Table 1 shows the parameters of experiments.

Table 1. Experimental platform and parameter setting

OS	Centos 6.3
Host memory	32 GB
CPU	Intel(R) Xeon(R) CPU E5-2609, 2.40 GHz, 8 cores
GPU	Tesla C2070 (4)
GPU memory	5 GB
The size of cell-data	256 M
The points number of sinc interpolation	16

4.1 Parellel Effect

CUDA Profiler is utilized to test the parallel effect of the method proposed in this paper. Figures 5 and 6 show some partial results of CSA using 2 GPUs. Obviously, task execution on GPU0 and GPU1 is almost concurrently. On each GPU, there are three streams that the time of kernel computation and data transmission is completely overlapped except the transmission time of the first cell-data and the last one. Figures 5 and 6 are the typical examples in the executing procedure of the three algorithms. Figure 5 represents the case that transmission time is greater than the calculation time of kernels. Figure 6 shows the opposite case. Step 1, 2, 3, 4 (Fig. 2) of RDA belongs to Fig. 5. Step 1, 2, 4 of CSA and ωKA belong to Fig. 5. Step 3 of CSA and ωKA belongs to Fig. 6. Step 1, 2, 4 contains only FFT/IFFT and complex multiplication and the execution is very short. Stolt interpolation in ωKA and three times of phase multiplication in CSA have longer execution time than transmission.

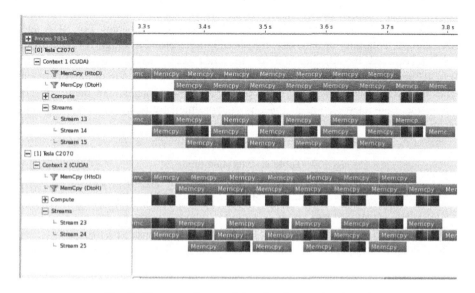

Fig. 5. The case of transmitting time longer than kernel

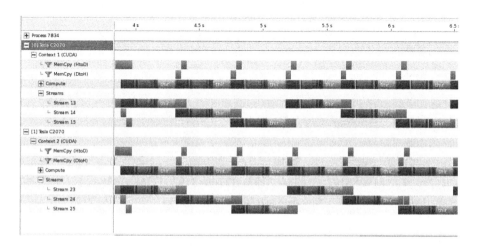

Fig. 6. The case of transmitting time shorter than kernel

4.2   Computational Time and Speedup Ratio on CPU/Single GPU

The computational time of RDA, CSA, ωKA on CPU and single GPU is summarized in Table 2. It must be pointed out that the timing results do not include I/O operations, space allocation and release. From the horizontal view, the execution time of these three algorithms from short to long is RDA, CSA and ωKA. The execution time of ωKA is much longer than other two algorithms. In the vertically view, as the increasing of SAR data size, the execution time has grown exponentially for these three algorithms. The main processing time of ωKA is 33.65 s on GPU and 18798.25 s on CPU, of which the data size is 32768*16384. On the whole, compared to CPU, the performance difference is dramatic on GPU.

Combine with Fig. 7, the difference of speedup ratio is apparent. For RDA and CSA, with the enlarging of data size, the speedup ratio promoted slightly which from 33 to 46. For ωKA, the speedup is about 300 times when the data size changing from 1G to 4G and reached 558 on the size of 8G. In general, the speedup of ωKA is much higher than RDA and CSA though the execution time is longer than them. This is because the stolt interpolation in ωKA is extraordinarily time consumption and the execution on CPU is very slow.

Table 2. Execution time

Data size	RDA (CPU/GPU)	CSA (CPU/GPU)	ωKA (CPU/GPU)
8192 × 8192	57.11 s/1.71 s	89.01 s/2.55 s	1277.98 s/4.42 s
16384 × 8192	116.94 s/3.08 s	178.33 s/4.62 s	2529.61 s/8.53 s
32768 × 8192	243.48 s/6.05 s	382.59 s/9.86 s	5084.54 s/16.91 s
32768 × 16384	556.51 s/11.85 s	781.02 s/18.28 s	18798.25 s/33.65 s

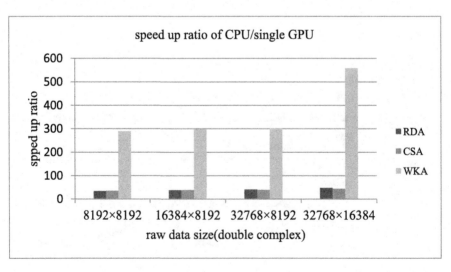

Fig. 7. Speedup ratio

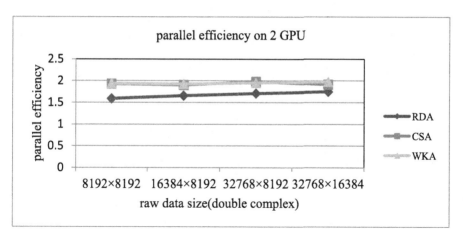

Fig. 8. Parallel efficiency on 2 GPU

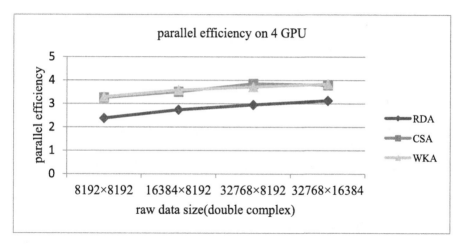

Fig. 9. Parallel efficiency on 4 GPU

4.3 Parallel Efficiency

Figures 8 and 9 illustrate the parallel efficiency on 2 GPU and 4 GPU respectively. The calculation of parallel efficiency is based on the follow formula. S represents the execution time of a single GPU and N represents the execution time of 2 or 4 GPUs.

$$parallel \cdot efficiency = \frac{S}{N}$$

As the increasing of the data size, the parallel efficiency increased gently. CSA and ωKA can reach 1.96, while RDA can only reach 1.75 on 2 GPU. On 4 GPU, CSA and ωKA could reach 3.84 and RDA reached 3.13. The reason is that the execution time of

RDA is very short and the average synchronization time between GPUs account for 8 % according to our statistics. While the effect of synchronization time on CSA and ωKA is very slightly that only 1 %. The parallel method could be extended to more GPUs without decreasing parallel efficiency.

Table 3. Processing rate

Algorithms	RDA	CSA	ωKA
1 GPU	691 MB/s	448 MB/s	224 MB/s
2 GPU	1208 MB/s	883 MB/s	480 MB/s
4 GPU	2163 MB/s	1698 MB/s	933 MB/s

4.4   Real-Time Analysis

Based on the analysis herein above, the processing speed of our method on single GPU could reach 691 MB/s on RDA, 448 MB/s on CSA and 224 MB/s in ωKA. Detailed processing speed on multi-GPUs is shown in Table 3. The processing speed is much greater than the downlink data rate of Envisat ASAS and RADARSAT-2 which are 100 MB/s and 105 MB/s respectively.

5   Conclusions and Future Work

RDA, CSA and ωKA are all reasonable approaches for SAR data to its precision processing. CSA is more complex and takes longer in its implementation but promises a better resolution in some extreme cases. CSA is more phase preserving and it avoids computationally extensive and complicated interpolation used by the RDA. While ωKA is the most complex and time consuming algorithm due to its stolt interpolation. Nevertheless, it can offer the best quality SAR images in most cases. The detailed comparison of algorithms for implementation on multi-GPU is shown in Table 4 (the data size is 8G). Researchers can select the most suitable algorithm according to our conclusions.

Table 4. Comparison diagram of RDA, CSA and ωKA

Algorithms		RDA	CSA	ωKA
Computation time on single GPU		11.85 s	18.28 s	33.65 s
Speedup ratio		47	44	558
Parallel efficiency	2 GPU	1.75	1.91	1.97
	4 GPU	3.12	3.79	3.83
Usage scenario		Small-squint, small-aperture	Wide-swath	Large-beam, large-squint

We also put forward some novel ideas about SAR imaging on GPU platform in the future work. Our experimental results have demonstrated that the actual time request of SAR imaging could be satisfied when using our on multi-GPU. That is to say the amount of calculation is no longer a problem thanks to the excellent computational power of GPU. We could design SAR imaging algorithms from another aspect. Such as in order to improve the resolution of SAR image, the interpolation points can be increased in ωKA. The precision implementation of RDA that combines with RCMC interpolation on GPU is no longer a complex question.

References

1. Soumekh, M.: Moving target detection in foliage using along track monopulse synthetic aperture radar imaging. IEEE Trans. Image Process. **6**(8), 1148–1163 (1997)
2. Koskinen, J.T., Pulliainen, J.T., Hallikainen, M.T.: The use of ERS-1 SAR data in snow melt monitoring. IEEE Trans. Geosci. Remote Sens. **35**(3), 60–610 (1997)
3. Sharma, R., Kumar, S.B., Desai, N.M., Gujraty, V.R.: SAR for disaster management. IEEE Aerosp. Electron. Syst. Mag. **23**(6), 4–9 (2008)
4. Liang, C., Teng, L.: Spaceborne SAR real-time quick-look system. Trans. Beijing Inst. Technol. **6**, 017 (2008)
5. Tang, Y.S., Zhang, C.Y.: Multi-DSPs and SAR real-time signal processing system based on cPCI bus. In: 2007 1st Asia and Pacific Conference on Synthetic Aperture Radar, pp. 661–663. IEEE (2007)
6. Xiong, J.J., Wang, Z.S., Yao, J.P.: The FPGA design of on board SAR real time imaging processor. Chin. J. Electron. **33**(6), 1070–1072 (2005)
7. Marchese, L., Doucet, M., Harnisch, B., Suess, M., Bourqui, P., Legros, M., Bergeron, A.: Real-time optical processor prototype for remote SAR applications. In: Proceedings of SPIE7477, Image and Signal Processing for Remote Sensing XV, pp. 74771H–74771H (2009)
8. Cumming, I.G., Wong, F.H.: Digital Processing of Synthetic Aperture Radar Data: Algorithms and Implementation. Artech House, Norwood (2005)
9. Zhang, S., Chu, Y.L.: GPU High Performance Computing: CUDA. Waterpower Press, Bejing (2009)
10. Meng, D.D., Hu, Y.X., Shi, T., Sun, R.: Airborne SAR real-time imaging algorithm design and implementation with CUDA on NVIDIA GPU. J. Radars **2**(4), 481–491 (2013)
11. Wu, Y.W., Chen, J., Zhang, H.Q.: A real-time SAR imaging system based on CPUGPU heterogeneous platform. In: 11th International Conference on Signal Processing, pp. 461–464. IEEE (2012)
12. Malanowski, M., Krawczyk, G., Samczynski, P., Kulpa, K., Borowiec, K., Gromek, D.: Real-time high-resolution SAR processor using CUDA technology. In: 2013 14th International Radar Symposium (IRS), pp. 673–678. IEEE (2013)
13. Bhaumik Pandya, D., Gajjar, N.: Parallelization of synthetic aperture radar (SAR) imaging algorithms on GPU. Int. J. Comput. Sci. Commun. (IJCSC) **5**, 143–146 (2014)
14. Song, M.C., Liu, Y.B., Zhao, F.J., Wang, R., Li, H. Y.: Processing of SAR data based on the heterogeneous architecture of GPU and CPU. In: IET International Radar Conference 2013, pp. 1–5. IET (2013)

15. Ning, X., Yeh C., Zhou, B., Gao, W., Yang, J.: Multiple-GPU accelerated range-doppler algorithm for synthetic aperture radar imaging. In: 2011 IEEE Radar Conference (RADAR), pp. 698–701. IEEE (2011)
16. Tiriticco, D., Fratarcangeli, M., Ferrara, R., Marra, S.: Near-real-time multi-GPU wk algorithm for SAR processing. In: Proceedings of the 2014 Conference on Big Data from Space, pp. 263–266. Publications Office of the European Union (2014)

An Extreme Learning Approach to Fast Prediction in the Reduce Phase of a Cloud Platform

Qi Liu[1], Weidong Cai[1], Jian Shen[1(✉)], Baowei Wang[1], Zhangjie Fu[1], and Nigel Linge[2]

[1] Nanjing University of Information Science and Technology,
219 Ningliu Road, Nanjing 210044, Jiangsu, China
S_shenjian@126.com
[2] The University of Salford, Salford, Greater Manchester M5 4WT, UK

Abstract. As a widely used programming model for the purposes of processing large data sets, MapReduce (MR) becomes inevitable in data clusters or grids, e.g. a Hadoop environment. However, experienced programmers are needed to decide the number of reducers used during the reduce phase of the MR, which makes the quality of MR scripts differ. In this paper, an extreme learning method is employed to recommend potential number of reducer a mapped task needs. Execution time is also predicted for user to better arrange their tasks. According to the results, our method can provide fast prediction than SVM with similar accuracy maintained.

Keywords: MapReduce · Extreme learning · Fast prediction

1 Introduction

MapReduce (MR) [1] has become the most popular distributed computing model used in a cloud environment, where large-scale datasets can be handled/processed using map and reduce procedures in the cloud infrastructure transparently. Two types of nodes are maintained in a cluster based on the MR framework; they are JobTracker and Task-Tracker nodes. The Jobtracker, which runs on the data node, coordinates MapReduce jobs.

The MR, as well as loud computing has become a hotspot in the academia [2]. Many people try to optimize it. Proposals in [3–6] may predict the execution states of mapreduce, but they cannot precisely predict it. In this paper, a novel prediction model based on the ELM algorithm is proposed to facilitate the execution of reduce operations in a cloud environment.

The rest sections are organized as followed. Related work is given in Sect. 2, followed by Sect. 3, where our prediction approach is detailed. In Sect. 4, testing environment and corresponding scenarios are design for the verification and evaluation. Finally, conclusion and future work are discussed in Sect. 5.

© Springer International Publishing Switzerland 2015
Z. Huang et al. (Eds.): ICCCS 2015, LNCS 9483, pp. 417–423, 2015.
DOI: 10.1007/978-3-319-27051-7_35

2   Related Work

Offline or online profiling has been proposed by previous work to predict application resource requirements by using benchmarks or real application workloads. Wood et al. [3] designed a general approach to estimate the resource requirements of applications running in a virtualized environment. They profiled different types of virtualization overhead and built a model to map file in the local system into the virtualized system. Their model focused on relating the resource requirements of real hardware platform to the virtual one. Islam et al. [4] studied the changing workload demands by starting new VM instances, and proposed a prediction model for adaptively resource provisioning in a cloud. Complex machine learning techniques were proposed in [5] to create accurate performance models of applications. They estimated the usage state of resource by an approach named PQR2. Jing et al. [6] presented a model that can predict the computing resource consumption of MapReduce applications based on a Classified and Regression Tree.

3   A Prediction Model Based on NO-ELM

Artificial neural networks (ANNs), as an effective method have been widely applied in applications involving classification or function approximation [7]. However, the training speed of ANNs is much slower than what a practical application needs. In order to overcome this drawback, the approximation capability of feed is employed to advance neural networks, especially in a limited training set. One of the most important achievement of this work is putting forward a novel learning algorithm in single hidden layer feed forward neural network (SLFNs) [8], i.e. ELM [8–13].

3.1   Number of Hidden Neurons Optimized ELM (NO-ELM)

In the basic ELM algorithm, the number noted as L, is usually generated through iterating. To find the min $RMSE$ or R^2 that is close to 1, L needs to be trained into the best value. However, original method is has the disadvantage that the number may be different through different experiments. An optimized algorithm is therefore introduced to achieve the process, as shown in Algorithm 1.

Algorithm 1. Generate the number of hidden neurons

Input:
    TS: size of the training set
    IT: times of iteration
    RT: times of running

Output: L: the number of hidden neurons

Steps:

    1.   While times of running is smaller than RT

    2.   While times of iteration is smaller than IT

    3.   If the accuracy Acc get this time is smaller the $RMSE$

    4.   RMSE = Acc

    5. L_{RT} equals the number of iteration

    6.   End While

    7.   If there is no L_{RT} in the Collection <K, V>

    8.   Add <L_{RT}, 1> to the result Collection <K, V>

    9.   else

    10.   Get the number of element *value* in Collection <K, V>

    11.   Add < L_{RT}, *value*+1> to the result Collection <K, V>

    12.   End If

    13. End While

    14. For each L_{RT} in Collection <K, V>

    15.   Find L_{RT} with the max *value*

    16.   Record L_{RT} as L

    17. End For

    18. Return L

In Algorithm 1, the size of training set, as well as the time of iteration and execution is collected as input parameters. The number L is generated as the output.

3.2   The Process to Build the Prediction Model Based on NO-ELM

The building progresses of the prediction model for the number of reducers and the execution time are as follows:

Step 1: **Data preprocessing.** First, samples that may contain great network congestion need to be removed. Then, the refined datasets will be split into training samples and test samples. The training samples are used for training prediction model and test samples are used to check if the prediction model has been well trained.

Step 2: **Model training.** To build the prediction model, training parameters of the model are obtained by using the training samples generated in Step1. The Specific processes include:

(a) randomly generate the weights between input layer and hidden layer, where hidden layer neurons w and the threshold b are set;
(b) calculate the output matrix H of hidden layer;
(c) work out output layer weights.

Step 3: **Data validation.** Use the data generated in Step 1 to validate the NO-ELM prediction model. According to the parameters trained in step 2 to get the predictive value of test set, and compare with the actual value to verify prediction performance of the model.

For the model to predict the number of reducers, the data format is set as *{reducer_no, execution_time, input_data_vol}*. Under the default circumstance, the prediction model recommends the number of reducers that can complete the task as soon as possible. The input format can then be simplified as *{reducer_no, input_data_vol}*. If the complete time of a task needs to be specified, the prediction model will recommend corresponding number of reducers. For doing that, the input format is as *{execution_time, input_data_vol}*.

4 Experiment and Analysis

In order to test the performance the new prediction model, a practical Hadoop environment was built consisting of personal computers and a server. Each personal computer has 12 GB of memory, a single 500 GB disk and dual-core processors. The server is equipped with 288 GB of memory, a 10 TB SATA driver. Eight virtual instances are therefore created in the server with same specification as personal computers, i.e. the same amount of memory and storage space, as well as the same number of processors. In terms of role configuration, the server suns as the name node, whilst the virtual machines and personal computers run as the data nodes.

A shared open dataset [6] was manipulated as the input workload containing 26 GB of text files. The dataset was further separated into 5 groups for testing purposes. A K-means (KM) clustering algorithm provided by Purdue MR Benchmarks Suite was used for partitioning operation in the cloud platform.

Before training the NO-ELM prediction model, the samples are prepared following the equation below in order to meet the requirement of the model:

$$h_t = (s_t - \bar{s})/(\bar{s}) \tag{1}$$

where $\bar{s}$ is the mean value of sample series, s_t is the value of one sample. Here, we remove s_t from the samples if h_t is greater than 5 % and s_t is greater than $\bar{s}$ considering the cases where these samples may be affected by the network congestion.

The sample data are then normalized following the equation below:

$$s_t = (s_t - s_{\min})/(s_{\max} - s_{\min}) \tag{2}$$

where $s_{\min}$ is the minimum value of sample series, $s_{\max}$ is the maximum value of samples. After normalization, the variation range of sample data is [0, 1].

In order to keep the generality, experiments in all performance evaluation parameters were run 50 times to get the average value. All the experiments bellow were operated under the circumstances that reduce tasks started when map tasks had finished using "Sigmoidal Function" as activation function. To verify the performance of the NO-ELM prediction model, we compare the predicted values of the NO-ELM prediction model with the test set samples (real values) and the SVM model.

4.1   NO-ELM for Predicting the Number of Reducers

The input data size varies from 1 GB to 23.5 GB, while the number of reducers is selected from 4 to 8. As seen in Fig. 1, the predicted values generated by NO-ELM show a better trend following the real results than the SVM.

In Table 1, 12 groups of the training time are depicted running the application with NO-ELM and SVM consumed, where the NO-ELM consumes less time than SVM in the train stage.

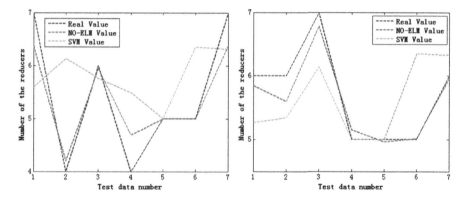

Fig. 1. Experiment comparison for prediction model on the number of reducers

Table 1. Comparison between NO-ELM and SVM in training time

	1	2	3	4	5	6	7	8	9	10	11	12
NO-ELM (ms)	32	47	36	45	54	32	33	43	47	40	41	39
SVM (ms)	384	446	415	394	363	347	407	396	341	387	471	468

4.2   NO-ELM for Predicting Execution Time

In this section, two samples are prepared in each group for training and testing purposes, as shown in Table 2. The simulation results are depicted in Fig. 2.

Table 2. Comparison between NO-ELM and SVM in training time

Group no.	Input data size	Number of split datasets	Number of training set	Number of test set
1	1 GB	68	66	2
2	2 GB	5	3	2
3	5 GB	63	61	2
4	8.5 GB	56	54	2
5	10 GB	15	13	2
6	12.5 GB	57	55	2
7	16 GB	53	51	2
8	17 GB	16	14	2
9	19.5 GB	54	52	2
10	23.5 GB	62	60	2
11	25 GB	8	6	2
12	26.5 GB	67	65	2

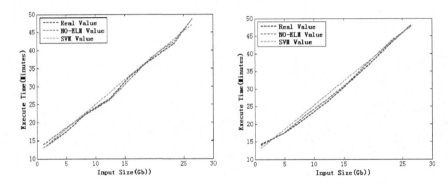

Fig. 2. Experiment comparison for prediction model of execution time

5 Conclusion

In this paper, an extreme learning machine with the number of hidden neurons optimized (NO-ELM) has been introduced to analyze and predict the data. The NO-ELM
method has been implemented in a real Hadoop environment, where the SVM algorithm has also been replicated for comparison purposes. Through the results, the
NO-ELM has depicted better performance in the prediction of execution time and the
number of reducers to be used.

Acknowledgement. This work is supported by the NSFC (61300238, 61232016, U1405254,
61373133), Basic Research Programs (Natural Science Foundation) of Jiangsu Province
(BK20131004), Scientific Support Program of Jiangsu Province (BE2012473) and Suzhou City
(SYG201315), and the PAPD fund.

References

1. Dean, J., Ghemawat, S.: MapReduce: simplified data processing on large clusters. Commun. ACM **51**(1), 107–113 (2008)
2. Fu, Z., Sun, X., Liu, Q., Zhou, L., Shu, J.: Achieving efficient cloud search services: multi-keyword ranked search over encrypted cloud data supporting parallel computing. IEICE Trans. Commun. **E98-B**(1), 190–200 (2015)
3. Wood, T., Cherkasova, L., Ozonat, K., Shenoy, P.D.: Profiling and modeling resource usage of virtualized applications. In: Issarny, V., Schantz, R. (eds.) Middleware 2008. LNCS, vol. 5346, pp. 366–387. Springer, Heidelberg (2008)
4. Islam, S., Keung, J., Lee, K., Liu, A.: Empirical prediction models for adaptive resource provisioning in the cloud. Future Gener. Comput. Syst. **28**(1), 155–162 (2012)
5. Matsunaga, A., Fortes, J.A.B.: On the use of machine learning to predict the time and resources consumed by applications. In: Proceedings of the 2010 10th IEEE/ACM International Conference on Cluster, Cloud and Grid Computing, pp. 495–504. IEEE Computer Society (2010)
6. Piao, J.T., Yan, J.: Computing resource prediction for MapReduce applications using decision tree. In: Sheng, Q.Z., Wang, G., Jensen, C.S., Xu, G. (eds.) APWeb 2012. LNCS, vol. 7235, pp. 570–577. Springer, Heidelberg (2012)
7. Oong, T.H., Isa, N.A.: Adaptive evolutionary artificial neural networks for pattern classification. IEEE Trans Neural Networks **22**, 1823–1836 (2011)
8. Huang, B., Zhu, Q.Y., Siew, C.K.: Extreme learning machine: theory and applications. Neurocomputing **70**, 489–501 (2006)
9. Samat, A., Du, P., Liu, S., Li, J., Cheng, L.: E2LMs: ensemble extreme learning machines for hyperspectral image classification. IEEE J. Sel. Topics Appl. Earth Observ. Remote Sens. **7**(4), 1060–1069 (2014)
10. Bianchini, M., Scarselli, F.: On the complexity of neural network classifiers: a comparison between shallow and deep architectures. IEEE Trans. Neural Netw. Learn. Syst. 1553–1565 (2013)
11. Wang, N., Er, M.J., Han, M.: Generalized single-hidden layer feedforward networks for regression problems. IEEE Trans. Neural Netw. Learn. Syst. **26**(6), 1161–1176 (2015)
12. Giusti, C., Itskov, V.: A no-go theorem for one-layer feedforward networks. IEEE Trans. Neural Netw. **26**(11), 2527–2540 (2014)
13. Huang, G., Zhou, H., Ding, X., Zhang, R.: Extreme learning machine for regression and multiclass classification. IEEE Trans. Syst. Man Cybern. B Cybern. **42**(2), 513–529 (2012)

Data Analysis in Cloud

Wind Speed and Direction Predictions Based on Multidimensional Support Vector Regression with Data-Dependent Kernel

Dingcheng Wang[✉], Yujia Ni, Beijing Chen, Zhili Cao,
Yuhang Tian, and Youzhi Zhao

School of Computer and Software, Nanjing University of Information Science
and Technology, Nanjing 210044, China
dcwang@nuist.edu.cn

Abstract. The development of wind power has a higher requirement for the accurate prediction of wind. In this paper, a trustworthy and practical approach, Multidimensional Support Vector Regression (MSVR) with Data-Dependent Kernel(DDK), is proposed. In the prediction model, we applied the longitudinal component and lateral component of the wind speed, changed from original wind speed and direction, as the input of this model. Then the Data-Dependent kernel is instead of classic kernels. In order to prove this model, actual wind data from NCEP/NCAR is used to test. MSVR with DDK model has higher accuracy comparing with MSVR without DDK, single SVR, Neural Networks.

Keywords: Wind forecasting · Multidimensional · Support vector regression · Data-dependent kernel

1 Introduction

As everyone knows, every walk of life is closely related to the wind. Therefore, accurate prediction of wind speed and direction is important and necessary. However, wind as a meteorological factor is an intermittent and non-dispatchable energy source, and then this research work is not going very well.

In literatures, many different techniques for predicting wind speed have been researched. The first is the physical method, which is used worldwidely for the large-scale weather [1]. Physical method does not apply to short-term prediction because it must use a long time to correction. The second is statistical method, including persistence method [2], time series [3], Kalman filter [4] and Grey forecasting [5]. Differ from physical method, it finds historical data's relevance to predict wind speed regardless of the wind physical speed. The third is learning method, like neural networks [6] and support vector regression [7]. The essence of learning method is extract the relationship between the input and output using artificial intelligence method instead of describing in the form of analytical expression.

In the above method, most studies concentrate on the wind speed prediction. However, direction is also an important influence factor to wind power. Forecasting the wind speed and direction simultaneously is more reasonable than forecasting respectively.

© Springer International Publishing Switzerland 2015
Z. Huang et al. (Eds.): ICCCS 2015, LNCS 9483, pp. 427–436, 2015.
DOI: 10.1007/978-3-319-27051-7_36

Therefore, the method of Multidimensional Support Vector Regression (MSVR) is presented to predict the wind speed and direction simultaneously in this paper.

2   The Method

2.1   Geometry of MSVR Kernel

When it comes to wind speed and direction prediction, two SVR models may be usually built [8]. In this paper, MSVR is proposed to predict the wind speed and wind direction at the same time.

The most important difference of SVR and MSVR is one output in SVR turned into multiple outputs in MSVR. Therefore, for regression problems, MSVR's task is constructing the correlation function between multiple inputs and multiple outputs.

For the minimum empirical risks and error on the predictions like classification problem [9], the multi-regression problem is transferred to an optimization problem. Based on the idea, the training of the MSVR is formulated directly as a second order cone programming in the primal space as follows:

$$
\min \sum_{j=1}^{n} ||\boldsymbol{w}_j||^2 + C \sum_{i=1}^{l} \xi_i^2
$$
$$
s.t. ||\boldsymbol{y}_i - \boldsymbol{W} \cdot \phi(\boldsymbol{x}_i) - \boldsymbol{B}|| \leq \varepsilon + \xi_i \tag{1}
$$
$$
\xi_i \geq 0
$$

To SVR, Eq. (1) could be solved by formulated in the dual space. But the method can't be used here directly since the inequality constraint is not affine. Therefore, a loss function defined in the hypersphere is lead up.

$$
L_\varepsilon(z) = \begin{cases} 0 & z \leq \varepsilon \\ (z - \varepsilon)^2 & z > \varepsilon \end{cases} \tag{2}
$$

After the above loss function introduced, the programming problem can be solved directly in the original space. The training of MSVR can be equivalently rewritten as an unconstrained optimization problem

$$
\min \sum_{j=1}^{n} ||\boldsymbol{w}_j||^2 + C \sum_{i=1}^{l} L_\varepsilon(||\boldsymbol{y}_i - \boldsymbol{W} \cdot \phi(\boldsymbol{x}_i) - \boldsymbol{B}||) \tag{3}
$$

Defining

$$
\beta_{i,j} = -\frac{2}{C} \cdot \frac{\partial}{\partial w_j} L_\varepsilon(||\boldsymbol{y}_i - \boldsymbol{W} \cdot \phi(\boldsymbol{x}_i) - \boldsymbol{B}||) \tag{4}
$$

then

$$w_j = \sum_{i=1}^{l} \phi(x_i)\beta_{i,j} \tag{5}$$

According to Eq. (5), the optimal solution w_j is represented as a linear combination of feature functions with Riemann-Stieltjes integral. We can get the unconstrained optimization problem (6) by substituting Eq. (5) into equation

$$\min\lambda \sum_{j=1}^{n} (\sum_{i,p=1}^{l} \beta_{i,j}\beta_{p,j}k(x_i,x_p)) + \sum_{i=1}^{l} L_\varepsilon(\|y_i - \sum_{p=1}^{l} \beta_p k(x_i,x_p) - B\|) \tag{6}$$

problem (3). The unconstrained formulation can be solved by the Newton-Raphson method [10].

2.2   A Data Dependent Way for Optimizing Kernel

For the reason of the practical data is noisy, one kernel function can never be suitable to all of data set. To improve the accuracy of prediction, a kernel function must be built on the basis of the training data set without breaking the construction of points. Support vector points determine the hyperplane of training results, so the space around support vector should be reduce and other area should be enlarged on the contrary. The literature [11] proposed a method that the conformal transformation $c(x)$ is used to improve the kernel function. The conformal transformation can refactor kernel function without changing the angle of whole space. With conformal mapping, the kernel function is reconstructed as:

$$\tilde{K}(x,x') = c(x)c(x')K(x,x'), \tag{7}$$

where $c(x)$ is the positive definite function about $\mathbf{x}$, $\tilde{K}(x,x')$ is the data dependent kernel function satisfying Mercer condition. It can be proved easily. Here we set

$$c(\mathbf{x}) = \sum_{x_i \in SV} h_i \exp(\|\mathbf{x} - \mathbf{x}_i\|^2 / 2\tau_i^2)$$

$$\tau_i^2 = \frac{1}{l}\sum_{p}^{l} \|\mathbf{x}_p - \mathbf{x}_i\|^2 \tag{8}$$

At the moment, if we choose RBF as the original kernel function, the scale factor can be written as

$$\sqrt{\tilde{g}(x)} = \frac{h_i^n}{\sigma^n}e^{nr^2/2\tau_i^2}\sqrt{1 + \frac{\sigma^2}{\tau_i^4}r^2}, \tag{9}$$

where $r = \|x - x_i\|$. From Eq. (9), the value of $\sqrt{\tilde{g}(x)}$ is smaller around x_i when $h_i < \sigma$ and $\tau < \sigma/\sqrt{n}$. Then $\sqrt{\tilde{g}(x)}$ is controlled by changing h_i. That is to say, we can compress the space by regulating h_i to improve the accuracy of regression.

3   Model

In this paper, a model used to predict the wind speed and direction is proposed, and it is shown as Fig. 1. In feature extraction, we choose wind speed, wind direction, air temperature, pressure, potential temperature, precipitable water, relative humidity and sea level pressure as features of data set.

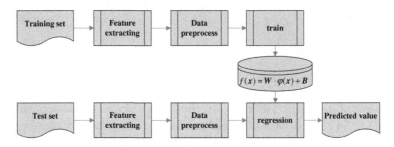

Fig. 1. The model of wind prediction

3.1   Data Preprocessing

The prediction method before is that construct two SVRs and forecast wind speed and wind direction respectively. Here we break the traditional thinking and use multi-output SVR. When using multi-output SVR, the influence between inputs have been considered. Wind speed and wind direction fluctuate greatly. Hence, we must make inputs have more dependency. Here a method that decomposes wind speed to two components according wind direction is proposed. The method can be called component method.

In this method, which is divided two steps, firstly, the prevailing direction is found out according the wind direction in data. Then wind speed can be divided into two component, portrait and landscape based on the prevailing wind direction. In order to find the prevailing wind direction, here a calculation way is shown:

$$\bar{\theta} = \begin{cases} \tan^{-1}(S/C) & S > 0, C > 0 \\ \tan^{-1}(S/C) + \pi & C < 0 \\ \tan^{-1}(S/C) + 2\pi & S < 0, C > 0 \end{cases}, \tag{10}$$

where, $S = \sum\limits_{i=1}^{l} \sin \theta_i$ and $C = \sum\limits_{i=1}^{l} \cos \theta_i$ θ is the angle between wind vector and north vector.

Secondly, the wind direction vector is divided into lateral component and longitudinal component. It can be achieved by the following formulas:

$$v_{iy} = v\cos(\theta_i - \bar{\theta})$$
$$v_{ix} = v\sin(\theta_i - \bar{\theta}) \qquad (11)$$

Dividing the wind speed into two components with above method can link wind speed and wind direction together more closer and the relationship can appear in the process of multi-output SVR.

3.2   MSVR with Data-Dependent Kernel

In this section, the new method that MSVR with Data-Dependent kernel would be shown. According the introduction above, We have known that MSVR is to find the variables W and B. We also have known solving the Eq. (6) can find the variables meeting the requirements. The unconstrained formulation can be solved by the Newton-Raphson method.

$$L(\boldsymbol{\beta}_{aug}) = \lambda \boldsymbol{\beta}_{aug}^T \boldsymbol{K}_{aug} \boldsymbol{\beta}_{aug} + \sum_{i=1}^{l} L_\varepsilon(\|\boldsymbol{y}_i - \boldsymbol{K}_i^T \boldsymbol{\beta}_{aug}\|). \qquad (12)$$

Using the Newton-Raphson method to minimize the Eq. (12), $\boldsymbol{G} = \frac{\partial L(\boldsymbol{\beta}_{aug})}{\partial \boldsymbol{\beta}_{aug}}$, $\boldsymbol{H} = \frac{\partial^2 L(\boldsymbol{\beta}_{aug})}{\partial^2 \boldsymbol{\beta}_{aug}}$. We can get the convergent result through the iterative formula:

$$\boldsymbol{\beta}_{aug}^{new} = \boldsymbol{\beta}_{aug}^{old} - \alpha \boldsymbol{H}^{-1}\boldsymbol{G}, \qquad (13)$$

where, α is the iteration step.

Leading the Data-Dependent kernel into the method, the Eq. (12) can be changed to

$$L(\boldsymbol{\beta}_{aug}) = \lambda \boldsymbol{\beta}_{aug}^T \tilde{\boldsymbol{K}}_{aug} \boldsymbol{\beta}_{aug} + \sum_{i=1}^{Msv} (\|\boldsymbol{y}_i - \tilde{\boldsymbol{K}}_i^T \boldsymbol{\beta}_{aug}\| - \varepsilon)^2, \qquad (14)$$

Where, Msv is the set of support vector when $\|\boldsymbol{y}_i - \boldsymbol{K}_i^T\boldsymbol{\beta}_{aug}\| > \varepsilon$.

Finally the convergent result $\hat{\boldsymbol{\beta}}_{aug}$ can be gained. Then the needed variables W and B can be calculated. Hence the regression model can be got.

The process of MSVR with Data-Dependent kernel is divided into two parts, the training samples set and test samples set.

The training and prediction process is described as follows:

Training Input: data set X;

Step 1: Choosing the classic kernel K as the original kernel and using X to learn a regression model with Eq. (12), we get Msv and $\boldsymbol{\beta}_{aug}$;

Step 2: Calculating the $c(x)$ with Eq. (8) utilizing the information of Msv, we get Data-Dependent kernel $\tilde{K}$;

Step 3: Relearning a regression model with Eq. (14), the Msv and β_{aug} are updated;

Step 4: If β_{aug} is not iterative, repeat from Step2 to Step 3. Otherwise calculating the variables W and B;

Training Output: regression model.

Prediction Input: test samples x;

Step 1: Bringing x to regression model with the last Msv, we get the predicted value;

Prediction Output: the predicted value y correspongding to x.

4   Experiment

In this section, a set of experiments is performed to compare the performances of MSVR with Data-Dependent kernel to some other regression algorithms, like MSVR without Data-Dependent kernel, single SVR, NN.

Here the data is extracted from the NCEP/NCAR Reanalysis project. We choose 8 features from the 4-times daily data, containing U-wind, V-wind, air temperature, potential temperature, pressure, precipitable water, relative humidity and sea level pressure. Figure 2 shows the 1464 data points of wind speed and direction at Wulu-muqi, China in 2000.

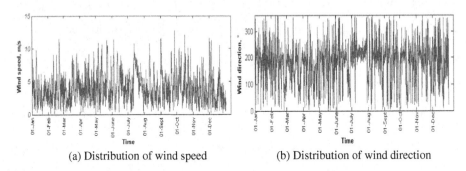

(a) Distribution of wind speed   (b) Distribution of wind direction

Fig. 2. Wind speed and direction during 1st January - 31th December

We can see the difference of magntiudes between wind speed and direction is large. Hence, the Eq. (10), (11) can change them to two wind speed components. By the calculation, the value of $\bar{\theta}$ is clockwise 210.6213° with the north axis. So the set of data can be reconstructed to the form like Fig. 3.

After the data preprocessing, the train process with MSVR with Data-Dependent kernel can be begun. The first 1100 data points is arranged to be training data, meanwhile, the next 100 data points is used to be testing data. We do it following the method mentioned in the last paragraph.

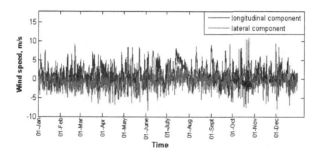

Fig. 3. Distribution of two wind speed components

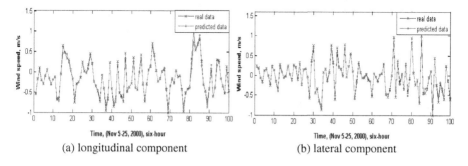

(a) longitudinal component   (b) lateral component

Fig. 4. Distribution of real and predicted wind speed

In the model, the parameter C is set to [1.00e + 003 1.00e + 005]. Here RBF kernel is chosen as the original kernel and the kernel parameter is set to [7500 1000]. Besides, the iteration step α and the iterative threshold value in the Newton-Raphson method are set to 1 and 0.001 respectively. The predicting result shows in Fig. 4.

The way of reasonable error analyze is very significant to result evaluation. This paper selects the root-mean-squares of errors (RMSE) and the mean absolute percentage error (MAPE) as the evaluation indicators.

$$MAPE = \frac{1}{M} \left[\sum_{i=1}^{M} \frac{|y_i - f(x_i)|}{y_i} \right] \times 100\%$$

$$RMSE = \sqrt{\frac{1}{M} \sum_{i=1}^{M} [y_i - f(x_i)]^2} \qquad (15)$$

We can know the errors of the predicted longitudinal component and lateral component wind speed used MSVR with Data-Dependent kernel from Table 1.

Table 1. Errors of two wind speed components

Component	MAPE(%)	RMSE(m/s)
Longitudinal component	10.42	0.0390
lateral component	10.16	0.0301

At present, the predicting error of wind speed time series can be almost 20 %. So the error 10.42 % and 10.16 % is rather small and the model MSVR with Data-Dependent kernel perform well. However, it may be a coincidence. Hence, we make several other methods to compare their performance to prove the ability of our method in predicting the wind speed and direction. Here, we choose three other methods, MSVR without Data-Dependent kernel, single SVR, Neural Network. These methods are all learning methods. Comparison with MSVR without Data-Dependent kernel can get the effect of data dependent kernel. Comparison with single SVR can prove the ideal forecasting simultaneously is right. Neural Network is used to compare with SVR and here we also choose it to contrast. Figure 5 shows their performance and Table 2 lists their prediction error.

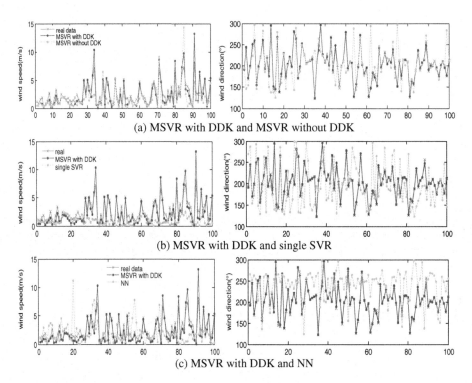

(a) MSVR with DDK and MSVR without DDK

(b) MSVR with DDK and single SVR

(c) MSVR with DDK and NN

Fig. 5. Distribution of wind speed and direction based on models

Table 2. Forecasting errors based on four models

	MAPE(%)		RMSE(m/s, °)	
	Speed	Direction	Speed	Direction
MSVR with DDK	16.81	18.59	0.2446	11.4595
MSVR without DDK	21.89	23.67	0.7755	17.8553
Single SVR	31.31	39.53	1.8904	37.8550
NN	50.37	41.53	1.6570	39.7905

From the error values in Table 2, we can see clearly that the model of MSVR with Data-Dependent kernel has relative small prediction error. The contrast experiment proves our model's ability in predicting the wind speed and direction.

5 Conclusion

In this paper, the MSVR with Data-Dependent kernel model for forecasting wind speed and direction at the same time is built. The next six-hour wind in the farm is predicted by four models, including our model. The error analysis shows that MSVR with Data-Dependent kernel model is the better model for wind speed and direction forecasting, due to the lowest MAPE (16.81 %, 18.59 %) and the RMSE (0.2246, 11.4595), 4-5 points lower than the second-lowest MSVR without Data-Dependent kernel. According the data, we can see the improvement of data dependent kernel. And it proves that forecasting two factors at the same time can get better result than respectively. Thus, it is an effective model for the wind speed and direction forecasting.

Acknowledgments. This work was supported in full by the Natural Science Foundation of JiangSu Province No. BK2012858, and supported in part by the National Natural Science Foundation of China under grant numbers 61103141.

References

1. Negnevitsky, M., Potter, C.W.: Innovative short-term wind generation prediction techniques. In: Power Engineer in Society General Meeting, pp. 60-65. IEEE Press, Montreal (2006)
2. Han, S., Yang, Y.P., Liu, Y.Q.: Application study of three methods in wind speed prediction. J. North China Electric Power Univ. **35**(3), 57–61 (2008)
3. Firat, U., Engin, S.N., Saralcar, M., Ertuzun, A.B.: Wind speed forecasting based on second order blind identification and autoregressive model. In: International Conference on Machine Learning and Applications (ICMLA), pp. 686-691 (2010)
4. Babazadeh, H., Gao, W.Z., Lin, C., Jin, L.: An hour ahead wind speed prediction by Kalman filter. In: Power Electronics and Machines in Wind Applications (PEMWA), pp. 1-6 (2012)
5. Huang, C.Y., Liu, Y.W., TZENG W.C., Wang, P.Y.: Short term wind speed predictions by using the grey prediction model based forecast method. In: Green Technologies Conference (IEEE-Green), pp. 1-5 (2011)
6. Ghanbarzadeh, A., Noghrehabadi, A.R., Behrang, M.A., Assareh, E.: Wind speed prediction based on simple meteorological data using artificial neural network. In: IEEE International Conference on Industrial Informatics, pp. 664-667 (2009)
7. Peng, H.W., Yang, X.F., Liu, F.R.: Short-term wind speed forecasting of wind farm based on SVM method. Power Syst. Clean Energy **07**, 48–52 (2009)
8. Wang, D.C., Ni, Y.J., Chen, B.J., Cao, Z.L.: A wind speed forecasting model based on support vector regression with data dependent kernel. J. Nanjing Normal Univ. (Nat. Sci. Edn.) **37**(3), 15–20 (2014)

9. Bin, G., Victor, S.: Feasibility and finite convergence analysis for accurate on-line v-support vector machine. IEEE Trans. Neural Netw. Learn. Syst. **24**(8), 1304–1315 (2013)
10. Crotes, C., Vapnik, V.: Support vector networks. Mach. Learn. **20**, 273–297 (1995)
11. Wu, I., Amari, S.: Conformal transformation of kernel functions: a data-dependent way to improve support vector machine classifiers. Neural Process. Lett. **15**(1), 59–67 (2002)

Research on Rootkit Detection Model Based on Intelligent Optimization Algorithm in the Virtualization Environment

Lei Sun[1(✉)], Zhiyuan Zhao[1], Feiran Wang[2], and Lei Jin[1]

[1] Zhengzhou Institute of Information Science and Technology,
Zhengzhou, China
zzy_taurus@foxmail.com, {759731637,984522340}@qq.com
[2] Mudanjiang 61112, China
1025878311@qq.com

Abstract. In order to solve the problems that the high misjudgment ratio of Rootkit detection and undetectable unknown Rootkit in the virtualization guest operating system, a Rootkit detecting model (QNDRM) based on intelligent optimization algorithm was proposed. The detecting model combines neural network with QPSO, which can take advantage of them. In the actual detection, QNDRM firstly captures the previously selected out Rootkit's typical characteristic behaviors. And then, the trained system detects the presence of Rootkit. The experimental results show that QNDRM can effectively reduce the misjudgment ratio and detect both known and unknown Rootkit.

Keywords: Virtualization · Neural network · QPSO · Rootkit

1 Introduction

Cloud computing technology has become another revolution of information technology after the Internet due to their advantages of dynamic extensions, on-demand services, and charging by volume [1], but the problem of information security in the cloud has attracted wide attention with more and more users moving their data into the cloud servers. The safety of the users' data is directly affected by virtualization technology which is the foundation of the cloud computing. The technology of safety monitoring is an important and efficient method to enhance the security of the system, however malicious code often avoid system monitoring by making use of the hidden ability of Rootkit [2]. Herein, realizing efficient detection of Rootkit is of great significance to enhance the security of virtualization environment.

However, the existing Rootkit detecting methods in virtualization environment are bad for detecting the unknown Rootkit and have lower efficiency. The Rootkit detecting model (QNDRM) based on intelligent optimization algorithm in this paper is proposed in light of the above problem. The model is based on QPSO and BP neural network in light of achieving the purpose of intelligent fast learning and detecting the unknown Rootkit.

Z. Huang et al. (Eds.): ICCCS 2015, LNCS 9483, pp. 437–447, 2015.
DOI: 10.1007/978-3-319-27051-7_37

2 Related Work

Attackers update attack technology constantly and develop the new Rootkit to attack the virtual machine in order to achieve their purpose. As a result, it is very important to improve the ability for detecting the unknown Rootkit. The artificial intelligence method of the system engineering can solve this problem very well. In recent years, a variety of artificial intelligence methods are applied to detect Rootkit.

Lu [3] studies a kind of using artificial immune algorithm to detect malicious program technology. The technology based on artificial immune optimization is applied to detect the malicious programs in computer and mobile phone. It improves the detection rate. Zhang [4] applies the artificial immune algorithm to the malicious code detection based on IRP in order to improve the efficiency and accuracy of the malicious code detection. Pan [5] studies the killing of malicious code technology based on expert system. This technology can accurately detect malicious behavior information existing in the knowledge library. But the detection rate of unknown malicious code is low, and the ability of acquiring knowledge is poor. Shirazi H M [6] applies the genetic algorithm to the malicious code detection system. It reduces the misjudgment rate. Abadeh M S [7] applies the ant colony algorithm to optimize the fuzzy classification algorithm in intrusion detection, and it effectively improves the classification precision and the accuracy of intrusion detection. Dastanpour A [8] achieves the purpose of detecting malicious code by prediction based on combining genetic algorithm and neural network. The method can effectively detect the samples in the CPU data.

3 Architecture

QNDRM detecting model inputs the Rootkit behavior features encoded through quantitative module to the BP network. The Rootkit behavior features encoded through quantitative module are stored in BP network through training, and they are as the expert system knowledge library. Finally, QNDRM completes the purpose of detecting the unknown Rootkit.

Cybenko proved that only a single hidden layer can distinguish any classification problem when each neuron using S function in 1988 [9]. BP neural network having only three layers can achieve arbitrary n to m dimensional vector map, while it uses tangent sigmoid transfer function between two connected layers and the hidden layer has enough neurons [10]. Therefore, the paper determines that QNDRM's transfer function uses the S tangent function and the network structure is 3 layers. QNDRM detection model structure based on BP neural network is shown in Fig. 1.

QNDRM detecting model includes quantitative module, subject learning inference engine (automatic knowledge acquisition, knowledge library and inference engine) and decoding module. Firstly, QNDRM detecting model codes the behavioral character-istics through the quantitative module. Then, the model implicitly expresses the behavioral characteristics as the weight value and threshold value of the network structure and indirectly expresses expert knowledge. Finally, the model stories the knowledge in the network structure as the expert knowledge library. QNDRM realizes

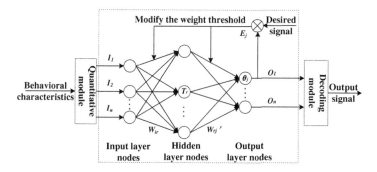

Fig. 1. QNDRM detection model structure

the reasoning mechanism based on the structure of the neural network, outputs non-numerical information through the decoding module, completes the Rootkit detection process.

3.1   Quantization Algorithm of Behavioral Characteristics

For QNDRM detection model, coding means that converts logic thinking of human rules into the thinking way of machine. Decoding means that converts the numerical value into the form of natural language that the users can understand. This section will code the Rootkit behavior characteristics based on the contribution value of detecting.

The behavioral characteristics of Rootkit can be expressed in a collection.

$$U = \{u_1, u_2, \ldots u_n\} \tag{1}$$

Among them, u_i expresses a behavior characteristic of Rootkit. n is the total number of behavior characteristics in the behavior feature library. A behavior characteristic can appear in Rootkit or normal procedures. As a result, the detecting model writes down the number of each behavior characteristic in Rootkit and ordinary procedures for more accurate expressing the contribution of the behavior characteristic correctly detecting Rootkit. And then the paper uses the binary group to express each behavior characteristic.

$$u_i = \langle R_i, N_i \rangle \tag{2}$$

Among them, R_i expresses the number of u_i occurred in Rootkit. N_i expresses the number of u_i occurred in the normal procedures.

If the number of u_i occurred in Rootkit is far beyond its amount in the normal procedures, then u_i is a classic feature of Rootkit. And it can play a more important role in detecting Rootkit process. Then U is gave the larger contribution value for improving the ability of detecting Rootkit. Contribution value of U is normalized and expressed as the form of vector:

$$V = \{v_1, v_2, \ldots v_n\} \tag{3}$$

The contribution value of detecting Rootkit of every behavior characteristic is defined as:

$$Con(u_i) = \frac{n \times R_i}{\sum R_i + \sum N_i} \times \left(1 - \frac{n \times N_i}{\sum R_i + \sum N_i}\right) \tag{4}$$

The contribution value is normalized, and inputs the BP neural network.

$$v_i = \frac{Con(u_i)}{\sum Con(u_i)} \tag{5}$$

3.2 Decoding Algorithm of Output Results

The output of QNDRM model is expressed by numerical logic, so it need be decoded. The decoding process is relatively simple. And it needs to convert logical numerical results of the actual results. The result is a Rootkit or a normal procedure according to the output. Therefore the output layer of QNDRM only needs a neuron. The relationship between ideal output values and the detecting results is shown in Table 1.

Table 1. The output value and the detecting results

The ideal output values	Test results
"0"	The normal procedure
"1"	Rootkit

However there is a certain error between actual output value and ideal output value of QNDRM, namely, the actual output value is not absolute "0" or "1". Therefore, we need to define a range of error. When the actual output is within the error range, we believe that the output is "0" or "1".

3.3 The Subject Learning Inference Engine

The subject learning inference engine based on QPSO optimizing the parameters of BP network in QNDRM detecting model is described as follows: First of all, it uses the improved QPSO to optimize the parameters of BP network, until the particle swarm got enough good fitness value or the maximum number of iterations. At this point, the parameters and the optimal value of the BP neural network are closed, and this narrowed the scope of the parameters of BP network training. Then the subject learning inference engine uses the BP algorithm to optimize the parameters obtained from the above, and gets the optimal weight values and threshold values. This method takes note of the advantages of both QPSO and BP algorithm at the same time, and makes use of the complementary advantages between them to avoid slow convergence speed, poor optimization precision and local minimum problem. That can greatly improve the training effect.

(1) Improved QPSO Algorithm.

The inertia weight is constant in standard QPSO algorithm, and this cannot effectively response the actual application. For the above situation, the random inertia weight β is put forward, and β is changed through the evolution algebra and random. In the algorithm, β is changed by the following formula:

$$\beta = \beta_{\max} - \frac{rand(\ )}{2} \cdot \frac{G_{current}}{G_{\max}} \qquad 0 \leq rand() \leq 1 \qquad (6)$$

Among them, $rand(\ )$ is the random number between 0 and 1. $\beta_{\max}$ is the maximum inertia weight, $\beta_{\max} = 0.9$. $G_{current}$ is the current generation, $G_{\max}$ is the maximum generation.

When the paper thinks $rand(\ )$ is a constant, $G_{current}$ will increase and β will decrease linear. Therefore, in the beginning, $G_{current}$ is the smaller, and $G_{current}/G_{\max}$ is the smaller, and β is the bigger. So the algorithm has strong global search ability, and gets proper particles, and is conducive to jump out of local minimum point in the beginning. When $G_{current}$ increases, $G_{current}/G_{\max}$ is the bigger, and β is the smaller. This increases the local search ability of the algorithm so that we can make particles gradually shrink to good areas to more detailed search. At the same time it can improve the convergence speed. $rand(\ )$ is random changed in fact. The overall trend is linear regressive, but β is changed nonlinear. This shows a complex change process and avoids the premature convergence phenomenon.

(2) Steps of Inference Engine.

The specific steps of inference engine are as follows:

Step1: Firstly, the BP network structure is determined and the training sample set is given.

Step2: The population size, the particle dimension and the number of iterations of the improved QPSO are set based on the BP network structure. Each particle represents a set of neural network parameters;

Step3: Initialization population of particles, and then setting the mean square error of BP network to particle fitness function.

Step4: Decoding each particle to obtain corresponding weight values and the threshold values of BP network;

Step5: The sample is input in QNDRM for obtaining the corresponding output, and then the fitness value of each particle is calculated through the mean square error function.

Step6: Comparing the mean square error E and the expected value ε. If $E < \varepsilon$, jumping to step 9, otherwise jumping to the step 7.

Step7: According to the algorithm to update the best position of particles and the global best position.

Step8: Increased the number of iterations k, if $k > k_{\max}$, executing the next step, otherwise jumping to step 4.

Step9: To map the global optimal particle for structure parameters of BP network, and parameters is the final results of the optimization.

Step10: End of the algorithm (Fig. 2).

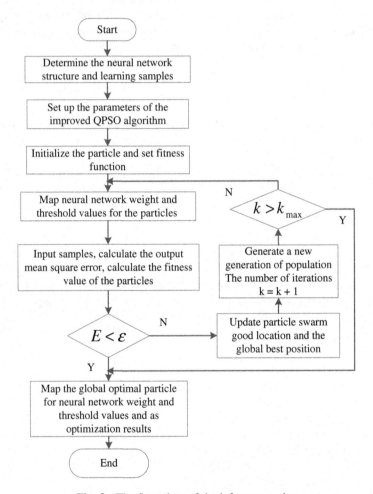

Fig. 2. The flow chart of the inference engine

4   Experiment and Results

4.1   Analysis the Behavior Characteristics

The input of QNDRM detecting model is behavior characteristics of Rootkit. So to complete the function verification and performance analysis, we must analyze the behavior characteristics of Rootkit, filter the input, and prepare for the next experiment.

Rootkit must be loaded into memory and leave a variety of behaviors for playing their functions. It is hopeful that find Rootkit through analyzing the behavior of traces in the system. In the process of the actual detection, behavior characteristics of Rootkit must be chosen for the input of QBDRM. To make a smaller amount of calculation, having a faster response speed, having a higher detection rate, the paper selects the representative and effective behavior characteristics of Rootkit based on the KDD CUP99 dataset [11] as the input of QNDRM. The KDD CUP99 dataset is the most authoritative testing data sets, and there are about 5 million records in it (Table 2).

Table 2. 18 typical behavior characteristics of rootkit

Number	Describing behavioral characteristics
1	The no-system process P1 writes in memory of another process P2, but P1 is not the parent process of P2
2	The behavior of creatin a process
3	The behavior of no-system process injecting into the thread of other process
4	The behavior of creating a service, drive and so on
5	The behavior of setting the key registry value
6	The behavior of creating a driver files and other sensitive
7	Modify import table or export table of the executable procedures for changing the function execution process
8	The behavior of the no-system process allocating memory across processes
9	The behavior of published table of system services being pubished again
10	The behavior of MSR Hook
11	The behavior of Inline Hook
12	The behavior of Derived Tables Hook
13	The behavior of hiding process
14	The behavior of hiding the driver
15	Setting itself to run automatically when restart and promoting a non-root user privileges associated to the root level
16	Establishing concealed information channel by looking for system vulnerabilities
17	Implanting malicious code into the kernel based on kernel drivers
18	Collecting password or other confidential information etc. by the way of keystroke sniffer and the packet sniffer and so on

4.2   Creation Network Structure and Selection Parameter

The method of determining the BP network structure does not have a set of complete theory. It is mainly based on prior knowledge and experiment to establish. The paper has selected the s-shaped function as transfer function. To make the algorithm to be simple and feasible, the paper chooses only a hidden layer and a neuron of output layer, and this can meet the needs of display the results. The number of input neurons is determining by input features of QNDRM detecting model, namely the input layer has 18 neurons.

There is no specific reference formula for solving the number of hidden layer neurons, so we can only accord to the characteristics of the network structure and the work of others to estimate the number of hidden layer neurons. Then the best value is selected according to the order of the valuation range through the experiment, and this can improve the efficiency of selection. In the network with three layers, two empirical formulas are used the most frequently as follow [12]:

$$N_{hidden} = \sqrt{N_{in} \times N_{out}} \tag{7}$$

$$N_{hidden} = (N_{in} + N_{out})/2 \tag{8}$$

The paper has identified that N_{in} is 18 and N_{out} is 1. So according to the above two formulas, N_{hidden} is:

$$N_{hidden} = \sqrt{N_{in} \times N_{out}} \approx 4 \tag{9}$$

$$N_{hidden} = (N_{in} + N_{out})/2 = 9.5 \approx 10 \tag{10}$$

According to the results of the above two formulas, the number of neurons in hidden layer is between 4 to 10. Under the condition of without considering the other parameters change, the number of hidden layer neurons within the scope of 4 to 10 is experimented, as shown in Table 3.

Table 3. The test results

The Number of Hidden Layer Node	Mean Square Error
4	0.00426281
5	0.00120495
6	0.00064653
7	0.00026821
8	0.00024276
9	0.00023672
10	0.00024012

Before the node number is 6, the mean square error and the error percentage has obvious drop. After the node number is 8, the trend of the value slowed down. It is considered that the number of hidden layer would increase the complexity of the calculation, therefore, this paper determines that the number of hidden layer neurons is 7. Detailed parameters are shown in Table 4.

Table 4. Parameter settings

The structural parameters	Specific indicators	Setting the value
The number of Neural node	The input layer N_{in}	18
	The hidden layer N_{hidden}	7
	The output layer N_{out}	1
The parameter settings of network structure	Transfer function of input layer to hidden layer	tansig
	Transfer function of hidden layer to output layer	tansig
	Learning function	trainlm
The parameter settings of network training	Training goal	0.01
	Interval	10
	Learning rate β	0.1
	Learning rate λ	0.01
QPSO related parameters	Particle dimension D	141
	Population size M	30
	The biggest inertia weight β_{max}	0.9
	Maximum generation number G_{max}	500

4.3   Detecting Results

Functional experiments include normal system and implanted Rootkit system detection. The system is to pure state before each experiment is repeated. The paper sets the output layer application error of 0.1. When the normal operation system is running, we execute office, browser and so on. Each experiment lasts for 30 s at a time, and the output value changes all around zero. It is shown in Fig. 3 with the point line. The online well-known Rootkit are selected as follow: hxdef, futo, ntrootkit, futo_enhanced, badrkdemo, and they are dealt by Themida to simulate unknown Rootkit. There are 10 samples. Rootkit is implanted in the system at T moment, and then look at the value of the output layer. It

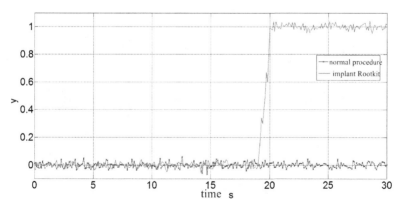

Fig. 3. The detecting results

is shown in Fig. 3 with smooth curve. Rootkit is implanted at 19 s, and the output value changes to 1. So QNDRM can effectively detect known and unknown Rootkit.

4.4   Performance Evaluation

(1)   Analysis the Effectiveness of QNDRM

The paper selects 20 normal procedures and 10 Rootkit for testing the effectiveness of QNDRM. And they are dealt by ACProtect, PE-Armor, Themida and Winlicense. So we can get 70 samples for testing. Then the samples are detected by XenPHD, Hyperchk, Livewire and QNDRM, the detecting results is shown in Table 5.

Table 5. The contrast table of detecting results

	XenPHD	Hyperchk	Livewire	QNDRM
Normal procedures	20	18	20	20
Rootkit	46	46	44	47
Detection rate	92 %	92 %	88 %	94 %
Misjudgment rate	5.7 %	8.6 %	8.6 %	4.3 %

Shown in Table 5, the detecting effect of QNDRM is superior to other detecting system.

(2)   Analysis the performance of QNDRM

In order to more clearly showing the performance of the detecting system, XenPHD, Hyperchk, Livewire and QNDRM are tested by UnixBench. The basis without any detecting system is 1, and system performance loss is calculated, as shown in Fig. 4.

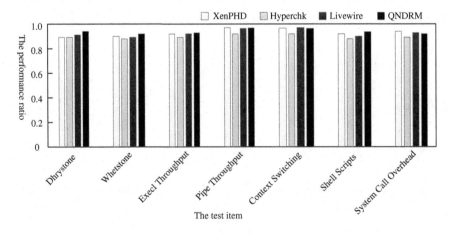

Fig. 4. The contrast of performance testing

As shown in Fig. 4, the Y coordinate represents the ratio of running each detecting system and without detecting system, and the X coordinate represents the test items. The method in this paper is better than the other methods in terms of performance loss. When QNDRM is running, the average performance loss is 5.7 %.

5 Conclusion

In this paper we have presented a novel approach of detecting Rootkit. To the best of our knowledge, there are no papers about such a kind of study to have been published. The Rootkit heuristic detecting model based on intelligent optimization algorithm in virtualization environment was proposed. The model improved the ability to detect known and unknown Rootkit and enhanced the security of the virtual machine by combining neural network and QPSO. Finally, it was proved that the detecting model could effectively find the Rootkit through the experiment. In a word, the method solves the problem in the virtualization environment by using intelligent optimization algorithm, which provides a new way for detecting Rootkit.

References

1. Vivek, K.: Guide to Cloud Computing for Business and Technology Managers: From Distributed Computing to Cloudware Applications. CRC Press, Boca Raton (2014)
2. Hoglund, G., Butler, J.: Rootkits: Subverting the Windows Kernel. Addison-Wesley Professional, Reading (2006)
3. Lu, T.: Research on Malcode Detection Technology Based on Artificial Immune System. Beijing University of Posts and Telecommunications (2013)
4. Zhang F.: Research on Artificial Immune Algorithms on Malware Detection. South China University of Technology (2012)
5. Jianfeng, Pan: Design and Implemetation of Host-Based Malcode Detection System. University of Science and Technology of China, Anhui (2009)
6. Shirazi, H.M.: An intelligent intrusion detection system using genetic algorithms and features selection. Majlesi J. Electr. Eng. 4(1), 33–43 (2010)
7. Abadeh, M.S., Habibi, J.A.: Hybridization of evolutionary fuzzy systems and ant colony optimization for intrusion detection. ISC Int. J. Inf. Secur. 2(1), 33–46 (2015)
8. Dastanpour, A., Ibrahim, S., Mashinchi, R.: Using genetic algorithm to supporting artificial neural network for intrusion detection system. In: The International Conference on Computer Security and Digital Investigation (ComSec2014). The Society of Digital Information and Wireless Communication, pp. 1–13 (2014)
9. Yuan, X., Li, H., Liu, S.: Neural Network and Genetic Algorithm Apply in Water Science. China Water & Power Press, Beijing (2002)
10. Zhu H.: Intrusion Detection System Research Based on Neural Network. Shandong University (2008)
11. Wan, T., Ma, J., Zeng, G.: Analysis of sample database for intelligence intrusion detection evaluation. South-Central Univ. Nationalities 2(29), 84–87 (2010)
12. Debar, H., Becker, M., Siboni, D.: A neural network component for an intrusion detection system. In: Proceedings of the 1992 IEEE Computer Society Symposium on Research in Security and Privacy, pp. 240–250. IEEE (1992)

Performance Analysis of (1+1)EA on the Maximum Independent Set Problem

Xue Peng[(✉)]

School of Computer Science and Engineering,
South China University of Technology, Guangzhou 510006, China
pxue2008@163.com

Abstract. The maximum independent set problem (MISP) is a classic graph combinatorial optimization problem and it is known to be NP-complete. In this paper, we investigate the performance of the (1+1)EA, which is a simple evolutionary algorithm, on MISP from a theoretical point of view. We showed that the (1+1)EA can obtain an approximation ratio of $\frac{\triangle+1}{2}$ on this problem in expected time $O(n^4)$, where $\triangle$ and n denote the maximum vertex degree and the number of nodes in a graph, respectively. Later on, we reveal that the (1+1)EA has better performances than the local search algorithm on an instance of MISP. We present that the local search algorithm with 3-flip neighborhood will be trapped in local optimum while the (1+1)EA can find the global optimum in expected running time $O(n^5)$.

Keywords: Maximum independent set · Performance analysis · Evolutionary algorithm · Approximation algorithm

1 Introduction

Evolutionary algorithms (EAs) are stochastic optimization techniques which are inspired from the principles of natural evolution and they have been successfully applied to solving combinatorial optimization problems for decades. Contrary to the success of EAs in applications, the theoretical foundation of EAs is at a lower level. It is commonly acknowledged that research on the theory of EAs helps give us a better understanding of how the algorithms work and directs the application of the algorithms. Therefore, a well theoretical foundation for such algorithms is required.

Running time analysis is one of the principal branch of theoretical analysis on EAs. In recent years, theoretical research on this field has attracted wide attention [1,2]. In the early research in this field, researchers [3,4] mainly concerned about a class of simple evolutionary algorithm, (1+1)EA, in which the running time analyses on some artificial functions are performed. By analyzing these functions which have special structure, we can have a better understanding of the behavior of EAs, and we can also obtain some useful mathematical methods and analysis tools for combinatorial optimization problems.

© Springer International Publishing Switzerland 2015
Z. Huang et al. (Eds.): ICCCS 2015, LNCS 9483, pp. 448–456, 2015.
DOI: 10.1007/978-3-319-27051-7_38

Afterwards, the running time analysis of EAs turns to some classic combinatorial optimization problems in P class such as the maximum matching [5], the minimum spanning tree [6], the shortest path problems [7] and so on. These theoretical studies show that though the EAs can not beat those classic problem-specific algorithms in general case, it can solve these problems within an expected running time which is close to those specific algorithms.

In practice, a lot of combinatorial optimization problems are NP-complete. Complexity theory tells us that unless $P = NP$, the maximum independent problem can not be solved by a deterministic polynomial time algorithm. A natural question is whether we can effectively find their approximation solutions.

Although EAs are a class of global optimization algorithms, we can not expect that they can solve any instance of NP-complete problems in polynomial time. Therefore, research and analysis on the approximation performance of EAs will be a meaningful work. Witt [8] presents the approximation performance of EAs on an NP-complete problem, the Partition problem. He proved that both the random local search algorithm and the $(1 + 1)$EA can obtain an approximation ratio of $\frac{4}{3}$ in an expected running time $O(n^2)$. Friedrich et al. [9] analyzed the approximation performance of a hybrid evolutionary algorithm on the vertex cover problem. They investigated some special instances to prove that EAs can improve the approximation solution.

Recently Yu et al. [10] proposed an evolutionary algorithm called SEIP (simple evolutionary algorithm with isolated population) and proved that for unbounded set cover problem this algorithm can get an approximation ratio of H_n, where $H_n = \sum_{i=1}^{n} \frac{1}{i}$ is a nth harmonic number. For k-set cover problem, they showed that SEIP can obtain an approximation ratio of $H_k - \frac{k-1}{8k^9}$. Later on, Zhou et al. [11–14] extended the approximation performance of EAs to other combinatorial optimization problems.

In this paper, we analyze a classic combinatorial optimization problem, the maximum independent set problem (MISP). Given an undirected graph, independent set refers to a set of vertices in a graph such that any two vertices in this set are adjacent. The goal is to find an independent set so that its size is maximized. With this paper, we investigate the approximation performance of the $(1 + 1)$EA on MISP from a theoretical point of view. We prove that by simulating the local search algorithm, the $(1 + 1)$EA can obtain the same approximation ratio $\frac{\Delta+1}{2}$ as that of the local search algorithm in expected running time $O(n^4)$, where Δ denotes the maximum degree in the graph. Further, by constructing an instance of MISP, we can show that the $(1 + 1)$EA outperforms the local search algorithm on it.

The remainder of this paper is structured as follows. In Sect. 2, we introduce the algorithms, problem and method; Sect. 3 presents the approximation performance of the $(1 + 1)$EA on MISP; Sect. 4 analyzes the performance of the (1+1)EA on an instance of MISP; Sect. 5 concludes the paper.

2   Related Algorithms and Problems

2.1   Local Search Algorithm

Local search is an iterative improvement method, and it is often used as a tool for solving combinatorial optimization problems. The main approach of local search is that starting from an initial solution, then, the neighborhood is searched for an improved solution in each iteration. If an improved solution is found then the search will be continued, otherwise the current solution is returned. Assume $f : S = \{0, 1\}^n \rightarrow R$ is the objective function or fitness function which needs to be maximized, where R is a set which consists of all different fitness values. The description of the local search algorithm is given as follows:

(1) Initialization: a solution $x_0 \in \{0, 1\}^n$ is generated and let $x = x_0$.
(2) While (termination condition is not satisfied) do
    a. find a new solution x' in the neighborhood of x.
    b. if $f(x) < f(x')$, then $x = x'$.
(3) End while.
(4) Return x.

Local search algorithm is a simple algorithm and it is easy to implement, but its drawbacks are that it is easy to get trapped in local optimum and the quality of the solution is closely related to the structure of the initial solution and the neighborhood. Here, the $(1 + 1)$EA makes up the deficiencies of local search algorithm.

2.2   (1+1)EA

The $(1 + 1)$EA, which uses mutation operator and selection operator, is a simple and effective evolutionary algorithm and it has a population size of 1. The description of the $(1+1)$EA is given as follows:

(1) Initialization: a solution $x_0 \in \{0, 1\}^n$ is generated and let $x = x_0$.
(2) While (termination condition is not satisfied) do
    a. generate a new solution x' by flipping a bit x_i independently with probability $\frac{1}{n}$.
    b. if $f(x) < f(x')$, then $x = x'$.
(3) End while.
(4) Return x.

2.3   Maximum Independent Set Problem

Now we give the definition of MISP:

Definition 1 *(MISP). Let $G(V, E)$ be an undirected graph, where E is the set of edges and V is the set of vertices. The aim is to find a subset $A \subseteq V$ such that the number of vertices which are included in A to be maximized and any two vertices in A has no edge in G, that is, $\forall v_i, v_j \in A, (v_i, v_j) \notin E$.*

In order to use the $(1 + 1)$EA to obtain the approximate optimal or optimal solution of MISP, we first need to encode solutions. For each subset $A \subseteq V$, we can use a string $(x_1, x_2, \ldots, x_n) \in \{0, 1\}^n$ to represent it, where n refers to the total number of vertices in graph $G(V, E)$, and a subset A is represented by $x = (x_1, x_2, \ldots, x_n)$. For each vertex v_i which is included in A, the corresponding bit x_i is set to 1, otherwise 0.

The fitness function is defined as follows:

$$f_1(x) = \sum_{i=1}^{n} x_i - n \sum_{i=1}^{n} x_i \sum_{j=1}^{n} x_j e_{ij}, \tag{1}$$

where edge e_{ij} connects vertices v_i and v_j, that is, $e_{ij} = (v_i, v_j)$.

Now we introduce the concepts of independent point and independent edge, which are relative to the subset of A. Independent point is a point that no edge connects to it or has an edge connecting to it but the point in the other endpoint of this edge is in A. Independent edge is an edge two endpoints of which are not in A. $\sum_{i=1}^{n} x_i \sum_{j=1}^{n} x_j e_{ij}$ in formula (1) is used to compute the number of non-independent edges contained in the current solution . Note that $\sum_{i=1}^{n} x_i \sum_{j=1}^{n} x_j e_{ij} \neq 0$ indicates that the current solution is not an independent set, while $\sum_{i=1}^{n} x_i \sum_{j=1}^{n} x_j e_{ij} = 0$ indicates that the current solution is an independent set. Our goal is to maximize the fitness function $f_1(x)$. In the case of non-independent set, algorithm accepts two operations: the first is to increase independence point, and the second is to reduce the non-independent point and thus reduce non-independent edges. In the case of independent set, algorithm only accepts the operation that increasing independence points. The second term of the fitness function gives a penalty to each non-independent point and we call it a penalty term.

2.4   Fitness Partitioning Methods

Fitness partitioning method is a powerful mathematical tool for the theoretical analysis of EAs. Due to its simplicity and practicality, it is commonly used to the running time analysis of EAs. In the following, we give the definition of fitness partitioning method.

Definition 2 *(f-partition). Let $f : L \to R$ be an objective function which needs to be maximized, where L is a limited search space. Let $f_0, f_1, \ldots, f_m$ be all possible different function values of f and satisfy $f_0 < f_1 < \ldots, < f_m$. We define $A_i = \{x \in L | f(x) = f_i\}$ $(i = 0, 1, \ldots, m)$. Then we call the set $\{A_0, A_1, \ldots, A_m\}$ a f-partition.*

Lemma 1 *[15]. Let set $\{A_0, A_1, \ldots, A_m\}$ be a f-partition. $P(A_i)$ be the probability that a search point which is selected randomly belongs to A_i, let $s(a)$ be the probability that $a \in A_i$ is mutated into $A_{i-1} \cup A_{i-2} \cup \ldots \cup A_0$, and let $s_i = min\{s(a) | a \in A_i\}$. We denote X_f by the running time of an algorithm on function f, then*

$$E(X_f) \leq s_1^{-1} + s_2^{-1} + \ldots + s_m^{-1} \tag{2}$$

3   The Approximation Performance of the $(1 + 1)$EA on MISP

The MISP is a NP-complete problem, and for this class of problem, an algorithm can obtain an approximation ratio α refers to that for any instance, algorithm can generate a solution with value at least $\frac{o}{\alpha}$, where α and o represent the value of the current solution and the value of the optimal solution, respectively. Thus, the algorithm is called α approximation algorithm.

For MISP, there are two kinds of algorithms which are precise algorithms and approximation algorithms. Currently, the best exact algorithm can obtain the MISP of a graph containing n vertices in expected running time $O(1.2^n)$ [17]. For the approximation algorithm, it can only obtain a constant approximation ratio on some special graphs. By using the greedy algorithm, Halldrsson et al. [18] obtained an approximation ratio of $\frac{\Delta+2}{3}$ on some graph with a vertex degree, which has a bound of constant Δ. Khanna et al. [16] presented the approximation performance analysis of a local search algorithm with 3-flip neighborhood on MISP. In this paper, we showed that by simulating the local search algorithm the $(1 + 1)$EA can and obtain an approximation ratio as that of the local search algorithm.

Lemma 2 *[16]. Local search algorithm with 3-flip neighborhood can obtain an approximation ratio of $\frac{\Delta+1}{2}$ on any instance of MISP with a vertex degree, which has a bound of constant Δ.*

In the following, we introduce 3-flip operation and the local search algorithm with 3-flip neighborhood.

Suppose that S is an independent set. The so-called 3-flip operation refers to an operation of adding a vertex to S or deleting a vertex in S and simultaneously increasing two vertices which are not in S.

At each step, the local search algorithm improves the current solution according to its neighbors. Suppose that S' is a new independent set which is obtained by executing a 3-flip operation on S. The framework of the local search algorithm with 3-flip neighborhood is as follows: starting from an initial solution S_0, algorithm finds a new solution S' in its neighbours by using the 3-flip operation. This process is repeated until it meets the stop condition of the algorithm.

By simulating the local search algorithm with 3-flip neighborhood, the $(1 + 1)$EA can obtain the same approximation ratio $\frac{\Delta+1}{2}$.

Theorem 1. *For any given instance I of MISP, which has a bound of constant Δ on any vertex, and let opt be the maximal number of vertices which are included in I. The $(1 + 1)$EA can find an independent set with the number of vertices at least $\frac{2opt}{\Delta+1}$ in expected running time $O(n^4)$.*

Proof. Proof We use the method of fitness partitioning to prove this theorem. We partition the solution space into three disjoint sets A_1, A_2, A_3 according to different fitness function values.

$A_1 = \{x \in \{0,1\}^n | x \text{ is an infeasible solution and satisfies } f_1(x) < 0\}$

$A_2 = \{x \in \{0,1\}^n | x \text{ is a feasible solution and satisfies } 0 \leq f_1(x) < \frac{2opt}{\Delta+1}\}$

$A_3 = \{x \in \{0,1\}^n | x \text{ is a feasible solution and satisfies } f_1(x) \geq \frac{2opt}{\Delta+1}\}$

Note that in the evolution process of the $(1 + 1)$EA, the fitness will never be decreased. Suppose the current solution x is generated at the t-th iteration by the $(1 + 1)$EA. If x belongs to A_1, x is not an independent set. At this moment algorithm only accepts the operation of increasing independent point or decreasing non-independent edge. Therefore, there exists at least one vertex in the current solution, and deleting this vertex from the current solution can decrease the fitness value by at least 1. The probability of deleting a specific vertex from the current solution is $\frac{1}{n}(1 - \frac{1}{n})^{n-1} \geq \frac{1}{en}$, hence the fitness value can be increased by at least 1 in expected running time $O(n)$. Note that the graph contains at most n points, therefore, a solution starting from set A_1 can enter set A_2 in expected running time $O(n^2)$.

Now we assume that the current solution x belongs to A_2. Following Lemma 1, we know that if $f_1(x) < \frac{2opt}{\Delta+1}$, there exists at least one 3-flip operation which can increase the fitness value by at least 1. The probability that the $(1 + 1)$EA performs a specific 3-flip operation is $\Omega(\frac{1}{n^3})$. In fact, the probability of deleting a specific vertex from the current solution while increasing two vertices to the current solution is $\frac{1}{n^3}\left(1 - \frac{1}{n}\right)^{n-1} \geq \frac{1}{en^3}$. Note that, by executing a 3-flip operation, the fitness value will be increased by at least 1. When $x \in A_2$, then we have $0 \leq f_1(x) \leq n$. Therefore, after n times 3-flip operations, the solution will enter set A_3. Thus, the running time of the $(1+1)$EA starting from A_2 to A_3 is bound above by $O(n^4)$.

Altogether, we complete the conclusion.

4 The $(1 + 1)$EA Beats the Local Search Algorithm on An Instance of MISP

By using local search algorithm with a 3-flip operation, Khanna et al. [16] have proven that this algorithm can obtain an approximation ratio of $\frac{\Delta+1}{2}$, and they also pointed out that this approximation ratio is tight.

In the following, we construct an instance I_1 and show that the local search algorithm with 3-flip neighborhood can be trapped in local optimum on this instance, while the $(1 + 1)$EA can obtain the global optimal solution in a polynomial time. The vertices of this instance are divided into two sets X and Y, where X contains d elements and Y contains $\frac{d(d-1)}{2}$ elements, and the set Y consists of subsets which contain one or two elements in set X. An example of instance I_1 is given in Fig. 1.

Obviously, the maximum independent set (global optimum solution) of I_1 is a solution which contains all of the elements in Y but does not contain any element in X. A solution containing all elements in X but does not contain any

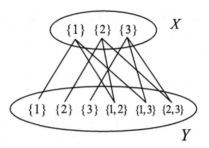

Fig. 1. An example of I_1 with $d = 3$.

element in Y is called a locally optimum solution with respect to the local search algorithm with 3-flip neighborhood, and by executing any single 3-flip operation the current solution can not be improved, thus the local search algorithm with 3-flip neighborhood is trapped in local optimum.

Theorem 2. *Starting from any initialized solution, the (1 + 1)EA can find the global optimal solution of instance I_1 in expected running time $O(n^5)$.*

Proof. Note that the elements in X from left to right are $\{1\}$, $\{2\}$, ..., $\{d\}$, and the elements in Y from left to right are $\{1\}$, $\{2\}$, ..., $\{d\},\{1,2\}$, $\{1,3\}$, ..., $\{d-1,d\}$. We also use the method of fitness partitioning to prove this theorem, and we partition the proof into two parts.

The first part: the current solution is a non-independent set. In this case, the algorithm accepts the operation which only reduces the number of non-independent point. Note that the maximum number of non-independent points is n ($n = d + d + \frac{d(d-1)}{2}$), while the algorithm only needs to remove a non-independent point in each step and the probability of executing this operation is $\Omega(\frac{1}{n})$. Therefore, in the first part, the expected running time of the (1+1)EA on instance I_1 is bounded above by $O(n^2)$.

The second part: in this part the current solution is an independent set and we can divide the solutions into four cases:

Case 1: If the current solution contains all elements in X, then it does not contain any solution in Y. By deleting two elements $\{i\}$ and $\{j\}$ randomly from X, and meanwhile adding elements $\{i\}$, $\{j\}$ and $\{i,j\}$, the fitness value will be increased by 1. Since the (1+1)EA accepts the solution with better fitness, for the solution that contains all elements in x, once the algorithm is left, it will never go back to this solution. Thus, the event that the solution contains all of the elements in X may occur at most once in the evolution process. Now we compute the probability that the (1+1)EA performs this operation. The probability of choosing one element from $\{1,2\}$, $\{1,3\}$, ..., $\{d-1,d\}$ is $\frac{d(d-1)}{2n}$, and if the chosen element is $\{i,j\}$, we need to delete two elements $\{i\}$ and $\{j\}$ from X, and meanwhile add two elements $\{i\}$ and $\{j\}$ in Y. The probability of executing this operation is $\frac{d(d-1)}{2n}\frac{1}{n^4}(1-\frac{1}{n})^{n-5} = \Omega(\frac{1}{n^4})$.

Case 2: If the number of element, which is chosen from X, in the current solution is less than d, and meanwhile the current solution does not contain any element in Y. Algorithm can increase the fitness value by adding the elements in X or adding elements in Y which are not incident to X. The probability of executing the above operation is $\Omega(\frac{1}{n})$.

Case 3: If the number of element, which is chosen from X, in the current solution is less than d, and meanwhile the current solution contains the element in Y, we divide this case into two subcases:

Case 3.1: If the number of element, which is choosing from X, in the current solution is less than $d-1$. W.l.o.g., we assume that the current solution does not contain elements $\{i\}$ and $\{j\}$ but contains $\{k\}$. Since the current solution is an independent set, thus, both elements $\{i,k\}$ and $\{j,k\}$ are not contained in the current solution. By deleting the element k from X and meanwhile adding two elements $\{i,k\}$ and $\{j,k\}$, the fitness value can be increased. The probability of operating this operation is $\Omega(\frac{1}{n^3})$.

Case 3.2: If the number of element, which is chosen from X, in the current solution is less than $d-1$, e.g., one element in X is not selected. W.l.o.g., we assume that the current solution does not contain the element i which is in X. Since the current solution is an independent set, the element $\{i,j\}$ is not included in the current solution, where $j \neq i$. By deleting the element j from X and adding two elements $\{j\}$ and $\{i,j\}$, the fitness value can be increased. The probability of doing this operation is $\frac{1}{n^3}$.

Case 4: If the current solution only contains the element in Y. The fitness value can be increased by adding any element in Y. The probability of doing the above operation is $\Omega(\frac{1}{n})$.

In the second part, the maximum fitness value is $\frac{d(d-1)}{2}$ and the minimum fitness value is 0, and we also note that the fitness value can be increased by at least 1 through any operation of increasing the fitness value. Following lemma 1, we can obtain that the (1+1)EA can find the optimum solution of instance I_1 in expected running time $O(n^5)$.

5   Conclusion

In this paper, we present the approximation performance analysis of EAs on MISP. For the graph which has a constraint on the vertex, we have proved that the (1+1)EA can obtain an approximation ratio of $\frac{\triangle+1}{2}$ in expected running time $O(n^4)$. Later on, we proved that the (1+1)EA has a better performance than the local search algorithm on an instance of MISP. It is natural to ask whether we can achieve better approximation ratios than the local search algorithm on MISP. In addition, it is also an interesting issue whether we can obtain an approximation ratio of weighted maximum independent set problem.

456   X. Peng

References

1. Oliveto, P.S., He, J., Yao, X.: Time complexity of evolutionary algorithms for combinatorial optimization: a decade of results. Int. J. Autom. Comput. **4**(3), 281–293 (2007)
2. Neumann, F., Witt, C.: Bioinspired Computation in Combinatorial Optimization Algorithms and Their Computational Complexity. Springer, Berlin (2010)
3. Droste, S., Jansen, T., Wegener, I.: On the analysis of the (1+1) evolutionary algorithm. Theor. Comput. Sci. **276**, 51–81 (2001)
4. He, J., Yao, X.: Drift analysis and average time complexity of evolutionary algorithms. Artif. Intell. **127**(1), 57–85 (2001)
5. Giel, O., Wegener, I.: Evolutionary algorithms and the maximum matching problem. In: Alt, H., Habib, M. (eds.) STACS 2003. LNCS, vol. 2607, pp. 415–426. Springer, Heidelberg (2003)
6. Neumann, F., Wegener, I.: Randomized local search, evolutionary algorithms and the minimum spanning tree problem. Theor. Comput. Sci. **378**(1), 32–40 (2007)
7. Doerr, B., Happ, E., Klein, C.: A tight analysis of the (1+1)-EA for the single source shortest path problem. In: Proceedings of the IEEE Congress on Evolutionary Computation (CEC 2007), pp. 1890–1895. IEEE Press (2007)
8. Witt, C.: Worst-case and average-case approximations by simple randomized search heuristics. In: Diekert, V., Durand, B. (eds.) STACS 2005. LNCS, vol. 3404, pp. 44–56. Springer, Heidelberg (2005)
9. Friedrich, T., He, J., Hebbinghaus, N., Neumann, F., Witt, C.: Analyses of simple hybrid evolutionary algorithms for the vertex cover problem. Evol. Comput. **17**(1), 3–20 (2009)
10. Yu, Y., Yao, X., Zhou, Z.H.: On the approximation ability of evolutionary optimization with application to minimum set cover. Artif. Intell. **180–181**, 20–33 (2012)
11. Zhou, Y.R., Lai, X.S., Li, K.S.: Approximation and parameterized runtime analysis of evolutionary algorithms for the maximum cut problem. IEEE Trans. Cyber. (2015, in press)
12. Zhou, Y.R., Zhang, J., Wang, Y.: Performance analysis of the (1+1) evolutionary algorithm for the multiprocessor scheduling problem. Algorithmica. (2015, in press)
13. Xia, X., Zhou, Y., Lai, X.: On the analysis of the (1+1) evolutionary algorithm for the maximum leaf spanning tree problem. Int. J. Comput. Math. **92**(10), 2023–2035 (2015)
14. Lai, X.S., Zhou, Y.R., He, J., Zhang, J.: Performance analysis on evolutionary algorithms for the minimum label spanning tree problem. IEEE Trans. Evol. Comput. **18**(6), 860–872 (2014)
15. Wegener, I.: Methods for the analysis of evolutionary algorithms on pseudo-boolean functions. In: Sarker, R., Mohammadian, M., Yao, X. (eds.) Evolutionary Optimization. Kluwer Academic Publishers, Boston (2001)
16. Khanna, S.: Motwani, R.: Sudan, M., Vazirani, U.: On syntactic versus computational views of approximability. In: Proceedings 35th Annual IEEE Symposium on Foundations of Computer Science, pp. 819–836 (1994)
17. Ming, Y.X., Hiroshi, N.: Confining sets and avoiding bottleneck cases: a simple maximum independent set algorithm in degree-3 graphs. Theor. Comput. Sci. **469**, 92–104 (2013)
18. Halldrsson, M.M., Radhakrishnan, J.: Greed is good: approximating independent sets in sparse and bounded-degree graphs. Algorithmica **18**(1), 145–163 (1997)

A Robust Iris Segmentation Algorithm Using Active Contours Without Edges and Improved Circular Hough Transform

Yueqing Ren$^{(\boxtimes)}$, Zhiyi Qu, and Xiaodong Liu

School of Information Science and Engineering,
Lanzhou University, Lanzhou, China
{renyql3,quzy,liuxdl4}@lzu.edu.cn

Abstract. Iris segmentation plays the most important role in iris biometric system and it determines the subsequent recognizing result. So far, there are still many challenges in this research filed. This paper proposes a robust iris segmentation algorithm using active contours without edges and improved circular Hough transform. Firstly, we adopt a simple linear interpolation model to remove the specular reflections. Secondly, we combine HOG features and Adaboost cascade detector to extract the region of interest from the original iris image. Thirdly, the active contours without edges model and the improved circular Hough transform model are used for the pupillary and limbic boundaries localization, respectively. Lastly, two iris databases CASIA-IrisV1 and CASIA-IrisV4-Lamp were adopted to prove the efficacy of the proposed method. The experimental results show that the performance of proposed method is effective and robust.

Keywords: Iris segmentation · Iris recognition · Adaboost · Histograms of oriented gradients · Active contours without edges · Hough transform

1 Introduction

The rapid development of science and technology brings us much convenience both in life and work, at the same time, however, it also brings more security risks, so a morereliable identity verify system is essential for proving that people are who they claim to be. The traditional authenticationsystems, based on passwords or ID/swipe cards that can be forgotten, lost or stolen, are not very reliable. On the other hand, the biometrics-based authentication systems through matching the physical or behavioral characteristics such as iris pattern, fingerprint or voice to determine the identity of individuals, whichhave a more highly reliability, because that people are impossible to forgot or lose their physical or behavioral characteristics and the characteristics are difficult to be achieved by others. As every iris pattern has a highly detailed and unique texture [1] and is stable during individuals' lifetime, thus iris recognition becomes the particularlyinteresting research field for identity authentication. Iris segmentation, whose goal is to separate out the valid region from original eye image, is the most important step for recognizing.

© Springer International Publishing Switzerland 2015
Z. Huang et al. (Eds.): ICCCS 2015, LNCS 9483, pp. 457–468, 2015.
DOI: 10.1007/978-3-319-27051-7_39

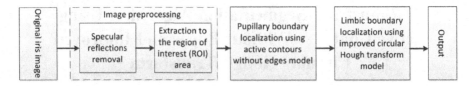

Fig. 1. Flow diagram of proposed algorithm.

In recent two decades, the researchers in this field have proposed many methods for iris segmentation. As early as 1993, John Daugman's work [1] described a feasible iris recognition system in detail and in 1997 Wilds [2] presented an iris biometrics system using an absolutely different method with that of Daugman. These two classical methods established the base of later studies. Shamsi et al. [3] improved the integral-differential operator [1] by restricting the space of potential circles to segment the iris region. Wang [4] proposed a surface integral-differential operator to detect the iris boundaries. Li et al. [5] first located the region which contains pupil by the information of specular high-lights, then detected the pupillary boundary using Canny edge detection and Hough transform. [2, 6, 7] are all Hough transform-based segmentation methods.

All the methods mentioned above are circular fitting model. Howeverthe facts are not always as we wish. In most instances, the pupil is not a circular area, so that it may has more or less errors if we try to approximate the boundary with a regular circle. To remedy this difficulty, there are also many researchers who have put forward viable ideas. Daugman [8] used active contours model, which based on discrete Fourier series expansions of the contour data, to segment the iris region. Ryan et al. [9] fitted the iris boundaries using ellipses, but, for extremely irregular iris boundaries, the result is not very ideal. Mehrabian et al. [10] detected the pupil boundary using graph cuts theory and their algorithm was only worked on the iris images of CASIA-IrisV1, which were pretreated. Shah and Ross [11] segmented the iris region using geodesic active contours, their work gave a better solution to thedistorted iris images, and however, the model may over-segment at the blurred iris boundaries.

In this paper we propose a robust iris segmentation algorithm that locates the iris boundaries based on active contours without edges and improved circular Hough transform, Fig. 1 illustrates the flow diagram of the proposed algorithm. The rest of this paper is organized as follows: Sect. 2 presents preprocessing of the original iris images through which to reduce the noises and computational burden. Section 3 describes the location details of pupillary boundary using active contour without edges model. In Sect. 4, improved circular Hough transform is used for limbic boundary locating. Experimental results are given in Sect. 5. Conclusions are provided in Sect. 6.

2   Image Preprocessing

2.1   Specular Reflections Removal

Generally, the iris images are collected under nearinfrared illumination, so these images inevitably contain specular reflections (See Fig. 2a, d) which may affect the following segmentation if we do not remove them. As the brightest area, specular reflections can be easily detected by binarizationwhen we use an adaptive threshold (See Fig. 2b, e).

Considering that the reflections cannot be located on the edge of the image, we adopt a simple linear interpolation model to interpolate them as shown in Fig. 3.

In processing, we orderly scan the pixel gray scales of each line of the binary image and record the left and rightboundary points p_{left} and p_{right} when detect the brightest regions (See Fig. 3), then we regard the correspondingregion in original image $[p_{left} - 5, p_{left} - 1]$ and $[p_{right} + 1, p_{right} + 5]$ as the left neighborhood and right neighborhood respectively. Presenting the average gray scales of neighborhoods as avg_{left} and avg_{right}, we can calculate the pixel gray scales in the reflection region of original image as follow:

$$p = \frac{d1}{d1 + d2} \tag{1}$$

$$I(x, y) = (1 - p) * avg_{left} + p * avg_{right} \tag{2}$$

Where $I(x, y)$ is the reflection pixel point in original image, $d1$ is the distance of $I(x, y)$ to the left boundary and $d2$ is the distance of $I(x, y)$ to the right boundary. The interpolating result can be seen in Fig. 2c, f.

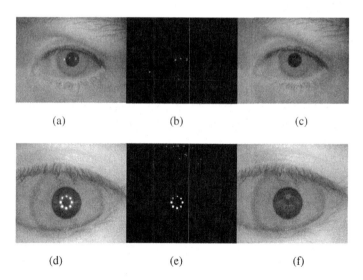

(a)   (b)   (c)

(d)   (e)   (f)

Fig. 2. Illustration of specular reflections removal. (a), (d) are original iris images. (b), (e) arebinary images in which the bright regions correspond with the reflections in (a) and (d), respectively. (c), (f) are the iris images after reflections removal.

2.2 Extraction to the Region of Interest (ROI) Area

Usually, the original images contain the whole region of eye, so it is relatively difficult and time-consuming to extract iris region from original image. Even though each

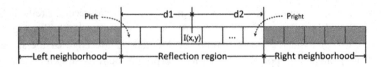

Fig. 3. The model of specular reflections interpolating. Each pixel value in reflection region is determined by the average gray scale values of left and right neighborhood regions.

individual's irises are different, they have a common structure (i.e., all the irises are ring-like structure). In [12], Friedman et al. have proved that boosting is particularly effective when the base models are simple and in recent years the adaptive boosting (Adaboost) cascade detector has been proven to have a good performance in detecting well-structured models, such as face [13], hand posture [14], etc. Here we adopt Adaboost-cascade detector to extract the region of interest.

In thestage of training process ofAdaboost-cascade detector, we collected 1,000 positive images and 1,520 negative images as the training set. Each positive image which contains the complete iris region is normalized with a size of 32*32, while the negative images (non-iris) without any further processing. Histograms of oriented gradients (HOG) [15] features are extracted from each training sample (after reflections removal) to serve as the input data of training system. The feature extraction is processed as follows:

1. *Gradient computation.* Here, [−1, 0, 1] and [−1, 0, 1]^T are used for getting the gradients of horizontal and vertical of the samples, respectively.
2. *Orientation binning.* Each sample is divided into 8*8 pixel cells, then vote the gradients in each cell into 9 orientation bins in 0°– 180°("unsigned" gradient). So each block can be got 4*9 features. The relation between cell and block is shown in Fig. 4. In addition, half of each block is overlapped by its adjacent blocks. 3*3*4*9 = 324 features are got from each positive sample.

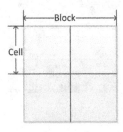

Fig. 4. The relation between block and cell. Each block is consisted of four cells.

The trained Adaboost-cascade detector contains 15 layers. In the execution process, if a specific sub-window of the input image can pass all 15 layers, then the input image is considered as an iris image and output the position and scale of the sub-window.

Otherwise, the input image is considered to be a non-iris image. Three images after iris detection are shown in Fig. 5a, b, c.

The advantages of this step are that: (1). The non-iris image can be eliminated at the beginning of processing so that the computational burden is reduced. (2). ROI is extracted from the original image making the subsequent processing more attentively.

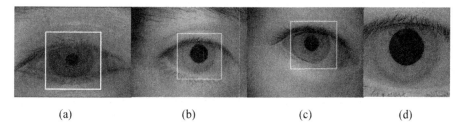

(a)   (b)   (c)   (d)

Fig. 5. Example images after Adaboost detection. (a) – (c) are the detection results in which the white boxes denote the ROI area. (d) is the ROI extracted from iris image.

3 The Pupillary Boundary Localization

The traditional image segmentation methods are gradient–based, considering the position where the gradient of image has a strong change as the edge point. However, for the images whose edges are smoothed, the segmentation results of traditional methods are not satisfying. In 2001, Chan and Vese [18] proposed an active contours without edges model, based on techniques of curve evolution, Mumford-Shah functional for segmentation and level sets, from energy minimizationperspective instead of searching gradient characters. In this section, the pupillary boundary localization is based on Chan-Vese segmentation algorithm.

The basic theory is described as follows: Assume that, the given image u_0 is consisted of two regions of approximately piecewise-constant intensities as shown in Fig. 6a. Here, we appoint that the black region in Fig. 6a is u_0^i and gray region is u_0^o. An evolving curve C in u_0 is defined as:

$$C = \{(x,y)|(x,y) \in u_0, \phi(x,y) = 0\} \qquad (3)$$

and

$$inside(C) = \{(x,y)|(x,y) \in u_0, \phi(x,y) > 0\} \qquad (4)$$

$$outside(C) = \{(x,y)|(x,y) \in u_0, \phi(x,y) < 0\} \qquad (5)$$

Consider the energy function:

$$E = F_1(C) + F_2(C) = \int\limits_{inside(C)} |u_0(x,y) - c_1|^2 dxdy + \int\limits_{outside(C)} |u_0(x,y) - c_2|^2 dxdy$$

(6)

Where:

$$c_1 = \frac{1}{N_i} \sum_{inside(C)} u_0(x,y)$$

(7)

$$c_2 = \frac{1}{N_o} \sum_{outside(C)} u_0(x,y)$$

(8)

Here, N_i is the pixels number inside C and N_o is the pixels number outside C. In Fig. 6b, c, d, e, we can see that only when the curve C on the boundary of u_i can the energy function get the minimum value, obviously. That is,

$$\inf_C \{F_1(C) + F_2(C)\} \approx 0 \approx F_1(C_0) + F_2(C_0)$$

(9)

Where C_0 is the boundary of u_i.

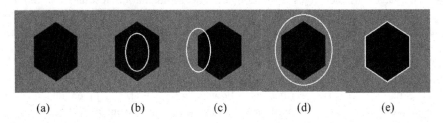

| (a) | (b) | (c) | (d) | (e) |

Fig. 6. (a)is the example image. (b) – (c) illustrate all the possible cases in the position of the curve. (b) $F_1(c) \approx 0, F_2(C) > 0, E > 0$. (c) $F_1(C) > 0, F_2(C) > 0, E > 0$. (d) $F_1(C) > 0$, $F_2(C) \approx 0, E > 0$. (e) $F_1(C) \approx 0, F_2(C) \approx 0, E \approx 0$.

In the active contours model of Chan and Vese [16] some regularizing terms such as the length of the curve C and area of the region inside C are added into the energy function. The function is shown as follow:

$$F(c_1, c_2, C) = \mu \cdot Length(C) + v \cdot Area(inside(C))$$
$$+ \lambda_1 \int\limits_{inside(C)} |u_0(x,y) - c_1|^2 dxdy + \lambda_2 \int\limits_{outside(C)} |u_0(x,y) - c_2|^2 dxdy$$

(10)

Where $\mu \geq 0, v \geq 0, \lambda_1, \lambda_2 \geq 0$.

Based on the energy function (10), we can get the level set formulation through introducing Heaviside function $H(\cdot)$ and Dirac function $\delta(\cdot)$. The formulation is given by:

$$F(c_1, c_2, \phi) = \mu \int_{u_0} \delta(\phi(x,y))|\nabla\phi(x,y)|dxdy + v \int_{u_0} H(\phi(x,y))dxdy$$

$$+ \lambda_1 \int_{u_0} |u_0(x,y) - c_1|^2 H(\phi(x,y))dxdy \qquad (11)$$

$$+ \lambda_2 \int_{u_0} |u_0(x,y) - c_2|^2 (1 - H(\phi(x,y)))dxdy$$

Where c_1 and c_2 can be written by:

$$c_1 = \frac{\int_{u_0} u_0(x,y)H(\phi(x,y))dxdy}{\int_{u_0} H(\phi(x,y))dxdy} \qquad (12)$$

$$c_2 = \frac{\int_{u_0} u_0(x,y)(1 - H(\phi(x,y)))dxdy}{\int_{u_0} (1 - H(\phi(x,y)))dxdy} \qquad (13)$$

In order to get the minimum of F, then the derivative of F is calculated and set to zero, as follow:

$$\frac{\partial\phi}{\partial t} = \delta(\phi)\left[\mu \cdot div\left(\frac{\nabla\phi}{|\nabla\phi|}\right) - v - \lambda_1(u_0 - c_1)^2 + \lambda_2(u_0 - c_2)^2\right] = 0 \qquad (14)$$

Where t is an artificial time and $t \geq 0$. In the implementation process we set $\mu = 0.01 * 255 * 255$, $v = 0$ and $\lambda_1 = \lambda_2 = 1$. We start the iteration at the center of the ROI which extracted by the Adaboost cascade detector in above section so as to locate the pupillary boundary in a high speed and accuracy. Figure 7 shows some samples of pupillary boundary localization results using active contours without edges model. We can obviously see that the pupil boundaries which are not regular circles can also be approximated accurately.

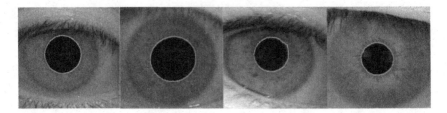

Fig. 7. Samples of pupillary boundary localization using active contour without edges model.

4   The Limbic Boundary Localization

As the definition of limbic boundary is not as strong as that of the pupillary boundary, in addition, the textures of iris near the limbic boundary are not so rich, therefore, the error is acceptable when we using an regular circle to approximate the limbic boundary-whilethe eye in frontal sate. In this section, an improved circular Hough transform is used for locating the limbic boundary. The detailed processing is as follows:

1. *Resizing.* Taking the ROI image as input and resize it with a predetermined scale, through which can greatly decrease the computing burden of subsequent processing. In experiment we set the scale = 0.3.
2. *Blurring.* In order to remove the noises that may affect the limbic boundary locating, here we adopt Gaussian filter to blur the output image of step 1. In Fig. 8 we can see that the edge detecting result after Gaussian filter processing (Fig. 8b) has fewer noises than the result without the processing (Fig. 8a).

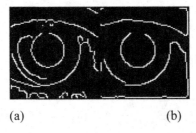

(a)   (b)

Fig. 8. Comparison between the results of edge detecting. (a) is the result without Gaussian filter processing. (b) is the result with Gaussian filter processing.

3. *Enhancing.* Here, histogram equalization is adopted to enhance the output of step 2. After this processing, the characteristics of the boundary will be more obvious.
4. *Edge detecting.* Here, we use Cannyedge detection method to detect the edges in the output of step 3. The detecting result is shown as Fig. 8b, in which the iris boundaries are very obvious and that there are very few noises.
5. *Limbic boundary Locating.* As the iris edges are detected roughly in step 4, here we adopt an improved circular Hough transform to locate the limbic boundary. Generally, the geometric center of the limbic boundary will be limited in the region of pupil, so we can avoid the circles whose center outside the pupil boundary, which is

located in Sect. 3, when searching the best-fit-circle. In this way, we can greatly improve the processing efficiency.

The locating process follows the improved circular Hough transform model. Here we define that the edge points detected by Canny are belong to the points set E, the coordinate points inside the pupil region are belong to the points set P and the radius of fit-circles which we search for is limited in theinterval $[r_{min}, r_{max}]$. So fit-circles are limited in a 3D space as (x_0, y_0, r), where $(x_0, y_0) \in P$ and $r \in [r_{min}, r_{max}]$. The circular Hough transform model is given as (15) and (16):

$$W_{(x_0,y_0,r)} = \sum_{(x,y)\in E} \sum_{\theta=0}^{359} (S(\sqrt{((x - r \cdot \cos(\frac{2\pi\theta}{360}) - x_0)^2 + ((y - r \cdot \sin(\frac{2\pi\theta}{360})) - y_0)^2} - \varepsilon))$$

$$(14)$$

$$(x_0, y_0) \in P, r \in [r_{min}, r_{max}] \tag{15}$$

$$S(x) = \begin{cases} 1, x<0 \\ 0, x\geq0 \end{cases} \tag{16}$$

Where $S(x)$ is a voting function, if $x<0$, the output is 1, otherwise the output is 0. So if the edge point fit the specified circle model (x_0, y_0, r), then adds 1 to the weight of the circle $W_{(x_0,y_0,r)}$. ε is a fixed and predefined small value, in experiment we set $\varepsilon = 3$.

After the voting process for each candidate circle model, we can get a set of weights of potential circles which is shown as (17).

$$Circle_{weight} = \{W(x_0, y_0, r)|(x_0, y_0) \in P, r \in [r_{min}, r_{max}]\} \tag{17}$$

The best-fit circle is the one whose weight is the largest in the set of $Circle_{weight}$, The best-fit circle is written by (18).

$$Circle_{best-fit}(x_0, y_0, r) = \max_{(x_0,y_0,r)} Circle_{weight} \tag{18}$$

Figure 9 shows some process results using improved circular Hough transform.

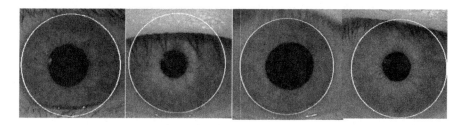

Fig. 9. Samples of limbic boundary locating results using improved circular Hough transform model.

5   Experimental Results

In order to evaluate the effectiveness of the proposed algorithm,CASIA-IrisV1 [17] and CASIA-IrisV4-Lamp [17] irisdatabases were adopted in our experiments. The CASIA-IrisV1 contains 756 iris images and all images arestored as BMP format with resolution 320*280. The images of CASIA-IrisV4-Lamp are stored as JPG format with resolution 640*480. We performed the proposed algorithm in Matlab R2012B environment and on a PC with Intel i3 CPU at 3.30 GHz speed and with 4.0G RAM.

As the pupil regions of all iris images in CASIA-IrisV1 were replaced with a circular region of constant intensity, we skipped the step of removing specular reflections when the algorithm performed on the database CASIA-IrisV1.

For comparison, in experiments we re-implemented the classical segmentation methods proposed by Daugman [18] and Wilds [2] in Matlab, respectively. The experimental analysis proved that the performance of the method proposed in this paper was better than that of Daugman and Wilds.

The experiment results for database CASIA-IrisV1 are shown in Table 1.

Table 1. The performance comparison for database CASIA-IrisV1

Method	Accuracy (%)	Mean elapsed time(s)
Daugman [18]	96.3 %	2.32
Wilds [2]	92.5 %	1.93
Proposed method	98.7 %	1.57

Some samples of segmentation results from database CASIA-IrisV1 are shown in Fig. 10.

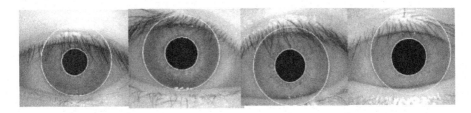

Fig. 10. Samples of iris segmentation results from database CASIA-IrisV1.

For database CASIA-IrisV4-Lamp, there are lots of iris samples that have long eyelashes. In order to improve the performance, 1D rank filter was adopted to process the eyelashes before segmentation. The experiment results for database CASIA-IrisV4-Lamp are shown in Table 2.

Some samples of segmentation results from database CASIA-IrisV4-Lamp are shown in Fig. 11.

Table 2. The performance comparison for database CASIA-IrisV4-Lamp

Method	Accuracy (%)	Mean elapsed time(s)
Daugman [18]	93.3 %	2.58
Wilds [2]	89.3 %	2.16
Proposed method	95.1 %	1.96

Fig. 11. Samples of iris segmentation results from database CASIA-IrisV4-Lamp.

The above two groups of experimental results demonstrate the effectiveness and robustness of the proposed method.

6 Conclusions

Iris segmentation is a critical module in iris recognition system and its accuracy will affect the recognition results seriously. In this paper we propose a robust iris segmentation method using active contours without edges and improved circular Hough transform. Firstly, we use a simple linear interpolation method to remove specular reflections and combine the HOG features and Adaboost-cascade detector to detect the region of interest. Secondly, the active contours without edges model is adopted to locate the pupillary boundary. Finally, improved circular Hough transform is used for limbic boundary locating. Experimental results show that the performance of proposed method in this paper is better than that of Daugman [18] and Wilds [2].

This paper does not involve the research about eyelids and eyelashes processing, which also is an important part in iris segmenting. So in the future work, we will pay more time to remove the interferences from eyelids and eyelashes and to extract out the most effective iris region for subsequence matching.

Acknowledgement. The authors wish to thank the Chinese Academy of Sciences' Institute of Automation (CASIA) for providing CASIA iris image databases

References

1. Daugman, J.G.: High confidence visual recognition of persons by a test of statistical independence. IEEE Trans. Pattern Anal. Mach. Intell. **15**, 1148–1161 (1993)
2. Wildes, R.P.: Iris recognition: an emerging biometric technology. Proc. IEEE **85**, 1348–1363 (1997)

3. Shamsi, M., Saad, P.B., Ibrahim, S.B., Kenari, A.R.: Fast algorithm for iris localization using daugman circular integro differential operator. In: International Conference of Soft Computing and Pattern Recognition, SOCPAR 2009, pp. 393–398 (2009)

4. Chunping, W.: Research on iris image recognition algorithm based on improved differential operator. J. Convergence Inf. Technol. **8**, 563–570 (2013)

5. Peihua, L., Xiaomin, L.: An incremental method for accurate iris segmentation. In: 19th International Conference on Pattern Recognition, 2008, ICPR 2008, pp. 1–4 (2008)

6. Bendale, A., Nigam, A., Prakash, S., Gupta, P.: Iris segmentation using improved hough transform. In: Huang, D.-S., Gupta, P., Zhang, X., Premaratne, P. (eds.) ICIC 2012. CCIS, vol. 304, pp. 408–415. Springer, Heidelberg (2012)

7. Mahlouji, M., Noruzi, A., Kashan, I.: Human iris segmentation for iris recognition in unconstrained environments. IJCSI Int. J. Comput. Sci. **9**, 149–155 (2012)

8. Daugman, J.: New methods in iris recognition. IEEE Trans. Syst. Man Cybern. Part B Cybern. **37**, 1167–1175 (2007)

9. Ryan, W.J., Woodard, D.L., Duchowski, A.T., Birchfield, S.T.: Adapting starburst for elliptical iris segmentation. In: 2nd IEEE International Conference on Biometrics: Theory, Applications and Systems, BTAS 2008, pp. 1–7 (2008)

10. Mehrabian, H., Hashemi-Tari, P.: Pupil boundary detection for iris recognition using graph cuts. In: Proceedings of Image and Vision Computing New Zealand 2007, pp. 77–82 (2007)

11. Shah, S., Ross, A.: Iris segmentation using geodesic active contours. IEEE Trans. Inf. Forensics Secur. **4**, 824–836 (2009)

12. Friedman, J., Hastie, T., Tibshirani, R.: Additive logistic regression: a statistical view of boosting (With discussion and a rejoinder by the authors). Ann. Stat. **28**, 337–407 (2000)

13. Viola, P., Jones, M.: Rapid object detection using a boosted cascade of simple features. In: Proceedings of the 2001 IEEE Computer Society Conference on Computer Vision and Pattern Recognition, CVPR 2001, vol.1, pp. I-511–I-518 (2001)

14. Yao, Y., Li, C.-T.: Hand posture recognition using SURF with adaptive boosting. In: Presented at the British Machine Vision Conference (BMVC), Guildford, United Kingdom (2012)

15. Dalal, N., Triggs, B.: Histograms of oriented gradients for human detection. In: IEEE Computer Society Conference on Computer Vision and Pattern Recognition, CVPR 2005, vol. 1, pp. 886–893 (2005)

16. Chan, T.F., Vese, L.A.: Active contours without edges. IEEE Trans. Image Process. **10**, 266–277 (2001)

17. CASIA iris image database: http://biometrics.idealtest.org/

18. Daugman, J.: How iris recognition works. In: Proceedings of 2002 International Conference on Image Processing, vol. 1, pp. I-33–I-36 (2002)

An Adaptive Hybrid PSO and GSA Algorithm for Association Rules Mining

Zhiping Zhou[✉], Daowen Zhang, Ziwen Sun, and Jiefeng Wang

School of Internet of Things Engineering, Jiangnan University,
Wuxi 214122, Jiangsu, China
{zzp,sunziwen}@jiangnan.edu.cn,
{18206181483,18352513420}@163.com

Abstract. Association rule mining is an interesting topic to extract hidden knowledge in data mining. Particle Swarm Optimization(PSO) has been used to mine Association rules, but it suffers from easily falling into local optimum. Gravitational search algorithm(GSA) has high performance in searching the global optimum but it suffers from running slowly especially in the last iterations. In order to resolve the aforementioned problem, in this paper a new hybrid algorithm called A_PSOGSA is proposed for association rules mining. Firstly, it integrates PSO and GSA. To make the idea simpler, PSO will browse the search space in such away to cover most of its regions and the local exploration of each particle is computed by GSA search. Secondly, the acceleration coefficients are controlled dynamically with the population distribution information during the process of evolution in order to provide a better balance between the ability of global and local searching. The experiments verify the accuracy and the effectiveness of the algorithm in this paper compared with the other algorithms for mining association rules.

Keywords: Association rules mining · Particle Swarm Optimization · Gravitational Search Algorithm · Dynamically updating approach

1 Introduction

The main goal of mining association rules is to find hidden relationship between items from a given transactional database. Since it was proposed, association rules had been attracted universal attention of scholars and deeply studied. And it has been successfully applied to many different fields, such as shopping cart analysis [1], stock market analysis and network attacks analysis [2] and so on.

Many algorithms have been proposed for association rules, such as FP-tree [3], the classic algorithm: Apriori [4, 5] and the other algorithms based on frequent itemsets. The current dataset is featured by big volumes of data. The classical association rules mining algorithms dealt with data sets somehow in an efficient way and in reasonable time. However they are difficult to be applicable to the current amount of data. Recent years, research on intelligent heuristic algorithms has got great progress. The intelligent algorithms have been used to solve non-convex and non-linear optimization problem. Hence, people are trying to use new intelligent algorithms to mine association rules, such as genetic algorithm [6], particle swarm algorithm [7], ant colony algorithm [8],

© Springer International Publishing Switzerland 2015
Z. Huang et al. (Eds.): ICCCS 2015, LNCS 9483, pp. 469–479, 2015.
DOI: 10.1007/978-3-319-27051-7_40

some hybrid algorithms [9, 10] and so on. In [9], the authors propose SARIC algorithm, which uses set particle swarm optimization to generate association rules from a database and considers both positive and negative occurrences of attributes. The experiments verify the efficiency of SARIC. In [10], a novel hybrid algorithm called HPSO-TS-ARM has been proposed for association rules mining. These algorithms are based three well known high-level procedures: Particle Swarm Optimization, Tabu Search and Apriori Algorithm. Particle swarm optimization (PSO) is a new evolutionary algorithm developed in recent years. It is also from the random solution, through the iterative search for the optimal solution, it is also through the fitness to evaluate the quality of the solution, but it is more simple than the genetic algorithm. This algorithm has attracted the attention of academic circles and has demonstrated its superiority in solving practical problems with its advantages of easy realization, high accuracy and fast convergence. PSO owns the ability of convergence speed, but it suffers from easily falling into local optimal especially for mining association rules. A novel heuristic optimization method called Gravitational Search Algorithm (GSA) based on the law of gravity and mass interactions is proposed in [11]. It has been proven that this algorithm has good ability to search for the global optimum, but it suffers from slow searching speed in the last iterations. Utilizing intelligent algorithms to resolve problems, some parameters need to be set in advance, such as the inertia and acceleration coefficients in PSO, mutation, selection probability in GA and so on. Researches have shown that parameters have great influence on the performance of the algorithms processing various problems. For example, Bergh et al. estimate the influence of parameters, such as the inertia term on the performance of the algorithm [12]. In the past few years, many approaches have been applied to investigate how to adapt suitable parameters. The acceleration coefficients in PSO algorithm are varied adaptively during iterations to improve solution quality of original PSO and avoid premature convergence [13]. According to the results of the experiments, the self-adaptive scheme proposed in [13] can well balance the capabilities of exploration and exploitation. In [14], An adaptive particle swarm optimization (APSO) based on the population distribution of information during the process of evolution state is presented to adaptively control the acceleration coefficients, Results show that APSO substantially enhances the performance of the PSO. Motivated by the hybrid idea of the algorithms and the adaptive approach to control the acceleration coefficients, in this paper, we propose a new algorithm called A_PSOGSA for association rules mining.

The rest of this paper is organized as follows. In Sect. 2, we introduce the related theory of the association rules and PSO, GSA. In Sect. 3, the new algorithm is proposed. Section 4 summarizes our experimental results. We demonstrate the good performance of the algorithm A_PSOGSA and compare it to the other ARM algorithms. In Sect. 5 we point out the innovation of the article and give a conclusion to this paper by some remarks.

2   Related Theory

This section mainly introduces the basic concept of association rules and the related theory of PSO and GSA.

2.1 Association Rules

Association Rules Mining (ARM) is an important branche of data mining which has been used in many areas. Formally, the association rules problem is as follows: Let I be a set of items or attributes $I = \{i_1, i_2, \ldots, i_m\}$, X is a subset of I, If there are k attributes in X, then X is called a k set; let D be a set of transactions. $D=\{t_1, t_2, \ldots, t_n\}$, an association rule is an expression of the form X =>Y, where $X \subset I, Y \subset I, X \cap Y = \emptyset$, the itemset X is called antecedent while the itemset Y is called consequent. Similarly, an fuzzy association rules is an implication of the form if X is M, then Y is N, where M, N are linguistic variables. Generally, association rules have two measures: Support and Confidence. Support is calculated by the equation of $Support(X => Y) = \frac{|X \cup Y|}{|D|}$, $|X \cup Y|$, is the number of transactions which contains both X and Y. Confidence is calculated by the equation of $Confidence(X \Rightarrow Y) = \frac{support(X \cup Y)}{support(Y)}$. The two threshold of fuzzy association rules have the same calculation method in the condition of converting quantitative data to fuzzy linguistic variables. Formally, the rules satisfying the minimum confidence are called strong fuzzy association rules.

2.2 Particle Swarm Optimization Algorithm

Particle swarm optimization algorithm(PSO) [15] is usually used to solve the nonlinear numerical problem, where every particle represents the candidate solution of the problem. In each iteration, particles update themselves by tracking the two extreme values: one is individual optimal solution, denoted by pbest; the other is a global optimal solution, denoted by gbest. Each particle in PSO should consider the current position, the current velocity, the distance to pbest, and the distance to gbest in order to modify its position. PSO was mathematically modelled as follows:

$$v_i(t+1) = w \times v_i(t+1) + c_1 \times r_1 \times [pbest_i - x_i(t)] + c_2 \times r_2 \times [gbest_i - x_i(t)] \quad (1)$$

$$x_i(t+1) = x_i(t) + v_i(t+1) \quad (2)$$

where w is the inertia weight, c1, c2 are two constants which are usually 2, r1, r2 are random numbers between 0–1. As shown in Eq. 1, the first part provides exploration ability for PSO, the second part represents individual cognition which lead particles to move toward the particles' optimal position experienced, the third part represents group cognition which lead particles to move toward the best position found by swarm.

PSO has the advantage of fast convergence speed, but it is easy to fall into local optimum, especially dealing with huge amount of data. Particles update their positions by tracking only two extreme values, without considering the interaction between particles. If considering the influence between particles, the probability of falling into local optimum will be reduced and efficiency will be improved.

2.3 Gravitational Search Algorithm

The gravitational search algorithm (GSA) [11] is inspired by Newton's law of universal gravitation. According to [11], suppose there is a system with n agents, every agent represents a candidate solutions to the problem, in this paper it represents a rule in association rules mining problems through special coding, related content about this will be introduced in the Sect. 3.

For n agents, each agent's position is $x_i, i = 1, 2, 3, \ldots, n$.

All agents are randomly initialized in a problem space. In iteration t, the forces of i from j are defined as follows:

$$F_{ij}(t) = G(t) \times \frac{M_{pi}(t) \times M_{pj}(t)}{R_{ij}(t) + \varepsilon} \times (x_j(t) - x_i(t)) \tag{3}$$

where G(t)is gravity coefficient at a specific time t, $R_{ij}(t)$ is the Euclidean distance between two agents, calculated as follows:

$$G(t) = G_0 \times \exp(-\alpha \times iter / maxiter) \tag{4}$$

$$R_{ij}(t) = \left\| x_i(t), x_j(t) \right\|_2 \tag{5}$$

where α a is the descending coefficient, G_0 is the initial gravitational constant, iter is the current iteration, and maxiter is the maximum number of iterations.

In the search space, the total gravitational force of agent i is represented by the following formula:

$$F_i(t) = \sum_{j=1, j \neq i}^{n} rand_j \times F_{ij}(t) \tag{6}$$

so the accelerations of all agents are calculated as follows:

$$a_i(t) = \frac{F_i(t)}{M_{ii}(t)} \tag{7}$$

The velocity and position of the agents are defined as follows:

$$v_i(t+1) = rand_i \times v_i(t) + a_i(t) \tag{8}$$

$$x_i(t+1) = x_i(t) + v_i(t+1) \tag{9}$$

The masses of all agents are updated using the following equations:

$$M_i(t) = \frac{fit_i(t) - worst_i(t)}{best_i(t) - worst_i(t)} \tag{10}$$

worst, best depends on the type of the problems studied, namely it is minimization problem or maximization problem.

GSA considers the interaction between particles, but without memory function, the agents can not observe global optimal. The main drawback is that the convergence speed of the algorithm is slow.

3   An Adaptive Hybrid PSO and GSA Algorithm

3.1   Hybrid PSO and GSA Algorithm

The basic idea of integration of PSO and GSA algorithm is to combine the local search ability of GSA and the global search ability of PSO. PSO does not consider the inter particle distance, while the GSA dose. Added memory capacity of PSO and inter particle force of GSA, the hybrid algorithm increases the interaction between particles, strengthen the local searching ability. Improvements are realized in the particle position and velocity updating formula, which are defined as follows:

$$v_i(t+1) = w \times v_i(t) + c_1 \times r_1 \times [a_i(t) + (pbest - x_i(t))] + c_2 \times r_2 \times (gbest - x_i(t)) \tag{11}$$

$$x_i(t+1) = x_i(t) + v_i(t+1) \tag{12}$$

where the parameters of w, c_1, c_2, r_1, r_2 have the same meaning as they are explained in PSO, $a_i(t)$ is the acceleration of the particle i at the iteration t which is calculated by GSA. In the combination algorithm, the updating of the velocity is not only dependent on the local optimum and global optimum, but also the acceleration of the particles which is calculated by GSA. That is to say, in the new updating method, the particles are affected by the full force of all the particles, which makes the algorithm more efficient when searching in the problem space as we can see in the following aspects: The fitness of particles is considered in the updating process of each iteration; Particles near the optimal value can be able to attract particles that attempt to explore other search space; The algorithm has the ability of memory to save the global optimum found so far, so we can get the best solution at any time, which is very useful for association rules mining; Any particle can perceive the global optimal solution and keep close to him.

When we use the proposed algorithm to mine association rules, some specific action must be taken on the particles.

The encoding solution: the coding method used in this paper is that a particle represents a rule, every particle S is a vector of n + 1 elements (n is the number of all attributes or items) where: S[1] is index separator between the consequent and the antecedent parts, S[2]-S[n + 1] is the position of the items consists with two parts which are attributes and the data point's linguistic values. The item position's value maybe 0, representing the attribute at this position does not exist in the rule.

The fitness function: the fitness function is the correlation between the algorithm and association rules, a good fitness function can help algorithms better dig. Minimum support, and minimum confidence are two threshold of the rule. The fitness is of rule S defined as follows:

$$fitness = w \times [\frac{SUP(A \cup B)}{SUP(A)}] \times [\frac{SUP(A \cup B)}{SUP(B)}] \times [1 - \frac{SUP(A \cup B)}{|D|}]$$ (13)

Where w is used to increase the number of meaningful rules, in this paper set w 2. $|D|$ is the total number of records in a transaction database.

3.2   Adaptive Approach

Inspired by the Literature [13, 14], in this section an approach is proposed to adaptively adjust the parameters during the process of the evolution. Know from Eq. (11), the performance of the hybrid algorithm is mainly influenced by three parameters, the inertia weight and two positive acceleration coefficients (c_1 and c_2). In most cases, the acceleration coefficients are set to be constant values, but, in fact, intelligent algorithm should dynamically adjust the value of the parameters depending on the evolution state in order to provide a better balance between the ability of global and local searching. Evolution state an be estimated based on the population distribution information. During the evolutionary process, the particles tend to the global optimum area, hence, the evolution state experienced can be determined according to the population distribution information. However, In [14], the algorithm does not put forward specific formula to calculate the acceleration coefficients (c_1 and c_2). Combined with [13], utilizing constriction factor, this paper proposes a specific method. The specific dynamic adjustment strategy of acceleration coefficients is detailed in the following part.

The evolution state is divided into four stages: exploration, exploitation, convergence, and jumping out. Determine the "evolutionary factor" using $f = \frac{d_g - d_{min}}{d_{max} - d_g}$, d_g is the mean distance of global best particle to all the other particles. d_{max} is the maximum distance and d_{min} is the minimum distance. $d_i = \frac{1}{N-1} \sum_{j=1, j \neq i}^{N} \sqrt{\sum_{k=1}^{A} (x_i^k - x_j^k)^2}$, indicates the mean distance of particle i to the other particles, where N is population size, A is number of attributes. Classify particles into one of the four aforementioned evolutionary states. At different evolutionary state, the acceleration coefficients are adaptively controlled and calculated according to the formula (14) and (15).

$$f = \left| \frac{2}{2 - \varphi - \sqrt{\varphi^2 - 4\varphi}} \right|, \varphi = c_1 + c_2$$ (14)

$$c_1 = c_{1i} + \frac{c_{1f} - c_{1i}}{max iter} \times iter$$ (15)

Where, c_{1f}, c_{1i} care initial and final values of cognitive and social components acceleration factors respectively.

Depending on population distribution information and constriction factor, acceleration coefficients (c_1 and c_2) are set different values during different evolutionary stage. The reason why we do this is that the function of acceleration factor is different in different stages of evolution. For example, in the exploration stage, the particles must have the ability to search the other regions of problem space not crowding at the same region.

The specific flow path of mining association rules with A_PSOGSA are shown as follows:

Step1: Randomly generate a certain size of population, initialize each particle and set C1, C2 to 2;

Step 2: Calculate the support and confidence, fitness of the rules;

Step 3: Update the G, pbest and gbest for the populations.

Step 4: Calculate M, forces and accelerations for all particles.

Step 5: Get the population distribution information to calculate evolutionary factor and then adaptively update c_1, c_2 as mentioned in Sect. 3.2

Step 6: Add the rules which meet the conditions in the gbest to the rules set, and delete duplicate rules.

Step 7: Update velocity and position of each particle.

Step 8: If meeting the conditions or reaching the maximum number of iterations,the algorithm terminates,if not, return to step 2.

4 The Experiment and Analysis

In order to verify the feasibility, accuracy and efficiency of the A-PSOGSA algorithm for mining association rules, the algorithm is programmed by matlab2009,which is running on the platform of ordinary Lenovo computer whose clocked is 1.78 GHz, memory is 3G. The test data sets are from the UCI public data set: Car Evaluation, Nursery, Page Block, Balance. The download address is http://archive.ics.uci.edu/ml/datasets.html. The features of the datasets are described in Table 1.

For A_PSOGSA algorithm, c1, c2 are initialized to 2 and adaptively controlled according to different evolutionary states. w decreases linearly from 0.9 to 0.4, the α and G_0 in GSA are set to be 20 and 1. The initial population size of particle is 100; the maximum number of iterations is 300.

4.1 The Experiment of Testing Fitness Function

Run the experiment 30 times, we calculate the fitness value according to the formula (13). Figures 1 and 2 shows the best, average, worst value of the fitness at different iteration in data set Car Evaluation and Nursery.

The experimental results proves the feasibility of A_PSOGSA algorithm in association rules mining.

Table 1. Dataset description

Dataset	Instances	Attributes	Types
Car Evaluation	1728	6	Categorical
Nursery	12960	8	Categorical
Page Block	5473	10	Integer
Balance	625	4	Categorical

4.2   Algorithm Comparison Experiment and Analysis

In order to prove the good performance of the algorithm, compare the algorithm in this paper with two well known algorithms: PSO algorithm, GA algorithm and the adaptive PSO(APSO) algorithm in [14]. For PSO, w is 0.8, acceleration coefficients are 2. For GA, Mutation rate is 0.02, choice rate is 0.8. Population size is 100, the maximum number of iterations is 300 in both PSO and GA. The algorithms are all running on data set Page Block. Figure 3 shows the mining result.

As shown in Fig. 3, the A_PSOGSA algorithm in this paper have good mining advantage especially dealing with huge amount of data. A_PSOGSA have the ability of mining rules at the beginning of iterations compared with the other two algorithms PSO and GA. The algorithm provides a better performance by using the adaptive approach. GSA considers the interaction between particles, but without memory function, the agents can not observe global optimal. The main drawback is that the convergence speed of the algorithm is slow. GA starts slowly caused by its own limitations. Like PSO, GA is also easy to fall into local optimum, which can not mine the rules fully. PSO has the advantage of fast convergence speed, but it is easy to fall into local optimum, especially dealing with huge amount of data. Particles update their positions by tracking only two extreme values, without considering the interaction between particles. If considering the influence between particles, the probability of falling into local optimum will be reduced and efficiency will be improved.

4.3   Mining Results of the Four Datasets

Table 2 shows the results of association rules mining when applying A_PSOGSA, PSO, GA and APSO algorithms on the four datasets. In the table, "Sup" is the average support and "Conf" is the average confidence of the rules. "Rules" represents the total number of the rules of different datasets.

As can be seen from the table, the proposed algorithm A_PSOGSA in this paper has better performance than the other two algorithms. A_PSOGSA has good ability of exploration, and exploitation due to the hybrid PSO and GSA. It provides a better balance between the ability of global and local searching. By adaptively adjusting the acceleration coefficients, the algorithm owns high convergence speed but not easily fall into local optimal. Hence, A_PSOGSA has been improved compared with PSO and GA.

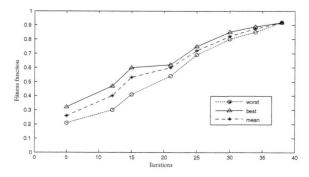

Fig. 1. The A_PSOGSA algorithm's running result on Car Evaluation.

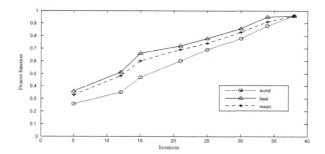

Fig. 2. The A_PSOGSA algorithm's running result on Nursery.

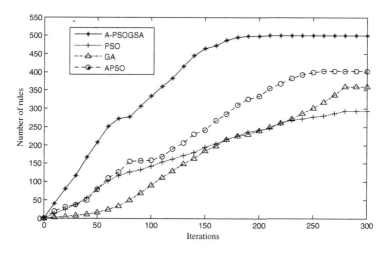

Fig. 3. The mining result comparison of A_PSOGSA, PSO, GA and APSO on Page Block

Table 2. The results of association rules mining of A_PSOGSA, PSO, GA and APSO

Data set	Algorithm	Sup	Conf	rules
Page Block	A_PSOGSA	0.68	0.93	500
	PSO	0.71	0.86	293
	GA	0.65	0.85	360
	APSO	0.70	0.90	402
Car Eva	A_PSOGSA	0.69	0.71	26
	PSO	0.64	0.68	21
	GA	0.60	0.70	24
	APSO	0.66	0.72	23
Nursery	A_PSOGSA	0.56	0.82	41
	PSO	0.53	0.80	41
	GA	0.54	0.79	38
	APSO	0.56	0.80	40
Balance	A_PSOGSA	0.38	0.75	36
	PSO	0.38	0.76	32
	GA	0.35	0.73	30
	APSO	0.37	0.76	32

5   Conclusion

In this paper, a novel algorithm called A_PSOGSA is proposed for mining association rules. This progress is made possible by integrating PSO and GSA, which utilizes the high convergence speed of PSO and global searching ability of GSA, by adaptively controlling the acceleration coefficient with the population distribution information., which provides a better balance between global exploration and local exploitation. The experiments demonstrate the feasibility of the presented algorithm when mining association rules. The mining results show that A_PSOGSA algorithm's performance has been improved compared with PSO and GA algorithm In summary, the algorithm is suitable to mine association rules and has good performance.

Acknowledgement. This work is supported by Jiangsu Province Joint Research Project Foundation(BY2013015-33) and Nature Science Foundation of Jiangsu Province(NO. BK20131107)

References

1. Cao, L., Zhao, Y., Zhang, H., et al.: Flexible frameworks for actionable knowledge discovery. J. Knowl. Data Eng. 22(9), 1299–1312 (2010)
2. Lan, G.C., Hong, T.P., Tseng, V.S.: A projection-based approach for discovering high average-utility itemsets. J. Inf. Sci. Eng. 28(1), 193–209 (2012)

3. Han, J., Pei, J., Yin, Y.: Mining frequent patterns without candidate generation. In: SIGMOD 2000, Proceedings of the 2000 ACM SIGMOD International Conference on Management of Data, pp. 1–12. ACM, New York (2000)
4. Agrawal, R., Imieliński, T., Swami, A.: Mining association rules between sets of items in large databases. In: SIGMOD 1993, Proceedings of the 1993 ACM SIGMOD International Conference on Management of Data, pp. 207–216. ACM, New York (1993)
5. Agrawal, R., Srikant, R.: Fast algorithms for mining association rules. In: Proceedings of the 20th International Conference on Very Large Data Bases, VLDB, pp. 487–499 (1994)
6. Minaei-Bidgoli, B., Barmaki, R., Nasiri, M.: Mining numerical association rules via multi-objective genetic algorithms. J. Inf. Sci. **233**, 15–24 (2013)
7. Beiranvand, V., Mobasher-Kashani, M., Bakar, A.A.: Multi-objective PSO algorithm for mining numerical association rules without a priori discretization. J. Expert Syst. Appl. **41** (9), 4259–4273 (2014)
8. Sundaramoorthy, S., Shantharajah, S.P.: An improved ant colony algorithm for effective mining of frequent items. J. Web Eng. **13**(3–4), 263–276 (2014)
9. Agrawal, J., Agrawal, S., Singhai, A., et al.: SET-PSO-based approach for mining positive and negative association rules. J. Knowl. Inf. Syst., 1–19 (2014)
10. Kaur, S., Goyal, M.: Fast and robust hybrid particle swarm optimization tabu search association rule mining (HPSO-ARM) algorithm for web data association rule mining (WDARM). J. Adv. Res. Comput. Sci. Manag. Stud. **2**, 448–451 (2014)
11. Rashedi, E., Nezamabadi-Pour, H., Saryazdi, S.: GSA: a gravitational search algorithm. J. Inf. Sci. **179**(13), 2232–2248 (2009)
12. Van den Bergh, F., Engelbrecht, A.P.: A study of particle swarm optimization particle trajectories. J. Inf. Sci. **176**(8), 937–971 (2006)
13. Mohammadi-Ivatloo, B., Moradi-Dalvand, M., Rabiee, A.: Combined heat and power economic dispatch problem solution using particle swarm optimization with time varying acceleration coefficients. J. Electr. Power Syst. Res. **95**, 9–18 (2013)
14. Zhan, Z.H., Zhang, J., Li, Y., et al.: Adaptive particle swarm optimization. J. Syst. Man Cybern. **39**(6), 1362–1381 (2009)
15. Sarath, K., Ravi, V.: Association rule mining using binary particle swarm optimization. J. Eng. Appl. Artif. Intell. **26**(8), 1832–1840 (2013)

Sequential Pattern Mining and Matching Method with Its Application on Earthquakes

Jiang Zhu[1(✉)], Dechang Pi[1], Pan Xiong[2], and Xuhui Shen[2]

[1] College of Computer Science and Technology,
Nanjing University of Aeronautics and Astronautics,
29 Yudao Street, Nanjing, 210016 Jiangsu, People's Republic of China
zhujiang_0910@yeah.net, dc.pi@nuaa.edu.cn
[2] Institute of Earthquake Science, China Earthquake Administration,
Beijing 100036, People's Republic of China
xiong.pan@gmail.com, shenxh@seis.ac.cn

Abstract. As one of the important methods on prediction, data mining plays a significant role specifically in the field of abnormal prediction to ensure security. Based on the remote sensing data of the sun-synchronous polar orbit EOS-AQUA satellite of USA, this paper proposes an abnormal pattern detection method with sequential pattern mining and matching. First of all, based on the selected observation area, abnormal sequential patterns are mined and frequent abnormal sequential patterns are formed. Then, seismic sequential pattern is generated, and the matching algorithm of earthquake is established. Finally, the accuracy rate and the false positive rate of prediction are worked out. All experiments are conducted with the remote sensing satellite from 2005 to 2014, and the experimental results are interesting. According to the carbon monoxide content, the accuracy rate is 65 % while the false positive rate is 15 % by using the data of 30 days before earthquake for prediction.

Keywords: Time series · Abnormal pattern · Data mining · Pattern matching

1 Introduction

It is widely concerned by international scholars to mine abnormal patterns by means of observing the changes of the contents of chemical gases on earth through satellite [1]. More importantly, as a perspective of abnormal mining and detection [2], studies on the changes of sequential pattern of chemical gases before the earthquake is a challenging topic worth further researching. Time series is one of the most typical data representations. Sequential pattern mining algorithm is mainly divided into two broad categories. One is based on the discovering association rules algorithm called Apriori, which was put forward by Agrawal R, Srikant R, et al. in 1995. And it includes not only AprioriAll, AprioriSome and DynamicSome algorithms, but also the derived Generalization algorithm for mining sequential patterns called Gsp, and SPADE [3] algorithm with vertical data format, etc. The other one is based on pattern growth proposed by Han, Pei, et al., including FreeSpan algorithm, PrefixSpan [4] algorithm,

© Springer International Publishing Switzerland 2015
Z. Huang et al. (Eds.): ICCCS 2015, LNCS 9483, pp. 480–490, 2015.
DOI: 10.1007/978-3-319-27051-7_41

which is quite different from the Apriori based algorithm and proved to be much more efficient.

In general, time series data has characteristics of high dimensions, and the choice of methods which represent the sequential pattern [5] is of great importance. The frequency domain representation maps time series to frequency domain space using the Discrete Fourier Transform (DFT), while Singular Value Decomposition [6] (SVD) represents the whole time series database integrally by dimensions reduction. Symbolic representation [7] is to map time series discretely to character string.

Studies on the emissions of chemical gas before the earthquake, such as, carbonic oxide (CO), methane (CH4), etc., are paid great attention to. Through the analysis of large area CO gas escaping from Qinghai Tibet Plateau on April 30, 2000, the Earth Observation System (EOS) reveals that there is anomalous layer structure in abnormal high CO content areas [8]. Supervised instances show that abnormal phenomenon before the earthquake exists objectively resulting from the increased emissions of greenhouse gases. According to the analysis of the 18 dimensions attributes of EOS-AQUA satellite data, it is shown through a large number of experiments that the CO content results of the abnormal sequence mining trend to be relatively good. Therefore, the experiments in the paper are based on the analysis CO content.

The rest of this paper is organized as follows. In Sect. 2, some related definitions are introduced. Section 3 is devoted to present the abnormal findings method upon sequence mining. The analysis of the experimental results is provided in Sect. 4. In final, the summary of this paper and future work are discussed in Sect. 5.

2   Related Definitions

Sequential pattern is viewed as a new method of earthquake prediction. For a more detailed understanding, some related definitions are given step by step as follows.

Definition 1 (Precursor time): We define precursor time as days before the day earthquake happened. So, the period of days is the precursor period of earthquake prediction. In order to find out the optimum prediction, precursor time of 30 days, 15 days and 7 days are adopted successively in this experiment.

Definition 2 (Precursor area): Precursor area is regarded as the region affected by seismic activities. For the sake of simplicity, the EOS-AQUA satellite data adopted in this experiment is partitioned into grids of 360 * 180. Besides, the distance between two points of the longitude is named level unit distance. By contrast, the distance between two points of the latitude is called vertical unit distance. Since there is no unified view on the division of precursor area, taking the length of level unit distance and level unit distance into consideration, we adopt two kinds of precursor area, namely $1° * 1°$ and $2° * 2°$, so as to find out the best one.

Definition 3 (Sequential pattern): If the support of sequence α, namely support(α) is no less than minsup, that is, $\alpha.\text{sup} \geq \text{minsup}$, sequence α is regarded as a sequential pattern in the sequence database. Moreover, sequential pattern with length of L is recorded as L-pattern.

Definition 4 (Sequence class): Sequences which is partly similar to each other are classified as a set, named sequence class. To be specific, Fig. 1 is the result of 10 seismic data sequential patterns, namely, the set of 10 sequential patterns. This sequence class is represented as $< S_1, S_2, S_3, S_4, S_5, S_6, S_7, S_8, S_9, S_{10} >$, where S_i stands for a mined frequent sequence of the data processed by symbolization.

```
a c c c c d
a a c c c c d d
c c c c c d
a c c c c c d d
a a c c c d d e
a a c c c c c d d e d
a a c c c c d
c c c d d
a c c c c c d d e
a c d d e d
```

Fig. 1. A collection of similar sequence-sequence class

Definition 5 (Sequence focus): The sequence, which gets the highest inclusive degree among all the sequences, is the focus of the sequences, referred to as sequence focus. Here, the inclusive degree of S_i is defined to be the ratio reflecting the degree how far the sequence S_i contains the other sequences in the same sequence class. Take sequence class in Fig. 1 for example, the sequence with the highest inclusive degree, which is 100 % here, is {a a c c c c c d d e d}, therefore we regard this sequence as the sequence focus of the sequence class.

Definition 6 (Difference set of sequential pattern): In view that seismic precursory data possibly contains non-seismic factors, we mine frequent sequences from both seismic data and non-seismic data. Then, difference set of sequential pattern is generated by subtracting the non-seismic sequence set from the seismic sequence set. That is, if one sequence from the frequent seismic sequence set occurs in the frequent non-seismic sequence set, the support of this sequence is subtracted and the sequence turns to be saved or abandoned depending on whether the subtracted support is no less than the initialized minimum support or not.

3   Sequential Pattern Mining and Matching Method

3.1   The Principle Diagram

In this paper, algorithms and experiments are proposed according to the following steps, with the flow chart depicted in Fig. 2.

Step 1. First of all, abnormal sequences are mined respectively from the processed seismic data and non-seismic data of the EOS-AQUA satellite. Meanwhile, frequent abnormal sequential patterns are generated accordingly, and marked as QuakeFreSet and NormalFreSet.

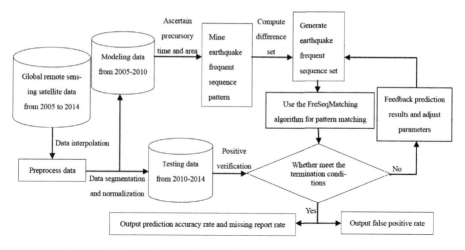

Fig. 2. The flow chart of abnormal findings method before earthquake

Step 2. In such a way that the frequent sequential patterns are generated, the specific sequential pattern before the earthquake is figured out. Moreover, sequence focuses meeting the defined conditions are located among the sequence class, after which the sets of sequence focus are formed as well as the matching algorithm.

Step 3. With the matching algorithm before the earthquake improved, the accuracy rate, the missing report rate and the false positive rate are computed to confirm the validity of this method.

3.2   Sequential Pattern Mining

In this experiment, PrefixSpan is adopted to mine frequent sequential patterns.

Algorithm PrefixSpan

Input : Sequence database S and the minimum support *min_support*

Output : A set of complete sequence pattern

1: Read in the sequence database S and the minimum support threshold *min_sup*.

2: Set sequence length $K = 1$ for the first time, and find out frequent sequence S with length of K from mapped database, where frequent sequence is no less than *min_sup* in the database.

3: By dividing the search space through S, respectively mine frequent sequnces, which obtain the *Prefix* and sequence length of $K+1$. If the result of the mining empty, step 3 is turned to step 5.

4: Increase k to k+1, L founded in step 3 is assigned to S, and turn to step 2.

5: Record and output all the mined frequet sequence.

In addition, as a kind of depth first search algorithm, it maps the data to a smaller database recursively in the process of projection. On account of no need to generate candidate sequential patterns, the search space is shrunk as well as the scale of the projection database. Thereby, the efficiency of mining is enhanced to a great extent.

3.3   FreSeqMatching Algorithm

In this paper, we proposed a new matching algorithm named FreSeqMatching, which is responding to the matching degree of time series. For the sake of describing the matching algorithm clearly, a definition of matching function is provided as follows. To describe the matching algorithm clearly, related definitions are provided as follows.

$$
match\_fun(F_i) = \begin{cases} 0, & isempty(LCS(\alpha, F_i)) = 1 \\ 1, & isempty(LCS(\alpha, F_i)) = 0 \end{cases} \tag{1}
$$

Where, α represents a time series like $<S_1, S_2, S_3 \dots S_n>$, and F is the set of all the sequence focus, namely, $\{F_1, F_2, F_3 \dots F_i\}$. The function $LCS(\alpha, F_i)$ is used to get the longest common subsequence between sequence α and sequence focus F_i. If the longest common subsequence is empty, that is, $isempty(LCS(\alpha, F_i)) = 1$, it means a failure match. Furthermore, the matching function is set to be 0, otherwise, to be 1.

The factors that influences the matching algorithm contain precursor time, precursor area, sequence support and data segment. In the case that the above parameters are set, matching degree can be further transformed to formula (2).

$$
f\_deg(\alpha) = \sum_{i=0}^{n} match\_fun(F_i) \div \sum_{i=0}^{n} F_i \tag{2}
$$

Here, α and F_i play the same role as the above formula (1). By means of a large number of experiments, it turns out that when the matching degree belongs to [0.4, 0.7], the predicting results trends to be better.

$$
f\_valid(F_i) = \begin{cases} 1, & f\_deg(\alpha) \geq sup\,Ratio \\ 0, & f\_deg(\alpha) < sup\,Ratio \end{cases} \tag{3}
$$

It is indicated in Formula (3) that when the matching degree is no less than the defined support, the data is valid, namely, $f\_valid(F_i) = 1$.

$$
match\_num(F) = \sum_{i=0}^{n} f\_valid(F_i) \tag{4}
$$

Formula (4) primarily aims to calculate the number of testing cases which is under certain condition, so as to work out both the accuracy rate and missing report rate.

The core concept of FreSeqMatching algorithm firstly is to positively verify seismic test set via the frequent sequence set, after which sequence matching degrees are figured out. Furthermore, seismic test data and non-seismic test data are matched by the mined frequent item sets.

Algorithm PreSeqMatching

Input : Frequent sequent set freqSeq, quake model data quakeModel,
quake test data quakeTest, normal test data normalTest
Output : Accuracy rate matchRatio and missing report rate falseRatio
1 : Read in frequent sequence set and data set of quakeModel, quakeTest, normalTest.
2 : Initialize and set support supRatio.
3 : Call function GetLFreq( ) to simplify freqSeq set.
4 : Work out the model matching ratio of quakeModel set by the formula of
modelMatchRatio = $MatchingDegree$ (freqSeq, quakeModel).
5 : If the result of modelMatchRatio meets the conditions, then turn to step 7.
6 : If not, reset the support and supRatio turn to step 4.
7 : For quakeTest set, calculate the matchRatio by the formula of
matchRatio = $MatchingDegree$ (freqSeq, quakeTest).
8 : While for normalTest set, calculate the falseRatio through this formula
falseRatio = $MatchingDegree$ (freqSeq, normalTest).

Analysis:

(1) Step 1 and step 2 is for initialization. Step 3 aims at simplifying frequent sequence sets by GetLFreq function. With the purpose of backward verification through the modeling data, step 4 to 6 is in demand. What's more, step 7 is to calculate the prediction accuracy rate. Meanwhile, the false positive rate is worked out in step 8.

(2) The GetLFreq function above is used for simplifying frequent sequence sets.

Function GetLfreq

Input : Frequent sequence set freqSeq
Output : Simplified frequent sequences
1 : Read in the number of freqSeq m.
2 : Initialize the min_sup of freqent sequence.
3 : For m frequent sequences, delete frequent sequences with support less
than min_sup , update m.
4 : For m frequent sequences, figure out the longest common sequence between
every two sequences by comSeq = LCS(freqSeq[i],freqSeq[j]), and finally turn to
step 8.
5 : If comSeq is a intersection of the two sequences or empty, turn to step 4.
6 : If comSeq = freqSeq[i], then mark freqSeq[i] as flag , turn to step 4.
7 : If comSeq = freqSeq[j], mark freqSeq[j] as flag, turn to step 4 as well.
8 : Delete sequences marked with flag in step 4 to 7, and gain simplified
frequent sequences.

(3) As an important function of FreSeqMatching algorithm, MatchingDegree function is repeatedly called in need, described as follows.

Function MatchingDegree

Input : Frequent sequence set freqSeq and quake test data quakeTest

Output : The accuracy rate matchRatio

1： For each quakeTest[i], for each simplified freqSeq[i], find out the longest
   common sequenct by the function LCS(quakeTest[i],freqSeq[j]).

2： Calculate the value of match_fun(freqSeq[i]) through formula (2) above.

3： For each earthquake case freqSeq[i] , figure out its matching degree based

   on formula (3), $f\_deg(\alpha)=\sum_{i=0}^{n} match\_fun\,(freqSeq[i]) \div \sum_{i=0}^{n} freqSeq[i]$.

4： For each matching degree, calculate the value of f_valid(quakeTest[i]) by
   formula (4).

5： According to given supRatio and formula (5), get the value of
   match_num(normalTest).

6： Figure out the accuracy rate on sequence matching by

   $matchRatio = match\_num(quakeTest) \div \sum_{i=0}^{n} quakeTest[i]$.

The LCS function in FreSeqMatching algorithm is a function with longest common subsequence and the content of sequence class and focus. Additionally, it is no longer described on this function in detail in this paper.

4   Experiments and Analysis

4.1   The Experimental Data Source

The experimental data covers EOS-AQUA satellite remote sensing data from the year 2005 to 2014, 217404000 data records in total. It contains 21 attributes, among which 18 attributes contribute to the seismic information.

Strong earthquake data with no less than 6.0 magnitudes is mainly adopted in this paper. The longitude of the selected earthquake area is from 73.5°E to 108.5°E, with the latitude from 20.5°N to 48.5°N. Mainly distributed in the western region in China, it covers the Qinghai-Tibet plateau seismic zone, etc. Moreover, it involves not only all or part of the Chinese provinces region, such as Tibet, Gansu, Yunnan, etc., and some part of neighbor countries, like Afghan, Pakistan, India, Bangladesh, Laos, etc.

4.2   Data Preprocessing

The remote sensing data of the EOS-AQUA satellite from 2005 to 2014 is divided into modeling data and test data. The classification of the satellite data is shown in Fig. 3.

As for the selection of test data, earthquakes with no less than 6 magnitudes are chosen from 2011 to 2014 as testing cases within the scope of 73.5°E to 108.5°E,

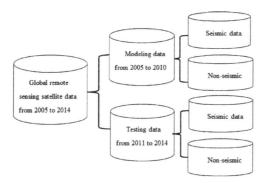

Fig. 3. Satellite data classification

20.5°N to 48.5°N. On account of the lack of enough earthquake cases, precursor area of 2°*2° is applied to obtain more earthquake samples in the experiment.

The main steps about data preprocessing are as follows.

(1) Data interpolation: among the remote sensing original data, outliers are represented by −9999, standing for the missing of the data. Nevertheless, it can be easily found that there is a certain amount of missing data. Therefore, data recovery is extremely necessary, namely, data interpolation. In this experiment, linear interpolation method is applied to take the place of the missing data appropriately.

(2) Data normalization: as a result of the influence of regional factors, remote sensing data are normalized in this paper. In view of the seasonal factors, the normalization in this experiment is corresponding to each month. That is, the mean values of all the historical data without earthquakes are computed in month, after which the percentage values divided by the average are figured out around 1. Hence, it can more effectively reflect the change trend of the data during the precursor time.

(3) Data segment: with the purpose of effectively representing the change trend of data, the linear segment method is applied on the basis of data normalization to turn into character representation. Consequently, it turns to be more convenient for mining sequential patterns. In order to gain better prediction results, different segments are adopted, such as 5, 7, 10 segments, to conduct experiments respectively.

4.3 Experimental Results and Analysis

Parameters Selection. The experiments are involved in a large number of parameters, with inclusive precursor time, precursor area, sequence support and the number of data segments, etc. Moreover, the selected parameters are briefly summarized in Table 1.

Table 1. Explanation of the selected parameters

Parameter list	Description of selected parameter
precursor time	Considering the best prediction effect, the experiment respectively selected 30 days, 15 days, 7 days before the earthquake as precursor time
precursor area	Taking the distance of level unit distance and vertical unit distance used in this experiment into account, two kinds of precursor area, 1°*1° and 2°*2, are adopted.
sequence support	In view of less earthquake cases, support of 0.3, 0.4, 0.5, 0.6 are set respectively.
data segment	On the basis of the normalization of data by month, segment of 5, 7, 10 are employed.

It is known from Table 1 that we have conducted 72 experiments to find out the better precursor time, precursor area, sequence support and data segments.

Analysis of Results. The prediction rate applied in the results is worked out as follows.

(1) SeismicData_CorrectRate, which is short for the correct rate of applying seismic data to predict earthquakes.

$$SeismicData\_CorrectRate = \frac{Tnum(SeismicDataTest\_True)}{Tnum(SeismicDataTest\_All)} \tag{5}$$

Where, Tnum(SeismicDataTest_True) refers to the number of correctly predicting earthquakes by seismic data, and Tnum(SeismicDataTest_All) points to the total number of the earthquake testing cases.

(2) SeismicData_FailureRate, standing for the failure rate of applying seismic data to predict earthquakes.

$$SeismicData\_FailureRate = 1 - SeismicData\_CorrectRate \tag{6}$$

(3) NormalData_FalseRate, which represents the false rate of using the normal data to predict earthquakes in this experiment

$$NormalData\_FalseRate = \frac{Tnum(NormalDataTest\_True)}{Tnum(NormalDataTest\_All)} \tag{7}$$

In formula (7), the number of correctly predicting earthquakes by non-seismic data is defined as Tnum(NormalDataTest_True), with Tnum(NormalDataTest_All) instead of the total number of the normal testing cases.

The accuracy rate, which comes from the carbon monoxide content (TOTCO_D) attribute with seismic data 30 days before the earthquake employed, is 65 % and the according missing report rate is 35 %. Meanwhile, non-seismic data 30 days before the earthquake is used to verify the experiments, and the false positive rate turns out to be

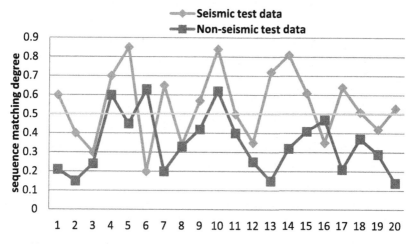

Fig. 4. Predicting results of the attribute of CO 30 days before earthquake

15 %. By contrast, the results are shown in Fig. 4, with X-axis to be the number of earthquake cases, and Y-axis to be the sequence matching support.

To explain Fig. 4 clearly, the sequence matching degree, which comes from the matching algorithm with the use of frequent patterns obtained from sequential pattern mining algorithm, reflects the similarity degrees between the testing cases and the mined earthquake frequent patterns. For seismic test data, it can be seen from the Fig. 4 that, when the matching support is set to be 0.5, the matching degree of NO.1 case is 0.6, greater than 0.5, so it is predicted to be seismic data. Whereas the matching degree of NO.2 case is 0.4, less than 0.5, it is conversely regarded as non-seismic data. As for non-seismic test data, NO.3 case is classified as non-seismic data, with matching degree of 0.24, obviously less than 0.5. Meanwhile, on account of the 0.63 matching degree, greater than 0.5, No.6 case is forecasted to be seismic data.

Hereby, there exist 13 cases of data with matching degree no less than 0.5 and 7 opposite cases among 20 cases of seismic data. Therefore, the accuracy rate is figured out to be 65 % based on Formula (5), with the missing report rate of 35 % on the basis of Formula (6). Besides, in 20 cases of non-seismic data, the number of cases with no less than 0.5 matching degree is 3, and the opposite is 17. Here comes the conclusive result that the false positive rate of prediction is 15 % in accordance with Formula (7).

5   Conclusions

It is an emerging direction of prediction to capture the exception rule by taking advantage of the technology of satellite for earth observation. From the perspective of time series, a method of abnormal pattern matching based on pattern mining is proposed in this paper, with the EOS-AQUA satellite data from 2005 to 2014. In final, after 72 times of experiments, it turns out that the predicting results of CO content is more satisfactory. Different from previous forecast model, it discovers abnormal regular pattern of remote sensing data from a new point of view. As a consequence, effective abnormal patterns implied in the history are mined to realize the prediction preferably by pattern matching.

The prediction before the earthquake upon sequential pattern matching still remains several aspects to be improved as follows.

(1) If a better interpolation method is considered when replacing the invalid data, the actual missing value could be reflected more precisely, which makes the mined sequential pattern to be much more accurate to a certain extent.
(2) With time factor involved in discovered sequential patterns, a real-time prediction could gain more actual application value.

Acknowledgments. This paper is supported by National Natural Science Foundation of China (U1433116), High resolution seismic monitoring and emergency application (31-Y30B09-9001-13/15).

References

1. Alvan, H.V., Azad, F.H., Omar, H.B.: Chlorophyll concentration and surface temperature changes associated with earthquakes. Nat. Hazards **64**(1), 691–706 (2012)
2. Dong, X., Pi, D.C.: Novel method for hurricane trajectory prediction based on data mining. Natural Hazards Earth Syst. Sci. **13**, 3211–3220 (2013)
3. Zaki, M.J.: SPADE: an efficient algorithm for mining frequent sequences. Mach. Learn. **42**(1–2), 31–60 (2001)
4. Pei, J., Han, J., Mortazavi-Asl, B., et al.: Prefixspan: Mining sequential patterns efficiently by prefix-projected pattern growth. In: 2013 IEEE 29th International Conference on Data Engineering (ICDE), pp. 0215–0215. IEEE Computer Society (2001)
5. Bettaiah, V., Ranganath, H.S.: An analysis of time series representation methods: data mining applications perspective. In: Proceedings of the 2014 ACM Southeast Regional Conference, p. 16. ACM (2014)
6. Tong, X.H., Ye, Z., Xu, Y.S., et al.: A novel subpixel phase correlation method using singular value decomposition and unified random sample consensus. IEEE Trans. Geosci. Remote Sens. **53**, 4143–4156 (2015)
7. Baydogan, M.G., Runger, G.: Learning a symbolic representation for multivariate time series classification. Data Min. Knowl. Discov. **29**, 1–23 (2014)
8. Yao, Q., Qiang, Z., Wang, Y.: CO release from the Tibetan plateau before earthquakes and increasing temperature anomaly showing in thermal infrared images of satellite. Advances in earth science **20**(5), 505–510 (2005)

Teaching Quality Assessment Model Based on Analytic Hierarchy Process and LVQ Neural Network

Shuai Hu$^{(\boxtimes)}$, Yan Gu, and Hua Jiang

Teaching and Research Institute of Foreign Languages,
Bohai University, Jinzhou, Liaoning, China
hushuai6@163.com

Abstract. To improve the accuracy of teaching quality assessment, an assessment model based on analytic hierarchy process (AHP) and learning vector quantization (LVQ) neural network is proposed in this paper. First a hierarchical model of teaching quality assessment was built by AHP. Then the weight of each assessment index was defined. All the indices involved were put into an LVQ neural network. The neural network model was trained and its generalization ability was also tested. The simulation result shows that compared with a traditional BP neural network, an AHP-LVQ network has simpler structure, better learning ability, faster convergence rate, higher assessment accuracy as well as better generalization ability.

Keywords: Analytic hierarchy process · LVQ neural network · BP neural network · Teaching quality assessment · Convergence rate · Generalization ability

1 Introduction

The quality of higher education has received increasingly more attention nowadays, and accordingly universities and colleges are trying to improve the teaching quality through various means. In the area of teaching quality assessment, manual assessment method used to be the predominant way to evaluate teachers' effectiveness in classroom teaching. However due to its innate limitations such as high subjectivity and low precision, gradually it has been almost out of use. Then an assessment method based on an expert system was introduced. It has higher evaluation precision compared with the traditional manual assessment method [1–3]. However teaching quality assessment is a comprehensive process which involves consideration of many factors, such as levels of assessment, targets and indices of assessment. Besides, in an expert system, the selection of indices is inevitably influenced by the designers' knowledge background as well as their personal preferences. All these undermine the objectivity and precision of an expert system.

With the development of information technology, new methods are applied in teaching quality assessment, including multiple linear regression (MLR), analytic hierarchy process (AHP), partial least squares (PLA), genetic algorithm (GA), support vector machines (SVM) and artificial neural networks (ANN). One study introduces an

© Springer International Publishing Switzerland 2015
Z. Huang et al. (Eds.): ICCCS 2015, LNCS 9483, pp. 491–500, 2015.
DOI: 10.1007/978-3-319-27051-7_42

assessment model based on a support vector machine. All the indices are put into the support vector machine after quantization. The parameters are improved by genetic algorithm. Although the assessment precision is improved, the convergence rate is still slow [4]. In another study, a multi-group genetic algorithm is employed to improve the parameters of a BP neural network too. The precision is improved, however the algorithm is complicate and the training speed of the network is not mentioned [5]. Researches also find out that when a BP network is employed to evaluate a comprehensive assessment system, it often fails to take a thorough consideration of the weights of all the indices [6, 7, 8, 9].

Currently, most of the studies focus on how to build an assessment model based on BP neural network and how to improve parameters of the BP network. Although a BP neural network is outstanding in nonlinear mapping, its shortcomings are not easy to overcome, like slow convergence rate and the local minimum [10]. Learning vector quantization (LVQ) neural network adopts a supervised learning algorithm. Sample clustering in the competing layer is easily obtained by computing the distances between the input sample vectors. Long training time, complicate computation and other problems of BP neural networks can be overcome by an LVQ neural network to a large degree [11].

In this paper, a teaching quality assessment system is established using analytic hierarchy process. The indices of the system are taken as the input variables of an LVQ network to build an AHP-LVQ network model. Its effectiveness is tested by comparing with that of a traditional BP network model.

2   Arithmetic Principle of Analytic Hierarchy Process

Analytic Hierarchy Process (AHP) is a systematic method which is used to compare a number of alternatives based on mathematics in almost all applications related with decision-making. Its essence is to create a matrix that expresses the relative values of a different attributes. AHP is helpful in capturing both subjective and objective evaluation measures, providing a consistency-checking mechanism of the assessment measures and alternatives, and it can reduce bias to the minimum.

It involves principles of decomposition, comparative judgments, and hierarchic composition or synthesis of priorities [12]. The decomposition principle simplifies a complex problem by making it into a hierarchy of clusters and sub-clusters. The comparative judgment principle can help to conduct pair-wise comparisons of all combinations of elements. The principle of hierarchic composition can help to multiply the local properties of the elements in every cluster. AHP combines qualitative analysis with quantitative analysis, and it is systematic and logical. Thus it is considered an effective way to solve problems of multi-level and multi-objective decision-makings [13].

2.1   Construction of Hierarchy Model of Teaching Quality Assessment

To assess teaching quality, the first and foremost is to build a framework that describes the core elements of effective teaching. In this paper, a three-leveled hierarchy model of teaching quality assessment is first built based on in-depth investigation into college English teachers, management departments, teaching supervisors as well as students.

Then a judgment matrix is built to conduct pair-wise comparisons among all the indices of the same level. All the indices are put in order when their weights are determined. A consistency test is also conducted [14]. The indices are classified into 3 levels. The higher level is a system of teaching quality assessment indices. The middle level subordinates to the higher level, and it consists of factors including teaching content, methods, attitude and effectiveness. The lower level consists of 12 specific indices that influence the middle level.

2.2   Determination of Assessment Index Weights

The indices in the hierarchical assessment model interact with one another, and their importance varies from one to another. To create a judgment matrix, the impact of indices of the same level upon its higher level is compared with each other. Weight coefficients are used to register the degrees of the importance of indices.

Set the final evaluation target to be Y, and set the weights of the four factors of the middle layer to be $w_i(i = 1, 2, 3, 4)$, then Eq. (1) is tenable. f_i in Eq. (1) stands for the four factors.

Pair-wise comparison is conducted among the four weight coefficients of the middle layer of target Y according to the degree of the coefficients' mutual influence. And Y is calculated as:

$$Y = w_1 \cdot f_1 + w_2 \cdot f_2 + w_3 \cdot f_3 + w_4 \cdot f_4 \tag{1}$$

Then a judgment matrix M is established.

$$M = \begin{pmatrix} w_1/w_1 & w_1/w_2 & w_1/w_3 & w_1/w_4 \\ w_2/w_1 & w_2/w_2 & w_2/w_3 & w_2/w_4 \\ w_3/w_1 & w_3/w_2 & w_3/w_3 & w_3/w_4 \\ w_4/w_1 & w_4/w_2 & w_4/w_3 & w_4/w_4 \end{pmatrix} \tag{2}$$

$$Y \cdot w = n \cdot w \tag{3}$$

If M meets the condition of consistency, f_1, f_2, f_3, and f_4, the four factors' weights of the middle layer of target Y, can be obtained by solving Eq. (3). All the weights of the 12 indices can be obtained in the same way. The eventually established teaching quality assessment system is shown in Table 1.

3   Arithmetic Principle of LVQ Neural Network

The arithmetic principle of LVQ neural network is as follows:

Step 1: Set variables and parameters. Let $\mathbf{X}(n) = [x_1(n), x_2(n), \cdots, x_N(n)]$ be the input vector, or the training sample. Let the weight vector be $\mathbf{W}_i(n) = [w_{i1}(n), w_{i2}(n), w_{i3}(n), \cdots, w_{iN}(n)]$, where $i = (1, 2, 3, \cdots, L)$. Choose the function of learning rate, $r(n)$. n is iteration times and L is the total iteration times.

Table 1. Teaching quality assessment system

Primary Index	Weight	Secondary Index	Weight
Teaching content	0.28	X_1. Clear and definite teaching objectives, good teaching organization	0.26
		X_2. Rich content, clear learning focuses	0.53
		X_3. Applicable theories, emphasis on development of learners' competence	0.10
		X_4. Introduction of new trends and achievements in the area of EFL	0.11
Teaching method	0.36	X_5. New and effective teaching methods	0.15
		X_6. Accordance with students' aptitudes in teaching	0.10
		X_7. Good lesson preparation	0.48
		X_8. Good command of modern technologies to facilitate teaching	0.27
Attitude	0.17	X_9. Compliance with regular class time	0.48
		X_{10}. Enthusiasm in classroom teaching	0.52
Effectiveness	0.19	X_{11}. Students' scores in mid-terms and final exams	0.82
		X_{12}. Students' interest and enthusiasm in learning	0.18

Step 2: Initialize the weight vector $\mathbf{W}_i(0)$ as well as the learning rate $r(0)$.

Step 3: Choose the input vector X from the training sample set.

Step 4: The winning neuron c can be obtained according to Eq. (4).

$$\|\mathbf{X} - \mathbf{W}_c\| = \min_i \|\mathbf{X} - \mathbf{W}_i\| \quad (i = 1, 2, 3, \cdots, L) \tag{4}$$

Step 5: Judge the classification is correct or not. Adjust the weight vector of the winning neuron according to the following rules:

Let $R_{\mathbf{W}_c}$ be the class related to the weight vector of the winning neuron, and R_{X_I} be the class that is associated with the input vector. If $R_{X_I} = R_{\mathbf{W}_c}$, then Eq. (5) is tenable.

$$\mathbf{W}_c(n+1) = \mathbf{W}_c(n) + r(n)[\mathbf{X} - \mathbf{W}_c(n)] \tag{5}$$

If $R_{X_I} \neq R_{\mathbf{W}_c}$, then Eq. (6) is tenable.

$$\mathbf{W}_c(n+1) = \mathbf{W}_c(n) - r(n)[\mathbf{X} - \mathbf{W}_c(n)] \tag{6}$$

Maintain the weight vectors as they are for the rest of the neurons.

Step 6: Adjust the learning rate $r(n)$, and it can be calculated Eq. (7) as:

$$r(n) = r(0) \cdot \left(1 - \frac{n}{N}\right) \tag{7}$$

Step 7: Judge whether n exceeds L. If $n \leq L$, then add 1 to the value of n, and go to step 3, otherwise end the iteration process.

4   Simulation Experiment

4.1   Collection of Original Sample Data

In this paper, an LVQ network is built on the platform of MATLAB R2013a to conduct a simulation experiment. Original assessment samples are descriptive statistics of 60 college English teachers' teaching. There are 12 indices assessed for each sample. The full score for each index is 10, and the grades of each teacher are given by teaching supervisors, the fellow teachers and students in the same university. Extreme data in the grades are deleted to ensure the objectivity and effectiveness of the grading. The average scores of each index of different teachers are computed and rated as *A, B, C* and *D*. The data are shown in Table 2.

Table 2. Original data of teaching quality assessment

Sample code	X_1	X_2	X_3	...	X_{10}	X_{11}	X_{12}	Assessment objective
1	9.34	9.57	9.68	...	8.74	9.38	9.00	1
2	9.44	9.46	9.79	...	8.89	9.11	9.13	1
3	9.28	9.62	9.73	...	8.63	9.29	8.98	1
4	9.38	9.66	9.76	...	8.51	8.44	9.01	2
5	9.27	9.37	9.61	...	8.71	8.55	8.32	2
6	9.60	9.47	9.43	...	8.96	8.77	8.05	2
7	9.76	8.98	8.86	...	7.99	8.11	8.09	2
8	8.63	8.30	9.26	...	8.06	8.23	6.49	2
9	8.47	9.18	8.92	...	8.22	8.18	6.71	2
10	9.12	8.26	9.08	...	8.49	7.12	7.24	2
...	...	...	...	...	...	...	...	...
52	8.80	8.19	8.67	...	7.46	7.06	7.07	3
53	8.09	7.71	8.94	...	7.10	7.14	6.55	3
54	9.31	8.02	9.1	...	6.92	7.21	7.26	3
55	7.01	8.29	7.56	...	5.99	7.11	6.09	3
56	7.24	7.11	8.85	...	7.02	6.93	8.28	4
57	7.18	7.16	7.38	...	6.95	6.71	7.87	4
58	7.05	7.02	8.74	...	6.97	6.32	8.15	4
59	6.84	8.21	8.42	...	7.10	6.95	8.31	4
60	6.49	7.10	6.79	...	6.72	6.55	8.06	4

4.2   Parameter Determination of the AHP-LVQ Network Model

There are 12 indices in the assessment system based on AHP, which determines the number of neurons in the LVQ network to be 12. And the neuron number of the output layer is 4. The four classification classes are labeled as *A, B, C* and *D*. The neuron number of a competing layer is usually an integral multiple of the neuron number of an output layer [15–17]. Accordingly, in the network training process in this paper, the number of neurons of the competing layer is set to be 4, 8, 1, 2, 16, 20 and 24.

When the neuron number is 16, the network achieves the utmost stability and the highest convergence speed. Therefore, the structure of the network model is 12-16-4. The learning function is learnlv1; the target precision is 0.01; the learning rate is 0.1.

4.3   Parameter Determination of the AHP-BP Network Model

A standard BP network assessment model is built to compare with the AHP-LVQ network model. A BP Network Model is featured with a typical, three-layered structure with a single hidden layer. The number of input layer nodes is equal to the dimension number of feature vectors of each sample, which is 12. Four different binary codes stand four evaluation classes. (0 0 0 1) stands for class A, (0 0 1 0) for class B, (0 1 0 0) for class C, and (1 0 0 0) for class D. Therefore, the number of output layer nodes is 4. The number of nodes of the hidden layer can be obtained according to Eq. (8), where I is the number of nodes of the input layer, O is the number of nodes of the output layer and h is the number of nodes of the hidden layer [18]. The number of hidden layer nodes is 20. So the topology of BP network model is 12-20-4. Standard gradient descent algorithm is employed to train the network. Its training function is *traingd* function; its conversion function is *sigmoid* function; its transfer function of the hidden layer is *tansig* function; its transfer function of the output layer is *logsig* function. The original sample data in Table 2 are first normalized to reduce the computation difficulty and the impact upon the training speed of the network model caused by the distinction among the original data.

$$h = \sqrt{I+O} + \beta, 1 < \beta < 10 \qquad (8)$$

4.4   Training of AHP-LVQ Network Model

The sample set in Table 2 is divided into two parts, with number 1 to number 40 being the training sample set and number 41 to number 60 being the testing sample set. The two network models are trained respectively when the target accuracy is 0.01, the training times is 20,000 and the learning rate is 0.1.

The distribution of training classes of the AHP-LVQ network is shown in Fig. 1. It can be seen that although the sample data in class A and class B are rather similar, only two samples in class A is wrongly classified into class B. The training accuracies of other classes are all100 %. And the final average training accuracy is 95 %.

The correlation curve between the real output and the target output of the AHP-BPNN can be seen in Fig. 2. It shows that the correlation coefficient R of linear regression between the output class and the target output class is 0.86176. This means the evaluation accuracy of the AHP-BPNN for the training sample set is just 86.176 %, which is significantly lower than the accuracy of the AHP-LVQ network model.

The error curves of the AHP-LVQ and AHP-BPNN are shown in Figs. 3 and 4. The above two figures show that the mean square errors of the two network models reduce with the increase of iteration times. And they come to an end when the target accuracy

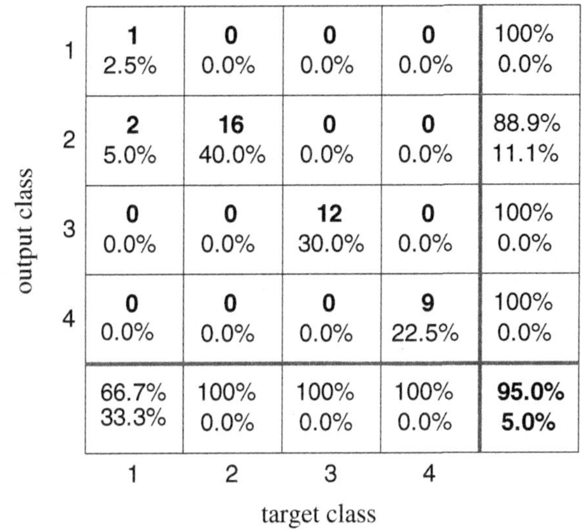

		1	2	3	4	
output class	1	**1** 2.5%	**0** 0.0%	**0** 0.0%	**0** 0.0%	100% 0.0%
	2	**2** 5.0%	**16** 40.0%	**0** 0.0%	**0** 0.0%	88.9% 11.1%
	3	**0** 0.0%	**0** 0.0%	**12** 30.0%	**0** 0.0%	100% 0.0%
	4	**0** 0.0%	**0** 0.0%	**0** 0.0%	**9** 22.5%	100% 0.0%
		66.7% 33.3%	100% 0.0%	100% 0.0%	100% 0.0%	**95.0%** **5.0%**
		1	2	3	4	

target class

Fig. 1. Distribution of training classes of AHP-LVQ network

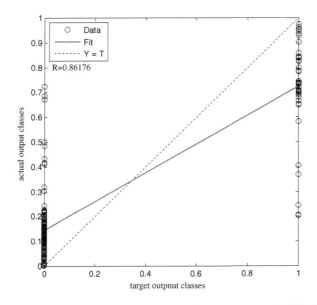

Fig. 2. Correlation curve of actual output and target output of AHP-BPNN

is achieved. For the AHP-LVQ network to achieve the target accuracy, only 581 iterations are needed, while the iteration times for the AHP-BPNN is 3669. The comparison indicates that the learning efficiency of the AHP-LVQ network is much higher.

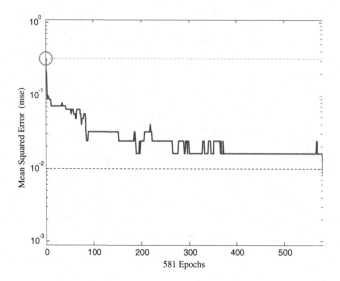

Fig. 3. Error curve of AHP-LVQ neural network training

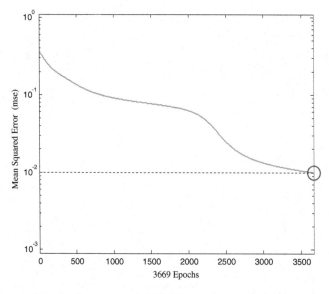

Fig. 4. Error curve of AHP-BP neural network training

4.5   Generalization Ability Test of AHP-LVQ Network Model

The comparison between the generalization abilities of the two networks is shown in Table 3. The table shows that the AHP-LVQ network is superior to the AHP-BPNN network in the classification of testing samples. The AHP-LVQ network performs with higher accuracy, faster convergence speed and better network structure.

Table 3. Comparison between the generalization abilities of the two networks

Network type	Amount of testing samples	Accuracy of each type of testing samples	Average accuracy
AHP-LVQ	20	85.71 100 100 100	96.42
AHP-BP	20	71.43 75 100 100	86.61

5 Conclusion

This paper proposes a teaching quality assessment model based on an AHP-LVQ neural network. This model performs with both the advantages of analytic hierarchy process and LVQ neural networks. A teaching quality assessment system is first built using analytic hierarchy process. On the one hand, compared with the current expert assessment system, the proposed system in this paper is more objective and can overcome the inherent subjectivity problem of the expert system. Thus this system makes it possible to objectively reflect teachers' actual teaching quality. One the other hand, compared with an AHP-BPNN network, the structure of an AHP-LVQ network is much simpler. Besides, it also has higher evaluation accuracy, faster training speed and better generalization ability.

Acknowledgements. The research work was supported by Social Science Foundation of Liaoning Provincial under Grant No. L14CYY022.

References

1. Ďurišová, M., Kucharčíková, A., Tokarčíková, E.: Assessment of higher education teaching outcomes (quality of higher education). J. Procedia-Soc. Behav. Sci. **174**, 2497–2502 (2015)
2. Yan, W.: Application research of data mining technology about teaching quality assessment in colleges and universities. J. Procedia Eng. **15**, 4241–4245 (2011)
3. Ghonji, M., Khoshnodifar, Z., Hosseini, S.M., Mazloumzadeh, S.M.: Analysis of the some effective teaching quality factors within faculty members of agricultural and natural resources colleges in Tehran University. J. Saudi Soc. Agric. Sci. **15**, 1–7 (2013)
4. Li, B.: Application of university's teaching quality evaluation based on support vector machine. J. Comput. Simul. **28**, 402–405 (2011)
5. Cai, Z., Chen, X., Shi, W.: Improved learning effect synthetic evaluation method based on back propagation neural network. J. Chongqing Univ. (Nat. Sci. Ed.) **30**, 96–99 (2007)
6. Wei, Z., Yan, K., Su, Y.: Model and simulation of maximum entropy neural network for teaching quality evaluation. J. Comput. Simul. **30**, 284–287 (2013)
7. Zhang, J., Liang, N.: Teaching quality appraisal model based on multivariate statistical-neural network. J. Nat. Sci. J. Hainan Univ. **28**, 188–192 (2010)
8. Zheng, Y., Chen, Y.: Research on evaluation model of university teachers' teaching quality based on BP neural network. J. Chongqing Inst. Technol. (Nat. Sci.) **29**, 85–90 (2015)
9. Sang, Q.: Study on bilingual teaching evaluation system based on neural network. J. Jiangnan Univ. (Nat. Sci. Ed.) **9**, 274–278 (2010)

10. Ding, S., Chang, X., Wu, Q.: Comparative study on application of LMBP and RBF neural networks in ECS characteristic curve fitting. J. Jilin Univ. (Inf. Sci. Ed.) **31**, 203–209 (2013)
11. Wang, K., Ren, Z., Gu, L., et al.: Research about mine ventilator fault diagnosis based on LVQ neural network. J. Coal Mine Mach. **32**, 256–258 (2011)
12. Satty, T.L.: Fundamentals of Decision Making and Priority Theory. RWS Publications, Pittsburgh (2001)
13. Feng, Y., Yu, G., Zhou, H.: Teaching quality evaluation model based on neural network and analytic hierarchy process. J. Comput. Eng. Appl. **49**, 235–238 (2013)
14. Ya-ni, Z.: Teaching quality evaluation based on intelligent optimization algorithms. J. Hangzhou Dianzi Univ. **34**, 66–70 (2014)
15. Ding, S., Chang, X., Wu, Q., et al.: Study on wind turbine gearbox fault diagnosis based on LVQ neural network. J Mod. Electron. Tech. **37**, 150–152 (2014)
16. Ding, S., Chang, X., Wu, Q.: A study on the application of learning vector quantization neural network in pattern classification. J. Appl. Mech. Mater. **525**, 657–660 (2014)
17. Zhao, P., Gu, L.: Diagnosis of vibration fault for asynchronous motors based on LVQ neural networks. J. Mach. Build. Autom. **39**, 172–174 (2010)
18. Ding, S., Wu, Q.: Performance comparison of function approximation based on improved BP neural network. J. Comput. Modernization **11**, 10–13 (2012)

Fast Sparse Representation Classification Using Transfer Learning

Qi Zhu[1,2(✉)], Baisheng Dai[3], Zizhu Fan[4], and Zheng Zhang[5]

[1] College of Computer Science and Technology, Nanjing University
of Aeronautics and Astronautics, Nanjing, China
zhuqi@nuaa.edu.cn
[2] Key Laboratory of Intelligent Perception and Systems for High-Dimensional
Information of Ministry of Education, Nanjing University
of Science and Technology, Nanjing, China
[3] School of Computing Science and Technology,
Harbin Institute of Technology, Harbin, China
csbsdai@gmail.com
[4] School of Basic Science, East China Jiaotong University, Nanchang, China
zzfan3@163.com
[5] Shenzhen Graduate School, Harbin Institute of Technology, Shenzhen, China
zhengzhang0812@163.com

Abstract. Under certain conditions, the sparsest solution to the combination coefficients can be achieved by L1-norm minimization. Many algorithms of L1-norm minimization have been studied in recent years, but they suffer from the expensive computational problem, which constrains the applications of SRC in large-scale problems. This paper aims to improve the computation efficiency of SRC by speeding up the learning of the combination coefficients. We show that the coupled representations in the original space and PCA space have the similar sparse representation model (coefficients). By using this trick, we successfully avoid the curse of dimensionality of SRC in computation and develop the Fast SRC (FSRC). Experimental results on several face datasets illustrate that FSRC has comparable classification accuracy to SRC. Compared to PCA +SRC, FSRC achieves higher classification accuracy.

Keywords: Biometrics · Sparse representation · Fast SRC · PCA

1 Introduction

Recently, by using compressed sensing, the sparse representation based classification (SRC) is proposed for face recognition [1], which has attracted much attention due to its good performance. The works [2–4] show SRC has better performance than the previous methods in robust face recognition. SRC needs to solve the l_1 norm optimization problem, which costs much computation time. Many researchers suggested solving the representation model with l_2 norm optimizer [5]. For example, Yanguses the whole training set to perform representation [4]. TPTSR is a local representation method [5]. The l_2 norm optimizer based methods are more efficient than SRC, but they cannot provide the sparse representation model, which plays important role in

© Springer International Publishing Switzerland 2015
Z. Huang et al. (Eds.): ICCCS 2015, LNCS 9483, pp. 501–509, 2015.
DOI: 10.1007/978-3-319-27051-7_43

classification. The computation efficiency of SRC constrains its applications. The main computation time of SRC is consumed in solving the sparse representation coefficients. This part of time increases greatly as the dimensionality of the sample increases. Consequently, the SRC is very time consuming or even unfeasible in many face recognition problems. Therefore, it is necessary to improve the classification efficiency of SRC. Learning the model from the other domain may be much easier and appropriate for classifying the data in the original domain, which is the main idea of transfer learning [6]. Transfer learning allows the domains used in training and test to be different, such as transfer via automatic mapping and revision (TAMAR) algorithm [7].

This paper aims to speed up the classification procedure of SRC by using transfer learning. Suppose that there exist coupled representations, i.e. high-dimensional representation (HR) and low-dimensional representation (LR), of the same image, the training samples in these two representations compose a pair of dictionaries. We assume the image has the similar sparse representation model on this pair of dictionaries. This assumption allows us to get the approximate solution of the coefficients in a low-dimensional space with a relatively low computation cost. In our method, we first convert the original (HR) test and training samples to the low high-dimensional space by K-L transform, and get the LR of the samples. The coefficients are learned by sparsely coding the LR test sample on the low-dimensional dictionary. Then, we reconstruct the HR test image by each class-specific HR face images with the obtained sparse coefficients. Finally, we classify the sample according to reconstruction error. It should be noted that our method is distinctly different from PCA+SRC that is the SRC performed in PCA space. Because the representation model of our method is learned in PCA space, the representation error of our method is calculated in original space. Otherwise, if representation error is directly calculated in the low-dimensional space, some discriminative features may be lost. This may explain why SRC after PCA, random-sampling or sub-sampling does not perform well shown in [6].

2 Preliminaries

2.1 SRC

Suppose there are n training samples from t classes. Class i has n_i training samples, and $n = \sum n_i$. Each image sample is stretched to column vector. Image sample is represented by $x_i \in \mathbf{R}^{m \times 1}$, m is the dimensionality of the sample. The test sample, e.g. $y \in \mathbf{R}^{m \times 1}$, is represented as:

$$y = XA \tag{1}$$

We can get the solution by:

$$a = \arg\min(||y - Xa||_2^2 + \mu||a||_1) \tag{2}$$

where, $X = [x_1, x_2, \ldots, x_n]$, μ is the regular parameter, $|| \; ||_1$ denotes the l_1 norm, and $|| \; ||_2$ denotes the l_2 norm. For example, for the vector $v = (v_1, v_2, \ldots, v_k)$, its l_1 norm is

$\sum_{i=1}^{k}|\mathbf{v}_i|$, and the l_2 norm is $\sqrt{\sum_{i=1}^{k}\mathbf{v}_i^2}$. After getting the coefficients, the representation error by each class can be derived by:

$$e_i = ||\mathbf{y} \text{ - } \mathbf{X}_i\mathbf{a}_i||_2^2 \qquad (i = 1,\ 2,\ \ldots,\ t) \tag{3}$$

where $\mathbf{X}_i \in \mathbf{R}^{m \times n_i}$, and $\mathbf{a}_i$ is the combination coefficient vector corresponding to $\mathbf{X}_i$. Finally, $\mathbf{y}$ is classified according to the representation error.

2.2 PCA

PCA or Karhunen-Loeve (KL) transform is a useful dimensionality reduction used in signal processing. PCA finds d directions in which the data has the largest variances, and projects the data along these directions. The covariance matrixis defined as:

$$\mathbf{C} = \sum_{j=1}^{n}(\mathbf{x}_j - \bar{\mathbf{x}})^T(\mathbf{x}_j - \bar{\mathbf{x}}), \qquad (j = 1,\ 2,\ldots,\ n) \tag{4}$$

where $\bar{\mathbf{x}} = \frac{1}{n}\sum_{j=1}^{n}x_j$. The transform projection vectors are d eigen-vectors, $\mathbf{p}_1, \mathbf{p}_2, \ldots, \mathbf{p}_d$, of the d largest eigen-values of the covariance matrix. PCA transform space is defined as $\Phi = span\{\mathbf{p}_1, \mathbf{p}_2, \ldots, \mathbf{p}_d\}$.

In many face recognition methods, PCA is usually used for dimensionality reduction before the classification. E.g., people often use the framework of PCA plus SRC. Indeed, performing PCA before SRC has the lower computational cost than SRC, and makes the solution of the combination sparser. But classifying the data using SRC in PCA space, i.e. PCA+SRC, cannot achieve promising accuracy, even much worse than that in original space. In next Section, we propose a novel framework than can speed up the classification of SRC without decrease of accuracy.

3 Fast SRC

SRC needs to solve l_1 norm minimization problem. Taking into account the very high dimensionality of the face image, SRC is very time consuming in face recognition. We aim to develop an efficient way to learn the representation model of SRC.

Proposition 1. The test image sample y can be coded by $\mathbf{Xa}$ in the original space, where $\mathbf{a} = \arg\min(||\mathbf{y} - \mathbf{Xa}||_2^2 + \mu||\mathbf{a}||_1)$. We use the function f to denote the transform from the original space to the new space, and then the test image in the new space, i.e., $f(\mathbf{y})$, can be coded by $f(\mathbf{X})\mathbf{a}'$, where $\mathbf{a}' = \arg\min(||f(\mathbf{y}) - f(\mathbf{X})\mathbf{a}'||_2^2 + \mu||\mathbf{a}'||_1)$. There exist some transforms from the original space to the new space, by which A is very close to A'.

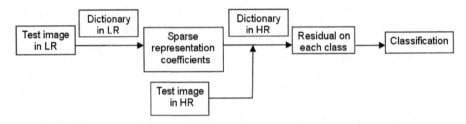

Fig. 1. Framework of the fast SRC

For example, with subsampling, the models in original space and sub-sampled space should be similar. By the l_1 norm optimizer, image y can be sparsely represented by $c_1\mathbf{x}_1 + c_2\mathbf{x}_2 + 0\mathbf{x}_3 + 0\mathbf{x}_4 + 0\mathbf{x}_5$, $(c_1 \neq 0$ and $c_2 \neq 0)$, and y' can be sparsely represented by $c'_1\mathbf{x}'_1 + c'_2\mathbf{x}'_2 + 0\mathbf{x}'_3 + 0\mathbf{x}'_4 + 0\mathbf{x}'_5$, $(c'_1 \neq 0$ and $c'_2 \neq 0)$. In the first model, if the representation coefficient vector $(c_1, c_2, 0, 0, 0)$ is replaced by $(c_1{}', c_2{}', 0, 0, 0)$, the representation result of y becomes $c'_1\mathbf{x}_1 + c'_2\mathbf{x}_2 + 0\mathbf{x}_3 + 0\mathbf{x}_4 + 0\mathbf{x}_5$. In this example, the coefficient vector in the sub-sampled space should be an approximate or suboptimal solution of the coefficient vector in the original space.

In many image classification problems, the original test and training samples are always in high-dimensional representation (HR) space. In framework shown in Fig. 1, we project them onto the subspace, and low-dimensional representation (LR) of the images. The test face image is reconstructed class by class using HR face images with the corresponding sparse representation coefficients learned on the LR dictionary. After devising the framework of Fast SRC, we need to find the transform (from dictionary in HR to dictionary in LR) having the following two properties: (1) computationally efficient to calculate the transform (low cost for getting the dictionary in LR) (2) the similar sparse representation model to that in the original space. In the next two subsections, we will demonstrate K-L transform (PCA) meets the above requirements.

We will show the relationship between the representation modelsin original space and K-L transformspace by the following intuitive explanation. It is reasonable to assume the prior probability distribution of the training samples coincides with the real probability distribution of the samples. Let $\mathbf{p}_1, \mathbf{p}_2, \ldots, \mathbf{p}_d$ be all the d orthonormal eigenvectors having non-zero eigenvalues obtained by PCA, and we denote $\mathbf{P} = (\mathbf{p}_1, \mathbf{p}_2, \ldots, \mathbf{p}_d)$. If y is coded by $\mathbf{Xa}$, where $\mathbf{a} = \arg\min(||\mathbf{y} - \mathbf{Xa}||_2^2 + \mu||\mathbf{a}||_1)$, we have $\mathbf{a} = \arg\min(||\mathbf{P}^T\mathbf{y} - \mathbf{P}^T\mathbf{Xa}||_2^2 + \mu_1||\mathbf{a}||_1)$, where μ_1 is the scalar constant.

Because, we know that the l_2 norm of the vector transformed into the K-L transform space is equal to that in original space. Then, if $||\mathbf{y} - \mathbf{Xa}||_2^2 > ||\mathbf{y} - \mathbf{Xa}'||_2^2$, we have $||\mathbf{P}^T\mathbf{y} - \mathbf{P}^T\mathbf{Xa}||_2^2 > ||\mathbf{P}^T\mathbf{y} - \mathbf{P}^T\mathbf{Xa}'||_2^2$. Hence, we can determine $\mathbf{a}$ is also a vector of the same test sample y in the K-L transform space.

The algorithm of FSRC:
Input: Training face image set X, test sample y, and projection number c.
Output:The prediction class of test sample
Step 1. Construct the covariance matrix of the training samples, and get the its c orthonormal eigenvectors $\tilde{\mathbf{P}} = (\mathbf{p}_1, \mathbf{p}_2, ..., \mathbf{p}_c)$ corresponding to the c largest eigen-values. Project the training and test samples onto the low dimensional space by $\tilde{\mathbf{P}}$.
Step2.Get the coefficient vector of y in PCA space: $\mathbf{b} = \arg\min(\|\tilde{\mathbf{P}}^T\mathbf{y} - \tilde{\mathbf{P}}^T\mathbf{Xb}\|_2^2 + \mu \|\mathbf{b}\|_1)$
Step 3. In original space, we calculate the representation error by each class $e_i = \|\mathbf{y} - \mathbf{X}_i\mathbf{b}_i\|_2^2$, where $i = 1,2,..., t$ and $\mathbf{b}_i$ is the combination coefficient vector corresponding to $\mathbf{X}_i$
Step 4. The FSRC classifies the sample according to reconstruction error

$\mathbf{p}_1, \mathbf{p}_2, ..., \mathbf{p}_c$ corresponding to the c largest non-zero eigen-values, where c is the integer smaller than d, play more important role than $\mathbf{p}_{c+1}, \mathbf{p}_{c+2}, ..., \mathbf{p}_d$ in the K-L transform. We use s_i to denote the eigen-value corresponding to the eigen-vector $\mathbf{p}_i$. In most face recognition problems, $\sum_{i=1}^{c} s_i / \sum_{i=1}^{d} s_i$ is close to 1, and we denote $V_c = \sum_{i=1}^{c} s_i / \sum_{i=1}^{d} s_i$. In most face recognition problems, $V_c = \sum_{i=1}^{c} s_i / \sum_{i=1}^{d} s_i$ is very close to 1, even though c is a very small integer. Denoted by the $m \times c$ matrix $\tilde{\mathbf{P}} = (\mathbf{p}_1, \mathbf{p}_2, ..., \mathbf{p}_c)$, we have $\|\tilde{\mathbf{P}}^T\mathbf{y} - \tilde{\mathbf{P}}^T\mathbf{Xa}\|_2^2$ is very close to $\|\mathbf{P}^T\mathbf{y} - \mathbf{P}^T\mathbf{Xa}\|_2^2$. Since the l_2 norm of the vector in the K-L transform space is equal to that in original space, i.e. $\|\mathbf{y} - \mathbf{Xa}\|_2^2 = \|\mathbf{P}^T\mathbf{y} - \mathbf{P}^T\mathbf{Xa}\|_2^2$, we have $\|\tilde{\mathbf{P}}^T\mathbf{y} - \tilde{\mathbf{P}}^T\mathbf{Xa}\|_2^2$ is very close to $\|\mathbf{y} - \mathbf{Xa}\|_2^2$. Therefore, we can get that the approximate solution of the sparse representation coefficient vector in c-dimensional PCA space, $(c << d \leq m)$. Based on the framework of fast SRC and the analysis of PCA, we proposed the FSRC algorithm.

As we know, the SRC can reconstruct the test sample $\mathbf{y}$ by $\mathbf{Xa}$. Although the sparse representation coefficient vector of FSRC is calculated in the low-dimensional space, FSRC also can reconstruct the test sample with the same dimensionality as that of original space by $\mathbf{Xb}$. Figure 2 shows some examples reconstructed by SRC and FSRC, respectively. In Fig. 2, the first row shows some images from ORL dataset, the second row shows the images reconstructed by SRC, and the third row shows the images reconstructed by FSRC.

From Algorithm 1, we find that the complexity of FSRC consists of three parts, feature extraction using PCA, sparse coding on the low-dimensional space, and calculating the representation error in original space. No matter how many test samples the test set has, the PCA transformation procedure in FSRC is performed only once. Supposing FSRC transforms the samples into c dimensional PCA for getting the sparse

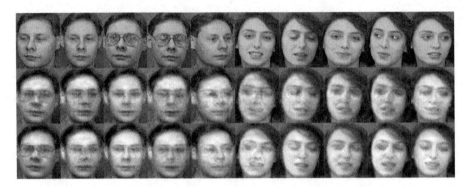

Fig. 2. Some face images and the reconstructed images by SRC and FSRC, respectively.

model, the time complexity of PCA procedure for each test sample can be considered as the $O(cm^2/t)$, where m and t denote dimensionality of the sample and test sample size, respectively. FSRC calculates representation error in original space, and the time complexity of this part is $O(mn)$. The first two columns of Table 1 give the computational complexity comparison between SRC and FSRC. Clearly, FSRC can reduce the computational complexity from $O(m^3)$ to $O(c^3 + cm^2/t)$, where c is much less than m.

4   Experiments

ORL, FERET, Extended Yale B and AR datasets were used in the experiments [8–11]. On ORL dataset, we randomly choose 5 images from each class for training, and the others are used as test samples. To fairly compare the performance, the experiments are repeated 30 times with 30 randomly possible selections of the training images. On FERET dataset, we randomly select 4 images from each subject for training. The experiments are repeated with 10 randomly possible selections. On the Extended Yale B dataset [10], 5 images of each subject were selected for training. The experiments are also repeated 10 times. The experiments are carried on the above three datasets, respectively. Two state-of-the-art methods CRC and SRC are employed as comparisons. Table 1 shows the classification accuracies of the methods SRC,CRC, PCAcFSRC and FSRC. From the results, we find our method achieves the comparable classification accuracy to SRC and CRC. Table 2 shows that the classification efficiency of FSRC is much higher than SRC on the first three datasets. In PCA+SRC, the representation error is directly calculated in the low-dimensional space. In the proposed method of FSRC, the representation error is calculated in the original space. For revealing the correlation between where the representation error is calculated and the accuracy, we also carried PCA+SRC on the datasets. Compared to the proposed method of FSRC, PCA+SRC always obtains a lower accuracy. In computation, FSRC achieves the higher classification efficiency than SRC. Each image of AR dataset is occupied by the Gaussian noise. The mean is 0 and variance is 0.01. Figure 3 gives the 26 noised images from the first subject.

Table 1. The classification accuracies (%) of the methods on four face datasets

	SRC	CRC	PCA+SRC	FSRC
ORL	92.08	91.72	88.53	92.62
FERET	65.00	58.83	54.53	64.50
Yale B	78.37	78.19	67.40	77.25
AR with noise	93.33	91.27	87.11	92.06

Table 2. The classification time (s) of the methods on four face datasets

	SRC	CRC	PCA+SRC	Random+SRC	Subsample+SRC	FSRC
ORL	1563.4	353.2	683.5	572.9	558.4	734.3
FERET	23752.1	894.3	2135.6	1443.2	1526.7	2556.3
Yale B	45958.0	2375.2	4772.4	3795.2	3419.5	5218.4
AR	21330.5	1372.7	4583.1	2836.8	2583.1	4036.7

Fig. 3. The noised images from the first subject

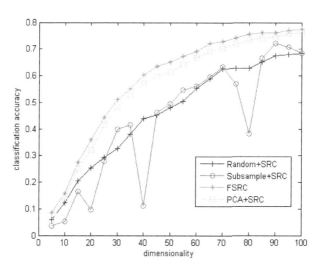

Fig. 4. The classification accuracies of the four fast SRC methods on AR dataset.

The classification accuracies and time of the methods SRC, CRC, PCA+SRC and FSRC on this dataset are shown in the last row of Tables 1 and 2, respectively. As we know, some feature selection or extraction plus SRC based methods, such as PCA +SRC, Random+SRC and Subsample+SRC [6], also have higher efficiency than SRC. Our method is distinctly different from the above methods. Seeing from step 4 of our algorithm, it is clear that all the features are participated in our classification method. PCA+SRC, Random+SRC and Subsample+SRC are also employed in the experiments for comparisons. The classification accuracies of our method, PCA+SRC, Random +SRC and Subsample+SRC, as their dimensionalities range from 5 to 100 with the interval of 5, are shown in Fig. 4. The Subsample+SRC case shows two significant drops in classification accuracy when the dimensionality is 40 and 80. We belive this phenomenon is led by the drawback of subsample method. When extracting the features, subsample method considers the position of the pixel rather than the discriminant information. Some pixels having discriminant information may be lost in sub-sample method. Then the features generated by sub-sample method may be not appropriate to classify using SRC. The results show that FSRC outperforms the other three methods with the same number of dimensionality. Table 2 also shows the running time of these four fast SRC methods on the noised AR dataset. Seeing form Fig. 4 and Table 2, we find that the four fast SRC methods cost the roughly equal running time, and our method achieves the best classification performance.

5 Conclusion

This paper proposed a fast sparse representation classification (FSRC) algorithm for face recognition. FSRC learns the approximate solution of the sparse representation coefficients in a low-dimensional space with a relatively low computation cost. Based on the idea of transfer learning, FSRCreconstructs the test image in original space rather than low-dimensional space. Therefore, FSRC can achieve the comparable accuracy to SRC, and much higher computational efficiency. It is necessary to point that the framework ofFSRC is independent on optimization algorithms. We evaluated the proposed method on four face datasets. Compared with SRC, FSRC is with significantly lower complexity and has very competitive accuracy. Compared with PCA +SRC and the other two SRC based fast classification frameworks, FSRC achieves the best classification results.

Acknowledgements. This article is partly supported by Nature Science Foundation of China under grants(Nos. 61375021, 61472138, 61362031and 61263032), China Postdoctoral Science Foundation funded project (No. 2015M570446), Jiangsu Planned Projects for Postdoctoral Research Funds (No.1402047B), Open Project Program of Key Laboratory of Intelligent Perception and Systems for High-Dimensional Information of Ministry of Education (No. JYB201503), and Natural Science Foundation ofJiangsu Province (No. BK20131365).

References

1. Wright, J., Yang, A.Y., Ganesh, A., Sastry, S.S., Ma, Y.: Robust face recognition via sparse representation. IEEE TPAMI **31**(2), 1–17 (2009)
2. Wagner, A., Wright, J., Ganesh, A., Zhou, Z., Ma, Y.: Towards a practical face recognition system: robust registration and illumination via sparse representation. IEEE Conference on Computer Vision and Pattern Recognition (CVPR), June 2009
3. Zhu, Q., Sun, H., Feng, Q.X., Wang, J.H.: CCEDA: building bridge between subspace projection learning and sparse representation-based classification. Electron. Lett. **50**(25), 1919–1921 (2014)
4. Yang, M., Zhang, L., Zhang, D., Wang, S.: Relaxed collaborative representation for pattern classification. In: CVPR (2012)
5. Xu, Y., Zhang, D., Yang, J., Yang, J.-Y.: A two-phase test sample sparse representation method for use with face recognition. IEEE Trans. Circ. Syst. Video Technol. **21**(9), 1255–1262 (2011)
6. Pan, SinnoJialin, Yang, Qiang: A survey on transfer learning. TKDE **22**(10), 1345–1359 (2010)
7. Yang, Qiang, Pan, SinnoJialin, Zheng, Vincent W.: Estimating location using Wi-Fi. IEEE Intell. Syst. **23**(1), 8–13 (2008)
8. http://www.uk.research.att.com/facedataset.html
9. Phillips, P.J., Moon, H., Rizvi, S.A., Rauss, P.: The FERET evaluation methodology for face recognition algorithms. IEEE TPAMI **22**, 1090–1104 (2000)
10. Lee, K., Ho, J., Kriegman, D.: Acquring linear subspaces for face recognition under variable lighting. IEEE TPAMI **27**, 684–698 (2005)
11. Martinez, A., Benavente, R.: The AR face database, The Computer Vision Center, Technical report (1998)

Probing the Scheduling Algorithms in the Cloud Based on OpenStack

Yang Luo[✉], Qingni Shen, Cong Li, Kang Chen, and Zhonghai Wu

School of Software and Microelectronics, Peking University, No. 5 Yiheyuan Road
Haidian District, Beijing, People's Republic of China
{veotax,lc8803188,chen_kang}@pku.edu.cn, {qingnishen,wuzh}@ss.pku.edu.cn

Abstract. Among modern cloud infrastructures, live migration of virtual machines offers many advantages like scalability and elasticity but also leads to risks in the meantime. Security issues of live migration have been studied and classified into three threats: control plane, data plane and migration module. Lots of work has focused on the latter two aspects. However, the security of control plane has yet to be analyzed. This paper starts by introducing three classes of control plane threats: load balancing, scheduling and transmission. We then elaborate how scheduling attack can subvert the VM scheduling algorithm via the proposed scheduling algorithm reverse approach (SARA). We evaluate the effects of SARA using datasets gathered from OpenStack. This work is a beneficial attempt to compromise the control plane of VM migration, which can be used as a self-test tool for cloud service providers to test the defences against network intruders.

Keywords: Cloud computing · Live migration · Scheduling algorithm

1 Introduction

Live virtual machine (VM) migration is the process of migrating a VM's memory content and processor states to another virtual machine monitor (VMM) even as the VM continues to execute without halting itself [1]. It has become a key selling point for recent clouds as it provides assistance for cloud service providers (CSPs) in load balancing [2], consolidated management, fault tolerance [3,4] and so on. Whereas, it as well introduces novel security threats, including aspects such as control plane, data plane and migration module [5], respectively referred to the securities of management commands, virtual machine data and migration mechanism itself. [5] has empirically demonstrated the importance of migration security, by implementing Xensploit to perform the data plane manipulation on Xen and VMware. Since then, the data plane issues have been fully researched by plenty of studies such as [6–8]. Opposite to data plane's popularity, the research on control plane related problems is very limited. [5] briefly investigated the possible loopholes at the control plane including incoming migration control, outgoing migration control and false resource advertising. Unfortunately, practical details were not offered in it. [9] extended trusted computing to virtualized

© Springer International Publishing Switzerland 2015
Z. Huang et al. (Eds.): ICCCS 2015, LNCS 9483, pp. 510–520, 2015.
DOI: 10.1007/978-3-319-27051-7_44

systems using vTPM, and [10–12] assumed that the destination is trustworthy and proposed secure transfer protocols based on vTPM for migration between identical platforms. These protocols are yet to be seen for practice use given their complexity. HyperSafe [13] is a lightweight approach that endows existing Type-I bare-metal hypervisors with a unique self-protection capability to provide lifetime control-flow integrity, this technique only supports to guarantee the hypervisors' integrity and network protection is not considered.

Given the increasing popularity of live VM migration, a comprehensive understanding of its security is essential. However, the security of its control plane has yet to be analyzed. This paper first explores threats against live virtual machine migration in the context of three control plane threats: load balancing, scheduling and transmission. We then present a scheduling algorithm reverse approach (SARA) against the functionality of VM scheduling. Effectiveness of SARA depends on the untrusted network assumption: the attacker is able to intercept the transmission channel of scheduling control commands by compromising the network or accessing as an insider. We provide a proof of concept for SARA by automating the exploiting recent OpenStack scheduling mechanism [14] during live migration, demonstrating that scheduling attack has become a realistic security issue. This PoC can be used as a self-test tool for CSPs to measure their defense strength against control plane attacks.

The remainder of the paper is organized as follows: Sect. 2 presents recent control plane threat classes. Section 3 details the proposed SARA technique for reversing scheduling algorithm. Section 4 presents the implementation and evaluation of the proposed technique. Lastly, conclusions and future work are presented in Sect. 5.

2 Control Plane Threat Classes

2.1 Overview

Despite the efforts of providing a threat model on VM migration control plane in [5], here we would like to present a more comprehensive taxonomy for control plane security issues based on working procedures.

1. **Load balancing.** In a production cloud, live migration is always automatically triggered by dynamic load balancing strategy instead of human decision. A collection phase of host running parameters is required before load balance decision-making. The transfer path of load balancing commands between controllers and hosts must be encrypted and authenticated. An attacker might be able to snoop or manipulate the source VM selection by compromising the load balancing command channel, which can cause false resource advertising attack [5].
2. **Scheduling.** A VM will be scheduled to a new host by the load balancer after being chosen as the source VM. The scheduling command channel must be secured and protected against sniffing and tampering. Passive sniffing might result in the compromise of the scheduling algorithm, yet active tampering

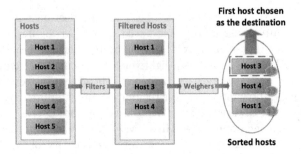

Fig. 1. Processing of scheduling algorithm

is able to cause arbitrary migration destinations, which would cause deny of service failures.

3. **Transmission.** Besides processor states and memory contents, control instructions are also required to be transmitted in order to manage the migration processing. At present, pre-copy [1] and post-copy [15] are the two most widely adopted techniques for live migration. By analyzing their control commands, an attacker can collect a bunch of memory pages of the migrated VM. Together with the processor states, the attacker is given the opportunity to analyze the dynamic execution of a critical process like decryption inside a VM, which is far more dangerous than leakage of a single memory snapshot.

This paper merely discusses about secure scheduling. Issues about load balancing and transmission are not within the scope of this article and will be addressed in next papers.

2.2   Scheduling Threat

Scheduling threat takes aim at compromising the cloud scheduling algorithm [14], an algorithm designed to determine to which host a VM should be migrated. The scheduling algorithm is commonly processed in two phases: filtering and weighing, as shown in Fig. 1.

1. **Filtering.** When the scheduler receives a VM migration request, it first applies filters to determine which hosts are eligible for consideration. A filter is binary and used to filtrate the hosts based on hosts' resources such as available cores, memory, storage and so on. A scheduling algorithm may contain multiple filters and merely hosts passing through all filters can stay on the list.
2. **Weighing.** Hosts accepted by filtering are weighed by each weigher, all weights for one single host are normalized and summed up. The scheduler then sorts the hosts and selects the one with the largest weight as the final scheduling destination.

Scheduling channels between controllers and VMMs must be secured, as even passive snooping against the scheduling algorithm can lead to security risks. Once an attacker gains access to the scheduling channels, by gathering and analyzing sufficient numbers of scheduling requests, the attacker is capable of restoring the scheduling law and leveraging it to predict a particular VM's migration destination. Specifically, damages are at least twofold.

1. **Compromised host threat.** An attacker can prepare an exactly suitable compromised host in advance for a particular migration request, advertise false resources and simply wait for the victim VM to enter the attacker's preset pitfall.
2. **Cross-VM threat.** In order to attack a victim VM protected in its VMM, an attacker might choose to bypass the VMM security mechanisms by preparing a suitable malicious VM and waiting it to be migrated into the hypervisor hosting the victim. Cross-VM threat [16] can subsequently be conducted to damage the victim machine.

3 Proposed Technique

This section details the innovative SARA technique to reverse the scheduling algorithm used during live migration in the cloud. As scheduling is performed in two stages, the proposed SARA technique is also comprised of two parts: filter determination and weigher determination. It takes VM migration requests, metadata of hosts and the destination host (the scheduling result) as inputs, the output is the decision result for filters and weighers.

3.1 Filter Determination

Before demonstrating how to determine the set of filters, we feel it essential to define the filter function first.

$$filter(r, f, h) = true \,/\, false, \tag{1}$$

where, r is the VM scheduling request, f is the filter, h is the host, and $filter()$ is the binary filter function, returning true if and only if the host h passes through the filter f under the request r. Given the specific r, f, h, the return value of $filter()$ can be figured out. It is notable that SARA relies on multiple times of scheduling, each of which is called an iteration. Assume that we have n iterations, this indicates there are also n migration requests and n destination hosts in the meantime.

Let F_{all} and F be the set of filters in total and the set of activated filters, respectively. Most filters are "constant", except some cases containing specific numbers: As the IoOpsFilter [14], it requires the simultaneous IO operation numbers of the destination host to be not over 8. There is much uncertainty about this filter as another CSP might modify the IO operation numbers to another value like 16 on its own behalf. We call these kinds of filters with exact figures Type-II filters (denoted as $F_{v,all}$), and the others Type-I filter (denoted as $F_{c,all}$).

The activated filters in $F_{c,all}$ and $F_{v,all}$ are F_c and F_v respectively. Obviously we have $F_{all} = F_{c,all} \cup F_{v,all}$ and $F = F_c \cup F_v$.

Type-I filters. In the following, we intend to discuss about how to gain the set of all activated Type-I filters at each iteration i, denoted as F_i.

$$F_i = \{f | f \in F_{i-1} \wedge filter(r_i, f, h_{dst,i}) = true\}, \tag{2}$$

where, r_i is the i-th migration request, $h_{dst,i}$ is the i-th destination host. Particularly for initial value, we have $F_0 = F_{c,all}$. F_i is calculated based on F_{i-1} because $h_{dst,i}$ for all iterations must pass through all activated filters. The final filter set will be the intersection of F_i at all iterations. For performance, we can just directly figure out F_i based on F_{i-1} and spare the intersection operations.

Through iteratively applying (2) for n times, F_n can be figured out. It is worth noting that the filters excluded from F_n cannot fulfill our scheduling requirements, doesn't mean that filters within F_n are all necessary. In fact, any subset of F_n is able to let all destination hosts pass through the filtering, thus strictly $F_c \subseteq F_n$ holds, in this work we will suppose $F_c \approx F_n$, as it occurs with the greatest probability. When request number rises to a very large value, the error between F_c and F_n is small enough and can be omitted.

Type-II filters. F_v is defined as filters with one exact figure, either appears in the request parameter (Type II-1) or the host parameter position (Type II-2). IoOpsFilter belongs to the former class, a case of the latter is not yet available in OpenStack [14], however this situation may change in future. The difficulty of calculating F_v lies in that we are unaware of the exact parameter value used by a Type-II filter. It needs to be estimated in some manner. For simplicity, we merely explore the Type II-1 condition, as Type II-2 ones can be resolved similarly. The filter function for Type II-1 filters is given in (3).

$$filter(f(x), h_{dst,i}(y_i)) = true / false, \tag{3}$$

where, $f(x)$ is the Type-II filter with exact value x in the place of the original request parameter, based on which, we do not need a request variable here. $h_{dst,i}(y_i)$ is the destination host for iteration i with host parameter y_i. As x and y_i are both figures, a common case is that the scheduler compares the value of x and y_i and decides whether the host can pass through this filter. The value of x must satisfy $filter(f(x), h_{dst,i}(y_i)) = true$ for each iteration i. Furthermore, we can reasonably suppose that $f(x)$ actually filtered some hosts out, as CSPs have no desire to deploy a filter that has no effects. Therefore, we have:

$$F_x = \{f(x) | \forall h_{dst,i}(y_i)(filter(f(x), h_{dst,i}(y_i)) = \\ true) \wedge \exists h_j(y_j)(filter(f(x), h_j(y_j)) = false)\}, \tag{4}$$

where, $h_j(y_j)$ is any non-destination host in each iteration, F_x is the set of all activated Type-II filters. (4) indicates that $f(x)$ belongs to F_x if and only if $f(x)$ passes through each $h_{dst,i}(y_i)$ and refuses at least one $h_j(y_j)$. Assume the filtering pattern for $f(x)$ is $x \geq y_i$ (similarly with $x \leq y_i$), obviously we have

$x \in [max(y_i), max(y_j) - 1]$ based on (4). If x exists, here we can suppose $f(x)$ filter exists and $x \approx max(y_i)$ because this assignment for x has the maximal probability to happen. If x does not exist, we believe this filter is deactivated. In this paper, we suppose $F_v \approx F_x$, and the error between F_v and F_x can be narrowed and omitted when requests reach certain scale.

Based on all the analysis above, activated filter set F can be figured out finally:

$$F = F_c \cup F_v \approx F_n \cup F_x \tag{5}$$

3.2   Weigher Determination

Weighers's contribution to scheduling is reflected in their multipliers. We do not have to determine whether a weigher is activated, as a weigher with 0 multiplier can be considered as disabled. The difficulty of weigher determination thus lies in how to obtain the multipliers of all weighers. As a result of the previous step, we suppose filtered hosts are already gained. Similar to filtering, first we bring forward some definitions of weighing.

$$weigh(w, h) = score, \tag{6}$$

where, w is the weigher, h is the host, and $weigh()$ is the weighing function, returning the weight score the weigher w gives the host h. The higher score a host can obtain, the larger possibility it will be accepted as the migration destination.

$$weight(h) = \sum_{i=1}^{p} m_i \times weigh(w_i, h), \tag{7}$$

where, p is the number of weighers, w_i is the i-th weigher, m_i is the multiplier for w_i, and $weight()$ is the weighted summation function that sums up weight scores from all weighers and returns the final weight for a host. After weighing step, the hosts will be sorted by final weights in descending order. Besides, we assume that the scheduling randomization is disabled in our scenario, as implemented in OpenStack by default, so migration destination will always be the top one in the host list.

We have come forward with a mathematical method to figure out the multipliers. First we need to group iterations with identical filtered host lists together. By observing the iterations in request timestamp ascending order, we discovered a pattern: the migration destination of the previous request tends to be selected again for the current request, and this will not change, until the favored host is consumed too much to maintain the first position in the host list (consumption of the host will cause degradation of its weight). We call the alteration happened between two destination hosts within a group a host shifting. Take the host shifting from h_A to h_B for instance, before shifting we have $weight(h_A) > weight(h_B)$, and after shifting we get $weight(h'_A) < weight(h'_B)$. Combining above two inequalities, we can roughly draw a conclusion:

$$weight(h_A) + weight(h'_A) \approx weight(h_B) + weight(h'_B) \tag{8}$$

As a cloud usually owns hosts on a massive scale, the error between two sides of (8) can be reasonably ignored, so it will be regarded as an equation here. Substitute (7) into (8), we have the host shifting equation:

$$\sum_{i=1}^{p} m_i \times (weigh(w_i, h_A) + weigh(w_i, h'_A)) =$$
$$\sum_{i=1}^{p} m_i \times (weigh(w_i, h_B) + weigh(w_i, h'_B)), \tag{9}$$

where, $m_i(i = 1, 2, \ldots, p)$ are the p unknown multipliers.

One host shifting corresponds to one equation like (9). And $(p - 1)$ host shiftings can produce $(p - 1)$ equations, together with the predefined equation $\sum_{i=1}^{p} m_i = 1$, we have got p equations for p unknowns, and the solution of p multipliers can be found by solving this linear system according to the linear algebra theory.

4   Implementation and Evaluation

We implemented a prototype in C++ based on our SARA approach. The experimental setup is as follows. The testbed adopts OpenStack Juno 2014.2 version and consists of a controller node and dozens of compute nodes. A malicious node running our prototype is injected into the management network of OpenStack, ensuring that all migration requests, scheduling results and host metadata are collected by our prototype. OpenStack components interact with each other via advanced message queuing protocol (AMQP) [17], and the TLS encryption feature of AMQP is disabled by default, which provides convenience for us to access the packet contents. Wireshark [18] dissectors are used to dissect the AMQP packets. Our prototype also integrates a scheduling engine containing 16 filters and 3 weighers [14] to simulate the behaviors of OpenStack's nova-scheduler (requests and host metadata are also simplified for easier simulation). 2 weighers are added by us to demonstrate the weigher determination. Besides, CLAPACK [19] and Armadillo [20] are utilized to solve linear equations. As CLAPACK supports figuring out approximate solutions via the least square approach, we can conveniently solve all host shifting equations one time, even when the number of equations exceeds the multiplier count. As the problem this paper trying to address is very novel, it's hard to find related work to compare the experimental results with.

We have evaluated SARA's filter determination on a variety of datasets, which are presented in the form of (r, h). r is the number of migration requests and h is the number of hosts in the cloud. These datasets are generated randomly and we configured the random parameters to make the datasets close to reality. We applied different filters on these datasets and corresponding determination results are summarized in Table 1. **T-I** and **T-II** columns show the Type-I and Type-II filters detected respectively and **Precision** column shows the ratios of the expected number of filters to the determined number.

Table 1. SARA's detected filters, per dataset

Dataset	Detected filters							Precision
	T-I					T-II		
(10, 20)	5	5	8	11	14	0	1	86.05 %
(50, 20)	4	4	8	11	14	0	1	90.24 %
(100, 20)	3	3	8	11	13	0	1	94.87 %
(200, 20)	2	3	8	11	13	0	1	97.37 %
(400, 20)	2	3	8	11	13	0	1	97.37 %
(600, 20)	1	3	8	11	13	0	1	100 %
*expected	1	3	8	11	13	0	1	100 %

Through observing the data in Table 1, we found that: (i) Precision is positively correlated with the dataset scale, so larger datasets can achieve better results. Precision can be 100 % if we have sufficient requests. (ii) Most deactivated filters are found by the first several requests, as the precision for the first 10 requests has reached 86.05 %. (iii) SARA approach works by eliminating impossible filters, thus the more filters a CSP has activated in the cloud, the less remaining filters are going to be determined, which makes it easier for SARA to achieve a good precision.

$$
(A, \beta) = \begin{pmatrix}
1.0000 & 1.0000 & 1.0000 & 1.0 \\
-0.6046 & 0.0859 & 0.6754 & 0.0 \\
0.0348 & 0.0176 & 0.0054 & 0.0 \\
1.8193 & -1.0514 & 0.0084 & 0.0 \\
2.0000 & -1.9663 & 1.9960 & 0.0 \\
0.6985 & 0.1145 & -1.3094 & 0.0 \\
2.0000 & -1.0000 & -2.0000 & 0.0 \\
-1.0000 & -1.0000 & -1.0000 & 0.0
\end{pmatrix}
\tag{10}
$$

To evaluate the effectiveness of SARA's weigher determination, we enabled three weighers: CoreWeigher, RamWeigher and DiskWeigher with multipliers $(m_1, m_2, m_3) = (0.3, 0.5, 0.2)$ for example. All filters are activated to avoid influences from different filter sets. Table 2 summarizes the calculation results of multipliers and corresponding errors on different datasets. The precision of calculated multipliers increases as the dataset scale grows. When dataset is reduced to (100, 20), solution is even unavailable because the host shifting number is too small to solve the linear equations. When request number nearly reaches the capacity limit, 20 times more than the number of hosts, the precision gets better but are not entirely satisfactory, as the errors of m_2 and m_3 are still not small enough to guess the expected values. Optimizations need to be introduced to get better results.

As our multiplier determination is actually an approximate method, improper equations in the final linear system would lead to coarse-grained results. We thus improved the accuracy of multiplier calculations by employing two optimizing

Table 2. SARA's calculated multipliers of weighers, per dataset

Dataset	m_1	m_2	m_3	Error
(100, 20)	N/A	N/A	N/A	N/A
(200, 20)	0.6610	1.1030	-0.7640	1.1930
(400, 20)	0.3868	0.5246	0.0886	0.1434
(600, 40)	0.2924	0.4370	0.2706	0.0949
(800, 40)	0.2947	0.4573	0.2480	0.0645
(100, 20)'	N/A	N/A	N/A	N/A
(200, 20)'	0.3839	0.6161	0.0000	0.2460
(400, 20)'	0.3070	0.5103	0.1827	0.0213
(600, 40)'	0.2926	0.5076	0.1998	0.0106
(800, 40)'	0.2912	0.4949	0.2139	0.0172
*expected	0.3000	0.5000	0.2000	0.0000

methods based on offloading unsuitable equations. The matrix in (10) presents the linear system of host shifting equations on the (600, 40) dataset. The left 3 columns are coefficients and the column on the right is the constant term. In this matrix we found two anomalies: (i) As the other side of the equation is zero, the factors for one equation cannot be totally positive or negative in the meantime, like row 3, as this implies the existence of a negative multiplier (which is impossible). (ii) Some equation coefficients only contain 0, ±1, ±2 like row 5, 7 and 8, this always happens when there are merely two hosts for weighing and they shift alternately to become the destination, which we call "bad" host shifting (shown as below, * indicates the destination). Resulting from the side effect of weigher's normalization, weights of these two hosts will be normalized to 0 and 1 respectively, enlarging the their value gap and affecting the accuracy of our method. Therefore, to minimize calculation errors, the above "flawed" equations have to be eliminated. Optimized result for dataset (600, 40) is (0.2926, 0.5076, 0.1998), which is very close to the expected arguments. The comparison results for other datasets can be found in Table 2 (optimized are denoted with ').

```
Good host shifting:
Hosts for request [175]: [8], [13], *[22], [24], [29]
Hosts for request [328]: *[8], [13], [22], [24], [29]
Bad host shifting:
Hosts for request [426]: [13], *[36]
Hosts for request [586]: *[13], [36]
```

5   Conclusions and Future Work

In this paper, a novel approach, SARA is presented to reverse the scheduling algorithm in clouds. SARA achieves its goal by two steps: filter determination and weigher determination. Experimental results on a number of migration request datesets show SARA can reliably determine the filters and weighers deployed by CSPs in OpenStack, indicating how vulnerable wide-spread cloud software is to network sniffing attacks. In order to secure migration between virtual machines, encryption should be enforced on not only the data plane, but also the control plane, such as the scheduling commands transmitting channel. In our ongoing work SARA technique will be improved by adding anti-randomizing support, and we are also exploring the security issues on load balancing, to investigate whether its algorithm can either be reversed through traffic analyzing.

Acknowledgments. We thank the reviewers for their help improving this paper. This work is supported by the National High Technology Research and Development Program ("863" Program) of China under Grant No. 2015AA016009, the National Natural Science Foundation of China under Grant No. 61232005, and the Science and Technology Program of Shen Zhen, China under Grant No. JSGG20140516162852628.

References

1. Clark, C., Fraser, K., Hand, S., Hansen, J.G., Jul, E., Limpach, C., Warfield, A.: Live migration of virtual machines. In: Proceedings of the 2nd Conference on Symposium on Networked Systems Design & Implementation, vol. 2, pp. 273–286. USENIX Association (2005)
2. Forsman, M., Glad, A., Lundberg, L., Ilie, D.: Algorithms for automated live migration of virtual machines. J. Syst. Softw. **101**, 110–126 (2015)
3. Meneses, E., Ni, X., Zheng, G., Mendes, C.L., Kale, L.V.: Using migratable objects to enhance fault tolerance schemes in supercomputers. IEEE Trans. Parallel Distrib. Syst. **26**(7), 2061–2074 (2014)
4. Yang, C.T., Liu, J.C., Hsu, C.H., Chou, W.L.: On improvement of cloud virtual machine availability with virtualization fault tolerance mechanism. J. Supercomputing **69**(3), 1103–1122 (2014)
5. Oberheide, J., Cooke, E., Jahanian, F.: Empirical exploitation of live virtual machine migration. In: Proceedings of BlackHat DC Convention 2008
6. Ver, M.: Dynamic load balancing based on live migration of virtual machines: security threats and effects. Rochester Institute of Technology (2011)
7. Perez-Botero, D.: A Brief Tutorial on Live Virtual Machine Migration From a Security Perspective. University of Princeton, USA (2011)
8. Duncan, A., Creese, S., Goldsmith, M., Quinton, J.S.: Cloud computing: insider attacks on virtual machines during migration. In: 2013 12th IEEE International Conference on Trust, Security and Privacy in Computing and Communications (TrustCom), pp. 493–500. IEEE (2013)
9. Perez, R., Sailer, R., van Doorn, L.: vTPM: virtualizing the trusted platform module. In: Proceedings of the 15th Conference on USENIX Security Symposium, pp. 305–320 (2006)
10. Zhang, F., Huang, Y., Wang, H., Chen, H., Zang, B.: PALM: security preserving VM live migration for systems with VMM-enforced protection. In: Third Asia-Pacific Trusted Infrastructure Technologies Conference, APTC 2008, pp. 9–18. IEEE (2008)
11. Masti, R.J.: On the security of virtual machine migration and related topics. Master Thesis, Eidgenossische Technische Hochschule Zurich (2010)

12. Aslam, M., Gehrmann, C., Bjorkman, M.: Security and trust preserving VM migrations in public clouds. In: 2012 IEEE 11th International Conference on Trust, Security and Privacy in Computing and Communications (TrustCom), pp. 869–876. IEEE (2012)
13. Wang, Z., Jiang, X.: Hypersafe: a lightweight approach to provide lifetime hypervisor control-flow integrity. In: 2010 IEEE Symposium on Security and Privacy (SP), pp. 380–395. IEEE (2010)
14. Scheduling - OpenStack Configuration Reference - juno. http://docs.openstack.org/juno/config-reference/content/section_compute-scheduler.html
15. Hines, M.R., Deshpande, U., Gopalan, K.: Post-copy live migration of virtual machines. ACM SIGOPS Oper. Syst. Rev. **43**(3), 14–26 (2009)
16. Zhang, Y., Juels, A., Reiter, M.K., Ristenpart, T.: Cross-VM side channels and their use to extract private keys. In: Proceedings of the 2012 ACM Conference on Computer and Communications Security, pp. 305–316. ACM (2012)
17. Vinoski, S.: Advanced message queuing protocol. IEEE Internet Comput. **6**, 87–89 (2006)
18. Baxter, J.H.: Wireshark Essentials. Packt Publishing Ltd, UK (2014)
19. Anderson, E., Bai, Z., Bischof, C., Blackford, S., Demmel, J., Dongarra, J., Sorensen, D.: LAPACK Users' Guide, vol. 9. SIAM, Philadelphia (1999)
20. Sanderson, C.: Armadillo: an open source C++ linear algebra library for fast prototyping and computationally intensive experiments (2010)

Top-k Distance-Based Outlier Detection on Uncertain Data

Ying Zhang, Hongyuan Zheng$^{(\boxtimes)}$, and Qiulin Ding

College of Computer Science and Technology, Nanjing University
of Aeronautics and Astronautics, Nanjing, China
984589338@qq.com, zixiayedu@126.com,
qlding@nuaa.edu.cn

Abstract. In recent years, more researchers are studying uncertain data with the development of Internet of Things. The technique of outlier detection is one of the significant branches of emerging uncertain database. In existing algorithms, parameters are difficult to set, and expansibility is poor when used in large data sets. Aimed at these shortcomings, a top-k distance-based outlier detection algorithm on uncertain data is proposed. This algorithm applies dynamic programming theory to calculate outlier possibility and greatly improves the efficiency. Furthermore, an efficient virtual grid-based optimization approach is also proposed to greatly improve our algorithm's efficiency. The theoretical analysis and experimental results fully prove that the algorithm is feasible and efficient.

Keywords: Uncertain data · Outlier detection · Dynamic programming theory · Optimization approach

1 Introduction

In the real world, data contains uncertainty for reasons that include poor precision of equipment, absence of data and transmission delay. The new data pattern has become a new research hotspot, outliers detection is one of them. Outlier detection is a fundamental issue in data mining. It has been applied in lots of areas including network intrusion detection [1], industrial sciences [2], environmental monitoring [3], credit card fraud detection [4], etc. The outlier is data with abnormal behavior or characteristic that obviously deviates from other sample data. The main task of outlier detection is to find outlier from a large number of complex dataset [5].

The outlier detection comes from the statistics, and later it was introduced into the data mining domain by Knorr [6, 7]. Some outlier detection algorithms are commonly used at present, such as distance-based outlier detection and density-based outlier detection. However, all these outlier detection algorithms mainly focus on deterministic data and cannot directly process uncertain data, most existing outlier detection algorithms on uncertain data are the improvement and innovation on the basis of the above algorithms.

At present, the outlier detection technology of deterministic data has matured and is used cosmically, but research about uncertain data is just beginning. The first definition of outlier on uncertain data was given by Aggarwal C C, Yu P S, et al. [8]. According to

© Springer International Publishing Switzerland 2015
Z. Huang et al. (Eds.): ICCCS 2015, LNCS 9483, pp. 521–535, 2015.
DOI: 10.1007/978-3-319-27051-7_45

them, an uncertain data that can be represented by a probability density function (PDF) is an outlier if its existential probability in some subspace with density at least η is less than δ. But their works only can detect local outlier and cannot be well applied to global outlier. Shaikh and S.A also proposed an outlier detection algorithm on uncertain data of the Gaussian distribution in [9]. According to them, for an uncertain data, if its expected number of neighbors that exist within its D-distance is less than or equal to threshold, it is a density-based outlier. However, in practice, parameter p is hard to set. Subsequently, aimed at the shortcomings of the proposed algorithms in [9], they proposed a fast top-k outlier detection algorithm on uncertain data in [10] and an approximate outlier detection algorithm in [11]. However, all of their works are based on an uncertain data model that Gaussian probability density function is used to describe uncertain data, which is different from the data model we will discuss in this paper. Wang et al. first proposed the concept of distance-based outlier detection. In [12], the definition of outliers is based on the possible world. They judge whether an object is an outlier by calculating the sum of the probabilities of possible world instances that consist of at least k objects. If the sum is less than a pre-defined value, the object is an outlier, which is then extended to outlier detection on the uncertain data stream in [13].

Existing distance-based outlier detection algorithms need user to set up several parameters in practical applications, but it is very difficult to set up reasonable parameters for users who are not familiar with data distribution. In order to decrease the difficulty of parameter setting, we use a constant parameter k that is independent of the dataset features to instead of probability threshold value. In this paper, we redefine the concept of outlier on uncertain data and propose a top-k distance-based outlier detection algorithm on uncertain data. We sort all objects in descending order of its probability of being outlier and the preceding k objects are our results. In order to reduce the computational cost, we apply dynamic programming theory to compute the possibility of being an outlier for an object and greatly improve the efficiency, then present an efficient virtual grid-based optimization method to achieve better effect.

The remainder of this paper is organized as follows. In the next section, we propose a basic algorithm of top-k distance-based outlier detection on uncertain data. A grid-based optimization approach was presented to improve the efficiency of the basic algorithm in Sect. 3. Section 4 contains experimental results that fully prove the efficiency of the proposed algorithms and Sect. 5 concludes our paper.

2 Top-K Distance-Based Outlier Detection on Uncertain Data

2.1 Related Concepts

In this paper, our works focus on tuple-level uncertain data. Given an uncertain dataset $D = \{x_0, x_1, \ldots, x_i, \ldots\}$, in which each tuple x_i has the form of $<\overline{xi}, pi>$, where $\overline{xi}$ is uncertain record of x_i, p_i is existential probability of x_i. $|D| = N$.

Definition 1 (ud-neighborhood [12]). ud is a distance parameter. An object is a neighbor of x_i if the distance between it and x_i is less than ud. $R(x_i)$ is ud-neighborhood of x_i, $R(xi) = \{xj | xj \in D, dist(\overline{xi}, \overline{xj}) \leq ud\}$.

The main difference between certain and uncertain data is that uncertain data contain uncertain record and their existential probability. So any combination of tuples in ud-neighborhood of the data needs to be unfolded. Then possible world model was built. There are many models of uncertain data, but possible world model is the most popular one [14].

Definition 2 (Probability of the possible world instance (PPW)). For uncertain data x_i, an arbitrary combination of tuples in $R(x_i)$ constitutes a possible world instance (PW), all possible world instances constitute possible world of x_i. We denote the possibility of possible world instance by PPW, can be computed as follows:

$$PPW = \prod_{xj \in R(xi) \wedge xj \in PW} pj \prod_{xk \in R(xi) \wedge xk \notin PW} (1 - pk) \tag{1}$$

Where x_j and x_k are objects in $R(x_i)$, x_j is in the possible world instance PW and x_k is not in PW, p_j and p_k are existential probability of x_j and x_k respectively.

When considering deterministic data, a distance-based outlier is a data who has not enough neighbors within a given distance threshold [15]. For uncertain data, however, existential probability needs to be taken into account in detection. We can only judge whether an object is an outlier through calculating the probability of the object to become an outlier.

Definition 3 (Outlier probability). For an uncertain data x_i, we define the sum of the probabilities of possible world instances that contain less than n tuples as its outlier probability. Then,

$$P_{outlier(xi)} = \sum_{PW_j \in Sn(xi,PW)} PPW_j \tag{2}$$

Where $P_{outlier(xi)}$ denotes the outlier probability of x_i. $S_n(x_i, PW)$ is the set of possible world instances that contain less than n tuples in possible world of x_i.

Definition 4 (Top-k Outlier). We sort all uncertain data in descending order of their outlier probability, and collect the preceding k objects as top-k outliers on uncertain data.

2.2 Dynamic Programming Algorithm

The key computation of top-k outlier detection is calculating outlier probability of each data. The basic method is to list all possible world instances, and calculates the sum of the probabilities of possible world instances that contain less than n tuples. But the time complexity of this method shows exponential growth with neighborhood scale.

A dynamic programming algorithm is proposed by Wang B in [12]. In this paper, we improve the dynamic programming algorithm to calculate outlier probability, which makes the time complexity of the probability calculation decrease to $O(nN)$ from $O(n \cdot 2^N)$.

If $R(x_i)$ is ud-neighborhood of uncertain data x_i, let $R(x_i) = \{x_0, x_1,...,x_{m-1}\}$. $[R(x_i), j]$ denotes event that only occurs j tuples in $R(x_i)$. We find all events in $[R(x_i), j]$ are exactly possible world instances that contain j tuples in $R(x_i)$. According to this, we can use a meaningful equivalent conversion for computing the outlier probability of an object. We list all the possible events. Then,

$$[R(xi) < n] = [R(xi), 0] \cup [R(xi), 1] \cup \cdots \cup [R(xi), n-1] \tag{3}$$

Where $[R(x_i) < n]$ denotes all events that occur less than n tuples in $R(x_i)$, $[R(x_i), j]$ ($j = 0, 1, ... ,n-1$) denotes the event that only occurs j tuples in $R(x_i)$.

Then, the outlier probability of x_i can be converted to another expression:

$$P_{outlier(xi)} = P[R(xi) < n] = P[R(xi), 0] + P[R(xi), 1] + \cdots + P[R(xi), n-1]$$
$$= \sum_{j=0}^{n-1} P[R(xi), j] \tag{4}$$

Where $P[R(x_i) < n]$ denotes the probability of event $[R(x_i) < n]$. $P[R(x_i), j]$ ($j = 0, 1, ... ,n-1$) denotes the probability of event $[R(x_i), j]$.

The problem becomes how to calculate $P[R(x_i), j]$ efficiently, $R(x_i)$ will be divided into two parts based on the dynamic programming theory: the last tuple and the rest of tuples. If the last tuple occurs, the next step is to calculate probability of the event that only occurs $j-1$ tuples in the rest of tuples; if the last tuple doesn't occur, the next step is to calculate probability of the event that occurs j tuples in the rest of tuples.

The order of tuples in $R(x_i)$ remains unchanged during the calculation. $|R(x_i)| = m$, probabilities of tuples in $R(x_i)$ are represented $p_0, p_1, ..., p_{m-1}$ respectively. In this paper, we use two-dimensional array to store the value of $P[R(x_i),j]$. We need to create a two-dimensional array T that contains m rows and n columns, $T[i][j]$ denotes the probability of event that only occurs j tuples in the dataset that consisted by the first i tuples of $R(x_i)$. So $P[R(x_i) < n]$ is the sum of values of the last row in T, then,

$$P_{outlier(xi)} = P[R(xi) < n] = \sum_{j=0}^{n-1} T[m][j] \tag{5}$$

The row number of array starts with 1 because it is meaningless when the formula $i = 0$. Solving formulas of two-dimensional array are as follows:

$$T[i][j] = \begin{cases} \overline{p_0} & if\ j = 0, i = 1 \\ p_0 & if\ j = 1, i = 1 \\ \overline{p_{i-1}} * T[i-1][0] & if\ j = 0, i > 1 \\ p_{i-1} * T[i-1][j-1] & if\ j = i, i > 1 \\ p_{i-1} * T[i-1][j-1] + \overline{p_{i-1}} * T[i-1][j] & if\ j \neq 0, j < i \\ 0 & if\ j > i \end{cases} \tag{6}$$

For instance, R_1 is ud-neighborhood of an uncertain object, let $R_1 = \{x_0,...,x_{m1-2}, x_{m1-1}\}$. Figure 1 shows the storage situation in two-dimensional array when calculating $P[R_1 < n]$ by formula(6).

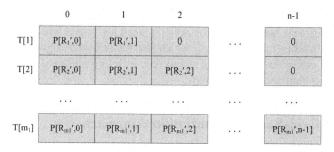

Fig. 1. Storage situation in two-dimensional array of R_1

Where R_i' $(i = 1,\ldots, m_1)$ is a data set that consists of the first i tuples appear of R_1. And $P[R_1 < n] = T[m_1][0] + \ldots + T[m_1][n-1]$.

In this paper, the above dynamic programming algorithm is represented by DPA.

2.3   Basic Algorithm

In this paper, k objects with maximum outlier probability in D are considered to be outliers. We need a data container to store k objects. Threshold δ has been always the minimum outlier probability in the data container. Considering that we need to find the minimum outlier probability in k objects every time, the minimum heap is used as the data container. The main idea of the algorithm is to search ud-neighborhood of each uncertain object x_i, and calculate the outlier probability of x_i by DPA, if the number of objects is less than k in the minimum heap, then insert x_i into the minimum heap, otherwise, assign outlier probability of the top object of the minimum heap to δ and replace the top object of the minimum heap with x_i if its outlier probability is greater than δ. The pseudo code is as follows:

```
Input: D, ud, n, k
Output: top-k outlier
1 δ=∞
2 for there exists at least one uncertain data x_i, x_i∈D
    Search for R(x_i) ;
    Calculate P_outlier(xi) by DPA;
    If (|minheap|<k)
      minheap.insert(x_i);
    Else
      δ=outlier probability of the top object;
      If P_outlier(xi)>δ
        minheap.erase(top object);
        minheap.insert(x_i);
      End if
    End if
  End for
3 output objects in minimum heap.
```

The above algorithm is called basic algorithm of top-k outlier detection or BA.

In the experiment, we find that BA needs to search ud-neighborhood and calculate the outlier probability for each object, which inevitably brings high time complexity. Then a virtual grid-based optimization algorithm is proposed to reduce the consumption of the algorithm and optimize BA.

3   Virtual Grid-Based Optimization Approach

3.1   Dynamic Increasing Calculation

Through further study on DPA, we find the following properties:

Property1: Outlier probability isn't affected by the order of tuples in $R(x_i)$.

Property2: Given two uncertain datasets U and U' ($|U| > n$ and $|U'| > n$), $P[U' < n] \geq P[U < n]$ holds, if $U' \subseteq U$.

Proof. We use $[U \geq n]$ to denote the event that at least n elements appear in U. Since $U' \subseteq U$, we get $U = U' \cup (U - U')$. Therefore, $[U' \geq n] \square [\, U - U' \geq 0]$ is a sub-event of $[U \geq n]$, Since elements are mutually independent, thus $P[U' \geq n] * P[U - U' \geq 0] \leq P[U \geq n]$

, where $[U - U' \geq 0]$ is a certain event and $P[U - U' \geq 0] = 1$.Therefore, $P[U' \geq n] \leq P[U \geq n]$

holds and $1 - P[U' \geq n] \geq 1 - P[U \geq n]$.Therefore, $P[U' < n] \geq P[U < n]$.

According to the above properties, For uncertain data x_i, R' is a partition of $R(x_i)$, x_i isn't an outlier if the value of $P[R' < n]$ is less than or equal to the threshold δ. So we needn't find all ud-neighborhood of x_i when detecting x_i. A pruning rule is proposed out of such point view in the next section.

In the process of judging whether uncertain data x_i is an outlier, we need to calculate $P[R' < n]$ many times. If we calculate $P[R' < n]$ by starting all over again, time cost will be undoubtedly huge. So we propose the dynamic increasing calculation, which doesn't increase the total time regardless of the times to calculate when detecting an object.

If R_2 is an intersection of R_1 (Sect. 2.2) and $\{x_0', x_1', \ldots, x_{m2-1}'\}$ ($R_2 = \{x_0, \ldots, x_{m_1-2}, x_{m_1-1}, x_0', x_1', \ldots x_{m_2-1}'\}$). Figure 2 shows the storage situation in array when calculating $P[R_2 < n]$.

Through comparison between Fig. 1 and Fig. 2, we don't need to calculate $P[R_2 < n]$ again from the very beginning, because the value of the first m_1 rows of Fig. 2 and Fig. 1 is completely identical, so we just need to calculate from $(m_1 + 1)_{th}$ row to $(m_1 + m_2)_{th}$ row.

The above method is called dynamic increasing calculation (DIC) which is proposed to reduce the amount of calculation of the pruning algorithm when used as an auxiliary algorithm in the second stage in the next section.

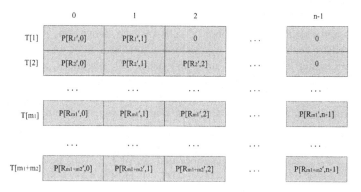

Fig. 2. Storage situation in two-dimensional array of R_2

3.2 Virtual Grid-Based Optimization Algorithm

Wang B proposed a pruning strategy based on grid in [12], and the transformation is speeded up. However, in the large data sets, the data distribution is relatively sparse, empty cells account for a large proportion of the grid, which wastes a lot of storage space and access time. In this paper, we introduce a virtual grid structure [16] that only stores nonempty cell to effectively avoid the happening of this kind of situation.

In this section, the outlier detection process is divided into two stages. In the first stage, dataset is simply clustered. In the second stage, detecting outlier for clustering results by pruning rule.

(1) The First Stage. In the first stage, we realize relatively simple cluster analysis for uncertain dataset. We needn't to seek the optimal clustering effect, the key is efficiency of the algorithm. In this paper, we only discuss and analyze uncertain data in a two-dimensional space.

(1) Virtual grid structure

In order to avoid storing and searching empty cells, this paper introduces the virtual grid structure (VG).

Cell structure: each cell structure consists of 5-tuple < X, *checked, info, down, right* > , as shown in Fig. 3.

Fig. 3. Cell structure

Where X is the coordinate value of the cell; *checked* denotes whether the cell is checked; *info* denotes information of tuples in the cell, such as tuple set, the number of tuples, the sum of probabilities of tuples; *down* point to the next cell in the same column; *right* point to the next cell in the same row.

For a given uncertain dataset D, we divide its domain into many mutual disjoint square cells and calculate the number of cells in each dimension. According to the number of cells in each dimension, we establish a total head node and two head nodes. Sequentially reading tuple x_i from uncertain dataset D, we add x_i into the cell and update information of the cell if the cell that contains x_i is already in VG; otherwise, we need to create a new cell node and insert it into cross list, then add x_i into the cell and update information of the cell. VG don't finish until all tuples are read. Its structure is shown in Fig. 4.

Each side of the cell is ud/2. Let $C_{x,y}$ be a cell of 2-D space. $L(C_{x,y}) = \{C_{u,v}|u = x\pm2,$ $v = y\pm2, C_{u,v} \neq C_{x,y}\}$ denotes the neighbor cell set of $C_{x,y}$. Cell holds the following natures: for $\forall xi \in C_{x,y}$, there is $R(x_i)\in(C_{x,y}\cup L(C_{x,y}))$, and $C_{x,y}\in R(x_i)$. So we only need to find ud-neighborhood of x_i in $L(C_{x,y})$ when searching $R(x_i)$.

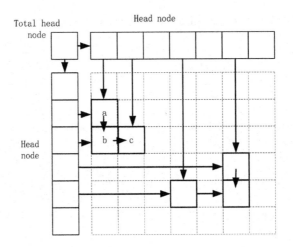

Fig. 4. The structure of VG

(2) Clustering

Once VG is constructed, we traverse the VG, and get a set of adjacent cells in the first column (such as a and b in Fig. 4), then store them into a temporary list and cluster set, then find adjacent cell in the same row (such as b and c in Fig. 4) of them and store adjacent cell which does not exist in temporary list into cluster set, finally clear temporary list. Repeat above steps until there is no cell in VG.

$LC = \{C_1,..., C_i,..., C_M\}$ denotes the set of clusters after clustering. Let $|C_i|$ is the number of tuples in C_i, $Count_i$ is the number of cells in C_i. According to the properties of the DPA, the outlier probability of an uncertain data is influenced by probability distribution and tuple density. The probability of containing outliers in C_i is larger when its sum of existential probability is smaller and the number of cells in C_i is larger. Considering the aforementioned factors, we measure the probability of containing outliers in C_i by the average probability of the cells in C_i. Let den be probability threshold. Then,

$$den = \frac{\sum_{j=1}^{|C_i|} p_j}{Count_i} \tag{7}$$

Where p_j is the existential probability of the object in C_i. The smaller den is, the greater the probability of containing outliers in C_i becomes.

In the process of the algorithm, δ is gradually increasing, the greater δ is, the more objects can be pruned. So, optimization algorithm prioritizes clusters whose den are minimum, then cells in the cluster are sorted by the sum of probabilities in ascending order, and detecting outlier from cell whose sum of probabilities is minimum, which makes δ rapidly increase.

(2) The Second Stage. In the second stage, we need to detect outlier for each cluster based on pruning rule.

In the process of neighbor search or calculation of a data, we can immediately interrupt the search or calculation if we can judge the non-outlier as early as possible. So the following pruning rule is presented. M is a dataset that stores neighbors of the object in the process of the algorithm.

Pruning rule: If $P[M < n] \leq \delta$, and M only contains part of the neighborhood of a query object, this query object can be pruned as non-outlier. A special case: If $P[M < n] \leq \delta$, and M only contains all objects of a cell, all objects in this cell can be pruned as non-outlier.

In the process of judging whether uncertain data x_i is an outlier, firstly, if the number of objects in the minimum heap is less than k, then calculate outlier probability of x_i and insert x_i into the minimum heap. Otherwise, all tuples in the cell that contains x_i are stored into M, then we calculate $P[M < n]$, if $P[M < n] \leq \delta$, all tuples in this cell can be pruned as non-outlier, otherwise, find a neighbor cell in the cluster that contains x_i, and search neighbors in the neighbor cell and store them into M, then calculate $P[M < n]$ (by DIC) when a cell is finished. If $P[M < n] \leq \delta$, x_i is not an outlier. If it still does not meet the pruning condition and has undetected neighbor cells when all neighbor cells in the cluster that contains x_i are detected, we need to find neighbor cells in VG, repeat above calculation and judgment. If all neighbor cells are evaluated, $P[M < n]$ is still greater than δ, then remove the top object in minimum heap and insert x_i into minimum heap, and outlier probability of the top object in minimum heap is assigned to δ, continue to test the next object.

The whole algorithm flowchart is shown in Fig. 5.

In the process of the algorithm, δ is gradually increasing, the vast majority of objects only need to search a small part of ud-neighborhood, which can judge whether the object is an outlier, thus save a lot of time.

Neighbor cells of the vast majority of objects are practically clustered in a same cluster, and only a few objects need to search VG when searching their ud-neighborhood in the first stage of the optimization algorithm.

In this paper, the above algorithm is called top-k virtual grid-based outlier detection algorithm on uncertain data (VGUOD for short).

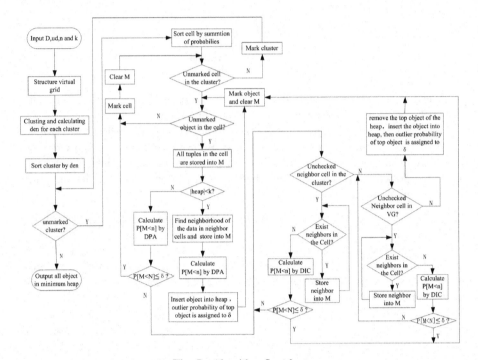

Fig. 5. Algorithm flowchart

4   Experiments

To evaluate the performance of the proposed algorithm objectively, in this chapter, the experiment is taken on two synthetic datasets SynDS1 and SynDS2 and mainly focuses on the influence of several parameters and comparisons in precision and running time between VGUOD and GPA that proposed in [12]. Software environment: 2.93GHZ CPU、2G main memory and Microsoft Windows7 Ultimate system. Experiment platform: Microsoft Visual Studio 2010. Language: C ++.

Synthetic datasets are generated by Matlab. Each dataset has 100000 uncertain records. Valued attributes are 2-dimensional and each dimension is floating point number that distribute in [0, 1000], SynDS1 and SynDS2 are composed respectively of several normal distributions and uniform distributions. Existential probability was randomly generated in the range of (0, 1).

4.1   Influence from Parameters

In order to analyze the influence of parameters on the performance of the algorithms, we evaluate the effectiveness of BA and VGUOD by using SynDS1. We need to set values for parameters before the experiments begin. Let $n = 4$, $ud = 20$, $k = 0.03*N$, $|D| = N$.

Firstly, we discussed the effect of the parameter k, we varied k from $0.01*N$ to $0.05*N$ with increment $0.01*N$ while keeping other parameters constant, then recorded the running time. The running time of BA and VGUOD is shown in Fig. 6.

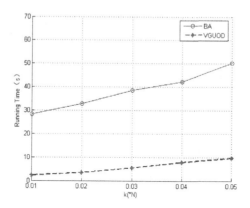

Fig. 6. Running time vs. k

The number of outliers was increasing as k grew, and running time of two approaches is increasing. However, as the Fig. 6 shows, the running time of VGUOD is far less than running time of BA, because virtual grid structure can filter all empty cells and find neighbors more easily, besides, pruning method based on virtual grid structure can trim most non-outliers, so VGUOD can effectively save running time.

The relationship between ud and running time is illustrated in Fig. 7. The number of ud-neighborhood of an object for different ud (ud is increasing from 10 to 28) is increasing. BA needs to search the whole dataset and calculates the outlier probability for each object, which inevitably costs more computation time. However, for VGUOD, the value of $P[M < n]$ in a cell is declining as ud grow. The smaller the value of $P[M < n]$ is, the greater the probability of meeting the pruning condition becomes. So VGUOD needs less running time than BA.

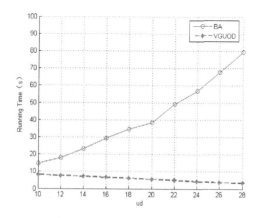

Fig. 7. Running time vs. ud

Then we analyzed the influence of parameter n on running time. The parameter n varied from 4 to 20 to test BA and VGUOD. The cost of calculating outlier probability is increasing as n gets larger, which increases running time. Since BA is running without any pruning strategy, it spends more time calculating outlier probability of all objects in dataset. VGUOD effectively reduces the impact of parameter n on running time by using pruning rule and DIC. As Fig. 8 shows, the running time of VGUOD is far less than running time of BA.

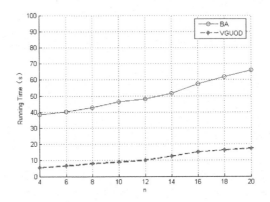

Fig. 8. Running time vs. n

Finally, the effects of the change of data size on the running time were discussed. We used ten datasets that generated by Matlab and the number of records of them varied from 20000 to 160000 to test BA and VGUOD. Figure 9. shows both the running time of BA and VGUOD in different datasets. The more the number of records in dataset, the more the amount of calculation and the running time consumption. BA needs to calculate all objects, its computational effort remarkably increases with the size of the dataset. The running time of VGUOD is far less than the time of BA because of its pruning ability.

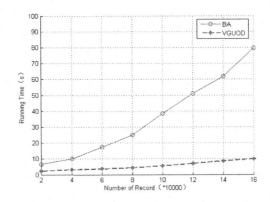

Fig. 9. Running time vs. Number of Record

4.2   Compared with Other Algorithm

In this section, we evaluate the precision and execution time cost of VGUOD compared with GPA. We use the ratio of the right number of outliers found by the algorithm to the total numbers of outliers found by the algorithm to evaluate the precision of the algorithm. Apparently, the higher the ratio, the higher the precision of the algorithm. So we run the GPA algorithm and the VGUOD algorithm on SynDS1 and SynDS2 and calculate the ratio Z by Eq. (8).

$$Z = \frac{b}{B} \tag{8}$$

Where B denotes the total number of outliers found by the algorithm, and b is the right number of outliers found by the algorithm.

Figures 10 and 11 respectively contrasts the precision and execution time cost of GPA and VGUOD when they run in the same dataset to detect the same number of outliers. Let $ud = 20$, $n = 4$.

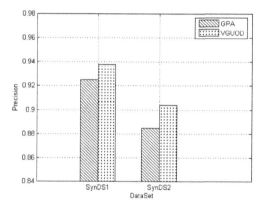

Fig. 10. Precision

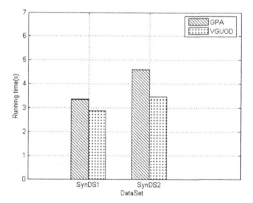

Fig. 11. Running time

By analyzing experimental results, we can observe that the VGUOD has advanced performance in both running time and precision than GPA. VGUOD algorithm gets top-k outliers, which guarantees it has a higher precision than GPA when detecting the same number of outliers. In terms of running time, VGUOD algorithm filters empty cells and judges whether an object is outlier by using less computation amounts, which greatly saves running time.

5 Conclusions

As a new but important research field, Outlier detection on uncertain data has a good extensive application prospect. In this paper, a new definition of outlier detection on uncertain data is put forward, and then we introduce the dynamic programming idea to efficiently calculate the outlier probability of the data, and propose an efficient virtual grid-based optimization method. The algorithm adapts to detect outliers in large dataset to a certain extent.

We will study more complex uncertain data model in the future work, and detecting outlier on uncertain data in high dimensional data space.

References

1. Zhang, J., Zulkernine, M.: Anomaly based network intrusion detection with unsupervised outlier detection. In: IEEE International Conference on Communications, ICC 2006, pp. 2388–2393. IEEE (2006)
2. Alaydie, N., Fotouhi, F., Reddy, C.K., Soltanian-Zadeh, H.: Noise and outlier filtering in heterogeneous medical data sources. In: 2012 23rd International Workshop on Database and Expert Systems Applications, pp. 115–119. IEEE (2010)
3. Knorr, E.M., Ng, R.T.: Algorithms for mining distance-based outliers in large datasets. In: Proceedings of the 24rd International Conference on Very Large Data Bases, pp. 392–403. Morgan Kaufmann Publishers Inc. (1998)
4. Wang, L., Zou, L.: Research on algorithms for mining distance-based outliers. J. Electron. **14**, 485–490 (2005)
5. Han, J., Kamber, M.: Data Mining–Concepts and Techniques 2nd ed. Data Mining Concepts Models Methods & Algorithms Second Edition 10(9),1–18 (2006)
6. Knorr, E.M., Ng, R.T.: Finding intensional knowledge of distance-based outliers. In: VLDB, pp. 211–222 (1999)
7. Knorr, E.M., Ng, R.T., Tucakov, V.: Distance-based outliers: algorithms and applications. VLDB J. — Int. J. Very Large Data Bases 8(3–4), 237–253 (2000)
8. Aggarwal, C.C., Yu, P.S.: Outlier detection with uncertain data. In: SDM (2008)
9. Shaikh, S.A., Kitagawa, H.: Distance-based outlier detection on uncertain data of Gaussian distribution. In: Sheng, Q.Z., Wang, G., Jensen, C.S., Xu, G. (eds.) APWeb 2012. LNCS, vol. 7235, pp. 109–121. Springer, Heidelberg (2012)
10. Shaikh, S.A., Kitagawa, H.: Fast top-k distance-based outlier detection on uncertain data. In: Wang, J., Xiong, H., Ishikawa, Y., Xu, J., Zhou, J. (eds.) WAIM 2013. LNCS, vol. 7923, pp. 301–313. Springer, Heidelberg (2013)

11. Shaikh, S.A., Kitagawa, H.: Top-k outlier detection from uncertain data. Int. J. Autom. Comput. **11**(2), 128–142 (2014)
12. Wang, B., Xiao, G., Yu, H., et al.: Distance-based outlier detection on uncertain data. In: IEEE Ninth International Conference on Computer & Information Technology, pp. 293–298. IEEE (2009)
13. Wang, B., Yang, X.-C., Wang, G.-R., Ge, Yu.: Outlier detection over sliding windows for probabilistic data streams. J. Comput. Sci. Technol. **25**(3), 389–400 (2010)
14. Abiteboul, S., Kanellakis, P., Grahne, G.: On the representation and querying of sets of possible worlds. In: PODS 2001, pp. 34–48 (1991)
15. Angiulli, F., Pizzuti, C.: Fast outlier detection in high dimensional spaces. In: Elomaa, T., Mannila, H., Toivonen, H. (eds.) PKDD 2002. LNCS (LNAI), vol. 2431, pp. 15–27. Springer, Heidelberg (2002)
16. Dong, J., Cao, M., Huang, G., Ren, J.: Virtual grid-based clustering of uncertain data on vulnerability database. J. Convergence Inf. Technol. **7**(20), 429–438 (2012)

An Airport Noise Prediction Model Based on Selective Ensemble of LOF-FSVR

Haiyan Chen[✉], Jiajia Deng, Bo Sun, and Jiandong Wang

College of Computer Science and Technology, Nanjing University of Aeronautics
and Astronautics, 29 Yudao Street, Nanjing 210016, China
chenhaiyan@nuaa.edu.cn

Abstract. Airport noise prediction is of vital importance to the planning and designing of airports and flights, as well as in controlling airport noise. Benefited from the development of the Internet of things, large-scale noise monitoring systems have been developed and applied to monitor the airport noise, thus a large amount of real-time noise data has been collected, making it possible to train an airport noise prediction model using an appropriate machine learning algorithm. Support vector machine (SVM) is a powerful machine learning algorithm and has been demonstrated to have better performance than many existing algorithms. Thus, we intend to adopt SVM as the base learning algorithm. However, in some cases, the monitored airport noise data contains many outliers, which degrades the prediction performance of the trained SVM. To enhance its outlier immunity, in this paper, we design a Local Outlier Factor based Fuzzy Support Vector Regression algorithm (LOF-FSVR) for airport noise prediction, in which we calculate the fuzzy membership of each sample based on a local outlier factor. In addition, ensemble learning has become a powerful paradigm to effectively improve the prediction performance of individual models, motivated by ensemble learning, we propose a LOF-FSVR based ensemble prediction model to improve the prediction accuracy and reliability of single LOF-FSVR airport noise prediction model. Conducted experiments on the monitored airport noise data demonstrate the good performance of the proposed airport noise prediction model.

Keywords: Airport noise prediction · Noise monitoring · Fuzzy support vector regression · Local outlier factor · Selective ensemble · Orientation ordering · Adaboost

1 Introduction

With the rapid development of China's civil aviation, the airport noise pollution problem is becoming more and more serious and becomes one of the obstacles affecting the sustainable and healthy development of the civil aviation industry. Therefore, how to effectively predict airport noise is of vital importance to the design of airports and flights. Currently, the airport noise is commonly predicted by some noise calculation models and noise prediction software [1], such

© Springer International Publishing Switzerland 2015
Z. Huang et al. (Eds.): ICCCS 2015, LNCS 9483, pp. 536–549, 2015.
DOI: 10.1007/978-3-319-27051-7_46

as INM [2], Noisemap [3] and Sound Plan [4]. However, each of these methods has some drawbacks. For example, Asensio [5] pointed out that the INM model does not consider the aircraft taxiing factor, leading to its prediction deviation; Yang [6] pointed out that the INM model sometimes can not provide accurate noise prediction for realistic environment. Thus, it is urgent to take advantage of advanced information technology to scientifically predict airport noise so as to provide decision support for civil aviation sector.

In recent years, owing to the development of wireless sensing technic and the Internet of things, some effective noise monitoring systems have been developed. In these systems, wireless sensors are located in the influence scope of airport noise to capture real-time noise data, on which we can make a comprehensive analysis and further provide decision support for related departments to control the airport noise pollution problem.

The large amount of monitored noise data provides a sufficient condition for applying machine learning algorithms to predict airport noise. Berg's study [7] indicated that we can effectively improve the noise prediction accuracy by combining the acoustic theory calculation model with the pattern learned from the actual noise data. Makarewicz et al. [8] studied the impact pattern of vehicle speed on noise prediction in a statistical way based on the historical data, and presented a method to calculate the annual average sound level of the road traffic noise. Yin [9] adopted a multi-layer neural network using L-M optimization algorithm to predict the road traffic noise. Wen et al. [10] analyzed the characteristic of the noise data and presented a time series prediction model based on GM and LSSVR algorithm. Xu et al. [11] applied a fast hierarchical clustering algorithm to predict the noise distribution of flight events. Chen et al. [12] applied an integrated BP neural network to build an observational learning model, which provides interactive predictions for the abnormal noise monitoring nodes. The above researches have indicated that noise prediction models trained on the monitored noise data have better prediction performance than general empirical noise calculation models.

As known, support vector machine (SVM)[13] is an excellent machine learning algorithm and has been demonstrated to have better prediction capacity than many existing algorithms. Thus, in this work, we adopt SVM as the base learning algorithm to train airport noise prediction model. However, in some cases, the monitored airport noise data contains many outliers, leading to the degraded performance of the trained SVM model. To improve the outlier immunity of SVM, we design a Local Outlier Factor based Fuzzy Support Vector Regression algorithm (LOF-FSVR), in which we present to calculate the fuzzy membership of each sample based on a local outlier factor (LOF) to better describe the deviation degree of each sample from the regression interval. Conducted experiments demonstrate the superiority of our LOF-FSVR to other closely-related algorithms.

In the past decade, ensemble learning [14] has become a powerful paradigm to improve the prediction performance of individual models, it first trains multiple diverse models, then combines their outputs using an appropriate combination method, e.g., the simple majority voting rule, to obtain the final prediction result.

Theoretical and empirical studies have indicated that an ensemble is significantly better than its component models if they are accurate and diverse [15, 16]. Many successful ensemble learning algorithms have been proposed, such as Bagging [17], AdaBoost [18], Decorate [19, 20], Random Forests [21], etc. Motivated by ensemble learning, we propose *a LOF-FSVR based selective ensemble model* to improve the prediction accuracy and reliability of a single LOF-FSVR prediction model, in which we adopt AdaBoost [18] to train many diverse LOF-FSVR models and then select a subset of them using Orientation Ordering (OO)[29] to compose the final prediction model. We conduct experiments on airport noise data to verify the effectiveness of our model.

The rest of this paper is organized as follows. Section 2 reviews SVR and FSVR that serve as the foundation of our LOF-FSVR. In Sect. 3, we first define the LOF based fuzzy membership function, then demonstrate the outlier identification ability of LOF, after that, we experimentally verify the effectiveness of the designed LOF-FSVR. In Sect. 4, we detail our LOF-FSVR based ensemble prediction model, then verify its effectiveness by carrying out experiments on airport noise data. Conclusions and future work are presented in Sect. 5.

2   SVR and FSVR

2.1   Support Vector Regression SVR

When support vector machine is utilized to solve a regression problem, we call it Support Vector Regression (SVR)[22, 23]. For the training set $T = \{(x_i, y_i)|x_i \in \mathbf{R}^n, y_i \in \mathbf{R}, i = 1, 2, \cdots, l\}$, the first step of SVR is to map the input space to a high-dimensional space through a nonlinear mapping function ϕ, the second step is to conduct a linear regression in the high-dimensional space, this problem can be transformed to a constrained optimization problem:

$$min \frac{1}{2} \|w\|^2 + C \sum_{i=1}^{l} (\zeta_i^- + \zeta_i^+)$$

$$s.t. \begin{cases} y_i - (w \cdot \phi(x_i)) - b \le \varepsilon + \zeta_i^- \\ (w \cdot \phi(x_i)) + b - y_i \le \varepsilon + \zeta_i^+ \\ \zeta_i^-, \zeta_i^+ \ge 0, \quad i = 1, 2, \cdots, l \end{cases} \tag{1}$$

In the above formula, ε is the insensitive loss function, ζ_i^- and ζ_i^+ are the relaxation factors describing the loss of the sample's deviation from the regression interval, and the constant C is the penalty to each relaxation factor determining the punishment to a sample when the SVR function estimation error is larger than ε. We call the samples deviating far away from the regression interval outliers. However, fixed penalty factor C will make the regression function very sensitive to the outliers, leading to the over-fitting of SVR as shown in Fig. 1, which demonstrate that the regression interval moves towards the outliers with the adding of outliers, thus affecting the accuracy of SVR.

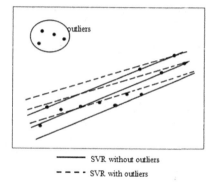

SVR without outliers
SVR with outliers

Fig. 1. Over-fitting caused by outliers in SVR

2.2 Fuzzy Support Vector Regression FSVR

In order to enhance the anti-noise capacity and regression accuracy of SVR, Lin [22] proposed a kind of SVR called fuzzy support vector machine FSVR. In FSVR, each sample is assigned to a fuzzy membership $\mu_i(0 < \mu_i < 1)$ denoting the degree of importance of this sample to the regression result, the input data set can be represented as: $T = \{(x_1, y_1, \mu_1), (x_2, y_2, \mu_2), \cdots, (x_l, y_l, \mu_l)\}$. Thus, the optimization problem expressed in formula (1) is transformed into the following form:

$$min \frac{1}{2}\|w\|^2 + C\frac{1}{l}\sum_{i=1}^{l}\mu_i(\zeta_i^- + \zeta_i^+)$$

$$s.t. \begin{cases} y_i - (w \cdot \phi(x_i)) - b \leq \varepsilon + \zeta_i^- \\ (w \cdot \phi(x_i)) + b - y_i \leq \varepsilon + \zeta_i^+ \\ \zeta_i^-, \zeta_i^+ \geq 0, \quad i = 1, 2, \cdots, l \end{cases} \tag{2}$$

Its Wolfe dual problem is expressed as:

$$maxW = \sum_{i=1}^{l}(\alpha_i + \alpha_i^*)y_i - \varepsilon\sum_{i=1}^{l}(\alpha_i + \alpha_i^*) - \frac{1}{2}\sum_{i,j=1}^{l}(\alpha_i - \alpha_i^*)(\alpha_j - \alpha_j^*)(x_i \cdot x_j),$$

$$s.t. \begin{cases} \sum_{i=1}^{l}(\alpha_i - \alpha_i^*) = 0 \\ 0 \leq \alpha_i, \alpha_i^* \leq \mu_i C, \quad i = 1, 2, \cdots, l. \end{cases} \tag{3}$$

Alphabets α_i and α_i^* in formula (3) are the lagrange multipliers obtained by solving the quadratic programming problem expressed in this formula. Then, we compute the bias variable b using α_i and α_i^*. Finally, we get the FSVR function:

$$f(x) = \sum_{i=1}^{l}(\alpha_i^* - \alpha_i)\langle x_i, x \rangle + b. \tag{4}$$

3   LOF Based FSVR

3.1   LOF Based Fuzzy Membership Function

The key problem of FSVR is to define a fuzzy membership function to measure the deviation degree of a sample with respect to the regression interval. In our study, we calculate the fuzzy membership based on a local outlier factor LOF [24], LOF describes the isolation degree of a sample with respect to its neighbors. In this way, the degree of a sample's deviation from the regression interval can be evaluated using its fuzzy membership. The following four concepts are defined to describe a sample's neighbors and the close relationship between a sample and its neighbors.

Definition 1 (k-distance). A sample's k-distance is calculated in this way: first, the sample's k nearest neighbors are determined, then the distance between this sample and each neighbor is calculated, the largest one among these k values is the sample's k-distance.

   The purpose of calculating a sample's k-distance is to determine its neighbors and the degree of sparsity around this sample. For instance, sample P_1's k-distance is shown in Fig. 2, it can be easily seen that P_1's 3-distance is 5 and its 5-distance is 8: $d_3(P_1) = 5, d_5(P_1) = 8$.

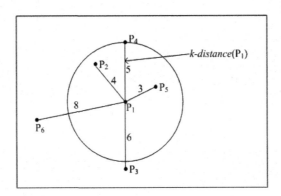

Fig. 2. Schematic diagram for sample P_1's k-distance

Definition 2 (k-distance neighbors). The k-distance neighbors of sample p are composed of the samples whose distance to sample p is no greater than p's k-distance, sample p's k-distance neighbors are expressed as follows:

$$N_k(p) = \{q|q \in D \setminus \{p\}, distance(p, q) \le d_k(p)\}, \tag{5}$$

   For instance, in Fig. 2, we can learn that sample P_1's 3-distance is 5, thus, its 3-distance neighbors are $N_3(P_1) = \{P_2, P_4, P_5\}$. A sample's isolation degree is calculated based on its k-distance neighbors instead of the whole data set D.

Definition 3 (reachable distance). The reachable distance of sample p with respect to sample o is the larger one of the two distances: the k-distance of sample o, the distance between p and o.

$$rd_k(p, o) = max\{d_k(o), distance(p, o)\}, \tag{6}$$

If the distance between p and o is smaller than the k-distance of o, the reachable distance of p is the k-distance of o, otherwise is the distance between p and o. For example, when k=3, the reachable distance of P_2, P_4 and P_5 with respect to P_1 is 5: $rd_3(P_{2,4,5}, P_1) = d_3(P_1) = 5$, and the reachable distance of P_3 and P_6 with respect to P_1 are 6 and 8, respectively. With this concept, it can be guaranteed that the members within a sample's k-distance neighbors have the same distance indicator, thus their isolation degrees are very approximate.

Definition 4 (local reachable density LRD). The local reachable density [25] of sample p is defined in Eq.(7):

$$lrd_k(p) = \frac{|N_k(p)|}{\sum_{o \in N_k(p)} rd_k(p, o)}, \tag{7}$$

where $|N_k(p)|$ denotes the number of k-distance neighbors of sample p, thus, sample p's local reachable density is calculated as the number of it k-distance neighbors divided by the sum of the reachable distances of p with respect to each of its k-distance neighbors, its practical meaning is the inverse ratio of the average reachable distance of p's k-distance neighbors.

Definition 5 (local outlier factor LOF). LOF is used to measure the isolation degree of a sample. The LOF of sample p is the ratio between the average LRD of p's k-distance neighbors and p's LRD, which is represented in the following formula:

$$lof_k(p) = \frac{1}{|N_k(p)|} \sum_{o \in N_k(p)} \frac{lrd_k(o)}{lrd_k(p)}, \tag{8}$$

If $lof_k(p)$ is near to 1, in this case, sample p has a good relation with its k-distance neighbors: very similar distribution and easily merged into the same class; If $lof_k(p)$ is greater than 1, it means that sample p has a higher degree of isolation than its k-distance neighbors. The more isolated a sample is, the more likely an outlier it is. The concept of membership degree can describe the degree of an object's belonging to a class. From the above analysis, it is easy to conclude that a sample's membership degree is in inverse proportion to its degree of isolation.

Definition 6 (LOF based membership function). The membership function based on LOF is defined as follows:

$$\mu_i = \begin{cases} (1-\theta)^m + \sigma, & \overline{lof} < lof_k(p) \le lof_{max} \\ 1-\theta, & lof_{min} \le lof_k(p) \le \overline{lof} \end{cases} \tag{9}$$

where $\theta = (lof_k(p) - lof_{min})/(lof_{max} - lof_{min})$, $lof_k(p)$ is the LOF of sample p; lof_{min}, lof_{max} and $\overline{lof}$ are the minimum, maximum and average values among

LOFs of all the samples, respectively; $\sigma < 1$ is a very small positive real number while $m \geq 2$. The LOF based membership function is shown in Fig. 3, which demonstrates that the larger LOF value a sample has, the more rapid decline its membership gets. If $lof_k(p)$ is close to lof_{max}, sample p' membership will be close to a very small positive real number σ, indicating that the higher isolation degree of a sample, the less impact it has on the regression model.

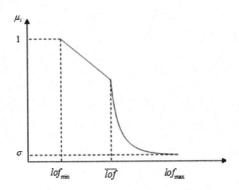

Fig. 3. Schematic diagram for LOF based membership function

3.2   Outlier Identification Ability of LOF

In this section we verify the outlier identification ability of LOF using airport noise data. The monitored airport noise data set contains the attributes of a monitoring node such as its coordinates; the attributes of single flight event such as flight amount in morning, afternoon and night; the attributes of weather such as temperature. According to the definition of LOF, we now calculate the value of LOF for each sample in the data set, and k is set to 50. After the execution of principle component analysis (PCA), the three-dimensional projection of the airport noise data is obtained as displayed in Fig. 4, where the larger points denote the samples whose LOF values are in top 100.

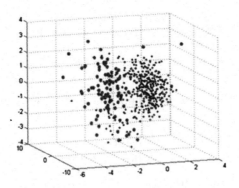

Fig. 4. Three-dimensional projection of the original data set

The distance, density and affinity based outlier factors, and the LOF of samples in the airport noise data are calculated, respectively. For each algorithm, the samples whose values of outlier factors are among the top 100 are determined, the number of real noise samples in these 100 samples is used to evaluate the outlier identification ability of an algorithm. Table 1 shows the numbers of the true outliers identified by these algorithms, it can be seen that the LOF algorithm has better outlier identification ability than other three algorithms, this is because LOF uses the concept of k-distance neighbors and can better identify the outliers lying on the class boundary. Thus, we believe that, using the LOF based fuzzy membership function, the FSVR algorithm will get better prediction accuracy.

Table 1. Outlier identification results of different algorithms

Algorithm	Samples	Outliers	Identified outliers	Hit rate
distance based	500	100	70	70 %
density based	500	100	62	62 %
affinity based	500	100	43	43 %
LOF	500	100	81	81 %

3.3 Performance of LOF Based FSVR

Experiments are carried out on the airport noise data to demonstrate the superiority of LOF-FSVR to other related SVR algorithms, such as ε-SVR without(or with) outliers, density based FSVR [25, 26] and affinity based FSVR [27]. In this study, the Radical Basis Function (RBF) represented in formula (10) is employed as the kernel function of all these algorithms, where σ is the bandwidth of RBF.

$$K(x, x_i) = exp\{-\frac{|x - x_i|^2}{\sigma^2}\}. \tag{10}$$

For all the algorithms, 10-fold Cross Validation is adopted to search the best values for parameters C and σ, the membership function parameter m is set to 10. Figures 5 and 6 display the prediction results of ε-SVR and LOF-FSVR, respectively, the Root Mean Squared Errors RMSEs (calculated according to formula (11)) of all the algorithms are listed in Table 2.

$$RMSE = \sqrt{\frac{1}{N}\sum_{i=1}^{N}(f(x_i) - y_i)^2}, \tag{11}$$

It can be seen from Figs. 5 and 6 that, with the adding of outliers, the regression interval of ε-SVR moves towards the outliers, which indicates that ε-SVR is very sensitive to the outliers and its prediction ability is greatly reduced. However, LOF-FSVR can reduce the impact of the outliers to some extent and

Table 2. RMSEs of different FSVR algorithms

Algorithm	ε-SVR without outlier	ε-SVR with outlier	density based $FSVR$	affinity based $FSVR$	LOF based $FSVR$
RMSE(dB)	8.0771	8.4151	7.8258	7.6790	7.4577

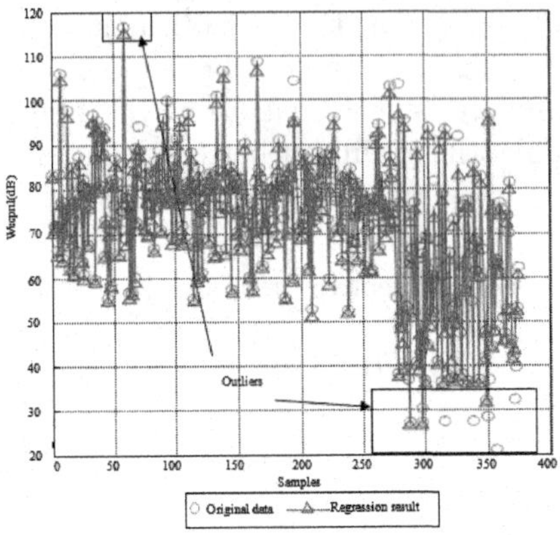

Fig. 5. Prediction results of ε-SVR

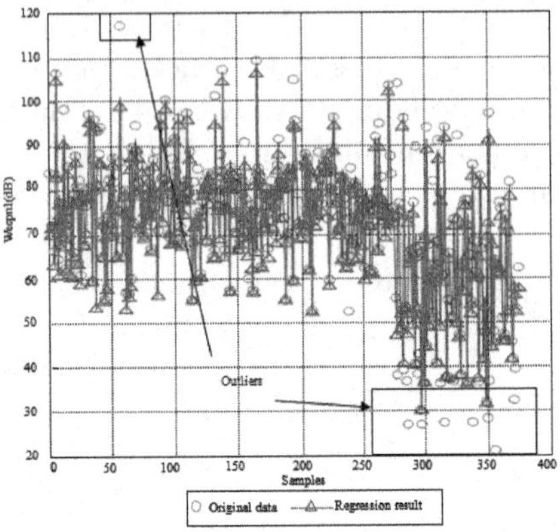

Fig. 6. Prediction results of LOF-FSVR

has better outlier immunity and more stable performance. From Table 2 we can learn that, with the adding of noisy samples, the accuracy of all the FSVR algorithms is significantly better than that of the ε-SVR algorithms, indicating that the immunity of FSVR algorithms is improved due to the incorporation of fuzzy membership. In addition, compared with the density based FSVR, the proposed LOF-FSVR can better describe the degree of samples' deviation from the regression interval, therefore, it has better generalization performance.

4   The LOF-FSVR Based Airport Noise Ensemble Prediction Model

4.1   LOF-FSVR Based Ensemble Prediction Model

A single prediction model may be unstable and not accurate enough in the prediction phase, as ensemble learning [14,15] has been proved to be an effective way of improving the performance of single models [16], thus, we employ ensemble learning to enhance the prediction capacity of a single LOF-FSVR model.

In the combination phase of ensemble learning, the traditional method is combining all the generated models, which results in a high time and space complexity and slows down the prediction speed. In the past decade, selective ensemble learning [28,29] has been proposed, which heuristically selects a subset of generated models and discards the inaccurate and redundant ones. Theoretical and empirical studies [29] have demonstrated that selective ensemble can reduce the ensemble size while maintaining or even improving the prediction performance. Therefore, in this study, selective ensemble is utilized to further improve the prediction performance. In our prediction model, we first adopt AdaBoost [18] to generate many diverse LOF-FSVR models, then adopt the simple and quick Orientation Ordering (OO)[29] selective approach to prune the generated models, finally we get an ensemble prediction model. The concrete steps of our prediction model are described in Algorithm 1 and the general process is displayed in Fig. 7.

- *Input*

training set $S = \{(x_1, y_1), \cdots, (x_N, y_N)\}$, the maximum iteration times T and the initial weights of training samples: $w_i^1 = 1/N, (i = 1, 2, \cdots, N)$;
- *Ensemble   generation   phase*

Step 1: resample the training set S using AdaBoost according to its current weight distribution $\{w_i^t\}_{i=1}^N$ and obtain the sampled training set S_t, where $t(1 \leq t \leq T)$ denotes the tth iteration;

Step 2: calculate the fuzzy membership μ_i of each sample $(x_i, y_i)(i = 1, 2, \cdots, N)$, the proposed LOF-FSVR is applied on the training set S_t to train a model h_t, then h_t is used to predict the original training set S and the prediction results are obtained: $f_t(x_i)$ $(i = 1, 2, \cdots, N)$;

Step 3: calculate the loss $l_i = 1 - exp\{-|f_t(x_i) - y_i|/D\}$ on each sample, where $D = max_{i=1,\cdots,N}(|f_t(x_i) - y_i|)$, and the average loss of the model: $L_t = \sum_{i=1}^N l_i w_i^t$. If $L_t \geq 0.5$, go to Step 2;

Step 4: set a threshold λ for the loss value l_i, assume that

$$c_t(i) = \begin{cases} 1, & l_i \leq \lambda \\ -1, & l_i > \lambda \end{cases},$$

and the signature vector of model h_t is: $C_t = [c_t(1)w_1^t, \cdots, c_t(N)w_N^t]^T$;

Step 5: compute the confidence value $\beta_t = L_t/(1 - L_t)$, update the weights of samples in S: $w_i^{t+1} = w_i^t \beta_t^{1-L_t}/Z_t, (i = 1, 2, \cdots, N)$, where Z_t is a normalization coefficient satisfying $\sum_{i=1}^N w_i^{t+1} = 1$;

Step 6: set the weight of the model h_t: $wh_t = log(1/\beta_t)$;

Step 7: repeat Steps 1 to 6 T times, then a set of diverse models $\{h_1, h_2, \cdots, h_T\}$ are generated.
- *Selective   ensemble   phase*

Step 8: calculate the signature vector of the ensemble that is composed of the T models: $H = 1/\sum_{t=1}^T wh_t(C_1 wh_1, \cdots, C_T wh_T)$, the reference vector $R = O + \alpha H$, where $R \perp H$, O is a unit matrix and has the same type with H, thus, we have $\alpha = \frac{-O \cdot H}{|H|^2}$;

Step 9: compute the angles between the reference vector R and each signature vector C_t: $\theta_t = arccos\frac{R \cdot C_t}{|R| \cdot |C_t|}$ $(t = 1, 2, \cdots, T)$, rank the T models in increasing order according to their angles, then select the models whose angles are less than $\frac{\pi}{2}$. In this way, we obtain a subset of models: $\{h_1', \cdots, h_S'\}, (1 \leq S < T)$;

- *Prediction   phase*

  Step 10: the selected S models are combined as the final ensemble prediction model $ES = \{h'_1, \cdots, h'_S\}$. ES predicts a new sample x in this manner: rank these S models in decreasing order according to their prediction results: $Y = \{g_1(x), g_2(x), \cdots, g_S(x)\}$, the corresponding weights of the reordered models are $\{wh_1, wh_2, \cdots, wh_S\}$, the final output of ES is:

$$G(x) = inf\{y \in Y, \sum_{t:g_t(x) \leq y} wh_t \geq \frac{1}{2} \sum_t wh_t\}. \tag{12}$$

Algorithm 1. Steps of the proposed ensemble prediction model

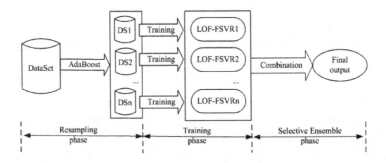

Fig. 7. The LOF-FSVR based airport noise ensemble prediction model

4.2   Performance of the Proposed Model on Airport Noise Data Set

To verify the effectiveness of our prediction model, we conduct experiments on airport noise data set whose characteristics have been described in Sect. 3.2. In these experiments, the kernel function and the values of C and ρ are the same as those in Sect. 3, and the number of LOF-FSVRs generated by Adaboost is 20. Figure 8 shows the prediction results of single LOF-FSVR and our ensemble model. Here we adopt RMSE and MAD to evaluate their prediction performances, where MAD (Mean Absolute Deviation) is calculated using formula (13). Similar to RMSE, the smaller the value of MAD, the lower the degree of average deviation of the predicted values and thus the better the prediction performance. The concrete experimental results are listed in Table 3.

$$MAD = \frac{1}{N} \sum_{i=1}^{N} |f(x_i) - y_i|. \tag{13}$$

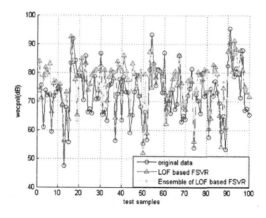

Fig. 8. Prediction results of the two compared methods

Table 3. RMSE and MAD of the two methods

	single LOF based FSVR	selective ensemble of LOF-FSVR
RMSE(dB)	7.4577	6.9182
MAD(dB)	6.0975	5.7775

From Fig. 8 and Table 3 we can learn that, the proposed ensemble prediction model improves the prediction performance of single LOF-FSVR to a large extent and the prediction error of each monitoring node is controlled at 6–7dB. In the model combination phase, since we adopt the quick Orientation Ordering method, the base models contained in the final ensemble account for 30 % to 50 % of the originally generated models, indicating that the proposed prediction model greatly improves the prediction efficiency and performance.

5 Conclusion and Future Work

Airport noise prediction is of vital importance to the design of airports and flights. As SVM has been proved to have good prediction capacity, we adopt it for airport noise prediction. However, in some cases, outliers contained in the monitored airport noise data degrade the prediction performance of the trained SVM. To solve this problem, we design a Local Outlier Factor based Fuzzy Support Vector Regression algorithm LOF-FSVR to improve the noise immunity of SVM. In addition, ensemble learning is an effective way to improve individual models, motivated by ensemble learning, we propose a LOF-FSVR based ensemble prediction model to improve the performance of a single LOF-FSVR model. Conducted experiments on airport noise data verify the effectiveness of our prediction model. In the future, we intend to apply our prediction model on larger practical airport noise data sets and expect that it will get satisfactory prediction performance.

Acknowledgments. This research is funded by the National Natural Science Foundation of China (No.61139002), the Fundamental Research Funds for the Central Universities (NO.NS2015091) and the Postdoctoral Funding Scheme of Jiangsu Province (NO.1301013A).

References

1. Lei, B., Yang, X., Yang, J.: Noise prediction and control of Pudong international airport expansion project. Environ. Monit. Assess. **151**(1–4), 1–8 (2009)
2. David, W.F., John, G, Dipardo, J.: Review of ensemble noise model (INM) equations and processes. Technical report, Washington University Forum (2003)
3. Wasmer, C.: The Data Entry Component for the Noisemap Suite of Aircraft Noise Models. http://wasmerconsulting.com/baseops.htm
4. GmdbH, B.: User's Manual SoundPLAN. Shelton, USA (2003)
5. Asensio, C., Ruiz, M.: Estimation of directivity and sound power levels emitted by aircrafts during taxiing for outdoor noise prediction purpose. Appl. Acoust. **68**(10), 1263–1279 (2007)
6. Yang, Y., Hinde C., Gillingwater, D.: Airport noise simulation using neural networks. In: IEEE International Joint Conference on Neural Networks, pp. 1917–1923. IEEE Press, Piscataway (2008)
7. Van Den Berg, F.: Criteria for wind farm noise: Lmax and Lden. J. Acoust. Soc. Am. **123**(5), 4043–4048 (2008)
8. Makarewicz, R., Besnardb, F., Doisyc, S.: Road traffic noise prediction based on speed-flow diagram. Appl. Acoust. **72**(4), 190–195 (2011)
9. Yin, Z.Y.: Study on traffic noise prediction based on L-M neural network. Environ. Monit. China **25**(4), 84–187 (2009)
10. Wen, D.Q., Wang, J.D., Zhang, X.: Prediction model of airport-noise time series based on GM-LSSVR (in Chinese). Comput. Sci. **40**(9), 198–220 (2013)
11. Xu, T., Xie, J.W., Yang, G.Q.: Airport noise data mining method based on hierarchical clustering. J. Nanjing Univ. Astronaut. Aeronaut. **45**(5), 715–721 (2013)
12. Chen, H.Y., Sun, B., Wang, J.D.: An interaction prediction model of monitoring node based on observational learning. Int. J. Inf. Electron. Eng. **5**(4), 259–264 (2014)
13. Vapnik, V.: The Nature of Statistical Learning Theory. Springer, New York (2000)
14. Zhou, Z.H.: Ensemble Methods: Foundations and Algorithms. CRC Press, Florida (2012)
15. Sun, B., Wang, J.D., Chen, H.Y., Wang, Y.T.: Diversity measures in ensemble learning (in Chinese). Control and Decis. **29**(3), 385–395 (2014)
16. Kuncheva, L.I., Whitaker, C.J.: Measures of diversity in classifier ensembles and their relationship with the ensemble accuracy. Mach. Learn. **51**(2), 181–207 (2003)
17. Breiman, L.: Bagging predictors. Mach. Learn. **24**(2), 123–140 (1996)
18. Freund, Y., Schapire, R.E., Tang, W.: A decision-theoretic generalization of online learning and an application to boosting. J. Comput. Syst. Sci. **55**(1), 119–139 (1997)
19. Melville, P., Mooney, R.J.: Creating diversity in ensembles using artificial data. Inf. Fusion **6**(1), 99–111 (2005)
20. Sun, B., Chen, H.Y., Wang, J.D.: An empirical margin explanation for the effectiveness of DECORATE ensemble learning algorithm. Knowl. Based Syst. **78**(1), 1–12 (2015)

21. Breiman, L.: Random forests. Mach. Learn. **45**(1), 5–32 (2001)
22. Lin, C.F., Wang, S.D.: Fuzzy support vector machines. IEEE Trans. Neural Netw. **13**(2), 464–471 (2002)
23. Smola, A.J., Scholkopf, B.: A tutorial on support vector regression. Stat. Comput. **14**(3), 199–222 (2004)
24. Gu, B., Wang, J.D.: Class of methods for calculating the threshold of local outlier factor. J. Chinese Comput. Syst. **29**(12), 2254–2257 (2008)
25. Breunig, M., Kriegel, H.P., Ng, R.T.: LOF: identifying density-based local outliers. In: Proceedings of the ACM SIGMOD International Conference on Management of Data, pp. 93–104. Assoc Computing Machinery, New York (2000)
26. An, J.L., Wang, Z.O., Ma, Z.P.: Fuzzy support vector machine based on density. J. Tianjin Univ. **37**(6), 544–548 (2004)
27. Zhang, X., Xiao, X.L., Xu, G.Y.: Fuzzy support vector machine based on affinity among samples. J. Softw. **17**(5), 951–958 (2006)
28. Guo, L., Boukir, S.: Margin-based ordered aggregation for ensemble pruning. Pattern Recogn. Lett. **34**(6), 603–609 (2013)
29. Martinez-Munoz, G., Suarez, A.: Pruning in ordered bagging ensembles. In: Proceedings of the 23rd International Conference on Machine Learning, pp. 609–616. ACM Press, New York (2006)
30. UCI Machine Learning Repository. http://www.ics.uci.edu/~mlearn/mlrepository.html
31. Libsvm: A Library for Support Vector Machines. http://www.csie.ntu.edu.tw/~cjlin/libsvmtools/datasets/

Application of Semantic-Based Laplacian Eigenmaps Method in 3D Model Classification and Retrieval

Xinying Wang[1(✉)], Fangming Gu[2], Gang Liu[1], and Zhiyu Chen[1]

[1] College of Computer Science and Engineering,
Changchun University of Technology, Changchun, China
wang_xinying1979@163.com
[2] College of Computer Science and Technology,
Jilin University, Changchun, China

Abstract. An effective way to solve the problem of semantic gap is to study of the semantic-based methods in the field of 3D model retrieval. Using multi-channel limited semantic information, we build a heterogeneous semantic network of 3D model, then convert the heterogeneous semantic network to the semantic features. On the base of that, we proposed a method of Semantic-based Laplacian Eigenmap (SBLE). We use the semantically nearest neighbor in heterogeneous semantic network instead of the distantly nearest neighbor in 3D model feature space, and embed the semantic relations in semantic space into the low dimensional feature space by feature mapping. The method retained massive semantic information of 3D models during the course of dimension reduction. Experiment results show the effectiveness of the proposed method for 3D model classification and retrieval on Princeton Shape Benchmark.

Keywords: Heterogeneous semantic network · Semantic features · Laplacian eigenmaps · 3D model classification and retrieval

1 Introduction

With the development of computer network and the universal application of 3D software, a lot of 3D models have been produced and widely disseminated [1, 2], so that the 3D model retrieval technology is becoming a hot topic in the field of multimedia information retrieval [3–5]. Content-based retrieval methods (CBIR) is the main contents of the 3D model retrieval technology, this method usually requires extracting shape features of 3D model, and these features are usually a high-dimensional vector. If they represent a point in the scale space, 3D model retrieval can be converted to the problem of finding the nearest point of a fixed point in the high dimensional scale space. However, for large-scale 3D model database, the distance calculation and storage in a high-dimensional vector space require very high computational complexity and space complexity. For this reason, people generally improve the retrieval efficiency by indexing technology or dimension reduction techniques. Dimension reduction technique maps set of points from high-dimensional scale space to low-dimensional scale space. This mapping generally requires maintaining their original structure

© Springer International Publishing Switzerland 2015
Z. Huang et al. (Eds.): ICCCS 2015, LNCS 9483, pp. 550–559, 2015.
DOI: 10.1007/978-3-319-27051-7_47

unchanged and removing redundant information, thus reduces the computation complexity and storage complexity and improve recognition speed of 3D model.

The traditional CBIR method uses physical information of 3D models, and does not consider the semantic information of 3D model. Because of the semantic gap [6], the retrieval results of traditional methods are generally similar in shape but the semantic expression are necessarily not identical. In this paper, a method of Semantic-based Laplacian Eigenmap (SBLE) is proposed. We use the semantically nearest neighbor in heterogeneous semantic network instead of the distantly nearest neighbor in 3D model feature space, and embed the semantic relations in semantic space into the low dimensional feature space by feature mapping. The method retained massive semantic information of 3D models during the course of dimension reduction. Experiment results show the effectiveness of the proposed method for 3D model classification and retrieval on Princeton Shape Benchmark [7].

2   Laplacian Eigenmap

Laplacian Eigenmap [8] is an effective manifold learning algorithm. The basic idea of Laplacian Eigenmap is that some points of near distance in the high dimensional space, which is projected into a low dimensional space, they should also be very close. Suppose W is the similarity matrix. Eigenvalues decomposition of the Laplacian matrix $L = D-W$:

$$Ly = \lambda Dy \tag{1}$$

where $D_{ii} = \sum_j W_{ji}$ is a diagonal weight matrix. The objective function of Laplacian Eigenmap is

$$Y_{opt} = \arg \min_Y \sum_{i,j} \left\| Y_i - Y_j \right\|^2 w_{ij} = tr(Y^T LY) \tag{2}$$

with the constraint

$$Y^T DY = I \tag{3}$$

Where $y_1,\dots,y_r$ are the first r smallest eigenvectors of Eq. (1). The i -th row of $Y = [y_1,\dots,y_r]$ is the new coordinate of point i.

3   Semantic-Based Laplacian Eigenmap Method

Laplacian Eigenmap method can effectively keep distance relationship of data in the original space, which is often used in a variety of multimedia information retrieval with a high-dimensional data, but the method is also subject to restrictions on the "semantic gap", data can not contain certain semantic information in dimensionality reduction process. A semantic-based Laplacian Eigenmap method is proposed, the method retained semantic information of 3D models greatly during the course of dimension reduction, thereby improve the efficiency of information retrieval.

3.1 Semantic Feature of 3D Model

There are several ways to obtain high-level semantic information of 3D models, for example: artificial classification information, semantic annotation for single model, text annotation, image description, user feedback, etc. In addition, we can build an ontology according to the limited semantic annotation information, and then adding the corresponding inference rules which can be further extend the semantic express ability [9]. These different forms of semantic information constitute a heterogeneous semantic network. The schematic diagram of 3D model heterogeneous semantic networks is as Fig. 1.

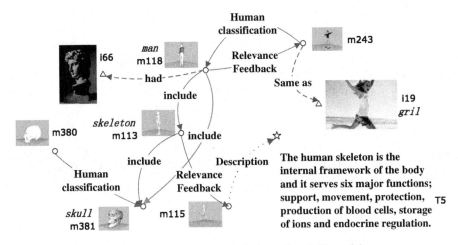

Fig. 1. Heterogeneous semantic networks of 3D model

The figure includes part of the semantic annotation Information of 3D models (text description); the relevance feedback information; artificial classified information and semantic ontology reasoning results (red line), etc.

Here we discuss several ways of semantic expression.

In the heterogeneous semantic network, for some 3D models with same annotation can be seen as the same category; for other 3D models with ontology relationship annotation, we only consider "same as" attribute of the model, namely "similar" relationship. Therefore, the definition of 3D models classification, annotation and ontology semantic information is as follows:

Definition 1. 3D model database $M = \{m_0, m_1, \ldots, m_n\}$. If m_i and m_j belong to the same category, m_i is directly semantic correlated with m_j, and the correlation times between m_i and m_j is termed as $Sem_I(m_i, m_j)$.

Relevance feedback technology is a common method in multimedia semantic retrieval. Results of feedback reflect semantic correlations of 3D models.

Definition 2. If 3D model m_k appeared in the relevance feedback of target model m_q, m_k is directly semantic correlated with m_q. And the times of the correlation between m_k and m_q is termed as $Sem_{II}(m_k, m_q)$.

Definition 3. Define matrix $D_{semantic} = [D_{ij}]_{n\times n}$ as **semantic correlation matrix**, where $D_{ij} = Sem_I(m_i, m_j) + Sem_{II}(m_i, m_j)$, if $i \neq j$, otherwise $D_{ij} = 0$.

We can use the different semantic information to construct the corresponding semantic correlation matrix. The Semantic Correlation Matrix contains many properties of Unified Relationship Matrix [10].

According to the matrix $D_{semantic}$, for any model m_i, $(D_{i1}, D_{i2}, ..., D_{iN})$ depicts the semantic correlation times between m_i and other models, which can be used as the semantic properties of the model m_i. The definition of semantic distance in $D_{semantic}$ is as follows:

$$Dis_{sem}(m_k, m_p) = \sqrt{\sum_{i=1}^{N}(D_{ki} - D_{pi})^2} \tag{4}$$

3.2 SBLE Algorithm

The SBLE algorithm has three main steps:

Step1. According to the matrix $D_{semantic}$, we can construct a 3D model semantic adjacency graph. If nodes X_i and X_j are close in the semantic space, put an edge between X_i and X_j. The semantic distance between two models can be calculated by the formula (4).

Step2. Choosing the weights W.

$$\begin{cases} w_{ij} = 1, & \text{if nodes } X_i \text{ and } X_j \text{ are connected} \\ w_{ij} = 0, & \text{otherwise} \end{cases}$$

Step3. Eigenvalues decomposition of the Laplacian matrix $L = D\text{-}W$: $Lf = \lambda Df$ where $D_{ii} = \sum_j w_{ij}$, it is a diagonal matrix.

Minimize the objective function:

$$\sum_{i=1}^{N}\sum_{j\neq i}\frac{1}{2}\|y_i - y_j\|^2 W_{ij} = tr(Y^T L Y)$$

Suppose, we obtain the eigenvector $f_0, f_1, ..., f_L$ corresponding to minimum $L + 1$ eigenvalues, then the final L-dimensional embedding eigenvectors is $Y_i = (f_1^i, ..., f_L^i)^T$ where $i = 1, 2, ..., N$, and $m = 1, 2, ..., L$.

4   3D Model Retrieval Based on SBLE

Using the SBLE method for 3D model retrieval, we need the content-based 3D model retrieval system to help the new system. The new system also needs the original 3D model database and the new database after dimension reduction with SBLE.

Retrieval process is as follows:

(1) Users need to provide a target model to be retrieved, the system first determines whether the 3D model in the original database or not, if it exists, the system will use the low dimensional feature vectors of the model as a new retrieval object, and retrieve the target models in the database after dimension reduction with SBLE directly.

(2) If the target 3D model is not in the database, the system needs to extract the features of 3D model and uses the traditional content-based method to retrieve the models from the database, and returns the retrieval results to the user for relevance feedback, and then using the method of SBLE to reduce the dimension of the models in the database.

(3) Finally, we use the low-dimensional feature vectors as the search target to retrieve in the database after dimension reduction with SBLE.

5   Experiment and Analysis

We choose the top 907 3D models in PSB Library as our experimental data set. There are 65 semantic classifications, feature extraction methods using depth-buffer method [11]. The dimensions of the 3D model features are 438. The classification standard adopts the basic manual classification of PSB.

In the aspect of semantic expression, we use relevance feedback and artificial semantic annotation (less than 5 %) and ontology reasoning method [9] to obtain the new semantic annotation information, then construct a 3D model semantic relationship matrix. In the relevance feedback process, in order to get the semantic relations of the 3D models, we let five people to participate in the test, and the goal is to retrieve the top 907 models in PSB library randomly, which is based on the content retrieval method, and feedback semantically related model.

Figure 2 shows the visual results of the final semantic relationship matrix.

5.1   Classification Experiment

In experiment, we use clustering technique for classification. *Entropy* and *purity* [12] are used to evaluate the classification performance. The definitions of them are as follows:

$$Entropy = \sum_{i=1}^{k} \frac{n_i}{N} (-\frac{1}{\log q} \sum_{j=1}^{q} \frac{n_i^j}{n_i} \log \frac{n_i^j}{n_i}) \tag{5}$$

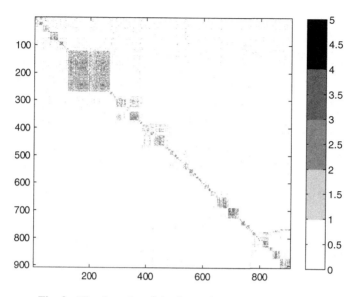

Fig. 2. Visual results of the Semantic Relationship Matrix

$$Purity = \sum_{i=1}^{k} \frac{1}{N} \max_{j}(n_i^j) \qquad (6)$$

Where q and k are the number of artificial classification and clusters respectively, n_i^j is the number of the data that belongs to the j-th class in original data set but appears in the i-th cluster. The smaller the *Entropy* value is and the bigger the *Purity* value is, the better the clustering effect performance.

X-means [13] clustering algorithm is used to cluster the original shape features in experiment, and set the number of clusters in the range of 60–70. Table 1 shows the comparison of clustering evaluation results between original features by X-means algorithm and the SBLE algorithm.

From Table 1 we can see that the results of proposed method were significantly better than the results of original features clustering.

Table 1. Clustering evaluation results.

Type	Number of clusters	Entropy	Purity
Original features	62	0.37576	0.45755
New features after SBLE	70	0.18464	0.69131

5.2 Retrieval Experiment

In the retrieval experiments, we compared the retrieval efficiency of the original features and the new features after using dimension reduction method of SBLE and the classical LE method. As shown below, the O907 represent the retrieval efficiency of the original 3D model features after Euclidean distance measure; LE20N12 and LE20N7 represent the retrieval efficiency after using classic LE method and the new features is 20 dimensions and the nearest neighbors (NN) is 12 and 7 respectively. SBLE20N12 and SBLE20N7 represent retrieval efficiency after using the proposed SBLE and the new features is 20 dimensions, the nearest semantic neighbors (NN) is 12 and 7 respectively.

The Fig. 3 shows that the retrieval efficiency of the proposed method was better than the other two methods.

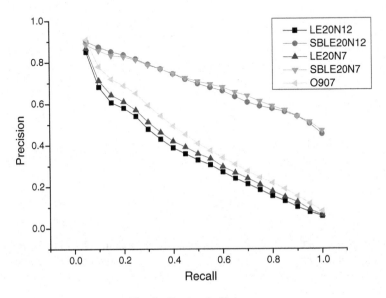

Fig. 3. Retrieval efficiency

Figure 4 shows the retrieval efficiency of four different categories of 3D models, in most cases, the proposed method is better than the other methods, but there are exceptions, for example, Fig. 4(4).watch model, the efficiency of the proposed method is lower than the above two methods.

The Table 2 lists the comparison of the retrieval actual effect about four types of 3D models. It is shown that the retrieval results obtained by the proposed method are generally better than the traditional method. But the "watch" model is an exception. From Table 2 we can see that if the target model is "watch", the system may return "watch" or "hourglass" or other models. Although the two kinds of models are completely different, they represent "timing tool" in semantic. We can see that the proposed method can retrieve some models have same semantic correlation.

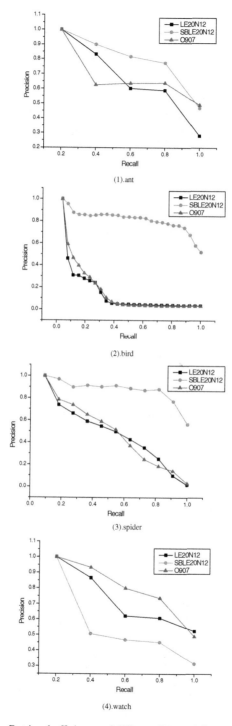

(1).ant

(2).bird

(3).spider

(4).watch

Fig. 4. Retrieval efficiency of different 3D model categories

Table 2. Retrieval results based on Euclidean distance comparison

6   Conclusion

In the field of multimedia information retrieval, the traditional CBIR (Content-based image retrieval) method is not satisfactory because of the limitation of semantic gap. In this paper, a semantic-based Laplacian Eigenmap method is proposed. This method can embed the semantic features of 3D model into a low dimensional feature space by feature mapping, which can preserve the semantic information during the process of feature dimension reduction. The experimental results on PSB (Princeton Shape Benchmark) have shown that the new method is effective in 3D model classification and retrieval.

This method also has some limitations. Because the method relies on semantic features, if the system contains the semantic information is very scarce, or user feedback and ontology reasoning results implied some unpredictable other semantic information resulting in retrieval accuracy difficult to define, 3D model retrieval effectiveness will be affected. The future work is using this semantic knowledge effectively and deeper study on 3D model semantic retrieval.

Acknowledgments. Our work is supported by the National Natural Science Foundation of China under Grant No. 61303132; The Science Foundation for Youths of the Science and Technology Department of Jilin Province under Grant No. 201201131.

References

1. Xu, B., Chang, W., Sheffer, A., et al.: True2Form: 3D curve networks from 2D sketches via selective regularization. ACM Trans. Graph. (Proc. SIGGRAPH 2014) **33**(4), 1–13 (2014)
2. Wang, Y., Feng, J., Wu, Z., Wang, J., Chang, S.-F.: From low-cost depth sensors to CAD: cross-domain 3D shape retrieval via regression tree fields. In: Fleet, D., Pajdla, T., Schiele, B., Tuytelaars, T. (eds.) ECCV 2014, Part I. LNCS, vol. 8689, pp. 489–504. Springer, Heidelberg (2014)
3. Thomas, F., Patrick, M., Misha, K., et al.: A search engine for 3D models. ACM Trans. Graph. J. **22**(1), 85–105 (2003)
4. Luo, S., Li, L., Wang, J.: Research on key technologies of 3D model retrieval based on semantic. J. Phy. Procedia **25**, 1445–1450 (2012)
5. Mangai, M.A., Gounden, N.A.: Subspace-based clustering and retrieval of 3-D objects. J. Comput. Electr. Eng. **39**(3), 809–817 (2013)
6. Zhao, R., Grosky, W.I.: Negotiating the semantic gap: from feature maps to semantic landscapes. J. Pattern Recogn. **35**(3), 51–58 (2002)
7. Shilane, P., et al. The princeton shape benchmark. In: The Shape Modeling International, pp. 388–399 (2004)
8. Belkin, M., Niyogi, P.: Laplacian eigenmaps for dimensionality reduction and data representation. Neural Comput. **15**(6), 1373–1396 (2003)
9. Wang, X.-y., Lv, T.-y., Wang, S.-s., Wang, Z.-x.: An ontology and SWRL based 3D model retrieval system. In: Li, H., Liu, T., Ma, W.-Y., Sakai, T., Wong, K.-F., Zhou, G. (eds.) AIRS 2008. LNCS, vol. 4993, pp. 335–344. Springer, Heidelberg (2008)
10. Xi, W., Fox, E.A., Zhang, B., et al.: SimFusion: measuring similarity using unified relationship matrix. In Proceedings of the 28th Annual International ACM SIGIR Conference on Research and Development in Information Retrieval (SIGIR 2005), Salvador, Brazil, pp. 130–137 (2005)
11. Heczko, M., Keim, D., Saupe, D., Vranic, D.V.: Methods for similarity search on 3D databases. J. German Datenbank-Spektrum **2**(2), 54–63 (2002)
12. Zhao, Y., Karypis, G.: Criterion functions for document clustering: experiment and analysis. Technical report, University of Minnesota, pp. 1–40 (2001)
13. Pelleg, D., Moore, A.: X-means: Extending K-means with efficient estimation of the number of clusters. In Proceedings of the 17th International Conference on Machine Learning (ICML 2000), Stanford University, pp. 89– 97 (2000)

Author Index

Aixiang, Zhu 49

Baosheng, Wang 181
Bin, Luo 101
Bo, Yu 181

Cai, Weidong 417
Cao, Xuehong 390
Cao, Zhili 427
Chang, Wenna 218
Chen, Beijing 427
Chen, Bing 206, 368
Chen, Haiyan 536
Chen, Kang 510
Chen, Lu 3
Chen, Taolue 192
Chen, Xianyi 123, 133
Chen, Zhiyu 550

Dai, Baisheng 501
Dai, Xuejun 3
Deng, Jiajia 536
Ding, Qiulin 259, 521
Du, Qingwei 332

Fan, Zizhu 501
Fang, Lei 356
Fang, Yuejian 74
Feng, Xiang-wen 321
Fengli, Zhang 62
Fu, Ping 206, 368
Fu, Zhangjie 417

Gu, Fangming 550
Gu, Jiayi 192
Gu, Yan 491

Haifeng, Zhao 101
Harit, Rohan 123
Hongshen, Liu 111
Hu, Aiqun 14
Hu, Shuai 491
Hu, Xiao-lin 321

Huabin, Wang 101
Huang, Yuhua 3

Ivanc, Blaž 230

Ji, Genlin 285
Jiali, Wang 111
Jiang, Guohua 244
Jiang, Hua 491
Jiang, Liu 88
Jin, Cancan 74
Jin, Lei 437

Klobučar, Tomaž 230

Lai, Haiguang 218
Lei, Weihua 356
Li, Chengye 380
Li, Cong 510
Li, Jing 147
Li, Miao 259
Linge, Nigel 417
Liu, Gang 550
Liu, Qi 417
Liu, Xiaodong 457
Lu, Ping 306
Lu, Tingting 3
Lu, Zeyuan 285
Luo, Yang 510

Ni, Siru 344
Ni, Yujia 427

Peng, Xue 448
Pi, Dechang 480

Qian, Cheng 25
Qian, Hongyan 206
Qian, Yuming 306
Qin, Xiaolin 306
Qu, Zhiyi 457

Ren, Yueqing 457
Rui, Xiongli 390

Shao, Nannan   157
Shen, Jian   417
Shen, Qingni   74, 510
Shen, Xuhui   480
Shen, Yao   306
Shi, Jiangyong   380
Shuwei, Wang   181
Su, Fei   3
Sun, Bo   536
Sun, Huiyu   123, 133
Sun, Lei   270, 437
Sun, Xingming   123, 133
Sun, Ziwen   157, 469

Tang, Yong   181
Tian, Yuhang   427
Ting, Zhong   49
Tobe, Yoshito   133

Wang, Baowei   417
Wang, Dingcheng   427
Wang, Feiran   437
Wang, Huanhuan   356
Wang, Jian   14, 25, 38, 169
Wang, Jiandong   536
Wang, Jiefeng   469
Wang, Jun   344
Wang, Sheng   306
Wang, Shuihua   285
Wang, Xiaolei   380
Wang, Xinying   550
Wang, Xue   404
Wang, Yinmeng   332
Wang, Youdong   14
Wang, Zhidan   169
Wang, Ziying   38
Wen, Zilong   74
Wu, Weigang   192
Wu, Zhonghai   74, 510

Xiao, Han   49
Xie, Qiang   259
Xinpeng, Zhang   101
Xiong, Pan   480

Xu, Chenhui   206
Xu, Feng   218
Xu, Jun   218
Xue, Mingfu   14

Yan, Xue-feng   321
Yang, Hanjie   368
Yang, Jie   270, 390
Yang, Jiquan   285
Yang, Qun   356
Yang, Yuexiang   380
Yijing, Bai   62
Yu, Xueyong   244
Yuan, Jiabin   404
Yue, Ruan   111
Yunshuo, Yang   49

Zhang, Daowen   469
Zhang, Fenglin   294
Zhang, Guangshuai   285
Zhang, Jingci   270
Zhang, Wenjun   294
Zhang, Xing   74
Zhang, Ying   521
Zhang, Yudong   285
Zhang, Zheng   285, 501
Zhao, Xingfang   404
Zhao, Yanfei   169
Zhao, Youzhi   427
Zhao, Zhiyuan   437
Zhaoxia, Yin   101
Zheng, Hongyuan   521
Zhou, Xingxing   285
Zhou, Yu   192
Zhou, Zhenliu   88
Zhou, Zhili   123, 133
Zhou, Zhiping   157, 469
Zhu, Jiang   480
Zhu, Qi   501
Zhu, Shidong   88
Zhu, Xianwei   270
Zhu, Zhiqiang   270
Zhuang, Yi   344

Printed in the United States
By Bookmasters